# DATA AND COMPUTER COMMUNICATIONS

## ISDN AND BROADBAND ISDN, WITH FRAME RELAY AND ATM: THIRD EDITION

An in-depth presentation of the technology and architecture of integrated services digital networks (ISDN). Covers the integrated digital network (IDN), ISDN services, architecture, signaling system no. 7 (SS7) and detailed coverage of the ITU-T standards. This new edition also provides detailed coverage of protocols and congestion control strategies for both frame relay and ATM.

## BUSINESS DATA COMMUNICATIONS SECOND EDITION

A comprehensive presentation of data communications and telecommunications from a business perspective. Covers voice, data, image, and video communications and applications technology and includes a number of case studies.

## COMPUTER ORGANIZATION AND ARCHITECTURE FOURTH EDITION

A unified view of this broad field. Covers fundamentals such as CPU, control unit, microprogramming, instruction set, I/O, and memory. Also covers advanced topics such as RISC, superscalar, and parallel organization. Awarded the Texty Award by the Text and Academic Authors Association for the best Computer Science and Engineering Textbook of 1996.

## PROTECT YOUR PRIVACY: A GUIDE FOR **PGP** USERS

Provides detailed step-by-step instructions on the use of PGP on the most important computer platforms. It explains the fundamentals of encryption and digital signatures so that the reader will know what PGP can do for him or her. Also provides explicit instructions on solving the all-important problem of obtaining trusted public keys of other users.

# The William Stallings Books
## on Computers and Data Communications Technology

### Data and Computer Communications
### Fifth Edition

A comprehensive survey, that has become the standard in the field, covering:

1. data communications, including transmission, media, signal encoding, link control, and multiplexing;
2. communication networks, including circuit- and packet-switched, frame relay, ATM, and LANs;
3. the TCP/IP protocol suite, including IPv6, TCP, SNMPv2, MIME, and HTTP, as well as a detailed treatment of network security.

### Network and Internetwork Security: Principles and Practice

A tutorial and survey on network security technology. Each of the basic building blocks of network security, including conventional and public-key cryptography, authentication, and digital signatures, are covered. In addition methods for countering hackers and viruses are explored. The book covers important network security applications, including PGP, PEM, Kerberos, and SNMPv2 security.

### Local and Metropolitan Area Networks
### Fifth Edition

An in-depth presentation of the technology and architecture of local and metropolitan area networks. Covers topology, transmission media, medium access control, standards, internetworking, and network management. Provides an up-to-date coverage of LAN/MAN systems, including Fast Ethernet, ATM LANs, Fibre Channel and wireless LANs.

### Operating Systems
### Second Edition

A state-of-the art survey of operating system principles. Covers fundamental technology as well as contemporary design issues, such as threads, real-time systems, multiprocessor scheduling, distributed systems, security, and object-oriented design.

# FIFTH EDITION

# DATA AND COMPUTER COMMUNICATIONS

## WILLIAM STALLINGS

PRENTICE-HALL INTERNATIONAL, INC.

© 1997 by Prentice-Hall, Inc.
Simon & Schuster / A Viacom Company
Upper Saddle River, New Jersey 07458

Printed in the United States of America

10   9   8

ISBN   0-13-571274-2

PRENTICE-HALL INTERNATIONAL (UK) LIMITED, *London*
PRENTICE-HALL OF AUSTRALIA PTY. LIMITED, *Sydney*
PRENTICE-HALL CANADA, INC., *Toronto*
PRENTICE-HALL HISPANOAMERICANA, S.A., *Mexico*
PRENTICE-HALL OF INDIA PRIVATE LIMITED, *New Delhi*
PRENTICE-HALL OF JAPAN, INC., *Tokyo*
SIMON & SCHUSTER ASIA PTE. LTD., *Singapore*
EDITORA PRENTICE-HALL DO BRASIL, LTDA., *Rio de Janeiro*
PRENTICE-HALL, INC., UPPER SADDLE RIVER, *New Jersey*

As always, for Antigone
and also for her constant
companion, Geoffroi, Chartreux nonpareil

# PREFACE

## Objectives

This book attempts to provide a unified overview of the broad field of data and computer communications. The organization of the book reflects an attempt to break this massive subject into comprehensible parts and to build, piece by piece, a survey of the state of the art. The book emphasizes basic principles and topics of fundamental importance concerning the technology and architecture of this field, as well as providing a detailed discussion of leading-edge topics.

The following basic themes serve to unify the discussion:

- *Principles:* Although the scope of this book is broad, there are a number of basic principles that appear repeatedly as themes and that unify this field. Examples are multiplexing, flow control, and error control. The book highlights these principles and contrasts their application in specific areas of technology.
- *Design Approaches:* The book examines alternative approaches to meeting specific communication requirements. The discussion is bolstered with examples from existing implementations.
- *Standards:* Standards have come to assume an increasingly important, indeed dominant, role in this field. An understanding of the current status and future direction of technology requires a comprehensive discussion of the role and nature of the related standards.

## Plan of the Text

The book is divided into four parts:

I  *Data Communications:* This part is concerned primarily with the exchange of data between two directly-connected devices. Within this restricted scope, the key aspects of transmission, interfacing, link control, and multiplexing are examined.

II  *Wide-Area Networks:* This part examines the internal mechanisms and technologies that have been developed to support voice, data, and multimedia communications over long-distance networks. The traditional technologies of packet switching and circuit switching are examined, as well as the more recent frame relay and ATM.

III *Local Area Networks:* This part explores the quite different technologies and architectures that have been developed for networking over shorter distances. The transmission media, topologies, and medium access control protocols that are the key ingredients of a LAN design are explored and specific standardized LAN systems examined.

IV *Communications Architecture and Protocols:* This part explores both the architectural principles and the mechanisms required for the exchange of data among computers, workstations, servers, and other data processing devices. Much of the material in this part relates to the TCP/IP protocol suite.

In addition, the book includes an extensive glossary, a list of frequently-used acronyms, and a a bibliography. Each chapter includes problems and suggestions for further reading.

The book is intended for both an academic and a professional audience. For the professional interested in this field, the book serves as a basic reference volume and is suitable for self-study.

As a textbook, it can be used for a one-semester or two-semester course. It covers the material in the Computer Communication Networks course of the joint ACM/IEEE Computing Curricula 1991. The chapters and parts of the book are sufficiently modular to provide a great deal of flexibility in the design of courses. The following are suggestions for course design:

- *Fundamentals of Data Communications*: Part I, Chapters 8 (circuit switching), 9 (packet switching), 12 (protocols and architecture).
- *Communications Networks*: If the student has a basic background in data communications, then this course could cover Parts II and III, and Appendix A.
- *Computer Networks*: If the student has a basic background in data communications, then this course could cover Chapters 5 (data communication interface), 6 (data link control), and Part IV.

In addition, a more streamlined course that covers the entire book is possible by eliminating certain chapters that are not essential on a first reading. Chapters that could be optional are: Chapters 2 (data transmission) and 3 (transmission media), if the student has a basic understanding of these topics, Chapter 7 (multiplexing), Chapter 10 (frame relay), Chapter 14 (bridges), and Chapter 18 (network security).

## INTERNET SERVICES FOR INSTRUCTORS AND STUDENTS

There is a web page for this book that provides support for students and instructors. The page includes links to relevant sites, transparency masters of figures in the book in PDF (Adobe Acrobat) format, and sign-up information for the book's internet mailing list. The mailing list has been set up so that instructors using this book can exchange information, suggestions, and questions with each other and with the author. The web page is at http://www.shore.net/~ws/DCC5e.html.

As soon as any typos or other errors are discovered, an errata list for this book will be available at http://www.shore.net/~ws/welcome.html.

## WHAT'S NEW IN THE FIFTH EDITION

This fifth edition is seeing the light of day less than a dozen years after the publication of the first edition. Much has happened during those years. Indeed, the pace of change, if anything, is increasing. The result is that this revision is more comprehensive and thorough than any of the previous ones. As an indication of this, about one-half of the figures (233 out of 343) and one-half of the tables (48 out of 91) in this edition are new. Every chapter has been revised, new chapters have been added, and the overall organization of the book has changed.

To begin this process of revision, the fourth edition of this book was extensively reviewed by a number of professors who taught from that edition. The result is that, in many places, the narrative has been clarified and tightened and illustrations have been improved. Also, a number of new "field-tested" problems have been added.

Beyond these refinements to improve pedagogy and user-friendliness, there have been major substantive changes throughout the book. Highlights include

- *ATM*: The coverage of ATM has been significantly expanded. There is now an entire chapter devoted to ATM and ATM congestion control (Chapter 11). New to this edition is the coverage of ATM LANs (Sections 13.4 and 14.3).
- *IPv6 (IPng) and IPv6 Security*: IPv6, also known as IPng (next generation), is the key to a greatly expanded use of TCP/IP both on the Internet and in other networks. This new topic is thoroughly covered. The protocol and its internetworking functions are discussed in Section 16.3, and the important material on IPv6 security is provided in Section 18.4.
- *Wireless and Spread Spectrum*: There is greater coverage of wireless technology (Section 3.2) and spread spectrum techniques (Section 4.5). New to this edition is treatment of the important topic of wireless LANs (Sections 12.5 and 13.6).
- *High-speed LANs*: Coverage of this important area is significantly expanded, and includes detailed treatment of leading-edge approaches, including Fast Ethernet (100BASE-T), 100VG-AnyLAN, ATM LANs, and Fibre Channel (Sections 13.1 through 13.5).
- *Routing*: The coverage of internetwork routing has been updated and expanded. There is a longer treatment of OSPF and a discussion of BGP has been added.
- *Frame Relay*: Frame relay also receives expanded coverage with Chapter 10 devoted to frame relay and frame relay congestion control.
- *Network Security*: Coverage of this topic has been expanded to an entire chapter (Chapter 18).
- *Network Management*: New developments in the specification of SNMPv2 are covered (Section 19.2).
- *SMTP and MIME*: Multimedia electronic mail combines the basic functionality of the Simple Mail Transfer Protocol with the Multi-purpose Internet Mail Extension.

- *HTTP*: (Hypertext Transfer Protocol): HTTP is the foundation of the operation of the worldwide web (www). Section 19.3 covers HTTP.
- *TCP/IP*: TCP/IP is now the focus of the protocol coverage in this book. Throughout the book, especially in Part IV, there is increased discussion of TCP/IP and related protocols and issues.

In addition, throughout the book, virtually every topic has been updated to reflect the developments in standards and technology that have occurred since the publication of the fourth edition.

## ACKNOWLEDGMENTS

This new edition has benefited from review by a number of people, who gave generously of their time and expertise. Kitel Albertson (Trondheim College of Engineering), Howard Blum (Pace University), Mike Borella (DePaul University), William Clark (University of Alaska, Anchorage), Joe Doupnik (Utah State University), Doug Jacobson (Iowa State University), Dave Mallya, Biswath Mukherjee (University of California, Davis), and Mark Pullen (George Mason University) reviewed all or part of the manuscript.

Steve Deering of Xerox PARC reviewed the material on IPv6. Ted Doty of Network Systems Corporation reviewed IP security. Henrik Nielson reviewed HTTP.

*William Stallings*

# BRIEF CONTENTS

# CONTENTS

# PART TWO
# Wide–Area Networks  229

# PART FOUR
## Communications Architecture and Protocols  497

# CHAPTER 1

# INTRODUCTION

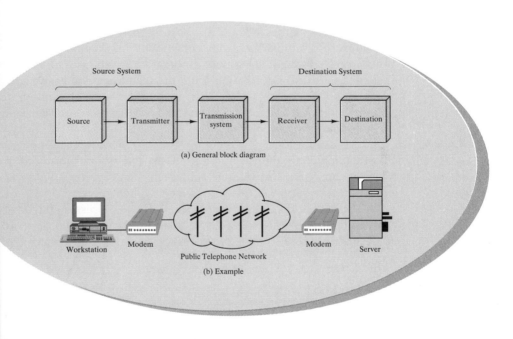

Source System

Destination System

Source → Transmitter → Transmission system → Receiver → Destination

(a) General block diagram

Workstation — Modem — Public Telephone Network — Modem — Server

(b) Example

The 1970s and 1980s saw a merger of the fields of computer science and data communications that profoundly changed the technology, products, and companies of the now-combined computer-communications industry. Although the consequences of this revolutionary merger are still being worked out, it is safe to say that the revolution has occurred, and any investigation of the field of data communications must be made within this new context.

The computer-communications revolution has produced several remarkable facts:

- There is no fundamental difference between data processing (computers) and data communications (transmission and switching equipment).
- There are no fundamental differences among data, voice, and video communications.
- The lines between single-processor computer, multi-processor computer, local network, metropolitan network, and long-haul network have blurred.

One effect of these trends has been a growing overlap of the computer and communications industries, from component fabrication to system integration. Another result is the development of integrated systems that transmit and process all types of data and information. Both the technology and the technical-standards organizations are driving toward a single public system that integrates all communications and makes virtually all data and information sources around the world easily and uniformly accessible.

It is the ambitious purpose of this book to provide a unified view of the broad field of data and computer communications. The organization of the book reflects an attempt to break this massive subject into comprehensible parts and to build, piece by piece, a survey of the state of the art. This introductory chapter begins with a general model of communications. Then, a brief discussion introduces each of the four major parts of this book. Next, the all-important role of standards is introduced. Finally, a brief outline of the rest of the book is provided.

## 1.1 A COMMUNICATIONS MODEL

We begin our study with a simple model of communications, illustrated by the block diagram in Figure 1.1a.

The fundamental purpose of a communications system is the exchange of data between two parties. Figure 1.1b presents one particular example, which is the communication between a workstation and a server over a public telephone network. Another example is the exchange of voice signals between two telephones over the same network. The key elements of the model are

**Source.** This device generates the data to be transmitted; examples are telephones and personal computers.

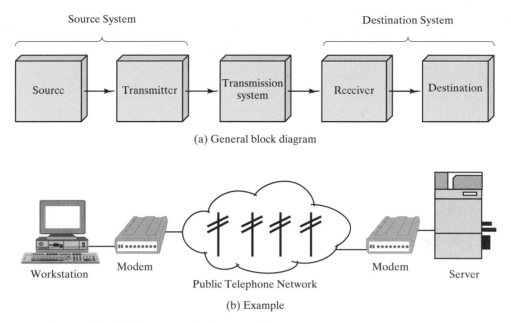

(a) General block diagram

(b) Example

**FIGURE 1.1** Simplified communications model.

- **Transmitter.** Usually, the data generated by a source system are not transmitted directly in the form in which they were generated. Rather, a transmitter transforms and encodes the information in such a way as to produce electromagnetic signals that can be transmitted across some sort of transmission system. For example, a modem takes a digital bit stream from an attached device such as a personal computer and transforms that bit stream into an analog signal that can be handled by the telephone network.
- **Transmission System.** This can be a single transmission line or a complex network connecting source and destination.
- **Receiver.** The receiver accepts the signal from the transmission system and converts it into a form that can be handled by the destination device. For example, a modem will accept an analog signal coming from a network or transmission line and convert it into a digital bit stream.
- **Destination.** Takes the incoming data from the receiver.

This simple narrative conceals a wealth of technical complexity. To get some idea of the scope of this complexity, Table 1.1 lists some of the key tasks that must be performed in a data communications system. The list is somewhat arbitrary: Elements could be added; items on the list could be merged; and some items represent several tasks that are performed at different "levels" of the system. However, the list as it stands is suggestive of the scope of this book.

**TABLE 1.1** Communications tasks.

| | |
|---|---|
| Transmission system utilization | Addressing |
| Interfacing | Routing |
| Signal generation | Recovery |
| Synchronization | Message formatting |
| Exchange management | Security |
| Error detection and correction | Network management |
| Flow control | |

The first item, **transmission system utilization**, refers to the need to make efficient use of transmission facilities that are typically shared among a number of communicating devices. Various techniques (referred to as multiplexing) are used to allocate the total capacity of a transmission medium among a number of users. Congestion control techniques may be required to assure that the system is not overwhelmed by excessive demand for transmission services.

In order to communicate, a device must **interface** with the transmission system. All the forms of communication discussed in this book depend, at bottom, on the use of electromagnetic signals propagated over a transmission medium. Thus, once an interface is established, **signal generation** is required for communication. The properties of the signal, such as form and intensity, must be such that they are (1) capable of being propagated through the transmission system, and (2) interpretable as data at the receiver.

Not only must the signals be generated to conform to the requirements of the transmission system and receiver, but there must be some form of **synchronization** between transmitter and receiver. The receiver must be able to determine when a signal begins to arrive and when it ends. It must also know the duration of each signal element.

Beyond the basic matter of deciding on the nature and timing of signals, there are a variety of requirements for communication between two parties that might be collected under the term **exchange management**. If data are to be exchanged in both directions over a period of time, the two parties must cooperate. For example, for two parties to engage in a telephone conversation, one party must dial the number of the other, causing signals to be generated that result in the ringing of the called phone. The called party completes a connection by lifting the receiver. For data processing devices, more will be needed than simply establishing a connection; certain conventions must be decided upon. These conventions may include whether both devices may transmit simultaneously or must take turns, the amount of data to be sent at one time, the format of the data, and what to do if certain contingencies, such as an error, arise.

The next two items might have been included under exchange management, but they are important enough to list separately. In all communications systems, there is a potential for error; transmitted signals are distorted to some extent before reaching their destination. **Error detection and correction** are required in circumstances where errors cannot be tolerated; this is usually the case with data processing systems. For example, in transferring a file from one computer to another, it is simply not acceptable for the contents of the file to be accidentally altered. **Flow control** is required to assure that the source does not overwhelm the destination by sending data faster than they can be processed and absorbed.

Next, we mention the related but distinct concepts of **addressing** and **routing**. When a transmission facility is shared by more than two devices, a source system must somehow indicate the identity of the intended destination. The transmission system must assure that the destination system, and only that system, receives the data. Further, the transmission system may itself be a network through which various paths may be taken. A specific route through this network must be chosen.

**Recovery** is a concept distinct from that of error correction. Recovery techniques are needed in situations in which an information exchange, such as a data base transaction or file transfer, is interrupted due to a fault somewhere in the system. The objective is either to be able to resume activity at the point of interruption or at least to restore the state of the systems involved to the condition prior to the beginning of the exchange.

**Message formatting** has to do with an agreement between two parties as to the form of the data to be exchanged or transmitted. For example, both sides must use the same binary code for characters.

Frequently, it is important to provide some measure of **security** in a data communications system. The sender of data may wish to be assured that only the intended party actually receives the data; and the receiver of data may wish to be assured that the received data have not been altered in transit and that the data have actually come from the purported sender.

Finally, a data communications facility is a complex system that cannot create or run itself. **Network management** capabilities are needed to configure the system, monitor its status, react to failures and overloads, and plan intelligently for future growth.

Thus we have gone from the simple idea of data communication between source and destination to a rather formidable list of data communications tasks. In this book, we further elaborate this list of tasks to describe and encompass the entire set of activities that can be classified under data and computer communications.

## 1.2  DATA COMMUNICATIONS

This book is organized into four parts. The first part deals with the most fundamental aspects of the communications function, focusing on the transmission of signals in a reliable and efficient manner. For want of a better name, we have given Part I the title "Data Communications," although that term arguably encompasses some or even all of the topics of Parts II, III, and IV.

To get some flavor for the focus of Part I, Figure 1.2 provides a new perspective on the communications model of Figure 1.1a. Let us trace through the details of this figure using electronic mail as an example.

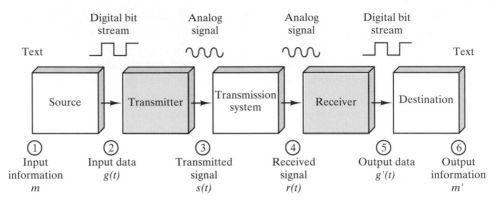

**FIGURE 1.2**    Simplified data communications model.

Consider that the input device and transmitter are components of a personal computer. The user of the PC wishes to send a message to another user—for example, "The meeting scheduled for March 25 is canceled" ($m$). The user activates the electronic mail package on the PC and enters the message via the keyboard (input device). The character string is briefly buffered in main memory. We can view it as a sequence of bits ($g$) in memory. The personal computer is connected to some transmission medium, such as a local network or a telephone line, by an I/O device (transmitter), such as a local network transceiver or a modem. The input data are transferred to the transmitter as a sequence of voltage shifts [$g(t)$] representing bits on some communications bus or cable. The transmitter is connected directly to the medium and converts the incoming stream [$g(t)$] into a signal [$s(t)$] suitable for transmission. Specific alternatives to this procedure will be described in Chapter 4.

The transmitted signal $s(t)$ presented to the medium is subject to a number of impairments, discussed in Chapter 2, before it reaches the receiver. Thus, the received signal $r(t)$ may differ to some degree from $s(t)$. The receiver will attempt to estimate the original $s(t)$, based on $r(t)$ and its knowledge of the medium, producing a sequence of bits $g'(t)$. These bits are sent to the output personal computer, where they are briefly buffered in memory as a block of bits ($g$). In many cases, the destination system will attempt to determine if an error has occurred and, if so, will cooperate with the source system to eventually obtain a complete, error-free block of data. These data are then presented to the user via an output device, such as a printer or a screen. The message ($m'$), as viewed by the user, will usually be an exact copy of the original message ($m$).

Now consider a telephone conversation. In this case, the input to the telephone is a message ($m$) in the form of sound waves. The sound waves are converted by the telephone into electrical signals of the same frequency. These signals are transmitted without modification over the telephone line. Hence, the input signal $g(t)$ and the transmitted signal $s(t)$ are identical. The signal $s(t)$ will suffer some distortion over the medium, so that $r(t)$ will not be identical to $s(t)$. Nevertheless, the signal $r(t)$ is converted back into a sound wave with no attempt at correction or improvement of signal quality. Thus $m'$ is not an exact replica of $m$. However, the received sound message is generally comprehensible to the listener.

The discussion so far does not touch on other key aspects of data communications, including data-link control techniques for controlling the flow of data and detecting and correcting errors, and multiplexing techniques for transmission efficiency. All of these topics are explored in Part I.

## 1.3  DATA COMMUNICATIONS NETWORKING

In its simplest form, data communication takes place between two devices that are directly connected by some form of point-to-point transmission medium. Often, however, it is impractical for two devices to be directly, point-to-point connected. This is so for one (or both) of the following contingencies:

- The devices are very far apart. It would be inordinately expensive, for example, to string a dedicated link between two devices thousands of miles apart.
- There is a set of devices, each of which may require a link to many of the others at various times. Examples are all of the telephones in the world and all of the terminals and computers owned by a single organization. Except for the case of a very few devices, it is impractical to provide a dedicated wire between each pair of devices.

The solution to this problem is to attach each device to a communications network. Figure 1.3 relates this area to the communications model of Figure 1.1a and also suggests the two major categories into which communications networks are traditionally classified: wide-area networks (WANs) and local-area networks (LANs). The distinction between the two, both in terms of technology and application, has become somewhat blurred in recent years, but it remains a useful way of organizing the discussion.

### Wide-Area Networks

Wide-area networks have been traditionally been considered to be those that cover a large geographical area, require the crossing of public right-of-ways, and rely at least in part on circuits provided by a common carrier. Typically, a WAN consists of a number of interconnected switching nodes. A transmission from any one device is routed through these internal nodes to the specified destination device. These nodes (including the boundary nodes) are not concerned with the content of the data; rather, their purpose is to provide a switching facility that will move the data from node to node until they reach their destination.

Traditionally, WANs have been implemented using one of two technologies: circuit switching and packet switching. More recently, frame relay and ATM networks have assumed major roles.

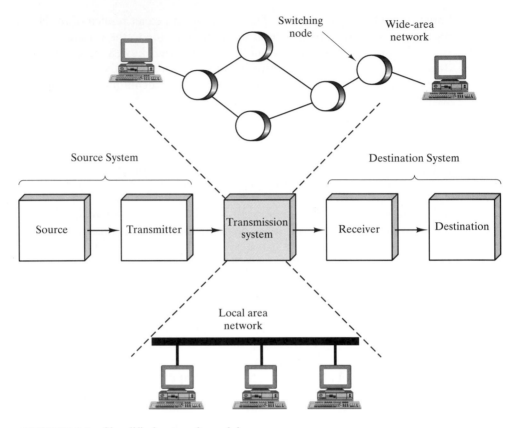

**FIGURE 1.3**  Simplified network models.

## Circuit Switching

In a circuit-switched network, a dedicated communications path is established between two stations through the nodes of the network. That path is a connected sequence of physical links between nodes. On each link, a logical channel is dedicated to the connection. Data generated by the source station are transmitted along the dedicated path as rapidly as possible. At each node, incoming data are routed or switched to the appropriate outgoing channel without delay. The most common example of circuit switching is the telephone network.

## Packet Switching

A quite different approach is used in a packet-switched network. In this case, it is not necessary to dedicate transmission capacity along a path through the network. Rather, data are sent out in a sequence of small chunks, called packets. Each packet is passed through the network from node to node along some path leading from source to destination. At each node, the entire packet is received, stored briefly, and then transmitted to the next node. Packet-switched networks are commonly used for terminal-to-computer and computer-to-computer communications.

### Frame Relay

Packet switching was developed at a time when digital long-distance transmission facilities exhibited a relatively high error rate compared to today's facilities. As a result, there is a considerable amount of overhead built into packet-switched schemes to compensate for errors. The overhead includes additional bits added to each packet to introduce redundancy and additional processing at the end stations and the intermediate switching nodes to detect and recover from errors.

With modern high-speed telecommunications systems, this overhead is unnecessary and counterproductive. It is unnecessary because the rate of errors has been dramatically lowered and any remaining errors can easily be caught in the end systems by logic that operates above the level of the packet-switching logic; it is counterproductive because the overhead involved soaks up a significant fraction of the high capacity provided by the network.

Frame relay was developed to take advantage of these high data rates and low error rates. Whereas the original packet-switching networks were designed with a data rate to the end user of about 64 kbps, frame relay networks are designed to operate efficiently at user data rates of up to 2 Mbps. The key to achieving these high data rates is to strip out most of the overhead involved with error control.

### ATM

Asynchronous transfer mode (ATM), sometimes referred to as cell relay, is a culmination of all of the developments in circuit switching and packet switching over the past 25 years.

ATM can be viewed as an evolution from frame relay. The most obvious difference between frame relay and ATM is that frame relay uses variable-length packets, called frames, and ATM uses fixed-length packets, called cells. As with frame relay, ATM provides little overhead for error control, depending on the inherent reliability of the transmission system and on higher layers of logic in the end systems to catch and correct errors. By using a fixed-packet length, the processing overhead is reduced even further for ATM compared to frame relay. The result is that ATM is designed to work in the range of 10s and 100s of Mbps, compared to the 2-Mbps target of frame relay.

ATM can also be viewed as an evolution from circuit switching. With circuit-switching, only fixed-data-rate circuits are available to the end system. ATM allows the definition of multiple virtual channels with data rates that are dynamically defined at the time the virtual channel is created. By using full, fixed-size cells, ATM is so efficient that it can offer a constant-data-rate channel even though it is using a packet-switching technique. Thus, ATM extends circuit switching to allow multiple channels with the data rate on each channel dynamically set on demand.

### ISDN and Broadband ISDN

Merging and evolving communications and computing technologies, coupled with increasing demands for efficient and timely collection, processing, and dissemination of information, are leading to the development of integrated systems that transmit and process all types of data. A significant outgrowth of these trends is the integrated services digital network (ISDN).

The ISDN is intended to be a worldwide public telecommunications network to replace existing public telecommunications networks and deliver a wide variety of services. The ISDN is defined by the standardization of user interfaces and implemented as a set of digital switches and paths supporting a broad range of traffic types and providing value-added processing services. In practice, there are multiple networks, implemented within national boundaries, but, from the user's point of view, there is intended to be a single, uniformly accessible, worldwide network.

Despite the fact that ISDN has yet to achieve the universal deployment hoped for, it is already in its second generation. The first generation, sometimes referred to as **narrowband ISDN**, is based on the use of a 64-kbps channel as the basic unit of switching and has a circuit-switching orientation. The major technical contribution of the narrowband ISDN effort has been frame relay. The second generation, referred to as **broadband ISDN**, supports very high data rates (100s of Mbps) and has a packet-switching orientation. The major technical contribution of the broadband ISDN effort has been asynchronous transfer mode (ATM), also known as cell relay.

## Local Area Networks

As with wide-area networks, a local-area network is a communications network that interconnects a variety of devices and provides a means for information exchange among those devices. There are several key distinctions between LANs and WANs:

1. The scope of the LAN is small, typically a single building or a cluster of buildings. This difference in geographic scope leads to different technical solutions, as we shall see.
2. It is usually the case that the LAN is owned by the same organization that owns the attached devices. For WANs, this is less often the case, or at least a significant fraction of the network assets are not owned. This has two implications. First, care must be taken in the choice of LAN, as there may be a substantial capital investment (compared to dial-up or leased charges for wide-area networks) for both purchase and maintenance. Second, the network management responsibility for a local network falls solely on the user.
3. The internal data rates of LANs are typically much greater than those of wide-area networks.

Traditionally, LANs make use of a broadcast network approach rather than a switching approach. With a broadcast communication network, there are no intermediate switching nodes. At each station, there is a transmitter/receiver that communicates over a medium shared by other stations. A transmission from any one station is broadcast to and received by all other stations. A simple example of this is a CB radio system, in which all users tuned to the same channel may communicate. We will be concerned with networks used to link computers, workstations, and other digital devices. In the latter case, data are usually transmitted in packets. Because the medium is shared, only one station at a time can transmit a packet.

More recently, examples of switched LANs have appeared. The two most prominent examples are ATM LANs, which simply use an ATM network in a local area, and Fibre Channel. We will examine these LANs, as well as the more common broadcast LANs, in Part III.

## 1.4 PROTOCOLS AND PROTOCOL ARCHITECTURE

When computers, terminals, and/or other data processing devices exchange data, the scope of concern is much broader than the concerns we have discussed in Sections 1.2 and 1.3. Consider, for example, the transfer of a file between two computers. There must be a data path between the two computers, either directly or via a communication network. But more is needed. Typical tasks to be performed are

1. The source system must either activate the direct data communication path or inform the communication network of the identity of the desired destination system.
2. The source system must ascertain that the destination system is prepared to receive data.
3. The file transfer application on the source system must ascertain that the file management program on the destination system is prepared to accept and store the file for this particular user.
4. If the file formats used on the two systems are incompatible, one or the other system must perform a format translation function.

It is clear that there must be a high degree of cooperation between the two computer systems. The exchange of information between computers for the purpose of cooperative action is generally referred to as *computer communications*. Similarly, when two or more computers are interconnected via a communication network, the set of computer stations is referred to as a *computer network*. Because a similar level of cooperation is required between a user at a terminal and one at a computer, these terms are often used when some of the communicating entities are terminals.

In discussing computer communications and computer networks, two concepts are paramount:

- Protocols
- Computer-communications architecture, or protocol architecture

A protocol is used for communication between entities in different systems. The terms "entity" and "system" are used in a very general sense. Examples of entities are user application programs, file transfer packages, data-base management systems, electronic mail facilities, and terminals. Examples of systems are computers, terminals, and remote sensors. Note that in some cases the entity and the system in which it resides are coextensive (e.g., terminals). In general, an entity is anything capable of sending or receiving information, and a system is a physically distinct object that contains one or more entities. For two entities to communicate successfully, they must "speak the same language." What is communicated, how it is communicated, and when it is communicated must conform to some mutually acceptable conventions between the entities involved. The conventions are referred to as a protocol, which may be defined as a set of rules governing the exchange of data between two entities. The key elements of a protocol are

- **Syntax.** Includes such things as data format and signal levels.
- **Semantics.** Includes control information for coordination and error handling.
- **Timing.** Includes speed matching and sequencing.

Having introduced the concept of a protocol, we can now introduce the concept of a protocol architecture. It is clear that there must be a high degree of cooperation between the two computers. Instead of implementing the logic for this as a single module, the task is broken up into subtasks, each of which is implemented separately. As an example, Figure 1.4 suggests the way in which a file transfer facility could be implemented. Three modules are used. Tasks 3 and 4 in the preceding list could be performed by a file transfer module. The two modules on the two systems exchange files and commands. However, rather than requiring the file transfer module to handle the details of actually transferring data and commands, the file transfer modules each rely on a communications service module. This module is responsible for making sure that the file transfer commands and data are reliably exchanged between systems. Among other things, this module would perform task 2. Now, the nature of the exchange between systems is independent of the nature of the network that interconnects them. Therefore, rather than building details of the network interface into the communications service module, it makes sense to have a third module, a network access module, that performs task 1 by interacting with the network.

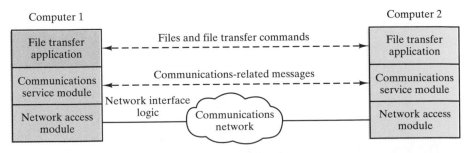

**FIGURE 1.4**  A simplified architecture for file transfer.

Let us try to summarize the motivation for the three modules in Figure 1.4. The file transfer module contains all of the logic that is unique to the file transfer application, such as transmitting passwords, file commands, and file records. There is a need to transmit these files and commands reliably. However, the same sorts of reliability requirements are relevant to a variety of applications (e.g., electronic mail, document transfer). Therefore, these requirements are met by a separate communications service module that can be used by a variety of applications. The communications service module is concerned with assuring that the two computer systems are active and ready for data transfer and for keeping track of the data that are being exchanged to assure delivery. However, these tasks are independent of the type of network that is being used. Therefore, the logic for actually dealing with the network is separated out into a separate network access module. That way, if the network to be used is changed, only the network access module is affected.

Thus, instead of a single module for performing communications, there is a structured set of modules that implements the communications function. That structure is referred to as a protocol architecture. In the remainder of this section, we generalize the preceding example to present a simplified protocol architecture. Following that, we look at more complex, real-world examples: TCP/IP and OSI.

## A Three-Layer Model

In very general terms, communications can be said to involve three agents: applications, computers, and networks. One example of an application is a file transfer operation. These applications execute on computers that can often support multiple simultaneous applications. Computers are connected to networks, and the data to be exchanged are transferred by the network from one computer to another. Thus, the transfer of data from one application to another involves first getting the data to the computer in which the application resides and then getting it to the intended application within the computer.

With these concepts in mind, it appears natural to organize the communication task into three relatively independent layers:

- Network access layer
- Transport layer
- Application layer

The **network access layer** is concerned with the exchange of data between a computer and the network to which it is attached. The sending computer must provide the network with the address of the destination computer, so that the network may route the data to the appropriate destination. The sending computer may wish to invoke certain services, such as priority, that might be provided by the network. The specific software used at this layer depends on the type of network to be used; different standards have been developed for circuit switching, packet switching, local area networks, and others. Thus, it makes sense to separate those functions having to do with network access into a separate layer. By doing this, the remainder of the communications software, above the network access layer, need not be concerned with the specifics of the network to be used. The same higher-layer software should function properly regardless of the particular network to which the computer is attached.

Regardless of the nature of the applications that are exchanging data, there is usually a requirement that data be exchanged reliably. That is, we would like to be assured that all of the data arrive at the destination application and that the data arrive in the same order in which they were sent. As we shall see, the mechanisms for providing reliability are essentially independent of the nature of the applications. Thus, it makes sense to collect those mechanisms in a common layer shared by all applications; this is referred to as the **transport layer**.

Finally, the **application layer** contains the logic needed to support the various user applications. For each different type of application, such as file transfer, a separate module is needed that is peculiar to that application.

Figures 1.5 and 1.6 illustrate this simple architecture. Figure 1.5 shows three computers connected to a network. Each computer contains software at the network access and transport layers and software at the application layer for one or more applications. For successful communication, every entity in the overall system must have a unique address. Actually, two levels of addressing are needed. Each computer on the network must have a unique network address; this allows the network to deliver data to the proper computer. Each application on a computer must have an address that is unique within that computer; this allows the transport layer to support multiple applications at each computer. These latter addresses are

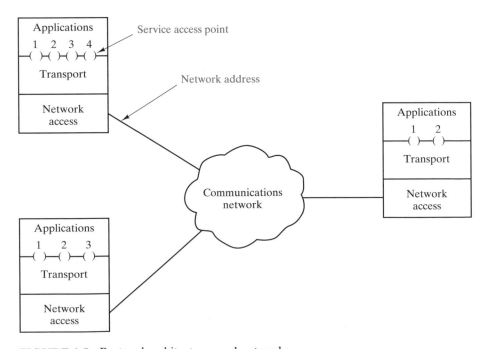

**FIGURE 1.5** Protocol architectures and networks.

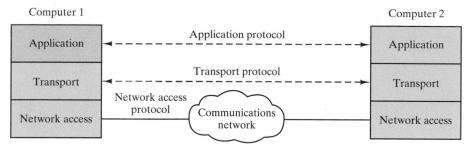

**FIGURE 1.6**   Protocols in a simplified architecture.

known as service access points (SAPs), connoting that each application is individually accessing the services of the transport layer.

Figure 1.6 indicates the way in which modules at the same level on different computers communicate with each other: by means of a protocol. A protocol is the set of rules or conventions governing the ways in which two entities cooperate to exchange data. A protocol specification details the control functions that may be performed, the formats and control codes used to communicate those functions, and the procedures that the two entities must follow.

Let us trace a simple operation. Suppose that an application, associated with SAP 1 at computer A, wishes to send a message to another application, associated with SAP 2 at computer B. The application at A hands the message over to its transport layer with instructions to send it to SAP 2 on computer B. The transport layer hands the message over to the network access layer, which instructs the network to send the message to computer B. Note that the network need not be told the identity of the destination service access point. All that it needs to know is that the data are intended for computer B.

To control this operation, control information, as well as user data, must be transmitted, as suggested in Figure 1.7. Let us say that the sending application generates a block of data and passes this to the transport layer. The transport layer may break this block into two smaller pieces to make it more manageable. To each of these pieces the transport layer appends a transport header, containing protocol control information. The combination of data from the next higher layer and control information is known as a protocol data unit (PDU); in this case, it is referred to as a transport protocol data unit. The header in each transport PDU contains control information to be used by the peer transport protocol at computer B. Examples of items that may be stored in this header include

- **Destination SAP.** When the destination transport layer receives the transport protocol data unit, it must know to whom the data are to be delivered.
- **Sequence number.** Because the transport protocol is sending a sequence of protocol data units, it numbers them sequentially so that if they arrive out of order, the destination transport entity may reorder them.

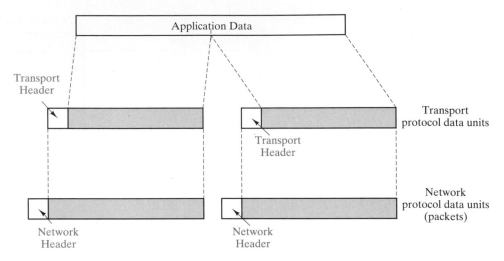

**FIGURE 1.7** Protocol data units.

- **Error-detection code.** The sending transport entity may include a code that is a function of the contents of the remainder of the PDU. The receiving transport protocol performs the same calculation and compares the result with the incoming code. A discrepancy results if there has been some error in transmission. In that case, the receiver can discard the PDU and take corrective action.

The next step is for the transport layer to hand each protocol data unit over to the network layer, with instructions to transmit it to the destination computer. To satisfy this request, the network access protocol must present the data to the network with a request for transmission. As before, this operation requires the use of control information. In this case, the network access protocol appends a network access header to the data it receives from the transport layer, creating a network-access PDU. Examples of the items that may be stored in the header include

- **Destination computer address.** The network must know to whom (which computer on the network) the data are to be delivered.
- **Facilities requests.** The network access protocol might want the network to make use of certain facilities, such as priority.

Figure 1.8 puts all of these concepts together, showing the interaction between modules to transfer one block of data. Let us say that the file transfer module in computer X is transferring a file one record at a time to computer Y. Each record is handed over to the transport layer module. We can picture this action as being in the form of a command or procedure call. The arguments of this procedure call include the destination computer address, the destination service access point, and

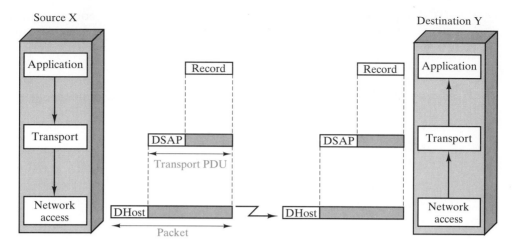

**FIGURE 1.8**   Operation of a protocol architecture.

the record. The transport layer appends the destination service access point and other control information to the record to create a transport PDU. This is then handed down to the network access layer by another procedure call. In this case, the arguments for the command are the destination computer address and the transport protocol data unit. The network access layer uses this information to construct a network PDU. The transport protocol data unit is the data field of the network PDU, and the network PDU header includes information concerning the source and destination computer addresses. Note that the transport header is not "visible" at the network access layer; the network access layer is not concerned with the contents of the transport PDU.

The network accepts the network PDU from X and delivers it to Y. The network access module in Y receives the PDU, strips off the header, and transfers the enclosed transport PDU to X's transport layer module. The transport layer examines the transport protocol data unit header and, on the basis of the SAP field in the header, delivers the enclosed record to the appropriate application, in this case the file transfer module in Y.

## The TCP/IP Protocol Architecture

Two protocol architectures have served as the basis for the development of interoperable communications standards: the TCP/IP protocol suite and the OSI reference model. TCP/IP is the most widely used interoperable architecture, and OSI has become the standard model for classifying communications functions. In the remainder of this section, we provide a brief overview of the two architectures; the topic is explored more fully in Chapter 15.

TCP/IP is a result of protocol research and development conducted on the experimental packet-switched network, ARPANET, funded by the Defense Advanced Research Projects Agency (DARPA), and is generally referred to as the

TCP/IP protocol suite. This protocol suite consists of a large collection of protocols that have been issued as Internet standards by the Internet Architecture Board (IAB).

There is no official TCP/IP protocol model as there is in the case of OSI. However, based on the protocol standards that have been developed, we can organize the communication task for TCP/IP into five relatively independent layers:

- Application layer
- Host-to-host, or transport layer
- Internet layer
- Network access layer
- Physical layer

The **physical layer** covers the physical interface between a data transmission device (e.g., workstation, computer) and a transmission medium or network. This layer is concerned with specifying the characteristics of the transmission medium, the nature of the signals, the data rate, and related matters.

The **network access layer** is concerned with the exchange of data between an end system and the network to which it is attached. The sending computer must provide the network with the address of the destination computer, so that the network may route the data to the appropriate destination. The sending computer may wish to invoke certain services, such as priority, that might be provided by the network. The specific software used at this layer depends on the type of network to be used; different standards have been developed for circuit-switching, packet-switching (e.g., X.25), local area networks (e.g., Ethernet), and others. Thus, it makes sense to separate those functions having to do with network access into a separate layer. By doing this, the remainder of the communications software, above the network access layer, need not be concerned about the specifics of the network to be used. The same higher-layer software should function properly regardless of the particular network to which the computer is attached.

The network access layer is concerned with access to and routing data across a network for two end systems attached to the same network. In those cases where two devices are attached to different networks, procedures are needed to allow data to traverse multiple interconnected networks. This is the function of the **internet layer**. The internet protocol (IP) is used at this layer to provide the routing function across multiple networks. This protocol is implemented not only in the end systems but also in routers. A router is a processor that connects two networks and whose primary function is to relay data from one network to the other on its route from the source to the destination end system.

Regardless of the nature of the applications that are exchanging data, there is usually a requirement that data be exchanged reliably. That is, we would like to be assured that all of the data arrive at the destination application and that the data arrive in the same order in which they were sent. As we shall see, the mechanisms for providing reliability are essentially independent of the nature of the applications. Thus, it makes sense to collect those mechanisms in a common layer shared by all applications; this is referred to as the **host-to-host layer**, or **transport layer**. The transmission control protocol (TCP) is the most commonly-used protocol to provide this functionality.

Finally, the **application layer** contains the logic needed to support the various user applications. For each different type of application, such as file transfer, a separate module is needed that is peculiar to that application.

Figure 1.9 shows how the TCP/IP protocols are implemented in end systems and relates this description to the communications model of Figure 1.1a. Note that the physical and network access layers provide interaction between the end system and the network, whereas the transport and application layers are what is known as end-to-end protocols; they support interaction between two end systems. The internet layer has the flavor of both. At this layer, the end system communicates routing information to the network but also must provide some common functions between the two end systems; these will be explored in Chapters 15 and 16.

## The OSI Model

The open systems interconnection (OSI) model was developed by the International Organization for Standardization (ISO) as a model for a computer communications architecture and as a framework for developing protocol standards. It consists of seven layers:

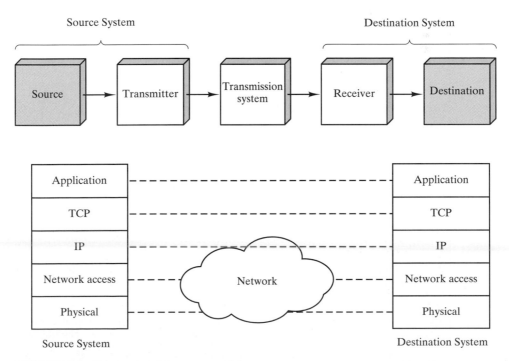

**FIGURE 1.9**  Protocol architecture model.

- Application
- Presentation
- Session
- Transport
- Network
- Data Link
- Physical

Figure 1.10 illustrates the OSI model and provides a brief definition of the functions performed at each layer. The intent of the OSI model is that protocols be developed to perform the functions of each layer.

The designers of OSI assumed that this model and the protocols developed within this model would come to dominate computer communications, eventually replacing proprietary protocol implementations and rival multivendor models such as TCP/IP. This has not happened. Although many useful protocols have been developed in the context of OSI, the overall seven-layer model has not flourished. Instead, it is the TCP/IP architecture that has come to dominate. Thus, our emphasis in this book will be on TCP/IP.

| **Application** |
| --- |
| Provides access to the OSI environment for users and also provides distributed information services. |
| **Presentation** |
| Provides independence to the application processes from differences in data representation (syntax). |
| **Session** |
| Provides the control structure for communication between applications; establishes, manages, and terminates connections (sessions) between cooperating applications. |
| **Transport** |
| Provides reliable, transparent transfer of data between end points; provides end-to-end error recovery and flow control. |
| **Network** |
| Provides upper layers with independence from the data transmission and switching technologies used to connect systems; responsible for establishing, maintaining, and terminating connections. |
| **Data Link** |
| Provides for the reliable transfer of information across the physical link; sends blocks of data (frames) with the necessary synchronization, error control, and flow control. |
| **Physical** |
| Concerned with transmission of unstructured bit stream over physical medium; deals with the mechanical, electrical, functional, and procedural characteristics to access the physical medium. |

**FIGURE 1.10** The OSI layers.

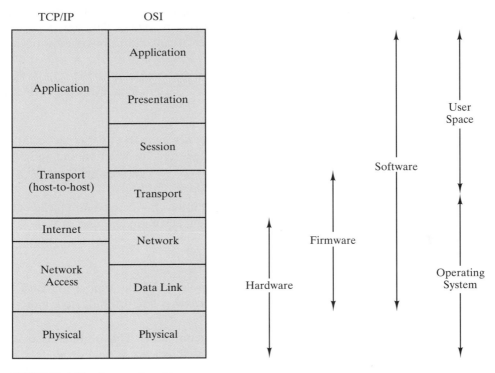

**FIGURE 1.11**   Protocol architectures.

Figure 1.11 illustrates the layers of the TCP/IP and OSI architectures, showing roughly the correspondence in functionality between the two. The figure also suggests common means of implementing the various layers.

## 1.5  STANDARDS

It has long been accepted in the communications industry that standards are required to govern the physical, electrical, and procedural characteristics of communication equipment. In the past, this view has not been embraced by the computer industry. Whereas communication-equipment vendors recognize that their equipment will generally interface to and communicate with other vendors' equipment, computer vendors have traditionally attempted to lock their customers into proprietary equipment; the proliferation of computers and distributed processing has made that an untenable position. Computers from different vendors must communicate with each other and, with the ongoing evolution of protocol standards, customers will no longer accept special-purpose protocol-conversion software development. The result is that standards now permeate all of the areas of technology discussed in this book.

Throughout the book we will describe the most important standards that are in use or that are being developed for various aspects of data and computer communications. Appendix 1A looks at the key organizations involved with the development of standards.

There are a number of advantages and disadvantages to the standards-making process. We list here the most striking ones. The principal advantages of standards are the following:

- A standard assures that there will be a large market for a particular piece of equipment or software. This encourages mass production and, in some cases, the use of large-scale-integration (LSI) or very-large-scale-integration (VLSI) techniques, resulting in lower costs.
- A standard allows products from multiple vendors to communicate, giving the purchaser more flexibility in equipment selection and use.

The principal disadvantages are these:

- A standard tends to freeze the technology. By the time a standard is developed, subjected to review and compromise, and promulgated, more efficient techniques are possible.
- There are multiple standards for the same thing. This is not a disadvantage of standards per se, but of the current way things are done. Fortunately, in recent years the various standards-making organizations have begun to cooperate more closely. Nevertheless, there are still areas where multiple conflicting standards exist.

## 1.6   OUTLINE OF THE BOOK

This chapter, of course, serves as an introduction to the entire book. A brief synopsis of the remaining chapters follows.

### Data Transmission

The principles of data transmission underlie all of the concepts and techniques presented in this book. To understand the need for encoding, multiplexing, switching, error control, and so on, the reader must understand the behavior of data signals propagated through a transmission medium. Chapter 2 provides an understanding of the distinction between digital and analog data and digital and analog transmission. Concepts of attenuation and noise are also examined.

### Transmission Media

Transmission media can be classified as either guided or wireless. The most commonly-used guided transmission media are twisted pair, coaxial cable, and optical fiber. Wireless techniques include terrestrial and satellite microwave, broadcast radio, and infrared. Chapter 3 covers all of these topics.

### Data Encoding

Data come in both analog (continuous) and digital (discrete) form. For transmission, input data must be encoded as an electrical signal that is tailored to the characteristics of the transmission medium. Both analog and digital data can be represented by either analog or digital signals; each of the four cases is discussed in Chapter 4. This chapter also covers spread-spectrum techniques.

### The Data Communications Interface

In Chapter 5 the emphasis shifts from data transmission to data communications. For two devices linked by a transmission medium to exchange digital data, a high degree of cooperation is required. Typically, data are transmitted one bit at a time over the medium. The timing (rate, duration, spacing) of these bits must be the same for transmitter and receiver. Two common communication techniques—asynchronous and synchronous—are explored. This chapter also looks at transmission line interfaces. Typically, digital data devices do not attach to and signal across a transmission medium directly. Rather, this process is mediated through a standardized interface.

### Data Link Control

True cooperative exchange of digital data between two devices requires some form of data link control. Chapter 6 examines the fundamental techniques common to all data link control protocols including flow control and error detection and correction, and then examines the most commonly used protocol, HDLC.

### Multiplexing

Transmission facilities are, by and large, expensive. It is often the case that two communication stations will not utilize the full capacity of a data link. For efficiency, it should be possible to share that capacity. The generic term for such sharing is multiplexing.

Chapter 7 concentrates on the three most common types of multiplexing techniques. The first, frequency-division multiplexing (FDM), is the most widespread and is familiar to anyone who has ever used a radio or television set. The second is a particular case of time-division multiplexing (TDM), often known as synchronous TDM. This is commonly used for multiplexing digitized voice streams. The third type is another form of TDM that is more complex but potentially more efficient than synchronous TDM; it is referred to as statistical or asynchronous TDM.

### Circuit Switching

Any treatment of the technology and architecture of circuit-switched networks must of necessity focus on the internal operation of a single switch. This is in contrast to packet-switched networks, which are best explained by the collective behavior of the set of switches that make up a network. Thus, Chapter 8 begins by examining digital-switching concepts, including space- and time-division switching. Then, the concepts of a multinode circuit-switched network are discussed; here, we are primarily concerned with the topics of routing and control signaling.

## Packet Switching

There are two main technical problems associated with a packet-switched network, and each is examined in Chapter 9:

- **Routing.** Because the source and destination stations are not directly connected, the network must route each packet, from node to node, through the network.
- **Congestion control.** The amount of traffic entering and transiting the network must be regulated for efficient, stable, and fair performance.

The key design issues in both of these areas are presented and analyzed; the discussion is supported by examples from specific networks. In addition, a key packet-switching interface standard, X.25, is described.

## Frame Relay

Chapter 10 examines the most important innovation to come out of the work on ISDN: frame relay. Frame relay provides a more efficient means of supporting packet switching than X.25 and is enjoying widespread use, not only in ISDN but in other networking contexts. This chapter looks at the data-transfer protocol and call-control protocol for frame relay and also looks at the related data link control protocol, LAPF.

A critical component for frame relay is congestion control. The chapter explains the nature of congestion in frame relay networks and both the importance and difficulty of controlling congestion. The chapter then describes a range of congestion control techniques that have been specified for use in frame relay networks.

## Asynchronous Transfer Mode (ATM)

Chapter 11 focuses on the transmission technology that is the foundation of broadband ISDN: asynchronous transfer mode (ATM). As with frame relay, ATM is finding widespread application beyond its use as part of broadband. This chapter begins with a description of the ATM protocol and format. Then the physical layer issues relating to the transmission of ATM cells and the ATM Adaptation Layer (AAL) are discussed.

Again, as with frame relay, congestion control is a vital component of ATM. This area, referred to as ATM traffic and congestion control, is one of the most complex aspects of ATM and is the subject of intensive ongoing research. This chapter surveys those techniques that have been accepted as having broad utility in

ATM environments.

## LAN Technology

The essential technology underlying all forms of local area networks comprises topology, transmission medium, and medium access control technique. Chapter 12 examines the first two of these elements. Four topologies are in common use: bus, tree, ring, star. The most common transmission media for local networking are twisted pair (unshielded and shielded), coaxial cable (baseband and broadband), and optical fiber. These topologies and transmission media are discussed, and the most promising combinations are described.

## LAN Systems

Chapter 13 looks in detail at the topologies, transmission media, and MAC protocols of the most important LAN systems in current use; all of these have been defined in standards documents. The discussion opens with what might be called traditional LANs, which typically operate at data rates of up to 10 Mbps and which have been in use for over a decade. These include Ethernet and related LANs and two token-passing schemes, token ring and FDDI (fiber distributed data interface). Then, more recent high-speed LAN systems are examined, including ATM LANs. Finally, the chapter looks at wireless LANs.

## Bridges

The increasing deployment of LANs has led to an increased need to interconnect LANs with each other and with wide-area networks. Chapter 14 focuses on a key device used in interconnection LANs: the bridges. Bridge operation involves two types of protocols: protocols for forwarding packets and protocols for exchanging routing information.

This chapter also returns to the topic of ATM LANs to look at the important concept of ATM LAN emulation, which relates to connecting other types of LANs to ATM networks.

## Protocols and Architecture

Chapter 15 introduces the subject of protocol architecture and motivates the need for a layered architecture with protocols defined at each layer. The concept of protocol is defined, and the important features of protocols are discussed.

The two most important communications architectures are introduced in this chapter. The open systems interconnection (OSI) model is described in some detail. Next, the TCP/IP model is examined. Although the OSI model is almost universally accepted as the framework for discourse in this area, it is the TCP/IP protocol suite that is the basis for most commercially available interoperable products.

### Internetworking

With the proliferation of networks, internetworking facilities have become essential components of network design. Chapter 16 begins with an examination of the requirements for an internetworking facility and the various design approaches that can be taken to satisfy those requirements. The remainder of the chapter explores the use of routers for internetworking. The internet protocol (IP) and the new IPv6, also known as IPng, are examined. Various routing protocols are also described, including the widely used OSPF and BGP.

### Transport Protocols

The transport protocol is the keystone of the whole concept of a computer communications architecture. It can also be one of the most complex of protocols. Chapter 17 examines in detail transport protocol mechanisms and then introduces two important examples: TCP and UDP.

### Network Security

Network security has become increasingly important with the growth in the number and importance of networks. Chapter 18 provides a survey of security techniques and services. The chapter begins with a look at encryption techniques for insuring privacy, which include the use of conventional and public-key encryption. Then, the area of authentication and digital signatures is explored. The two most important encryption algorithms, DES and RSA, are examined, as well as MD5, a one-way hash function important in a number of security applications.

### Distributed Applications

The purpose of a communications architecture is to support distributed applications. Chapter 19 examines three of the most important of these applications; in each case, general principles are discussed and are followed by a specific example. The applications discussed are network management, world-wide web (WWW) exchanges, and electronic mail. The corresponding examples are SNMPv2, HTTP, and SMTP/MIME. Before getting to these examples, the chapter opens with an examination of Abstract Syntax Notation One (ASN.1), which is the standardized language for defining distributed applications.

### ISDN and Broadband ISDN

The integrated-services digital network (ISDN) is a projected worldwide public telecommunications network that is designed to service a variety of user needs. Broadband ISDN is an enhancement of ISDN that can support very high data rates. Appendix A looks at the architecture, design principles, and standards for ISDN and broadband ISDN.

**1 A** **APPENDIX**

## STANDARDS ORGANIZATIONS

THROUGHOUT THIS BOOK, we describe the most important standards in use or being developed for various aspects of data and computer communications. Various organizations have been involved in the development or promotion of these standards. This appendix provides a brief description of the most important (in the current context) of these organizations:

- IETF
- ISO
- ITU-T

### Internet Standards and the IETF

Many of the protocols that make up the TCP/IP protocol suite have been standardized or are in the process of standardization. By universal agreement, an organization known as the Internet Architecture Board (IAB) is responsible for the development and publication of these standards, which are published in a series of documents called Requests for Comments (RFCs).

This section provides a brief description of the way in which standards for the TCP/IP protocol suite are developed.

#### The Internet and Internet Standards

The Internet is a large collection of interconnected networks, all of which use the TCP/IP protocol suite. The Internet began with the development of ARPANET and the subsequent support by the Defense Advanced Research Projects Agency (DARPA) for the development of additional networks to support military users and government contractors.

The IAB is the coordinating committee for Internet design, engineering, and management. Areas covered include the operation of the Internet itself and the standardization of protocols used by end systems on the Internet for interoperability. The IAB has two principle subsidiary task forces:

- Internet Engineering Task Force (IETF)
- Internet Research Task Force (IRTF)

The actual work of these task forces is carried out by working groups. Membership in a working group is voluntary; any interested party may participate.

It is the IETF that is responsible for publishing the RFCs. The RFCs are the working notes of the Internet research and development community. A document in this series may be on essentially any topic related to computer communications, and may be anything from a meeting report to the specification of a standard.

The final decision of which RFCs become Internet standards is made by the IAB, on the recommendation of the IETF. To become a standard, a specification must meet the following criteria:

- Be stable and well-understood
- Be technically competent
- Have multiple, independent, and interoperable implementations with operational experience

- Enjoy significant public support
- Be recognizably useful in some or all parts of the Internet

The key difference between these criteria and those used for international standards is the emphasis here on operational experience.

### The Standardization Process

Figure 1.12 shows the series of steps, called the *standards track*, that a specification goes through to become a standard. The steps involve increasing amounts of scrutiny and testing. At each step, the IETF must make a recommendation for advancement of the protocol, and the IAB must ratify it.

The white boxes in the diagram represent temporary states, which should be occupied for the minimum practical time. However, a document must remain a proposed standard for at least six months and a draft standard for at least four months to allow time for review and comment. The gray boxes represent long-term states that may be occupied for years.

A protocol or other specification that is not considered ready for standardization may be published as an experimental RFC. After further work, the specification may be resubmitted. If the specification is generally stable, has resolved known design choices, is believed to be well-understood, has received significant community review, and appears to enjoy enough community interest to be considered valuable, then the RFC will be designated a proposed standard.

For a specification to be advanced to draft-standard status, there must be at least two independent and interoperable implementations from which adequate operational experience has been obtained.

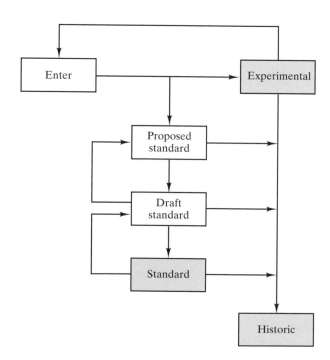

**FIGURE 1.12**   Standards track diagram.

After significant implementation and operational experience has been obtained, a specification may be elevated to standard. At this point, the specification is assigned an STD number as well as an RFC number.

Finally, when a protocol becomes obsolete, it is assigned to the historic state.

## The International Organization for Standardization (ISO)

ISO is an international agency for the development of standards on a wide range of subjects. It is a voluntary, nontreaty organization whose members are designated standards bodies of participating nations, plus nonvoting observer organizations. Although ISO is not a governmental body, more than 70 percent of ISO member bodies are governmental standards institutions or organizations incorporated by public law. Most of the remainder have close links with the public administrations in their own countries. The United States member body is the American National Standards Institute.

ISO was founded in 1946 and has issued more than 5000 standards in a broad range of areas. Its purpose is to promote the development of standardization and related activities to facilitate international exchange of goods and services and to develop cooperation in the sphere of intellectual, scientific, technological, and economic activity. Standards have been issued to cover everything from screw threads to solar energy. One important area of standardization deals with the open systems interconnection (OSI) communications architecture and the standards at each layer of the OSI architecture.

In the areas of interest in this book, ISO standards are actually developed in a joint effort with another standards body, the International Electrotechnical Commission (IEC). IEC is primarily concerned with electrical and electronic engineering standards. In the area of information technology, the interests of the two groups overlap, with IEC emphasizing hardware and ISO focusing on software. In 1987, the two groups formed the Joint Technical Committee 1 (JTC 1). This committee has the responsibility of developing the documents that ultimately become ISO (and IEC) standards in the area of information technology.

The development of an ISO standard from first proposal to actual publication of the standard follows a seven-step process. The objective is to ensure that the final result is acceptable to as many countries as possible. The steps are briefly described here. (Time limits are the minimum time in which voting could be accomplished, and amendments require extended time.)

1. A new work item is assigned to the appropriate technical committee, and within that technical committee, to the appropriate working group. The working group prepares the technical specifications for the proposed standard and publishes these as a draft proposal (DP). The DP is circulated among interested members for balloting and technical comment. At least three months are allowed, and there may be iterations. When there is substantial agreement, the DP is sent to the administrative arm of ISO, known as the Central Secretariat.

2. The DP is registered at the Central Secretariat within two months of its final approval by the technical committee.

3. The Central Secretariat edits the document to ensure conformity with ISO practices; no technical changes are made. The edited document is then issued as a draft international standard (DIS).

4. The DIS is circulated for a six-month balloting period. For approval, the DIS must receive a majority approval by the technical committee members and 75 percent approval of all voting members. Revisions may occur to resolve any negative vote. If more than two negative votes remain, it is unlikely that the DIS will be published as a final standard.

5. The approved, possibly revised, DIS is returned within three months to the Central Secretariat for submission to the ISO Council, which acts as the board of directors of ISO.

6. The DIS is accepted by the Council as an international standard (IS).
7. The IS is published by ISO.

As can be seen, the process of issuing a standard is a slow one. Certainly, it would be desirable to issue standards as quickly as the technical details can be worked out, but ISO must ensure that the standard will receive widespread support.

## ITU Telecommunications Standardization Sector

The ITU Telecommunications Standardization Sector (ITU-T) is a permanent organ of the International Telecommunication Union (ITU), which is itself a United Nations specialized agency. Hence, the members of ITU-T are governments. The U.S. representation is housed in the Department of State. The charter of the ITU is that it "is responsible for studying technical, operating, and tariff questions and issuing Recommendations on them with a view to standardizing telecommunications on a worldwide basis." Its primary objective is to standardize, to the extent necessary, techniques and operations in telecommunications to achieve end-to-end compatibility of international telecommunication connections, regardless of the countries of origin and destination.

The ITU-T was created on March 1, 1993, as one consequence of a reform process within the ITU. It replaces the International Telegraph and Telephone Consultative Committee (CCITT), which had essentially the same charter and objectives as the new ITU-T.

ITU-T is organized into 15 study groups that prepare Recommendations:

1. Service Description
2. Network Operation
3. Tariff and Accounting Principles
4. Network Maintenance
5. Protection Against Electromagnetic Environment Effects
6. Outside Plant
7. Data Network and Open Systems Communications
8. Terminal Equipment and Protocols for Telematic Services
9. Television and Sound Transmission
10. Languages for Telecommunication Applications
11. Switching and Signalling
12. End-to-End Transmission Performance
13. General Network Aspects
14. Modems and Transmission Techniques for Data, Telegraph, and Telematic Services
15. Transmission Systems and Equipment

Work within ITU-T is conducted in four-year cycles. Every four years, a World Telecommunications Standardization Conference is held. The work program for the next four years is established at the assembly in the form of questions submitted by the various study groups, based on requests made to the study groups by their members. The conference assesses the questions, reviews the scope of the study groups, creates new or abolishes existing study groups, and allocates questions to these groups.

Based on these questions, each study group prepares draft Recommendations. A draft Recommendation may be submitted to the next conference, four years hence, for approval. Increasingly, however, Recommendations are approved when they are ready, without having to wait for the end of the four-year Study Period. This accelerated procedure was adopted after the study period that ended in 1988. Thus, 1988 was the last time that a large batch of documents was published at one time as a set of Recommendations.

## 1B  APPENDIX

### INTERNET RESOURCES

THERE ARE A number of resources available on the Internet for keeping up with developments in this field.

### USENET Newsgroups

A number of USENET newsgroups are devoted to some aspect of data communications and networking. As with virtually all USENET groups, there is a high noise-to-signal ratio, but it is worth experimenting to see if any meet your needs. Here is a sample:

- comp.dcom.lans, comp.dcom.lans.misc: General discussions of LANs.
- comp.std.wireless: General discussion of wireless networks, including wireless LANs.
- comp.security.misc: Computer security and encryption.
- comp.dcom.cell-relay: Covers ATM and ATM LANs.
- comp.dcom.frame-relay: Covers frame-relay networks.
- comp.dcom.net-management: Discussion of network-management applications, protocols, and standards.
- comp.protocols.tcp-ip: The TCP/IP protocol suite.

### Web Sites for This Book

A special web page has been set up for this book at http://www.shore.net/~ws/DCC5e.html The site includes the following:

- Links to other web sites, including the sites listed in this book, provide a gateway to relevant resources on the web.
- Links to papers and reports available via the Internet provide additional, up-to-date material for study.
- We also hope to include links to home pages for courses based on the book; these pages may be useful to other instructors in providing ideas about how to structure the course.
- Additional problems, exercises, and other activities for classroom use are also planned.

As soon as any typos or other errors are discovered, an errata list for this book will be available at http://www.shore.net/~ws/welcome.html. The file will be updated as needed. Please email any errors that you spot to ws@shore.net. Errata sheets for other books are at the same web site, as well as discount ordering information for the books.

### Other Web Sites

There are numerous web sites that provide some sort of information related to the topics of this book. Here is a sample:

- http://www.soc.hawaii.edu/con/com-resources.html: Information and links to resources about data communications and networking.
- http://www.internic.net/ds/dspg01.html: Maintains archives that relate to the Internet and IETF activities. Includes keyword-indexed library of RFCs and draft documents as well as many other documents related to the Internet and related protocols.

- http://www.ronin.com/SBA: Links to over 1500 hardware and software vendors who currently have WWW sites, as well as a list of thousands of computer and networking companies in a Phone Directory.
- http://liinwww.ira.uka.de/bibliography/index.html: The Computer Science Bibliography Collection, a collection of hundreds of bibliographies with hundreds of thousands of references.

In subsequent chapters, pointers to more specific web sites can be found in the "Recommended Reading" section.

# PART ONE Data Communications

# CHAPTER 2

# DATA TRANSMISSION

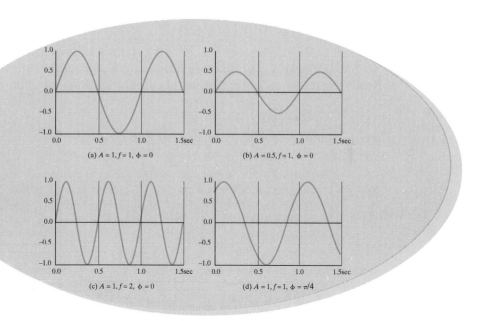

(a) $A = 1, f = 1, \phi = 0$

(b) $A = 0.5, f = 1, \phi = 0$

(c) $A = 1, f = 2, \phi = 0$

(d) $A = 1, f = 1, \phi = \pi/4$

Τhe successful transmission of data depends principally on two factors: the quality of the signal being transmitted and the characteristics of the transmission medium. The objective of this chapter and the next is to provide the reader with an intuitive feeling for the nature of these two factors.

The first section presents some concepts and terms from the field of electrical engineering; this should provide sufficient background for the remainder of the chapter. Section 2.2 clarifies the use of the terms *analog* and *digital*. Either analog or digital data may be transmitted using either analog or digital signals. Furthermore, it is common for intermediate processing to be performed between source and destination, and this processing has either an analog or digital character.

Section 2.3 looks at the various impairments that may introduce errors into the data during transmission. The chief impairments are attenuation, delay distortion, and the various forms of noise.

## 2.1 CONCEPTS AND TERMINOLOGY

In this section we introduce some concepts and terms that will be referred to throughout the rest of the chapter and, indeed, throughout Part I.

### Transmission Terminology

Data transmission occurs between transmitter and receiver over some transmission medium. Transmission media may be classified as guided or unguided. In both cases, communication is in the form of electromagnetic waves. With guided media, the waves are guided along a physical path; examples of guided media are twisted pair, coaxial cable, and optical fiber. Unguided media provide a means for transmitting electromagnetic waves but do not guide them; examples are propagation through air, vacuum, and sea water.

The term *direct link* is used to refer to the transmission path between two devices in which signals propagate directly from transmitter to receiver with no intermediate devices, other than amplifiers or repeaters used to increase signal strength. Both parts of Figure 2.1 depict a direct link. Note that this term can apply to both guided and unguided media.

A guided transmission medium is point-to-point if, first, it provides a direct link between two devices and, second, those are the only two devices sharing the medium (Figure 2.1a). In a multipoint guided configuration, more than two devices share the same medium (Figure 2.1b).

A transmission may be simplex, half-duplex, or full-duplex. In simplex transmission, signals are transmitted in only one direction; one station is the transmitter and the other is the receiver. In half-duplex operation, both stations may transmit, but only one at a time. In full-duplex operation, both stations may transmit simultaneously. In the latter case, the medium is carrying signals in both directions at the same time. How this can be is explained in due course.

We should note that the definitions just given are the ones in common use in the United States (ANSI definitions). In Europe (ITU-T definitions), the term

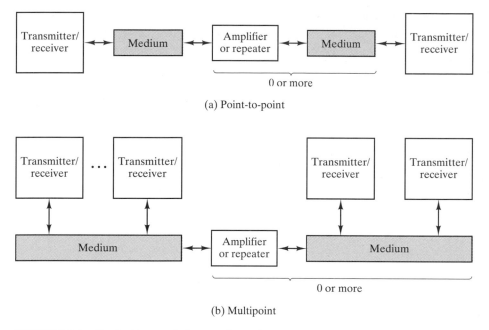

**FIGURE 2.1**  Guided transmission configurations.

"simplex" is used to correspond to half-duplex, as defined above, and "duplex" is used to correspond to full-duplex, as also defined above.

## Frequency, Spectrum, and Bandwidth

In this book, we are concerned with electromagnetic signals, used as a means to transmit data. At point 3 in Figure 1.2, a signal is generated by the transmitter and transmitted over a medium. The signal is a function of time, but it can also be expressed as a function of frequency; that is, the signal consists of components of different frequencies. It turns out that the *frequency-domain* view of a signal is far more important to an understanding of data transmission than a *time-domain* view. Both views are introduced here.

### Time-Domain Concepts

Viewed as a function of time, an electromagnetic signal can be either continuous or discrete. A continuous signal is one in which the signal intensity varies in a smooth fashion over time. In other words, there are no breaks or discontinuities in the signal.[1] A discrete signal is one in which the signal intensity maintains a constant level for some period of time and then changes to another constant level. Figure 2.2 shows examples of both kinds of signals. The continuous signal might represent speech, and the discrete signal might represent binary 1s and 0s.

The simplest sort of signal is a *periodic signal*, in which the same signal pattern repeats over time. Figure 2.3 shows an example of a periodic analog signal (sine

---

[1] A mathematical definition: A signal $s(t)$ is continuous if $\lim_{t \to a} s(t) = s(a)$ for all $a$.

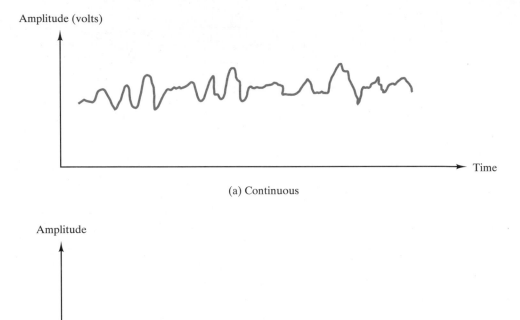

**(a) Continuous**

**(b) Discrete**

**FIGURE 2.2** Continuous and discrete signals.

wave) and a periodic digital signal (square wave). Mathematically, a signal $s(t)$ is defined to be periodic if and only if

$$s(t + T) = s(t) \qquad -\infty < t < +\infty$$

where the constant $T$ is the period of the signal. ($T$ is the smallest value that satisfies the equation.) Otherwise, a signal is aperiodic.

The sine wave is the fundamental continuous signal. A general sine wave can be represented by three parameters: amplitude ($A$), frequency ($f$), and phase ($\phi$). The *amplitude* is the peak value or strength of the signal over time; typically, this value is measured in volts or watts. The *frequency* is the rate (in cycles per second, or Hertz (Hz)) at which the signal repeats. An equivalent parameter is the *period* ($T$) of a signal, which is the amount of time it takes for one repetition; therefore, $T = 1/f$. *Phase* is a measure of the relative position in time within a single period of a signal, as illustrated below.

The general sine wave can be written

$$s(t) = A \sin(2\pi f t + \phi)$$

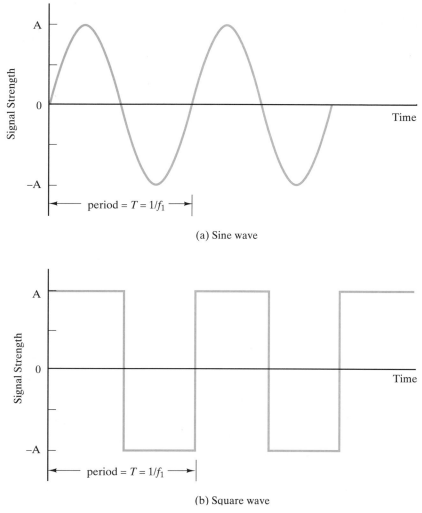

(a) Sine wave

(b) Square wave

**FIGURE 2.3** Example of periodic signals.

Figure 2.4 shows the effect of varying each of the three parameters. In part (a) of the figure, the frequency is 1 Hz; thus, the period is $T = 1$ second. Part (b) has the same frequency and phase but an amplitude of 1/2. In part (c), we have $f = 2$, which is equivalent to $T = 1/2$. Finally, part (d) shows the effect of a phase shift of $\pi/4$ radians, which is 45 degrees ($2\pi$ radians = 360° = 1 period).

In Figure 2.4, the horizontal axis is time; the graphs display the value of a signal at a given point in space as a function of time. These same graphs, with a change of scale, can apply with horizontal axes in space. In this case, the graphs display the value of a signal at a given point in time as a function of distance. For example, for a sinusoidal transmission (say an electromagnetic radio wave some distance from a radio antenna, or sound some distance from a loudspeaker), at a particular instant of time, the intensity of the signal varies in a sinusoidal way as a function of distance from the source.

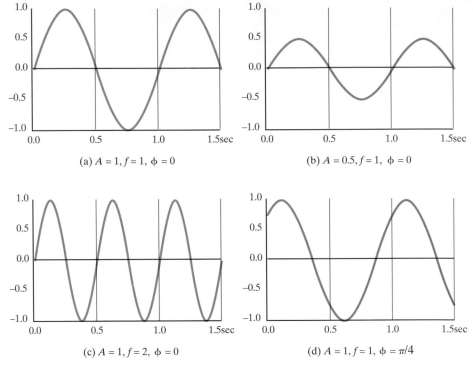

FIGURE 2.4  $A \sin (2\pi f t + \phi)$.

There are two simple relationships between the two sine waves, one in time and one in space. Define the *wavelength*, $\lambda$, of a signal as the distance occupied by a single cycle, or, put another way, as the distance between two points of corresponding phase of two consecutive cycles. Assume that the signal is traveling with a velocity $v$. Then the wavelength is related to the period as follows: $\lambda = vT$. Equivalently, $\lambda f = v$. Of particular relevance to this discussion is the case where $v = c$, the speed of light in free space, which is $3 \times 10^8$ m/s.

### Frequency Domain Concepts

In practice, an electromagnetic signal will be made up of many frequencies. For example, the signal

$$s(t) = \sin (2\pi f_1 t) + \frac{1}{3} \sin (2\pi(3f_1)t)$$

is shown in Figure 2.5. The components of this signal are just sine waves of frequencies $f_1$ and $3f_1$; parts a and b of the figure show these individual components. There are several interesting points that can be made about this figure:

- The second frequency is an integer multiple of the first frequency. When all of the frequency components of a signal are integer multiples of one fre-

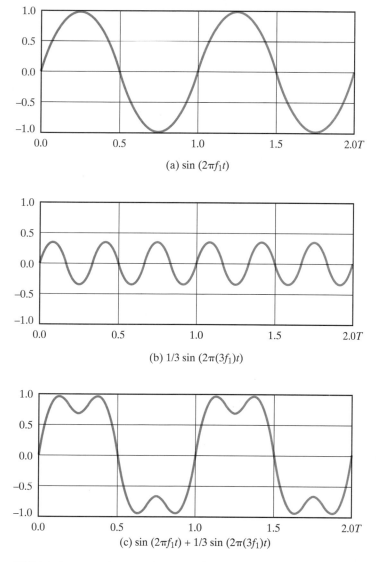

(a) $\sin (2\pi f_1 t)$

(b) $1/3 \sin (2\pi(3f_1)t)$

(c) $\sin (2\pi f_1 t) + 1/3 \sin (2\pi(3f_1)t)$

**FIGURE 2.5**   Addition of frequency components ($T = 1/f_1$).

quency, the latter frequency is referred to as the fundamental frequency.

- The period of the total signal is equal to the period of the fundamental frequency. The period of the component $\sin (2\pi f_1 t)$ is $T = 1/f_1$, and the period of $s(t)$ is also $T$, as can be seen from Figure 2.5c.

It can be shown, using a discipline known as Fourier analysis, that any signal is made up of components at various frequencies, in which each component is a sinusoid. This result is of tremendous importance, because the effects of various transmission media on a signal can be expressed in terms of frequencies, as is dis-

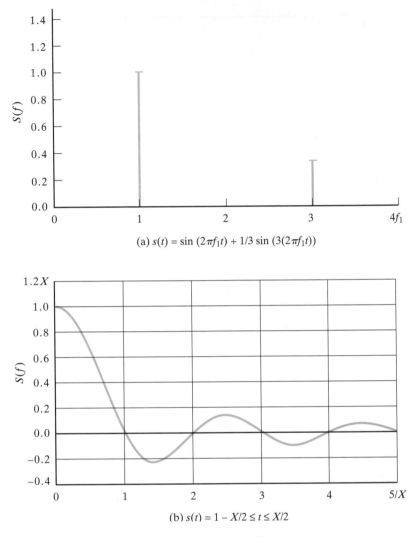

(a) $s(t) = \sin(2\pi f_1 t) + 1/3 \sin(3(2\pi f_1 t))$

(b) $s(t) = 1 - X/2 \le t \le X/2$

**FIGURE 2.6** Frequency-domain representations.

cussed later in this chapter. For the interested reader, the subject of Fourier analysis is introduced in Appendix 2A at the end of this chapter.

So, we can say that for each signal, there is a time-domain function $s(t)$ that specifies the amplitude of the signal at each instant in time. Similarly, there is a frequency-domain function $S(f)$ that specifies the constituent frequencies of the signal. Figure 2.6a shows the frequency-domain function for the signal in Figure 2.5c. Note that, in this case, $S(f)$ is discrete. Figure 2.6b shows the frequency domain function for a single square pulse that has the value 1 between $-X/2$ and $X/2$, and is 0 elsewhere. Note that in this case $S(f)$ is continuous, and that it has nonzero values indefinitely, although the magnitude of the frequency components becomes smaller for larger $f$. These characteristics are common for real signals.

The *spectrum* of a signal is the range of frequencies that it contains. For the signal in Figure 2.5c, the spectrum extends from $f_1$ to $3f_1$. The *absolute bandwidth* of

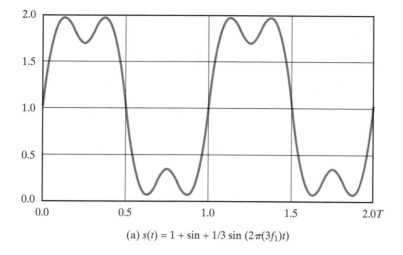

(a) $s(t) = 1 + \sin + 1/3 \sin (2\pi(3f_1)t)$

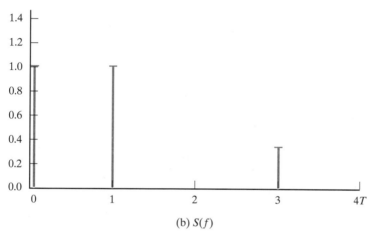

(b) $S(f)$

**FIGURE 2.7**   Signal with dc component.

a signal is the width of the spectrum. In the case of Figure 2.5c, the bandwidth is $2f_1$. Many signals, such as that of Figure 2.6b, have an infinite bandwidth. However, most of the energy in the signal is contained in a relatively narrow band of frequencies. This band is referred to as the *effective bandwidth*, or just *bandwidth*.

One final term to define is *dc component*. If a signal includes a component of zero frequency, that component is a direct current (dc) or constant component. For example, Figure 2.7 shows the result of adding a dc component to the signal of Figure 2.6. With no dc component, a signal has an average amplitude of zero, as seen in the time domain. With a dc component, it has a frequency term at $f = 0$ and a nonzero average amplitude.

### Relationship Between Data Rate and Bandwidth

The concept of effective bandwidth is a somewhat fuzzy one. We have said that it is the band within which most of the signal energy is confined. The term "most" in this context is somewhat arbitrary. The important issue here is that, although a given waveform may contain frequencies over a very broad range, as a practical matter any transmission medium that is used will be able to accommodate only a limited band of frequencies. This, in turn, limits the data rate that can be carried on the transmission medium.

To try to explain these relationships, consider the square wave of Figure 2.3b. Suppose that we let a positive pulse represent binary 1 and a negative pulse represent binary 0. Then, the waveform represents the binary stream 1010 . . . . The duration of each pulse is $1/2f_1$; thus, the data rate is $2f_1$ bits per second (bps). What are the frequency components of this signal? To answer this question, consider again Figure 2.5. By adding together sine waves at frequencies $f_1$ and $3f_1$, we get a waveform that resembles the square wave. Let us continue this process by adding a sine wave of frequency $5f_1$, as shown in Figure 2.8a, and then adding a sine wave of frequency $7f_1$, as shown in Figure 2.8b. As we add additional odd multiples of $f_1$, suitably scaled, the resulting waveform approaches more and more closely that of a square wave.

Indeed, it can be shown that the frequency components of the square wave can be expressed as follows:

$$s(t) = A \times \sum_{k \text{ odd}, k=1}^{\infty} \frac{1}{k} \sin(2\pi k f_1 t)$$

Thus, this waveform has an infinite number of frequency components and, hence, an infinite bandwidth. However, the amplitude of the $k$th frequency component, $kf_1$, is only $1/k$, so most of the energy in this waveform is in the first few frequency components. What happens if we limit the bandwidth to just the first three frequency components? We have already seen the answer, in Figure 2.8a. As we can see, the shape of the resulting waveform is reasonably close to that of the original square wave.

We can use Figures 2.5 and 2.8 to illustrate the relationship between data rate and bandwidth. Suppose that we are using a digital transmission system that is capable of transmitting signals with a bandwidth of 4 MHz. Let us attempt to transmit a sequence of alternating 1s and 0s as the square wave of Figure 2.8c. What data rate can be achieved? Let us approximate our square wave with the waveform of Figure 2.8a. Although this waveform is a "distorted" square wave, it is sufficiently close to the square wave that a receiver should be able to discriminate between a binary 0 and a binary 1. Now, if we let $f_1 = 10^6$ cycles/second = 1 MHz, then the bandwidth of the signal

$$s(t) = \sin((2\pi \times 10^6)t) + \frac{1}{3}\sin((2\pi \times 3 \times 10^6)t) + \frac{1}{5}\sin((2\pi \times 5 \times 10^6)t)$$

is $(5 \times 10^6) - 10^6 = 4$ MHz. Note that for $f_1 = 1$ MHz, the period of the fundamental frequency is $T = 1/10^6 = 10^{-6} = 1$ μsec. Thus, if we treat this waveform as a bit string of 1s and 0s, one bit occurs every 0.5 μsec, for a data rate of $2 \times 10^6 =$ 2 Mbps. Thus, for a bandwidth of 4 Mhz, a data rate of 2 Mbps is achieved.

Now suppose that we have a bandwidth of 8 MHz. Let us look again at Figure 2.8a, but now with $f_1 = 2$ MHz. Using the same line of reasoning as before,

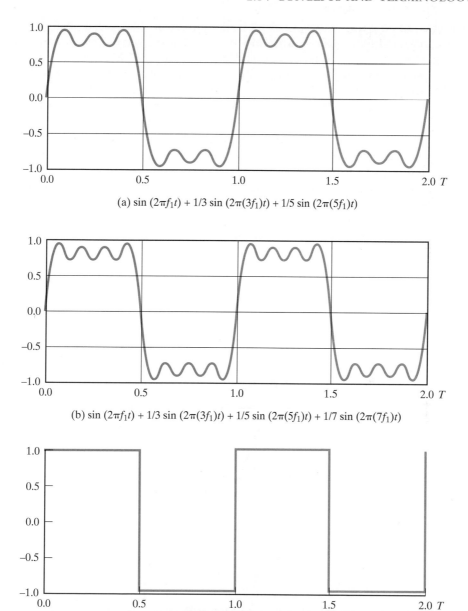

(a) $\sin (2\pi f_1 t) + 1/3 \sin (2\pi(3f_1)t) + 1/5 \sin (2\pi(5f_1)t)$

(b) $\sin (2\pi f_1 t) + 1/3 \sin (2\pi(3f_1)t) + 1/5 \sin (2\pi(5f_1)t) + 1/7 \sin (2\pi(7f_1)t)$

(c) $\Sigma \ 1/k \ \sin (2\pi k f_1 t)$

**FIGURE 2.8**   Frequency components of a square wave $(T = 1/f_1)$.

the bandwidth of the signal is $(5 \times 2 \times 10^6) - (2 \times 10^6) = 8$ MHz. But in this case $T = 1/f_1 = 0.5$ μsec. As a result, one bit occurs every 0.25 μsec for a data rate of 4 Mbps. Thus, other things being equal, by doubling the bandwidth, we double the potential data rate.

But now suppose that the waveform in Figure 2.5c is considered adequate for approximating a square wave. That is, the difference between a positive and negative pulse in Figure 2.5c is sufficiently distinct that the waveform can be successfully used to represent a sequence of 1s and 0s. Now, let $f_1 = 2$ MHz. Using the same line of reasoning as before, the bandwidth of the signal in Figure 2.5c is $(3 \times 2 \times 10^6) - (2 \times 10^6) = 4$ MHz. But, in this case, $T = 1/f_1 = 0.5$ μsec. As a result, one bit occurs every 0.25 μsec, for a data rate of 4 Mbps. Thus, a given bandwidth can support various data rates depending on the requirements of the receiver.

We can draw the following general conclusions from the above observations. In general, any digital waveform will have infinite bandwidth. If we attempt to transmit this waveform as a signal over any medium, the nature of the medium will limit the bandwidth that can be transmitted. Furthermore, for any given medium, the greater the bandwidth transmitted, the greater the cost. Thus, on the one hand, economic and practical reasons dictate that digital information be approximated by a signal of limited bandwidth. On the other hand, limiting the bandwidth creates

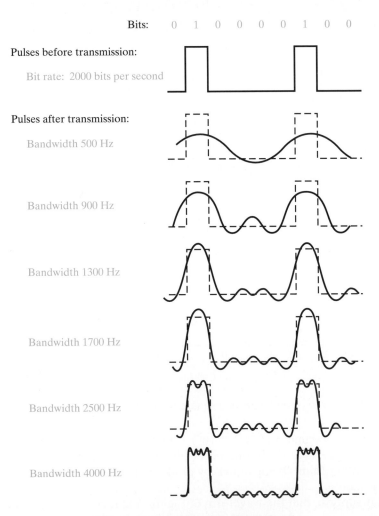

**FIGURE 2.9** Effect of bandwidth on a digital signal.

distortions, which makes the task of interpreting the received signal more difficult. The more limited the bandwidth, the greater the distortion, and the greater the potential for error by the receiver.

One more illustration should serve to reinforce these concepts. Figure 2.9 shows a digital bit stream with a data rate of 2000 bits per second. With a bandwidth of 1700 to 2500 Hz, the representation is quite good. Furthermore, we can generalize these results. If the data rate of the digital signal is $W$ bps, then a very good representation can be achieved with a bandwidth of $2W$ Hz; however, unless noise is very severe, the bit pattern can be recovered with less bandwidth than this.

Thus, there is a direct relationship between data rate and bandwidth: the higher the data rate of a signal, the greater is its effective bandwidth. Looked at the other way, the greater the bandwidth of a transmission system, the higher is the data rate that can be transmitted over that system.

Another observation worth making is this: If we think of the bandwidth of a signal as being centered about some frequency, referred to as the *center frequency*, then the higher the center frequency, the higher the potential bandwidth and therefore the higher the potential data rate. Consider that if a signal is centered at 2 MHz, its maximum bandwidth is 4 MHz.

We return to a discussion of the relationship between bandwidth and data rate later in this chapter, after a consideration of transmission impairments.

## 2.2 ANALOG AND DIGITAL DATA TRANSMISSION

In transmitting data from a source to a destination, one must be concerned with the nature of the data, the actual physical means used to propagate the data, and what processing or adjustments may be required along the way to assure that the received data are intelligible. For all of these considerations, the crucial question is whether we are dealing with analog or digital entities.

The terms *analog* and *digital* correspond, roughly, to *continuous* and *discrete*, respectively. These two terms are used frequently in data communications in at least three contexts:

- Data
- Signaling
- Transmission

We can define data as entities that convey meaning. Signals are electric or electromagnetic encoding of data. Signaling is the act of propagating the signal along a suitable medium. Finally, transmission is the communication of data by the propagation and processing of signals. In what follows, we try to make these abstract concepts clear by discussing the terms *analog* and *digital* in these three contexts.

### Data

The concepts of analog and digital data are simple enough. Analog data take on continuous values on some interval. For example, voice and video are continuously varying patterns of intensity. Most data collected by sensors, such as temperature

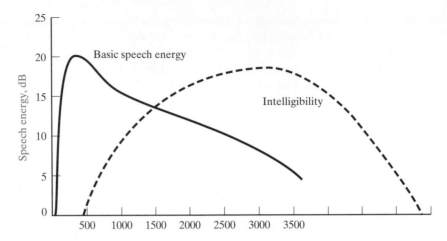

**FIGURE 2.10** Acoustic spectrum for speech. *Source: [FREE89]*

and pressure, are continuous-valued. Digital data take on discrete values; examples are text and integers.

The most familiar example of analog data is audio or acoustic data, which, in the form of sound waves, can be perceived directly by human beings. Figure 2.10 shows the acoustic spectrum for human speech. Frequency components of speech may be found between 20 Hz and 20 kHz. Although much of the energy in speech is concentrated at the lower frequencies, tests have shown that frequencies up to 600 to 700 Hz add very little to the intelligibility of speech to the human ear. The dashed line more accurately reflects the intelligibility or emotional content of speech.

Another common example of analog data is video. Here it is easier to characterize the data in terms of the viewer (destination) of the TV screen rather than the original scene (source) that is recorded by the TV camera. To produce a picture on the screen, an electron beam scans across the surface of the screen from left to right and top to bottom. For black-and-white television, the amount of illumination produced (on a scale from black to white) at any point is proportional to the intensity of the beam as it passes that point. Thus, at any instant in time, the beam takes on an analog value of intensity to produce the desired brightness at that point on the screen. Further, as the beam scans, the analog value changes. The video image, then, can be viewed as a time-varying analog signal.

Figure 2.11a depicts the scanning process. At the end of each scan line, the beam is swept rapidly back to the left (horizontal retrace). When the beam reaches the bottom, it is swept rapidly back to the top (vertical retrace). The beam is turned off (blanked out) during the retrace intervals.

To achieve adequate resolution, the beam produces a total of 483 horizontal lines at a rate of 30 complete scans of the screen per second. Tests have shown that this rate will produce a sensation of flicker rather than smooth motion. However, the flicker is eliminated by a process of interlacing, as depicted in Figure 2.11b. The electron beam scans across the screen starting at the far left, very near the top. The beam reaches the bottom at the middle after 241½ lines. At this point, the beam is

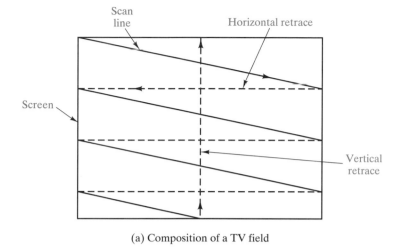

(a) Composition of a TV field

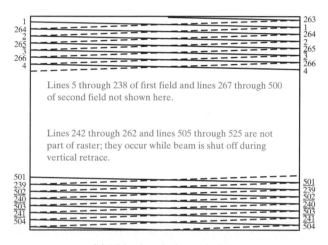

Lines 5 through 238 of first field and lines 267 through 500 of second field not shown here.

Lines 242 through 262 and lines 505 through 525 are not part of raster; they occur while beam is shut off during vertical retrace.

(b) Video interlacing technique

**FIGURE 2.11** TV picture production.

quickly repositioned at the top of the screen and, beginning in the middle, produces an additional 241½ lines interlaced with the original set. Thus, the screen is refreshed 60 times per second rather than 30, and flicker is avoided. Note that the total count of lines is 525. Of these, 42 are blanked out during the vertical retrace interval, leaving 483 actually visible on the screen.

A familiar example of digital data is text or character strings. While textual data are most convenient for human beings, they cannot, in character form, be easily stored or transmitted by data processing and communications systems. Such systems are designed for binary data. Thus, a number of codes have been devised by which characters are represented by a sequence of bits. Perhaps the earliest common example of this is the Morse code. Today, the most commonly used code in the United States is the ASCII (American Standard Code for Information Interchange) (Table 2.1) promulgated by ANSI. ASCII is also widely used outside the United

**TABLE 2.1**   The American Standard Code for Information Interchange (ASCII).

bit position

| b7 | b6 | b5 | b4 | b3 | b2 | b1 | 0 0 0 | 0 0 1 | 0 1 0 | 0 1 1 | 1 0 0 | 1 0 1 | 1 1 0 | 1 1 1 |
|----|----|----|----|----|----|----|-----|-----|-----|-----|-----|-----|-----|-----|
|    |    |    | 0  | 0  | 0  | 0  | NUL | DLE | SP  | 0   | @   | P   | '   | p   |
|    |    |    | 0  | 0  | 0  | 1  | SOH | DC1 | !   | 1   | A   | Q   | a   | q   |
|    |    |    | 0  | 0  | 1  | 0  | STX | DC2 | "   | 2   | B   | R   | b   | r   |
|    |    |    | 0  | 0  | 1  | 1  | ETX | DC3 | #   | 3   | C   | S   | c   | s   |
|    |    |    | 0  | 1  | 0  | 0  | EOT | DC4 | $   | 4   | D   | T   | d   | t   |
|    |    |    | 0  | 1  | 0  | 1  | ENQ | NAK | %   | 5   | E   | U   | e   | u   |
|    |    |    | 0  | 1  | 1  | 0  | ACK | SYN | &   | 6   | F   | V   | f   | v   |
|    |    |    | 0  | 1  | 1  | 1  | BEL | ETB | '   | 7   | G   | W   | g   | w   |
|    |    |    | 1  | 0  | 0  | 0  | BS  | CAN | (   | 8   | H   | X   | h   | x   |
|    |    |    | 1  | 0  | 0  | 1  | HT  | EM  | )   | 9   | I   | Y   | i   | y   |
|    |    |    | 1  | 0  | 1  | 0  | LF  | SUB | *   | :   | J   | Z   | j   | z   |
|    |    |    | 1  | 0  | 1  | 1  | VT  | ESC | +   | ;   | K   | [   | k   | {   |
|    |    |    | 1  | 1  | 0  | 0  | FF  | FS  | ,   | <   | L   | \   | l   | |   |
|    |    |    | 1  | 1  | 0  | 1  | CR  | GS  | –   | =   | M   | ]   | m   | }   |
|    |    |    | 1  | 1  | 1  | 0  | SO  | RS  | .   | >   | N   | ^   | n   | ~   |
|    |    |    | 1  | 1  | 1  | 1  | SI  | US  | /   | ?   | O   | _   | o   | DEL |

This is the U.S. national version of CCITT International Alphabet Number 5 (T.50). Control characters are explained in Table 2.

States. Each character in this code is represented by a unique 7-bit pattern; thus, 128 different characters can be represented. This is a larger number than is necessary, and some of the patterns represent "control" characters (Table 2.2). Some of these control characters have to do with controlling the printing of characters on a page. Others are concerned with communications procedures and will be discussed later. ASCII-encoded characters are almost always stored and transmitted using 8 bits per character (a block of 8 bits is referred to as an octet or a byte). The eighth bit is a parity bit used for error detection. This bit is set such that the total number of binary 1s in each octet is always odd (odd parity) or always even (even parity). Thus, a transmission error that changes a single bit can be detected.

## Signals

In a communications system, data are propagated from one point to another by means of electric signals. An analog signal is a continuously varying electromagnetic

**TABLE 2.2**   ASCII control characters. (*Continued on next page.*)

### Format control

**BS** (Backspace): Indicates movement of the printing mechanism or display cursor backward one position.

**HT** (Horizontal Tab): Indicates movement of the printing mechanism or display cursor forward to the next preassigned 'tab' or stopping position.

**LF** (Line Feed): Indicates movement of the printing mechanism or display cursor to the start of the next line.

**VT** (Vertical Tab): Indicates movement of the printing mechanism or display cursor to the next of a series preassigned printing lines.

**FF** (Form Feed): Indicates movement of the printing mechanism or display cursor to the starting position of the next page, form, or screen.

**CR** (Carriage Return): Indicates movement of the printing mechanism or display cursor to the starting position of the same line.

### Transmission control

**SOH** (Start of Heading): Used to indicate the start of a heading, which may contain address or routing information.

**STX** (Start of Text): Used to indicate the start of the text and so also indicates the end of the heading.

**ETX** (End of Text): Used to terminate the text that was started with STX.

**EOT** (End of Transmission): Indicates the end of a transmission, which may have included one or more 'texts' with their headings.

**ENQ** (Enquiry): A request for a response from a remote station. It may be used as a 'WHO ARE YOU' request for a station to identify itself.

**ACK** (Acknowledge): A character transmitted by a receiving device as an affirmation response to a sender. It is used as a positive response to polling messages.

**NAK** (Negative Acknowledgment): A character transmitted by a receiving device as a negative response to a sender. It is used as a negative response to polling messages.

**SYN** (Synchronous/Idle): Used by a synchronous transmission system to achieve synchronization. When no data are being sent, a synchronous transmission system may send SYN characters continuously.

**ETB** (End of Transmission Block): Indicates the end of a block of data for communication purposes. It is used for blocking data where the block structure is not necessarily related to the processing format.

### Information separator

**FS** (File Separator)
**GS** (Group Separator)
**RS** (Record Separator)
**US** (United Separator)

Information separators to be used in an optional manner except that their hierarchy shall be FS (the most inclusive) to US (the least inclusive).

---

wave that may be propagated over a variety of media, depending on spectrum; examples are wire media, such as twisted pair and coaxial cable, fiber optic cable, and atmosphere or space propagation. A digital signal is a sequence of voltage pulses that may be transmitted over a wire medium; for example, a constant positive voltage level may represent binary 1, and a constant negative voltage level may represent binary 0.

In what follows, we look first at some specific examples of signal types and then discuss the relationship between data and signals.

## Examples

Let us return to our three examples of the preceding subsection. For each example, we will describe the signal and estimate its bandwidth.

**TABLE 2.2** (*Continued*).

### Miscellaneous

**NUL** (Null): No character. Used for filling in time or filling space on tape when there are no data.

**BEL** (Bell): Used when there is need to call human attention. It may control alarm or attention devices.

**SO** (Shift Out): Indicates that the code combinations that follow shall be interpreted as outside of the standard character set until an SI character is reached.

**SI** (Shift In): Indicates that the code combinations that follow shall be interpreted according to the standard character set.

**DEL** (Delete): Used to obliterate unwanted characters, for example, by overwriting.

**SP** (Space): A nonprinting character used to separate words, or to move the printing mechanism or display cursor forward by one position.

**DLE** (Data Link Escape): A character that shall change the meaning of one or more contiguously following characters. It can provide supplementary controls or permit the sending of data characters having any bit combination.

**DC1, DC2, DC3, DC4** (Device Controls): Characters for the control of ancillary devices or special terminal features.

**CAN** (Cancel): Indicates that the data that precede it in a message or block should be disregarded (usually because an error has been detected).

**EM** (End of Medium): Indicates the physical end of a tape or other medium, or the end of the required or used portion of the medium.

**SUB** (Substitute): Substituted for a character that is found to be erroneous or invalid.

**ESC** (Escape): A character intended to provide code extension in that it gives a specified number of continuously following characters an alternate meaning.

In the case of acoustic data (voice), the data can be represented directly by an electromagnetic signal occupying the same spectrum. However, there is a need to compromise between the fidelity of the sound, as transmitted electrically, and the cost of transmission, which increases with increasing bandwidth. Although, as mentioned, the spectrum of speech is approximately 20 Hz to 20 kHz, a much narrower bandwidth will produce acceptable voice reproduction. The standard spectrum for a voice signal is 300 to 3400 Hz. This is adequate for voice reproduction, it minimizes required transmission capacity, and it allows for the use of rather inexpensive telephone sets. Thus, the telephone transmitter converts the incoming acoustic voice signal into an electromagnetic signal over the range 300 to 3400 Hz. This signal is then transmitted through the telephone system to a receiver, which reproduces an acoustic signal from the incoming electromagnetic signal.

Now, let us look at the video signal, which, interestingly, consists of both analog and digital components. To produce a video signal, a TV camera, which performs similar functions to the TV receiver, is used. One component of the camera is a photosensitive plate, upon which a scene is optically focused. An electron beam sweeps across the plate from left to right and top to bottom, in the same fashion as depicted in Figure 2.11 for the receiver. As the beam sweeps, an analog electric signal is developed proportional to the brightness of the scene at a particular spot.

Now we are in a position to describe the video signal. Figure 2.12a shows three lines of a video signal; in this diagram, white is represented by a small positive voltage, and black by a much larger positive voltage. So, for example, line 3 is at a medium gray level most of the way across with a blacker portion in the middle. Once the beam has completed a scan from left to right, it must retrace to the left

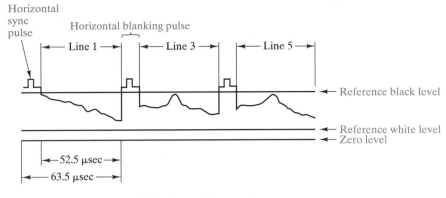

(a) Horizontal lines of video

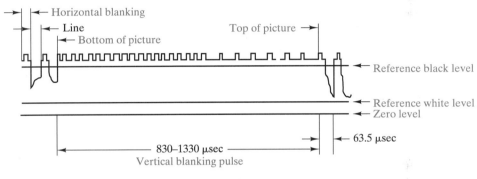

(b) Vertical blanking signal

**FIGURE 2.12**  Video signal (different scales for a and b).

edge to scan the next line. During this period, the picture should be blanked out (on both camera and receiver). This is done with a digital "horizontal blanking pulse." Also, to maintain transmitter-receiver synchronization, a synchronization (sync) pulse is sent between every line of video signal. This horizontal sync pulse rides on top of the blanking pulse, creating a staircase-shaped digital signal between adjacent analog video signals. Finally, when the beam reaches the bottom of the screen, it must return to the top, with a somewhat longer blanking interval required. This is shown in Figure 2.12b. The vertical blanking pulse is actually a series of synchronization and blanking pulses, whose details need not concern us here.

Next, consider the timing of the system. We mentioned that a total of 483 lines are scanned at a rate of 30 complete scans per second. This is an approximate number taking into account the time lost during the vertical retrace interval. The actual U.S. standard is 525 lines, but of these about 42 are lost during vertical retrace. Thus, the horizontal scanning frequency is $\dfrac{525 \text{ lines}}{1/30 \text{ s/scan}} = 15{,}750$ lines per second, or 63.5 μs/line. Of this 63.5 μs, about 11 μs are allowed for horizontal retrace, leaving a total of 52.5 μs per video line.

Finally, we are in a position to estimate the bandwidth required for the video signal. To do this, we must estimate the upper (maximum) and lower (minimum) frequency of the band. We use the following reasoning to arrive at the maximum frequency: The maximum frequency would occur during the horizontal scan if the scene were alternating between black and white as rapidly as possible. We can estimate this maximum value by considering the resolution of the video image. In the vertical dimension, there are 483 lines, so the maximum vertical resolution would be 483. Experiments have shown that the actual subjective resolution is about 70 percent of that number, or about 338 lines. In the interest of a balanced picture, the horizontal and vertical resolutions should be about the same. Because the ratio of width to height of a TV screen is 4:3, the horizontal resolution should be about $4/3 \times 338 = 450$ lines. As a worst case, a scanning line would be made up of 450 elements alternating black and white. The scan would result in a wave, with each cycle of the wave consisting of one higher (black) and one lower (white) voltage level. Thus, there would be $450/2 = 225$ cycles of the wave in 52.5 μs, for a maximum frequency of about 4 MHz. This rough reasoning, in fact, is fairly accurate. The maximum frequency, then, is 4 MHz. The lower limit will be a dc or zero frequency, where the dc component corresponds to the average illumination of the scene (the average value by which the signal exceeds the reference white level). Thus, the bandwidth of the video signal is approximately 4 MHz − 0 = 4 MHz.

The foregoing discussion did not consider color or audio components of the signal. It turns out that, with these included, the bandwidth remains about 4 MHz.

Finally, the third example described above is the general case of binary digital data. A commonly used signal for such data uses two constant (dc) voltage levels, one level for binary 1 and one level for binary 0. (In Chapter 3, we shall see that this is but one alternative, referred to as NRZ.) Again, we are interested in the bandwidth of such a signal. This will depend, in any specific case, on the exact shape of the waveform and on the sequence of 1s and 0s. We can obtain some understanding by considering Figure 2.9 (compare Figure 2.8). As can be seen, the greater the bandwidth of the signal, the more faithfully it approximates a digital pulse stream.

### Data and Signals

In the foregoing discussion, we have looked at analog signals used to represent analog data and digital signals used to represent digital data. Generally, analog data are a function of time and occupy a limited frequency spectrum; such data can be represented by an electromagnetic signal occupying the same spectrum. Digital data can be represented by digital signals, with a different voltage level for each of the two binary digits.

As Figure 2.13 illustrates, these are not the only possibilities. Digital data can also be represented by analog signals by use of a modem (modulator/demodulator). The modem converts a series of binary (two-valued) voltage pulses into an analog signal by encoding the digital data onto a carrier frequency. The resulting signal occupies a certain spectrum of frequency centered about the carrier and may be propagated across a medium suitable for that carrier. The most common modems represent digital data in the voice spectrum and, hence, allow those data to be prop-

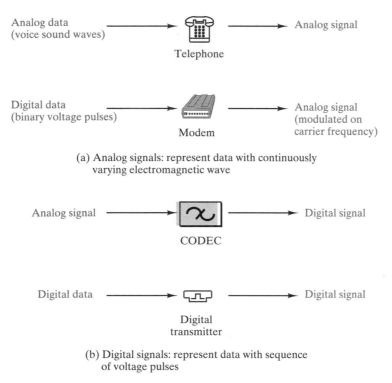

**FIGURE 2.13** Analog and digital signaling of analog and digital data.

agated over ordinary voice-grade telephone lines. At the other end of the line, the modem demodulates the signal to recover the original data.

In an operation very similar to that performed by a modem, analog data can be represented by digital signals. The device that performs this function for voice data is a codec (coder-decoder). In essence, the codec takes an analog signal that directly represents the voice data and approximates that signal by a bit stream. At the receiving end, the bit stream is used to reconstruct the analog data.

Thus, Figure 2.13 suggests that data may be encoded into signals in a variety of ways. We will return to this topic in Chapter 4.

## Transmission

A final distinction remains to be made. Both analog and digital signals may be transmitted on suitable transmission media. The way these signals are treated is a function of the transmission system. Table 2.3 summarizes the methods of data transmission. Analog transmission is a means of transmitting analog signals without regard to their content; the signals may represent analog data (e.g., voice) or digital data (e.g., binary data that pass through a modem). In either case, the analog signal will become weaker (attenuated) after a certain distance. To achieve longer distances, the analog transmission system includes amplifiers that boost the energy in the signal. Unfortunately, the amplifier also boosts the noise components. With

**TABLE 2.3**   Analog and digital transmission.

|  | **Analog signal** | **Digital signal** |
|---|---|---|
| **Analog data** | Two alternatives: (1) signal occupies the same spectrum as the analog data; (2) analog data are encoded to occupy a different portion of spectrum. | Analog data are encoded using a codec to produce a digital bit stream. |
| **Digital data** | Digital data are encoded using a modem to produce analog signal. | Two alternatives: (1) signal consists of two voltage levels to represent the two binary values; (2) digital data are encoded to produce a digital signal with desired properties. |

(a) Data and signals

|  | **Analog transmission** | **Digital transmission** |
|---|---|---|
| **Analog signal** | Is propagated through amplifiers; same treatment whether signal is used to represent analog data or digital data. | Assumes that the analog signal represents digital data. Signal is propagated through repeaters; at each repeater, digital data are recovered from inbound signal and used to generate a new analog outbound signal. |
| **Digital signal** | Not used | Digital signal represents a stream of 1s and 0s, which may represent digital data or may be an encoding of analog data. Signal is propagated through repeaters; at each repeater, stream of 1s and 0s is recovered from inbound signal and used to generate a new digital outbound signal. |

(b) Treatment of signals

amplifiers cascaded to achieve long distances, the signal becomes more and more distorted. For analog data, such as voice, quite a bit of distortion can be tolerated and the data remain intelligible. However, for digital data, cascaded amplifiers will introduce errors.

Digital transmission, in contrast, is concerned with the content of the signal. A digital signal can be transmitted only a limited distance before attenuation endangers the integrity of the data. To achieve greater distances, repeaters are used. A repeater receives the digital signal, recovers the pattern of 1s and 0s, and retransmits a new signal, thereby overcoming the attenuation.

The same technique may be used with an analog signal if it is assumed that the signal carries digital data. At appropriately spaced points, the transmission system has repeaters rather than amplifiers. The repeater recovers the digital data from the analog signal and generates a new, clean analog signal. Thus, noise is not cumulative.

The question naturally arises as to which is the preferred method of transmission; the answer being supplied by the telecommunications industry and its customers is digital, this despite an enormous investment in analog communications facilities. Both long-haul telecommunications facilities and intrabuilding services are gradually being converted to digital transmission and, where possible, digital signaling techniques. The most important reasons are

- **Digital technology.** The advent of large-scale integration (LSI) and very large-scale integration (VLSI) technology has caused a continuing drop in the cost and size of digital circuitry. Analog equipment has not shown a similar drop.
- **Data integrity.** With the use of repeaters rather than amplifiers, the effects of noise and other signal impairments are not cumulative. It is possible, then, to transmit data longer distances and over lesser quality lines by digital means while maintaining the integrity of the data. This is explored in Section 2.3.
- **Capacity utilization.** It has become economical to build transmission links of very high bandwidth, including satellite channels and connections involving optical fiber. A high degree of multiplexing is needed to effectively utilize such capacity, and this is more easily and cheaply achieved with digital (time-division) rather than analog (frequency-division) techniques. This is explored in Chapter 7.
- **Security and privacy.** Encryption techniques can be readily applied to digital data and to analog data that have been digitized.
- **Integration.** By treating both analog and digital data digitally, all signals have the same form and can be treated similarly. Thus, economies of scale and convenience can be achieved by integrating voice, video, and digital data.

## 2.3  TRANSMISSION IMPAIRMENTS

With any communications system, it must be recognized that the received signal will differ from the transmitted signal due to various transmission impairments. For analog signals, these impairments introduce various random modifications that degrade the signal quality. For digital signals, bit errors are introduced: A binary 1 is transformed into a binary 0 and vice versa. In this section, we examine the various impairments and comment on their effect on the information-carrying capacity of a communication link; the next chapter looks at measures to compensate for these impairments.

The most significant impairments are

- Attenuation and attenuation distortion
- Delay distortion
- Noise

## Attenuation

The strength of a signal falls off with distance over any transmission medium. For guided media, this reduction in strength, or attenuation, is generally logarithmic and is thus typically expressed as a constant number of decibels per unit distance. For unguided media, attenuation is a more complex function of distance and of the makeup of the atmosphere. Attenuation introduces three considerations for the transmission engineer. First, a received signal must have sufficient strength so that the electronic circuitry in the receiver can detect and interpret the signal. Second, the signal must maintain a level sufficiently higher than noise to be received without error. Third, attenuation is an increasing function of frequency.

The first and second problems are dealt with by attention to signal strength and by the use of amplifiers or repeaters. For a point-to-point link, the signal strength of the transmitter must be strong enough to be received intelligibly, but not so strong as to overload the circuitry of the transmitter, which would cause a distorted signal to be generated. Beyond a certain distance, the attenuation is unacceptably great, and repeaters or amplifiers are used to boost the signal from time to time. These problems are more complex for multipoint lines where the distance from transmitter to receiver is variable.

The third problem is particularly noticeable for analog signals. Because the attenuation varies as a function of frequency, the received signal is distorted, reducing intelligibility. To overcome this problem, techniques are available for equalizing attenuation across a band of frequencies. This is commonly done for voice-grade telephone lines by using loading coils that change the electrical properties of the line; the result is to smooth out attenuation effects. Another approach is to use amplifiers that amplify high frequencies more than lower frequencies.

An example is shown in Figure 2.14a, which shows attenuation as a function of frequency for a typical leased line. In the figure, attenuation is measured relative to the attenuation at 1000 Hz. Positive values on the y axis represent attenuation greater than that at 1000 Hz. A 1000-Hz tone of a given power level is applied to the input, and the power, $P_{1000}$, is measured at the output. For any other frequency $f$, the procedure is repeated and the relative attenuation in decibels is

$$N_f = -10 \log_{10} \frac{P_f}{P_{1000}}$$

The solid line in Figure 2.14a shows attenuation without equalization. As can be seen, frequency components at the upper end of the voice band are attenuated much more than those at lower frequencies. It should be clear that this will result in a distortion of the received speech signal. The dashed line shows the effect of equalization. The flattened response curve improves the quality of voice signals. It also allows higher data rates to be used for digital data that are passed through a modem.

Attenuation distortion is much less of a problem with digital signals. As we have seen, the strength of a digital signal falls off rapidly with frequency (Figure 2.6b); most of the content is concentrated near the fundamental frequency, or bit rate, of the signal.

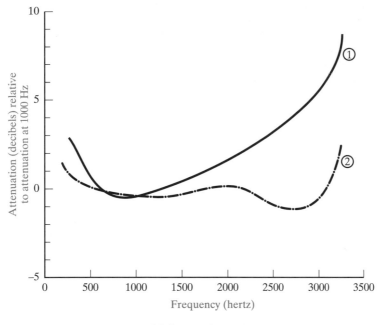

(a) Attenuation

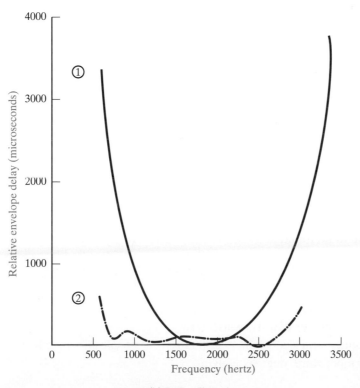

(b) Delay distortion

**FIGURE 2.14**
Attenuation and delay distortion curves for a voice channel.

## Delay Distortion

Delay distortion is a phenomenon peculiar to guided transmission media. The distortion is caused by the fact that the velocity of propagation of a signal through a guided medium varies with frequency. For a bandlimited signal, the velocity tends to be highest near the center frequency and lower toward the two edges of the band. Thus, various frequency components of a signal will arrive at the receiver at different times.

This effect is referred to as delay distortion, as the received signal is distorted due to variable delay in its components. Delay distortion is particularly critical for digital data. Consider that a sequence of bits is being transmitted, using either analog or digital signals. Because of delay distortion, some of the signal components of one bit position will spill over into other bit positions, causing intersymbol interference, which is a major limitation to maximum bit rate over a transmission control.

Equalizing techniques can also be used for delay distortion. Again using a leased telephone line as an example, Figure 2.14b shows the effect of equalization on delay as a function of frequency.

## Noise

For any data transmission event, the received signal will consist of the transmitted signal, modified by the various distortions imposed by the transmission system, plus additional unwanted signals that are inserted somewhere between transmission and reception; the latter, undesired signals are referred to as noise—a major limiting factor in communications system performance.

Noise may be divided into four categories:

- Thermal noise
- Intermodulation noise
- Crosstalk
- Impulse noise

Thermal noise is due to thermal agitation of electrons in a conductor. It is present in all electronic devices and transmission media and is a function of temperature. Thermal noise is uniformly distributed across the frequency spectrum and hence is often referred to as white noise; it cannot be eliminated and therefore places an upper bound on communications system performance. The amount of thermal noise to be found in a bandwidth of 1 Hz in any device or conductor is

$$N_0 = kT$$

where

$N_0$ = noise power density, watts/hertz
$k$ = Boltzmann's constant = $1.3803 \times 10^{-23}$ Joules/degrees Kelvin (J/°K)
$T$ = temperature, degrees Kelvin

The noise is assumed to be independent of frequency. Thus, the thermal noise, in watts, present in a bandwidth of W hertz can be expressed as

$$N = kTW$$

or, in decibel-watts,

$$N = 10 \log k + 10 \log T + 10 \log W$$
$$= -228.6 \text{ dBW} + 10 \log T + 10 \log W$$

When signals at different frequencies share the same transmission medium, the result may be intermodulation noise. The effect of intermodulation noise is to produce signals at a frequency that is the sum or difference of the two original frequencies, or multiples of those frequencies. For example, the mixing of signals at frequencies $f_1$ and $f_2$ might produce energy at the frequency $f_1 + f_2$. This derived signal could interfere with an intended signal at the frequency $f_1 + f_2$.

Intermodulation noise is produced when there is some nonlinearity in the transmitter, receiver, or intervening transmission system. Normally, these components behave as linear systems; that is, the output is equal to the input, times a constant. In a nonlinear system, the output is a more complex function of the input. Such nonlinearity can be caused by component malfunction or the use of excessive signal strength. It is under these circumstances that the sum and difference terms occur.

Crosstalk has been experienced by anyone who, while using the telephone, has been able to hear another conversation; it is an unwanted coupling between signal paths. It can occur by electrical coupling between nearby twisted pair or, rarely, coax cable lines carrying multiple signals. Crosstalk can also occur when unwanted signals are picked up by microwave antennas; although highly directional, microwave energy does spread during propagation. Typically, crosstalk is of the same order of magnitude (or less) as thermal noise.

All of the types of noise discussed so far have reasonably predictable and reasonably constant magnitudes; it is thus possible to engineer a transmission system to cope with them. Impulse noise, however, is noncontinuous, consisting of irregular pulses or noise spikes of short duration and of relatively high amplitude. It is generated from a variety of causes, including external electromagnetic disturbances, such as lightning, and faults and flaws in the communications system.

Impulse noise is generally only a minor annoyance for analog data. For example, voice transmission may be corrupted by short clicks and crackles with no loss of intelligibility. However, impulse noise is the primary source of error in digital data communication. For example, a sharp spike of energy of 0.01-second duration would not destroy any voice data, but would wash out about 50 bits of data being transmitted at 4800 bps. Figure 2.15 is an example of the effect on a digital signal. Here the noise consists of a relatively modest level of thermal noise plus occasional spikes of impulse noise. The digital data are recovered from the signal by sampling

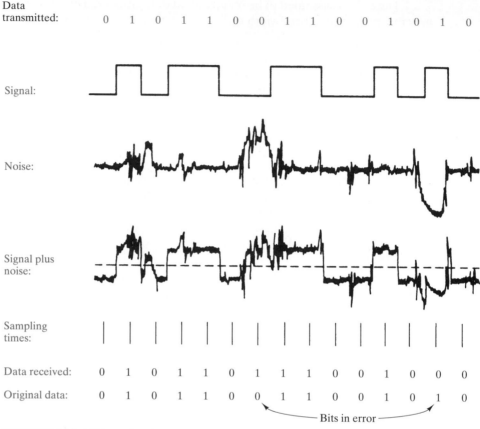

**FIGURE 2.15**   Effect of noise on a digital signal.

the received waveform once per bit time. As can be seen, the noise is occasionally sufficient to change a 1 to a 0 or a 0 to a 1.

## Channel Capacity

We have seen that there are a variety of impairments that distort or corrupt a signal. For digital data, the question that then arises is to what extent these impairments limit the data rate that can be achieved. The rate at which data can be transmitted over a given communication path, or channel, under given conditions, is referred to as the channel capacity.

There are four concepts here that we are trying to relate to one another:

- **Data rate.** This is the rate, in bits per second (bps), at which data can be communicated.
- **Bandwidth.** This is the bandwidth of the transmitted signal as constrained by the transmitter and by the nature of the transmission medium, expressed in cycles per second, or hertz.

- **Noise.** The average level of noise over the communications path.
- **Error rate.** The rate at which errors occur, where an error is the reception of a 1 when a 0 was transmitted, or the reception of a 0 when a 1 was transmitted.

The problem we are addressing is this: Communications facilities are expensive, and, in general, the greater the bandwidth of a facility, the greater the cost. Furthermore, all transmission channels of any practical interest are of limited bandwidth. The limitations arise from the physical properties of the transmission medium or from deliberate limitations at the transmitter on the bandwidth to prevent interference from other sources. Accordingly, we would like to make as efficient use as possible of a given bandwidth. For digital data, this means that we would like to get as high a data rate as possible at a particular limit of error rate for a given bandwidth. The main constraint on achieving this efficiency is noise.

To begin, let us consider the case of a channel that is noise-free. In this environment, the limitation on data rate is simply the bandwidth of the signal. A formulation of this limitation, due to Nyquist, states that if the rate of signal transmission is $2W$, then a signal with frequencies no greater than $W$ is sufficient to carry the data rate. The converse is also true: Given a bandwidth of $W$, the highest signal rate that can be carried is $2W$. This limitation is due to the effect of intersymbol interference, such as is produced by delay distortion. The result is useful in the development of digital-to-analog encoding schemes and is derived in Appendix 4A.

Note that in the last paragraph, we referred to signal rate. If the signals to be transmitted are binary (two voltage levels), then the data rate that can be supported by $W$ Hz is $2W$ bps. As an example, consider a voice channel being used, via modem, to transmit digital data. Assume a bandwidth of 3100 Hz. Then the capacity, $C$, of the channel is $2W = 6200$ bps. However, as we shall see in Chapter 4, signals with more than two levels can be used; that is, each signal element can represent more than one bit. For example, if four possible voltage levels are used as signals, then each signal element can represent two bits. With multilevel signaling, the Nyquist formulation becomes

$$C = 2W \log_2 M$$

where $M$ is the number of discrete signal or voltage levels. Thus, for $M = 8$, a value used with some modems, $C$ becomes 18,600 bps.

So, for a given bandwidth, the data rate can be increased by increasing the number of different signals. However, this places an increased burden on the receiver: Instead of distinguishing one of two possible signals during each signal time, it must distinguish one of $M$ possible signals. Noise and other impairments on the transmission line will limit the practical value of $M$.

Thus, all other things being equal, doubling the bandwidth doubles the data rate. Now consider the relationship between data rate, noise, and error rate. This can be explained intuitively by again considering Figure 2.15. The presence of noise can corrupt one or more bits. If the data rate is increased, then the bits become "shorter" so that more bits are affected by a given pattern of noise. Thus, at a given noise level, the higher the data rate, the higher the error rate.

All of these concepts can be tied together neatly in a formula developed by the mathematician Claude Shannon. As we have just illustrated, the higher the data rate, the more damage that unwanted noise can do. For a given level of noise, we would expect that a greater signal strength would improve the ability to correctly receive data in the presence of noise. The key parameter involved in this reasoning is the signal-to-noise ratio (S/N), which is the ratio of the power in a signal to the power contained in the noise that is present at a particular point in the transmission. Typically, this ratio is measured at a receiver, as it is at this point that an attempt is made to process the signal and eliminate the unwanted noise. For convenience, this ratio is often reported in decibels:

$$(\text{S/N})_{\text{dB}} = 10 \log \frac{\text{signal power}}{\text{noise power}}$$

This expresses the amount, in decibels, that the intended signal exceeds the noise level. A high S/N will mean a high-quality signal and a low number of required intermediate repeaters.

The signal-to-noise ratio is important in the transmission of digital data because it sets the upper bound on the achievable data rate. Shannon's result is that the maximum channel capacity, in bits per second, obeys the equation

$$C = W \log_2\left(1 + \frac{S}{N}\right)$$

where $C$ is the capacity of the channel in bits per second and $W$ is the bandwidth of the channel in hertz. As an example, consider a voice channel being used, via modem, to transmit digital data. Assume a bandwidth of 3100 Hz. A typical value of S/N for a voice-grade line is 30 dB, or a ratio of 1000:1. Thus,

$$C = 3100 \log_2(1 + 1000)$$

$$= 30{,}894 \text{ bps}$$

This represents the theoretical maximum that can be achieved. In practice,however, only much lower rates are achieved. One reason for this is that the formula assumes white noise (thermal noise). Impulse noise is not accounted for, nor are attenuation or delay distortion.

The capacity indicated in the preceding equation is referred to as the error-free capacity. Shannon proved that if the actual information rate on a channel is less than the error-free capacity, then it is theoretically possible to use a suitable signal code to achieve error-free transmission through the channel. Shannon's theorem unfortunately does not suggest a means for finding such codes, but it does provide a yardstick by which the performance of practical communication schemes may be measured.

The measure of efficiency of a digital transmission is the ratio of $C/W$, which is the bps per hertz that is achieved. Figure 2.16 illustrates the theoretical efficiency

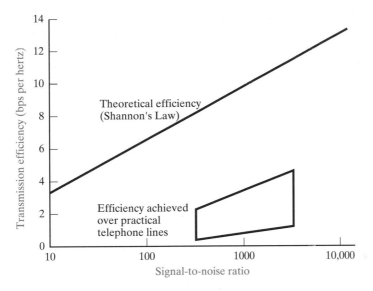

**FIGURE 2.16**  Theoretical and actual transmission efficiency.

of a transmission. It also shows the actual results obtained on a typical voice-grade line.

Several other observations concerning the above equation may be instructive. For a given level of noise, it would appear that the data rate could be increased by increasing either signal strength or bandwidth. However, as the signal strength increases, so do nonlinearities in the system, leading to an increase in inter-modulation noise. Note also that, because noise is assumed to be white, the wider the bandwidth, the more noise is admitted to the system. Thus, as $W$ increases, S/N decreases.

Finally, we mention a parameter related to S/N that is more convenient for determining digital data rates and error rates. The parameter is the ratio of signal energy per bit to noise-power density per hertz, $E_b/N_0$. Consider a signal, digital or analog, that contains binary digital data transmitted at a certain bit rate $R$. Recalling that 1 watt = 1 joule/s, the energy per bit in a signal is given by $E_b = ST_b$, where $S$ is the signal power and $T_b$ is the time required to send one bit. The data rate $R$ is just $R = 1/T_b$. Thus,

$$\frac{E_b}{N_0} = \frac{S/R}{N_0} = \frac{S}{kTR}$$

or, in decibel notation,

$$\frac{E_b}{N_0} = S - 10 \log R + 228.6 \text{ dBW} - 10 \log T$$

The ratio $E_b/N_0$ is important because the bit error rate for digital data is a (decreasing) function of this ratio. Given a value of $E_b/N_0$ needed to achieve a desired error rate, the parameters in the preceding formula may be selected. Note that as the bit rate $R$ increases, the transmitted signal power, relative to noise, must increase to maintain the required $E_b/N_0$.

Let us try to grasp this result intuitively by considering again Figure 2.15. The signal here is digital, but the reasoning would be the same for an analog signal. In several instances, the noise is sufficient to alter the value of a bit. Now, if the data rate were doubled, the bits would be more tightly packed together, and the same passage of noise might destroy two bits. Thus, for constant signal and noise strength, an increase in data rate increases the error rate.

### Example

For binary phase-shift keying (defined in Chapter 4), $E_b/N_0 = 8.4$ dB is required for a bit error rate of $10^{-4}$ (probability of error $= 10^{-4}$). If the effective noise temperature is 290°K (room temperature) and the data rate is 2400 bps, what received signal level is required?

We have

$$8.4 = S(\text{dBW}) - 10 \log 2400 + 228.6 \text{ dBW} - 10 \log 290$$

$$= S(\text{dBW}) - (10)(3.38) + 228.6 - (10)(2.46)$$

$$S = -161.8 \text{ dBW}$$

## 2.4   RECOMMENDED READING

There are many books that cover the fundamentals of analog and digital transmission. [COUC95] is quite thorough. Other excellent treatments include the three-volume [BELL90], [PROA94], and [HAYK94].

BELL90   Bellcore (Bell Communications Research). *Telecommunications Transmission Engineering, Third Edition*. Three volumes. 1990.

COUC95   Couch, L. *Modern Communication Systems: Principles and Applications*. Englewood Cliffs, NJ: Prentice Hall, 1994.

HAYK94   Haykin, S. *Communication Systems*. New York: Wiley, 1994.

PROA94   Proakis, J. and Salehi, M. *Communication Systems Engineering*. Englewood Cliffs, NJ: Prentice Hall, 1994.

## 2.5   PROBLEMS

2.1   a. For the multipoint configuration of Figure 2.1, only one device at a time can transmit. Why?

b. There are two methods of enforcing the rule that only one device can transmit. In the centralized method, one station is in control and can either transmit or allow a specified other station to transmit. In the decentralized method, the stations jointly cooperate in taking turns. What do you see as the advantages and disadvantages of the two methods?

**2.2** Figure 2.6b shows the frequency-domain function for a single square pulse. The single pulse could represent a digital 1 in a communication system. Note that an infinite number of higher frequencies of decreasing magnitudes are needed to represent the single pulse. What implication does that have for a real digital transmission system?

**2.3** Suppose that data are stored on 800-kbyte floppy diskettes that weigh 1 ounce each. Suppose that a Boeing 747 carries 10 tons of these floppies at a speed of 600 mph over a distance of 3000 miles. What is the data transmission rate in bits per second of this system?

**2.4** ASCII is a 7-bit code that allows 128 characters to be defined. In the 1970s, many newspapers received stories from the wire services in a 6-bit code called TTS. This code carried upper- and lower-case characters as well as many special characters and formatting commands. The typical TTS character set allowed over 100 characters to be defined. How do you think this could be accomplished?

**2.5** Figure 2.12 indicates that the vertical blanking pulse has a duration of 830 to 1330 μs. What is the total number of visible lines for each of these two figures?

**2.6** For a video signal, what increase in horizontal resolution is possible if a bandwidth of 5 MHz is used? What increase in vertical resolution is possible? Treat the two questions separately; that is, the increased bandwidth is to be used to increase either horizontal or vertical resolution, but not both.

**2.7** **a.** Suppose that a digitized TV picture is to be transmitted from a source that uses a matrix of $480 \times 500$ picture elements (pixels), where each pixel can take on one of 32 intensity values. Assume that 30 pictures are sent per second. (This digital source is roughly equivalent to broadcast TV standards that have been adopted.) Find the source rate $R$ (bps).

**b.** Assume that the TV picture is to be transmitted over a channel with 4.5-MHz bandwidth and a 35-dB signal-to-noise ratio. Find the capacity of the channel (bps).

**c.** Discuss how the parameters given in part (a) could be modified to allow transmission of color TV signals without increasing the required value for $R$.

**2.8** Figure 2.5 shows the effect of eliminating higher-harmonic components of a square wave and retaining only a few lower-harmonic components. What would the signal look like in the opposite case—that is, retaining all higher harmonics and eliminating a few lower harmonics?

**2.9** What is the channel capacity for a teleprinter channel with a 300-Hz bandwidth and a signal-to-noise ratio of 3 dB?

**2.10** A digital signaling system is required to operate at 9600 bps.

**a.** If a signal element encodes a 4-bit word, what is the minimum required bandwidth of the channel?

**b.** Repeat part (a) for the case of 8-bit words.

**2.11** What is the thermal noise level of a channel with a bandwidth of 10 kHz carrying 1000 watts of power operating at 50° C?

**2.12** Study the works of Shannon and Nyquist on channel capacity. Each places an upper limit on the bit rate of a channel, based on two different approaches. How are the two related?

**2.13** Given a channel with an intended capacity of 20 Mbps. The bandwidth of the channel is 3 MHz. What signal-to-noise ratio is required in order to achieve this capacity?

**2.14** The square wave of Figure 2.8c, with $T = 1$ msec, is transmitted through a low-pass filter that passes frequencies up to 8 kHz with no attenuation.

**a.** Find the power in the output waveform.

**b.** Assuming that at the filter input there is a thermal noise voltage with $N_0 = 0.1$ μWatt/Hz, find the output signal-to-noise ratio in dB.

2.15 A periodic bandlimited signal has only three frequency components: dc, 100 Hz, and 200 Hz. In sine-cosine form,

$$x(t) = 12 + 15 \cos 200\pi t + 20 \sin 200\pi t - 5 \cos 400\pi t - 12 \sin 400\pi t$$

Express the signal in amplitude/phase form.

2.16 If an amplifier has a 30-dB gain, what voltage ratio does the gain represent?

2.17 An amplifier has an output of 20W. What is its output in dBW?

> **2A**     **APPENDIX**

### FOURIER ANALYSIS

IN THIS APPENDIX, we provide an overview of key concepts in Fourier Analysis.

## Fourier Series Representation of Periodic Signals

With the aid of a good table of integrals, it is a remarkably simple task to determine the frequency-domain nature of many signals. We begin with periodic signals. Any periodic signal can be represented as a sum of sinusoids, known as a Fourier series:

$$x(t) = \sum_{n=0}^{\infty} a_n \cos(2\pi n f_0 t) + \sum_{n=1}^{\infty} b_n \sin(2\pi n f_0 t)$$

where $f_0$ is the inverse of the period of the signal ($f_0 = 1/T$). The frequency $f_0$ is referred to as the *fundamental frequency*; multiples of $f_0$ are referred to as *harmonics*. Thus, a periodic signal with period $T$ consists of the fundamental frequency $f_0 = 1/T$ plus harmonics of that frequency. If $a_0 \neq 0$, then $x(t)$ has a *dc component*.

The values of the coefficients are calculated as follows:

$$a_0 = \frac{1}{T} \int_0^T x(t)dt$$

$$a_n = \frac{2}{T} \int_0^T x(t)\cos(2\pi f_0 t)dt$$

$$b_n = \frac{2}{T} \int_0^T x(t)\sin(2\pi f_0 t)dt$$

This form of representation, known as the sine-cosine representation, is the easiest form to compute, but suffers from the fact that there are two components at each frequency. A more meaningful representation, the amplitude-phase representation, takes the form

$$x(t) = c_0 + \sum_{n=1}^{\infty} c_n \cos(2\pi n f_0 t + \theta_n)$$

This relates to the earlier representation, as follows:

$$c_0 = a_0$$

$$c_n = \sqrt{a_n^2 + b_n^2}$$

$$\theta_n = -\tan^{-1}\left(\frac{b_n}{a_n}\right)$$

Examples of the Fourier series for periodic signals are shown in Figure 2.17.

## Fourier Transform Representation of Aperiodic Signals

For a periodic signal, we have seen that its spectrum consists of discrete frequency components, at the fundamental frequency and at its harmonics. For an aperiodic signal, the spec-

Fourier series

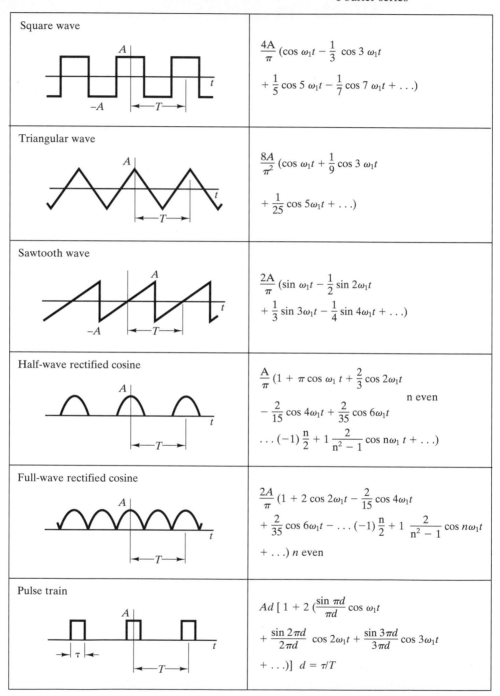

| Square wave | $\dfrac{4A}{\pi} (\cos \omega_1 t - \dfrac{1}{3} \cos 3\,\omega_1 t$ $+ \dfrac{1}{5} \cos 5\,\omega_1 t - \dfrac{1}{7} \cos 7\,\omega_1 t + \ldots)$ |
|---|---|
| Triangular wave | $\dfrac{8A}{\pi^2} (\cos \omega_1 t + \dfrac{1}{9} \cos 3\,\omega_1 t$ $+ \dfrac{1}{25} \cos 5\omega_1 t + \ldots)$ |
| Sawtooth wave | $\dfrac{2A}{\pi} (\sin \omega_1 t - \dfrac{1}{2} \sin 2\omega_1 t$ $+ \dfrac{1}{3} \sin 3\omega_1 t - \dfrac{1}{4} \sin 4\omega_1 t + \ldots)$ |
| Half-wave rectified cosine | $\dfrac{A}{\pi} (1 + \pi \cos \omega_1 t + \dfrac{2}{3} \cos 2\omega_1 t$ $n \text{ even}$ $- \dfrac{2}{15} \cos 4\omega_1 t + \dfrac{2}{35} \cos 6\omega_1 t$ $\ldots (-1)\dfrac{n}{2} + 1 \dfrac{2}{n^2 - 1} \cos n\omega_1 t + \ldots)$ |
| Full-wave rectified cosine | $\dfrac{2A}{\pi} (1 + 2 \cos 2\omega_1 t - \dfrac{2}{15} \cos 4\omega_1 t$ $+ \dfrac{2}{35} \cos 6\omega_1 t - \ldots (-1)\dfrac{n}{2} + 1 \dfrac{2}{n^2 - 1} \cos n\omega_1 t$ $+ \ldots) \; n \text{ even}$ |
| Pulse train | $Ad\,[\,1 + 2\,(\dfrac{\sin \pi d}{\pi d} \cos \omega_1 t$ $+ \dfrac{\sin 2\pi d}{2\pi d} \cos 2\omega_1 t + \dfrac{\sin 3\pi d}{3\pi d} \cos 3\omega_1 t$ $+ \ldots)\,] \;\; d = \tau/T$ |

**FIGURE 2.17** Some common periodic signals and their Fourier series.

trum consists of a continuum of frequencies. This spectrum can be defined by the Fourier transform. For a signal $x(t)$ with a spectrum $X(=f)$, the following relationships hold:

$$x(t) = \int_{-\infty}^{\infty} X(f)e^{j2\pi ft}df$$

$$X(f) = \int_{-\infty}^{\infty} x(t)e^{j2\pi ft}dt$$

Figure 2.18 presents some examples of Fourier transform pairs.

## Power Spectral Density and Bandwidth

The absolute bandwidth of any time-limited signal is infinite. In practical terms, however, most of the power in a signal will be concentrated in some finite band, and the effective bandwidth will consist of that portion of the spectrum that contains most of the power. To make this concept precise, we need to define the power spectral density.

First, we observe the power in the time domain. A function $x(t)$ usually specifies a signal in terms of either voltage or current. In either case, the instantaneous power in the signal is proportional to $|x(t)|^2$. We define the average power of a time-limited signal as

$$P = \frac{1}{t_2 - t_1} \int_{t_1}^{t_2} |x(t)|^2 \, dt$$

For a periodic signal, the average power in one period is

$$P = \frac{1}{T} \int_0^T |x(t)|^2 \, dt$$

We would like to know the distribution of power as a function of frequency. For periodic signals, this is easily expressed in terms of the coefficients of the exponential Fourier series. The power spectral density $S(f)$ obeys

$$S(f) = \sum_{n=-\infty}^{\infty} |X_n|^2 \, \delta(f - nf_0)$$

The power spectral density $S(f)$ for aperiodic functions is more difficult to define. In essence, it is obtained by defining a "period" $T_0$ and allowing $T_0$ to increase without limit.

For a continuous valued function $S(f)$, the power contained in a band of frequencies, $f_1 < f < f_2$, is

$$P = 2 \int_{f_1}^{f_2} S(f)df$$

For a periodic waveform, the power through the first $j$ harmonics is

$$P = \frac{1}{2} \sum_{n=0}^{j} |c_n|^2$$

With these concepts, we can now define the half-power bandwidth, which is perhaps the most common bandwidth definition. The half-power bandwidth is the interval between frequencies at which $S(f)$ has dropped to half of its maximum value of power, or 3 dB below the peak value.

| Signal $x(t)$ | Spectrum $X(f)$ |
|---|---|

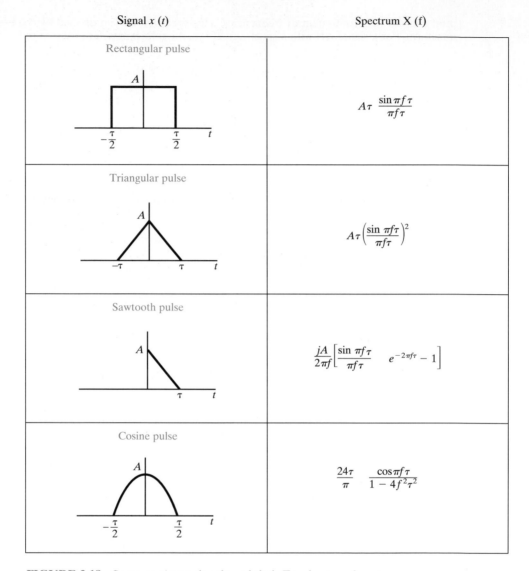

| | |
|---|---|
| Rectangular pulse | $A\tau \; \dfrac{\sin \pi f \tau}{\pi f \tau}$ |
| Triangular pulse | $A\tau \left( \dfrac{\sin \pi f \tau}{\pi f \tau} \right)^2$ |
| Sawtooth pulse | $\dfrac{jA}{2\pi f}\left[ \dfrac{\sin \pi f \tau}{\pi f \tau} \quad e^{-2\pi f \tau} - 1 \right]$ |
| Cosine pulse | $\dfrac{24\tau}{\pi} \quad \dfrac{\cos \pi f \tau}{1 - 4f^2\tau^2}$ |

**FIGURE 2.18**   Some common signals and their Fourier transforms.

**2B** **APPENDIX**

## DECIBELS AND SIGNAL STRENGTH

AN IMPORTANT PARAMETER in any transmission system is the strength of the signal being transmitted. As a signal propagates along a transmission medium, there will be a loss, or *attenuation*, of signal strength. Additional losses occur at taps and splitters. To compensate, amplifiers may be inserted at various points to impart a gain in signal strength.

It is customary to express gains, losses, and relative levels in decibels, because

- Signal strength often falls off logarithmically, so loss is easily expressed in terms of the decibel, which is a logarithmic unit.
- The net gain or loss in a cascaded transmission path can be calculated with simple addition and subtraction.

The decibel is a measure of the difference in two signal levels:

$$N_{dB} = 10 \log_{10} \frac{P_1}{P_2}$$

where

$N_{dB}$ = number of decibels
$P_{1,2}$ = power values
$\log_{10}$ = logarithm to the base 10 (from now on, we will simply use log to mean $\log_{10}$)

For example, if a signal with a power level of 10 *mW* is inserted onto a transmission line and the measured power some distance away is 5 *mW*, the loss can be expressed as

$$\text{LOSS} = 10 \log(5/10) = 10(-0.3) = -3 \text{ dB}$$

Note that the decibel is a measure of relative, not absolute difference. A loss from 1000 *mW* to 500 *mW* is also a –3 dB loss. Thus, a loss of 3 dB halves the voltage level; a gain of 3 dB doubles the magnitude.

The decibel is also used to measure the difference in voltage, taking into account that power is proportional to the square of the voltage:

$$P = \frac{V^2}{R}$$

where

$P$ = power dissipated across resistance $R$
$V$ = voltage across resistance $R$

Thus,

$$N_{dB} = 10 \log \frac{P_1}{P_2} = 10 \log \frac{V_1^2/R}{V_2^2/R} = 20 \log \frac{V_1}{V_2}$$

Decibel values refer to relative magnitudes or changes in magnitude, not to an absolute level. It is convenient to be able to refer to an absolute level of power or voltage in decibels so that gains and losses with reference to an initial signal level may easily be calculated. Thus, several derived units are in common use.

The dBW (decibel-Watt) is used extensively in microwave applications. The value of 1 $W$ is selected as a reference and defined to be 0 dB$W$. The absolute decibel level of power in dB$W$ is defined as

$$\text{Power(dBW)} = 10 \log \frac{\text{Power(W)}}{1\text{ W}}$$

For example, a power of 1000 W is 30 dBW, and a power of 1 mW is –30 dBW.

A unit in common use in cable television and broadband LAN applications is the dBmV (decibel-millivolt). This is an absolute unit with 0 dBmV equivalent to 1 mV. Thus,

$$\text{Voltage(dBmV)} = 20 \log \frac{\text{Voltage(mV)}}{1\text{ mV}}$$

The voltage levels are assumed to be across a 75-ohm resistance.

The decibel is convenient for determining overall gain or loss in a signal path. The amplifier gain, and the losses due to the cables, tap, and splitter are expressed in decibels. By using simple addition and subtraction, the signal level at the outlet is easily calculated. For example, consider a point-to-point link that consists of a transmission line with a single amplifier partway along. If the loss on the first portion of line is 13 dB, the gain of the amplifier is 30 dB, and the loss on the second portion of line is 40 dB, then the overall gain (loss) is –13 +30 –40 = –23 dB. If the original signal strength is –30 dBW, the received signal strength is –53 dBW.

# CHAPTER 3

# TRANSMISSION MEDIA

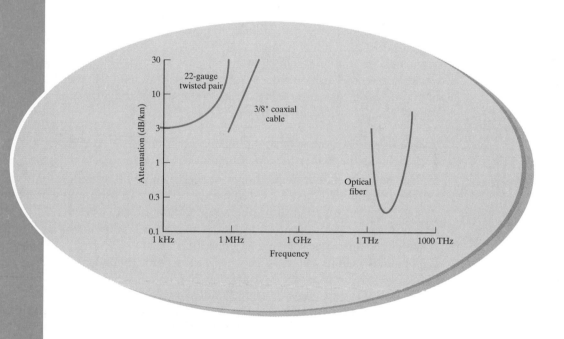

T

he transmission medium is the physical path between transmitter and receiver in a data transmission system. Transmission media can be classified as guided or unguided. In both cases, communication is in the form of electromagnetic waves. With guided media, the waves are guided along a solid medium, such as copper twisted pair, copper coaxial cable, and optical fiber. The atmosphere and outer space are examples of unguided media that provide a means of transmitting electromagnetic signals but do not guide them; this form of transmission is usually referred to as *wireless transmission*.

The characteristics and quality of a data transmission are determined both by the characteristics of the medium and the characteristics of the signal. In the case of guided media, the medium itself is more important in determining the limitations of transmission.

For unguided media, the bandwidth of the signal produced by the transmitting antenna is more important than the medium in determining transmission characteristics. One key property of signals transmitted by antenna is directionality. In general, signals at lower frequencies are omnidirectional; that is, the signal propagates in all directions from the antenna. At higher frequencies, it is possible to focus the signal into a directional beam.

In considering the design of data transmission systems, a key concern, generally, is data rate and distance: the greater the data rate and distance, the better. A number of design factors relating to the transmission medium and to the signal determine the data rate and distance:

- **Bandwidth.** All other factors remaining constant, the greater the bandwidth of a signal, the higher the data rate that can be achieved.
- **Transmission impairments.** Impairments, such as attenuation, limit the distance. For guided media, twisted pair generally suffer more impairment than coaxial cable, which in turn suffers more than optical fiber.
- **Interference.** Interference from competing signals in overlapping frequency bands can distort or wipe out a signal. Interference is of particular concern for unguided media, but it is also a problem with guided media. For guided media, interference can be caused by emanations from nearby cables. For example, twisted pair are often bundled together, and conduits often carry multiple cables. Interference can also be experienced from unguided transmissions. Proper shielding of a guided medium can minimize this problem.
- **Number of receivers.** A guided medium can be used to construct a point-to-point link or a shared link with multiple attachments. In the latter case, each attachment introduces some attenuation and distortion on the line, limiting distance and/or data rate.

Figure 3.1 depicts the electromagnetic spectrum and indicates the frequencies at which various guided media and unguided transmission techniques operate. In this chapter, we examine these guided and unguided alternatives. In all cases, we describe the systems physically, briefly discuss applications, and summarize key transmission characteristics.

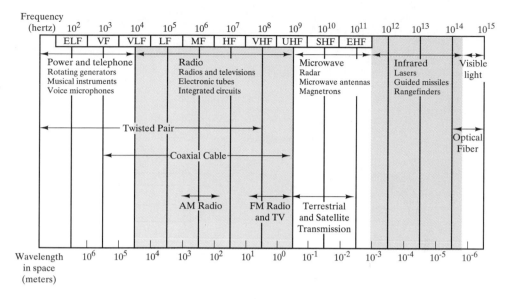

**FIGURE 3.1**    Electromagnetic spectrum for telecommunications.

## 3.1 GUIDED TRANSMISSION MEDIA

For guided transmission media, the transmission capacity, in terms of either data rate or bandwidth, depends critically on the distance and on whether the medium is point-to-point or multipoint, such as in a local area network (LAN). Table 3.1 indicates the type of performance typical for the common guided medium for long-distance point-to-point applications; we defer a discussion of the use of these media for LANs to Part III.

The three guided media commonly used for data transmission are twisted pair, coaxial cable, and optical fiber (Figure 3.2). We examine each of these in turn.

### Twisted Pair

The least-expensive and most widely-used guided transmission medium is twisted pair.

**TABLE 3.1**    Point-to-point transmission characteristics of guided media.

| Transmission medium | Total data rate | Bandwidth | Repeater spacing |
| --- | --- | --- | --- |
| Twisted pair | 4 Mbps | 3 MHz | 2 to 10 km |
| Coaxial cable | 500 Mbps | 350 MHz | 1 to 10 km |
| Optical fiber | 2 Gbps | 2 GHz | 10 to 100 km |

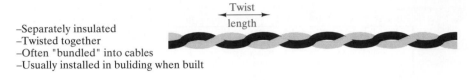

–Separately insulated
–Twisted together
–Often "bundled" into cables
–Usually installed in buliding when built

(a) Twisted pair

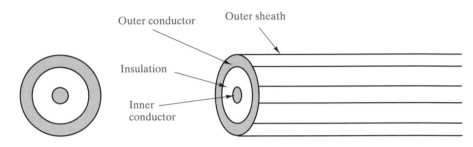

–Outer conductor is braided shield
–Inner conductor is solid metal
–Separated by insulating material
–Covered by padding

(b) Coaxial cable

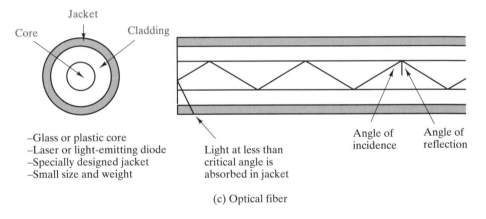

–Glass or plastic core
–Laser or light-emitting diode
–Specially designed jacket
–Small size and weight

(c) Optical fiber

**FIGURE 3.2**   Guided transmission media.

## Physical Description

A twisted pair consists of two insulated copper wires arranged in a regular spiral pattern. A wire pair acts as a single communication link. Typically, a number of these pairs are bundled together into a cable by wrapping them in a tough protective sheath. Over longer distances, cables may contain hundreds of pairs. The twisting tends to decrease the crosstalk interference between adjacent pairs in a cable. Neighboring pairs in a bundle typically have somewhat different twist lengths to reduce the crosstalk interference. On long-distance links, the twist length typically varies from two to six inches. The wires in a pair have thicknesses of from 0.016 to 0.036 inches.

## Applications

By far the most common transmission medium for both analog and digital signals is twisted pair. It is the most commonly used medium in the telephone network as well as being the workhorse for communications within buildings.

In the telephone system, individual residential telephone sets are connected to the local telephone exchange, or "end office," by twisted-pair wire. These are referred to as *subscriber loops*. Within an office building, each telephone is also connected to a twisted pair, which goes to the in-house private branch exchange (PBX) system or to a Centrex facility at the end office. These twisted-pair installations were designed to support voice traffic using analog signaling. However, by means of a modem, these facilities can handle digital data traffic at modest data rates.

Twisted pair is also the most common medium used for digital signaling. For connections to a digital data switch or digital PBX within a building, a data rate of 64 kbps is common. Twisted pair is also commonly used within a building for local area networks supporting personal computers. Data rates for such products are typically in the neighborhood of 10 Mbps. However, recently, twisted-pair networks with data rates of 100 Mbps have been developed, although these are quite limited in terms of the number of devices and geographic scope of the network. For long-distance applications, twisted pair can be used at data rates of 4 Mbps or more.

Twisted pair is much less expensive than the other commonly used guided transmission media (coaxial cable, optical fiber) and is easier to work with. It is more limited in terms of data rate and distance.

## Transmission Characteristics

Twisted pair may be used to transmit both analog and digital signals. For analog signals, amplifiers are required about every 5 to 6 km. For digital signals, repeaters are required every 2 or 3 km.

Compared to other commonly used guided transmission media (coaxial cable, optical fiber), twisted pair is limited in distance, bandwidth, and data rate. As Figure 3.3 shows, the attenuation for twisted pair is a very strong function of frequency. Other impairments are also severe for twisted pair. The medium is quite susceptible to interference and noise because of its easy coupling with electromagnetic fields. For example, a wire run parallel to an ac power line will pick up 60-Hz energy. Impulse noise also easily intrudes into twisted pair. Several measures are taken to reduce impairments. Shielding the wire with metallic braid or sheathing reduces interference. The twisting of the wire reduces low-frequency interference, and the use of different twist lengths in adjacent pairs reduces crosstalk.

For point-to-point analog signaling, a bandwidth of up to about 250 kHz is possible. This accommodates a number of voice channels. For long-distance digital point-to-point signaling, data rates of up to a few Mbps are possible; for very short

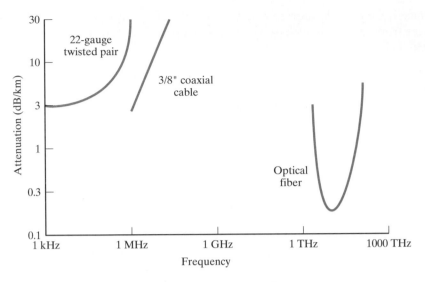

**FIGURE 3.3**   Attenuation of typical guided media.

distances, data rates of up to 100 Mbps have been achieved in commercially available products.

### Unshielded and Shielded Twisted Pair

Twisted pair comes in two varieties: unshielded and shielded. Unshielded twisted pair (UTP) is ordinary telephone wire. Office buildings, by universal practice, are pre-wired with a great deal of excess unshielded twisted pair, more than is needed for simple telephone support. This is the least expensive of all the transmission media commonly used for local area networks, and is easy to work with and simple to install.

Unshielded twisted pair is subject to external electromagnetic interference, including interference from nearby twisted pair and from noise generated in the environment. A way to improve the characteristics of this medium is to shield the twisted pair with a metallic braid or sheathing that reduces interference. This shielded twisted pair (STP) provides better performance at lower data rates. However, it is more expensive and more difficult to work with than unshielded twisted pair.

### Category 3 and Category 5 UTP

Most office buildings are prewired with a type of 100-ohm twisted pair cable commonly referred to as voice-grade. Because voice-grade twisted pair is already installed, it is an attractive alternative for use as a LAN medium. Unfortunately, the data rates and distances achievable with voice-grade twisted pair are limited.

In 1991, the Electronic Industries Association published standard EIA-568, Commercial Building Telecommunications Cabling Standard, that specified the use of voice-grade unshielded twisted pair as well as shielded twisted pair for in-building data applications. At that time, the specification was felt to be adequate for the range of frequencies and data rates found in office environments. Up to that time, the principal interest for LAN designs was in the range of data rates from 1 Mbps to 16 Mbps. Subsequently, as users migrated to higher-performance workstations and applications, there was increasing interest in providing LANs that could operate up to 100 Mbps over inexpensive cable. In response to this need, EIA-568-A was issued in 1995. The new standard reflects advances in cable and connector design and test methods. It covers 150-ohm shielded twisted pair and 100-ohm unshielded twisted pair.

EIA-568-A recognizes three categories of UTP cabling:

- **Category 3.** UTP cables and associated connecting hardware whose transmission characteristics are specified up to 16 MHz.
- **Category 4.** UTP cables and associated connecting hardware whose transmission characteristics are specified up to 20 MHz.
- **Category 5.** UTP cables and associated connecting hardware whose transmission characteristics are specified up to 100 MHz.

Of these, it is Category 3 and Category 5 cable that have received the most attention for LAN applications. Category 3 corresponds to the voice-grade cable found in abundance in most office buildings. Over limited distances, and with proper design, data rates of up to 16 Mbps should be achievable with Category 3. Category 5 is a data-grade cable that is becoming increasingly common for pre-installation in new office buildings. Over limited distances, and with proper design, data rates of up to 100 Mbps should be achievable with Category 5.

A key difference between Category 3 and Category 5 cable is the number of twists in the cable per unit distance. Category 5 is much more tightly twisted—typically 3 to 4 twists per inch, compared to 3 to 4 twists per foot for Category 3. The tighter twisting is more expensive but provides much better performance than Category 3.

Table 3.2 summarizes the performance of Category 3 and 5 UTP, as well as the STP specified in EIA-568-A. The first parameter used for comparison, attenuation, is fairly straightforward. The strength of a signal falls off with distance over any transmission medium. For guided media, attenuation is generally logarithmic and is therefore typically expressed as a constant number of decibels per unit distance. Attenuation introduces three considerations for the designer. First, a received signal must have sufficient magnitude so that the electronic circuitry in the receiver can detect and interpret the signal. Second, the signal must maintain a level sufficiently higher than noise to be received without error. Third, attenuation is an increasing function of frequency.

Near-end crosstalk, as it applies to twisted pair wiring systems, is the coupling of the signal from one pair of conductors to another pair. These conductors may be the metal pins in a connector or the wire pairs in a cable. The near end refers to coupling that takes place when the transmit signal entering the link couples back to the

TABLE 3.2 Comparison of shielded and unshielded twisted pair.

| Frequency (MHz) | Attenuation (dB per 100 m) | | | Near-end crosstalk (dB) | | |
|---|---|---|---|---|---|---|
| | Category 3 UTP | Category 5 UTP | 150 Ω STP | Category 3 UTP | Category 5 UTP | 150 Ω STP |
| 1 | 2.6 | 2.0 | 1.1 | 41 | 62 | 58 |
| 4 | 5.6 | 4.1 | 2.2 | 32 | 53 | 58 |
| 16 | 13.1 | 8.2 | 4.4 | 23 | 44 | 50.4 |
| 25 | — | 10.4 | 6.2 | — | 32 | 47.5 |
| 100 | — | 22.0 | 12.3 | — | — | 38.5 |
| 300 | — | — | 21.4 | — | — | 31.3 |

receive conductor pair at that same end of the link; in other words, the near-transmitted signal is picked up by the near-receive pair.

## Coaxial Cable

### Physical Description

Coaxial cable, like twisted pair, consists of two conductors, but is constructed differently to permit it to operate over a wider range of frequencies. It consists of a hollow outer cylindrical conductor that surrounds a single inner wire conductor (Figure 3.2b). The inner conductor is held in place by either regularly spaced insulating rings or a solid dielectric material. The outer conductor is covered with a jacket or shield. A single coaxial cable has a diameter of from 0.4 to about 1 in. Because of its shielded, concentric construction, coaxial cable is much less susceptible to interference and crosstalk than is twisted pair. Coaxial cable can be used over longer distances and supports more stations on a shared line than twisted pair.

### Applications

Coaxial cable is perhaps the most versatile transmission medium and is enjoying widespread use in a wide variety of applications; the most important of these are

- Television distribution
- Long-distance telephone transmission
- Short-run computer system links
- Local area networks

Coaxial cable is spreading rapidly as a means of distributing TV signals to individual homes—cable TV. From its modest beginnings as Community Antenna Television (CATV), designed to provide service to remote areas, cable TV will eventually reach almost as many homes and offices as the telephone. A cable TV system can carry dozens or even hundreds of TV channels at ranges up to a few tens of miles.

Coaxial cable has traditionally been an important part of the long-distance telephone network. Today, it faces increasing competition from optical fiber, terrestrial microwave, and satellite. Using frequency-division multiplexing (FDM, see Chapter 7), a coaxial cable can carry over 10,000 voice channels simultaneously.

Coaxial cable is also commonly used for short-range connections between devices. Using digital signaling, coaxial cable can be used to provide high-speed I/O channels on computer systems.

Another application area for coaxial cable is local area networks (Part Three). Coaxial cable can support a large number of devices with a variety of data and traffic types, over distances that encompass a single building or a complex of buildings.

### Transmission Characteristics

Coaxial cable is used to transmit both analog and digital signals. As can be seen from Figure 3.3, coaxial cable has frequency characteristics that are superior to those of twisted pair, and can hence be used effectively at higher frequencies and data rates. Because of its shielded, concentric construction, coaxial cable is much less susceptible to interference and crosstalk than twisted pair. The principal constraints on performance are attenuation, thermal noise, and intermodulation noise. The latter is present only when several channels (FDM) or frequency bands are in use on the cable.

For long-distance transmission of analog signals, amplifiers are needed every few kilometers, with closer spacing required if higher frequencies are used. The usable spectrum for analog signaling extends to about 400 MHz. For digital signaling, repeaters are needed every kilometer or so, with closer spacing needed for higher data rates.

## Optical Fiber

### Physical Description

An optical fiber is a thin (2 to 125 µm), flexible medium capable of conducting an optical ray. Various glasses and plastics can be used to make optical fibers. The lowest losses have been obtained using fibers of ultrapure fused silica. Ultrapure fiber is difficult to manufacture; higher-loss multicomponent glass fibers are more economical and still provide good performance. Plastic fiber is even less costly and can be used for short-haul links, for which moderately high losses are acceptable.

An optical fiber cable has a cylindrical shape and consists of three concentric sections: the core, the cladding, and the jacket (Figure 3.2c). The *core* is the innermost section and consists of one or more very thin strands, or fibers, made of glass or plastic. Each fiber is surrounded by its own *cladding*, a glass or plastic coating that has optical properties different from those of the core. The outermost layer, surrounding one or a bundle of cladded fibers, is the *jacket*. The jacket is composed of plastic and other material layered to protect against moisture, abrasion, crushing, and other environmental dangers.

## Applications

One of the most significant technological breakthroughs in data transmission has been the development of practical fiber optic communications systems. Optical fiber already enjoys considerable use in long-distance telecommunications, and its use in military applications is growing. The continuing improvements in performance and decline in prices, together with the inherent advantages of optical fiber, have made it increasingly attractive for local area networking. The following characteristics distinguish optical fiber from twisted pair or coaxial cable:

- **Greater capacity.** The potential bandwidth, and hence data rate, of optical fiber is immense; data rates of 2 Gbps over tens of kilometers have been demonstrated. Compare this capability to the practical maximum of hundreds of Mbps over about 1 km for coaxial cable and just a few Mbps over 1 km or up to 100 Mbps over a few tens of meters for twisted pair.
- **Smaller size and lighter weight.** Optical fibers are considerably thinner than coaxial cable or bundled twisted-pair cable—at least an order of magnitude thinner for comparable information-transmission capacity. For cramped conduits in buildings and underground along public rights-of-way, the advantage of small size is considerable. The corresponding reduction in weight reduces structural support requirements.
- **Lower attenuation.** Attenuation is significantly lower for optical fiber than for coaxial cable or twisted pair (Figure 3.3) and is constant over a wide range.
- **Electromagnetic isolation.** Optical fiber systems are not affected by external electromagnetic fields. Thus, the system is not vulnerable to interference, impulse noise, or crosstalk. By the same token, fibers do not radiate energy, thereby causing little interference with other equipment and thus providing a high degree of security from eavesdropping. In addition, fiber is inherently difficult to tap.
- **Greater repeater spacing.** Fewer repeaters means lower cost and fewer sources of error. The performance of optical fiber systems from this point of view has been steadily improving. For example, AT&T has developed a fiber transmission system that achieves a data rate of 3.5 Gbps over a distance of 318 km [PARK92] without repeaters. Coaxial and twisted-pair systems generally have repeaters every few kilometers.

Five basic categories of application have become important for optical fiber:

- Long-haul trunks
- Metropolitan trunks
- Rural-exchange trunks

- Subscriber loops
- Local area networks

Long-haul fiber transmission is becoming increasingly common in the telephone network. Long-haul routes average about 900 miles in length and offer high capacity (typically 20,000 to 60,000 voice channels). These systems compete economically with microwave and have so underpriced coaxial cable in many developed countries that coaxial cable is rapidly being phased out of the telephone network in such areas.

Metropolitan trunking circuits have an average length of 7.8 miles and may have as many as 100,000 voice channels in a trunk group. Most facilities are installed in underground conduits and are repeaterless, joining telephone exchanges in a metropolitan or city area. Included in this category are routes that link long-haul microwave facilities that terminate at a city perimeter to the main telephone exchange building downtown.

Rural exchange trunks have circuit lengths ranging from 25 to 100 miles that link towns and villages. In the United States, they often connect the exchanges of different telephone companies. Most of these systems have fewer than 5,000 voice channels. The technology in these applications competes with microwave facilities.

Subscriber loop circuits are fibers that run directly from the central exchange to a subscriber. These facilities are beginning to displace twisted pair and coaxial cable links as the telephone networks evolve into full-service networks capable of handling not only voice and data, but also image and video. The initial penetration of optical fiber in this application is for the business subscriber, but fiber transmission into the home will soon begin to appear.

A final important application of optical fiber is for local area networks. Recently, standards have been developed and products introduced for optical fiber networks that have a total capacity of 100 Mbps and can support hundreds or even thousands of stations in a large office building or in a complex of buildings.

The advantages of optical fiber over twisted pair and coaxial cable become more compelling as the demand for all types of information (voice, data, image, video) increases.

**Transmission Characteristics**

Optical fiber systems operate in the range of about $10^{14}$ to $10^{15}$ Hz; this covers portions of the infrared and visible spectrums. The principle of optical fiber transmission is as follows. Light from a source enters the cylindrical glass or plastic core. Rays at shallow angles are reflected and propagated along the fiber; other rays are absorbed by the surrounding material. This form of propagation is called *multimode*, referring to the variety of angles that will reflect. When the fiber core radius is reduced, fewer angles will reflect. By reducing the radius of the core to the order of a wavelength, only a single angle or mode can pass: the axial ray. This single-mode propagation provides superior performance for the following reason: With multimode transmission, multiple propagation paths exist, each with a different path length and, hence, time to traverse the fiber; this causes signal elements to spread out in time, which limits the rate at which data can be accurately received. Because there is a single transmission path with single-mode transmission, such distortion cannot occur. Finally, by varying the index of refraction of the core, a third type of transmission, known as multimode graded index, is possible. This type is intermediate between the other two in characteristics. The variable refraction has the effect of focusing the rays more efficiently than ordinary multimode, also known as multimode step index. Table 3.3 compares the three fiber transmission modes.

Two different types of light source are used in fiber optic systems: the light-emitting diode (LED) and the injection laser diode (ILD). Both are semiconductor devices that emit a beam of light when a voltage is applied. The LED is less costly, operates over a greater temperature range, and has a longer operational life. The ILD, which operates on the laser principle, is more efficient and can sustain greater data rates.

There is a relationship among the wavelength employed, the type of transmission, and the achievable data rate. Both single mode and multimode can support several different wavelengths of light and can employ laser or LED light source. In optical fiber, light propagates best in three distinct wavelength "windows," centered on 850, 1300, and 1550 nanometers (nm). These are all in the infrared portion of the frequency spectrum, below the visible-light portion, which is 400 to 700 nm. The loss is lower at higher wavelengths, allowing greater data rates over longer distances (Table 3.3). Most local applications today use 850-nm LED light sources. Although this combination is relatively inexpensive, it is generally limited to data rates under 100 Mbps and distances of a few kilometers. To achieve higher data rates and longer distances, a 1300-nm LED or laser source is needed. The highest data rates and longest distances require 1500-nm laser sources.

**TABLE 3.3**   Typical fiber characteristics [STER93].

| Fiber type | Core diameter (μm) | Cladding diameter (μm) | Attenuation (dB/km) (Max) | | | Bandwidth (MHz/km) (Max) |
|---|---|---|---|---|---|---|
| | | | 850 nm | 1300 nm | 1500 nm | |
| Single Mode | 5.0 | 85 or 125 | 2.3 | | | 5000 @ 850 nm |
| | 8.1 | 125 | | 0.5 | 0.25 | |
| Graded-index | 50 | 125 | 2.4 | 0.6 | 0.5 | 600 @ 850 nm |
| | | | | | | 1500 @ 1300 nm |
| | 62.5 | 125 | 3.0 | 0.7 | 0.3 | 200 @ 850 nm |
| | | | | | | 1000 @ 1300 nm |
| | 100 | 140 | 3.5 | 1.5 | 0.9 | 300 @ 850 nm |
| | | | | | | 500 @ 1300 nm |
| Step-index | 200 or 300 | 380 or 440 | 6.0 | | | 6 |

## 3.2  WIRELESS TRANSMISSION

For unguided media, transmission and reception are achieved by means of an antenna. For transmission, the antenna radiates electromagnetic energy into the medium (usually air), and for reception, the antenna picks up electromagnetic waves from the surrounding medium. There are basically two types of configurations for wireless transmission: directional and omnidirectional. For the directional configuration, the transmitting antenna puts out a focused electromagnetic beam; the transmitting and receiving antennas must therefore be carefully aligned. In the omnidirectional case, the transmitted signal spreads out in all directions and can be received by many antennas. In general, the higher the frequency of a signal, the more it is possible to focus it into a directional beam.

Three general ranges of frequencies are of interest in our discussion of wireless transmission. Frequencies in the range of about 2 GHz (gigahertz = $10^9$ Hz) to 40 GHz are referred to as microwave frequencies. At these frequencies, highly directional beams are possible, and microwave is quite suitable for point-to-point transmission. Microwave is also used for satellite communications. Frequencies in the range of 30 MHz to 1 GHz are suitable for omnidirectional applications. We will refer to this range as the broadcast radio range. Table 3.4 summarizes characteristics[1] of unguided transmission at various frequency bands. Microwave covers part of the UHF and all of the SHF band, and broadcast radio covers the VHF and part of the UHF band.

Another important frequency range, for local applications, is the infrared portion spectrum. This covers, roughly, from $3 \times 10^{11}$ to $2 \times 10^{14}$ Hz. Infrared is useful to local point-to-point and multipoint applications within confined areas, such as a single room.

### Terrestrial Microwave

### Physical Description

The most common type of microwave antenna is the parabolic "dish." A typical size is about 10 feet in diameter. The antenna is fixed rigidly and focuses a narrow beam to achieve line-of-sight transmission to the receiving antenna. Microwave antennas are usually located at substantial heights above ground level in order to extend the range between antennas and to be able to transmit over intervening obstacles. With no intervening obstacles, the maximum distance between antennas conforms to

$$d = 7.14\sqrt{Kh} \qquad (2\text{-}1)$$

where d is the distance between antennas in kilometers, h is the antenna height in meters, and K is an adjustment factor to account for the fact that microwaves are bent or refracted with the curvature of the earth and will, hence, propagate farther

---

[1] The various modulation techniques are explained in Chapter 4.

**TABLE 3.4** Characteristics of unguided communications bands

| Frequency band | Name | Analog data | | Digital data | | Principal applications |
| --- | --- | --- | --- | --- | --- | --- |
| | | Modulation | Bandwidth | Modulation | Data rate | |
| 30–300 kHz | LF (low frequency) | Generally not practical | | ASK, FSK, MSK | 0.1–100 bps | Navigation |
| 300–3000 kHz | MF (medium frequency) | AM | To 4 kHz | ASK, FSK, MSK | 10–1000 bps | Commercial AM radio |
| 3–30 MHz | HF (high frequency) | AM, SSB | To 4 kHz | ASK, FSK, MSK | 10–3000 bps | Shortwave radio CB radio |
| 30–300 MHz | VHF (very high frequency) | AM, SSB; FM | 5 kHz to 5 MHz | FSK, PSK | To 100 kbps | VHF television FM radio |
| 300–3000 MHz | UHF (ultra high frequency) | FM, SSB | To 20 MHz | PSK | To 10 Mbps | UHF television Terrestrial microwave |
| 3–30 GHz | SHF (super high frequency) | FM | To 500 MHz | PSK | To 100 Mbps | Terrestrial microwave Satellite microwave |
| 30–300 GHz | EHF (extremely high frequency) | FM | To 1 GHz | PSK | To 750 Mbps | Experimental short point-to-point |

than the optical line of sight. A good rule of thumb is $K = \frac{4}{3}$ [VALK93]. For example, two microwave antennas at a height of 100 m may be as far as $7.14 \times \sqrt{133} = 82$ km apart.

To achieve long-distance transmission, a series of microwave relay towers is used; point-to-point microwave links are strung together over the desired distance.

## Applications

The primary use for terrestrial microwave systems is in long-haul telecommunications service, as an alternative to coaxial cable or optical fiber. The microwave facility requires far fewer amplifiers or repeaters than coaxial cable over the same distance, but requires line-of-sight transmission. Microwave is commonly used for both voice and television transmission.

Another increasingly common use of microwave is for short point-to-point links between buildings; this can be used for closed-circuit TV or as a data link between local area networks. Short-haul microwave can also be used for the so-called bypass application. A business can establish a microwave link to a long-distance telecommunications facility in the same city, bypassing the local telephone company.

## Transmission Characteristics

Microwave transmission covers a substantial portion of the electromagnetic spectrum. Common frequencies used for transmission are in the range 2 to 40 GHz. The higher the frequency used, the higher the potential bandwidth and therefore the higher the potential data rate. Table 3.5 indicates bandwidth and data rate for some typical systems.

As with any transmission system, a main source of loss is attenuation. For microwave (and radio frequencies), the loss can be expressed as

$$L = 10\log\left(\frac{4\pi d}{\lambda}\right)^2 \text{ dB} \qquad (2\text{-}2)$$

where $d$ is the distance and $\lambda$ is the wavelength, in the same units. Loss varies as the square of the distance. In contrast, for twisted pair and coaxial cable, loss varies logarithmically with distance (linear in decibels). Repeaters or amplifiers, then, may be

**TABLE 3.5**  Typical digital microwave performance.

| Band (GHz) | Bandwidth (MHz) | Data rate (Mbps) |
|:----------:|:---------------:|:----------------:|
| 2          | 7               | 12               |
| 6          | 30              | 90               |
| 11         | 40              | 90               |
| 18         | 220             | 274              |

**TABLE 3.6** Principal microwave bands authorized for fixed telecommunications in the United States (1979).

| Band name | Range (GHz) | Maximum channel bandwidth (MHz) | Necessary spectral efficiency (bits/Hz) | Type of service |
|---|---|---|---|---|
| 2 GHz | 1.71 – 1.85 | — | | Federal government |
| 2 GHz | 1.85 – 1.99 | 8 | | Private; local government |
| 2 GHz | 2.11 – 2.13 | 3.5 | 2 | Common carrier (shared) |
| 2 GHz | 2.13 – 2.15 | 0.8/1.6 | | Private; local government |
| 2 GHz | 2.15 – 2.16 | 10 | | Private; multipoint |
| 2 GHz | 2.16 – 2.18 | 3.5 | 2 | Common carrier |
| 2 GHz | 2.18 – 2.20 | 0.8/1.6 | | Private; local government |
| 2 GHz | 2.20 – 2.29 | — | | Federal government |
| 2 GHz | 2.45 – 2.50 | 0.8 | | Private; local government (shared) |
| 4 GHz | 3.70 – 4.20 | 20 | 4.5 | Common carrier; satellite |
| 6 GHz | 5.925 – 6.425 | 30 | 3 | Common carrier; satellite |
| 6 GHz | 6.525 – 6.875 | 5/10 | | Private; shared |
| 7–8 GHz | 7.125 – 8.40 | — | | Federal government |
| 10 GHz | 10.550 – 10.680 | 25 | | Private |
| 11 GHz | 10.7 – 11.7 | 50 | 2.25 | Common carrier |
| 12 GHz | 12.2 – 12.7 | 10/20 | | Private; local government |
| 13 GHz | 13.2 – 13.25 | 25 | | Common carrier; private |
| 14 GHz | 14.4 – 15.25 | — | | Federal government |
| 18 GHz | 17.7 – 19.7 | 220 | | Common carrier; shared |
| 18 GHz | 18.36 – 19.04 | 50/100 | | Private; local government |
| 22 GHz | 21.2 – 23.6 | 50/100 | | Private; common carrier |
| 31 GHz | 31.0 – 31.2 | 50/100 | | Private; common carrier |
| 38 GHz | 36.0 – 38.6 | — | | Federal government |
| 40 GHz | 38.6 – 40.0 | 50 | | Private; common carrier |
| | Above 40.0 | — | | Developmental |

placed farther apart for microwave systems—10 to 100 km is typical. Attenuation increases with rainfall, the effects of which become especially noticeable above 10 GHz. Another source of impairment is interference. With the growing popularity of microwave, transmission areas overlap and interference is always a danger. As a result, the assignment of frequency bands is strictly regulated.

Table 3.6 shows the authorized microwave frequency bands as regulated by the Federal Communications Commission (FCC). The most common bands for long-haul telecommunications are the 4 GHz to 6 GHz bands. With increasing congestion at these frequencies, the 11 GHz band is now coming into use. The 12 GHz band is used as a component of cable TV systems. Microwave links are used to provide TV signals to local CATV installations; the signals are then distributed to individual subscribers via coaxial cable. Higher-frequency microwave is being used for short point-to-point links between buildings; typically, the 22 GHz band is used. The higher microwave frequencies are less useful for longer distances because of increased attenuation but are quite adequate for shorter distances. In addition, at the higher frequencies, the antennas are smaller and cheaper.

## Satellite Microwave

### Physical Description

A communication satellite is, in effect, a microwave relay station. It is used to link two or more ground-based microwave transmitter/receivers, known as earth stations, or ground stations. The satellite receives transmissions on one frequency band (uplink), amplifies or repeats the signal, and transmits it on another frequency (downlink). A single orbiting satellite will operate on a number of frequency bands, called *transponder channels*, or simply *transponders*.

Figure 3.4 depicts, in a general way, two common configurations for satellite communication. In the first, the satellite is being used to provide a point-to-point link between two distant ground-based antennas. In the second, the satellite provides communications between one ground-based transmitter and a number of ground-based receivers.

For a communication satellite to function effectively, it is generally required that it remain stationary with respect to its position over the earth; otherwise, it would not be within the line of sight of its earth stations at all times. To remain stationary, the satellite must have a period of rotation equal to the earth's period of rotation. This match occurs at a height of 35,784 km.

Two satellites using the same frequency band, if close enough together, will interfere with each other. To avoid this problem, current standards require a 4° spacing (angular displacement as measured from the earth) in the 4/6 GHz band and a 3° spacing at 12/14 GHz. Thus, the number of possible satellites is quite limited.

### Applications

The communication satellite is a technological revolution as important as fiber optics. Among the most important applications for satellites are

- Television distribution
- Long-distance telephone transmission
- Private business networks

Because of their broadcast nature, satellites are well suited to television distribution and are being used extensively in the United States and throughout the world for this purpose. In its traditional use, a network provides programming from a central location. Programs are transmitted to the satellite and then broadcast down to a number of stations, which then distribute the programs to individual viewers. One network, the Public Broadcasting Service (PBS), distributes its television programming almost exclusively by the use of satellite channels. Other commercial networks also make substantial use of satellite, and cable television systems are receiving an ever-increasing proportion of their programming from satellites. The most recent application of satellite technology to television distribution is direct broadcast satellite (DBS), in which satellite video signals are transmitted directly to the home user. The dropping cost and size of receiving antennas have made DBS economically feasible, and a number of channels are either already in service or in the planning stage.

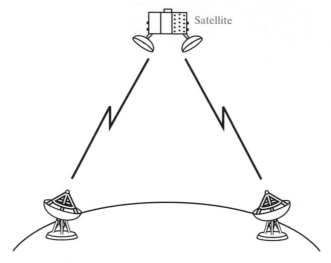

(a) Point-to-point link via satellite microwave

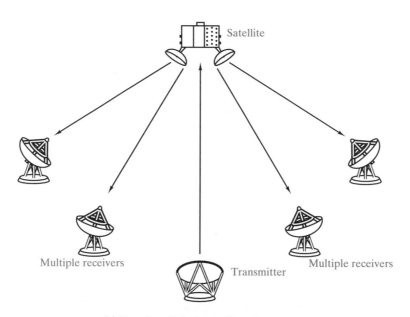

(b) Broadcast link via satellite microwave

**FIGURE 3.4** Satellite communications configurations.

Satellite transmission is also used for point-to-point trunks between telephone exchange offices in public telephone networks. It is the optimum medium for high-usage international trunks and is competitive with terrestrial systems for many long-distance intranational links.

Finally, there are a number of business data applications for satellite. The satellite provider can divide the total capacity into a number of channels and lease these channels to individual business users. A user equipped with the antennas at a

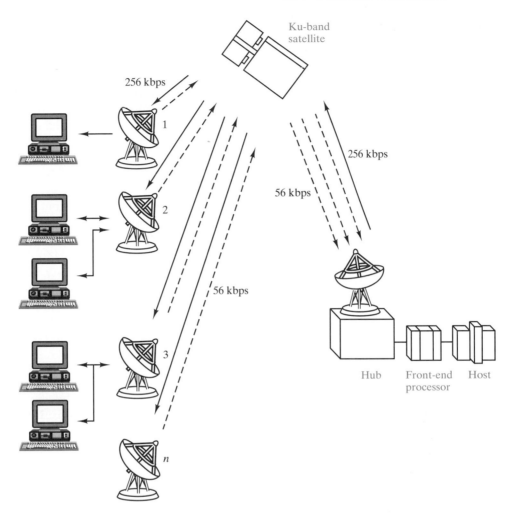

**FIGURE 3.5**   VSAT configuration.

number of sites can use a satellite channel for a private network. Traditionally, such applications have been quite expensive and limited to larger organizations with high-volume requirements. A recent development is the very small aperture terminal (VSAT) system, which provides a low-cost alternative. Figure 3.5 depicts a typical VSAT configuration. A number of subscriber stations are equipped with low-cost VSAT antennas (about $400 per month per VSAT). Using some protocol, these stations share a satellite transmission capacity for transmission to a hub station. The hub station can exchange messages with each of the subscribers as well as relay messages between subscribers.

**Transmission Characteristics**

The optimum frequency range for satellite transmission is 1 to 10 GHz. Below 1 GHz, there is significant noise from natural sources, including galactic, solar, and atmospheric noise, and human-made interference from various electronic devices. Above 10 GHz, the signal is severely attenuated by atmospheric absorption and precipitation.

Most satellites providing point-to-point service today use a frequency bandwidth in the range 5.925 to 6.425 GHz for transmission from earth to satellite (uplink) and a bandwidth in the range 3.7 to 4.2 GHz for transmission from satellite to earth (downlink). This combination is referred to as the 4/6 GHz band. Note that the uplink and downlink frequencies differ. For continuous operation without interference, a satellite cannot transmit and receive on the same frequency. Thus, signals received from a ground station on one frequency must be transmitted back on another.

The 4/6 GHz band is within the optimum zone of 1 to 10 GHz but has become saturated. Other frequencies in that range are unavailable because of sources of interference, usually terrestrial microwave. Therefore, the 12/14 GHz band has been developed (uplink: 14 to 14.5 GHz; downlink: 11.7 to 12.2 GHz). At this frequency band, attenuation problems must be overcome. However, smaller and cheaper earth-station receivers can be used. It is anticipated that this band will also saturate, and use is projected for the 19/29 GHz band (uplink: 27.5 to 31.0 Ghz; downlink: 17.7 to 21.2 GHz). This band experiences even greater attenuation problems but will allow greater bandwidth (2500 MHz versus 500 MHz) and even smaller and cheaper receivers.

Several properties of satellite communication should be noted. First, because of the long distances involved, there is a propagation delay of about a quarter second between transmission from one earth station and reception by another earth station. This delay is noticeable in ordinary telephone conversations. It also introduces problems in the areas of error control and flow control, which we discuss in later chapters. Second, satellite microwave is inherently a broadcast facility. Many stations can transmit to the satellite, and a transmission from a satellite can be received by many stations.

## Broadcast Radio

### Physical Description

The principal difference between broadcast radio and microwave is that the former is omnidirectional and the latter is directional. Thus, broadcast radio does not require dish-shaped antennas, and the antennas need not be rigidly mounted to a precise alignment.

### Applications

Radio is a general term used to encompass frequencies in the range of 3 kHz to 300 GHz. We are using the informal term *broadcast radio* to cover the VHF and part of the UHF band: 30 MHz to 1 GHz. This range covers FM radio as well as UHF and VHF television. This range is also used for a number of data-networking applications.

### Transmission Characteristics

The range 30 MHz to 1 GHz is an effective one for broadcast communications. Unlike the case for lower-frequency electromagnetic waves, the ionosphere is transparent to radio waves above 30 MHz. Transmission is limited to line of sight, and distant transmitters will not interfere with each other due to reflection from the atmosphere. Unlike the higher frequencies of the microwave region, broadcast radio waves are less sensitive to attenuation from rainfall.

As a line-of-sight propagation technique, radio obeys Equation (2-1); that is, the maximum distance between transmitter and receiver is slightly more than the optical line of sight, or $7.14 \sqrt{Kh}$. As with microwave, the amount of attenuation due to distance obeys Equation (2-2), namely, $10\log\left(\frac{4\pi d}{\lambda}\right)^2$ dB. Because of the longer wavelength, radio waves suffer relatively less attenuation.

A prime source of impairment for broadcast radio waves is multipath interference. Reflection from land, water, and natural or human-made objects can create multiple paths between antennas. This effect is frequently evident when TV reception displays multiple images as an airplane passes by.

## Infrared

Infrared communications is achieved using transmitters/receivers (transceivers) that modulate noncoherent infrared light. Transceivers must be in line of sight of each other, either directly or via reflection from a light-colored surface such as the ceiling of a room.

One important difference between infrared and microwave transmission is that the former does not penetrate walls. Thus, the security and interference problems encountered in microwave systems are not present. Furthermore, there is no frequency allocation issue with infrared, because no licensing is required.

## 3.3 RECOMMENDED READING

Detailed descriptions of the transmission characteristics of the transmission media discussed in this chapter can be found in [FREE91]. [REEV95] provides an excellent treatment of twisted pair and optical fiber. Two good treatments of optical fiber are [GREE93] and [STER93]. [STAL97] discusses the characteristics of transmission media for LANs in greater detail.

**FREE91** Freeman, R. *Telecommunication Transmission Handbook.* New York: Wiley, 1991.

**GREE93** Green, P. *Fiber Optic Networks.* Englewood Cliffs, NJ: Prentice Hall, 1993.

**REEV95** Reeve, W. *Subscriber Loop Signaling and Transmission Handbook.* Piscataway, NJ: IEEE Press, 1995.

**STAL97** Stallings, W. *Local and Metropolitan Area Networks, Fifth Edition.* Englewood Cliffs, NJ: Prentice Hall, 1997.

**STER93** Sterling, D. *Technician's Guide to Fiber Optics.* Albany, NY: Delmar Publications, 1993.

**One web site to recommend:**

•http://snapple.cs.washington.edu:600/mobile/mobile_html: Source for information about wireless technology, products, conferences, and publications.

## 3.4 PROBLEMS

3.1 Explain the logical flaw in the following argument:

According to Table 3.1, a twisted pair can carry a digital data rate of 4 Mbps. Home computers can use a modem with the telephone network to communicate across networks. The telephone outlet is connected to the central exchange by a subscriber loop, which is twisted pair. It is difficult to establish communication by this method at a data rate higher than 28.8 kbps, which is much lower then 4 Mbps. Therefore, there must be a mistake in Table 3.1.

3.2 A twisted-pair line is approximated as a filter with the characteristics shown in Figure 3.6. The figure shows the amount of attenuation of the signal as a function of frequency. Assuming that a square wave signal, such as Figure 2.8c, with $T = 0.1$ μsec and $A = \pi/4$ is fed to the cable, find the sine wave components, with their magnitudes, that would appear at the output.

3.3 A telephone line with a bandwidth of 100 kHz is known to have a loss of 20 dB. The input signal power is measured as 0.5 watt, and the output signal noise level is measured as 2.5 μwatt. Using this information, calculate the output signal-to-noise ratio.

3.4 A transmitter-receiver pair is connected across a coaxial cable. The signal power measured at the receiver is 0.1 watt. Signal levels change 1000 times per second. Noise energy is 0.05 μJoules for every 1 millisecond. If $E_b/N_0 = 10$ dB is desired, determine how many levels must be accommodated in the signal to encode the bits. What would be the bit rate?

3.5 Given a 100-watt power source, what is the maximum allowable length for the following transmission media if a signal of 1 watt is to be received?
   a. 22-gauge twisted pair operating at 300 kHz
   b. 22-gauge twisted pair operating at 1 MHz
   c. 0.375-inch coaxial cable operating at 1 MHz
   d. 0.375-inch coaxial cable operating at 25 MHz
   e. optical fiber operating at its optimal frequency

3.6 Coaxial cable is a two-wire transmission system. What is the advantage of connecting the outer conductor to ground?

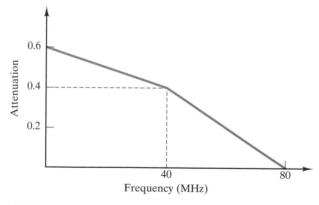

**FIGURE 3.6** Filter characteristics of a twisted-pair line.

# CHAPTER 4

# DATA ENCODING

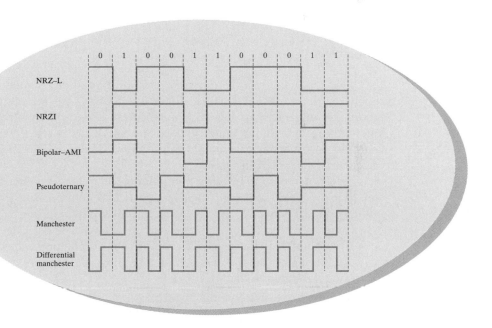

I n Chapter 2, a distinction was made between analog and digital data, and analog and digital signals. Figure 2.13 suggested that either form of data could be encoded into either form of signal.

Figure 4.1 is another depiction that emphasizes the process involved. For digital signaling, a data source $g(t)$, which may be either digital or analog, is encoded into a digital signal $x(t)$. The actual form of $x(t)$ depends on the encoding technique, and is chosen to optimize use of the transmission medium. For example, the encoding may be chosen to either conserve bandwidth or to minimize errors.

The basis for analog signaling is a continuous, constant-frequency signal known as the carrier signal. The frequency of the carrier signal is chosen to be compatible with the transmission medium being used. Data may be transmitted using a carrier signal by modulation. Modulation is the process of encoding source data onto a carrier signal with frequency $f_c$. All modulation techniques involve operation on one or more of the three fundamental frequency-domain parameters:

- Amplitude
- Frequency
- Phase

The input signal $m(t)$ may be analog or digital and is called the modulating signal, or baseband signal. The result of modulating the carrier signal is called the modulated signal $s(t)$. As Figure 4.1b indicates, $s(t)$ is a bandlimited (bandpass) signal. The location of the bandwidth on the spectrum is related to $f_c$ and is often centered on $f_c$. Again, the actual form of the encoding is chosen to optimize some characteristic of the transmission.

Each of the four possible combinations depicted in Figure 4.1 is in widespread use. The reasons for choosing a particular combination for any given communication task vary. We list here some representative reasons:

- **Digital data, digital signal.** In general, the equipment for encoding digital data into a digital signal is less complex and less expensive than digital-to-analog modulation equipment.
- **Analog data, digital signal.** Conversion of analog data to digital form permits the use of modern digital transmission and switching equipment. The advantages of the digital approach were outlined in Section 2.2.
- **Digital data, analog signal.** Some transmission media, such as optical fiber and the unguided media, will only propagate analog signals.
- **Analog data, analog signal.** Analog data in electrical form can be transmitted as baseband signals easily and cheaply; this is done with voice transmission over voice-grade lines. One common use of modulation is to shift the bandwidth of a baseband signal to another portion of the spectrum. In this way, multiple signals, each at a different position on the spectrum, can share the same transmission medium; this is known as frequency-division multiplexing.

We now examine the techniques involved in each of these four combinations and then look at spread spectrum, which fits into several categories.

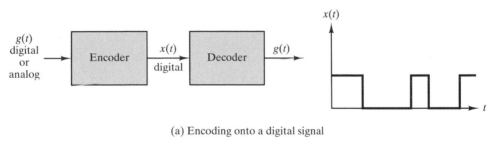

(a) Encoding onto a digital signal

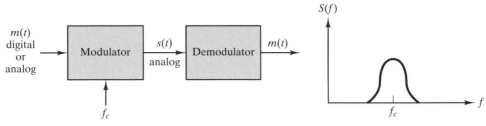

(b) Modulation onto an analog signal

**FIGURE 4.1**   Encoding and modulation techniques.

## 4.1  DIGITAL DATA, DIGITAL SIGNALS

A digital signal is a sequence of discrete, discontinuous voltage pulses. Each pulse is a signal element. Binary data are transmitted by encoding each data bit into signal elements. In the simplest case, there is a one-to-one correspondence between bits and signal elements. An example is shown in Figure 2.15, in which binary 0 is represented by a lower voltage level and binary 1 by a higher voltage level. As we shall see in this section, a variety of other encoding schemes are also used.

First, we define some terms. If the signal elements all have the same algebraic sign, that is, all positive or negative, then the signal is unipolar. In polar signaling, one logic state is represented by a positive voltage level, and the other by a negative voltage level. The data signaling rate, or just data rate, of a signal is the rate, in bits per second, that data are transmitted. The duration or length of a bit is the amount of time it takes for the transmitter to emit the bit; for a data rate R, the bit duration is $1/R$. The modulation rate, in contrast, is the rate at which signal level is changed; this will depend on the nature of the digital encoding, as explained below. The modulation rate is expressed in *bauds*, which means signal elements per second. Finally, the terms *mark* and *space*, for historical reasons, refer to the binary digits 1 and 0, respectively. Table 4.1 summarizes key terms; these should be clearer when we see an example later in this section.

The tasks involved in interpreting digital signals at the receiver can be summarized by again referring to Figure 2.15. First, the receiver must know the timing

**TABLE 4.1** Key data transmission terms.

| Term | Units | Definition |
|---|---|---|
| Data element | bits | A single binary one or zero. |
| Data rate | bits per second (bps) | The rate at which data elements are transmitted. |
| Signal element | Digital: a voltage pulse of constant amplitude. | That part of a signal that occupies the shortest interval of a signaling code. |
| | Analog: a pulse of constant frequency, phase, and amplitude. | |
| Signaling rate or modulation rate | Signal elements per second (baud) | The rate at which signal elements are transmitted |

of each bit. That is, the receiver must know with some accuracy when a bit begins and ends. Second, the receiver must determine whether the signal level for each bit position is high (1) or low (0). In Figure 2.15, these tasks are performed by sampling each bit position in the middle of the interval and comparing the value to a threshold. Because of noise and other impairments, there will be errors, as shown.

What factors determine how successful the receiver will be in interpreting the incoming signal? We saw in Chapter 2 that three factors are important: the signal-to-noise ratio (or, better, $E_b/N_0$), the data rate, and the bandwidth. With other factors held constant, the following statements are true:

- An increase in data rate increases bit error rate (the probability that a bit is received in error).
- An increase in S/N decreases bit error rate.
- An increase in bandwidth allows an increase in data rate.

There is another factor that can be used to improve performance, and that is the encoding scheme: the mapping from data bits to signal elements. A variety of encoding schemes are in use. In what follows, we describe some of the more common ones; they are defined in Table 4.2 and depicted in Figure 4.2.

Before describing these techniques, let us consider the following ways of evaluating or comparing the various techniques.

- **Signal spectrum.** Several aspects of the signal spectrum are important. A lack of high-frequency components means that less bandwidth is required for transmission. In addition, lack of a direct-current (dc) component is also desirable. With a dc component to the signal, there must be direct physical attachment of transmission components; with no dc component, ac-coupling via transformer is possible; this provides excellent electrical isolation, reducing interference. Finally, the magnitude of the effects of signal distortion and interference depend on the spectral properties of the transmitted signal. In practice, it usually happens that the transfer function of a channel is worse

TABLE 4.2 Definition of digital signal encoding formats.

**Nonreturn-to-Zero-Level (NRZ-L)**
  0 = high level
  1 = low level
**Nonreturn to Zero Inverted (NRZI)**
  0 = no transition at beginning of interval (one bit time)
  1 = transition at beginning of interval
**Bipolar-AMI**
  0 = no line signal
  1 = positive or negative level, alternating for successive ones
**Pseudoternary**
  0 = positive or negative level, alternating for successive zeros
  1 = no line signal
**Manchester**
  0 = transition from high to low in middle of interval
  1 = transition from low to high in middle of interval
**Differential Manchester**
  Always a transition in middle of interval
  0 = transition at beginning of interval
  1 = no transition at beginning of interval
**B8ZS**
  Same as bipolar AMI, except that any string of eight zeros is replaced by a string with
    two code violations
**HDB3**
  Same as bipolar AMI, except that any string of four zeros is replaced by a string with
    one code violation

near the band edges. Therefore, a good signal design should concentrate the transmitted power in the middle of the transmission bandwidth. In such a case, a smaller distortion should be present in the received signal. To meet this objective, codes can be designed with the aim of shaping the spectrum of the transmitted signal.

- **Clocking.** We mentioned the need to determine the beginning and end of each bit position. This is no easy task. One rather expensive approach is to provide a separate clock-lead to synchronize the transmitter and receiver. The alternative is to provide some synchronization mechanism that is based on the transmitted signal; this can be achieved with suitable encoding.

- **Error detection.** We will discuss various error-detection techniques in Chapter 6 and show that these are the responsibility of a layer of logic above the signaling level known as data link control. However, it is useful to have some error-detection capability built into the physical signaling-encoding scheme; this permits errors to be detected more quickly.

- **Signal interference and noise immunity.** Certain codes exhibit superior performance in the presence of noise. This ability is usually expressed in terms of a bit error rate.

- **Cost and complexity.** Although digital logic continues to drop in price, expense should not be ignored. In particular, the higher the signaling rate to

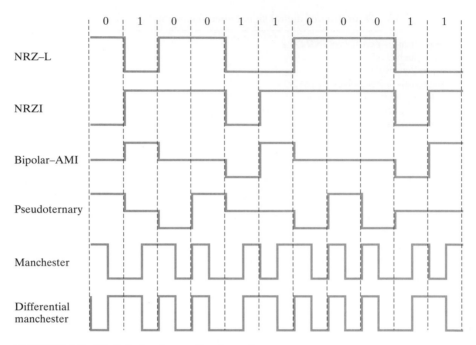

**FIGURE 4.2**   Digital signal encoding formats.

achieve a given data rate, the greater the cost. We will see that some codes require a signaling rate that is, in fact, greater than the actual data rate.

We now turn to a discussion of various techniques.

## Nonreturn to Zero (NRZ)

The most common, and easiest, way to transmit digital signals is to use two different voltage levels for the two binary digits. Codes that follow this strategy share the property that the voltage level is constant during a bit interval; there is no transition (no return to a zero voltage level). For example, the absence of voltage can be used to represent binary 0, with a constant positive voltage used to represent binary 1. More commonly, a negative voltage is used to represent one binary value and a positive voltage is used to represent the other. This latter code, known as **Nonreturn-to-Zero-Level** (NRZ-L), is illustrated[1] in Figure 4.2. NRZ-L is generally the code used to generate or interpret digital data by terminals and other devices. If a different code is to be used for transmission, it is typically generated from an NRZ-L signal by the transmission system. (In terms of Figure 1.2, NRZ-L is $g(t)$ and the encoded signal is $s(t)$.)

A variation of NRZ is known as **NRZI** (Nonreturn to zero, invert on ones). As with NRZ-L, NRZI maintains a constant voltage pulse for the duration of a bit

---

[1] In this figure, a negative voltage is equated with binary 1 and a positive voltage with binary 0. This is the opposite of the definition used in virtually all other textbooks. However, there is no "standard" definition of NRZ-L, and the definition here conforms to the use of NRZ-L in data communications interfaces and the standards that govern those interfaces.

time. The data themselves are encoded as the presence or absence of a signal transition at the beginning of the bit time. A transition (low-to-high or high-to-low) at the beginning of a bit time denotes a binary 1 for that bit time; no transition indicates a binary 0.

NRZI is an example of **differential encoding**. In differential encoding, the signal is decoded by comparing the polarity of adjacent signal elements rather than determining the absolute value of a signal element. One benefit of this scheme is that it may be more reliable to detect a transition in the presence of noise than to compare a value to a threshold. Another benefit is that with a complex transmission layout, it is easy to lose the sense of the polarity of the signal. For example, on a multidrop twisted-pair line, if the leads from an attached device to the twisted pair are accidentally inverted, all 1s and 0s for NRZ-L will be inverted; this cannot happen with differential encoding.

The NRZ codes are the easiest to engineer and, in addition, make efficient use of bandwidth. This latter property is illustrated in Figure 4.3, which compares the spectral density of various encoding schemes. In the figure, frequency is normalized to the data rate. As can be seen, most of the energy in NRZ and NRZI signals is between dc and half the bit rate. For example, if an NRZ code is used to generate a signal with a data rate of 9600 bps, most of the energy in the signal is concentrated between dc and 4800 Hz.

The main limitations of NRZ signals are the presence of a dc component and the lack of synchronization capability. To picture the latter problem, consider that with a long string of 1s or 0s for NRZ-L, or a long string of 0s for NRZI, the output is a constant voltage over a long period of time. Under these circumstances, any drift between the timing of transmitter and receiver will result in a loss of synchronization between the two.

Because of their simplicity and relatively low frequency response characteristics, NRZ codes are commonly used for digital magnetic recording. However, their limitations make these codes unattractive for signal transmission applications.

## Multilevel Binary

A category of encoding techniques known as multilevel-binary address some of the deficiencies of the NRZ codes. These codes use more than two signal levels. Two examples of this scheme are illustrated in Figure 4.2: bipolar-AMI (alternate mark inversion) and pseudoternary.[2]

In the case of the **bipolar-AMI** scheme, a binary 0 is represented by no line signal, and a binary 1 is represented by a positive or negative pulse. The binary 1 pulses must alternate in polarity. There are several advantages to this approach. First, there will be no loss of synchronization if a long string of 1s occurs. Each 1 introduces a transition, and the receiver can resynchronize on that transition. A long string of 0s would still be a problem. Second, because the 1 signals alternate in voltage from positive to negative, there is no net dc component. Also, the

---

[2] These terms are not consistently used in the literature. In some books, these two terms are used for different encoding schemes than those defined here, and a variety of terms have been used for the two schemes illustrated in Figure 4.2. The nomenclature used here corresponds to the usage in various ITU-T standards documents.

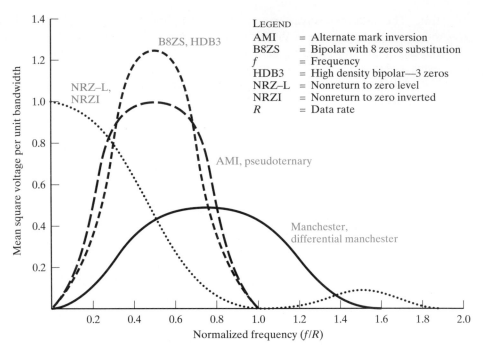

**FIGURE 4.3**   Spectral density of various signal encoding schemes.

bandwidth of the resulting signal is considerably less than the bandwidth for NRZ (Figure 4.3). Finally, the pulse-alternation property provides a simple means of error detection. Any isolated error, whether it deletes a pulse or adds a pulse, causes a violation of this property.

The comments of the previous paragraph also apply to **pseudoternary**. In this case, it is the binary 1 that is represented by the absence of a line signal, and the binary 0 by alternating positive and negative pulses. There is no particular advantage of one technique over the other, and each is the basis of some applications.

Although a degree of synchronization is provided with these codes, a long string of 0s in the case of AMI or 1s in the case of pseudoternary still presents a problem. Several techniques have been used to address this deficiency. One approach is to insert additional bits that force transitions. This technique is used in ISDN for relatively low data-rate transmission. Of course, at a high data rate, this scheme is expensive, as it results in an increase in an already high signal-transmission rate. To cope with this problem at high data rates, a technique that involves scrambling the data is used; we will look at two examples of the technique later in this section.

Thus, with suitable modification, multilevel binary schemes overcome the problems of NRZ codes. Of course, as with any engineering design decision, there is a tradeoff. With multilevel binary coding, the line signal may take on one of three levels, but each signal element, which could represent $\log_2 3 = 1.58$ bits of information, bears only one bit of information, making multilevel binary not as efficient as NRZ coding. Another way to state this is that the receiver of multilevel binary signals has to distinguish between three levels $(+A, -A, 0)$ instead of just two levels

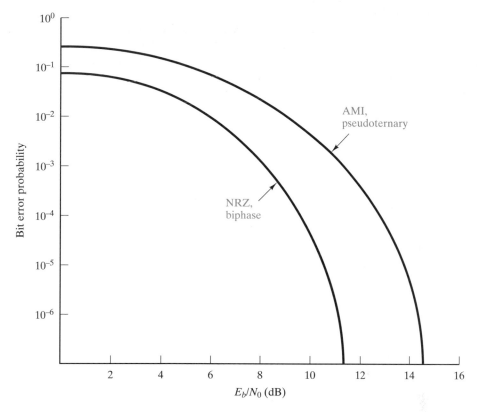

**FIGURE 4.4**    Theoretical bit error rate for various digital encoding schemes.

in the other signaling formats previously discussed. Because of this, the multilevel binary signal requires approximately 3 dB more signal power than a two-valued signal for the same probability of bit error; this is illustrated in Figure 4.4. Put another way, the bit error rate for NRZ codes, at a given signal-to-noise ratio, is significantly less than that for multilevel binary.

## Biphase

There is another set of alternative coding techniques, grouped under the term *biphase*, which overcomes the limitations of NRZ codes. Two of these techniques, Manchester and Differential Manchester, are in common use.

In the **Manchester** code, there is a transition at the middle of each bit period. The mid-bit transition serves as a clocking mechanism and also as data: a low-to-high transition represents a 1, and a high-to-low transition represents a 0.[3] In **Dif-**

---

[3] The definition of Manchester presented here conforms to its usage in local area networks. In this definition, a binary 1 corresponds to a low-to-high transition, and a binary 0 to a high-to-low transition. Unfortunately, there is no official standard for Manchester, and a number of respectable textbooks (e.g., [TANF88], [COUC95], [FREE91], [SKLA88], [PEEB87], [BERT92], and the first two editions of this textbook) use the inverse, in which a low-to-high transition defines a binary 0 and a high-to-low transition defines a binary 1. Here, we conform to industry practice and to the definition used in the various LAN standards.

**ferential Manchester**, the mid-bit transition is used only to provide clocking. The encoding of a 0 is represented by the presence of a transition at the beginning of a bit period, and a 1 is represented by the absence of a transition at the beginning of a bit period. Differential Manchester has the added advantage of employing differential encoding.

All of the biphase techniques require at least one transition per bit time and may have as many as two transitions. Thus, the maximum modulation rate is twice that for NRZ; this means that the bandwidth required is correspondingly greater. On the other hand, the biphase schemes have several advantages:

- **Synchronization.** Because there is a predictable transition during each bit time, the receiver can synchronize on that transition. For this reason, the biphase codes are known as self-clocking codes.
- **No dc component.** Biphase codes have no dc component, yielding the benefits described earlier.
- **Error detection.** The absence of an expected transition can be used to detect errors. Noise on the line would have to invert both the signal before and after the expected transition to cause an undetected error.

As can be seen from Figure 4.3, the bulk of the energy in biphase codes is between one-half and one times the bit rate. Thus, the bandwidth is reasonably narrow and contains no dc component; however, it is wider than the bandwidth for the multilevel binary codes.

Biphase codes are popular techniques for data transmission. The more common Manchester code has been specified for the IEEE 802.3 standard for baseband coaxial cable and twisted-pair CSMA/CD bus LANs. Differential Manchester has been specified for the IEEE 802.5 token ring LAN, using shielded twisted pair.

## Modulation Rate

When signal encoding techniques are used, a distinction needs to be made between data rate (expressed in bits per second), and modulation rate (expressed in baud). The data rate, or bit rate, is $1/t_B$, where $t_B$ = bit duration. The modulation rate is the rate at which signal elements are generated. Consider, for example, Manchester encoding. The minimum size signal element is a pulse of one-half the duration of a bit interval. For a string of all binary zeroes or all binary ones, a continuous stream of such pulses is generated. Hence, the maximum modulation rate for Manchester is $2/t_B$. This situation is illustrated in Figure 4.5, which shows the transmission of a stream of 1 bits at a data rate of 1 Mbps using NRZI and Manchester. In general,

$$D = \frac{R}{b} = \frac{R}{\log_2 L}$$

where

$D$ = modulation rate, baud
$R$ = data rate, bps

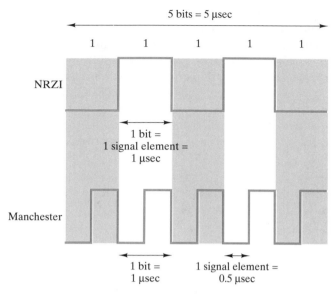

FIGURE 4.5   A stream of ones at 1 Mbps.

$L$ = number of different signal elements

$b$ = number of bits per signal element

One way of characterizing the modulation rate is to determine the average number of transitions that occur per bit time. In general, this will depend on the exact sequence of bits being transmitted. Table 4.3 compares transition rates for various techniques. It indicates the signal transition rate in the case of a data stream of alternating 1s and 0s, and for the data stream that produces the minimum and maximum modulation rate.

## Scrambling Techniques

Although the biphase techniques have achieved widespread use in local-area-network applications at relatively high data rates (up to 10 Mbps), they have not been widely used in long-distance applications. The principal reason for this is that they

TABLE 4.3   Normalized signal transition rate of various digital signal encoding rates.

| | Minimum | 101010. . . | Maximum |
|---|---|---|---|
| NRZ-L | 0 (all 0's or 1's) | 1.0 | 1.0 |
| NRZI | 0 (all 0's) | 0.5 | 1.0 (all 1's) |
| Binary-AMI | 0 (all 0's) | 1.0 | 1.0 |
| Pseudoternary | 0 (all 1's) | 1.0 | 1.0 |
| Manchester | 1.0 (1010 . . .) | 1.0 | 2.0 (all 0's or 1's) |
| Differential Manchester | 1.0 (all 1's) | 1.5 | 2.0 (all 0's) |

require a high signaling rate relative to the data rate. This sort of inefficiency is more costly in a long-distance application.

Another approach is to make use of some sort of scrambling scheme. The idea behind this approach is simple: sequences that would result in a constant voltage level on the line are replaced by filling sequences that will provide sufficient transitions for the receiver's clock to maintain synchronization. The filling sequence must be recognized by the receiver and replaced with the original data sequence. The filling sequence is the same length as the original sequence, so there is no data-rate increase. The design goals for this approach can be summarized as follows:

- No dc component
- No long sequences of zero-level line signals
- No reduction in data rate
- Error-detection capability

Two techniques are commonly used in long-distance transmission services; these are illustrated in Figure 4.6.

A coding scheme that is commonly used in North America is known as **bipolar with 8-zeros substitution (B8ZS)**. The coding scheme is based on a bipolar-AMI. We have seen that the drawback of the AMI code is that a long string of zeros may

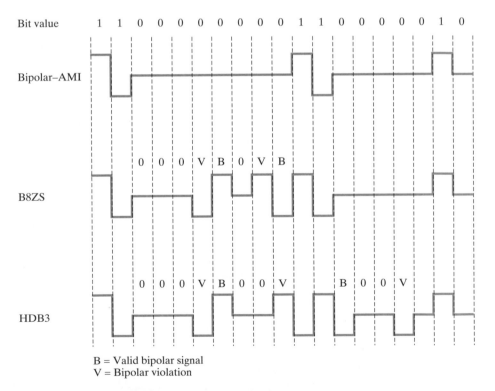

B = Valid bipolar signal
V = Bipolar violation

**FIGURE 4.6**   Encoding rules for B8ZS and HDB3.

TABLE 4.4   HDB3 substitution rules.

| Polarity of preceding pulse | Number of bipolar pulses (ones) since last substitution | |
| --- | --- | --- |
| | Odd | Even |
| − | 000− | +00+ |
| + | 000+ | −00− |

result in loss of synchronization. To overcome this problem, the encoding is amended with the following rules:

- If an octet of all zeros occurs and the last voltage pulse preceding this octet was positive, then the eight zeros of the octet are encoded as 000+–0–+.
- If an octet of all zeros occurs and the last voltage pulse preceding this octet was negative, then the eight zeros of the octet are encoded as 000–+0+–.

This technique forces two code violations (signal patterns not allowed in AMI) of the AMI code, an event unlikely to be caused by noise or other transmission impairment. The receiver recognizes the pattern and interprets the octet as consisting of all zeros.

A coding scheme that is commonly used in Europe and Japan is known as the **high-density bipolar-3 zeros (HDB3)** code (Table 4.4). As before, it is based on the use of AMI encoding. In this case, the scheme replaces strings of four zeros with sequences containing one or two pulses. In each case, the fourth zero is replaced with a code violation. In addition, a rule is needed to ensure that successive violations are of alternate polarity so that no dc component is introduced. Thus, if the last violation was positive, this violation must be negative, and vice versa. The table shows that this condition is tested for by knowing whether the number of pulses since the last violation is even or odd and the polarity of the last pulse before the occurrence of the four zeros.

Figure 4.3 shows the spectral properties of these two codes. As can be seen, neither has a dc component. Most of the energy is concentrated in a relatively sharp spectrum around a frequency equal to one-half the data rate. Thus, these codes are well suited to high data-rate transmission.

## 4.2 DIGITAL DATA, ANALOG SIGNALS

We turn now to the case of transmitting digital data using analog signals. The most familiar use of this transformation is for transmitting digital data through the public telephone network. The telephone network was designed to receive, switch, and transmit analog signals in the voice-frequency range of about 300 to 3400 Hz. It is not at present suitable for handling digital signals from the subscriber locations (although this is beginning to change). Thus, digital devices are attached to the network via a modem (modulator-demodulator), which converts digital data to analog signals, and vice versa.

For the telephone network, modems are used that produce signals in the voice-frequency range. The same basic techniques are used for modems that produce signals at higher frequencies (e.g., microwave). This section introduces these techniques and provides a brief discussion of the performance characteristics of the alternative approaches.

## Encoding Techniques

We mentioned that modulation involves operation on one or more of the three characteristics of a carrier signal: amplitude, frequency, and phase. Accordingly, there are three basic encoding or modulation techniques for transforming digital data into analog signals, as illustrated in Figure 4.7:

- Amplitude-shift keying (ASK)
- Frequency-shift keying (FSK)
- Phase-shift keying (PSK)

In all these cases, the resulting signal occupies a bandwidth centered on the carrier frequency.

In **ASK**, the two binary values are represented by two different amplitudes of the carrier frequency. Commonly, one of the amplitudes is zero; that is, one binary digit is represented by the presence, at constant amplitude, of the carrier, the other by the absence of the carrier. The resulting signal is

$$s(t) = \begin{cases} A \cos(2\pi f_c t) & \text{binary 1} \\ 0 & \text{binary 0} \end{cases}$$

where the carrier signal is $A \cos(2\pi f_c t)$. ASK is susceptible to sudden gain changes and is a rather inefficient modulation technique. On voice-grade lines, it is typically used only up to 1200 bps.

The ASK technique is used to transmit digital data over optical fiber. For LED transmitters, the equation above is valid. That is, one signal element is represented by a light pulse while the other signal element is represented by the absence of light. Laser transmitters normally have a fixed "bias" current that causes the device to emit a low light level. This low level represents one signal element, while a higher-amplitude lightwave represents another.

In **FSK**, the two binary values are represented by two different frequencies near the carrier frequency. The resulting signal is

$$s(t) = \begin{cases} A \cos(2\pi f_1 t) & \text{binary 1} \\ A \cos(2\pi f_2 t) & \text{binary 0} \end{cases}$$

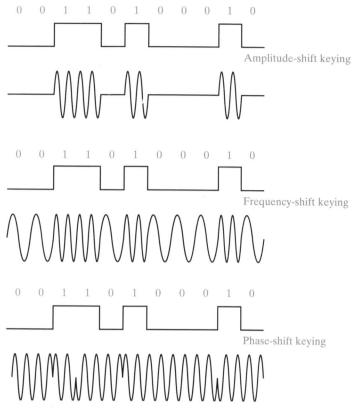

**FIGURE 4.7**   Modulation of analog signals for digital data.

where $f_1$ and $f_2$ are typically offset from the carrier frequency $f_c$ by equal but opposite amounts.

Figure 4.8 shows an example of the use of FSK for full-duplex operation over a voice-grade line. The figure is a specification for the Bell System 108 series modems. Recall that a voice-grade line will pass frequencies in the approximate range of 300 to 3400 Hz, and that full-duplex means that signals are transmitted in both directions at the same time. To achieve full-duplex transmission, this bandwidth is split at 1700 Hz. In one direction (transmit or receive), the frequencies used to represent 1 and 0 are centered on 1170 Hz, with a shift of 100 Hz on either side. The effect of alternating between those two frequencies is to produce a signal whose spectrum is indicated as the shaded area on the left in Figure 4.8. Similarly, for the other direction (receive or transmit) the modem uses frequencies shifted 100 Hz to each side of a center frequency of 2125 Hz. This signal is indicated by the shaded area on the right in Figure 4.8. Note that there is little overlap and, consequently, little interference.

FSK is less susceptible to error than ASK. On voice-grade lines, it is typically used up to 1200 bps. It is also commonly used for high-frequency (3 to 30 MHz)

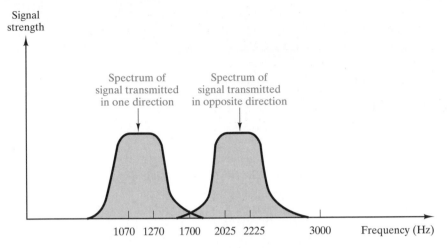

**FIGURE 4.8** Full-duplex FSK transmission on a voice-grade line.

radio transmission. It can also be used at even higher frequencies on local area networks that use coaxial cable.

In **PSK**, the phase of the carrier signal is shifted to represent data. The bottom of Figure 4.7 is an example of a two-phase system. In this system, a binary 0 is represented by sending a signal burst of the same phase as the previous signal burst. A binary 1 is represented by sending a signal burst of opposite phase to the preceding one; this is known as differential PSK, as the phase shift is with reference to the previous bit transmitted rather than to some constant reference signal. The resulting signal is

$$s(t) = \begin{cases} A\cos(2\pi f_c t + \pi) & \text{binary 1} \\ A\cos(2\pi f_c t) & \text{binary 0} \end{cases}$$

with the phase measured relative to the previous bit interval.

More efficient use of bandwidth can be achieved if each signaling element represents more than one bit. For example, instead of a phase shift of 180°, as allowed in PSK, a common encoding technique, known as quadrature phase-shift keying (QPSK) uses phase shifts of multiples of 90°:

$$s(t) = \begin{cases} A\cos(2\pi f_c t + 45°) & 11 \\ A\cos(2\pi f_c t + 135°) & 10 \\ A\cos(2\pi f_c t + 225°) & 00 \\ A\cos(2\pi f_c t + 315°) & 01 \end{cases}$$

Thus, each signal element represents two bits rather than one.

This scheme can be extended. It is possible to transmit bits three at a time using eight different phase angles. Further, each angle can have more than one amplitude. For example, a standard 9600 bps modem uses 12 phase angles, four of which have two amplitude values (Figure 4.9).

This latter example points out very well the difference between the data rate R (in bps) and the modulation rate D (in bauds) of a signal. Let us assume that this scheme is being employed with NRZ-L digital input. The data rate is $R = 1/t_B$ where $t_B$ is the width of each NRZ-L bit. However, the encoded signal contains b = 4 bits in each signal element using L = 16 different combinations of amplitude and phase. The modulation rate can be seen to be R/4, as each change of signal element communicates four bits. Thus, the line signaling speed is 2400 bauds, but the data rate is 9600 bps. This is the reason that higher bit rates can be achieved over voice-grade lines by employing more complex modulation schemes.

To repeat

$$D = \frac{R}{b} = \frac{R}{\log_2 L}$$

where

$D$ = modulation rate, bauds

$R$ = data rate, bps

$L$ = number of different signal elements

$b$ = number of bits per signal element

The above is complicated when an encoding technique other than NRZ is used. For example, we saw that the maximum modulation rate for biphase signals is $2/t_B$. Thus, D for biphase is greater than D for NRZ. This, to some extent, counteracts the reduction in D achieved by using multilevel signal modulation techniques.

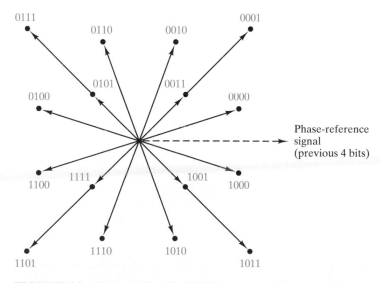

**FIGURE 4.9**   Phase angles for 9600 bit-per-second transmission.

## Performance

In looking at the performance of various digital-to-analog modulation schemes, the first parameter of interest is the bandwidth of the modulated signal. This depends on a variety of factors, including the definition of bandwidth used and the filtering technique used to create the bandpass signal. We will use some straightforward results from [COUC95].

The transmission bandwidth $B_T$ for ASK is of the form

$$B_T = (1 + r)R$$

where $R$ is the bit rate and $r$ is related to the technique by which the signal is filtered to establish a bandwidth for transmission; typically, $0 < r < 1$. The bandwidth, then, is directly related to the bit rate. The formula above is also valid for PSK.

For FSK, the bandwidth can be expressed as

$$B_T = 2\Delta F + (1 + r)R$$

where $\Delta F = f_2 - f_c = f_c - f_1$ is the offset of the modulated frequency from the carrier frequency. When very high frequencies are used, the $\Delta F$ term dominates. For example, one of the standards for FSK signaling on a coaxial cable multipoint local network uses $\Delta F = 1.25$ MHz, $f_c = 5$ MHz, and $R = 1$ Mbps. In this case, $B_T \approx 2\Delta F = 2.5$ MHz. In the example of the preceding section for the Bell 108 modem, $\Delta F = 100$ Hz, $f_c = 1170$ Hz (in one direction), and $R = 300$ bps. In this case, $B_T \approx (1 + r)R$, which is the range from 300 to 600 Hz.

With multilevel signaling, significant improvements in bandwidth can be achieved. In general

$$B_T = \left(\frac{1 + r}{l}\right)R = \left(\frac{1 + r}{\log_2 L}\right)R$$

where $l$ is the number of bits encoded per signal element and $L$ is the number of different signal elements.

Table 4.5 shows the ratio of data rate, $R$, to transmission bandwidth for various schemes. This ratio is also referred to as the bandwidth efficiency. As the name suggests, this parameter measures the efficiency with which bandwidth can be used to transmit data. The advantage of multilevel signaling methods now becomes clear.

Of course, the discussion above refers to the spectrum of the input signal to a communications line. Nothing has yet been said of performance in the presence of noise. Figure 4.10 summarizes some results based on reasonable assumptions concerning the transmission system [COUC95]. Here, bit error rate is plotted as a function of the ratio $E_b/N_0$ defined in Chapter 2. Of course, as that ratio increases, the bit-error rate drops. Further, PSK and QPSK are about 3 dB superior to ASK and FSK.

This information can now be related to bandwidth efficiency. Recall that

$$\frac{E_b}{N_0} = \frac{S}{N_0 R}$$

**TABLE 4.5**  Data rate to transmission bandwidth ratio for various digital-to-analog encoding schemes.

|  | $r = 0$ | $r = 0.5$ | $r = 1$ |
|---|---|---|---|
| ASK | 1.0 | 0.67 | 0.5 |
| FSK |  |  |  |
|   Wideband ($\Delta F >> R$) | ~0 | ~0 | ~0 |
|   Narrowband ($\Delta F \approx f_c$) | 1.0 | 0.67 | 0.5 |
| PSK | 1.0 | 0.67 | 0.5 |
| Multilevel signaling |  |  |  |
|   $L = 4, l = 2$ | 2.00 | 1.33 | 1.00 |
|   $L = 8, l = 3$ | 3.00 | 2.00 | 1.50 |
|   $L = 16, l = 4$ | 4.00 | 2.67 | 2.00 |
|   $L = 32, l = 5$ | 5.00 | 3.33 | 2.50 |

The parameter $N_0$ is the noise-power density in watts/hertz. Hence, the noise in a signal with bandwidth $B_T$ is $N = N_0 B_T$. Substituting, we have

$$\frac{E_b}{N_0} = \frac{S}{N} \frac{B_T}{R}$$

For a given signaling scheme, the bit error rate can be reduced by increasing $E_b/N_0$,

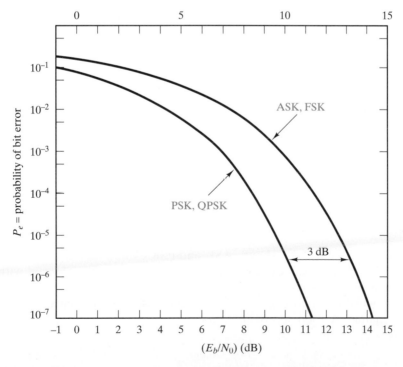

**FIGURE 4.10**  Bit error rate of various digital-to-analog encoding schemes.

which can be accomplished by increasing the bandwidth or decreasing the data rate—in other words, by reducing bandwidth efficiency.

### Example

What is the bandwidth efficiency for FSK, ASK, PSK, and QPSK for a bit error rate of $10^{-7}$ on a channel with an S/N of 12 dB?

We have

$$\frac{E_b}{N_0} = 12 \text{ dB} - \left(\frac{R}{B_T}\right)\text{dB}$$

For FSK and ASK, from Figure 4.10,

$$\frac{E_b}{N_0} = 14.2 \text{ dB}$$

$$\left(\frac{R}{B_T}\right)\text{dB} = -2.2 \text{ dB}$$

$$\frac{R}{B_T} = 0.6$$

For PSK, from Figure 4.10

$$\frac{E_b}{N_0} = 11.2 \text{ dB}$$

$$\left(\frac{R}{B_T}\right)\text{dB} = -0.8 \text{ dB}$$

$$\frac{R}{B_T} = 1.2$$

The result for QPSK must take into account that the baud rate $D = R/2$. Thus,

$$\frac{R}{B_T} = 2.4$$

As the example above shows, ASK and FSK exhibit the same bandwidth efficiency; PSK is better, and even greater improvement can be achieved with multi-level signaling.

It is worthwhile to compare these bandwidth requirements with those for digital signaling. A good approximation is

$$B_T = 0.5(1 + r)D$$

where $D$ is the modulation rate. For NRZ, $D = R$, and we have

$$\frac{R}{B} = \frac{2}{1 + r}$$

Thus, digital signaling is in the same ballpark, in terms of bandwidth efficiency, as ASK, FSK, and PSK. Significant advantage for analog signaling is seen with multi-level techniques.

## 4.3  ANALOG DATA, DIGITAL SIGNALS

In this section we examine the process of transforming analog data into digital signals. Strictly speaking, it might be more correct to refer to this as a process of converting analog data into digital data, a process known as digitization. Once analog data have been converted into digital data, a number of things can happen; the three most common are

1. The digital data can be transmitted using NRZ-L. In this case, we have gone directly from analog data to a digital signal.
2. The digital data can be encoded as a digital signal using a code other than NRZ-L. Thus, an extra step is required.
3. The digital data can be converted into an analog signal, using one of the modulation techniques discussed in Section 4.2.

This last, seemingly curious procedure is illustrated in Figure 4.11, which shows voice data that are digitized and then converted to an analog ASK signal; this allows digital transmission in the sense defined in Chapter 2. The voice data, because they have been digitized, can be treated as digital data, even though transmission requirements (e.g., use of microwave) dictate that an analog signal be used.

The device used for converting analog data into digital form for transmission, and subsequently recovering the original analog data from the digital, is known, as a codec (coder-decoder). In this section, we examine the two principal techniques used in codecs, pulse code modulation, and delta modulation. The section closes with a discussion of comparative performance.

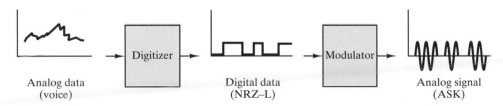

**FIGURE 4.11**   Digitizing analog data.

### Pulse Code Modulation

Pulse Code Modulation (PCM) is based on the sampling theorem, which states

> If a signal $f(t)$ is sampled at regular intervals of time and at a rate higher than twice the highest significant signal frequency, then the samples contain all the

information of the original signal. The function $f(t)$ may be reconstructed from these samples by the use of a low-pass filter.

For the interested reader, a proof is provided in Appendix 4A. If voice data are limited to frequencies below 4000 Hz, a conservative procedure for intelligibility, 8000 samples per second would be sufficient to completely characterize the voice signal. Note, however, that these are analog samples.

This is illustrated in Figure 4.12a and b. The original signal is assumed to be bandlimited with a bandwidth of $B$. Samples are taken at a rate $2B$, or once every $1/2B$ seconds. These samples are represented as narrow pulses whose amplitude is proportional to the value of the original signal. This process is known as pulse

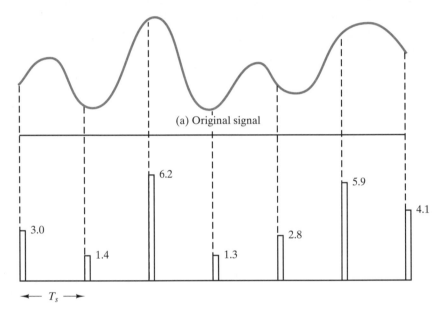

(a) Original signal

(b) PAM pulses

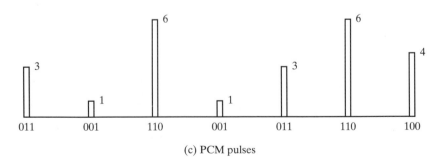

(c) PCM pulses

0110011100010111110100

(d) PCM output

**FIGURE 4.12**   Pulse-code modulation.

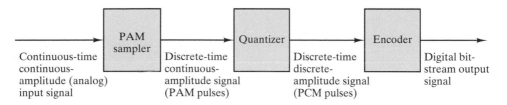

**FIGURE 4.13**   Analog-to-digital conversion.

amplitude modulation (PAM). By itself, this technique has commercial applicability. It is used, for example, in some of AT&T's Dimension PBX products.

However, the most significant fact about PAM is that it is the first step toward PCM, as depicted in Figure 4.12c. To produce PCM data, the PAM samples are quantized. That is, the amplitude of each PAM pulse is approximated by an $n$-bit integer. In the example, $n = 3$. Thus, $8 = 2^3$ levels are available for approximating the PAM pulses.

Figure 4.13 illustrates the process, starting with a continuous-time, continuous-amplitude (analog) signal, in which a digital signal is produced. The digital signal consists of blocks of $n$ bits, where each $n$-bit number is the amplitude of a PCM pulse. On reception, the process is reversed to reproduce the analog signal. Notice, however, that this process violates the terms of the sampling theorem. By quantizing the PAM pulse, the original signal is now only approximated and cannot be recovered exactly. This effect is known as quantizing error or quantizing noise. The signal-to-noise ratio for quantizing noise can be expressed as

$$\frac{S}{N} = 6n + 1.8 \text{ dB}$$

Each additional bit used for quantizing increases S/N by 6 dB, which is a factor of 4.

Typically, the PCM scheme is refined using a technique known as nonlinear encoding, which means, in effect, that the quantization levels are not equally spaced. The problem with equal spacing is that the mean absolute error for each sample is the same, regardless of signal level. Consequently, lower amplitude values are relatively more distorted. By using a greater number of quantizing steps for signals of low amplitude, and a smaller number of quantizing steps for signals of large amplitude, a marked reduction in overall signal distortion is achieved (e.g., see Figure 4.14).

The same effect can be achieved by using uniform quantizing but companding (compressing-expanding) the input analog signal. Companding is a process that compresses the intensity range of a signal by imparting more gain to weak signals than to strong signals on input. At output, the reverse operation is performed. Figure 4.15 is a typical companding function.

Nonlinear encoding can significantly improve the PCM S/N ratio. For voice signals, improvements of 24 to 30 dB have been achieved.

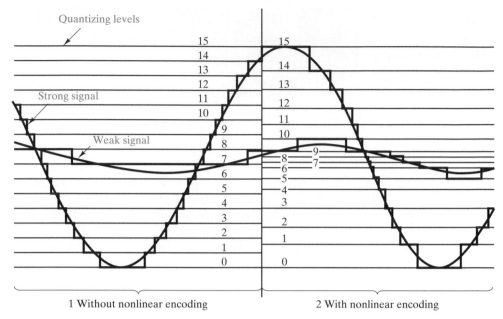

**FIGURE 4.14**   Effect of nonlinear coding.

## Delta Modulation (DM)

A variety of techniques have been used to improve the performance of PCM or to reduce its complexity. One of the most popular alternatives to PCM is delta modulation (DM).

With delta modulation, an analog input is approximated by a staircase function that moves up or down by one quantization level ($\delta$) at each sampling interval ($T_S$). An example is shown in Figure 4.16, where the staircase function is overlaid on the original analog waveform. The important characteristic of this staircase function is that its behavior is binary: At each sampling time, the function moves up or down a constant amount $\delta$. Thus, the output of the delta modulation process can be

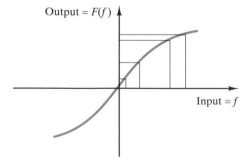

**FIGURE 4.15**   Typical companding function.

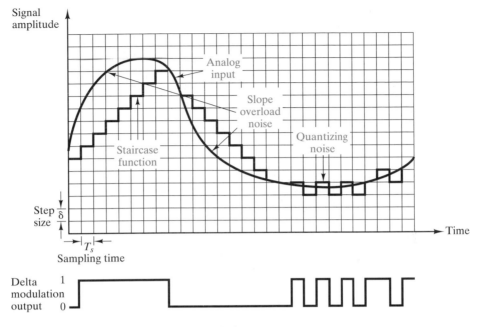

**FIGURE 4.16**    Example of delta modulation.

represented as a single binary digit for each sample. In essence, a bit stream is produced by approximating the derivative of an analog signal rather than its amplitude. A 1 is generated if the staircase function is to go up during the next interval; a 0 is generated otherwise.

The transition (up or down) that occurs at each sampling interval is chosen so that the staircase function tracks the original analog waveform as closely as possible. Figure 4.17 illustrates the logic of the process, which is essentially a feedback mechanism. For transmission, the following occurs: At each sampling time, the analog input is compared to the most recent value of the approximating staircase function. If the value of the sampled waveform exceeds that of the staircase function, a 1 is generated; otherwise, a 0 is generated. Thus, the staircase is always changed in the direction of the input signal. The output of the DM process is therefore a binary sequence that can be used at the receiver to reconstruct the staircase function. The staircase function can then be smoothed by some type of integration process or by passing it through a low-pass filter to produce an analog approximation of the analog input signal.

There are two important parameters in a DM scheme: the size of the step assigned to each binary digit, $\delta$, and the sampling rate. As Figure 4.16 illustrates, $\delta$ must be chosen to produce a balance between two types of errors or noise. When the analog waveform is changing very slowly, there will be quantizing noise, which increases as $\delta$ is increased. On the other hand, when the analog waveform is changing rapidly enough such that the staircase can't follow, there is slope-overload noise. This noise increases as $\delta$ is decreased.

It should be clear that the accuracy of the scheme can be improved by increasing the sampling rate; however, this increases the data rate of the output signal.

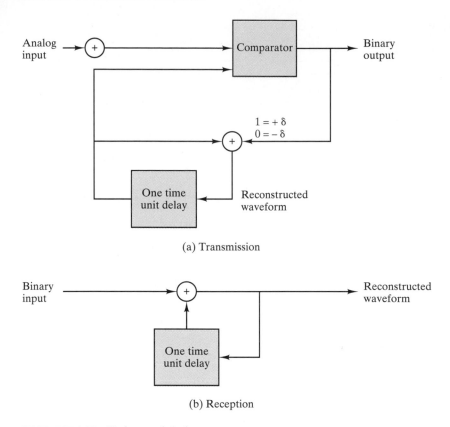

FIGURE 4.17   Delta modulation.

The principal advantage of DM over PCM is the simplicity of its implementation. In general, PCM exhibits better S/N characteristics at the same data rate.

## Performance

Good voice reproduction via PCM can be achieved with 128 quantization levels, or 7-bit coding ($2^7 = 128$). A voice signal, conservatively, occupies a bandwidth of 4 kHz. Thus, according to the sampling theorem, samples should be taken at a rate of 8000 per second. This implies a data rate of $8000 \times 7 = 56$ kbps for the PCM-encoded digital data.

Consider what this means from the point of view of bandwidth requirement. An analog voice signal occupies 4 kHz. A 56-kbps digital signal will require on the order of at least 28 kHz! Even more severe differences are seen with higher bandwidth signals. For example, a common PCM scheme for color television uses 10-bit codes, which works out to 92 Mbps for a 4.6-MHz bandwidth signal. In spite of these numbers, digital techniques continue to grow in popularity for transmitting analog data. The principal reasons for this are

- Because repeaters are used instead of amplifiers, there is no additive noise.

- As we shall see, time-division multiplexing (TDM) is used for digital signals instead of the frequency-division multiplexing (FDM) used for analog signals. With TDM, there is no intermodulation noise, whereas we have seen that this is a concern for FDM.
- The conversion to digital signaling allows the use of the more efficient digital switching techniques.

Furthermore, techniques are being developed to provide more efficient codes. In the case of voice, a reasonable goal appears to be in the neighborhood of 4 kbps. With video, advantage can be taken of the fact that from frame to frame, most picture elements will not change. Interframe coding techniques should allow the video requirement to be reduced to about 15 Mbps, and for slowly changing scenes, such as found in a video teleconference, down to 64 kbps or less.

As a final point, we mention that in many instances, the use of a telecommunications system will result in both digital-to-analog and analog-to-digital processing. The overwhelming majority of local terminations into the telecommunications network are analog, and the network itself uses a mixture of analog and digital techniques. As a result, digital data at a user's terminal may be converted to analog by a modem, subsequently digitized by a codec, and perhaps suffer repeated conversions before reaching its destination.

Because of the above, telecommunication facilities handle analog signals that represent both voice and digital data. The characteristics of the waveforms are quite different. Whereas voice signals tend to be skewed to the lower portion of the bandwidth (Figure 2.10), analog encoding of digital signals has a more uniform spectral content and therefore contains more high-frequency components. Studies have shown that, because of the presence of these higher frequencies, PCM-related techniques are preferable to DM-related techniques for digitizing analog signals that represent digital data.

## 4.4   ANALOG DATA, ANALOG SIGNALS

Modulation has been defined as the process of combining an input signal $m(t)$ and a carrier at frequency $f_c$ to produce a signal $s(t)$ whose bandwidth is (usually) centered on $f_c$. For digital data, the motivation for modulation should be clear: When only analog transmission facilities are available, modulation is required to convert the digital data to analog form. The motivation when the data are already analog is less clear. After all, voice signals are transmitted over telephone lines at their original spectrum (referred to as baseband transmission). There are two principal reasons:

- A higher frequency may be needed for effective transmission. For unguided transmission, it is virtually impossible to transmit baseband signals; the required antennas would be many kilometers in diameter.
- Modulation permits frequency-division multiplexing, an important technique explored in Chapter 7.

In this section, we look at the principal techniques for modulation using ana-log data: amplitude modulation (AM), frequency modulation (FM), and phase modulation (PM). As before, the three basic characteristics of a signal are used for modulation.

## Amplitude Modulation

Amplitude modulation (AM) is the simplest form of modulation, and is depicted in Figure 4.18. Mathematically, the process can be expressed as

$$s(t) = [1 + n_a x(t)]\cos 2\pi f_c t$$

where $\cos 2\pi f_c t$ is the carrier and $x(t)$ is the input signal (carrying data), both nor-malized to unity amplitude. The parameter $n_a$, known as the modulation index, is the ratio of the amplitude of the input signal to the carrier. Corresponding to our previous notation, the input signal is $m(t) = n_a x(t)$. The 1 in the preceding equation is a dc component that prevents loss of information, as explained subsequently. This scheme is also known as double-sideband transmitted carrier (DSBTC).

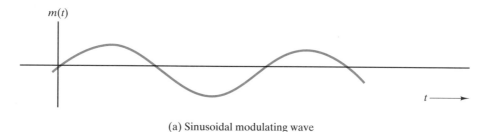

(a) Sinusoidal modulating wave

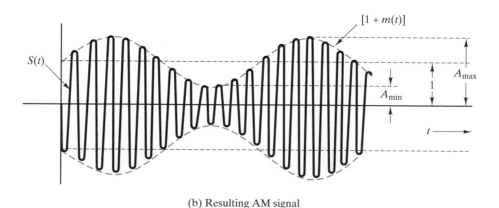

(b) Resulting AM signal

**FIGURE 4.18** Amplitude modulation.

## Example

Derive an expression for $s(t)$ if $x(t)$ is the amplitude-modulating signal $\cos 2\pi f_m t$. We have

$$s(t) = [1 + n_a \cos 2\pi f_m t] \cos 2\pi f_c t$$

By trigonometric identity, this may be expanded to

$$s(t) = \cos 2\pi f_c t + \frac{n_a}{2} \cos 2\pi (f_c - f_m)t + \frac{n_a}{2} \cos 2\pi (f_c + f_m)t$$

The resulting signal has a component at the original carrier frequency plus a pair of components, each spaced $f_m$ hertz from the carrier.

From the equation above and Figure 4.18, it can be seen that AM involves the multiplication of the input signal by the carrier. The envelope of the resulting signal is $[1 + n_a x(t)]$ and, as long as $n_a < 1$, the envelope is an exact reproduction of the original signal. If $n_a > 1$, the envelope will cross the time axis and information is lost.

It is instructive to look at the spectrum of the AM signal. An example is shown in Figure 4.19. The spectrum consists of the original carrier plus the spectrum of the input signal translated to $f_c$. The portion of the spectrum for $|f| > |f_c|$ is the *upper sideband*, and the portion of the spectrum for $|f| < |f_c|$ is the *lower sideband*. Both the upper and lower sidebands are replicas of the original spectrum $M(f)$, with the lower sideband being frequency-reversed. As an example, consider a voice signal

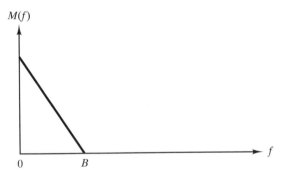

(a) Spectrum of modulating signal

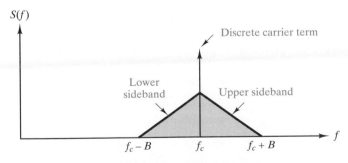

(b) Spectrum of AM signal with carrier at $f_c$

**FIGURE 4.19**   Spectrum of an AM signal.

with a bandwidth that extends from 300 to 3000 Hz being modulated on a 60-kHz carrier. The resulting signal contains an upper sideband of 60.3 to 63 kHz, a lower sideband of 57 to 59.7 kHz, and the 60-Hz carrier. An important relationship is

$$P_t = P_c\left(1 + \frac{n_a^2}{2}\right)$$

where $P_t$ is the total transmitted power in $s(t)$ and $P_c$ is the transmitted power in the carrier. We would like $n_a$ as large as possible so that most of the signal power is used to actually carry information. However, $n_a$ must remain below 1.

It should be clear that $s(t)$ contains unnecessary components, as each of the sidebands contains the complete spectrum of $m(t)$. A popular variant of AM, known as single sideband (SSB), takes advantage of this fact by sending only one of the sidebands, eliminating the other sideband and the carrier. The principal advantages of this approach are

- Only half the bandwidth is required; that is, $B_T = B$, where $B$ is the bandwidth of the original signal. For DSBTC, $B_T = 2B$.
- Less power is required because no power is used to transmit the carrier or the other sideband.

Another variant is double-sideband suppressed carrier (DSBSC), which filters out the carrier frequency and sends both sidebands. This saves some power but uses as much bandwidth as DSBTC.

The disadvantage of suppressing the carrier is that the carrier can be used for synchronization purposes. For example, suppose that the original analog signal is an ASK waveform encoding digital data. The receiver needs to know the starting point of each bit time to interpret the data correctly. A constant carrier provides a clocking mechanism by which to time the arrival of bits. A compromise approach is vestigial sideband (VSB), which uses one sideband and a reduced-power carrier.

### Angle Modulation

Frequency modulation (FM) and phase modulation (PM) are special cases of angle modulation. The modulated signal is expressed as

$$s(t) = A_c \cos[2\pi f_c t + \phi(t)]$$

For phase modulation, the phase is proportional to the modulating signal:

$$\phi(t) = n_p m(t)$$

where $n_p$ is the phase modulation index.

For frequency modulation, the derivative of the phase is proportional to the modulating signal,

$$\phi'(t) = n_f m(t)$$

where $n_f$ is the frequency modulation index.

The definitions above may be clarified if we consider the following. The phase of $s(t)$ at any instant is just $2\pi f_c t + \phi(t)$. The instantaneous phase deviation from the carrier signal is $\phi(t)$. In PM, this instantaneous phase deviation is proportional to $m(t)$. Because frequency can be defined as the rate of change of phase of a signal, the instantaneous frequency of $s(t)$ is

$$2\pi f_i(t) = \frac{d}{dt}[2\pi f_c t + \phi(t)]$$

$$f_i(t) = f_c + \frac{1}{2\pi}\phi'(t)$$

and the instantaneous frequency deviation from the carrier frequency is $\phi'(t)$, which in FM is proportional to $m(t)$.

Figure 4.20 illustrates amplitude, phase, and frequency modulation by a sine wave. The shapes of the FM and PM signals are very similar. Indeed, it is impossible to tell them apart without knowledge of the modulation function.

Several observations about the FM process are in order. The peak deviation $\Delta F$ can be seen to be

$$\Delta F = \frac{1}{2\pi} n_f A_m \text{ Hz}$$

where $A_m$ is the maximum value of $m(t)$. Thus, an increase in the magnitude of $m(t)$ will increase $\Delta F$, which, intuitively, should increase the transmitted bandwidth $B_T$. However, as should be apparent from Figure 4.20, this will not increase the average power level of the FM signal, which is $A_c^2/2$; this is distinctly different from AM, where the level of modulation affects the power in the AM signal but does not affect its bandwidth.

## Example

Derive an expression for $s(t)$ if $\phi(t)$ is the phase-modulating signal $n_p \cos 2\pi f_m t$. Assume that $A_c = 1$. This can be seen directly to be

$$s(t) = \cos[2\pi f_c t + n_p \cos 2\pi f_m t]$$

The instantaneous phase deviation from the carrier signal is $n_p \cos \pi f_m t$. The phase angle of the signal varies from its unmodulated value in a simple sinusoidal fashion, with the peak phase deviation equal to $n_p$.

The expression above can be expanded using Bessel's trigonometric identities:

$$s(t) = \sum_{n=-\infty}^{\infty} J_n(n_p)\cos\left(2\pi f_c t + 2\pi f_m t + \frac{n\pi}{2}\right)$$

where $J_n(n_p)$ is the $n$th order Bessel function of the first kind. Using the property

$$J_{-n}(x) = (-1)^n J_n(x)$$

Carrier

Modulating sine-wave signal

Amplitude-modulated (DSBTC) wave

Phase-modulated wave

Frequency-modulated wave

**FIGURE 4.20** Amplitude, phase, and frequency modulation of a sine-wave carrier by a sine-wave signal.

this can be rewritten as

$$s(t) = J_0(n_p)\cos 2\pi f_c t +$$

$$\sum_{n=-\infty}^{\infty} J_n(n_p)\left[\cos\left(2\pi(f_c + nf_m)t + \frac{n\pi}{2}\right) + \cos\left(2\pi(f_c - nf_m)t + \frac{(n+2)\pi}{2}\right)\right]$$

The resulting signal has a component at the original carrier frequency plus a set of sidebands displaced from $f_c$ by all possible multiples of $f_m$. For $n_p \ll 1$, the higher-order terms fall off rapidly.

## Example

Derive an expression for $s(t)$ if $\phi'(t)$ is the frequency-modulating signal $-n_f \sin 2\pi f_m t$. The form of $\phi'(t)$ was chosen for convenience. We have

$$X_s(f) = \sum_{n=-\infty}^{\infty} P_n X(f - nf_s) \quad \phi(t) = -\int n_f \sin 2\pi f_m t \, dt = \frac{n_f}{2\pi f_m} \cos 2\pi f_m t$$

Thus,

$$s(t) = \cos\left[2\pi f_c t + \frac{n_f}{2\pi f_m} \cos 2\pi f_m t\right]$$

$$= \cos\left[2\pi f_c t + \frac{\Delta F}{f_m} \cos 2\pi f_m t\right]$$

The instantaneous frequency deviation from the carrier signal is $-n_f \sin 2\pi f_m t$. The frequency of the signal varies from its unmodulated value in a simple sinusoidal fashion, with the peak frequency deviation equal to $n_f$ radians/second.

The equation for the FM signal has the identical form as for the PM signal, with $\Delta F/f_m$ substituted for $n_p$. Thus, the Bessel expansion is the same.

As with AM, both FM and PM result in a signal whose bandwidth is centered at $f_c$. However, we can now see that the magnitude of that bandwidth is very different. Amplitude modulation is a linear process and produces frequencies that are the sum and difference of the carrier signal and the components of the modulating signal. Hence, for AM

$$B_T = 2B$$

However, angle modulation includes a term of the form $\cos(\phi(t))$, which is non-linear and will produce a wide range of frequencies. In essence, for a modulating sinusoid of frequency $f_m$, $s(t)$ will contain components at $f_c + f_m$, $f_c + 2f_m$, and so on. In the most general case, infinite bandwidth is required to transmit an FM or PM signal. As a practical matter, a very good rule of thumb, known as Carson's rule [COUC95], is

$$B_T = 2(\beta + 1)B$$

where

$$\beta = \begin{cases} n_p A_m & \text{for PM} \\[2mm] \dfrac{\Delta F}{B} = \dfrac{n_f A_m}{2\pi B} & \text{for FM} \end{cases}$$

We can rewrite the formula for FM as

$$B_T = 2\Delta F + 2B$$

Thus, both FM and PM require greater bandwidth than AM.

## 4.5   SPREAD SPECTRUM

An increasingly popular form of communications is known as spread spectrum. This technique does not fit neatly into the categories defined in this chapter, as it can be used to transmit either analog or digital data, using an analog signal.

The spread spectrum technique was developed initially for military and intelligence requirements. The essential idea is to spread the information signal over a wider bandwidth in order to make jamming and interception more difficult. The first type of spread spectrum developed became known as frequency-hopping.[4] A more recent version is direct-sequence spread spectrum. Both of these techniques are used in various wireless data-network products. They also find use in other communications applications, such as cordless telephones.

Figure 4.21 highlights the key characteristics of any spread spectrum system. Input is fed into a channel encoder that produces an analog signal with a relatively narrow bandwidth around some center frequency. This signal is further modulated using a sequence of seemingly random digits known as a pseudorandom sequence. The effect of this modulation is to significantly increase the bandwidth (spread the spectrum) of the signal to be transmitted. On the receiving end, the same digit sequence is used to demodulate the spread spectrum signal. Finally, the signal is fed into a channel decoder to recover the data.

A comment about pseudorandom numbers is in order. These numbers are generated by an algorithm using some initial value called the *seed*. The algorithm is deterministic and therefore produces sequences of numbers that are not statistically random. However, if the algorithm is good, the resulting sequences will pass many reasonable tests of randomness. Such numbers are often referred to as pseudorandom numbers.[5] The important point is that unless you know the algorithm and

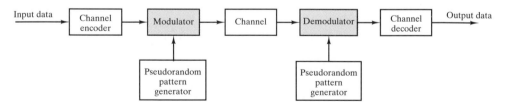

**FIGURE 4.21**   General model of spread spectrum digital communication system.

---

[4] Spread spectrum (using frequency-hopping) was invented, believe it or not, by Hollywood screen siren Hedy Lamarr in 1940 at the age of 26. She and a partner who later joined her effort were granted a patent in 1942 (U.S. Patent 2,292,387; 11 August 1942). Lamarr considered this her contribution to the war effort and never profited from her invention. For an interesting account, see [MEEK90].

[5] See [STAL95b] for a more detailed discussion of pseudorandom numbers.

the seed, it is impractical to predict the sequence. Hence, only a receiver that shares this information with a transmitter will be able to successfully decode the signal.

## Frequency–Hopping

Under this scheme, the signal is broadcast over a seemingly random series of radio frequencies, hopping from frequency to frequency at split-second intervals. A receiver, hopping between frequencies in synchronization with the transmitter, picks up the message. Would-be eavesdroppers hear only unintelligible blips. Attempts to jam the signal succeed only at knocking out a few bits of it.

A typical block diagram for a frequency-hopping system is shown in Figure 4.22. For transmission, binary data is fed into a modulator using some digital-to-

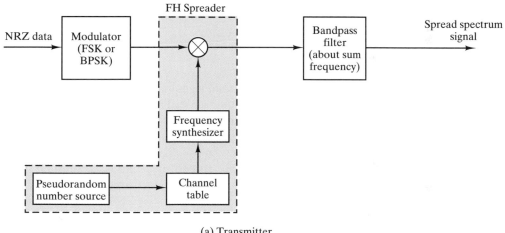

(a) Transmitter

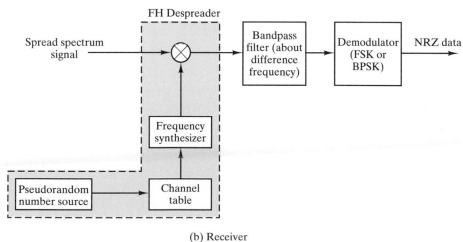

(b) Receiver

**FIGURE 4.22** Frequency-hopping spread spectrum system.

analog encoding scheme, such as frequency-shift keying (FSK) or binary-phase shift keying (BPSK). The resulting signal is centered around some base frequency. A pseudorandom number source serves as an index into a table of frequencies. At each successive interval, a new frequency is selected from the table. This frequency is then modulated by the signal produced from the initial modulator to produce a new signal with the same shape but now centered on the frequency chosen from the table.

On reception, the spread-spectrum signal is demodulated using the same sequence of table-derived frequencies and then demodulated to produce the output data.

For example, if FSK is employed, the modulator selects one of two frequencies, say $f_0$ or $f_1$, corresponding to the transmission of binary 0 or 1. The resulting binary FSK signal is translated in frequency by an amount determined by the output sequence from the pseudorandom number generator. Thus, if the frequency selected at time $i$ is $f_i$, then the signal at time $i$ is either $f_i + f_0$ or $f_i + f_1$.

### Direct Sequence

Under this scheme, each bit in the original signal is represented by multiple bits in the transmitted signal, known as a chipping code. The chipping code spreads the signal across a wider frequency band in direct proportion to the number of bits used. Therefore, a 10-bit chipping code spreads the signal across a frequency band that is 10 times greater than a 1-bit chipping code.

One technique with direct-sequence spread spectrum is to combine the digital information stream with the pseudorandom bit stream using an exclusive-or. Figure

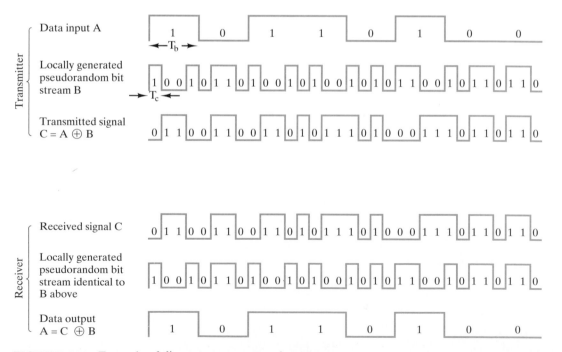

**FIGURE 4.23** Example of direct sequence spread spectrum.

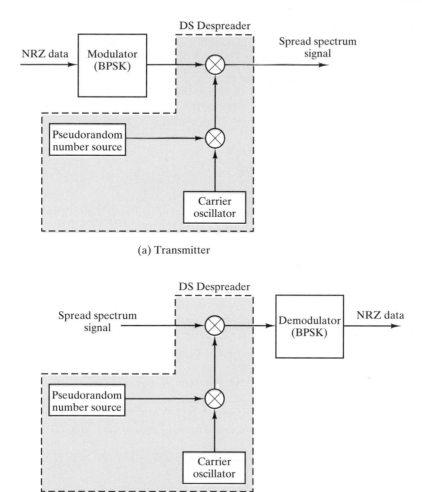

(a) Transmitter

(b) Receiver

**FIGURE 4.24** Direct sequence spread spectrum system.

4.23 shows an example. Note that an information bit of 1 inverts the pseudorandom bits in the combination, while an information bit of 0 causes the pseudorandom bits to be transmitted without inversion. The combination bit stream has the data rate of the original pseudorandom sequence, so it has a wider bandwidth than the information stream. In this example, the pseudorandom bit stream is clocked at four times the information rate.

Figure 4.24 shows a typical direct sequence implementation. In this case, the information stream and the pseudorandom stream are both converted to analog signals and then combined, rather than performing the exclusive-or of the two streams and then modulating.

The spectrum spreading achieved by the direct sequence technique is easily determined. For example, suppose the information signal has a bit width of $T_b$, which is equivalent to a data rate of $1/T_b$. In that case, the bandwidth of the signal, depending on encoding technique, is roughly $2/T_b$. Similarly, the bandwidth of the pseudorandom signal is $2/T_c$, where $T_c$ is the bit width of the pseudorandom input. The bandwidth of the combined signal is approximately the sum of the two bandwidths, or $2/(T_b + T_c)$. The amount of spreading that is achieved is a direct result of the data rate of the pseudorandom stream; the greater the data rate of the pseudorandom input, the greater the amount of spreading.

## 4.6  RECOMMENDED READING

It is difficult, for some reason, to find solid treatments of digital-to-digital encoding schemes. [PEEB87] provides one of the best analyses. [SKLA88] and [BENE87] also provide some insights. On the other hand, there are many good references on analog modulation schemes for digital data. Good choices are [COUC95], [HAYK94], and [PROA94]; these three also provide comprehensive treatment of digital and analog modulation schemes for analog data.

An exceptionally clear exposition that covers digital-to-analog, analog-to-digital, and analog-to-analog techniques is [PEAR92].

Both [PETE95] and [DIXO94] provide comprehensive treatment of spread spectrum.

BENE87    Benedetto, S., Biglieri, E., and Castellani, V. *Digital Transmission Theory.* Englewood Cliffs, NJ: Prentice Hall, 1987.

COUC95    Couch, L. *Modern Communication Systems: Principles and Applications.* Englewood Cliffs, NJ: Prentice Hall, 1995.

DIXO94    Dixon, R. *Spread Spectrum Systems with Commercial Applications.* New York: Wiley, 1994.

HAYK94    Haykin, S. *Communication Systems.* New York: Wiley, 1994.

PEAR92    Pearson, J. *Basic Communication Theory.* Englewood Cliffs, NJ: Prentice Hall, 1992.

PEEB87    Peebles, P. *Digital Communication Systems.* Englewood Cliffs, NJ: Prentice Hall, 1987.

PETE95    Peterson, R., Ziemer, R., and Borth, D. *Introduction to Spread Spectrum Communications.* Englewood Cliffs, NJ: Prentice Hall, 1995.

PROA94    Proakis, J., and Salehi, M. *Communication Systems Engineering.* Englewood Cliffs, NJ: Prentice Hall, 1994.

SKLA88    Sklar, B. *Digital Communications: Fundamentals and Applications.* Englewood Cliffs, NJ: Prentice Hall, 1988.

## 4.7  PROBLEMS

4.1    Which of the signals of Table 4.2 use differential encoding?

4.2    Develop algorithms for generating each of the codes of Table 4.2 from NRZ-L.

4.3    A modified NRZ code known as enhanced-NRZ (E-NRZ) is sometimes used for high density magnetic tape recording. E-NRZ encoding entails separating the NRZ-L data stream into 7-bit words; inverting bits 2, 3, 6, and 7; and adding one parity bit to each word. The parity bit is chosen to make the total number of 1s in the 8-bit word an odd count. What are the advantages of E-NRZ over NRZ-L? Any disadvantages?

4.4    Develop a state diagram (finite-state machine) representation of pseudoternary coding.

**4.5** Consider the following signal encoding technique. Binary data are presented as input, $a_m$, for $m = 1, 2, 3, \ldots$ Two levels of processing occur. First, a new set of binary numbers are produced:

$$b_m = (a_m + b_{m-1}) \bmod 2$$

These are then encoded as

$$c_m = b_m - b_{m-1}$$

On reception, the original data is recovered by

$$a_m = c_m \bmod 2$$

a. Verify that the received values of $a_m$ equal the transmitted values of $a_m$.
b. What sort of encoding is this?

**4.6** For the bit stream 01001110, sketch the waveforms for each of the codes of Table 4.2.

**4.7** The waveform of Figure 4.25 belongs to a Manchester encoded binary data stream. Determine the beginning and end of bit periods (i.e., extract clock information) and give the data sequence.

**FIGURE 4.25** A Manchester stream.

**4.8** A sine wave is to be used for two different signaling schemes: (a) PSK; (b) QPSK. The duration of a signal element is $10^{-5}$ sec. If the received signal is of the following form,

$$s(t) = 0.005 \sin (2\pi 10^6 t + \theta) \text{ volts}$$

and if the measured noise power at the receiver is $2.5 \times 10^{-8}$ watts, determine the $E_b/N_0$ (in dB) for each case.

**4.9** Consider Figure 4.9. Eight of the phases use only a single level of amplitude. The system shown encodes only 4 bits. How many bits could be encoded if the single amplitude phase were made to be double amplitude?

**4.10** Derive an expression for baud rate $D$ as a function of bit rate $R$ for QPSK using the digital encoding techniques of Table 4.2.

**4.11** What S/N ratio is required to achieve a bandwidth efficiency of 5.0 for ASK, FSK, PSK, and QPSK? Assume that the required bit error rate is $10^{-6}$.

**4.12** An NRZ-L signal is passed through a filter with $r = 0.5$ and then modulated onto a carrier. The data rate is 2400 bps. Evaluate the bandwidth for ASK and FSK. For FSK assume that the two frequencies used are 50 kHz and 55 kHz.

**4.13** Assume that a telephone-line channel is equalized to allow bandpass data transmission over a frequency range of 600 to 3000 Hz. The available bandwidth is 2400 Hz with a center frequency of 1800 Hz. For $r = 1$, evaluate the required bandwidth for 2400 bps QPSK and 4800-bps, eight-level multilevel signaling. Is the bandwidth adequate?

**4.14** Why should PCM be preferable to DM for encoding analog signals that represent digital data?

**4.15** Are the modem and the codec functional inverses (i.e., could an inverted modem function as a codec, or vice versa)?

**4.16** The signal of Problem 2.15 is quantized using 10-bit PCM. Find the signal-to-quantization noise ratio.

**4.17** Consider an audio signal with spectral components in the range 300 to 3000 Hz. Assume that a sampling rate of 7 kHz will be used to generate a PCM signal.
a. For S/N = 30 dB, what is the number of uniform quantization levels needed? Assume $a = 0.1$
b. What data rate is required?

**4.18**  Find the step size $\delta$ required to prevent slope-overload noise as a function of the frequency of the highest-frequency component of the signal. Assume that all components have amplitude $A$.

**4.19**  A PCM encoder accepts a signal with a full-scale voltage of 10 V and generates 8-bit codes using uniform quantization. The maximum normalized quantized voltage is $1 - 2^{-8}$. Determine: (a) normalized step size, (b) actual step size in volts, (c) actual maximum quantized level in volts, (d) normalized resolution, (e) actual resolution, and (f) percentage resolution.

**4.20**  The analog waveform shown in Figure 4.26 is to be delta-modulated. The sampling period and the step size are indicated by the grid on the figure. The first DM output and the staircase function for this period are also shown. Show the rest of the staircase function and give the DM output. Indicate regions where slope-overload distortion exists.

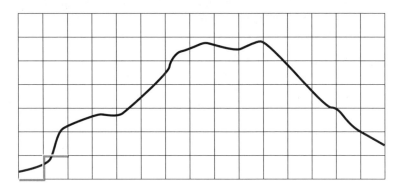

DM output

**FIGURE 4.26**  Delta modulation example.

**4.21**  By far, the most widely used technique for pseudorandom number generation is the linear congruential method. The algorithm is parameterized with four numbers, as follows:

| | | |
|---|---|---|
| $m$ | the modulus | $m > 0$ |
| $a$ | the multiplier | $0 \leq a < m$ |
| $c$ | the increment | $0 \leq c < m$ |
| $X_0$ | the starting value, or seed | $0 \leq X_0 < m$ |

The sequence of pseudorandom numbers $\{X_n\}$ is obtained via the following iterative equation:

$$X_{n+1} = (aX_n + c) \bmod m$$

If $m$, $a$, $c$, and $X_0$ are integers, then this technique will produce a sequence of integers with each integer in the range $0 \leq X_n < m$. An essential characteristic of a pseudorandom number generator is that the generated sequence should appear random. Although the sequence is not random, because it is generated deterministically, there is a variety of statistical tests that can be used to assess the degree to which a sequence exhibits randomness. Another desirable characteristic is that the function should be a full-period generating function. That is, the function should generate all the numbers between 0 and $m$ before repeating.

With the linear congruential algorithm, a choice of parameters that provides a full period does not necessarily provide a good randomization. For example, consider the two generators

$$X_{n+1} = (6X_n) \bmod 13$$

$$X_{n+1} = (7X_n) \bmod 13$$

Write out the two sequences to show that both are full-period. Which one appears more random to you?

4.22   We would like $m$ to be very large, so that there is the potential for producing a long series of distinct random numbers. A common criterion is that $m$ be nearly equal to the maximum representable nonnegative integer for a given computer. Thus, a value of $m$ near to or equal to $2^{31}$ is typically chosen. Many experts recommend a value of $2^{31}$ –1. You may wonder why one should not simply use $2^{31}$, as this latter number can be represented with no additional bits, and the mod operation should be easier to perform. In general, the modulus $2^k - 1$ is preferable to $2^k$. Why is this so?

4.23   In any use of pseudorandom numbers, whether for encryption, simulation, or statistical design, it is dangerous to blindly trust the random number generator that happens to be available in your computer's system library. One recent study found that many contemporary textbooks and programming packages make use of flawed algorithms for pseudorandom number generation. This exercise will enable you to test your system:

The test is based on a theorem attributed to Ernesto Cesaro, which states that the probability is equal to $6/\pi^2$ that the greatest common divisor of two randomly chosen integers is 1. Use this theorem in a program to determine statistically the value of $\pi$. The main program should call three subprograms: the random-number generator from the system library to generate the random integers; a subprogram to calculate the greatest common divisor of two integers using Euclid's Algorithm (found in all books on number theory), and a subprogram that calculates square roots. If these latter two programs are not available, you will have to write them as well. The main program should loop through a large number of random numbers to give an estimate of the probability referenced above. From this, it is a simple matter to solve for your estimate of $\pi$.

If the result is close to 3.14, congratulations! If not, then the result is probably low, usually a value of around 2.7. Why would such an inferior result be obtained?

•

**4A** **APPENDIX**

## Proof of the Sampling Theorem

The sampling theorem can be restated as follows. Given that

- $x(t)$ is a bandlimited signal with bandwidth $f_h$.
- $p(t)$ is a sampling signal consisting of pulses at intervals $T_s = 1/f_s$, where $f_s$ is the sampling frequency.
- $x_s(t) = x(t)p(t)$ is the sampled signal.

Then, $x(t)$ can be recovered exactly from $x_s(t)$ if and only if $f_s \geq 2f_h$.

*Proof:*
Because $p(t)$ consists of a uniform series of pulses, it is a periodic signal and can be represented by a Fourier series:

$$p(t) = \sum_{n=-\infty}^{\infty} P_n e^{j2\pi nf_s t}$$

We have

$$x_s(t) = x(t)p(t)$$
$$= \sum_{n=-\infty}^{\infty} P_n x(t) e^{j2\pi nf_s t}$$

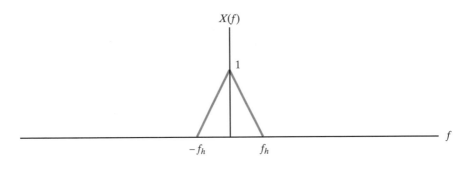

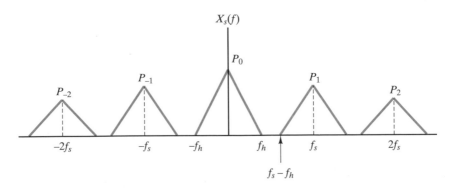

**FIGURE 4.27** Spectrum of a sampled signal.

Now consider the Fourier transform of $x_s(t)$:

$$X_s(f) = \int_{-\infty}^{\infty} x(t)e^{-j2\pi ft}dt$$

Substituting for $x_s(t)$, we have

$$X_s(f) = \int_{-\infty}^{\infty} \sum_{n=-\infty}^{\infty} P_n x(t)e^{j2\pi nf_s t}dt$$

Rearranging yields

$$X_s(f) = \sum_{n=-\infty}^{\infty} P_n \int_{-\infty}^{\infty} x(t)e^{-j2\pi(f-nf_s)t}dt$$

From the definition of the Fourier transform, we can write

$$X(f - nf_s) = \int_{-\infty}^{\infty} x(t)e^{-j2\pi(f-nf_s)t}dt$$

where $X(f)$ is the Fourier transform of $x(t)$; substituting this into the preceding equation, we have

$$X_s(f) = \sum_{n=-\infty}^{\infty} P_n X(f - nf_s)$$

This last equation has an interesting interpretation, which is illustrated in Figure 4.27, where we assume without loss of generality that the bandwidth of $x(t)$ is in the range 0 to $f_h$. The spectrum of $x_s(t)$ is composed of the spectrum of $x(t)$ plus the spectrum of $x(t)$ translated to each harmonic of the sampling frequency. Each of the translated spectra is multiplied by the corresponding coefficient of the Fourier series of $p(t)$. Now, if $f_s > 2f_h$, these various translations do not overlap, and the spectrum of $x(t)$, multiplied by $P_0$, appears in $X_s(f)$. By passing $X_s(f)$ through a bandpass filter with $f < f_s$, the spectrum of $x(t)$ is recovered. In equation form,

$$X_s(f) = P_0 X(f) \qquad -fs < f < fs$$

# CHAPTER 5

# THE DATA COMMUNICATIONS INTERFACE

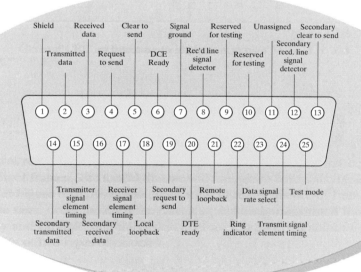

n the preceding chapters, we have been concerned primarily with the attributes of data transmission, such as the characteristics of data signals and transmission media, the encoding of signals, and transmission performance. In this chapter, we shift our emphasis to the interface between data communicating devices and the data transmission system.

For two devices linked by a transmission medium to exchange data, a high degree of cooperation is required. Typically, data are transmitted one bit at a time over the medium. The timing (rate, duration, spacing) of these bits must be the same for transmitter and receiver. Two common techniques for controlling this timing—asynchronous and synchronous—are explored in Section 5.1. Next, we look at the physical interface between data transmitting devices and the transmission line. Typically, digital data devices do not attach to and signal across the medium directly. Instead, this process is mediated through a standardized interface that provides considerable control over the interaction between the transmitting/receiving devices and the transmission line.

## 5.1  ASYNCHRONOUS AND SYNCHRONOUS TRANSMISSION

In this book, we are concerned with serial transmission of data; that is, data rate transferred over a single signal path rather than a parallel set of lines, as is common with I/O devices and internal computer signal paths. With serial transmission, signaling elements are sent down the line one at a time. Each signaling element may be

- **Less than one bit.** This is the case, for example, with Manchester coding.
- **One bit.** NRZ-L and FSK are digital and analog examples, respectively.
- **More than one bit.** QPSK is an example.

For simplicity in the following discussion, we assume one bit per signaling element unless otherwise stated. The discussion is not materially affected by this simplification.

Recall from Figure 2.15 that the reception of digital data involves sampling the incoming signal once per bit time to determine the binary value. One of the difficulties encountered in such a process is that various transmission impairments will corrupt the signal so that occasional errors will occur. This problem is compounded by a timing difficulty: In order for the receiver to sample the incoming bits properly, it must know the arrival time and duration of each bit that it receives.

Suppose that the sender simply transmits a stream of data bits. The sender has a clock that governs the timing of the transmitted bits. For example, if data are to be transmitted at one million bits per second (1 Mbps), then one bit will be transmitted every $1/10^6 = 1$ microsecond ($\mu$s), as measured by the sender's clock. Typically, the receiver will attempt to sample the medium at the center of each bit-time. The receiver will time its samples at intervals of one bit-time. In our example, the sampling would occur once every 1 $\mu$s. If the receiver times its samples based on its own clock, then there will be a problem if the transmitter's and receiver's clocks are not precisely aligned. If there is a drift of 1 percent (the receiver's clock is 1 percent faster or slower than the transmitter's clock), then the first sampling will be 0.01 of a bit-time (0.01 μs) away from the center of the bit (center of bit is .5 μs from beginning and end of bit). After 50 or more samples, the receiver may be in error because it is sampling in the wrong bit-time ($50 \times .01 = .5$ μs). For smaller timing differences, the error would occur later, but, eventually, the receiver will be out of step with the transmitter if the transmitter sends a sufficiently long stream of bits and if no steps are taken to synchronize the transmitter and receiver.

## Asynchronous Transmission

Two approaches are common for achieving the desired synchronization. The first is called, oddly enough, asynchronous transmission. The strategy with this scheme is to avoid the timing problem by not sending long, uninterrupted streams of bits. Instead, data are transmitted one character at a time, where each character is five to eight bits in length.[1] Timing or synchronization must only be maintained within each character; the receiver has the opportunity to resynchronize at the beginning of each new character.

The technique is easily explained with reference to Figure 5.1. When no character is being transmitted, the line between transmitter and receiver is in an *idle* state. The definition of idle is equivalent to the signaling element for binary 1. Thus, for NRZ-L signaling (see Figure 4.2), which is common for asynchronous transmission, idle would be the presence of a negative voltage on the line. The beginning of a character is signaled by a *start-bit* with a value of binary 0. This is followed by the five to eight bits that actually make up the character. The bits of the character are transmitted beginning with the least significant bit. For example, for ASCII characters, the first bit transmitted is the bit labeled $b_1$ in Table 2.1. Usually, this is followed by a parity bit, which therefore is in the most significant bit position. The parity bit is set by the transmitter such that the total number of ones in the character, including the parity bit, is even (even parity) or odd (odd parity), depending on the convention being used. This bit is used by the receiver for error detection, as discussed in Chapter 6. The final element is a *stop*, which is a binary 1. A minimum length for the stop is specified, and this is usually 1, 1.5, or 2 times the duration of an ordinary bit. No maximum value is specified. Because the stop is the same as the idle state, the transmitter will continue to transmit the stop signal until it is ready to send the next character.

If a steady stream of characters is sent, the interval between two characters is uniform and equal to the stop element. For example, if the stop is one bit-time and the ASCII characters ABC are sent (with even parity bit), the pattern is 01000001010010000101011000011111 . . . 111.[2] The start bit (0) starts the timing sequence for the next nine elements, which are the 8-bit ASCII code and the stop

---

[1] The number of bits that comprise a character depends on the code used. We have already seen one common example, the ASCII code, which uses seven bits per character (Table 4-1). Another common code is the Extended Binary Coded Decimal Interchange Code (EBCDIC), which is an 8-bit character code used on all IBM machines except for their personal computers.

[2] In the text, the transmission is shown from left (first bit transmitted) to right (last bit transmitted).

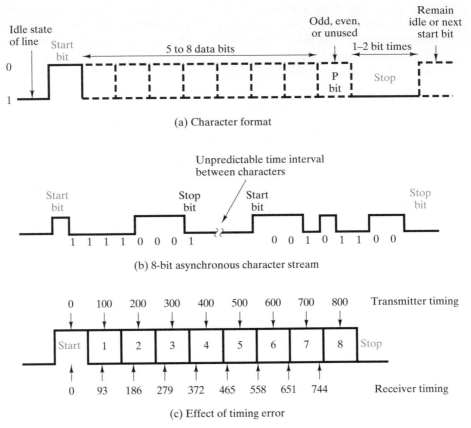

(a) Character format

(b) 8-bit asynchronous character stream

(c) Effect of timing error

**FIGURE 5.1**   Asynchronous transmission.

bit. In the idle state, the receiver looks for a transition from 1 to 0 to signal the beginning of the next character and then samples the input signal at one-bit intervals for seven intervals. It then looks for the next 1-to-0 transition, which will occur no sooner than one more bit-time.

The timing requirements for this scheme are modest. For example, ASCII characters are typically sent as 8-bit units, including the parity bit. If the receiver is 5 percent slower or faster than the transmitter, the sampling of the eighth information bit will be displaced by 45 percent and still be correctly sampled. Figure 5.1c shows the effects of a timing error of sufficient magnitude to cause an error in reception. In this example we assume a data rate of 10,000 bits per second (10 kbps); therefore, each bit is of 0.1 millisecond (ms), or 100 μs, duration. Assume that the receiver is off by 7 percent, or 7 μs per bit-time. Thus, the receiver samples the incoming character every 93 μs (based on the transmitter's clock). As can be seen, the last sample is erroneous.

An error such as this actually results in two errors. First, the last sampled bit is incorrectly received. Second, the bit count may now be out of alignment. If bit 7 is a 1 and bit 8 is a 0, bit 8 could be mistaken for a start bit. This condition is termed a *framing error*, as the character plus start and stop bits are sometimes referred to as a frame. A framing error can also occur if some noise condition causes the false appearance of a start bit during the idle state.

Asynchronous transmission is simple and cheap but requires an overhead of two to three bits per character. For example, for an 8-bit code, using a 1-bit-long stop bit, two out of every ten bits convey no information but are there merely for synchronization; thus the overhead is 20%. Of course, the percentage overhead could be reduced by sending larger blocks of bits between the start and stop bits. However, as Figure 5.1c indicates, the larger the block of bits, the greater the cumulative timing error. To achieve greater efficiency, a different form of synchronization, known as synchronous transmission, is used.

## Synchronous Transmission

With synchronous transmission, a block of bits is transmitted in a steady stream without start and stop codes. The block may be many bits in length. To prevent timing drift between transmitter and receiver, their clocks must somehow be synchronized. One possibility is to provide a separate clock line between transmitter and receiver. One side (transmitter or receiver) pulses the line regularly with one short pulse per bit-time. The other side uses these regular pulses as a clock. This technique works well over short distances, but over longer distances the clock pulses are subject to the same impairments as the data signal, and timing errors can occur. The other alternative is to embed the clocking information in the data signal; for digital signals, this can be accomplished with Manchester or Differential Manchester encoding. For analog signals, a number of techniques can be used; for example, the carrier frequency itself can be used to synchronize the receiver based on the phase of the carrier.

With synchronous transmission, there is another level of synchronization required, so as to allow the receiver to determine the beginning and end of a block of data; to achieve this, each block begins with a *preamble* bit pattern and generally ends with a *postamble* bit pattern. In addition, other bits are added to the block that convey control information used in the data link control procedures discussed in Chapter 6. The data plus preamble, postamble, and control information are called a **frame**. The exact format of the frame depends on which data link control procedure is being used.

Figure 5.2 shows, in general terms, a typical frame format for synchronous transmission. Typically, the frame starts with a preamble called a flag, which is eight bit-long. The same flag is used as a postamble. The receiver looks for the occurrence of the flag pattern to signal the start of a frame. This is followed by some number of control fields, then a data field (variable length for most protocols), more control fields, and finally the flag is repeated.

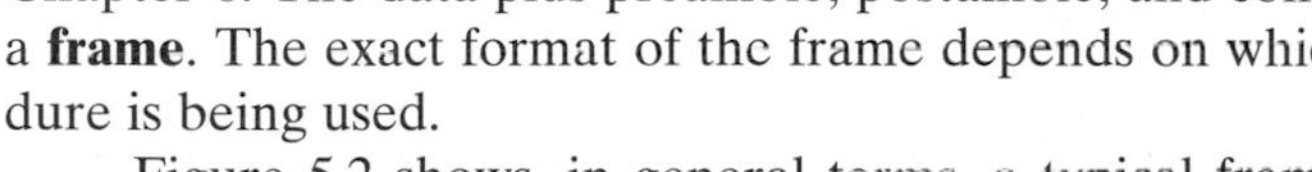

| 8-bit flag | Control fields | Data field | Control fields | 8-bit flag |
|---|---|---|---|---|

**FIGURE 5.2** Synchronous frame format.

For sizable blocks of data, synchronous transmission is far more efficient than asynchronous. Asynchronous transmission requires 20 percent or more overhead. The control information, preamble, and postamble in synchronous transmission are typically less than 100 bits. For example, one of the more common schemes, HDLC, contains 48 bits of control, preamble, and postamble. Thus, for a 1000-character block of data, each frame consists of 48 bits of overhead and $1000 \times 8 = 8,000$ bits of data, for a percentage overhead of only $48/8048 \times 100\% = 0.6\%$.

## 5.2   LINE CONFIGURATIONS

Two characteristics that distinguish various data link configurations are topology and whether the link is half duplex or full duplex.

### Topology

The topology of a data link refers to the physical arrangement of stations on a transmission medium. If there are only two stations, (e.g., a terminal and a computer or two computers), the link is point-to-point. If there are more than two stations, then it is a multipoint topology. Traditionally, a multipoint link has been used in the case of a computer (primary station) and a set of terminals (secondary stations). In today's environments, the multipoint topology is found in local area networks.

Traditional multipoint topologies are made possible when the terminals are only transmitting a fraction of the time. Figure 5.3 illustrates the advantages of the multipoint configuration. If each terminal has a point-to-point link to its computer, then the computer must have one I/O port for each terminal. Also, there is a sepa-

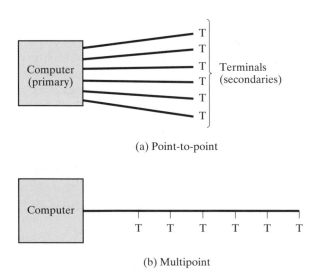

(a) Point-to-point

(b) Multipoint

**FIGURE 5.3**   Traditional computer/terminal configurations.

rate transmission line from the computer to each terminal. In a multipoint configuration, the computer needs only a single I/O port, thereby saving hardware costs. Only a single transmission line is needed, which also saves costs.

### Full Duplex and Half Duplex

Data exchanges over a transmission line can be classified as full duplex or half duplex. With *half-duplex transmission*, only one of two stations on a point-to-point link may transmit at a time. This mode is also referred to as *two-way alternate*, suggestive of the fact that two stations must alternate in transmitting; this can be compared to a one-lane, two-way bridge. This form of transmission is often used for terminal-to-computer interaction. While a user is entering and transmitting data, the computer is prevented from sending data, which would appear on the terminal screen and cause confusion.

For *full-duplex transmission*, two stations can simultaneously send and receive data from each other. Thus, this mode is known as *two-way simultaneous* and may be compared to a two-lane, two-way bridge. For computer-to-computer data exchange, this form of transmission is more efficient than half-duplex transmission.

With digital signaling, which requires guided transmission, full-duplex operation usually requires two separate transmission paths (e.g., two twisted pairs), while half duplex requires only one. For analog signaling, it depends on frequency; if a station transmits and receives on the same frequency, it must operate in half-duplex mode for wireless transmission, although it may operate in full-duplex mode for guided transmission using two separate transmission lines. If a station transmits on one frequency and receives on another, it may operate in full-duplex mode for wireless transmission and in full-duplex mode with a single line for guided transmission.

## 5.3  INTERFACING

Most digital data-processing devices have limited data-transmission capability. Typically, they generate a simple digital signal, such as NRZ-L, and the distance across which they can transmit data is limited. Consequently, it is rare for such a device (terminal, computer) to attach directly to a transmission or networking facility. The more common situation is depicted in Figure 5.4. The devices we are discussing, which include terminals and computers, are generically referred to as *data terminal equipment (DTE)*. A DTE makes use of the transmission system through the mediation of *data circuit-terminating equipment (DCE)*. An example of the latter is a modem.

On one side, the DCE is responsible for transmitting and receiving bits, one at a time, over a transmission medium or network. On the other side, the DCE must interact with the DTE. In general, this requires both data and control information to be exchanged. This is done over a set of wires referred to as *interchange circuits*. For this scheme to work, a high degree of cooperation is required. The two DCEs that exchange signals over the transmission line or network must understand each

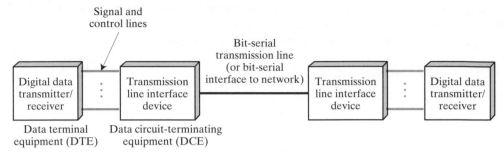

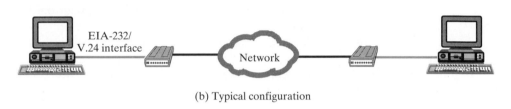

**FIGURE 5.4** Data communications interfacing.

other. That is, the receiver of each must use the same encoding scheme (e.g., Manchester, PSK) and data rate as the transmitter of the other. In addition, each DTE-DCE pair must be designed to interact cooperatively. To ease the burden on data-processing equipment manufacturers and users, standards have been developed that specify the exact nature of the interface between the DTE and the DCE. Such an interface has four important characteristics:

- Mechanical
- Electrical
- Functional
- Procedural

The *mechanical characteristics* pertain to the actual physical connection of the DTE to the DCE. Typically, the signal and control interchange circuits are bundled into a cable with a terminator plug, male or female, at each end. The DTE and DCE must present plugs of opposite genders at one end of the cable, effecting the physical connection; this is analogous to the way residential electrical power is produced. Power is provided via a socket or wall outlet, and the device to be attached must have the appropriate male plug (two-pronged, two-pronged polarized, or three-pronged) to match the socket.

The *electrical characteristics* have to do with the voltage levels and timing of voltage changes. Both DTE and DCE must use the same code (e.g., NRZ-L), must use the same voltage levels to mean the same things, and must use the same duration of signal elements. These characteristics determine the data rates and distances that can be achieved.

*Functional characteristics* specify the functions that are performed by assigning meanings to each of the interchange circuits. Functions can be classified into the broad categories of data, control, timing, and electrical ground.

*Procedural characteristics* specify the sequence of events for transmitting data, based on the functional characteristics of the interface. The examples that follow should clarify this point.

A variety of standards for interfacing exists; this section presents two of the most important: V.24/EIA-232-E, and the ISDN Physical Interface.

## V.24/EIA-232-E

The most widely used interface is one that is specified in the ITU-T standard, V.24. In fact, this standard specifies only the functional and procedural aspects of the interface; V.24 references other standards for the electrical and mechanical aspects. In the United States, there is a corresponding specification, virtually identical, that covers all four aspects: EIA-232. The correspondence is as follows:

- Mechanical: ISO 2110
- Electrical: V.28
- Functional: V.24
- Procedural: V.24

EIA-232 was first issued by the Electronic Industries Association in 1962, as RS-232. It is currently in its fifth revision EIA-232-E, issued in 1991. The current V.24 and V.28 specifications were issued in 1993. This interface is used to connect DTE devices to voice-grade modems for use on public analog telecommunications systems. It is also widely used for many other interconnection applications.

### Mechanical Specification

The mechanical specification for EIA-232-E is illustrated in Figure 5.5. It calls for a 25-pin connector, defined in ISO 2110, with a specific arrangement of leads. This connector is the terminating plug or socket on a cable running from a DTE (e.g., terminal) or DCE (e.g., modem). Thus, in theory, a 25-wire cable could be used to connect the DTE to the DCE. In practice, far fewer interchange circuits are used in most applications.

### Electrical Specification

The electrical specification defines the signaling between DTE and DCE. Digital signaling is used on all interchange circuits. Depending on the function of the interchange circuit, the electrical values are interpreted either as binary or as control signals. The convention specifies that, with respect to a common ground, a voltage more negative than −3 volts is interpreted as binary 1 and a voltage more positive than +3 volts is interpreted as binary 0; this is the NRZ-L code illustrated in Figure 4.2. The interface is rated at a signal rate of <20 kbps and a distance of <15 meters.

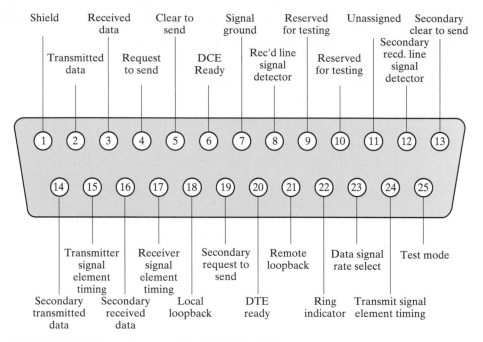

**FIGURE 5.5** Pin assignments for V.24/EIA-232.

Greater distances and data rates are possible with good design, but it is prudent to assume that these limits apply in practice as well as in theory.

The same voltage levels apply to control signals; a voltage more negative than –3 volts is interpreted as an OFF condition and a voltage more positive than +3 volts is interpreted as an ON condition.

### Functional Specification

Table 5.1 summarizes the functional specification of the interchange circuits, and Figure 5.5 illustrates the placement of these circuits on the plug. The circuits can be grouped into the categories of data, control, timing, and ground. There is one data circuit in each direction, so full-duplex operation is possible. In addition, there are two secondary data circuits that are useful when the device operates in a half-duplex fashion. In the case of half-duplex operation, data exchange between two DTEs (via their DCEs and the intervening communications link) is only conducted in one direction at a time. However, there may be a need to send a halt or flow-control message to a transmitting device; to accommodate this, the communication link is equipped with a reverse channel, usually at a much lower data rate than the primary channel. At the DTE-DCE interface, the reverse channel is carried on a separate pair of data circuits.

There are fifteen control circuits. The first ten of these listed in Table 5.1 relate to the transmission of data over the primary channel. For asynchronous transmission, six of these circuits are used (105, 106, 107, 108.2, 125, 109). The use of these circuits is explained in the subsection on procedural specifications. In addition to these six circuits, three other control circuits are used in synchronous transmis-

**TABLE 5.1**  V.24/EIA-232-E interchange circuits.

| V.24 | EIA-232 | Name | Direction to: | Function |
|------|---------|------|---------------|----------|
| | | **DATA SIGNALS** | | |
| 103 | BA | Transmitted data | DCE | Transmitted by DTE |
| 104 | BB | Received data | DTE | Received by DTE |
| 118 | SBA | Secondary transmitted data | DCE | Transmitted by DTE |
| 104 | SBB | Secondary received data | DTE | Received by DTE |
| | | **CONTROL SIGNALS** | | |
| 105 | CA | Request to send | DCE | DTE wishes to transmit |
| 106 | CB | Clear to send | DTE | DCE is ready to receive; response to Request to send |
| 107 | CC | DCE ready | DTE | DCE is ready to operate |
| 108.2 | CD | DTE ready | DCE | DTE is ready to operate |
| 125 | CE | Ring indicator | DTE | DCE is receiving a ringing signal on the channel line |
| 109 | CF | Received line signal detector | DTE | DCE is receiving a signal within appropriate limits on the channel line |
| 110 | CG | Signal quality detector | DTE | Indicates whether there is a high probability of error in the data received |
| 111 | CH | Data signal rate selector | DCE | Selects one of two data rates |
| 112 | CI | Data signal rate selector | DTE | Selects one of two data rates |
| 133 | CJ | Ready for receiving | DCE | On/off flow control |
| 120 | SCA | Secondary request to send | DCE | DTE wishes to transmit on reverse channel |
| 121 | SCB | Secondary clear to send | DTE | DCE is ready to receive on reverse channel |
| 122 | SCF | Secondary received line signal detector | DTE | Same as 109, for reverse channel |
| 140 | RL | Remote loopback | DCE | Instructs remote DCE to loop back signals |
| 141 | LL | Local loopback | DCE | Instructs DCE to loop back signals |
| 142 | TM | Test mode | DTE | Local DCE is in a test condition |
| | | **TIMING SIGNALS** | | |
| 113 | DA | Transmitter signal element timing | DCE | Clocking signal; transitions to ON and OFF occur at center of each signal element |
| 114 | DB | Transmitter signal element timing | DTE | Clocking signal; both 113 and 114 relate to signals on circuit 103 |
| 115 | DD | Receiver signal element timing | DTE | Clocking signal for circuit 104 |
| | | **GROUND** | | |
| 102 | AB | Signal ground/common return | | Common ground reference for all circuits |

sion. The Signal Quality Detector circuit is turned ON by the DCE to indicate that the quality of the incoming signal over the telephone line has deteriorated beyond some defined threshold. Most high-speed modems support more than one transmission rate so that they can fall back to a lower speed if the telephone line becomes noisy. The Data Signal Rate Selector circuits are used to change speeds; either the DTE or DCE may initiate the change. The next three control circuits (120, 121, 122) are used to control the use of the secondary channel, which may be used as a reverse channel or for some other auxiliary purpose.

The last group of control signals relate to loopback testing. These circuits allow the DTE to cause the DCE to perform a loopback test. These circuits are only valid if the modem or other DCE supports loopback control; this is now a common modem feature. In the local loopback function, the transmitter output of the modem is connected to the receiver input, disconnecting the modem from the transmission line. A stream of data generated by the user device is sent to the modem and looped back to the user device. For remote loopback, the local modem is connected to the transmission facility in the usual fashion, and the receiver output of the remote modem is connected to the modem's transmitter input. During either form of test, the DCE turns ON the Test Mode circuit. Table 5.2 shows the settings for all of the circuits related to loopback testing, and Figure 5.6 illustrates the use.

Loopback control is a useful fault-isolation tool. For example, suppose that a user at a personal computer is communicating with a server by means of a modem connection and communication suddenly ceases. The problem could be with the local modem, the communications facility, the remote modem, or the remote server. A network manager can use loopback tests to isolate the fault. Local loopback checks the functioning of the local interface and the local DCE. Remote loopback tests the operation of the transmission channel and the remote DCE.

The timing signals provide clock pulses for synchronous transmission. When the DCE is sending synchronous data over the Received Data circuit (104), it also sends 1-0 and 0-1 transitions on Receiver Element Signal Timing (115), with transitions timed to the middle of each BB signal element. When the DTE is sending synchronous data, either the DTE or DCE can provide timing pulses, depending on the circumstances.

Finally, the signal ground/common return (102) serves as the return circuit for all data leads. Hence, transmission is unbalanced, with only one active wire. Balanced and unbalanced transmission are discussed in the section on the ISDN interface.

**TABLE 5.2**   Loopback circuit settings for V.24/EIA-232.

| Local loopback | | Remote loopback | | |
| --- | --- | --- | --- | --- |
| Circuit | Condition | Circuit | Local interface | Remote interface |
| DCE ready | ON | DCE ready | ON | OFF |
| Local loopback | ON | Local loopback | OFF | OFF |
| Remote loopback | OFF | Remote loopback | ON | OFF |
| Test mode | ON | Test mode | ON | ON |

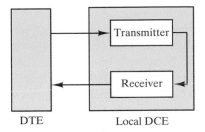

DTE          Local DCE

(a) Local loopback Testing

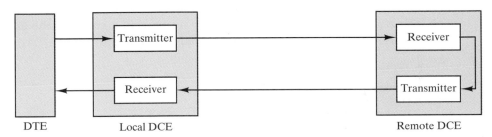

DTE          Local DCE                    Remote DCE

(b) Remote loopback testing

**FIGURE 5.6**   Local and remote loopback.

## Procedural Specification

The procedural specification defines the sequence in which the various circuits are used for a particular application. We give a few examples.

The first example is a very common one for connecting two devices over a short distance within a building. It is known as an asynchronous private line modem, or a limited-distance modem. As the name suggests, the limited-distance modem accepts digital signals from a DTE, such as a terminal or computer, converts these to analog signals, and then transmits these over a short length of medium, such as twisted pair. On the other end of the line is another limited-distance modem, which accepts the incoming analog signals, converts them to digital, and passes them on to another terminal or computer. Of course, the exchange of data is two-way. For this simple application, only the following interchange circuits are actually required:

- Signal ground (102)
- Transmitted data (103)
- Received data (104)
- Request to send (105)
- Clear to send (106)
- DCE ready (107)
- Received-Line Signal Detector (109)

When the modem (DCE) is turned on and is ready to operate, it asserts (applies a constant negative voltage to) the DCE Ready line. When the DTE is ready to send data (e.g., the terminal user has entered a character), it asserts Request to Send. The modem responds, when ready, by asserting Clear to Send, indicating that data may be transmitted over the Transmitted Data line. If the arrangement is half-duplex, then Request to Send also inhibits the receive mode. The DTE may now transmit data over the Transmitted Data line. When data arrive from the remote modem, the local modem asserts Received-Line Signal Detector to indicate that the remote modem is transmitting and delivers the data on the Received Data line. Note that it is not necessary to use timing circuits, as this is asynchronous transmission.

The circuits just listed are sufficient for private line point-to-point modems, but additional circuits are required to use a modem to transmit data over the telephone network. In this case, the initiator of a connection must call the destination device over the network. Two additional leads are required:

- DTE ready (108.2)
- Ring indicator (125)

With the addition of these two lines, the DTE-modem system can effectively use the telephone network in a way analogous to voice telephone usage. Figure 5.7 depicts the steps involved in dial-up half-duplex operation. When a call is made, either manually or automatically, the telephone system sends a ringing signal. A telephone set would respond by ringing its bell; a modem responds by asserting Ring Indicator. A person answers a call by lifting the handset; a DTE answers by asserting Data Terminal Ready. A person who answers a call will listen for another's voice, and, if nothing is heard, hang up. A DTE will listen for Carrier Detect, which will be asserted by the modem when a signal is present; if this circuit is not asserted, the DTE will drop Data Terminal Ready. You might wonder how this last contingency might arise; one common way is if a person accidentally dials the number of a modem. This activates the modem's DTE, but when no carrier tone comes through, the problem is resolved.

It is instructive to consider situations in which the distances between devices are so close as to allow two DTEs to directly signal each other. In this case, the V.24/EIA-232 interchange circuits can still be used, but no DCE equipment is provided. For this scheme to work, a null modem is needed, which interconnects leads in such a way as to fool both DTEs into thinking that they are connected to modems. Figure 5.8 is an example of a null modem configuration; the reasons for the particular connections should be apparent to the reader who has grasped the preceding discussion.

## ISDN Physical Interface

The wide variety of functions available with V.24/EIA-232 is provided by the use of a large number of interchange circuits. This is a rather expensive way to achieve results. An alternative would be to provide fewer circuits but to add more logic at the DTE and DCE interfaces. With the dropping costs of logic circuitry, this is an attractive approach. This approach was taken in the X.21 standard for interfacing to public circuit-switched networks, specifying a 15-pin connector. More recently, the

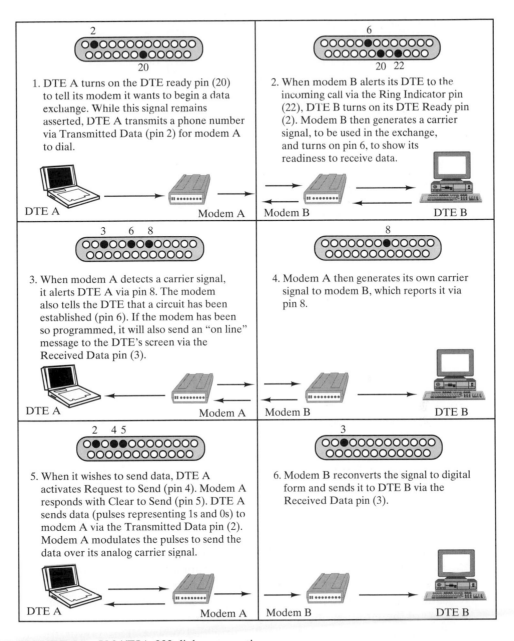

**FIGURE 5.7**  V.24/EIA-232 dial-up operation.

trend has been carried further with the specification of an 8-pin physical connector to an Integrated Services Digital Network (ISDN). ISDN, which is an all-digital replacement for existing public telephone and analog telecommunications networks, is discussed further in Appendix A. In this section, we look at the physical interface defined for ISDN.

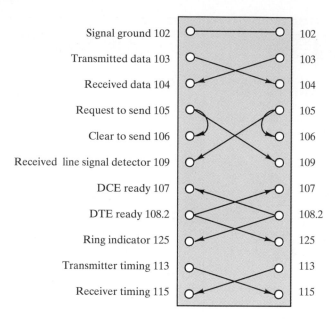

Signal ground 102 — 102
Transmitted data 103 — 103
Received data 104 — 104
Request to send 105 — 105
Clear to send 106 — 106
Received line signal detector 109 — 109
DCE ready 107 — 107
DTE ready 108.2 — 108.2
Ring indicator 125 — 125
Transmitter timing 113 — 113
Receiver timing 115 — 115

**FIGURE 5.8**   Example of a null modem.

## Physical Connection

In ISDN terminology, a physical connection is made between terminal equipment (TE) and network-terminating equipment (NT). For purposes of our discussion, these terms correspond, rather closely, to DTE and DCE, respectively. The physical connection, defined in ISO 8877, specifies that the NT and TE cables shall terminate in matching plugs that provide for 8 contacts.

Figure 5.9 illustrates the contact assignments for each of the 8 lines on both the NT and TE sides. Two pins are used to provide data transmission in each direction. These contact points are used to connect twisted-pair leads coming from the NT and TE devices. Because there are no specific functional circuits, the transmit/receive circuits are used to carry both data and control signals. The control information is transmitted in the form of messages.

The specification provides for the capability to transfer power across the interface. The direction of power transfer depends on the application. In a typical application, it may be desirable to provide for power transfer from the network side toward the terminal in order, for example, to maintain a basic telephony service in the event of failure of the locally provided power. This power transfer can be accomplished using the same leads used for digital signal transmission (c, d, e, f), or on additional wires, using access leads g-h. The remaining two leads are not used in the ISDN configuration but may be useful in other configurations.

## Electrical Specification

The ISDN electrical specification dictates the use of balanced transmission. With *balanced transmission*, signals are carried on a line, such as twisted pair, consisting

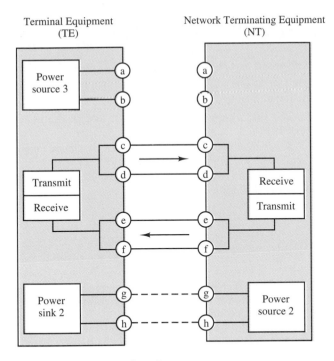

**FIGURE 5.9** ISDN interface.

of two conductors. Signals are transmitted as a current that travels down one conductor and returns on the other, the two conductors forming a complete circuit. For digital signals, this technique is known as *differential signaling*,[3] as the binary value depends on the direction of the voltage difference between the two conductors. *Unbalanced transmission*, which is used on older interfaces such as EIA-232, uses a single conductor to carry the signal, with ground providing the return path.

The balance mode tolerates more, and produces less, noise than unbalanced mode. Ideally, interference on a balanced line will act equally on both conductors and not affect the voltage difference. Because unbalanced transmission does not possess these advantages, it is generally limited to use on coaxial cable; when it is used on interchange circuits, such as EIA-232, it is limited to very short distances.

The data encoding format used on the ISDN interface depends on the data rate. For the *basic rate* of 192 kbps, the standard specifies the use of pseudoternary coding (Figure 4.2). Binary one is represented by the absence of voltage, and binary zero is represented by a positive or negative pulse of 750 mV ±10%. For the *primary rate*, there are two options: 1.544 Mbps using alternate mark inversion (AMI) with B8ZS (Figure 4.6) and 2.049 Mbps using AMI with HDB3. The reason for the different schemes for the two different primary rates is simply historical; neither has a particular advantage.

---

[3] Not to be confused with differential encoding; see Section 4.1.

## 5.4 RECOMMENDED READING

[BLAC95a] provides detailed, broad coverage of many physical-layer interface standards.

[BLAC95b] focuses on the ITU-T V series recommendations. [SEYE91] is an easy-to-read and thorough introduction to EIA-232.

BLAC95a   Black, U. *Physical Level Interfaces and Protocols*. Los Alamitos, CA: IEEE Computer Society Press, 1995.

BLAC95b   Black, U. *The V Series Recommendations: Standards for Data Communications Over the Telephone Network*. New York: McGraw-Hill, 1995.

SEYE91   Seyer, M. *RS-232 Made Easy: Connecting Computers, Printers, Terminals, and Modems*. Englewood Cliffs, NJ: Prentice Hall, 1991.

## 5.5 PROBLEMS

5.1   A data source produces 8-bit ASCII characters. Derive an expression for the maximum data rate (rate of ASCII data bits) over a $B$-bps line for the following:
   **a.** Asynchronous transmission with a 1.5-unit stop bit.
   **b.** Synchronous transmission, with a frame consisting of 48 control bits and 128 information bits. The information field contains 8-bit ASCII characters.
   **c.** Same as (b), but with an information field of 1024 bits.

5.2   Demonstrate by example (write down a few dozen arbitrary bit patterns with start and stop bits) that a receiver that suffers a framing error on asynchronous transmission will eventually become realigned.

5.3   Suppose that the sender and receiver agree not to use any stop bits. Could this work? If so, explain any necessary conditions.

5.4   Consider a transmission system that is clocked by a master clock running at 8 MHz. This clock has a maximum error of 30 seconds per month. Transmission is asynchronous serial consisting of characters containing one start bit, seven data bits, one parity bit, and one stop bit. If characters are transmitted in a continuous stream as rapidly as possible (a burst mode), how many characters could be sent before a transmission error caused by the master clock error occurs? Assume that each bit must be sampled within 40% of its center position. Note that the transmission rate is not a factor, as both the bit period and the absolute timing error decrease proportionately at higher transmission rates.

5.5   An asynchronous transmission uses 8 data bits, an even parity bit, and 2 stop bits. What percentage of clock inaccuracy can be tolerated at the receiver with respect to the framing error? Assume that the bit samples are taken at the middle of the clock period. Also assume that, at the beginning of the start bit, the clock and incoming bits are in phase.

5.6   Suppose that a synchronous serial data transmission is clocked by two 8-MHz clocks (one at the sender and one at the receiver) that each have a drift of 1 minute in one year. How long a sequence of bits can be sent before possible clock drift could cause a problem? Assume that a bit waveform will be good if it is sampled within 40% of its center and that the sender and receiver are resynchronized at the beginning of each frame.

5.7   Draw a timing diagram showing the state of all EIA-232 leads between two DTE-DCE pairs during the course of a data call on the switched telephone network.

5.8   Explain the operation of each null modem connection in Figure 5.8.

5.9   For the V.24/EIA-232 Remote Loopback circuit to function properly, what circuits must be logically connected?

# CHAPTER 6

# DATA LINK CONTROL

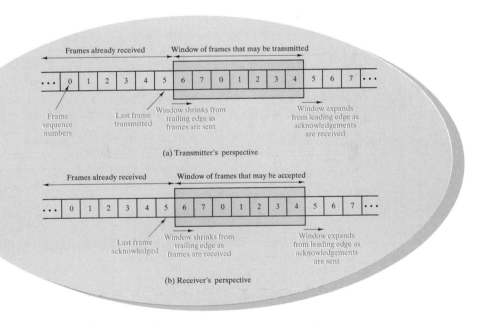

Frames already received | Window of frames that may be transmitted

Frame sequence numbers

Last frame transmitted

Window shrinks from trailing edge as frames are sent

Window expands from leading edge as acknowledgements are received

(a) Transmitter's perspective

Frames already received | Window of frames that may be accepted

Last frame acknowledged

Window shrinks from trailing edge as frames are received

Window expands from leading edge as acknowledgements are sent

(b) Receiver's perspective

Our discussion so far has concerned *sending signals over a transmission link*. For effective digital data communications, much more is needed to control and manage the exchange. In this chapter, we shift our emphasis to that of *sending data over a data communications link*. To achieve the necessary control, a layer of logic is added above the physical interfacing discussed in Chapter 5; this logic is referred to as *data link control* or a *data link control protocol*. When a data link control protocol is used, the transmission medium between systems is referred to as a *data link*.

To see the need for data link control, we list some of the requirements and objectives for effective data communication between two directly connected transmitting-receiving stations:

- **Frame synchronization.** Data are sent in blocks called frames. The beginning and end of each frame must be recognizable. We briefly introduced this topic with the discussion of synchronous frames (Figure 5.2).

- **Flow control.** The sending station must not send frames at a rate faster then the receiving station can absorb them.

- **Error control.** Any bit errors introduced by the transmission system must be corrected.

- **Addressing.** On a multipoint line, such as a local area network (LAN), the identity of the two stations involved in a transmission must be specified.

- **Control and data on same link.** It is usually not desirable to have a physically separate communications path for control information. Accordingly, the receiver must be able to distinguish control information from the data being transmitted.

- **Link management.** The initiation, maintenance, and termination of a sustained data exchange requires a fair amount of coordination and cooperation among stations. Procedures for the management of this exchange are required.

None of these requirements is satisfied by the physical interfacing techniques described in Chapter 6. We shall see in this chapter that a data link protocol that satisfies these requirements is a rather complex affair. We begin by looking at three key mechanisms that are part of data link control: flow control, error detection, and error control. Following this background information, we look at the most important example of a data link control protocol: HDLC (high-level data link control). This protocol is important for two reasons: First, it is a widely used standardized data link control protocol. And secondly, HDLC serves as a baseline from which virtually all other important data link control protocols are derived. Following a detailed examination of HDLC, these other protocols are briefly surveyed. Finally, an appendix to this chapter addresses some performance issues relating to data link control.

## 6.1 FLOW CONTROL

Flow control is a technique for assuring that a transmitting entity docs not overwhelm a receiving entity with data. The receiving entity typically allocates a data buffer of some maximum length for a transfer. When data are received, the receiver must do a certain amount of processing before passing the data to the higher-level software. In the absence of flow control, the receiver's buffer may fill up and overflow while it is processing old data.

To begin, we examine mechanisms for flow control in the absence of errors. The model we will use is depicted in Figure 6.1a, which is a vertical-time sequence diagram. It has the advantages of showing time dependencies and illustrating the correct send-receive relationship. Each arrow represents a single frame transiting a data link between two stations. The data are sent in a sequence of frames with each frame containing a portion of the data and some control information. For now, we

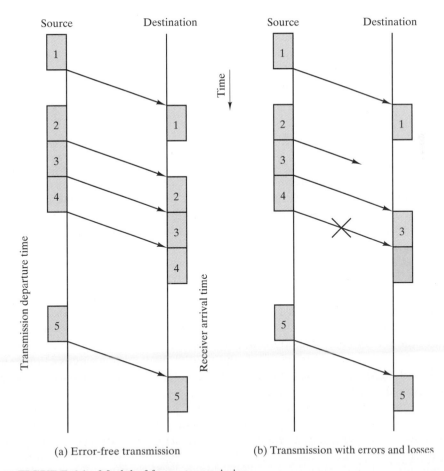

(a) Error-free transmission  (b) Transmission with errors and losses

**FIGURE 6.1**  Model of frame transmission.

assume that all frames that are transmitted are successfully received; no frames are lost and none arrive with errors. Furthermore, frames arrive in the same order in which they are sent. However, each transmitted frame suffers an arbitrary and variable amount of delay before reception.

### Stop-and-Wait Flow Control

The simplest form of flow control, known as stop-and-wait flow control, works as follows. A source entity transmits a frame. After reception, the destination entity indicates its willingness to accept another frame by sending back an acknowledgment to the frame just received. The source must wait until it receives the acknowledgment before sending the next frame. The destination can thus stop the flow of data by simply withholding acknowledgment. This procedure works fine and, indeed, can hardly be improved upon when a message is sent in a few large frames. However, it is often the case that a source will break up a large block of data into smaller blocks and transmit the data in many frames. This is done for the following reasons:

- The buffer size of the receiver may be limited.
- The longer the transmission, the more likely that there will be an error, necessitating retransmission of the entire frame. With smaller frames, errors are detected sooner, and a smaller amount of data needs to be retransmitted.
- On a shared medium, such as a LAN, it is usually desirable not to permit one station to occupy the medium for an extended period, as this causes long delays at the other sending stations.

With the use of multiple frames for a single message, the stop-and-wait procedure may be inadequate. The essence of the problem is that only one frame at a time can be in transit. In situations where the bit length of the link is greater than the frame length, serious inefficiencies result; this is illustrated in Figure 6.2. In the figure, the transmission time (the time it takes for a station to transmit a frame) is normalized to one, and the propagation delay (the time it takes for a bit to travel from sender to receiver) is expressed as the variable $a$. In other words, when $a$ is less than 1, the propagation time is less than the transmission time. In this case, the frame is sufficiently long that the first bits of the frame have arrived at the destination before the source has completed the transmission of the frame. When $a$ is greater than 1, the propagation time is greater than the transmission time. In this case, the sender completes transmission of the entire frame before the leading bits of that frame arrive at the receiver. Put another way, larger values of $a$ are consistent with higher data rates and/or longer distances between stations. Appendix 6A discusses $a$ and data link performance.

Both parts of the figure (a and b) consist of a sequence of snapshots of the transmission process over time. In both cases, the first four snapshots show the process of transmitting a frame containing data, and the last snapshot shows the return of a small acknowledgment frame. Note that for $a > 1$, the line is always underutilized, and, even for $a < 1$, the line is inefficiently utilized. In essence, for very high data rates, or for very long distances between sender and receiver, stop-and-wait flow control provides inefficient line utilization.

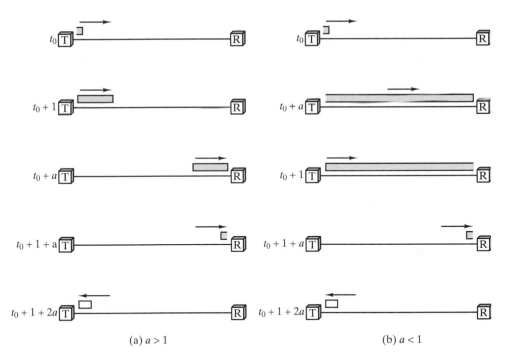

(a) $a > 1$ (b) $a < 1$

**FIGURE 6.2** Stop-and-wait link utilization (transmission time = 1; propagation time = a).

## Sliding-Window Flow Control

The essence of the problem described so far is that only one frame at a time can be in transit. In situations where the bit length of the link is greater than the frame length ($a > 1$), serious inefficiencies result. Efficiency can be greatly improved by allowing multiple frames to be in transit at the same time.

Let us examine how this might work for two stations, $A$ and $B$, connected via a full-duplex link. Station $B$ allocates buffer space for $n$ frames. Thus, $B$ can accept $n$ frames, and $A$ is allowed to send $n$ frames without waiting for any acknowledgments. To keep track of which frames have been acknowledged, each is labeled with a sequence number. $B$ acknowledges a frame by sending an acknowledgment that includes the sequence number of the next frame expected. This acknowledgment also implicitly announces that $B$ is prepared to receive the next $n$ frames, beginning with the number specified. This scheme can also be used to acknowledge multiple frames. For example, $B$ could receive frames 2, 3, and 4, but withhold acknowledgment until frame 4 has arrived; by then returning an acknowledgment with sequence number 5, $B$ acknowledges frames 2, 3, and 4 at one time. $A$ maintains a list of sequence numbers that it is allowed to send, and $B$ maintains a list of sequence numbers that it is prepared to receive. Each of these lists can be thought of as a *window* of frames. The operation is referred to as sliding-window flow control.

Several additional comments need to be made. Because the sequence number to be used occupies a field in the frame, it is clearly of bounded size. For example, for a 3-bit field, the sequence number can range from 0 to 7. Accordingly, frames are numbered modulo 8; that is, after sequence-number 7, the next number is 0. In general, for a $k$-bit field the range of sequence numbers is 0 through $2^k - 1$, and frames are numbered modulo $2^k$; with this in mind, Figure 6.3 is a useful way of depicting the sliding-window process. It assumes the use of a 3-bit sequence number, so that frames are numbered sequentially from 0 through 7, and then the same numbers are reused for subsequent frames. The shaded rectangle indicates that the sender may transmit 7 frames, beginning with frame 6. Each time a frame is sent, the shaded window shrinks; each time an acknowledgment is received, the shaded window grows.

The actual window size need not be the maximum possible size for a given sequence-number length. For example, using a 3-bit sequence number, a window size of 4 could be configured for the stations using the sliding-window flow control protocol.

An example is shown in Figure 6.4. The example assumes a 3-bit sequence number field and a maximum window size of seven frames. Initially, A and B have windows indicating that A may transmit seven frames, beginning with frame 0 (F0). After transmitting three frames (F0, F1, F2) without acknowledgment, A has shrunk its window to four frames. The window indicates that A may transmit four frames, beginning with frame number 3. B then transmits an RR (receive-ready) 3, which means: "I have received all frames up through frame number 2 and am ready

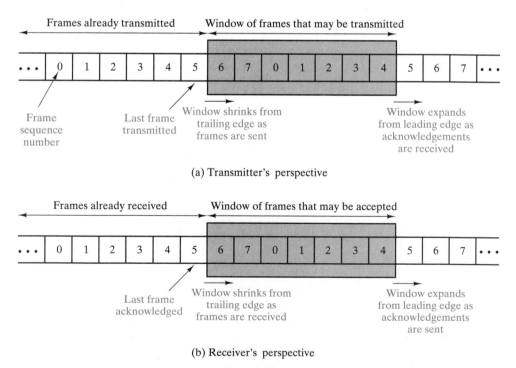

(a) Transmitter's perspective

(b) Receiver's perspective

**FIGURE 6.3** Sliding-window depiction.

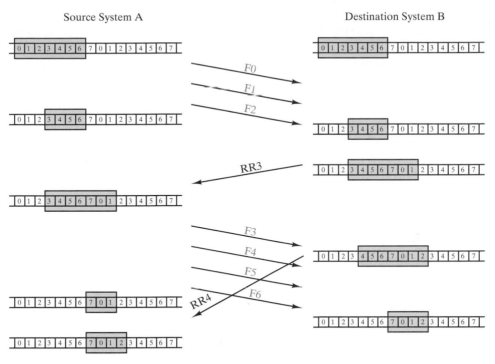

**FIGURE 6.4** Example of a sliding-window protocol.

to receive frame number 3; in fact, I am prepared to receive seven frames, beginning with frame number 3." With this acknowledgment, A is back up to permission to transmit seven frames, still beginning with frame 3. A proceeds to transmit frames 3, 4, 5, and 6. B returns an RR 4, which allows A to send up to and including frame F2.

The mechanism so far described does indeed provide a form of flow control: The receiver must only be able to accommodate 7 frames beyond the one it has last acknowledged; to supplement this, most protocols also allow a station to completely cut off the flow of frames from the other side by sending a Receive-Not-Ready (RNR) message, which acknowledges former frames but forbids transfer of future frames. Thus, RNR 5 means: "I have received all frames up through number 4 but am unable to accept any more." At some subsequent point, the station must send a normal acknowledgment to reopen the window.

So far, we have discussed transmission in one direction only. If two stations exchange data, each needs to maintain two windows, one for transmit and one for receive, and each side needs to send the data and acknowledgments to the other. To provide efficient support for this requirement, a feature known as *piggybacking* is typically provided. Each *data frame* includes a field that holds the sequence number of that frame plus a field that holds the sequence number used for acknowledgment. Thus, if a station has data to send and an acknowledgment to send, it sends both together in one frame, thereby saving communication capacity. Of course, if a station has an acknowledgment but no data to send, it sends a separate *acknowledgment frame*. If a station has data to send but no new acknowledgment to send, it must repeat the last acknowledgment that it sent; this is because the data frame includes a field for the acknowledgment number, and some value must be put into that field. When a station receives a duplicate acknowledgment, it simply ignores it.

It should be clear from the discussion that sliding-window flow control is potentially much more efficient than stop-and-wait flow control. The reason is that, with sliding-window flow control, the transmission link is treated as a pipeline that may be filled with frames in transit. In contrast, with stop-and-wait flow control, only one frame may be in the pipe at a time. Appendix 6A quantifies the improvement in efficiency.

## 6.2  ERROR DETECTION

In earlier chapters, we talked about transmission impairments and the effect of data rate and signal-to-noise ratio on bit error rate. Regardless of the design of the transmission system, there will be errors, resulting in the change of one or more bits in a transmitted frame.

Let us define these probabilities with respect to errors in transmitted frames:

$P_b$: Probability of a single bit error; also known as the bit error rate.

$P_1$: Probability that a frame arrives with no bit errors.

$P_2$: Probability that a frame arrives with one or more undetected bit errors.

$P_3$: Probability that a frame arrives with one or more detected bit errors but no undetected bit errors.

First, consider the case when no means are taken to detect errors; the probability of detected errors ($P_3$), then, is zero. To express the remaining probabilities, assume that the probability that any bit is in error ($P_b$) is constant and independent for each bit. Then we have

$$P_1 = (1 - P_b)^F$$
$$P_2 = 1 - P_1$$

where $F$ is the number of bits per frame. In words, the probability that a frame arrives with no bit errors decreases when the probability of a single bit error increases, as you would expect. Also, the probability that a frame arrives with no bit errors decreases with increasing frame length; the longer the frame, the more bits it has and the higher the probability that one of these is in error.

Let us take a simple example to illustrate these relationships. A defined object for ISDN connections is that the bit error rate on a 64-kbps channel should be less than $10^{-6}$ on at least 90% of observed 1-minute intervals. Suppose now that we have the rather modest user requirement that at most one frame with an undetected bit error should occur per day on a continuously used 64-kbps channel, and let us assume a frame length of 1000 bits. The number of frames that can be transmitted in a day comes out to $5.529 \times 10^6$, which yields a desired frame error rate of

$P_2 = 1/(5.529 \times 10^6) = 0.18 \times 10^{-6}$. But, if we assume a value of $P_b$ of $10^{-6}$, then $P_1 = (0.999999)^{1000} = 0.999$ and, therefore, $P_2 = 10^{-3}$, which is about three orders of magnitude too large to meet our requirement.

This is the kind of result that motivates the use of error-detection techniques. All of these techniques operate on the following principle (Figure 6.5). For a given frame of bits, additional bits that constitute an error-detecting code are added by the transmitter. This code is calculated as a function of the other transmitted bits. The receiver performs the same calculation and compares the two results. A detected error occurs if and only if there is a mismatch. Thus, $P_3$ is the probability that if a frame contains errors, the error-detection scheme will detect that fact. $P_2$ is known as the residual error rate, and is the probability that an error will be undetected despite the use of an error-detection scheme.

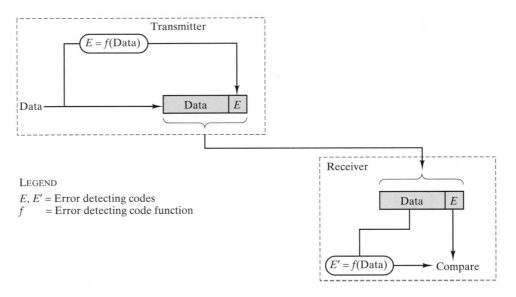

FIGURE 6.5   Error detection.

## Parity Check

The simplest error-detection scheme is to append a parity bit to the end of a block of data. A typical example is ASCII transmission, in which a parity bit is attached to each 7-bit ASCII character. The value of this bit is selected so that the character has an even number of 1s (even parity) or an odd number of 1s (odd parity). So, for example, if the transmitter is transmitting an ASCII G (1110001) and using odd parity, it will append a 1 and transmit 11100011. The receiver examines the received character and, if the total number of 1s is odd, assumes that no error has occurred. If one bit (or any odd number of bits) is erroneously inverted during transmission (for example, 11000011), then the receiver will detect an error. Note, however, that if two (or any even number) of bits are inverted due to error, an undetected error occurs. Typically, even parity is used for synchronous transmission and odd parity for asynchronous transmission.

The use of the parity bit is not foolproof, as noise impulses are often long enough to destroy more than one bit, particularly at high data rates.

### Cyclic Redundancy Check (CRC)

One of the most common, and one of the most powerful, error-detecting codes is the cyclic redundancy check (CRC), which can be described as follows. Given a $k$-bit block of bits, or message, the transmitter generates an $n$-bit sequence, known as a frame check sequence (FCS), so that the resulting frame, consisting of $k + n$ bits, is exactly divisible by some predetermined number. The receiver then divides the incoming frame by that number and, if there is no remainder, assumes there was no error.

To clarify this, we present the procedure in three ways: modulo 2 arithmetic, polynomials, and digital logic.

#### Modulo 2 Arithmetic

Modulo 2 arithmetic uses binary addition with no carries, which is just the exclusive-or operation. For example:

$$
\begin{array}{r}
1111 \\
+1010 \\
\hline
0101
\end{array}
\qquad
\begin{array}{r}
11001 \\
\times\ \ 11 \\
\hline
11001 \\
11001\ \ \\
\hline
101011
\end{array}
$$

Now define:

$T = (k + n)$-bit frame to be transmitted, with $n < k$
$M = k$-bit message, the first $k$ bits of $T$
$F = n$-bit FCS, the last $n$ bits of $T$
$P = $ pattern of $n + 1$ bits; this is the predetermined divisor

We would like $T/P$ to have no remainder. It should be clear that

$$T = 2^n M + F$$

That is, by multiplying $M$ by $2^n$, we have, in effect, shifted it to the left by $n$ bits and padded out the result with zeroes. Adding $F$ yields the concatenation of $M$ and $F$, which is $T$. We want $T$ to be exactly divisible by P. Suppose that we divided $2^n M$ by $P$:

$$\frac{2^n M}{P} = Q + \frac{R}{P} \qquad (6.1)$$

There is a quotient and a remainder. Because division is modulo 2, the remainder is always at least one bit less than the divisor. We will use this remainder as our FCS. Then

$$T = 2^n M + R$$

Question: Does this $R$ satisfy our condition that $T/P$ have no remainder? To see that it does, consider

$$\frac{T}{P} = \frac{2^n M + R}{P}$$

Substituting Equation (6.1), we have

$$\frac{T}{P} = Q + \frac{R}{P} + \frac{R}{P}$$

However, any binary number added to itself (modulo 2) yields zero. Thus,

$$\frac{T}{P} = Q + \frac{R + R}{P} = Q$$

There is no remainder, and, therefore, $T$ is exactly divisible by $P$. Thus, the FCS is easily generated: Simply divide $2^n M$ by $P$ and use the remainder as the FCS. On reception, the receiver will divide $T$ by $P$ and will get no remainder if there have been no errors.

Let us now consider a simple example.

1. Given
   Message $M = 1010001101$ (10 bits)
   Pattern $P = 110101$ (6 bits)
   FCS $R = $ to be calculated (5 bits)
2. The message $M$ is multiplied by $2^5$, yielding 101000110100000.
3. This product is divided by P:

```
                        1101010110←Q
      P→110101 )101000110100000←2ⁿM
               110101
               111011
               110101
                111010
                110101
                 111110
                 110101
                  101100
                  110101
                   110010
                   110101
                    01110←R
```

4. The remainder ($R = 01110$) is added to $2^n M$ to give $T = 101000110101110$, which is transmitted.
5. If there are no errors, the receiver receives T intact. The received frame is divided by P:

```
                                    1101010110←Q
              P→110101 101000110101110←T
                       110101
                       111011
                       110101
                        111010
                        110101
                         111110
                         110101
                          101111
                          110101
                           110101
                           110101
                           00000←R
```

Because there is no remainder, it is assumed that there have been no errors.

The pattern $P$ is chosen to be one bit longer than the desired FCS, and the exact bit pattern chosen depends on the type of errors expected. At minimum, both the high- and low-order bits of $P$ must be 1.

The occurrence of an error is easily expressed. An error results in the reversal of a bit. This is equivalent to taking the exclusive-or of the bit and 1 (modulo 2 addition of 1 to the bit): $0 + 1 = 1$; $1 + 1 = 0$. Thus, the errors in an $(n + k)$-bit frame can be represented by an $(n + k)$-bit field with 1s in each error position. The resulting frame $T_r$ can be expressed as

$$T_r = T + E$$

where

$T$ = transmitted frame
$E$ = error pattern with 1s in positions where errors occur
$T_r$ = received frame

The receiver will fail to detect an error if and only if $T_r$ is divisible by $P$, which is equivalent to $E$ divisible by $P$. Intuitively, this seems an unlikely occurrence.

### Polynomials

A second way of viewing the CRC process is to express all values as polynomials in a dummy variable $X$, with binary coefficients. The coefficients correspond to the bits in the binary number. Thus, for $M = 110011$, we have $M(X) = X^5 + X^4 + X + 1$, and, for $P = 11001$, we have $P(X) = X^4 + X^3 + 1$. Arithmetic operations are again modulo 2. The CRC process can now be described as

$$\frac{X^n M(X)}{P(X)} = Q(X) + \frac{R(X)}{P(X)}$$

$$T(X) = X^n M(X) + R(X)$$

An error $E(X)$ will only be undetectable if it is divisible by $P(X)$. It can be shown [PETE61] that all of the following errors are not divisible by a suitably chosen $P(X)$ and, hence, are detectable:

- All single-bit errors.
- All double-bit errors, as long as $P(X)$ has at least three 1s.
- Any odd number of errors, as long as $P(X)$ contains a factor $(X + 1)$.
- Any burst error for which the length of the burst is less than the length of the divisor polynomial; that is, less than or equal to the length of the FCS.
- Most larger burst errors.

In addition, it can be shown that if all error patterns are considered equally likely, then for a burst error of length $r + 1$, the probability that $E(X)$ is divisible by $P(X)$ is $1/2^{r-1}$, and for a longer burst, the probability is $1/2^r$, where $r$ is the length of the FCS.

Three versions of $P(X)$ are widely used:

$$
\begin{aligned}
\text{CRC-16} \quad &= X^{16} + X^{15} + X^2 + 1 \\
\text{CRC-CCITT} &= X^{16} + X^{12} + X^5 + 1 \\
\text{CRC-32} \quad &= X^{32} + X^{26} + X^{23} + X^{22} + X^{16} + X^{12} + X^{11} + X^{10} \\
&\quad + X^8 + X^7 + X^5 + X^4 + X^2 + X + 1
\end{aligned}
$$

## Digital Logic

The CRC process can be represented by, and indeed implemented as, a dividing circuit consisting of exclusive-or gates and a shift register. The shift register is a string of 1-bit storage devices. Each device has an output line, that indicates the value currently stored, and an input line. At discrete time instants, known as clock times, the value in the storage device is replaced by the value indicated by its input line. The entire register is clocked simultaneously, causing a 1-bit shift along the entire register.

The circuit is implemented as follows:

1. The register contains $n$ bits, equal to the length of the FCS.
2. There are up to n exclusive-or gates.
3. The presence or absence of a gate corresponds to the presence or absence of a term in the divisor polynomial, $P(X)$.

The architecture of this circuit is best explained by first considering an example, which is illustrated in Figure 6.6. In this example, we use

$$
\begin{aligned}
\text{Message } M &= 1010001101; & M(X) &= X^9 + X^7 + X^3 + X^2 + 1 \\
\text{Divisor } P &= 110101; & P(X) &= X^5 + X^4 + X^2 + 1
\end{aligned}
$$

which were used earlier in the discussion.

Part (a) of the figure shows the shift register implementation. The process begins with the shift register cleared (all zeros). The message, or dividend, is then

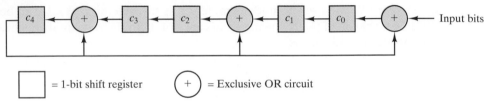

= 1-bit shift register $\quad\bigoplus$ = Exclusive OR circuit

(a) Shift-register implementation

|  | $c_4$ | $c_3$ | $c_2$ | $c_1$ | $c_0$ | $c_4 \oplus c_3$ | $c_4 \oplus c_1$ | $c_4 \oplus$ input | input |
|---|---|---|---|---|---|---|---|---|---|
| Initial | 0 | 0 | 0 | 0 | 0 | 0 | 0 | 1 | 1 |
| Step 1 | 0 | 0 | 0 | 0 | 1 | 0 | 0 | 0 | 0 |
| Step 2 | 0 | 0 | 0 | 1 | 0 | 0 | 1 | 1 | 1 |
| Step 3 | 0 | 0 | 1 | 0 | 1 | 0 | 0 | 0 | 0 |
| Step 4 | 0 | 1 | 0 | 1 | 0 | 1 | 1 | 0 | 0 |
| Step 5 | 1 | 0 | 1 | 0 | 0 | 1 | 1 | 1 | 0 |
| Step 6 | 1 | 1 | 1 | 0 | 1 | 0 | 1 | 0 | 1 |
| Step 7 | 0 | 1 | 1 | 1 | 0 | 1 | 1 | 1 | 1 |
| Step 8 | 1 | 1 | 1 | 0 | 1 | 0 | 1 | 1 | 0 |
| Step 9 | 0 | 1 | 1 | 1 | 1 | 1 | 1 | 1 | 1 |
| Step 10 | 1 | 1 | 1 | 1 | 1 | 0 | 0 | 1 | 0 |
| Step 11 | 0 | 1 | 0 | 1 | 1 | 1 | 1 | 0 | 0 |
| Step 12 | 1 | 0 | 1 | 1 | 0 | 1 | 0 | 1 | 0 |
| Step 13 | 1 | 1 | 0 | 0 | 1 | 0 | 1 | 1 | 0 |
| Step 14 | 0 | 0 | 1 | 1 | 1 | 0 | 1 | 0 | 0 |
| Step 15 | 0 | 1 | 1 | 1 | 0 | 1 | 1 | 0 | — |

Message to be sent: Steps 4–9. Five zeros added: Steps 10–14.

**FIGURE 6.6** Circuit with shift registers for dividing by the polynomial $X^5 + X^4 + X^2 + 1$.

entered, one bit at a time, starting with the most significant bit. Part (b) is a table that shows the step-by-step operation as the input is applied one bit at a time. Each row of the table shows the values currently stored in the five shift-register elements. In addition, the row shows the values that appear at the outputs of the three exclusive-or circuits. Finally, the row shows the value of the next input bit, which is available for the operation of the next step.

Because no feedback occurs until a 1-dividend bit arrives at the most significant end of the register, the first five operations are simple shifts. Whenever a 1 bit arrives at the left end of the register ($c_4$), a 1 is subtracted (exclusive-or) from the second ($c_3$), fourth ($c_1$), and sixth (input) bits on the next shift. This is identical to the binary long-division process illustrated earlier. The process continues through all the bits of the message, plus five zero bits. These latter bits account for shifting M to the left five position to accommodate the FCS. After the last bit is processed, the shift register contains the remainder (FCS), which can then be transmitted.

At the receiver, the same logic is used. As each bit of M arrives, it is inserted into the shift register. If there have been no errors, the shift register should contain the bit pattern for $R$ at the conclusion of $M$. The transmitted bits of $R$ now begin to arrive, and the effect is to zero-out the register so that, at the conclusion of reception, the register contains all 0s.

Figure 6.7 indicates the general architecture of the shift register implementation of a CRC for the polynomial $P(X) = \sum\limits_{i=0}^{n} a_i X^i$ where $a_0 = a_n = 1$ and all other $a_i$ equal either 0 or 1.

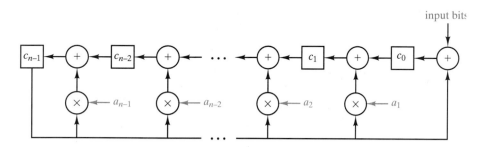

**FIGURE 6.7**    General CRC architecture to implement divisor $1 + a_1 X + a_2 X^2 + \cdots + a_{n-1} X^{n-1} + X^n$.

## 6.3  ERROR CONTROL

Error control refers to mechanisms to detect and correct errors that occur in the transmission of frames. The model that we will use, which covers the typical case, is illustrated in Figure 6.1b. As before, data are sent as a sequence of frames; frames arrive in the same order in which they are sent; and each transmitted frame suffers an arbitrary and variable amount of delay before reception. In addition, we admit the possibility of two types of errors:

- **Lost frame.** A frame fails to arrive at the other side. For example, a noise burst may damage a frame to the extent that the receiver is not aware that a frame has been transmitted.
- **Damaged frame.** A recognizable frame does arrive, but some of the bits are in error (have been altered during transmission).

The most common techniques for error control are based on some or all of the following ingredients:

- **Error detection.** As discussed in the preceding section.
- **Positive acknowledgment.** The destination returns a positive acknowledgment to successfully received, error-free frames.

- **Retransmission after timeout.** The source retransmits a frame that has not been acknowledged after a predetermined amount of time.
- **Negative acknowledgment and retransmission.** The destination returns a negative acknowledgment to frames in which an error is detected. The source retransmits such frames.

Collectively, these mechanisms are all referred to as **automatic repeat request** (ARQ); the effect of ARQ is to turn an unreliable data link into a reliable one. Three versions of ARQ have been standardized:

- Stop-and-wait ARQ
- Go-back-N ARQ
- Selective-reject ARQ

All of these forms are based on the use of the flow control technique discussed in Section 6.1. We examine each in turn.

### Stop-and-Wait ARQ

Stop-and-wait ARQ is based on the stop-and-wait flow-control technique outlined previously and is depicted in Figure 6.8. The source station transmits a single frame and then must await an acknowledgment (ACK). No other data frames can be sent until the destination station's reply arrives at the source station.

Two sorts of errors could occur. First, the frame that arrives at the destination could be damaged; the receiver detects this by using the error detection technique referred to earlier and simply discards the frame. To account for this possibility, the source station is equipped with a timer. After a frame is transmitted, the source station waits for an acknowledgment. If no acknowledgment is received by the time the timer expires, then the same frame is sent again. Note that this method requires that the transmitter maintain a copy of a transmitted frame until an acknowledgment is received for that frame.

The second sort of error is a damaged acknowledgment. Consider the following situation. Station $A$ sends a frame. The frame is received correctly by station $B$, which responds with an acknowledgment (ACK). The ACK is damaged in transit and is not recognizable by $A$, which will therefore time-out and resend the same frame. This duplicate frame arrives and is accepted by $B$, which has therefore accepted two copies of the same frame as if they were separate. To avoid this problem, frames are alternately labeled with 0 or 1, and positive acknowledgments are of the form ACK0 and ACK1. In keeping with the sliding-window convention, an ACK0 acknowledges receipt of a frame numbered 1 and indicates that the receiver is ready for a frame numbered 0.

The principal advantage of stop-and-wait ARQ is its simplicity. Its principal disadvantage, as discussed in Section 6.1, is that stop-and-wait is an inefficient mechanism. The sliding-window flow control technique can be adapted to provide more efficient line use; in this context, it is sometimes referred to as *continuous ARQ*.

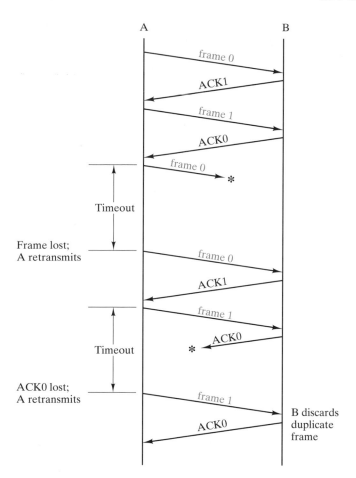

**FIGURE 6.8**    Stop-and-wait ARQ.

## Go-back-N ARQ

The form of error control based on sliding-window flow control that is most commonly used is called go-back-N ARQ.

In go-back-N ARQ, a station may send a series of frames sequentially numbered modulo some maximum value. The number of unacknowledged frames outstanding is determined by window size, using the sliding-window flow control technique. While no errors occur, the destination will acknowledge (RR = receive-ready) incoming frames as usual. If the destination station detects an error in a frame, it sends a negative acknowledgment (REJ = reject) for that frame. The destination station will discard that frame and all future incoming frames until the frame in error is correctly received. Thus, the source station, when it receives an REJ, must retransmit the frame in error plus all succeeding frames that were transmitted in the interim.

Consider that station $A$ is sending frames to station $B$. After each transmission, $A$ sets an acknowledgment timer for the frame just transmitted. The go-back-N technique takes into account the following contingencies:

1. **Damaged frame.** There are three subcases:
   a) $A$ transmits frame $i$. $B$ detects an error and has previously successfully received frame $(i - 1)$. $B$ sends REJ $i$, indicated that frame $i$ is rejected. When $A$ receives the REJ, it must retransmit frame $i$ and all subsequent frames that it has transmitted since the original transmission of frame $i$.
   b) Frame $i$ is lost in transit. $A$ subsequently sends frame $(i + 1)$. $B$ receives frame $(i + 1)$ out of order and sends an REJ $i$. $A$ must retransmit frame $i$ and all subsequent frames.
   c) Frame $i$ is lost in transit, and $A$ does not soon send additional frames. $B$ receives nothing and returns neither an RR nor an REJ. When $A$'s timer expires, it transmits an RR frame that includes a bit known as the P bit, which is set to 1. $B$ interprets the RR frame with a P bit of 1 as a command that must be acknowledged by sending an RR indicating the next frame that it expects. When $A$ receives the RR, it retransmits frame $i$.

2. **Damaged RR.** There are two subcases:
   a) $B$ receives frame $i$ and sends RR $(i + 1)$, which is lost in transit. Because acknowledgments are cumulative (e.g., RR 6 means that all frames through 5 are acknowledged), it may be that $A$ will receive a subsequent RR to a subsequent frame and that it will arrive before the timer associated with frame $i$ expires.
   b) If $A$'s timer expires, it transmits an RR command as in Case 1c. It sets another timer, called the P-bit timer. If $B$ fails to respond to the RR command, or if its response is damaged, then $A$'s P-bit timer will expire. At this point, $A$ will try again by issuing a new RR command and restarting the P-bit timer. This procedure is tried for a number of iterations. If $A$ fails to obtain an acknowledgment after some maximum number of attempts, it initiates a reset procedure.

3. **Damaged REJ.** If an REJ is lost, this is equivalent to Case 1c.

Figure 6.9 is an example of the frame flow for go-back-N ARQ. Because of the propagation delay on the line, by the time that an acknowledgment (positive or negative) arrives back at the sending station, it has already sent two additional frames beyond the one being acknowledged. Thus, when an REJ is received to frame 5, not only frame 5, but frames 6 and 7, must be retransmitted. Thus, the transmitter must keep a copy of all unacknowledged frames.

In Section 6.1, we mentioned that for a $k$-bit sequence number field, which provides a sequence number range of $2^k$, the maximum window size is limited to $2^k - 1$. This has to do with the interaction between error control and acknowledgment. Consider that if data are being exchanged in both directions, station $B$ must send piggybacked acknowledgments to station $A$'s frames in the data frames being transmitted by $B$, even if the acknowledgment has already been sent; as we have mentioned, this is because $B$ must put some number in the acknowledgment field of

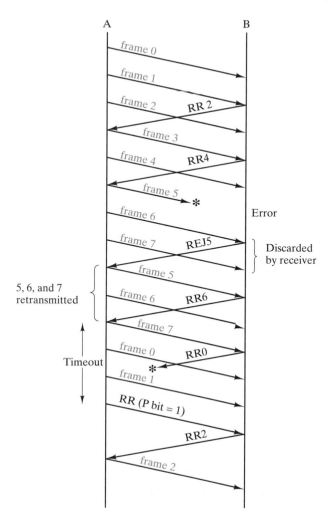

**FIGURE 6.9**   Go-back-N ARQ.

its data frame. As an example, assume a 3-bit sequence number (sequence-number space = 8). Suppose a station sends frame 0 and gets back an RR 1, and then sends frames 1, 2, 3, 4, 5, 6, 7, 0 and gets another RR 1. This could mean that all eight frames were received correctly and the RR 1 is a cumulative acknowledgment. It could also mean that all eight frames were damaged or lost in transit, and the receiving station is repeating its previous RR 1. The problem is avoided if the maximum window size is limited to 7 ($2^3 - 1$).

### Selective-reject ARQ

With selective-reject ARQ, the only frames retransmitted are those that receive a negative acknowledgment, in this case called SREJ, or that time-out. This would appear to be more efficient than go-back-N, because it minimizes the amount of retransmission. On the other hand, the receiver must maintain a buffer large enough to save post-SREJ frames until the frame in error is retransmitted, and it must contain logic for reinserting that frame in the proper sequence. The transmitter, too, requires more complex logic to be able to send a frame out of sequence. Because of such complications, select-reject ARQ is much less used than go-back-N ARQ.

The window-size limitation is more restrictive for selective-reject than for go-back-N. Consider the case of a 3-bit sequence-number size for selective-reject. Allow a window size of seven, and consider the following scenario [TANE88]:

1. Station *A* sends frames 0 through 6 to station *B*.
2. Station *B* receives all seven frames and cumulatively acknowledges with RR 7.
3. Because of a noise burst, the RR 7 is lost.
4. *A* times out and retransmits frame 0.
5. *B* has already advanced its receive window to accept frames 7, 0, 1, 2, 3, 4, and 5. Thus, it assumes that frame 7 has been lost and that this is a new frame 0, which it accepts.

The problem with the foregoing scenario is that there is an overlap between the sending and receiving windows. To overcome the problem, the maximum window size should be no more than half the range of sequence numbers. In the scenario above, if only four unacknowledged frames may be outstanding, no confusion can result. In general, for a k-bit sequence number field, which provides a sequence number range of $2^k$, the maximum window size is limited to $2^{k-1}$.

## 6.4 HIGH-LEVEL DATA LINK CONTROL (HDLC)

The most important data link control protocol is HDLC (ISO 33009, ISO 4335). Not only is HDLC widely used, but it is the basis for many other important data link control protocols, which use the same or similar formats and the same mechanisms as employed in HDLC. Accordingly, in this section we provide a detailed discussion of HDLC. Section 6.5 surveys related protocols.

### Basic Characteristics

To satisfy a variety of applications, HDLC defines three types of stations, two link configurations, and three data-transfer modes of operation. The three station types are

- **Primary station.** Has the responsibility for controlling the operation of the link. Frames issued by the primary are called *commands*.
- **Secondary station.** Operates under the control of the primary station. Frames

issued by a secondary are called *responses*. The primary maintains a separate logical link with each secondary station on the line.

- **Combined station.** Combines the features of primary and secondary. A combined station may issue both commands and responses.

The two link configurations are

- **Unbalanced configuration.** Consists of one primary and one or more secondary stations and supports both full-duplex and half-duplex transmission.
- **Balanced configuration.** Consists of two combined stations and supports both full-duplex and half-duplex transmission.

The three data transfer modes are

- **Normal response mode (NRM).** Used with an unbalanced configuration. The primary may initiate data transfer to a secondary, but a secondary may only transmit data in response to a command from the primary.
- **Asynchronous balanced mode (ABM).** Used with a balanced configuration. Either combined station may initiate transmission without receiving permission from the other combined station.
- **Asynchronous response mode (ARM).** Used with an unbalanced configuration. The secondary may initiate transmission without explicit permission of the primary. The primary still retains responsibility for the line, including initialization, error recovery, and logical disconnection.

NRM is used on mulitdrop lines, in which a number of terminals are connected to a host computer. The computer polls each terminal for input. NRM is also sometimes used on point-to-point links, particularly if the link connects a terminal or other peripheral to a computer. ABM is the most widely used of the three modes; it makes more efficient use of a full-duplex point-to-point link as there is no polling overhead. ARM is rarely used; it is applicable to some special situations in which a secondary may need to initiate transmission.

## Frame Structure

HDLC uses synchronous transmission. All transmissions are in the form of frames, and a single frame format suffices for all types of data and control exchanges.

Figure 6.10a depicts the structure of the HDLC frame. The flag, address, and control fields that precede the information field are known as a header. The FCS and flag fields following the data field are referred to as a *trailer*.

### Flag Fields

Flag fields delimit the frame at both ends with the unique pattern 01111110. A single flag may be used as the closing flag for one frame and the opening flag for the next. On both sides of the user-network interface, receivers are continuously hunting for the flag sequence to synchronize on the start of a frame. While receiving a

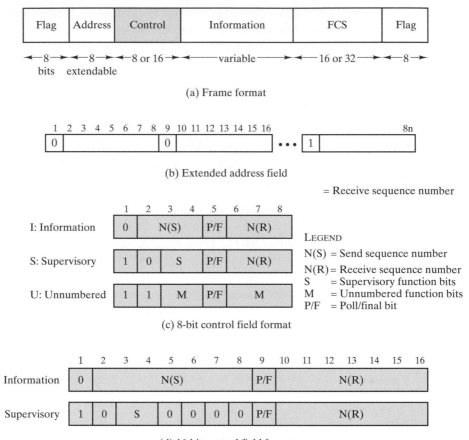

(a) Frame format

(b) Extended address field

(c) 8-bit control field format

(d) 16-bit control field format

**FIGURE 6.10**   HDLC frame structure.

frame, a station continues to hunt for that sequence to determine the end of the frame. However, it is possible that the pattern 01111110 will appear somewhere inside the frame, thus destroying frame-level synchronization. To avoid this, a procedure known as *bit stuffing* is used. Between the transmission of the starting and ending flags, the transmitter will always insert an extra 0 bit after each occurrence of five 1s in the frame. After detecting a starting flag, the receiver monitors the bit stream. When a pattern of five 1s appears, the sixth bit is examined. If this bit is 0, it is deleted. If the sixth bit is a 1 and the seventh bit is a 0, the combination is accepted as a flag. If the sixth and seventh bits are both 1, the sender is indicating an abort condition.

With the use of bit stuffing, arbitrary bit patterns can be inserted into the data field of the frame. This property is known as *data transparency*.

Figure 6.11a shows an example of bit stuffing. Note that in the first two cases, the extra 0 is not strictly necessary for avoiding a flag pattern, but is necessary for the operation of the algorithm. The pitfalls of bit stuffing are also illustrated in this

Original pattern

111111111111011111101111110

After bit-stuffing

11111011111011011111101011111010

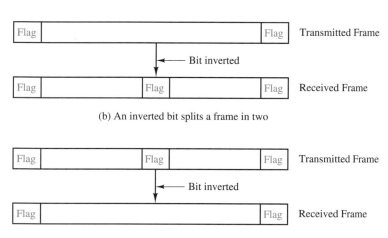

(a) Example

(b) An inverted bit splits a frame in two

(c) An inverted bit merges two frames

**FIGURE 6.11**   Bit stuffing.

figure. When a flag is used as both an ending and a starting flag, a 1-bit error merges two frames into one; conversely, a 1-bit error inside the frame could split it in two.

### Address Field

The address field identifies the secondary station that transmitted or is to receive the frame. This field is not needed for point-to-point links, but is always included for the sake of uniformity. The address field is usually eight bits long but, by prior agreement, an extended format may be used in which the actual address length is a multiple of seven bits (Figure 6.10b). The least significant bit of each octet is 1 or 0, depending on whether it is or is not the last octet of the address field. The remaining seven bits of each octet form part of the address. The single-octet address of 11111111 is interpreted as the all-stations address in both basic and extended formats. It is used to allow the primary to broadcast a frame for reception by all secondaries.

### Control Field

HDLC defines three types of frames, each with a different control field format. *Information frames* (I-frames) carry the data to be transmitted for the user (the logic above HDLC that is using HDLC). Additionally, flow- and error-control data, using the ARQ mechanism, are piggybacked on an information frame. *Supervisory frames* (S-frames) provide the ARQ mechanism when piggybacking is not used. *Unnumbered frames* (U-frames) provide supplemental link control functions. The first one or two bits of the control field serves to identify the frame type. The remaining bit positions are organized into subfields as indicated in Figure 6.10c and d. Their use is explained below in the discussion of HDLC operation.

Note that the basic control field for S- and I-frames uses 3-bit sequence numbers. With the appropriate set-mode command, an extended control field can be used for S- and I-frames that employs 7-bit sequence numbers. U-frames always contain an 8-bit control field.

### Information Field

The information field is present only in I-frames and some U-frames. The field can contain any sequence of bits but must consist of an integral number of octets. The length of the information field is variable up to some system-defined maximum.

### Frame Check Sequence Field

The frame check sequence (FCS) is an error-detecting code calculated from the remaining bits of the frame, exclusive of flags. The normal code is the 16-bit CRC-CCITT defined in Section 6.2. An optional 32-bit FCS, using CRC-32, may be employed if the frame length or the line reliability dictates this choice.

## Operation

HDLC operation consists of the exchange of I-frames, S-frames, and U-frames between two stations. The various commands and responses defined for these frame types are listed in Table 6.1. In describing HDLC operation, we will discuss these three types of frames.

The operation of HDLC involves three phases. First, one side or another initializes the data link so that frames may be exchanged in an orderly fashion. During this phase, the options that are to be used are agreed upon. After initialization, the two sides exchange user data and the control information to exercise flow and error control. Finally, one of the two sides signals the termination of the operation.

### Initialization

Initialization may be requested by either side by issuing one of the six set-mode commands. This command serves three purposes:

1. It signals the other side that initialization is requested.
2. It specifies which of the three modes (NRM, ABM, ARM) is requested.
3. It specifies whether 3- or 7-bit sequence numbers are to be used.

If the other side accepts this request, then the HDLC module on that end transmits an unnumbered acknowledged (UA) frame back to the initiating side. If the request is rejected, then a disconnected mode (DM) frame is sent.

**TABLE 6.1**   HDLC Commands and responses.

| Name | Command/response | Description |
|---|---|---|
| Information (I) | C/R | Exchange user data |
| Supervisory (S) | | |
| Receive ready (RR) | C/R | Positive acknowledgment; ready to receive I-frame |
| Receive not ready (RNR) | C/R | Positive acknowledgment; not ready to receive |
| Reject (REJ) | C/R | Negative acknowledgment; go back N |
| Selective reject (SREJ) | C/R | Negative acknowledgment; selective reject |
| Unnumbered (U) | | |
| Set normal response/extended mode (SNRM/SNRME) | C | Set mode; extended = 7-bit sequence numbers |
| Set asynchronous response/extended mode (SARM/SARME) | C | Set mode; extended = 7-bit sequence numbers |
| Set asynchronous balanced/extended mode (SABM, SABME) | C | Set mode; extended = 7-bit sequence numbers |
| Set initialization mode (SIM) | C | Initialize link control functions in addressed station |
| Disconnect (DISC) | C | Terminate logical link connection |
| Unnumbered acknowledgment (UA) | R | Acknowledge acceptance of one of the set-mode commands |
| Disconnected mode (DM) | C | Terminate logical link connection |
| Request disconnect (RD) | R | Request for DISC command |
| Request initialization mode (RIM) | R | Initialization needed; request for SIM command |
| Unnumbered information (UI) | C/R | Used to exchange control information |
| Unnumbered poll (UP) | C | Used to solicit control information |
| Reset (RSET) | C | Used for recovery; resets $N(R)$, $N(S)$ |
| Exchange identification (XID) | C/R | Used to request/report status |
| Test (TEST) | C/R | Exchange identical information fields for testing |
| Frame reject (FRMR) | R | Reports receipt of unacceptable frame |

## Data Transfer

When the initialization has been requested and accepted, then a logical connection is established. Both sides may begin to send user data in I-frames, starting with sequence number 0. The $N(S)$ and $N(R)$ fields of the I-frame are sequence numbers that support flow control and error control. An HDLC module sending a sequence of I-frames will number them sequentially, modulo 8 or 128, depending on whether 3- or 7-bit sequence numbers are used, and place the sequence number in $N(S)$. $N(R)$ is the acknowledgment for I-frames received; it enables the HDLC module to indicate which number I-frame it expects to receive next.

S-frames are also used for flow control and error control. The receive-ready (RR) frame is used to acknowledge the last I-frame received by indicating the next I-frame expected. The RR is used when there is no reverse-user data traffic (I-frames) to carry an acknowledgment. Receive-not-ready (RNR) acknowledges an I-frame, as with RR, but also asks the peer entity to suspend transmission of I-frames. When the entity that issued RNR is again ready, it sends an RR. REJ initiates the go-back-N ARQ. It indicates that the last I-frame received has been rejected and that retransmission of all I-frames beginning with number N(R) is required. Selective reject (SREJ) is used to request retransmission of just a single frame.

### Disconnect

Either HDLC module can initiate a disconnect, either on its own initiative if there is some sort of fault, or at the request of its higher-layer user. HDLC issues a disconnect by sending a disconnect (DISC) frame. The other side must accept the disconnect by replying with a UA.

### Examples of Operation

In order to better understand HDLC operation, several examples are presented in Figure 6.12. In the example diagrams, each arrow includes a legend that specifies the frame name, the setting of the P/F bit, and, where appropriate, the values of N(R) and N(S). The setting of the P or F bit is 1 if the designation is present and 0 if absent.

Figure 6.12a shows the frames involved in link setup and disconnect. The HDLC protocol entity for one side issues an SABM command to the other side and starts a timer. The other side, upon receiving the SABM, returns a UA response and sets local variables and counters to their initial values. The initiating entity receives the UA response, sets its variables and counters, and stops the timer. The logical connection is now active, and both sides may begin transmitting frames. Should the timer expire without a response, the originator will repeat the SABM, as illustrated. This would be repeated until a UA or DM is received or until, after a given number of tries, the entity attempting initiation gives up and reports failure to a management entity. In such a case, higher-layer intervention is necessary. The same figure (Figure 6.12a) shows the disconnect procedure. One side issues a DISC command, and the other responds with a UA response.

Figure 6.12b illustrates the full-duplex exchange of I-frames. When an entity sends a number of I-frames in a row with no incoming data, then the receive sequence number is simply repeated (e.g., I, 1, 1; I, 2, 1 in the A-to-B direction). When an entity receives a number of I-frames in a row with no outgoing frames, then the receive sequence number in the next outgoing frame must reflect the cumulative activity (e.g., I, 1, 3 in the B-to-A direction). Note that, in addition to I-frames, data exchange may involve supervisory frames.

Figure 6.12c shows an operation involving a busy condition. Such a condition may arise because an HDLC entity is not able to process I-frames as fast as they are

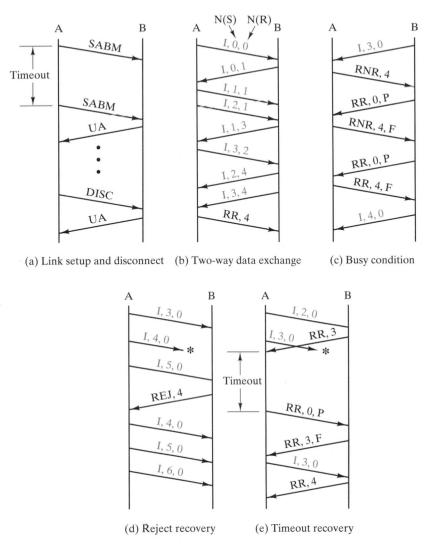

FIGURE 6.12 Examples of HDLC operation.

arriving, or the intended user is not able to accept data as fast as they arrive in I-frames. In either case, the entity's receive buffer fills up and it must halt the incoming flow of I-frames, using an RNR command. In this example, A issues an RNR, which requires B to halt transmission of I-frames. The station receiving the RNR will usually poll the busy station at some periodic interval by sending an RR with the P-bit set; this requires the other side to respond with either an RR or an RNR. When the busy condition has cleared, A returns an RR, and I-frame transmission from B can resume.

An example of error recovery using the REJ command is shown in Figure 6.12d. In this example, A transmits I-frames numbered 3, 4, and 5. Number 4 suffers an error and is lost. When B receives I-frame number 5, it discards this frame

| Flag | Address | Control | Information | FCS | Flag |
|------|---------|---------|-------------|-----|------|
| 8 | 8n | 8 or 16 | Variable | 16 or 32 | 8 |

(a) HDLC, LAPB

| Flag | Address | Control | Information | FCS | Flag |
|------|---------|---------|-------------|-----|------|
| 8 | 16 | 16* | Variable | 16 | 8 |

(b) LAPD

| MAC control | Dest. MAC address | Source MAC address | DSAP | SSAP | LLC control | Information | FCS |
|-------------|-------------------|--------------------|------|------|-------------|-------------|-----|
| Variable | 16 or 48 | 16 or 48 | 8 | 8 | 16* | Variable | 32 |

(c) LLC/MAC

| Flag | Address | Control | Information | FCS | Flag |
|------|---------|---------|-------------|-----|------|
| 8 | 16 or 32 | 16* | Variable | 16 or 32 | 8 |

(d) LAPF (control)

| Flag | Address | Information | FCS | Flag |
|------|---------|-------------|-----|------|
| 8 | 16 to 32 | Variable | 16 | 8 |

(e) LAPF (core)

| General flow control | Virtual path identifier | Virtual channel identifier | Control bits | Header error control | Information |
|----------------------|-------------------------|----------------------------|--------------|----------------------|------------|
| 4 | 8 | 16 | 4 | 8 | 384 |

(f) ATM

* = 16-bit control field (7 bit sequence numbers) for I- and S-frames; 8 bit for U-frames.

**FIGURE 6.13**   Data link control frame formats.

because it is out of order and sends an REJ with an N(R) of 4. This causes A to initiate retransmission of all I-frames sent, beginning with frame 4. It may continue to send additional frames after the retransmitted frames.

An example of error recovery using a timeout is shown in Figure 6.12e. In this example, A transmits I-frame number 3 as the last in a sequence of I-frames. The frame suffers an error. B detects the error and discards it. However, B cannot send an REJ; this is because there is no way to know if this was an I-frame. If an error is detected in a frame, all of the bits of that frame are suspect, and the receiver has no way to act upon it. A, however, would have started a timer as the frame was transmitted. This timer has a duration long enough to span the expected response time. When the timer expires, A initiates recovery action; this is usually done by polling the other side with an RR command with the P bit set, to determine the status of the other side. Because the poll demands a response, the entity will receive a frame containing an N(R) field and be able to proceed. In this case, the response indicates that frame 3 was lost, which A retransmits.

These examples are not exhaustive. However, they should give the reader a good feel for the behavior of HDLC.

## 6.5 OTHER DATA LINK CONTROL PROTOCOLS

In addition to HDLC, there are a number of other important data link control protocols. Figure 6.13 illustrates the frame formats, and this section provides a brief overview.

### LAPB

LAPB (Link Access Procedure, Balanced) was issued by ITU-T as part of its X.25 packet-switching network-interface standard. It is a subset of HDLC that provides only the asynchronous balanced mode (ABM); it is designed for the point-to-point link between a user system and a packet-switching network node. Its frame format is the same as that of HDLC.

### LAPD

LAPD (Link Access Procedure, D-Channel) was issued by ITU-T as part of its set of recommendations on ISDN (Integrated Services Digital Network). LAPD provides data link control over the D channel, which is a logical channel at the user-ISDN interface.

There are several key differences between LAPD and HDLC. Like LAPB, LAPD is restricted to ABM. LAPD always uses 7-bit sequence numbers; 3-bit sequence numbers are not allowed. The FCS for LAPD is always the 16-bit CRC. Finally, the address field for LAPD is a 16-bit field that actually contains two sub-addresses: one is used to identify one of possibly multiple devices on the user side of the interface, and the other is used to identify one of possibly multiple logical users of LAPD on the user side of the interface.

### Logical Link Control (LLC)

LLC is part of the IEEE 802 family of standards for controlling operation over a local area network (LAN). LLC is lacking some features found in HDLC and also has some features not found in HDLC.

The most obvious difference between LLC and HDLC is the difference in frame format. Link control functions in the case of LLC are actually divided between two layers: a medium access control (MAC) layer, and the LLC layer, which operates on top of the MAC layer.

Figure 6.13c shows the structure of the combined MAC/LLC frame; the shaded portion corresponds to the fields produced at the LLC layer, and the unshaded portions are the header and trailer of the MAC frame. The MAC layer includes source and destination addresses for devices attached to the LAN. Two addresses are needed as there is no concept of primary and secondary in the LAN environment; therefore, both the sender and receiver must be identified. Error detection is done at the MAC level, using a 32-bit CRC. Finally, there are some control functions peculiar to medium-access control that may be included in a MAC control field.

At the LLC layer, there are four fields. The destination and source service access points (DSAP and SSAP), identify the logical user of LLC at the source and destination systems. The LLC control field has the same format as that of HDLC, limited to 7-bit sequence numbers.

Operationally, LLC offers three forms of *service*. The connection-mode service is the same as the ABM of HDLC. The other two services, unacknowledged connectionless and acknowledged connectionless, are described in Part II.

### Frame Relay

Frame relay is a data link control facility designed to provide a streamlined capability for use over high-speed packet-switched networks. It is used in place of X.25, which consists of both a data link control protocol (LAPB) and a network-layer protocol (called X.25 packet layer). Frame relay is examined in detail in Part II.

The data link control protocol defined for frame relay is LAPF (Link Access Procedure for Frame-Mode Bearer Services). There are actually two protocols: a *control protocol*, which has similar features to HDLC, and a *core protocol*, which is a subset of the control protocol.

There are several key differences between the LAPF control protocol and HDLC. Like LAPB, LAPF control is restricted to ABM. LAPF control always uses 7-bit sequence numbers; 3-bit sequence numbers are not allowed. The FCS for LAPF control is always the 16-bit CRC. Finally, the address field for LAPF control is two, three, or four octets long, containing a 10-bit, 16-bit, or 23-bit DLCI (data link connection identifier). The DLCI identifies a logical connection between a source and destination system. In addition, the address field contains some control bits that are useful for flow control purposes.

The LAPF core consists of the same flag, address, information, and FCS fields as LAPF control. The difference is that there is no control field for LAPF core. Thus, there is no means of doing flow and error control, which results in a more streamlined operation.

### Asynchronous Transfer Mode (ATM)

Like frame relay, ATM is designed to provide a streamlined data-transfer capability across high-speed networks. Unlike frame relay, ATM is not based on HDLC. Instead, ATM is based on a completely new frame format, known as a cell, that provides minimum processing overhead.

The cell has a fixed length of 53 octets, or 424 bits. The details of the ATM cell fields are discussed in Part II.

## 6.6 RECOMMENDED READING

An excellent and very detailed treatment of flow control and error control is to be found in [BERT92]. A good survey of data link control protocols is [BLAC93].

BERT92   Bertsekas, D. and Gallager, R. *Data Networks*. Englewood Cliffs, NJ: Prentice Hall, 1992.

BLAC93    Black, U. *Data Link Protocols*. Englewood Cliffs, NJ: Prentice Hall, 1993.

## 6.7  PROBLEMS

**6.1**  Consider a half-duplex point-to-point link using a stop-and-wait scheme.
  **a.** What is the effect on line utilization of increasing the message size so that fewer messages will be required? Other factors remain constant.
  **b.** What is the effect on line utilization of increasing the number of frames for a constant message size?
  **c.** What is the effect on line utilization of increasing frame size?

**6.2**  A channel has a data rate of 4 kbps and a propagation delay of 20 ms. For what range of frame sizes does stop-and-wait give an efficiency of at least 50%?

**6.3**  Consider the use of 1000-bit frames on a 1-Mbps satellite channel with a 270-ms delay. What is the maximum link utilization for
  **a.** Stop-and-wait flow control?
  **b.** Continuous flow control with a window size of 7?
  **c.** Continuous flow control with a window size of 127?
  **d.** Continuous flow control with a window size of 255?

**6.4**  In Figure 6.14, frames are generated at node $A$ and sent to node $C$ through node $B$. Determine the minimum transmission rate required between nodes $B$ and $C$ so that the buffers of node $B$ are not flooded, based on the following:

  - The data rate between $A$ and $B$ is 100 kbps.
  - The propagation delay is 10 μsec/mile for both lines.
  - There are full duplex lines between the nodes.
  - All data frames are 1000 bits long; ACK frames are separate frames of negligible length.
  - Between $A$ and $B$, a sliding-window protocol with a window size of 3 is used.
  - Between $B$ and $C$, stop-and-wait is used.
  - There are no errors.

  **Hint**: In order not to flood the buffers of $B$, the average number of frames entering and leaving $B$ must be the same over a long interval.

**6.5**  A channel has a data rate of $R$ bps and a propagation delay of $t$ seconds per kilometer. The distance between the sending and receiving nodes is $L$ kilometers. Nodes

**FIGURE 6.14**    Configuration for problem 6.4

exchange fixed-size frames of $B$ bits. Find a formula that gives the minimum sequence field size of the frame as a function of $R$, $t$, $B$, and $L$ (considering maximum utilization). Assume that ACK frames are negligible in size and the processing at the nodes is instantaneous.

**6.6**  Would you expect that the inclusion of a parity bit with each character would change the probability of receiving a correct message?

**6.7**  What is the purpose of using modulo 2 arithmetic rather than binary arithmetic in computing an FCS?

**6.8**  Consider a frame consisting of two characters of four bits each. Assume that the probability of bit error is $10^{-3}$ and that it is independent for each bit.

      **a.** What is the probability that the received frame contains at least one error?

      **b.** Now add a parity bit to each character. What is the probability?

**6.9** Using the CRC-CCITT polynomial, generate the 16-bit CRC code for a message consisting of a 1 followed by 15 0s.

      **a.** Use long division.

      **b.** Use the shift register mechanism shown in Figure 6.6.

**6.10** Explain in words why the shift register implementation of CRC will result in all 0s at the receiver if there are no errors. Demonstrate by example.

**6.11** For $P = 110011$ and $M = 11100011$, find the CRC.

**6.12** A CRC is constructed to generate a 4-bit FCS for an 11-bit message. The generator polynomial is $X^4 + X^3 + 1$.

      **a.** Draw the shift register circuit that would perform this task (see Figure 6.6).

      **b.** Encode the data bit sequence 10011011100 (leftmost bit is the least significant) using the generator polynomial and give the code word.

      **c.** Now assume that bit 7 (counting from the LSB) in the code word is in error and show that the detection algorithm detects the error.

**6.13** A modified CRC procedure is commonly used in communications standards. It is defined as follows:

$$\frac{X^{16}M(X) = X^k L(X)}{P(X)} = Q + \frac{R(X)}{P(X)}$$
$$\text{FCS} = L(X) + R(X)$$

where

$$L(X) = X^{15} + X^{14} + X^{13} + \ldots + X + 1$$

      **a.** Describe in words the effect of this procedure.

      **b.** Explain the potential benefits.

**6.14** Why is it not necessary to have NAK0 and NAK1 for stop-and-wait ARQ?

**6.15** Suppose that a selective-reject ARQ is used where $N = 4$. Show, by example, that a 3-bit sequence number is needed.

**6.16** Using the same assumptions that are used for Figure 6.17 in Appendix 6A, plot line utilization as a function of $P$, the probability that a single frame is in error for the following error-control techniques:

      **a.** Stop-and-wait.

      **b.** Go-back-N with N = 7.

      **c.** Go-back-N with N = 127.

      **d.** Selective reject with N = 7.

      **e.** Selective reject with N = 127.

      Do all of the preceding for the following values of $a$: 0.1, 1, 10, 100. Draw conclusions about which technique is appropriate for various ranges of $a$.

**6.17** Two neighboring nodes (A and B) use a sliding-window protocol with a 3-bit sequence number. As the ARQ mechanism, Go-back-N is used with a window size of 4. Assuming A is transmitting and B is receiving, show the window positions for the following succession of events:

      **a.** Before A sends any frames.

      **b.** After A sends frames 0, 1, 2 and B acknowledges 0, 1 and the ACKs are received by A.

      **c.** After A sends frames 3, 4, and 5 and B acknowledges 4 and the ACK is received by A.

**6.18** It was stated in Section 6.3 that out-of-sequence acknowledgment could not be used for selective-reject ARQ. That is, if frame $i$ is rejected by station X, all subsequent I-frames and RR frames sent by X must have $N(R) = i$ until frame $i$ is successfully received, even if other frames with $N(S) > i$ are successfully received in the meantime.

One possible refinement is the following: $N(R) = j$ in an I-frame or an RR frame is interpreted to mean that frame $j - 1$ and all preceding frames are accepted except for those that have been explicitly rejected using an SREJ frame. Comment on any possible drawback to this scheme.

6.19   The ISO standard for HDLC procedures (ISO 4335) includes the following definitions: (1) an REJ condition is considered cleared upon the receipt of an incoming I-frame with an $N(S)$ equal to the $N(R)$ of the outgoing REJ frame; and (2) an SREJ condition is considered cleared upon the receipt of an I-frame with an $N(S)$ equal to the $N(R)$ of the SREJ frame. The standard includes rules concerning the relationship between REJ and SREJ frames. These rules indicate what is allowable (in terms of transmitting REJ and SREJ frames) if an REJ condition has not yet been cleared and what is allowable if an SREJ condition has not yet been cleared. Deduce the rules and justify your answer.

6.20   Two stations communicate via a 1-Mbps satellite link with a propagation delay of 270 ms. The satellite serves merely to retransmit data received from one station to another, with negligible switching delay. Using HDLC frames of 1024 bits with 3-bit sequence numbers, what is the maximum possible data throughput (not counting overhead bits)?

6.21   It is clear that bit stuffing is needed for the address, data, and FCS fields of an HDLC frame. Is it needed for the control field?

6.22   Suggest improvements to the bit stuffing-algorithm to overcome the problems of single-bit errors.

6.23   Using the example bit string of Figure 6.11, show the signal pattern on the line using NRZ-L coding; does this suggest a side benefit of bit stuffing?

6.24   Assume that the primary HDLC station in NRM has sent six I-frames to a secondary. The primary's $N(S)$ count was three (011 binary) prior to sending the six frames. If the poll bit is on in the sixth frame, what will be the $N(R)$ count back from the secondary after the last frame? Assume error-free operation.

6.25   Consider that several physical links connect two stations. We would like to use a "multilink HDLC" that makes efficient use of these links by sending frames on an FIFO basis on the next available link. What enhancements to HDLC are needed?

## 6A APPENDIX

### PERFORMANCE ISSUES

IN THIS APPENDIX, we examine some of the performance issues related to the use of sliding-window flow-control.

### Stop-and-Wait Flow Control

Let us determine the maximum potential efficiency of a half-duplex point-to-point line using the stop-and-wait scheme described in Section 6.1. Suppose that a long message is to be sent as a sequence of frames $f_1, f_2, \ldots, f_n$, in the following fashion:

- Station $S_1$ sends $f_1$.
- Station $S_2$ sends an acknowledgment.
- Station $S_1$ sends $f_2$.
- Station $S_2$ sends an acknowledgment.

   •

   •

   •

- Station $S_1$ sends $f_n$.
- Station $S_2$ sends an acknowledgment.

The total time to send the data, $T$, can be expressed as $T = nT_F$, where $T_F$ is the time to send one frame and receive an acknowledgment. We can express $T_F$ as follows:

$$T_F = t_{prop} + t_{frame} + t_{proc} + t_{prop} + t_{ack} + t_{proc}$$

where

   $t_{prop}$ = propagation time from $S_1$ to $S_2$
   $t_{frame}$ = time to transmit a frame (time for the transmitter to send out all of the bits of the frame)
   $t_{proc}$ = processing time at each station to react to an incoming event
   $t_{ack}$ = time to transmit an acknowledgment

Let us assume that the processing time is relatively negligible, and that the acknowledgment frame is very small compared to a data frame, both of which are reasonable assumptions. Then we can express the total time to send the data as

$$T = n(2t_{prop} + t_{frame})$$

Of that time, only $n \times t_{frame}$ is actually spent transmitting data and the rest is overhead. The utilization, or efficiency, of the line is

$$U = \frac{n \times t_{frame}}{n(2t_{prop} + t_{frame})}$$

$$= \frac{t_{frame}}{2t_{prop} + t_{frame}}$$

It is useful to define the parameter $a = t_{prop}/t_{frame}$. Then,

$$U = \frac{1}{1 + 2a} \tag{6.2}$$

This is the maximum possible utilization of the link. Because the frame contains overhead bits, actual utilization is lower. The parameter $a$ is constant if both $t_{prop}$ and $t_{frame}$ are constants, which is typically the case. Fixed length frames are often used for all except the last frame in a sequence, and the propagation delay is constant for point-to-point links.

To get some insight into Equation (6.2), let us derive a different expression for $a$. We have

$$a = \frac{\text{Propagation Time}}{\text{Transmission Time}} \tag{6.3}$$

The propagation time is equal to the distance $d$ of the link divided by the velocity of propagation $V$. For unguided transmission through air or space, $V$ is the speed of light, $3 \times 10^8$ m/sec. For guided transmission, $V$ is approximately the speed of light for optical fiber and about 0.67 times the speed of light for copper media. The transmission time is equal to the length of the frame in bits, $L$, divided by the data rate $R$. Therefore,

$$a = \frac{d/V}{L/R} = \frac{Rd}{VL}$$

Thus, for fixed-length frames and a fixed distance between stations, $a$ is proportional to the data rate times the length of the medium. A useful way of looking at a is that it represents the length of the medium in bits $(R \times {}^d/_V)$ compared to the frame length $(L)$.

With this interpretation in mind, Figure 6.2 illustrates equation (6.2). In this figure, transmission time is normalized to 1 and, hence, the propagation time, by Equation (6.3), is $a$. For the case of $a < 1$, the link's bit length is less than that of the frame. The station $T$ begins transmitting a frame at time $t_0$. At $t_0 + a$, the leading edge of the frame reaches the receiving station $R$, while $T$ is still in the process of transmitting the frame. At $t_0 + 1$, $T$ completes transmission. At $t_0 + 1 + a$, $R$ has received the entire frame and immediately transmits a small acknowledgment frame. This acknowledgment arrives back at $T$ at $t_0 + 1 + 2a$. Total elapsed time: $1 + 2a$. Total transmission time: 1. Hence, utilization is $1/(1 + 2a)$. The same result is achieved with a $> 1$, as illustrated in Figure 6.2.

Let us consider a few examples. First, consider a wide-area network (WAN) using ATM (asynchronous transfer mode, described in Part II), with the two stations a thousand kilometers apart. The standard ATM frame size (called a cell) is 424 bits and one of the standardized data rates is 155.52 Mbps. Thus, transmission time equals $424/(155.52 \times 10^6) = 2.7 \times 10^{-6}$ seconds. If we assume an optical fiber link, then the propagation time is $(10^6 \text{ meters})/(3 \times 10^8 \text{ m/sec}) = 0.33 \times 10^{-2}$ seconds. Thus, $a = (0.33 \times 10^{-2})/(2.7 \times 10^{-6}) = 1222$, and efficiency is only $1/2445 = 0.0004$!

At the other extreme, in terms of distance, is the local area network (LAN). Distances range from 0.1 to 10 km, with data rates of 10 to 100 Mbps; higher data rates tend to be associated with shorter distances. Using a value of $V = 2 \times 10^8$ m/sec, a frame size of 1000 bits, and a data rate of 10 Mbps, the value of $a$ is in the range of 0.005 to 0.5; this yields a utilization in the range of 0.5 to 0.99. For a 100-Mbps LAN, given the shorter distances, comparable utilizations are possible.

We can see that LANs are typically quite efficient, whereas high-speed WANs are not. As a final example, let us consider digital data transmission via modem over a voice-grade line. A practical upper bound on data rate is 28.8 kbps. Again, let us consider a 1000-bit frame. The link distance can be anywhere from a few tens of meters to thousands of kilometers. If we pick, say, as a short distance, $d = 1000$ m, then $a = (28{,}800 \text{ bps} \times 1000 \text{ m})/(2 \times 10^8 \text{ m/sec} \times 1000 \text{ bits}) = 1.44 \times 10^{-4}$, and utilization is effectively 1.0. Even in a long-distance case, such as $d = 5000$ km, we have $a = (28{,}800 \times 5 \times 10^6)/(2 \times 10^8 \times 1000 \text{ bits}) = 0.72$ and efficiency equals 0.4.

### Sliding–Window Control

For sliding-window flow control, the efficiency of the line depends on both the window size, $N$, and the value of $a$. For convenience, let us again normalize frame transmission time to a value of 1; thus, the propagation time is $a$. Figure 6.15 illustrates the efficiency of a full-duplex point-to-point line. Station $A$ begins to emit a sequence of frames at time $t_0$. The leading edge

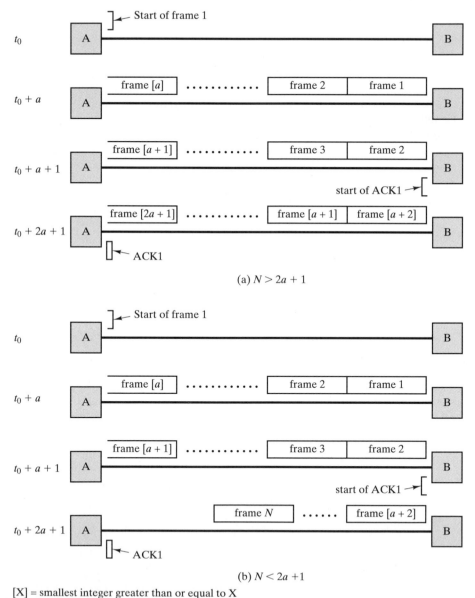

(a) $N > 2a + 1$

(b) $N < 2a + 1$

$[X]$ = smallest integer greater than or equal to X

**FIGURE 6.15**   Timing of a sliding-window protocol.

of the first frame reaches station $B$ at $t_0 + a$. The first frame is entirely absorbed by $t_0 + a + 1$. Assuming negligible processing time, $B$ can immediately acknowledge the first frame (ACK1). Let us also assume that the acknowledgment frame is so small that transmission time is negligible. Then the ACK1 reaches $A$ at $t_0 + 2a + 1$. To evaluate performance, we need to consider two cases:

- Case 1: $N \geq 2a + 1$. The acknowledgment for frame 1 reaches $A$ before $A$ has exhausted its window. Thus, $A$ can transmit continuously with no pause, and utilization is 1.0.
- Case 2: $N < 2a + 1$. $A$ exhausts its window at $t_0 + N$ and cannot send additional frames until $t_0 + 2a + 1$. Thus, line utilization is $N$ time units out of a period of $(2a + 1)$ time units.

Therefore, we can state that

$$U = \begin{cases} 1 & N \geq 2a + 1 \\ \dfrac{N}{2a + 1} & N < 2a + 1 \end{cases} \qquad (6.4)$$

Typically, the sequence number is provided for in an $n$-bit field, and the maximum window size is $N = 2^n - 1$ (not $2^n$; this is explained in Section 6.3). Figure 6.16 shows the maximum efficiency achievable for window sizes of 1, 7, and 127 as a function of a. A window size of 1 corresponds to stop-and-wait. A window size of 7 (3 bits) is adequate for many applications. A window size of 127 (7 bits) is adequate for larger values of $a$, such as may be found in high-speed WANs.

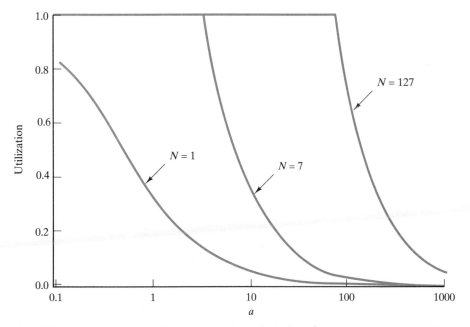

**FIGURE 6.16** Line utilization as a function of window size.

### ARQ

We have seen that sliding-window flow control is more efficient than stop-and-wait flow control. We would expect that when error-control functions are added, this would still be true—that is, that go-back-N and selective-reject ARQ are more efficient than stop-and-wait ARQ. Let us develop some approximations to determine the degree of improvement to be expected.

First, consider stop-and-wait ARQ. With no errors, the maximum utilization is $1/(1 + 2a)$ as shown in Equation (6.2). We want to account for the possibility that some frames are repeated because of bit errors. To start, note that the utilization U can be defined as

$$U = \frac{T_f}{T_t} \tag{6.5}$$

where

$T_f$ = time for transmitter to emit a single frame
$Tt$ = total time that line is engaged in the transmission of a single frame

For error-free operation using stop-and-wait ARQ,

$$U = \frac{T_f}{T_f + 2T_p}$$

where $T_p$ is the propagation time. Dividing by $T_f$ and remembering that $a = T_p/T_f$, we again have Equation (6.2). If errors occur, we must modify Equation (6.5) to

$$U = \frac{T_f}{N_r T_t}$$

where $N_r$ is the expected number of transmissions of a frame. Thus, for stop-and-wait ARQ, we have

$$U = \frac{1}{N_r(1 + 2a)}$$

A simple expression for $N_r$ can be derived by considering the probability $P$ that a single frame is in error. If we assume that ACKs and NAKs are never in error, the probability that it will take exactly $k$ attempts to transmit a frame successfully is $P^{k-1}(1 - P)$. That is, we have $(k - 1)$ unsuccessful attempts followed by one successful attempt; the probability of this occurring is just the product of the probability of the individual events occurring. Then,[1]

$$N_r = \text{E[transmissions]} = \sum_{i=1}^{\infty} (i \times P_r[i \text{ transmissions}])$$
$$= \sum_{i=1}^{\infty} (iP^{i-1}(1 - P)) = \frac{1}{1 - P}$$

So we have

$$\textit{Stop-and-Wait:} \qquad U = \frac{1 - P}{1 + 2a}$$

---

[1] This derivation uses the equality $\sum_{i=1}^{\infty} (iX^{i-1}) = \frac{1}{(1 - X)^2}$ for $(-1 < X < 1)$

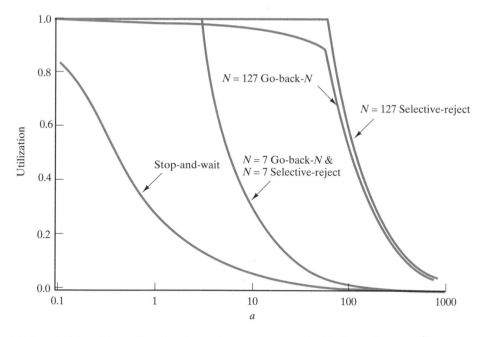

**FIGURE 6.17**   Line utilization for various error-control techniques ($P = 10^{-3}$).

For the sliding-window protocol, Equation (6.4) applies for error-free operation. For selective-reject ARQ, we can use the same reasoning as applied to stop-and-wait ARQ. That is, the error-free equations must be divided by $N_r$. Again, $N_r = 1/(1 - P)$. So,

$$\textit{Selective reject:} \qquad U = \begin{cases} 1 - P & N > 2a + 1 \\ \dfrac{N(1 - P)}{2a + 1} & N < 2a + 1 \end{cases}$$

The same reasoning applies for go-back-N ARQ, but we must be more careful in approximating $N_r$. Each error generates a requirement to retransmit K frames rather than just one frame. Thus,

$$N_r = E[\textit{number of transmitted frames to successfully transmit one frame}]$$

$$= \sum_{i=1}^{\infty} f(i)P^{i-1}(1 - P)$$

where $f(i)$ is the total number of frames transmitted if the original frame must be transmitted $i$ times. This can be expresses as

$$f(i) = 1 + (i - 1)K$$
$$= (1 - K) + Ki$$

Substituting yields[2]

---

[2] This derivation uses the equality $\displaystyle\sum_{i=1}^{\infty} X^{i-1} = \dfrac{1}{1 - X}$ for $(-1 < X < 1)$.

$$N_r = (1 - K) \sum_{i=1}^{\infty} P^{i-1}(1 - P) + K \sum_{i=1}^{\infty} iP^{i-1}(1 - P)$$

$$= 1 - K + \frac{K}{1 - P}$$

$$= \frac{1 - P + KP}{1 - P}$$

By studying Figure 6.15, the reader should conclude that $K$ is approximately equal to $(2a + 1)$ for $N \geqslant (2a + 1)$, and $K = N$ for $N < (2a + 1)$. Thus,

$$\text{Go-back-N:} \qquad U = \begin{cases} \dfrac{1 - P}{1 + 2aP} & N \geqslant 2a + 1 \\[3mm] \dfrac{N(1 - P)}{(2a + 1)(1 - P + NP)} & N < 2a + 1 \end{cases}$$

Note that for $N = 1$, both selective-reject and go-back-N ARQ reduce to stop-and-wait. Figure 6.17 compares these three error-control techniques for a value of $P = 10^{-3}$. [3] This figure and the equations are only approximations. For example, we have ignored errors in acknowledgment frames and, in the case of go-back-N, we have also ignored errors in retransmitted frames other than the frame initially in error. However, the results do give an indication of the relative performance of the three techniques.

---

[3] For $N = 7$, the curves for go-back-N and selective-reject are so close that they appear to be identical in the figure.

# CHAPTER 7

# MULTIPLEXING

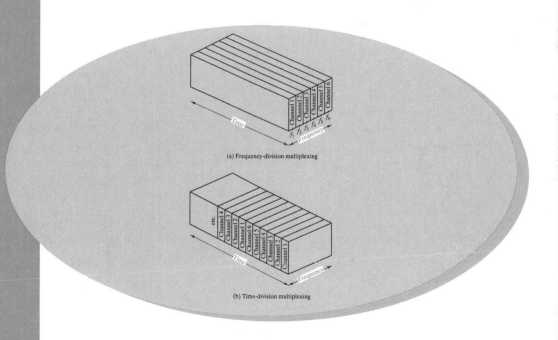

(a) Frequency-division multiplexing

(b) Time-division multiplexing

I n Chapter 6, we described efficient techniques for utilizing a data link under heavy load. Specifically, with two devices connected by a point-to-point link, it is generally desirable to have multiple frames outstanding so that the data link does not become a bottleneck between the stations. Now consider the opposite problem. Typically, two communicating stations will not utilize the full capacity of a data link. For efficiency, it should be possible to share that capacity. A generic term for such sharing is multiplexing.

A common application of multiplexing is in long-haul communications. Trunks on long-haul networks are high-capacity fiber, coaxial, or microwave links. These links can carry large numbers of voice and data transmissions simultaneously using multiplexing.

Figure 7.1 depicts the multiplexing function in its simplest form. There are $n$ inputs to a multiplexer. The multiplexer is connected by a single data link to a demultiplexer. The link is able to carry $n$ separate channels of data. The multiplexer combines (multiplexes) data from the $n$ input lines and transmits over a higher-capacity data link. The demultiplexer accepts the multiplexed data stream, separates (demultiplexes) the data according to channel, and delivers them to the appropriate output lines.

**FIGURE 7.1**   Multiplexing.

The widespread use of multiplexing in data communications can be explained by the following:

1. The higher the data rate, the more cost-effective the transmission facility. That is, for a given application and over a given distance, the cost per kbps declines with an increase in the data rate of the transmission facility. Similarly, the cost of transmission and receiving equipment, per kbps, declines with increasing data rate.

2. Most individual data-communicating devices require relatively modest data-rate support. For example, for most terminal and personal computer applications, a data rate of between 9600 bps and 64 kbps is generally adequate.

The preceding statements were phrased in terms of data communicating devices. Similar statements apply to voice communications; that is, the greater the capacity of a transmission facility, in terms of voice channels, also, the less the cost per individual voice channel; so, the capacity required for a single voice channel is modest.

This chapter concentrates on three types of multiplexing techniques. The first, frequency-division multiplexing (FDM), is the most heavily used and is familiar to anyone who has ever turned on a radio or television set. The second is a particular case of time-division multiplexing (TDM) known as synchronous TDM. This is commonly used for multiplexing digitized voice streams and data streams. The third type seeks to improve on the efficiency of synchronous TDM by adding complexity to the multiplexer. It is known by a variety of names, including statistical TDM, asynchronous TDM, and intelligent TDM. This book uses the term statistical TDM, which highlights one of its chief properties.

## 7.1  FREQUENCY-DIVISION MULTIPLEXING

### Characteristics

FDM is possible when the useful bandwidth of the transmission medium exceeds the required bandwidth of signals to be transmitted. A number of signals can be carried simultaneously if each signal is modulated onto a different carrier frequency and the carrier frequencies are sufficiently separated that the bandwidths of the signals do not overlap. A general case of FDM is shown in Figure 7.2a. Six signal sources are fed into a multiplexer, which modulates each signal onto a different frequency $(f_1, \ldots, f_6)$. Each modulated signal requires a certain bandwidth centered around its carrier frequency, referred to as a *channel*. To prevent interference, the channels are separated by guard bands, which are unused portions of the spectrum.

The composite signal transmitted across the medium is analog. Note, however, that the input signals may be either digital or analog. In the case of digital input, the input signals must be passed through modems to be converted to analog. In either case, each input analog signal must then be modulated to move it to the appropriate frequency band.

A familiar example of FDM is broadcast and cable television. The television signal discussed in Chapter 2 fits comfortably into a 6-MHz bandwidth. Figure 7.3 depicts the transmitted TV signal and its bandwidth. The black-and-white video signal is AM modulated on a carrier signal $f_{cv}$. Because the baseband video signal has a bandwidth of 4 MHz, we would expect the modulated signal to have a bandwidth of 8 MHz centered on $f_{cv}$. To conserve bandwidth, the signal is passed through a sideband filter so that most of the lower sideband is suppressed. The resulting signal extends from about $f_{cv} - 0.75$ MHz to $f_{cv} + 4.2$ MHz. A separate color subcarrier, $f_{cc}$, is used to transmit color information. This is spaced far enough from $f_{cv}$ that there is essentially no interference. Finally, the audio portion of the signal is modulated on $f_{ca}$, outside the effective bandwidth of the other two signals. A bandwidth of 50 kHz is allocated for the audio signal. The composite signal fits into a 6-MHz bandwidth with the video, color, and audio signal carriers at 1.25 MHz, 4.799545 MHz, and 5.75 MHz, respectively, above the lower edge of the band. Thus, multiple TV signals can be frequency-division multiplexed on a CATV cable, each with a bandwidth of 6 MHz. Given the enormous bandwidth of coaxial cable (as much as 500 MHz), dozens of TV signals can be simultaneously carried using FDM. Of course, using radio-frequency propagation through the atmosphere is also a form of FDM; Table 7.1 shows the frequency allocation in the United States for broadcast television.

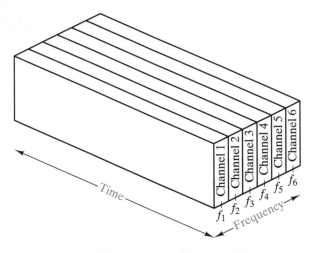

(a) Frequency-division multiplexing

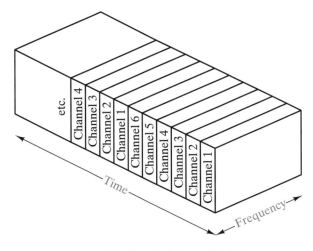

(b) Time-division multiplexing

**FIGURE 7.2** FDM and TDM.

A generic depiction of an FDM system is shown in Figure 7.4. A number of analog or digital signals $[m_i(t), i = 1, N]$ are to be multiplexed onto the same transmission medium. Each signal $m_i(t)$ is modulated onto a carrier $f_{sci}$; because multiple carriers are to be used, each is referred to as a subcarrier. Any type of modulation may be used. The resulting modulated analog signals are then summed to produce a composite signal $m_c(t)$. Figure 7.4b shows the result. The spectrum of signal $m_i(t)$ is shifted to be centered on $f_{sci}$. For this scheme to work, $f_{sci}$ must be chosen so that the bandwidths of the various signals do not overlap; otherwise, it will be impossible to recover the original signals.

The composite signal may then be shifted as a whole to another carrier frequency by an additional modulation step. We will see examples of this below. This second modulation step need not use the same modulation technique as the first.

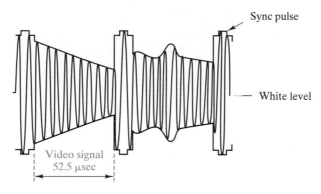

(a) Amplitude modulation with video signal

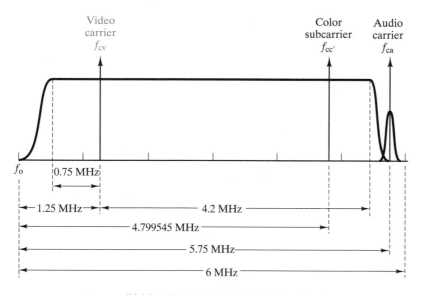

(b) Magnitude spectrum of RF video signal

**FIGURE 7.3**   Transmitted TV signal.

The composite signal has a total bandwidth $B$, where $B > \sum_{i=1}^{N} B_{sci}$. This ana-log signal may be transmitted over a suitable medium. At the receiving end, the composite signal is passed through $N$ bandpass filters, each filter centered on $f_{sci}$ and having a bandwidth $B_{sci}$, for $1 < i < N$; in this way, the signal is again split into its component parts. Each component is then demodulated to recover the original signal.

Let us consider a simple example of transmitting three voice signals simulta-neously over a medium. As was mentioned, the bandwidth of a voice signal is gen-erally taken to be 4 kHz, with an effective spectrum of 300 to 3400 Hz (Figure 7.5a). If such a signal is used to amplitude-modulate a 64-kHz carrier, the spectrum of Fig-

**TABLE 7.1** Broadcast television channel frequency allocation.

| Channel number | Band (MHz) | Channel number | Band (MHz) | Channel number | Band (MHz) |
|---|---|---|---|---|---|
| 2 | 54–60 | 25 | 536–542 | 48 | 674–680 |
| 3 | 60–66 | 26 | 542–548 | 49 | 680–686 |
| 4 | 66–72 | 27 | 548–554 | 50 | 686–692 |
| 5 | 76–82 | 28 | 554–560 | 51 | 692–698 |
| 6 | 82–88 | 29 | 560–566 | 52 | 698–704 |
| 7 | 174–180 | 30 | 566–572 | 53 | 704–710 |
| 8 | 180–186 | 31 | 572–578 | 54 | 710–716 |
| 9 | 186–192 | 32 | 578–584 | 55 | 716–722 |
| 10 | 192–198 | 33 | 584–590 | 56 | 722–728 |
| 11 | 198–204 | 34 | 590–596 | 57 | 728–734 |
| 12 | 204–210 | 35 | 596–602 | 58 | 734–740 |
| 13 | 210–216 | 36 | 602–608 | 59 | 740–746 |
| 14 | 470–476 | 37 | 608–614 | 60 | 746–752 |
| 15 | 476–482 | 38 | 614–620 | 61 | 752–758 |
| 16 | 482–488 | 39 | 620–626 | 62 | 758–764 |
| 17 | 488–494 | 40 | 626–632 | 63 | 764–770 |
| 18 | 494–500 | 41 | 632–638 | 64 | 770–776 |
| 19 | 500–506 | 42 | 638–644 | 65 | 776–782 |
| 20 | 506–512 | 43 | 644–650 | 66 | 782–788 |
| 21 | 512–518 | 44 | 650–656 | 67 | 788–794 |
| 22 | 518–524 | 45 | 656–662 | 68 | 794–800 |
| 23 | 524–530 | 46 | 662–668 | 69 | 800–806 |
| 24 | 530–536 | 47 | 668–674 | | |

ure 7.5b results. The modulated signal has a bandwidth of 8 kHz, extending from 60 to 68 kHz. To make efficient use of bandwidth, we elect to transmit only the lower sideband. Now, if three voice signals are used to modulate carriers at 64, 68, and 72 kHz, and only the lower sideband of each is taken, the spectrum of Figure 7.5c results.

This figure points out two problems that an FDM system must cope with. The first is crosstalk, which may occur if the spectra of adjacent component signals overlap significantly. In the case of voice signals, with an effective bandwidth of only 3100 Hz (300 to 3400), a 4-kHz bandwidth is adequate. The spectra of signals produced by modems for voiceband transmission also fit well in this bandwidth. Another potential problem is intermodulation noise, which was discussed in Chapter 2. On a long link, the nonlinear effects of amplifiers on a signal in one channel could produce frequency components in other channels.

## Analog Carrier Systems

The long-distance carrier system provided in the United States and throughout the world is designed to transmit voiceband signals over high-capacity transmission links, such as coaxial cable and microwave systems. The earliest, and still most common, technique for utilizing high-capacity links is FDM. In the United States, AT&T has designated a hierarchy of FDM schemes to accommodate transmission systems of various capacities. A similar, but unfortunately not identical, system has been adopted internationally under the auspices of ITU-T (Table 7.2).

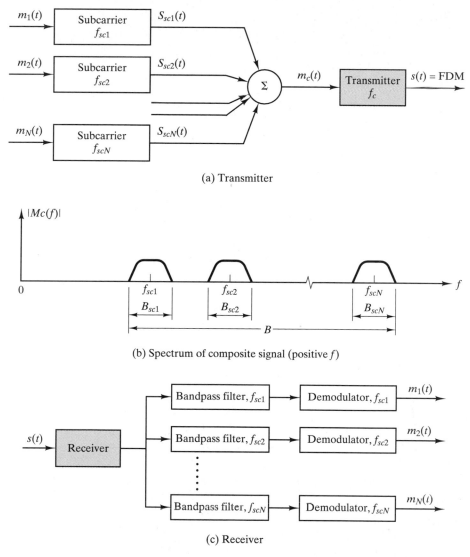

(a) Transmitter

(b) Spectrum of composite signal (positive $f$)

(c) Receiver

**FIGURE 7.4**   Frequency division multiplexing.

At the first level of the AT&T hierarchy, 12 voice channels are combined to produce a group signal with a bandwidth of $12 \times 4$ kHz = 48 kHz, in the range 60 to 108 kHz. The signals are produced in a fashion similar to that described above, using subcarrier frequencies of from 64 to 108 kHz in increments of 4 kHz. The next basic building block is the 60-channel supergroup, which is formed by frequency-division multiplexing five-group signals. At this step, each group is treated as a single signal with a 48-kHz bandwidth and is modulated by a subcarrier. The subcarriers have frequencies from 420 to 612 kHz in increments of 48 kHz. The resulting signal occupies 312 to 552 kHz.

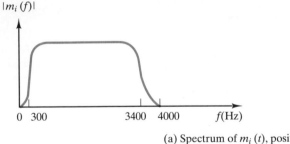

(a) Spectrum of $m_i(t)$, positive $f$

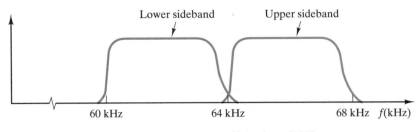

(b) Spectrum of $S_{sc1}(t)$ for $f_{sc1} = 64$ kHz

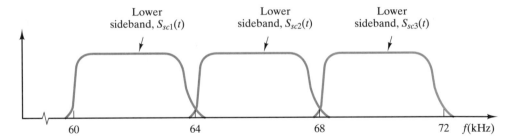

(c) Spectrum of composite signal using subcarriers at 64 kHz, 68 kHz, and 72 kHz

**FIGURE 7.5** FDM of three voiceband signals.

There are several variations to supergroup formation. Each of the five inputs to the supergroup multiplexer may be a group channel containing 12 multiplexed voice signals. In addition, any signal up to 48 kHz wide whose bandwidth is contained within 60 to 108 kHz may be used as input to the supergroup multiplexer. As another variation, it is possible to directly combine 60 voiceband channels into a supergroup; this may reduce multiplex costs where an interface with existing-group multiplex is not required.

The next level of the hierarchy is the mastergroup that combines 10 supergroup inputs. Again, any signal with a bandwidth of 240 kHz in the range 312 to 552 kHz can serve as input to the mastergroup multiplexer. The mastergroup has a bandwidth of 2.52 MHz and can support 600 voice-frequency (VF) channels. Higher-level multiplexing is defined above the mastergroup, as shown in Table 7.2.

Note that the original voice or data signal may be modulated many times. For example, a data signal may be encoded using QPSK to form an analog voice signal.

**TABLE 7.2**   North American and international FDM carrier standards.

| Number of voice channels | Bandwidth | Spectrum | AT&T | ITU-T |
|---|---|---|---|---|
| 12 | 48 kHz | 60–108 kHz | Group | Group |
| 60 | 240 kHz | 312–552 kHz | Supergroup | Supergroup |
| 300 | 1.232 MHz | 812–2044 kHz | | Mastergroup |
| 600 | 2.52 MHz | 564–3084 kHz | Mastergroup | |
| 900 | 3.872 MHz | 8.516–12.388 MHz | | Supermaster group |
| $N \times 600$ | | | Mastergroup multiplex | |
| 3,600 | 16.984 MHz | 0.564–17.548 MHz | Jumbogroup | |
| 10,800 | 57.442 MHz | 3.124–60.566 MHz | Jumbogroup multiplex | |

This signal could then be used to modulate a 76-kHz carrier to form a component of a group signal. This group signal could then be used to modulate a 516-kHz carrier to form a component of a supergroup signal. Each stage can distort the original data; this is so, for example, if the modulator/multiplexer contains nonlinearities or if it introduces noise.

## 7.2   SYNCHRONOUS TIME-DIVISION MULTIPLEXING

### Characteristics

Synchronous time-division multiplexing is possible when the achievable data rate (sometimes, unfortunately, called bandwidth) of the medium exceeds the data rate of digital signals to be transmitted. Multiple digital signals (or analog signals carrying digital data) can be carried on a single transmission path by interleaving portions of each signal in time. The interleaving can be at the bit level or in blocks of bytes or larger quantities. For example, the multiplexer in Figure 7.2b has six inputs which might each be, say, 9.6 kbps. A single line with a capacity of at least 57.6 kbps (plus overhead capacity) could accommodate all six sources.

A generic depiction of a synchronous TDM system is provided in Figure 7.6. A number of signals $[m_i(t), i = 1, N]$ are to be multiplexed onto the same transmission medium. The signals carry digital data and are generally digital signals. The incoming data from each source are briefly buffered. Each buffer is typically one bit or one character in length. The buffers are scanned sequentially to form a composite digital data stream $m_c(t)$. The scan operation is sufficiently rapid so that each buffer is emptied before more data can arrive. Thus, the data rate of $m_c(t)$ must at least equal the sum of the data rates of the $m_i(t)$. The digital signal $m_c(t)$ may be transmitted directly or passed through a modem so that an analog signal is transmitted. In either case, transmission is typically synchronous.

The transmitted data may have a format something like Figure 7.6b. The data are organized into frames. Each frame contains a cycle of time slots. In each frame,

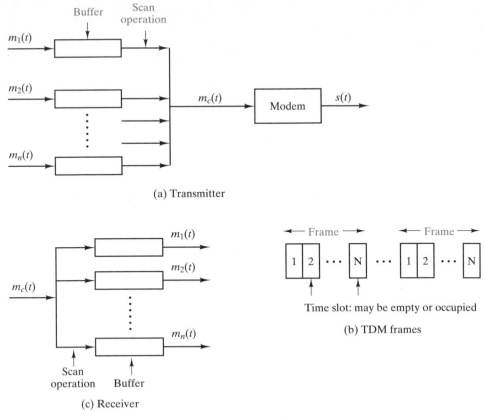

FIGURE 7.6 Synchronous time-division multiplexing.

one or more slots is dedicated to each data source. The sequence of slots dedicated to one source, from frame to frame, is called a channel. The slot length equals the transmitter buffer length, typically a bit or a character.

The character-interleaving technique is used with asynchronous sources. Each time slot contains one character of data. Typically, the start and stop bits of each character are eliminated before transmission and reinserted by the receiver, thus improving efficiency. The bit-interleaving technique is used with synchronous sources and may also be used with asynchronous sources. Each time slot contains just one bit.

At the receiver, the interleaved data are demultiplexed and routed to the appropriate destination buffer. For each input source $m_i(t)$, there is an identical output source which will receive the input data at the same rate at which it was generated.

Synchronous TDM is called synchronous not because synchronous transmission is used, but because the time slots are preassigned to sources and fixed. The time slots for each source are transmitted whether or not the source has data to send; this is, of course, also the case with FDM. In both cases, capacity is wasted to achieve simplicity of implementation. Even when fixed assignment is used, however, it is possible for a synchronous TDM device to handle sources of different data rates. For example, the slowest input device could be assigned one slot per cycle, while faster devices are assigned multiple slots per cycle.

## TDM Link Control

The reader will note that the transmitted data stream depicted in Figure 7.6 does not contain the headers and trailers that we have come to associate with synchronous transmission. The reason is that the control mechanisms provided by a data link protocol are not needed. It is instructive to ponder this point, and we do so by considering two key data link control mechanisms: flow control and error control. It should be clear that, as far as the multiplexer and demultiplexer (Figure 7.1) are concerned, flow control is not needed. The data rate on the multiplexed line is fixed, and the multiplexer and demultiplexer are designed to operate at that rate. But suppose that one of the individual output lines attaches to a device that is temporarily unable to accept data? Should the transmission of TDM frames cease? Clearly not, as the remaining output lines are expecting to receive data at predetermined times. The solution is for the saturated output device to cause the flow of data from the corresponding input device to cease. Thus, for a while, the channel in question will carry empty slots, but the frames as a whole will maintain the same transmission rate.

The reasoning for error control is the same. It would not do to request retransmission of an entire TDM frame because an error occurs on one channel. The devices using the other channels do not want a retransmission nor would they know that a retransmission has been requested by some other device on another channel. Again, the solution is to apply error control on a per-channel basis.

How are flow control, error control, and other good things to be provided on a per-channel basis? The answer is simple: Use a data link control protocol such as HDLC on a per-channel basis. A simplified example is shown in Figure 7.7. We

(a) Configuration

Input₁ ········ $F_1$ $f_1$ $f_1$ $d_1$ $d_1$ $d_1$ $C_1$ $A_1$ $F_1$ $f_1$ $f_1$ $d_1$ $d_1$ $d_1$ $C_1$ $A_1$ $F_1$

Input₂ ··· $F_2$ $f_2$ $f_2$ $d_2$ $d_2$ $d_2$ $d_2$ $C_2$ $A_2$ $F_2$ $f_2$ $f_2$ $d_2$ $d_2$ $d_2$ $d_2$ $C_2$ $A_2$ $F_2$

(b) Input data stream

··· $f_2$ $F_1$ $d_2$ $f_1$ $d_2$ $f_1$ $d_2$ $d_1$ $d_2$ $d_1$ $C_2$ $d_1$ $A_2$ $C_1$ $F_2$ $A_1$ $f_2$ $F_1$ $f_2$ $f_1$ $d_2$ $f_1$ $d_2$ $d_1$ $d_2$ $d_1$ $d_2$ $d_1$ $C_2$ $C_1$ $A_2$ $A_1$ $F_2$ $F_1$

(c) Multiplexed data stream

LEGEND

$F$ = flag field        $d$ = one octet of data field
$A$ = address field     $f$ = one octet of FCS field
$C$ = control field

**FIGURE 7.7**    Use of data link control on TDM channels.

assume two data sources, each using HDLC. One is transmitting a stream of HDLC frames containing three octets of data; the other is transmitting HDLC frames containing four octets of data. For clarity, we assume that character-interleaved multiplexing is used, although bit interleaving is more typical. Notice what is happening. The octets of the HDLC frames from the two sources are shuffled together for transmission over the multiplexed line. The reader may initially be uncomfortable with this diagram, as the HDLC frames have lost their integrity in some sense. For example, each frame check sequence (FCS) on the line applies to a disjointed set of bits. Even the FCS is not in one piece! However, the pieces are reassembled correctly before they are seen by the device on the other end of the HDLC protocol. In this sense, the multiplexing/demultiplexing operation is transparent to the attached stations; to each communicating pair of stations, it appears that they have a dedicated link.

One refinement is needed in Figure 7.7. Both ends of the line need to be a combination multiplexer/demultiplexer with a full-duplex line in between. Then each channel consists of two sets of slots, one traveling in each direction. The individual devices attached at each end can, in pairs, use HDLC to control their own channel. The multiplexer/demultiplexers need not be concerned with these matters.

### Framing

So we have seen that a link control protocol is not needed to manage the overall TDM link. There is, however, a basic requirement for framing. Because we are not providing flag or SYNC characters to bracket TDM frames, some means is needed to assure frame synchronization. It is clearly important to maintain framing synchronization because, if the source and destination are out of step, data on all channels are lost.

Perhaps the most common mechanism for framing is known as added-digit framing. In this scheme, typically, one control bit is added to each TDM frame. An identifiable pattern of bits, from frame to frame, is used on this "control channel." A typical example is the alternating bit pattern, 101010 . . . . This is a pattern unlikely to be sustained on a data channel. Thus, to synchronize, a receiver compares the incoming bits of one frame position to the expected pattern. If the pattern does not match, successive bit positions are searched until the pattern persists over multiple frames. Once framing synchronization is established, the receiver continues to monitor the framing bit channel. If the pattern breaks down, the receiver must again enter a framing search mode.

### Pulse Stuffing

Perhaps the most difficult problem in the design of a synchronous time-division multiplexer is that of synchronizing the various data sources. If each source has a separate clock, any variation among clocks could cause loss of synchronization. Also, in some cases, the data rates of the input data streams are not related by a simple rational number. For both these problems, a technique known as pulse stuffing is an effective remedy. With pulse stuffing, the outgoing data rate of the multiplexer, excluding framing bits, is higher than the sum of the maximum instantaneous incoming rates. The extra capacity is used by stuffing extra dummy bits or pulses into each incoming signal until its rate is raised to that of a locally-generated clock signal. The stuffed pulses are inserted at fixed locations in the multiplexer frame format so that they may be identified and removed at the demultiplexer.

## Example

An example, from [COUC95], illustrates the use of synchronous TDM to multiplex digital and analog sources. Consider that there are 11 sources to be multiplexed on a single link:

- Source 1: Analog, 2-kHz bandwidth.
- Source 2: Analog, 4-kHz bandwidth.
- Source 3: Analog, 2-kHz bandwidth.
- Sources 4–11: Digital, 7200 bps synchronous.

As a first step, the analog sources are converted to digital using PCM. Recall from Chapter 4 that PCM is based on the sampling theorem, which dictates that a signal be sampled at a rate equal to twice its bandwidth. Thus, the required sampling rate is 4000 samples per second for sources 1 and 3, and 8000 samples per second for source 2. These samples, which are analog (PAM), must then be quantized or digitized. Let us assume that 4 bits are used for each analog sample. For convenience, these three sources will be multiplexed first, as a unit. At a scan rate of 4 kHz, one PAM sample each is taken from sources 1 and 3, and two PAM samples are taken from source 2 per scan. These four samples are interleaved and converted to 4-bit PCM samples. Thus, a total of 16 bits is generated at a rate of 4000 times per second, for a composite bit rate of 64 kbps.

For the digital sources, pulse stuffing is used to raise each source to a rate of 8 kbps, for an aggregate data rate of 64 kbps. A frame can consist of multiple cycles of 32 bits, each containing 16 PCM bits and two bits from each of the eight digital sources. Figure 7.8 depicts the result.

## Digital Carrier Systems

The long-distance carrier system provided in the United States and throughout the world was designed to transmit voice signals over high-capacity transmission links, such as optical fiber, coaxial cable, and microwave. Part of the evolution of these telecommunications networks toward digital technology has been the adoption of synchronous TDM transmission structures. In the United States, AT&T developed a hierarchy of TDM structures of various capacities; this structure is used in Canada and Japan as well as in the United States. A similar, but unfortunately not identical, hierarchy has been adopted internationally under the auspices of ITU-T (Table 7.3).

The basis of the TDM hierarchy (in North America and Japan) is the DS-1 transmission format (Figure 7.9), which multiplexes 24 channels. Each frame contains 8 bits per channel plus a framing bit for $24 \times 8 + 1 = 193$ bits. For voice transmission, the following rules apply. Each channel contains one word of digitized voice data. The original analog voice signal is digitized using pulse code modulation

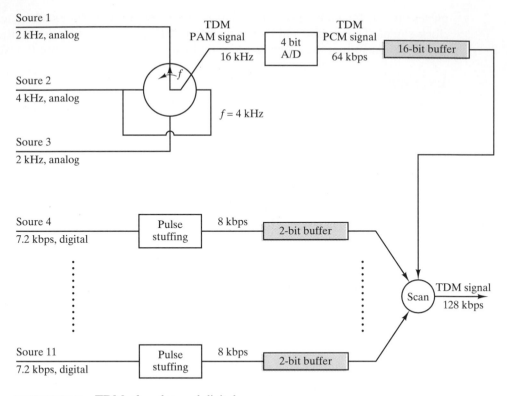

**FIGURE 7.8** TDM of analog and digital sources.

(PCM) at a rate of 8000 samples per second. Therefore, each channel slot and, hence, each frame must repeat 8000 times per second. With a frame length of 193 bits, we have a data rate of 8000 × 193 = 1.544 Mbps. For five of every six frames, 8-bit PCM samples are used. For every sixth frame, each channel contains a 7-bit PCM word plus a *signaling bit*. The signaling bits form a stream for each voice channel that contains network control and routing information. For example, control signals are used to establish a connection or to terminate a call.

The same DS-1 format is used to provide digital data service. For compatibility with voice, the same 1.544-Mbps data rate is used. In this case, 23 channels of

**TABLE 7.3** North American and international TDM carrier standards.

| (a) North American | | | (b) International (ITU-T) | | |
|---|---|---|---|---|---|
| Digital signal number | Number of voice channels | Data rate (Mbps) | Level number | Number of voice channels | Data rate (Mbps) |
| DS-1 | 24 | 1.544 | 1 | 30 | 2.048 |
| DS-1C | 48 | 3.152 | 2 | 120 | 8.448 |
| DS-2 | 96 | 6.312 | 3 | 480 | 34.368 |
| DS-3 | 672 | 44.736 | 4 | 1920 | 139.264 |
| DS-4 | 4032 | 274.176 | 5 | 7680 | 565.148 |

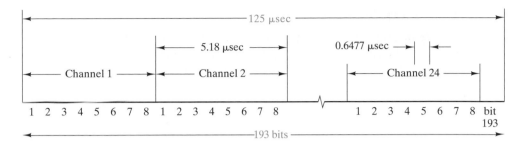

**Notes:**

1. Bit 193 is a framing bit, used for synchronization.
2. Voice channels:
   • 8-bit PCM used on five of six frames.
   • 7-bit PCM used on every sixth frame. Bit 8 of each channel is a signaling bit.
3. Data channels:
   • Channel 24 used for signaling only in some schemes.
   • Bit 8 is a control bit.
   • Bits 1–7 used for 56 kbps service.
   • Bits 2–7 used for 9.6 kbps, 4.8 kbps, and 2.4 kbps service.

**FIGURE 7.9**    DS-1 transmission format.

data are provided. The twenty-fourth channel position is reserved for a special sync byte, which allows faster and more reliable reframing following a framing error. Within each channel, seven bits per frame are used for data, with the eighth bit used to indicate whether the channel, for that frame, contains user data or system control data. With seven bits per channel, and because each frame is repeated 8000 times per second, a data rate of 56 kbps can be provided per channel. Lower data rates are provided using a technique known as subrate multiplexing. For this technique, an additional bit is robbed from each channel to indicate which subrate multiplexing rate is being provided; this leaves a total capacity per channel of $6 \times 8000 = 48$ kbps. This capacity is used to multiplex five 9.6-kbps channels, ten 4.8-kbps channels, or twenty 2.4-kbps channels. For example, if channel 2 is used to provide 9.6-kbps service, then up to five data subchannels share this channel. The data for each subchannel appear as six bits in channel 2 every fifth frame.

Finally, the DS-1 format can be used to carry a mixture of voice and data channels. In this case, all 24 channels are utilized; no sync byte is provided.

Above this basic data rate of 1.544 Mbps, higher-level multiplexing is achieved by interleaving bits from DS-1 inputs. For example, the DS-2 transmission system combines four DS-1 inputs into a 6.312-Mbps stream. Data from the four sources are interleaved 12 bits at a time. Note that $1.544 \times 4 = 6.176$ Mbps. The remaining capacity is used for framing and control bits.

## ISDN User–Network Interface

ISDN enables the user to multiplex traffic from a number of devices on the user's premises over a single line into an ISDN (Integrated Services Digital Network). Two interfaces are defined: a basic interface and a primary interface.

## Basic ISDN Interface

At the interface between the subscriber and the network terminating equipment, digital data are exchanged using full-duplex transmission. A separate physical line is used for the transmission in each direction. The line coding specification for the interface dictates the use of a pseudoternary coding scheme.[1] Binary one is represented by the absence of voltage; binary zero is represented by a positive or negative pulse of 750 mV ±10%. The data rate is 192 kbps.

The basic access structure consists of two 64-kbps B channels and one 16-kbps D channel. These channels, which produce a load of 144 kbps, are multiplexed over a 192-kbps interface at the S or T reference point. The remaining capacity is used for various framing and synchronization purposes.

The B channel is the basic user channel. It can be used to carry digital data (e.g., a personal computer connection), PCM-encoded digital voice (e.g., a telephone connection), or any other traffic that can fit into a 64-kbps channel. At any given time, a logical connection can be set up separately for each B channel to separate ISDN destinations. The D channel can be used for a data-transmission connection at a lower data rate. It is also used to carry control information needed to set up and terminate the B-channel connections. Transmission on the D channel consists of a sequence of LAPD frames.

As with any synchronous time-division multiplexed (TDM) scheme, basic access transmission is structured into repetitive, fixed-length frames. In this case, each frame is 48 bits long; at 192 kbps, frames must repeat at a rate of one frame every 250 μsec. Figure 7.10 shows the frame structure; the upper frame is transmitted by the subscriber's terminal equipment (TE) to the network (NT); the lower frame is transmitted from the NT to the TE.

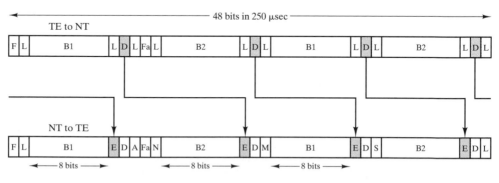

LEGEND

| | | |
|---|---|---|
| F = Framing bit | Fa = Auxiliary framing bit | B2 = B channel bits (16 per frame) |
| L = dc balancing bit | N = Set to opposite of Fa | D = D channel bits (4 per frame) |
| E = D-echo channel bit | M = Multiframing bit | S = Spare bits |
| A = Activation bit | B1= B channel bits (16 per frame) | |

**FIGURE 7.10** Frame structure for ISDN basic rate access.

---

[1] See Section 4.1.

Each frame of 48 bits includes 16 bits from each of the two B channels and 4 bits from the D channel. The remaining bits have the following interpretation. Let us first consider the frame structure in the TE-to-NT direction. Each frame begins with a framing bit (F) that is always transmitted as a positive pulse. This is followed by a dc balancing bit (L) that is set to a negative pulse to balance the voltage. The F-L pattern thus acts to synchronize the receiver on the beginning of the frame. The specification dictates that, following these first two bit positions, the first occurrence of a zero bit will be encoded as a negative pulse. After that, the pseudoternary rules are observed. The next eight bits (B1) are from the first B channel; this is followed by another dc balancing bit (L). Next comes a bit from the D channel, followed by its balancing bit. This is followed by the auxiliary framing bit ($F_A$), which is set to zero unless it is to be used in a multiframe structure. There follows another balancing bit (L), eight bits (B2) from the second B channel, and another balancing bit (L); this is followed by bits from the D channel, first B channel, D channel again, second B channel, and the D channel yet again, with each group of channel bits followed by a balancing bit.

The frame structure in the NT-to-TE direction is similar to the frame structure for transmission in the TE-to-NT direction. The following new bits replace some of the dc balancing bits. The D-channel echo bit (E) is a retransmission by the NT of the most recently received D bit from the TE; the purpose of this echo is explained below. The activation bit (A) is used to activate or deactivate a TE, allowing the device to come on line or, when there is no activity, to be placed in low-power-consumption mode. The N bit is normally set to binary one. The N and M bits may be used for multiframing. The S bit is reserved for other future standardization requirements.

The E bit in the TE-to-NT direction comes into play to support a contention resolution function, which is required when multiple TE1 terminals share a single physical line (i.e., a multipoint line). There are three types of traffic to consider:

- **B-channel traffic.** No additional functionality is needed to control access to the two B channels, as each channel is dedicated to a particular TE at any given time.
- **D-channel traffic.** The D channel is available for use by all the subscriber devices for both control signaling and packet transmission, so the potential for contention exists. There are two subcases:
  - □ *Incoming traffic:* The LAPD addressing scheme is sufficient to sort out the proper destination for each data unit.
  - □ *Outgoing traffic:* Access must be regulated so that only one device at a time transmits. This is the purpose of the contention-resolution algorithm.

The D-channel contention-resolution algorithm has the following elements:

1. When a subscriber device has no LAPD frames to transmit, it transmits a series of binary ones on the D channel; using the pseudoternary encoding scheme, this corresponds to the absence of line signal.
2. The NT, on receipt of a D-channel bit, reflects back the binary value as a D-channel echo bit.

3. When a terminal is ready to transmit an LAPD frame, it listens to the stream of incoming D-channel echo bits. If it detects a string of 1-bits equal in length to a threshold value $X_i$, it may transmit; otherwise, the terminal must assume that some other terminal is transmitting, and wait.

4. It may happen that several terminals are monitoring the echo stream and begin to transmit at the same time, causing a collision. To overcome this condition, a transmitting TE monitors the E bits and compares them to its transmitted D bits. If a discrepancy is detected, the terminal ceases to transmit and returns to a listen state.

The electrical characteristics of the interface (i.e., 1-bit = absence of signal) are such that any user equipment transmitting a 0-bit will override user equipment transmitting a 1-bit at the same instant. This arrangement ensures that one device will be guaranteed successful completion of its transmission.

The algorithm includes a primitive priority mechanism based on the threshold value $X_i$. Control information is given priority over user data. Within each of these two priority classes, a station begins at normal priority and then is reduced to lower priority after a transmission. It remains at the lower priority until all other terminals have had an opportunity to transmit. The values of $X_i$ are as follows:

- Control Information
  - Normal priority $\quad X_1 = 8$
  - Lower priority $\quad X_1 = 9$
- User Data
  - Normal priority $\quad X_2 = 10$
  - Lower priority $\quad X_2 = 11$

## Primary ISDN Interface

The primary interface, like the basic interface, multiplexes multiple channels across a single transmission medium. In the case of the primary interface, only a point-to-point configuration is allowed. Typically, the interface supports a digital PBX or other concentration device controlling multiple TEs and providing a synchronous TDM facility for access to ISDN. Two data rates are defined for the primary interface: 1.544 Mbps and 2.048 Mbps.

The ISDN interface at 1.544 Mbps is based on the North American DS-1 transmission structure, which is used on the T1 transmission service. Figure 7.11a illustrates the frame format for this data rate. The bit stream is structured into repetitive 193-bit frames. Each frame consists of 24 8-bit time slots and a framing bit, which is used for synchronization and other management purposes. The same time slot repeated over multiple frames constitutes a channel. At a data rate of 1.544 Mbps, frames repeat at a rate of one every 125 $\mu$sec, or 8000 frames per second. Thus, each channel supports 64 kbps. Typically, the transmission structure is used to support 23 B channels and 1 64-kbps D channel.

The line coding for the 1.544-Mbps interface is AMI (Alternate Mark Inversion) using B8ZS.

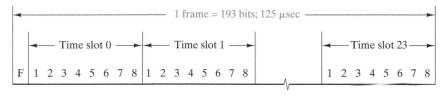

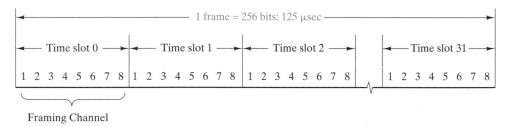

(a)  Interface at 1.544 Mbps

Framing Channel

(b)  Interface at 2.048 Mbps

**FIGURE 7.11**   ISDN primary access frame formats.

The ISDN interface at 2.048 Mbps is based on the European transmission structure of the same data rate. Figure 7.11b illustrates the frame format for this data rate. The bit stream is structured into repetitive 256-bit frames. Each frame consists of 32 8-bit time slots. The first time slot is used for framing and synchronization purposes; the remaining 31 time slots support user channels. At a data rate of 2.048 Mbps, frames repeat at a rate of one every 125 $\mu$sec, or 8000 frames per second. Thus, each channel supports 64 kbps. Typically, the transmission structure is used to support 30 B channels and 1 D channel.

The line coding for the 2.048-Mbps interface is AMI using HDB3.

## SONET/SDH

SONET (Synchronous Optical Network) is an optical transmission interface originally proposed by BellCore and standardized by ANSI. A compatible version, referred to as Synchronous Digital Hierarchy (SDH), has been published by ITU-T in Recommendations G.707, G.708, and G.709.[2] SONET is intended to provide a specification for taking advantage of the high-speed digital transmission capability of optical fiber.

### Signal Hierarchy

The SONET specification defines a hierarchy of standardized digital data rates (Table 7.4). The lowest level, referred to as STS-1 (Synchronous Transport Signal,

---

[2] In what follows, we will use the term SONET to refer to both specifications. Differences that exist will be addressed.

**TABLE 7.4** SONET/SDH signal hierarchy.

| SONET designation | CCITT designation | Data rate (Mbps) | Payload rate (Mbps) |
|---|---|---|---|
| STS-1/OC-1 | | 51.84 | 50.112 |
| STS-3/OC-3 | STM-1 | 155.52 | 150.336 |
| STS-9/OC-9 | STM-3 | 466.56 | 451.008 |
| STS-12/OC-12 | STM-4 | 622.08 | 601.344 |
| STS-18/OC-18 | STM-6 | 933.12 | 902.016 |
| STS-24/OC-24 | STM-8 | 1244.16 | 1202.688 |
| STS-36/OC-36 | STM-12 | 1866.24 | 1804.032 |
| STS-48/OC-48 | STM-16 | 2488.32 | 2405.376 |

level 1) or OC-1 (Optical Carrier level 1),[3] is 51.84 Mbps. This rate can be used to carry a single DS-3 signal or a group of lower-rate signals, such as DS1, DS1C, DS2, plus ITU-T rates (e.g., 2.048 Mbps).

Multiple STS-1 signals can be combined to form an STS-N signal. The signal is created by interleaving bytes from N STS-1 signals that are mutually synchronized.

For the ITU-T Synchronous Digital Hierarchy, the lowest rate is 155.52 Mbps, which is designated STM-1. This corresponds to SONET STS-3. The reason for the discrepancy is that STM-1 is the lowest-rate signal that can accommodate an ITU-T level 4 signal (139.264 Mbps).

## Frame Format

The basic SONET building block is the STS-1 frame, which consists of 810 octets and is transmitted once every 125 $\mu$s, for an overall data rate of 51.84 Mbps (Figure 7.12a). The frame can logically be viewed as a matrix of 9 rows of 90 octets each, with transmission being one row at a time, from left to right and top to bottom.

The first three columns (3 octets $\times$ 9 rows = 27 octets) of the frame are devoted to overhead octets. Nine octets are devoted to section-related overhead and 18 octets are devoted to line overhead. Figure 7.13a shows the arrangement of overhead octets, and Table 7.5 defines the various fields.

The remainder of the frame is payload, which is provided by the path layer. The payload includes a column of path overhead, which is not necessarily in the first available column position; the line overhead contains a pointer that indicates where the path overhead starts. Figure 7.13b shows the arrangement of path overhead octets, and Table 7.5 defines these.

Figure 7.12b shows the general format for higher-rate frames, using the ITU-T designation.

---

[3] An OC-N rate is the optical equivalent of an STS-N electrical signal. End user devices transmit and receive electrical signals; these must be converted to and from optical signals for transmission over optical fiber.

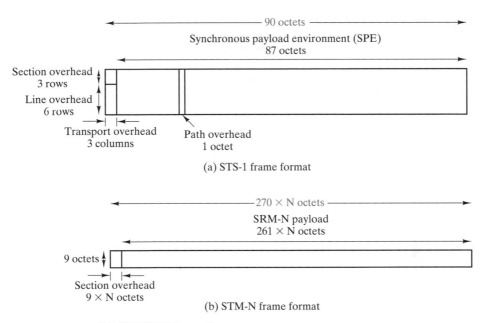

(a) STS-1 frame format

(b) STM-N frame format

**FIGURE 7.12**  SONET/SDH frame formats.

| | Framing<br>A1 | Framing<br>A2 | STS-ID<br>C1 | | Trace<br>J1 |
|---|---|---|---|---|---|
| Section<br>Overhead | BIP-8<br>B1 | Orderwire<br>E1 | User<br>F1 | | BIP-8<br>B3 |
| | Data Com<br>D1 | Data Com<br>D2 | Data Com<br>D3 | | Signal Label<br>C2 |
| | Pointer<br>H1 | Pointer<br>H2 | Pointer Action<br>H3 | | Path Status<br>G1 |
| | BIP-8<br>B2 | APS<br>K1 | APS<br>K2 | | User<br>F2 |
| Line<br>Overhead | Data Com<br>D4 | Data Com<br>D5 | Data Com<br>D6 | | Multiframe<br>H4 |
| | Data Com<br>D7 | Data Com<br>D8 | Data Com<br>D9 | | Growth<br>Z3 |
| | Data Com<br>D10 | Data Com<br>D11 | Data Com<br>D12 | | Growth<br>Z4 |
| | Growth<br>Z1 | Growth<br>Z2 | Orderwire<br>E2 | | Growth<br>Z5 |

(a) Section overhead          (b) Path overhead

**FIGURE 7.13**  SONET STS-1 overhead octets.

**TABLE 7.5** STS-1 Overhead bits.

| Section overhead | |
| --- | --- |
| A1, A2: | Framing bytes = F6,28 hex; used to synchronize the beginning of the frame. |
| C1: | STS-1 ID identifies the STS-1 number (1 to N) for each STS-1 within an STS-*N* multiplex. |
| B1: | Bit-interleaved parity byte providing even parity over previous STS-*N* frame after scrambling; the *i*th bit of this octet contains the even parity value calculated from the ith bit position of all octets in the previous frame. |
| E1: | Section level 64-kbps PCM orderwire; optional 64 Kbps voice channel to be used between section terminating equipment, hubs, and remote terminals. |
| F1: | 64-kbps channel set aside for user purposes. |
| D1–D3: | 192-kbps data communications channel for alarms, maintenance, control, and administration between sections. |

| Line overhead | |
| --- | --- |
| H1–H3: | Pointer bytes used in frame alignment and frequency adjustment of payload data. |
| B2: | Bit-interleaved parity for line level error monitoring. |
| K1, K2: | Two byes allocated for signaling between line level automatic protection switching equipment; uses a bit-oriented protocol that provides for error protection and management of the SONET optical link. |
| D4–D12: | 576-kbps data communications channel for alarms, maintenance, control, monitoring, and administration at the line level. |
| Z1, Z2 | Reserved for future use. |
| E2: | 64-kbps PCM voice channel for line level orderwire. |

| Path overhead | |
| --- | --- |
| J1: | 64-kbps channel used to repetitively send a 64-octet fixed-length string so a receiving terminal can continuously verify the integrity of a path; the contents of the message are user programmable. |
| B3: | Bit-interleaved parity at the path level, calculated over all bits of the previous SPE. |
| C2: | STS path signal label to designate equipped versus unequipped STS signals. Unequipped means the the line connection is complete but there is no path data to send. For equipped signals, the label can indicate the specific STS payload mapping that might be needed in receiving terminals to interpret the payloads. |
| G1: | Status byte sent from path terminating equipment back to path originating equipment to convey status of terminating equipment and path error performance. |
| F2: | 64-kbps channel for path user. |
| H4: | Multiframe indicator for payloads needing frames that are longer than a single STS frame; multiframe indicators are used when packing lower rate channels (virtual tributaries) into the SPE. |
| Z3–Z5: | Reserved for future use. |

## 7.3 STATISTICAL TIME-DIVISION MULTIPLEXING

### Characteristics

In a synchronous time-division multiplexer, it is generally the case that many of the time slots in a frame are wasted. A typical application of a synchronous TDM involves linking a number of terminals to a shared computer port. Even if all terminals are actively in use, most of the time there is no data transfer at any particular terminal.

An alternative to synchronous TDM is statistical TDM, also known as asynchronous TDM and intelligent TDM. The statistical multiplexer exploits this common property of data transmission by dynamically allocating time slots on demand. As with a synchronous TDM, the statistical multiplexer has a number of I/O lines on one side and a higher-speed multiplexed line on the other. Each I/O line has a buffer associated with it. In the case of the statistical multiplexer, there are $n$ I/O lines, but only $k$, where $k < n$, time slots available on the TDM frame. For input, the function of the multiplexer is to scan the input buffers, collecting data until a frame is filled, and then send the frame. On output, the multiplexer receives a frame and distributes the slots of data to the appropriate output buffers.

Because statistical TDM takes advantage of the fact that the attached devices are not all transmitting all of the time, the data rate on the multiplexed line is less than the sum of the data rates of the attached devices. Thus, a statistical multiplexer can use a lower data rate to support as many devices as a synchronous multiplexer. Alternatively, if a statistical multiplexer and a synchronous multiplexer both use a link of the same data rate, the statistical multiplexer can support more devices.

Figure 7.14 contrasts statistical and synchronous TDM. The figure depicts four data sources and shows the data produced in four time epochs ($t_0$, $t_1$, $t_2$, $t_3$). In the case of the synchronous multiplexer, the multiplexer has an effective output rate of four times the data rate of any of the input devices. During each epoch, data are collected from all four sources and sent out. For example, in the first epoch, sources C and D produce no data. Thus, two of the four time slots transmitted by the multiplexer are empty.

In contrast, the statistical multiplexer does not send empty slots if there are data to send. Thus, during the first epoch, only slots for A and B are sent. However, the positional significance of the slots is lost in this scheme. It is not known ahead of time which source's data will be in any particular slot. Because data arrive from

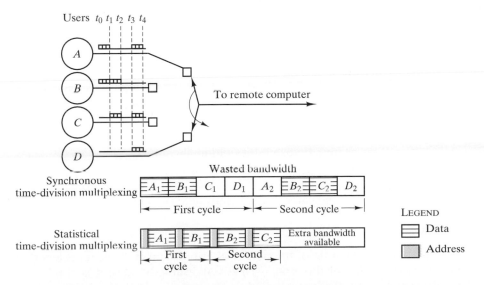

**FIGURE 7.14** Synchronous TDM contrasted with statistical TDM.

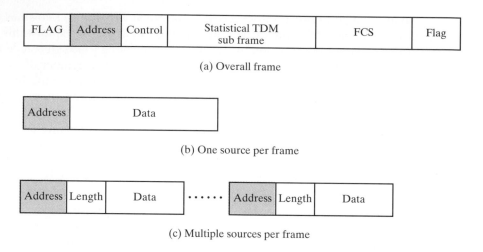

FIGURE 7.15   Statistical TDM frame formats.

and are distributed to I/O lines unpredictably, address information is required to assure proper delivery. As a result, there is more overhead per slot for statistical TDM as each slot carries an address as well as data.

The frame structure used by a statistical multiplexer has an impact on performance. Clearly, it is desirable to minimize overhead bits to improve throughput. Generally, a statistical TDM system will use a synchronous protocol such as HDLC. Within the HDLC frame, the data frame must contain control bits for the multiplexing operation. Figure 7.15 shows two possible formats. In the first case, only one source of data is included per frame. That source is identified by an address. The length of the data field is variable, and its end is marked by the end of the overall frame. This scheme can work well under light load, but is quite inefficient under heavy load.

A way to improve efficiency is to allow multiple data sources to be packaged in a single frame. Now, however, some means is needed to specify the length of data for each source. Thus, the statistical TDM subframe consists of a sequence of data fields, each labeled with an address and a length. Several techniques can be used to make this approach even more efficient. The address field can be reduced by using relative addressing. That is, each address specifies the number of the current source relative to the previous source, modulo the total number of sources. So, for example, instead of an 8-bit address field, a 4-bit field might suffice.

Another refinement is to use a two-bit label with the length field. A value of 00, 01, or 10 corresponds to a data field of one, two, or three bytes; no length field is necessary. A value of 11 indicates that a length field is included.

## Performance

We have said that the data rate of the output of a statistical multiplexer is less than the sum of the data rates of the inputs. This is allowable because it is anticipated that the average amount of input is less than the capacity of the multiplexed line.

The difficulty with this approach is that, while the average aggregate input may be less than the multiplexed line capacity, there may be peak periods when the input exceeds capacity.

The solution to this problem is to include a buffer in the multiplexer to hold temporary excess input. Table 7.6 gives an example of the behavior of such systems. We assume 10 sources, each capable of 1000 bps, and we assume that the average input per source is 50% of its maximum. Thus, on average, the input load is 5000 bps. Two cases are shown: multiplexers of output capacity 5000 bps and 7000 bps. The entries in the table show the number of bits input from the 10 devices each millisecond and the output from the multiplexer. When the input exceeds the output, backlog develops that must be buffered.

There is a trade-off between the size of the buffer used and the data rate of the line. We would like to use the smallest possible buffer and the smallest possible data rate, but a reduction in one requires an increase in the other. Note that we are not so much concerned with the cost of the buffer—memory is cheap—as we are with the fact that the more buffering there is, the longer the delay. Thus, the trade-off is really one between system response time and the speed of the multiplexed line. In this section, we present some approximate measures that examine this trade-off. These are sufficient for most purposes.

Let us define the following parameters for a statistical time-division multiplexer:

**TABLE 7.6**   Example of statistical multiplexer performance.

| Input[a] | Capacity = 5000 bps | | Capacity = 7000 bps | |
| | Output | Backlog | Output | Backlog |
|---|---|---|---|---|
| 6 | 5 | 1 | 6 | 0 |
| 9 | 5 | 5 | 7 | 2 |
| 3 | 5 | 3 | 5 | 0 |
| 7 | 5 | 5 | 7 | 0 |
| 2 | 5 | 2 | 2 | 0 |
| 2 | 4 | 0 | 2 | 0 |
| 2 | 2 | 0 | 2 | 0 |
| 3 | 3 | 0 | 3 | 0 |
| 4 | 4 | 0 | 4 | 0 |
| 6 | 5 | 1 | 6 | 0 |
| 1 | 2 | 0 | 1 | 0 |
| 10 | 5 | 5 | 7 | 3 |
| 7 | 5 | 7 | 7 | 3 |
| 5 | 5 | 7 | 7 | 1 |
| 8 | 5 | 10 | 7 | 2 |
| 3 | 5 | 8 | 5 | 0 |
| 6 | 5 | 9 | 6 | 0 |
| 2 | 5 | 6 | 2 | 0 |
| 9 | 5 | 10 | 7 | 2 |
| 5 | 5 | 10 | 7 | 0 |

[a] Input − 10 sources, 1000 bps/source; average input rate = 50% of maximum.

$N$ = number of input sources

$R$ = data rate of each source, bps

$M$ = effective capacity of multiplexed line, bps

$\alpha$ = mean fraction of time each source is transmitting, $0 < \alpha < 1$

$K = \dfrac{M}{NR}$ = ratio of multiplexed line capacity to total maximum input

In the above, we have defined $M$ taking into account the overhead bits introduced by the multiplexer. That is, $M$ represents the maximum rate at which data bits can be transmitted.

The parameter $K$ is a measure of the compression achieved by the multiplexer. For example, for a given data rate $M$, if $K = 0.25$, there are four times as many devices being handled as by a synchronous time-division multiplexer using the same link capacity. The value of $K$ can be bounded:

$$\alpha < K < 1$$

A value of $K = 1$ corresponds to a synchronous time-division multiplexer, as the system has the capacity to service all input devices at the same time. If $K < \alpha$, the input will exceed the multiplexer's capacity.

Some results can be obtained by viewing the multiplexer as a single-server queue. A queuing situation arises when a "customer" arrives at a service facility and, finding it busy, is forced to wait. The delay incurred by a customer is the time spent waiting in the queue plus the time for the service. The delay depends on the pattern of arriving traffic and the characteristics of the server. Table 7.7 summarizes results for the case of random (Poisson) arrivals and constant service time. This model is easily related to the statistical multiplexer:

**TABLE 7.7**   Single-server queues with constant service times and poisson (random) arrivals.

---

**Parameters**

$\lambda$ = mean number of arrivals per second

$s$ = service time for each arrival

$\rho$ = utilization, fraction of time the server is busy

$q$ = mean number of items in system (waiting and being served)

$t_q$ = mean time an item spends in system

$\sigma q$ = standard deviation of q

**Formulas**

$$\rho = \lambda s$$

$$q = \frac{\rho^2}{2(1 - \rho)} + \rho$$

$$t_q = \frac{s(2 - \rho)}{2(1 - \rho)}$$

$$\sigma q = \frac{1}{1 - p} \sqrt{\rho - \frac{3\rho^2}{2} + \frac{5\rho^3}{6} - \frac{\rho^4}{12}}$$

---

$$\lambda = \alpha NR$$

$$S = \frac{1}{M}$$

The average arrival rate $\lambda$, in bps, is the total potential input ($NR$) times the fraction of time $\alpha$ that each source is transmitting. The service time $S$, in seconds, is the time it takes to transmit one bit, which is $1/M$. Note that

$$\rho = \lambda s = \frac{\alpha NR}{M} = \frac{\alpha}{K} = \frac{\lambda}{M}$$

The parameter $\rho$ is the utilization or fraction of total link capacity being used. For example, if the capacity $M$ is 50 kbps and $\rho = 0.5$, the load on the system is 25 kbps. The parameter $q$ is a measure of the amount of buffer space being used in the multiplexer. Finally, $t_q$ is a measure of the average delay encountered by an input source.

Figure 7.16 gives some insight into the nature of the trade-off between system response time and the speed of the multiplexed line. It assumes that data are being transmitted in 1000-bit frames. Part (a) of the figure shows the average number of frames that must be buffered as a function of the average utilization of the multiplexed line. The utilization is expressed as a percentage of the total line capacity. Thus, if the average input load is 5000 bps, the utilization is 100 percent for a line capacity of 5000 bps and about 71 percent for a line capacity of 7000 bps. Part (b) of the figure shows the average delay experienced by a frame as a function of utilization and data rate. Note that as the utilization rises, so do the buffer requirements and the delay. A utilization above 80 percent is clearly undesirable.

Note that the average buffer size being used depends only on $\rho$, and not directly on $M$. For example, consider the following two cases:

| Case I | Case II |
| --- | --- |
| $N = 10$ | $N = 100$ |
| $R = 100\text{bps}$ | $R = 100 \text{ bps}$ |
| $\alpha = 0.4$ | $\alpha = 0.4$ |
| $M = 500 \text{ bps}$ | $M = 5000 \text{ bps}$ |

In both cases, the value of $\rho$ is 0.8 and the mean buffer size is 2.4. Thus, proportionately, a smaller amount of buffer space per source is needed for multiplexers that handle a larger number of sources. Figure 7.16b also shows that the average delay will be smaller as the link capacity increases, for constant utilization.

So far, we have been considering average queue length, and, hence, the average amount of buffer capacity needed. Of course, there will be some fixed upper bound on the buffer size available. The variance of the queue size grows with utilization. Thus, at a higher level of utilization, a larger buffer is needed to hold the

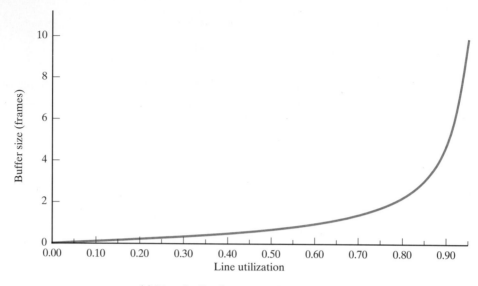

(a) Mean buffer size versus utilization

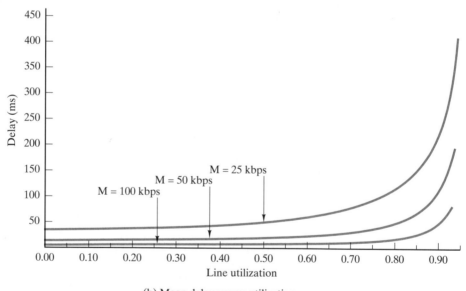

(b) Mean delay versus utilization

**FIGURE 7.16** Buffer size and delay for a statistical multiplexer.

backlog. Even so, there is always a finite probability that the buffer will overflow. Figure 7.17 shows the strong dependence of overflow probability on utilization. This figure, plus Figure 7.16, suggest that utilization above about 0.8 is undesirable.

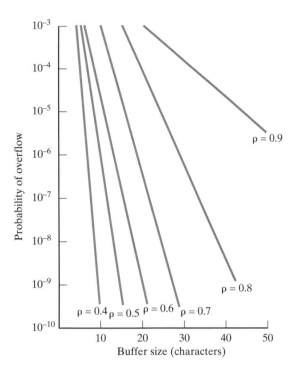

**FIGURE 7.17** Probability of overflow as a function of buffer size.

## 7.4 RECOMMENDED READING

A discussion of FDM and TDM carrier systems can be found in [BELL90] and [FREE94]. More detailed description and analysis of TDM carrier systems is provided by [POWE90]. ISDN interfaces and SONET are treated in greater depth in [STAL95].

**BELL90** Bellcore (Bell Communications Research). *Telecommunications Transmission Engineering*. Three volumes. 1990.

**FREE94** Freeman, R. *Reference Manual for Telecommunications Engineering*. New York: Wiley, 1994.

**POWE90** Powers, J. and Stair, H. *Megabit Data Communications*. Englewood Cliffs, NJ: Prentice Hall, 1990.

**STAL95** Stallings, W. *ISDN and Broadband ISDN, with Frame Relay and ATM*. Englewood Cliffs, NJ: Prentice Hall, 1995.

**Recommended Web Site**

- http://www.atis.org/sif/sifhom.html: SONET Interoperability Forum site. Discusses current projects and technology.

## 7.5 PROBLEMS

7.1 The information in four analog signals is to be multiplexed and transmitted over a telephone channel that has a 400- to 3100-Hz bandpass. Each of the analog baseband signals is bandlimited to 500 Hz. Design a communication system (block diagram) that will allow the transmission of these four sources over the telephone channel using
   **a.** Frequency-division multiplexing with SSB (single sideband) subcarriers.
   **b.** Time-division multiplexing using PCM.

   Show the block diagrams of the complete system, including the transmission, channel, and reception portions. Include the bandwidths of the signals at the various points in the systems.

7.2 To paraphrase Lincoln, All of the channel some of the time, some of the channel all of the time. Refer to Figure 7.2 and relate the preceding to the figure.

7.3 Consider a transmission system using frequency-division multiplexing. What cost factors are involved in adding one more pair of stations to the system?

7.4 Ten analog signals that are bandlimited to frequencies below 16 kHz are sampled at the Nyquist rate. The digitizing error is to be held below 0.2%. The signals are to travel on a synchronous TDM channel. What is the data rate required for the channel?

7.5 In Synchronous TDM, it is possible to interleave bits, one bit from each channel participating in a cycle. If the channel is using a self-clocking code in order to assist synchronization, might this bit interleaving introduce problems, as there is not a continuous stream of bits from one source?

7.6 Why is it that the start and stop bits can be eliminated when character interleaving is used in synchronous TDM?

7.7 Explain in terms of data link control and physical-layer concepts how error and flow control are accomplished in synchronous time-division multiplexing.

7.8 Bit 193 in the DS-1 transmission format is used for frame synchronization. Explain its use.

7.9 In the DS-1 format, what is the control signal data rate for each voice channel?

7.10 Twenty-four voice signals are to be multiplexed and transmitted over twisted pair. What is the bandwidth required for FDM? Assuming a bandwidth efficiency of 1 bps/Hz, what is the bandwidth required for TDM using PCM?

7.11 Draw a block diagram similar to Figure 7.8 for a TDM PCM system that will accommodate four 300-bps, synchronous, digital inputs and one analog input with a bandwidth of 500 Hz. Assume that the analog samples will be encoded into 4-bit PCM words.

7.12 A character-interleaved time-division multiplexer is used to combine the data streams of a number of 110-bps asynchronous terminals for data transmission over a 2400-bps digital line. Each terminal sends characters consisting of 7 data bits, 1 parity bit, 1 start bit, and 2 stop bits. Assume that one synchronization character is sent every 19 data characters and, in addition, at least 3% of the line capacity is reserved for pulse stuffing to accommodate speed variations from the various terminals.
   **a.** Determine the number of bits per character.
   **b.** Determine the number of terminals that can be accommodated by the multiplexer.
   **c.** Sketch a possible framing pattern for the multiplexer.

7.13 Assume that two 600-bps terminals, five 300-bps terminals, and a number of 150-bps terminals are to be time-multiplexed in a character-interleaved format over a 4800-bps digital line. The terminals send 10 bits/character, and one synchronization character is inserted for every 99 data characters. All the terminals are asynchronous, and 3% of the line capacity is allocated for pulse stuffing to accommodate variations in the terminal clock rates.

a. Determine the number of 150-bps terminals that can be accommodated.

b. Sketch a possible framing pattern for the multiplexer.

7.14 Find the number of the following devices that could be accommodated by a T1-type TDM line if 1% of the line capacity is reserved for synchronization purposes.

a. 110-bps teleprinter terminals.

b. 300-bps computer terminals.

c. 1200-bps computer terminals.

d. 9600-bps computer output ports.

e. 64-kbps PCM voice-frequency lines.

How would these numbers change if each of the sources were operational an average of 10% of the time?

7.15 Ten 9600-bps lines are to be multiplexed using TDM. Ignoring overhead bits, what is the total capacity required for synchronous TDM? Assuming that we wish to limit average line utilization of 0.8, and assuming that each line is busy 50% of the time, what is the capacity required for statistical TDM?

7.16 For a statistical time-division multiplexer, define the following parameters:

$F$ = frame length, bits
$OH$ = overhead in a frame, bits
$L$ = load of data in the frame, bps
$C$ = capacity of link, bps

a. Express $F$ as a function of the other parameters. Explain why $F$ can be viewed as a variable rather than a constant.

b. Plot $F$ versus $L$ for $C$ = 9.6 kbps and values of $OH$ = 40, 80, 120. Comment on the results and compare to Figure 7.16.

c. Plot $F$ versus $L$ for $OH$ = 40 and values of $C$ = 9.6 kbps and 7.2 kbps. Comment on the results and compare to Figure 7.16.

7.17 The Clambake Zipper Company has two locations. The international headquarters is located at Cut and Shoot, Texas, while the factory is at Conroe, about 25 miles away. The factory has four 300-bps terminals that communicate with the central computer facilities at headquarters over leased voice grade lines. The company is considering installing time-division multiplexing equipment so that only one line will be needed. What cost factors should be considered in the decision?

7.18 In statistical TDM, there may be a length field. What alternative could there be to the inclusion of a length field? What problem might this solution cause and how could it be solved?

7.19 In synchronous TDM, the I/O lines serviced by the two multiplexers may be either synchronous or asynchronous, although the channel between the two multiplexers must be synchronous. Is there any inconsistency in this? Why or why not?

7.20 Assume that you are to design a TDM carrier—say, DS-489 —to support 30 voice channels using 6 bit samples and a structure similar to DS-1. Determine the required bit rate.

# CHAPTER 8

# CIRCUIT SWITCHING

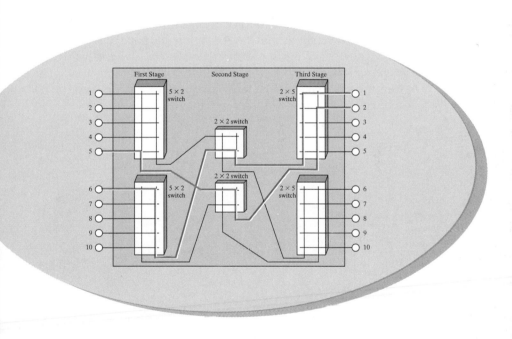

ince the invention of the telephone, circuit switching has been the dominant technology for voice communications, and it will remain so well into the ISDN era. This chapter begins with an introduction to the concept of a switched communications network and then looks at the key characteristics of a circuit-switching network.

## 8.1  SWITCHING NETWORKS

For transmission of data[1] beyond a local area, communication is typically achieved by transmitting data from source to destination through a network of intermediate switching nodes; this switched-network design is sometimes used to implement LANs and MANs as well. The switching nodes are not concerned with the content of the data; rather, their purpose is to provide a switching facility that will move the data from node to node until they reach their destination. Figure 8.1 illustrates a simple network. The end devices that wish to communicate may be referred to as *stations*. The stations may be computers, terminals, telephones, or other communicating devices. We will refer to the switching devices whose purpose is to provide communication as *nodes*, which are connected to each other in some topology by transmission links. Each station attaches to a node, and the collection of nodes is referred to as a *communications network*.

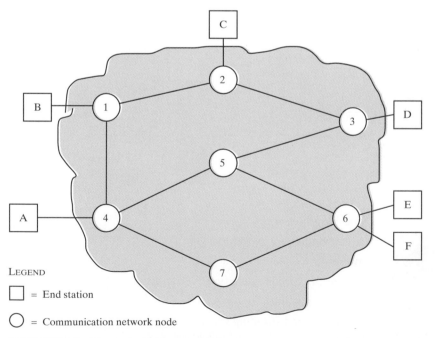

LEGEND

☐ = End station

◯ = Communication network node

**FIGURE 8.1**  Simple switching network.

---

[1] We use this term here in a very general sense to include voice, image, and video, as well as ordinary data (e.g., numerical, text).

The types of networks that are discussed in this and the next three chapters are referred to as *switched communication networks*. Data entering the network from a station are routed to the destination by being switched from node to node. For example, in Figure 8.1, data from station A intended for station F are sent to node 4. They may then be routed via nodes 5 and 6 or nodes 7 and 6 to the destination. Several observations are in order:

1. Some nodes connect only to other nodes (e.g., 5 and 7). Their sole task is the internal (to the network) switching of data. Other nodes have one or more stations attached as well; in addition to their switching functions, such nodes accept data from and deliver data to the attached stations.
2. Node-node links are usually multiplexed, using either frequency-division multiplexing (FDM) or time-division multiplexing (TDM).
3. Usually, the network is not fully connected; that is, there is not a direct link between every possible pair of nodes. However, it is always desirable to have more than one possible path through the network for each pair of stations; this enhances the reliability of the network.

Two quite different technologies are used in wide-area switched networks: circuit switching and packet switching. These two technologies differ in the way the nodes switch information from one link to another on the way from source to destination. In this chapter, we look at the details of circuit switching; packet switching is pursued in Chapter 9. Two approaches that evolved from packet switching, namely frame relay and ATM, are explored in Chapters 10 and 11, respectively.

## 8.2 CIRCUIT-SWITCHING NETWORKS

Communication via circuit switching implies that there is a dedicated communication path between two stations. That path is a connected sequence of links between network nodes. On each physical link, a logical channel is dedicated to the connection. Communication via circuit switching involves three phases, which can be explained with reference to Figure 8.1.

1. *Circuit establishment.* Before any signals can be transmitted, an end-to-end (station-to-station) circuit must be established. For example, station *A* sends a request to node 4 requesting a connection to station *E*. Typically, the link from *A* to 4 is a dedicated line, so that part of the connection already exists. Node 4 must find the next leg in a route leading to node 6. Based on routing information and measures of availability and, perhaps, cost, node 4 selects the link to node 5, allocates a free channel (using frequency-division multiplexing, FDM, or time-division multiplexing, TDM) on that link and sends a message requesting connection to *E*. So far, a dedicated path has been established from A through 4 to 5. Because a number of stations may attach to 4, it must be able to establish internal paths from multiple stations to multiple nodes. The remainder of the process proceeds similarly. Node 5 dedicates a channel to node 6 and internally ties that channel to the channel from node 4. Node 6

completes the connection to $E$. In completing the connection, a test is made to determine if $E$ is busy or is prepared to accept the connection.

2. *Data transfer.* Information can now be transmitted from A through the network to $E$. The data may be analog or digital, depending on the nature of the network. As the carriers evolve to fully integrated digital networks, the use of digital (binary) transmission for both voice and data is becoming the dominant method. The path is $A$-4 link, internal switching through 4, 4-5 channel, internal switching through 5, 5-6 channel, and internal switching through 6, 6-$E$ link. Generally, the connection is full-duplex.

3. *Circuit disconnect.* After some period of data transfer, the connection is terminated, usually by the action of one of the two stations. Signals must be propagated to nodes 4, 5, and 6 to deallocate the dedicated resources.

Note that the connection path is established before data transmission begins. Thus, channel capacity must be reserved between each pair of nodes in the path, and each node must have available internal switching capacity to handle the requested connection. The switches must have the intelligence to make these allocations and to devise a route through the network.

Circuit switching can be rather inefficient. Channel capacity is dedicated for the duration of a connection, even if no data are being transferred. For a voice connection, utilization may be rather high, but it still does not approach 100 percent. For a terminal-to-computer connection, the capacity may be idle during most of the time of the connection. In terms of performance, there is a delay prior to signal transfer for call establishment. However, once the circuit is established, the network is effectively transparent to the users. Information is transmitted at a fixed data rate with no delay other than that required for propagation through the transmission links. The delay at each node is negligible.

Circuit switching was developed to handle voice traffic but is now also used for data traffic. The best-known example of a circuit-switching network is the public telephone network (Figure 8.2); this is actually a collection of national networks interconnected to form the international service. Although originally designed and implemented to service analog telephone subscribers, the network handles substantial data traffic via modem and is gradually being converted to a digital network. Another well-known application of circuit switching is the private branch exchange (PBX), used to interconnect telephones within a building or office. Circuit switching is also used in private networks—corporations or other large organizations interconnecting their various sites; these usually consist of PBX systems at each site interconnected by dedicated, leased lines obtained from one of the carriers, such as AT&T. A final common example of the application of circuit switching is the data switch. The data switch is similar to the PBX but is designed to interconnect digital data-processing devices, such as terminals and computers.

A public telecommunications network can be described using four generic architectural components:

- **Subscribers:** The devices that attach to the network. It is still the case that most subscriber devices to public telecommunications networks are telephones, but the percentage of data traffic increases year by year.

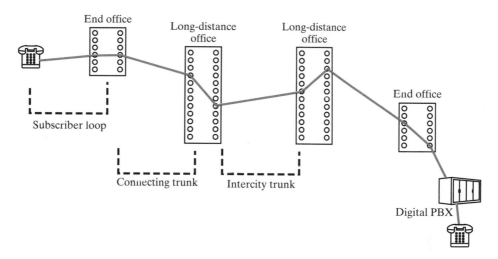

**FIGURE 8.2**  Public circuit-switching network.

- **Local loop:** The link between the subscriber and the network, also referred to as the *subscriber loop*. Almost all local loop connections used twisted-pair wire. The length of a local loop is typically in a range from a few kilometers to a few tens of kilometers.
- **Exchanges:** The switching centers in the network. A switching center that directly supports subscribers is known as an *end office*. Typically, an end office will support many thousands of subscribers in a localized area. There are over 19,000 end offices in the United States, so it is clearly impractical for each end office to have a direct link to each of the other end offices; this would require on the order of $2 \times 10^8$ links. Rather, intermediate switching nodes are used.
- **Trunks:** The branches between exchanges. Trunks carry multiple voice-frequency circuits using either FDM or synchronous TDM. Earlier, these were referred to as carrier systems.

Subscribers connect directly to an end office, which switches traffic between subscribers and between a subscriber and other exchanges. The other exchanges are responsible for routing and switching traffic between end offices; this distinction is shown in Figure 8.3. To connect two subscribers attached to the same end office, a circuit is set up between them in the same fashion as described before. If two subscribers connect to different end offices, a circuit between them consists of a chain of circuits through one or more intermediate offices. In the figure, a connection is established between lines *a* and *b* by simply setting up the connection through the end office. The connection between *c* and *d* is more complex. In *c*'s end office, a connection is established between line *c* and one channel on a TDM trunk to the intermediate switch. In the intermediate switch, that channel is connected to a channel on a TDM trunk to *d*'s end office. In that end office, the channel is connected to line *d*.

Circuit-switching technology has been driven by those applications that handle voice traffic. One of the key requirements for voice traffic is that there must be

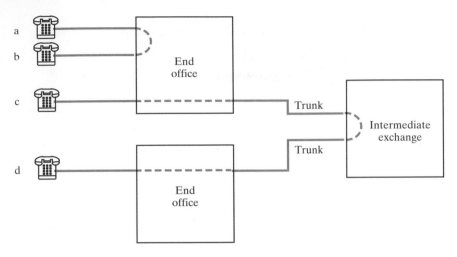

**FIGURE 8.3**    Circuit establishment.

virtually no transmission delay and certainly no variation in delay. A constant signal transmission rate must be maintained, as transmission and reception occur at the same signal rate. These requirements are necessary to allow normal human conversation. Further, the quality of the received signal must be sufficiently high to provide, at a minimum, intelligibility.

Circuit switching achieved its widespread, dominant position because it is well suited to the analog transmission of voice signals; in today's digital world, its inefficiencies are more apparent. However, despite the inefficiency, circuit switching will remain an attractive choice for both local-area and wide-area networking. One of its key strengths is that it is transparent. Once a circuit is established, it appears as a direct connection to the two attached stations; no special networking logic is needed at either point.

## 8.3  SWITCHING CONCEPTS

The technology of circuit switching is best approached by examining the operation of a single circuit-switched node. A network built around a single circuit-switching node consists of a collection of stations attached to a central switching unit. The central switch establishes a dedicated path between any two devices that wish to communicate. Figure 8.4 depicts the major elements of such a one-node network. The dotted lines inside the switch symbolize the connections that are currently active.

The heart of a modern system is a *digital switch*. The function of the digital switch is to provide a transparent signal path between any pair of attached devices. The path is transparent in that it appears to the attached pair of devices that there is a direct connection between them. Typically, the connection must allow full-duplex transmission.

The *network-interface* element represents the functions and hardware needed to connect digital devices, such as data processing devices and digital telephones, to

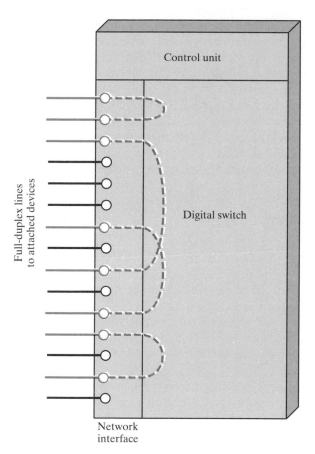

**FIGURE 8.4**    Elements of a circuit-switch node.

the network. Analog telephones can also be attached if the network interface contains the logic for converting to digital signals. Trunks to other digital switches carry TDM signals and provide the links for constructing multiple-node networks.

The *control unit* performs three general tasks. First, it establishes connections. This is generally done on demand—that is, at the request of an attached device. To establish the connection, the control unit must handle and acknowledge the request, determine if the intended destination is free, and construct a path through the switch. Second, the control unit must maintain the connection. Because the digital switch uses time-division principles, this may require ongoing manipulation of the switching elements. However, the bits of the communication are transferred transparently (from the point of view of the attached devices). Third, the control unit must tear down the connection, either in response to a request from one of the parties or for its own reasons.

An important characteristic of a circuit-switching device is whether it is blocking or nonblocking. Blocking occurs when the network is unable to connect two stations because all possible paths between them are already in use. A *blocking network* is one in which such blocking is possible. Hence, a *nonblocking network* permits all stations to be connected (in pairs) at once and grants all possible connection requests as long as the called party is free. When a network is supporting only voice traffic, a blocking configuration is generally acceptable, as it is expected that most phone calls are of short duration and that therefore only a fraction of the telephones will be engaged at any time. However, when data processing devices are involved, these assumptions may be invalid. For example, for a data-entry application, a terminal may be continuously connected to a computer for hours at a time. Hence, for data applications, there is a requirement for a nonblocking or "nearly nonblocking" (very low probability of blocking) configuration.

We turn now to an examination of the switching techniques internal to a single circuit-switching node.

### Space-division Switching

Space-division switching was originally developed for the analog environment and has been carried over into the digital realm. The fundamental principles are the same, whether the switch is used to carry analog or digital signals. As its name implies, a space-division switch is one in which the signal paths are physically separate from one another (divided in space). Each connection requires the establishment of a physical path through the switch that is dedicated solely to the transfer of signals between the two endpoints. The basic building block of the switch is a metallic crosspoint or semiconductor gate that can be enabled and disabled by a control unit.

Figure 8.5 shows a simple crossbar matrix with 10 full-duplex I/O lines. The matrix has 10 inputs and 10 outputs; each station attaches to the matrix via one input and one output line. Interconnection is possible between any two lines by enabling the appropriate crosspoint. Note that a total of 100 crosspoints is required. The crossbar switch has a number of limitations:

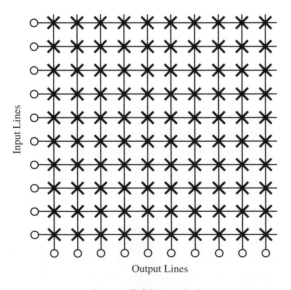

**FIGURE 8.5** Space-division switch.

- The number of crosspoints grows with the square of the number of attached stations. This is costly for a large switch.
- The loss of a crosspoint prevents connection between the two devices whose lines intersect at that crosspoint.
- The crosspoints are inefficiently utilized; even when all of the attached devices are active, only a small fraction of the crosspoints are engaged.

To overcome these limitations, multiple-stage switches are employed. Figure 8.6 is an example of a three-stage switch. This type of arrangement has several advantages over a single-stage crossbar matrix:

- The number of crosspoints is reduced, increasing crossbar utilization. In this example, the total number of crosspoints for 10 stations is reduced from 100 to 48.
- There is more than one path through the network to connect two endpoints, increasing reliability.

Of course, a multistage network requires a more complex control scheme. To establish a path in a single-stage network, it is only necessary to enable a single gate. In a multistage network, a free path through the stages must be determined and the appropriate gates enabled.

A consideration with a multistage space-division switch is that it may be blocking. It should be clear from Figure 8.5 that a single-stage crossbar matrix is nonblocking; that is, a path is always available to connect an input to an output; that this may not be the case with a multiple-stage switch can be seen in Figure 8.6. The

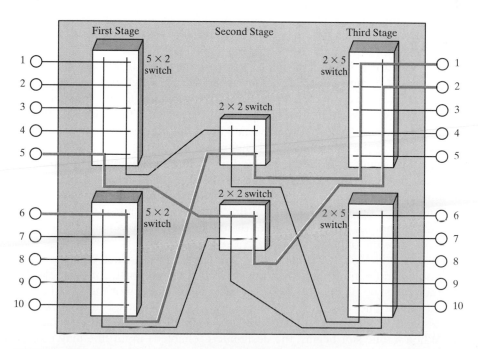

**FIGURE 8.6**  Three-stage space-division switch.

heavier lines indicate ones already in use. In this state, input line 10, for example, cannot be connected to output line 3, 4, or 5, even though all of these output lines are available. A multiple-stage switch can be made nonblocking by increasing the number or size of the intermediate switches, but of course this increases the cost.

### Time-division Switching

The technology of switching has a long history, most of it covering an era when analog signal switching predominated. With the advent of digitized voice and synchronous time-division multiplexing techniques, both voice and data can be transmitted via digital signals; this has led to a fundamental change in the design and technology of switching systems. Instead of relatively dumb space-division systems, modern digital systems rely on intelligent control of space- and time-division elements.

Virtually all modern circuit switches use digital time-division techniques for establishing and maintaining "circuits." Time-division switching involves the partitioning of a lower-speed bit stream into pieces that share a higher-speed stream with other bit streams. The individual pieces, or slots, are manipulated by control logic to route data from input to output. There are a number of variations on this basic concept. To give the reader some feel for time-division switching, we examine one of the simplest but most popular techniques, referred to as TDM bus switching.

TDM bus switching, and indeed all digital switching techniques, are based on the use of synchronous time-division multiplexing (TDM). As we saw in Figure 7.6, synchronous TDM permits multiple low-speed bit streams to share a high-speed line. A set of inputs is sampled in turn. The samples are organized serially into slots (channels) to form a recurring frame of slots, with the number of slots per frame equal to the number of inputs. A slot may be a bit, a byte, or some longer block. An important point to note is that with synchronous TDM, the source and destination of the data in each time slot are known. Hence, there is no need for address bits in each slot.

Figure 8.7 shows a simple way in which this technique can be adapted to achieve switching. Each device attaches to the switch through a full-duplex line. These lines are connected through controlled gates to a high-speed digital bus. Each line is assigned a time slot for providing input. For the duration of the slot, that line's gate is enabled, allowing a small burst of data onto the bus. For that same time slot, one of the other line gates is enabled for output. Thus, during that time slot, data are switched from the enabled input line to the enabled output line. During successive time slots, different input/output pairings are enabled, allowing a number of connections to be carried over the shared bus. An attached device achieves full-duplex operation by transmitting during one assigned time slot and receiving during another. The other end of the connection is an I/O pair for which these time slots have the opposite meanings.

Let us look at the timing involved more closely. First, consider a nonblocking implementation of Figure 8.7. For a switch that supports, for example, 100 devices, there must be 100 repetitively occurring time slots, each one assigned to an input and an output line. One iteration for all time slots is referred to as a *frame*. The input assignment may be fixed; the output assignments vary to allow various connections. When a time slot begins, the designated (enabled) input line may insert a burst of data onto the line, where it will propagate to both ends past all other output lines.

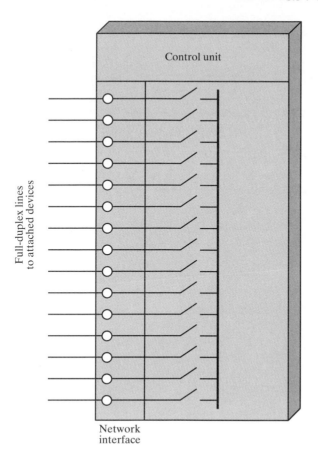

**FIGURE 8.7** TDM bus switching.

The designated (enabled) output line, during that time, copies the data, if present, as they go by. The time slot, therefore, must equal the transmission time of the input plus the propagation delay between input and output across the bus. In order to keep successive time slots uniform, time-slot length is defined as transmission time plus the end-to-end bus propagation delay.

To keep up with the input lines, the data rate on the bus must be high enough that the slots recur sufficiently frequently. For example, consider a system connecting 100 full-duplex lines at 19.2 kbps. Input data on each line are buffered at the gate. Each buffer must be cleared, by enabling the gate, quickly enough to avoid overrun. Thus, the data rate on the bus in this example must be greater than 1.92 Mbps. The actual data rate must be high enough to also account for the wasted time due to propagation delay.

The above considerations determine the traffic-carrying capacity of a blocking switch, as well, where there is no fixed assignment of input lines to time slots; they are allocated on demand. The data rate on the bus dictates how many connections can be made at a time. For a system with 200 devices at 19.2 kbps and a bus at 2 Mbps, about half of the devices can be connected at any one time.

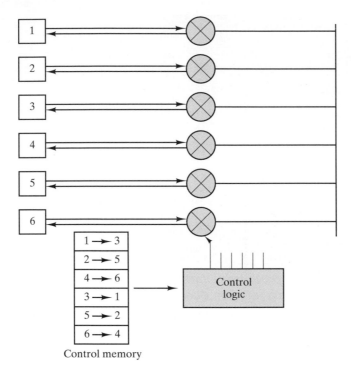

**FIGURE 8.8**  Control of a TDM bus switch.

The TDM bus-switching scheme can accommodate lines of varying data rates. For example, if a 9600-bps line gets one slot per frame, a 19.2-kbps line would get two slots per frame. Of course, only lines of the same data rate can be connected.

Figure 8.8 is an example that suggests how the control for a TDM bus switch can be implemented. Let us assume that the propagation time on the bus is 0.01 μsec. Time on the bus is organized into 30.06-μsec frames of six 5.01-μsec time slots each. A control memory indicates which gates are to be enabled during each time slot. In this example, six words of memory are needed. A controller cycles through the memory at a rate of one cycle every 30.06 μsec. During the first time slot of each cycle, the input gate from device 1 and the output gate to device 3 are enabled, allowing data to pass from device 1 to device 3 over the bus. The remaining words are accessed in succeeding time slots and treated accordingly. As long as the control memory contains the contents depicted in Figure 8.8, connections are maintained between 1 and 3, 2 and 5, and 4 and 6.

## 8.4  ROUTING IN CIRCUIT-SWITCHED NETWORKS

In a large circuit-switched network, such as the AT&T long-distance telephone network, many of the circuit connections will require a path through more than one switch. When a call is placed, the network must devise a route through the network from calling subscriber to called subscriber that passes through some number of switches and trunks. There are two main requirements for the network's architecture that bear on the routing strategy: efficiency and resilience. First, it is desirable to minimize the amount of equipment (switches and trunks) in the network subject to the ability to handle the expected load. The load requirement is usually expressed in terms of a *busy-hour traffic load*; this is simply the average load expected over the course of the busiest hour of use during the course of a day. From a functional point of view, it is necessary to handle that amount of load. From a cost point of view, we would like to handle that load with minimum equipment. However, there is another requirement, namely, resilience. Although the network may be sized for the busy hour load, it is possible for the traffic to temporarily surge above that level (for example, during a major storm). It will also be the case that, from time to time, switches and trunks will fail and be temporarily unavailable (unfortunately, maybe during the same storm). We would like the network to provide a reasonable level of service under such conditions.

The key design issue that determines the nature of the tradeoff between efficiency and resilience is the routing strategy. Traditionally, the routing function in public telecommunications networks has been quite simple. In essence, the switches of a network were organized into a tree structure, or hierarchy. A path was constructed by starting at the calling subscriber, tracing up the tree to the first common node, and then tracing down the tree to the called subscriber. To add some resilience to the network, additional high-usage trunks were added that cut across the tree structure to connect exchanges with high volumes of traffic between them; in general, this is a static approach. The addition of high-usage trunks provides redundancy and extra capacity, but limitations remain both in efficiency and resilience. Because this routing scheme is not able to adapt to changing conditions, the network must be designed to meet some typical heavy demand. As an example of the problems raised by this approach, the busy hours for east-west traffic and those for north-south traffic do not coincide; they each place different demands on the system. It is difficult to analyze the effects of these variables, which leads to oversizing and, ultimately, inefficiency. In terms of resilience, the fixed hierarchical structure with supplemental trunks may respond poorly to failures. Typically in such designs, the result of a failure is a major local congestion at that location.

To cope with the growing demands on public telecommunications networks, virtually all providers have moved away from the static hierarchical approach to a dynamic approach. A dynamic routing approach is one in which routing decisions are influenced by current traffic conditions. Typically, the circuit-switching nodes have a peer relationship with each other rather than a hierarchical one. All nodes are capable of performing the same functions. In such an architecture, routing is both more complex and more flexible. It is more complex because the architecture does not provide a "natural" path or set of paths based on hierarchical structure; but it is also more flexible, as more alternative routes are available.

Two broad classes of dynamic routing algorithms have been implemented: alternate routing and adaptive routing.

## Alternate Routing

The essence of alternate-routing schemes is that the possible routes to be used between two end offices are predefined. It is the responsibility of the originating switch to select the appropriate route for each call. Each switch is given a set of pre-planned routes for each destination, in order of preference. The preferred choice is a direct trunk connection between two switches. If this trunk is unavailable, then the second choice is to be tried, and so on. The routing sequences (sequence in which the routes in the set are tried) reflect an analysis based on historical traffic patterns, and are designed to optimize the use of network resources.

If there is only one routing sequence defined for each source-destination pair, the scheme is known as a fixed alternate-routing scheme. More commonly, a dynamic alternate-routing scheme is used. In the latter case, a different set of pre-planned routes is used for different time periods, to take advantage of the differing traffic patterns in different time zones and at different times of day. Thus, the routing decision is based both on current traffic status (a route is rejected if busy) and historical traffic patterns (which determine the sequence of routes to be considered).

A simple example is shown in Figure 8.9. The originating switch, X, has four possible routes to the destination switch, Y. The direct route (a) will always be tried first. If this trunk is unavailable (busy, out of service), the other routes will be tried in a particular order, depending on the time period. For example, during weekday mornings, route b is tried next.

A form of the dynamic alternate-routing technique is employed by the Bell Operating Companies for providing local and regional telephone service [BELL90]; it is referred to as multialternate routing (MAR). This approach is also used by AT&T in its long-distance network [ASH90], and is referred to as dynamic non-hierarchical routing (DNHR).

## Adaptive Routing

An adaptive-routing scheme is designed to enable switches to react to changing traffic patterns on the network. Such schemes require greater management overhead, as the switches must exchange information to learn of network conditions. However, compared to an alternate-routing scheme, an adaptive scheme has the potential for more effectively optimizing the use of network resources. In this subsection, we briefly describe an important example of an adaptive-routing scheme.

Dynamic traffic management (DTM) is a routing capability developed by Northern Telecom and used in the Canadian national and local telephone networks [REGN90].

DTM uses a central controller to find the best alternate route choices depending on congestion in the network. The central controller collects status data from each switch in the network every 10 seconds to determine preferred alternate routes. Each call is first attempted on the direct path, if any exists, between source and destination switches. If the call is blocked, it is attempted on a two-link alternate path.

Each switch $i$ communicates the following traffic measurements to the central controller:

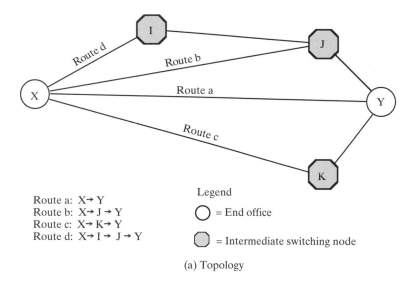

Route a: X→ Y
Route b: X→ J → Y
Route c: X→ K→ Y
Route d: X→ I → J → Y

Legend

◯ = End office

⬡ = Intermediate switching node

(a) Topology

| Time Period | First route | Second route | Third route | Fourth and final route |
|---|---|---|---|---|
| Morning | a | b | c | d |
| Afternoon | a | d | b | c |
| Evening | a | d | c | b |
| Weekend | a | c | b | d |

(b) Routing table

**FIGURE 8.9**    Alternate routes from end office X to end office.

$I_{ij}$ = The number of idle trunks on the link to switch $j$, for all switches in the network

$CPU_i$ = The CPU utilization of switch $i$

$O_{ij}$ = A measure of the traffic sent by $i$ to $j$ that overflowed the direct route.

Based on this information, the central controller periodically returns to each switch $i$, for each possible destination switch $j$:

$r_{ij}$ = The identifier of the switch through which $i$ should direct its calls to $j$ when the direct link is full.

The selection of $r_{ij}$ depends on whether or not a direct link exists between $i$ and $j$. If a direct link exists, which is the case for the vast majority of the calls, then $r_{ij}$ is determined as that switch $t$ that achieves the maximum in

$$\text{Max } \{A_t \times \text{Min } [I_{it} - PA_{it}, I_{tj} - PA_{tj}]\} \quad t \neq i,j$$

If there is no direct link between $i$ and $j$, then $r_{ij}$ is determined as that switch $t$ that achieves the maximum in

$$\text{Max } \{A_t \times \text{Min } [I_{it}, I_{tj}]\} \qquad t \neq i,j$$

where

$A_t$ = Parameter in the range [0,1] that reflects the availability of switch $t$. It is 1 if $t$ functions normally, but it is less if $t$ is overloaded; its role is to make alternative routes that transit through overloaded switches less attractive and, hence, less likely to be chosen by the network controller.

$PA_{xy}$ = Protective-allowance parameter for the direct traffic on link $x$-$y$; its role is to divert traffic away from the link when it is nearly fully occupied.

The second equation is the same as the first, except that protective allowances are not considered. The rationale is the following: If there is no direct link between switches $i$ and $j$, then traffic from $i$ to $j$ should not concede priority to direct traffic over links on potential alternate routes.

Figure 8.10 illustrates the selection process. If the link from $i$ to $j$ is saturated, the recommended alternate route is $i$-$y$-$j$. Although route $i$-$x$-$j$ has the largest idle capacity, it is not recommended because switch $x$ is overloaded.

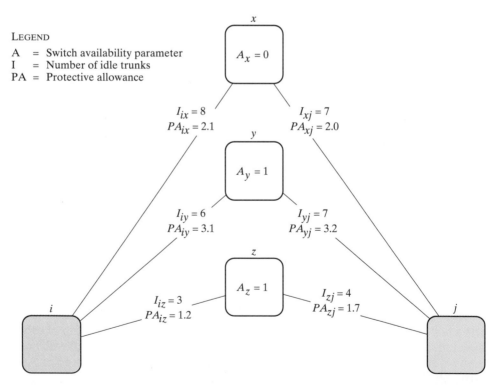

**FIGURE 8.10** Adaptive route selection in DTM.

The use of a set of parameters based on network status provides a powerful routing capability. Furthermore, it becomes an easy matter to experiment with various ways of determining the values of parameters and assessing their effect on performance. For example, the parameter $PA_{xy}$ can be set to a fixed value in a relatively stable network, or the overflow measurement $O_{xy}$ can be used.

## 8.5 CONTROL SIGNALING

In a circuit-switched network, control signals are the means by which the network is managed and by which calls are established, maintained, and terminated. Both call management and overall network management require that information be exchanged between subscriber and switch, among switches, and between switch and network management center. For a large public telecommunications network, a relatively complex control-signaling scheme is required. In this section, we provide a brief overview of control-signal functionality and then look at the technique that is the basis of modern integrated digital networks: common channel signaling.

### Signaling Functions

Control signals affect many aspects of network behavior, including both network services visible to the subscriber and internal mechanisms. As networks become more complex, the number of functions performed by control signaling necessarily grows. The following functions, listed in [MART90], are among the most important:

1. Audible communication with the subscriber, including dial tone, ringing tone, busy signal, and so on.
2. Transmission of the number dialed to switching offices that will attempt to complete a connection.
3. Transmission of information between switches indicating that a call cannot be completed.
4. Transmission of information between switches indicating that a call has ended and that the path can be disconnected.
5. A signal to make a telephone ring.
6. Transmission of information used for billing purposes.
7. Transmission of information giving the status of equipment or trunks in the network. This information may be used for routing and maintenance purposes.
8. Transmission of information used in diagnosing and isolating system failures.
9. Control of special equipment such as satellite channel equipment.

As an example of the use of control signaling, consider a typical telephone connection sequence from one line to another in the same central office:

1. Prior to the call, both telephones are not in use (on-hook). The call begins when one subscriber lifts the receiver (off-hook); this action is automatically signaled to the end office switch.
2. The switch responds with an audible dial tone, signaling the subscriber that the number may be dialed.
3. The caller dials the number, which is communicated as a called address to the switch.
4. If the called subscriber is not busy, the switch alerts that subscriber to an incoming call by sending a ringing signal, which causes the telephone to ring.
5. Feedback is provided to the calling subscriber by the switch:
   a) If the called subscriber is not busy, the switch returns an audible ringing tone to the caller while the ringing signal is being sent to the called subscriber.
   b) If the called subscriber is busy, the switch sends an audible busy signal to the caller.
   c) If the call cannot be completed through the switch, the switch sends an audible "reorder" message to the caller.
6. The called party accepts the call by lifting the receiver (off-hook), which is automatically signaled to the switch.
7. The switch terminates the ringing signal and the audible ringing tone, and establishes a connection between the two subscribers.
8. The connection is released when either subscriber hangs up.

When the called subscriber is attached to a different switch than that of the calling subscriber, the following switch-to-switch trunk signaling functions are required:

1. The originating switch seizes an idle interswitch trunk, sends an off-hook indication on the trunk, and requests a digit register at the far end, so that the address may be communicated.
2. The terminating switch sends an off-hook followed by an on-hook signal, known as a "wink." This indicates a register-ready status.
3. The originating switch sends the address digits to the terminating switch.

This example illustrates some of the functions performed using control signals.

Figure 8.11, based on a presentation in [FREE94], indicates the origin and destination of various control signals. Signaling can also be classified functionally as supervisory, address, call-information, and network-management.

The term *supervisory* is generally used to refer to control functions that have a binary character (true/false; on/off), such as request for service, answer, alerting, and return to idle; they deal with the availability of the called subscriber and of the needed network resources. Supervisory control signals are used to determine if a needed resource is available and, if so, to seize it; they are also used to communicate the status of requested resources.

*Address* signals identify a subscriber. Initially, an address signal is generated by a calling subscriber when dialing a telephone number. The resulting address may

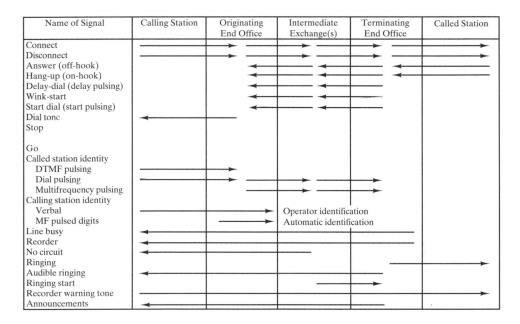

| Name of Signal | Calling Station | Originating End Office | Intermediate Exchange(s) | Terminating End Office | Called Station |
|---|---|---|---|---|---|
| Connect | | | | | |
| Disconnect | | | | | |
| Answer (off-hook) | | | | | |
| Hang-up (on-hook) | | | | | |
| Delay-dial (delay pulsing) | | | | | |
| Wink-start | | | | | |
| Start dial (start pulsing) | | | | | |
| Dial tone | | | | | |
| Stop | | | | | |
| | | | | | |
| Go | | | | | |
| Called station identity | | | | | |
| DTMF pulsing | | | | | |
| Dial pulsing | | | | | |
| Multifrequency pulsing | | | | | |
| Calling station identity | | | | | |
| Verbal | | | Operator identification | | |
| MF pulsed digits | | | Automatic identification | | |
| Line busy | | | | | |
| Reorder | | | | | |
| No circuit | | | | | |
| Ringing | | | | | |
| Audible ringing | | | | | |
| Ringing start | | | | | |
| Recorder warning tone | | | | | |
| Announcements | | | | | |

Note: A broken line indicates repetition of a signal at each office, whereas
      a solid line indicates direct transmittal through intermediate offices.

**FIGURE 8.11**    Control signaling through a circuit-switched telephone network.

be propagated through the network to support the routing function and to locate and ring the called subscriber's phone.

The term *call-information* refers to those signals that provide information to the subscriber about the status of a call. This is in contrast to internal control signals between switches used in call establishment and termination. Such internal signals are analog or digital electrical messages. In contrast, call information signals are audible tones that can be heard by the caller or an operator with the proper phone set.

Supervisory, address, and call-information control signals are directly involved in the establishment and termination of a call. In contrast, *network-management* signals are used for the maintenance, troubleshooting, and overall operation of the network. Such signals may be in the form of messages, such as a list of preplanned routes being sent to a station to update its routing tables. These signals cover a broad scope, and it is this category that will expand most with the increasing complexity of switched networks.

## Location of Signaling

Control signaling needs to be considered in two contexts: signaling between a subscriber and the network, and signaling within the network. Typically, signaling operates differently within these two contexts.

The signaling between a telephone or other subscriber device and the switching office to which it attaches is, to a large extent, determined by the characteristics of the subscriber device and the needs of the human user. Signals within the network are entirely computer-to-computer. The internal signaling is concerned not only with the management of subscriber calls but with the management of the network itself. Thus, for internal signaling, a more complex repertoire of commands, responses, and set of parameters is needed.

Because two different signaling techniques are used, the local switching office to which the subscriber is attached must provide a mapping between the relatively less complex signaling technique used by the subscriber and the more complex technique used within the network.

## Common Channel Signaling

Traditional control signaling in circuit-switched networks has been on a per-trunk or inchannel basis. With *inchannel signaling*, the same channel is used to carry control signals as is used to carry the call to which the control signals relate. Such signaling begins at the originating subscriber and follows the same path as the call itself. This process has the merit that no additional transmission facilities are needed for signaling; the facilities for voice transmission are shared with control signaling.

Two forms of inchannel signaling are in use: inband and out-of-band. *Inband signaling* uses not only the same physical path as the call it serves; it also uses the same frequency band as the voice signals that are carried. This form of signaling has several advantages. Because the control signals have the same electromagnetic properties as the voice signals, they can go anywhere that the voice signals go. Thus, there are no limits on the use of inband signaling anywhere in the network, including places where analog-to-digital or digital-to-analog conversion takes place. In addition, it is impossible to set up a call on a faulty speech path, as the control signals that are used to set up that path would have to follow the same path.

*Out-of-band signaling* takes advantage of the fact that voice signals do not use the full 4-kHz bandwidth allotted to them. A separate narrow signaling band within the 4 kHZ is used to send control signals. The major advantage of this approach is that the control signals can be sent whether or not voice signals are on the line, thus allowing continuous supervision and control of a call. However, an out-of-band scheme needs extra electronics to handle the signaling band, and the signaling rates are slower because the signal has been confined to a narrow bandwidth.

As public telecommunications networks become more complex and provide a richer set of services, the drawbacks of inchannel signaling become more apparent. The information transfer rate is quite limited with inchannel signaling. With inband signals, the voice channel being used is only available for control signals when there are no voice signals on the circuit. With out-of-band signals, a very narrow bandwidth is available. With such limits, it is difficult to accommodate, in a timely fashion, any but the simplest form of control messages. However, to take advantage of the potential services and to cope with the increasing complexity of evolving network technology, a richer and more powerful control signal repertoire is needed.

A second drawback of inchannel signaling is the amount of delay from the time a subscriber enters an address (dials a number) to when the connection is established. The requirement to reduce this delay is becoming more important as the network is used in new ways. For example, computer-controlled calls, such as with transaction processing, use relatively short messages; therefore, the call setup time represents an appreciable part of the total transaction time.

Both of these problems can be addressed with *common-channel signaling*, in which control signals are carried over paths completely independent of the voice channels (Table 8.1). One independent control signal path can carry the signals for a number of subscriber channels, and, hence, is a common control channel for these subscriber channels.

**TABLE 8.1**  Signaling techniques for circuit-switched networks.

| | Description | Comment |
|---|---|---|
| **Inchannel** | | |
| **Inband** | Transmit control signals in the same band of frequencies used by the voice signals. | The simplest technique. It is necessary for call information signals and may be used for other control signals. Inband can be used over any type of subscriber line interface. |
| **Out-of-band** | Transmit control signals over the same facilities as the voice signal but a different part of the frequency band. | Unlike inband, out-of-band provides continuous supervision for the duration of a connection. |
| **Common Channel** | Transmit control signals over signaling channels that are dedicated to control signals and are common to a number of voice channels. | Reduces call setup time compared with inchannel methods. It is also more adaptable to evolving functional needs. |

The principle of common-channel signaling is illustrated and contrasted with inchannel signaling in Figure 8.12. As can be seen, the signal path for common-channel signaling is physically separate from the path for voice or other subscriber signals. The common channel can be configured with the bandwidth required to carry control signals for a rich variety of functions. Thus, both the signaling protocol and the network architecture to support that protocol are more complex than inchannel signaling. However, the continuing drop in computer hardware costs makes common-channel signaling increasingly attractive. The control signals are messages that are passed between switches as well as between a switch and the network management center. Thus, the control-signaling portion of the network is, in effect, a distributed computer network carrying short messages.

Two modes of operation are used in common-channel signaling (Figure 8.13). In the *associated mode,* the common channel closely tracks along its entire length the interswitch trunk groups that are served between endpoints. The control signals are on different channels from the subscriber signals, and, inside the switch, the control signals are routed directly to a control signal processor. A more complex, but more powerful, mode is the *nonassociated mode*; with this, the network is augmented by additional nodes, known as signal transfer points. There is now no close or simple assignment of control channels to trunk groups. In effect, there are now two separate networks, with links between them so that the control portion of the

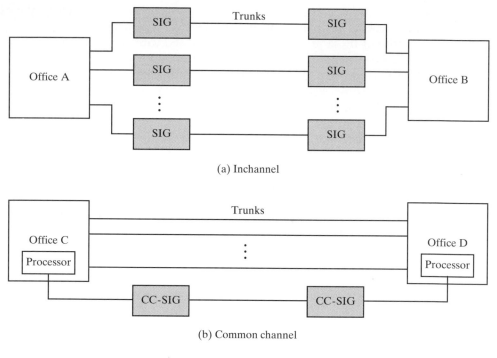

(a) Inchannel

(b) Common channel

LEGEND
SIG       = Per-trunk signaling equipment
CC-SIG = Common-channel signaling equipment

**FIGURE 8.12**   Inchannel and common-channel signaling.

network can exercise control over the switching nodes that are servicing the subscriber calls. Network management is more easily exerted in the nonassociated mode as control channels can be assigned to tasks in a more flexible manner. The nonassociated mode is the mode used in ISDN.

With inchannel signaling, control signals from one switch are originated by a control processor and switched onto the outgoing channel. On the receiving end, the control signals must be switched from the voice channel into the control processor. With common-channel signaling, the control signals are transferred directly from one control processor to another, without being tied to a voice signal; this is a simpler procedure, and one of the main motivations for common-channel signaling as it is less susceptible to accidental or intentional interference between subscriber and control signals. Another key motivation for common-channel signaling is that call-setup time is reduced. Consider the sequence of events for call setup with inchannel signaling when more than one switch is involved. A control signal will be sent from one switch to the next in the intended path. At each switch, the control signal cannot be transferred through the switch to the next leg of the route until the associated circuit is established through that switch. With common-channel signaling, forwarding of control information can overlap the circuit-setup process.

With nonassociated signaling, a further advantage emerges: One or more central control points can be established. All control information can be routed to a

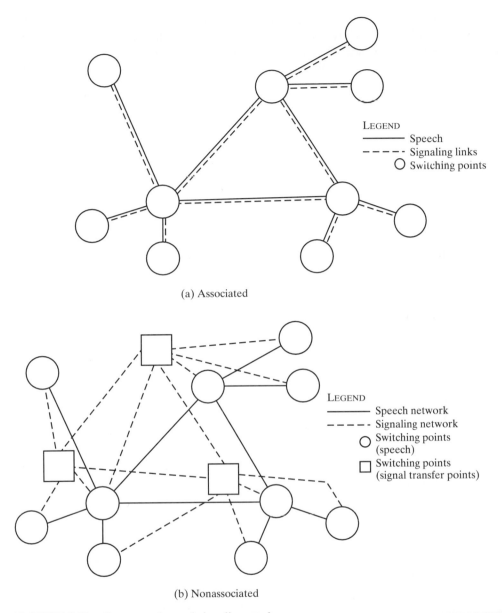

(a) Associated

(b) Nonassociated

**FIGURE 8.13**   Common-channel signaling modes.

network control center where requests are processed and from which control signals are sent to switches that handle subscriber traffic; in this way, requests can be
processed with a more global view of network conditions.

Of course, there are disadvantages to common-channel signaling; these primarily have to do with the complexity of the technique. However, the dropping cost
of digital hardware and the increasingly digital nature of telecommunication networks makes common-channel signaling the appropriate technology.

All of the discussion in this section has dealt with the use of common-channel signaling inside the network—that is, to control switches. Even in a network that is completely controlled by common-channel signaling, inchannel signaling is needed for at least some of the communication with the subscriber. For example, dial tone, ringback, and busy signals must be inchannel to reach the user. In a simple telephone network, the subscriber does not have access to the common-channel signaling portion of the network and does not employ the common-channel signaling protocol. However, in more sophisticated digital networks, including ISDN, a common-channel signaling protocol is employed between subscriber and network, and is mapped to the internal-signaling protocol.

## 8.6 RECOMMENDED READING

As befits its age, circuit switching has inspired a voluminous literature. Two good books on the subject are [BELL91] and [FREE96]. [MART90] also has a highly readable treatment.

The October 1990 issue of IEEE Communications magazine is devoted to the topic of routing in circuit-switched networks. [GIRA90] provides good coverage. Discussions of control signaling can be found in [FREE96] and [FREE94].

BELL91  Bellamy, J. *Digital Telephony*. New York: Wiley, 1991.

FREE96  Freeman, R. *Telecommunication System Engineering*. New York: Wiley, 1996.

FREE94  Freeman, R. *Reference Manual for Telecommunications Engineering*. New York: Wiley, 1994.

GIRA90  Girard, A. *Routing and Dimensioning in Circuit-Switched Networks*. Reading, MA: Addison-Wesley, 1990.

MART90  Martin, J. *Telecommunications and the Computer*. Englewood Cliffs, NJ: Prentice Hall, 1990.

## 8.7 PROBLEMS

8.1  Assume that the velocity of propagation on a TDM bus is 0.8 c, its length is 10 m, and the data rate is 500 Mbps. How many bits should be transmitted in a time slot to achieve a bus efficiency of 99%?

8.2  Consider a simple telephone network consisting of two end offices and one intermediate switch with a 1-MHz full-duplex trunk between each end office and the intermediate switch. The average telephone is used to make four calls per 8-hour workday, with a mean call duration of six minutes. Ten percent of the calls are long distance, What is the maximum number of telephones an end office can support?

# CHAPTER 9

# PACKET SWITCHING

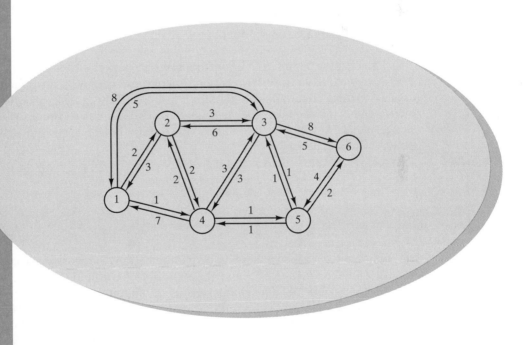

round 1970, research began on a new form of architecture for long-distance digital data communications: packet switching. Although the technology of packet switching has evolved substantially since that time, it is remarkable that (1) the basic technology of packet switching is fundamentally the same today as it was in the early-1970s networks, and (2) packet switching remains one of the few effective technologies for long-distance data communications.

This chapter provides an overview of packet-switching technology. We will see that many of the advantages of packet switching (flexibility, resource sharing, robustness, responsiveness) come with a cost. The packet-switching network is a distributed collection of packet-switching nodes. Ideally, all packet-switching nodes would always know the state of the entire network. Unfortunately, because the nodes are distributed, there is always a time delay between a change in status in one portion of the network and the knowledge of that change elsewhere. Furthermore, there is overhead involved in communicating status information. As a result, a packet-switching network can never perform "perfectly," and so elaborate algorithms are used to cope with the time delay and overhead penalties of network operation. These same issues will appear again when we discuss internetworking in Part IV.

The chapter begins with an introduction to packet-switching network principles. Next, we look at the internal operation of these networks, introducing the concepts of virtual circuits and datagrams. Following this, the key technologies of routing and congestion control are examined. The chapter concludes with an introduction to X.25, which is the standard interface between an end system and a packet-switching network.

## 9.1   PACKET-SWITCHING PRINCIPLES

The long-haul circuit-switching telecommunications network was orginally designed to handle voice traffic, and the majority of traffic on these networks continues to be voice. A key characteristic of circuit-switching networks is that resources within the network are dedicated to a particular call. For voice connections, the resulting circuit will enjoy a high percentage of utilization because, most of the time, one party or the other is talking. However, as the circuit-switching network began to be used increasingly for data connections, two shortcomings became apparent:

- In a typical user/host data connection (e.g., personal computer user logged on to a database server), much of the time the line is idle. Thus, with data connections, a circuit-switching approach is inefficient.
- In a circuit-switching network, the connection provides for transmission at constant data rate. Thus, each of the two devices that are connected must transmit and receive at the same data rate as the other; this limits the utility of the network in interconnecting a variety of host computers and terminals.

To understand how packet switching addresses these problems, let us briefly summarize packet-switching operation. Data are transmitted in short packets. A typical upper bound on packet length is 1000 octets (bytes). If a source has a longer message to send, the message is broken up into a series of packets (Figure 9.1). Each packet contains a portion (or all for a short message) of the user's data plus some control information. The control information, at a minimum, includes the information that the network requires in order to be able to route the packet through the network and deliver it to the intended destination. At each node en route, the packet is received, stored briefly, and passed on to the next node.

Let us return to Figure 8.1, but now assume that it depicts a simple packet-switching network. Consider a packet to be sent from station $A$ to station $E$. The packet will include control information that indicates that the intended destination is $E$. The packet is sent from $A$ to node 4. Node 4 stores the packet, determines the next leg of the route (say 5), and queues the packet to go out on that link (the 4-5 link). When the link is available, the packet is transmitted to node 5, which will forward the packet to node 6, and finally to $E$. This approach has a number of advantages over circuit switching:

- Line efficiency is greater, as a single node-to-node link can be dynamically shared by many packets over time. The packets are queued up and transmitted as rapidly as possible over the link. By contrast, with circuit switching, time on a node-to-node link is preallocated using synchronous time-division multiplexing. Much of the time, such a link may be idle because a portion of its time is dedicated to a connection which is idle.
- A packet-switching network can perform data-rate conversion. Two stations of different data rates can exchange packets because each connects to its node at its proper data rate.

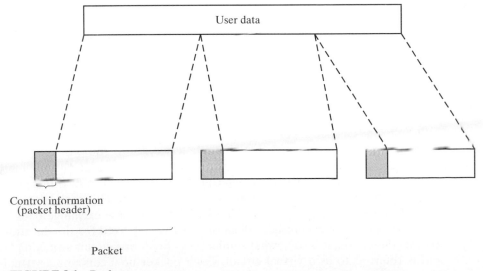

Control information
(packet header)

Packet

**FIGURE 9.1**  Packets.

- When traffic becomes heavy on a circuit-switching network, some calls are blocked; that is, the network refuses to accept additional connection requests until the load on the network decreases. On a packet-switching network, packets are still accepted, but delivery delay increases.
- Priorities can be used. Thus, if a node has a number of packets queued for transmission, it can transmit the higher-priority packets first. These packets will therefore experience less delay than lower-priority packets.

## Switching Technique

A station has a message to send through a packet-switching network that is of length greater than the maximum packet size. It therefore breaks the message up into packets and sends these packets, one at a time, to the network. A question arises as to how the network will handle this stream of packets as it attempts to route them through the network and deliver them to the intended destination; there are two approaches that are used in contemporary networks: datagram and virtual circuit.

In the datagram approach, each packet is treated independently, with no reference to packets that have gone before. Let us consider the implication of this approach. Suppose that station *A* in Figure 8.1 has a three-packet message to send to E. It transmits the packets, 1-2-3, to node 4. On each packet, node 4 must make a routing decision. Packet 1 arrives for delivery to *E*. Node 4 could plausibly forward this packet to either node 5 or node 7 as the next step in the route. In this case, node 4 determines that its queue of packets for node 5 is shorter than for node 7, so it queues the packet for node 5. Ditto for packet 2. But for packet 3, node 4 finds that its queue for node 7 is now shorter and so queues packet 3 for that node. So the packets, each with the same destination address, do not all follow the same route. As a result, it is possible that packet 3 will beat packet 2 to node 6. Thus, it is also possible that the packets will be delivered to *E* in a different sequence from the one in which they were sent. It is up to *E* to figure out how to reorder them. Also, it is possible for a packet to be destroyed in the network. For example, if a packet-switching node crashes momentarily, all of its queued packets may be lost. If this were to happen to one of the packets in our example, node 6 has no way of knowing that one of the packets in the sequence of packets has been lost. Again, it is up to *E* to detect the loss of a packet and figure out how to recover it. In this technique, each packet, treated independently, is referred to as a datagram.

In the virtual-circuit approach, a preplanned route is established before any packets are sent. For example, suppose that *A* has one or more messages to send to *E*. It first sends a special control packet, referred to as a Call-Request packet, to 4, requesting a logical connection to *E*. Node 4 decides to route the request and all subsequent packets to 5, which decides to route the request and all subsequent packets to 6, which finally delivers the Call-Request packet to *E*. If *E* is prepared to accept the connection, it sends a Call-Accept packet to 6. This packet is passed back through nodes 5 and 4 to *A*. Stations *A* and *E* may now exchange data over the route that has been established. Because the route is fixed for the duration of the logical connection, it is somewhat similar to a circuit in a circuit-switching network, and is referred to as a virtual circuit. Each packet now contains a virtual-circuit identifier as well as data. Each node on the preestablished route knows where to direct such packets; no routing decisions are required. Thus, every data packet from A intended for E traverses nodes 4, 5, and 6; every data packet from E intended for A traverses nodes 6, 5, and 4. Eventually, one of the stations terminates the connection with a Clear-Request packet. At any time, each station can have more than one virtual circuit to any other station and can have virtual circuits to more than one station.

So, the main characteristic of the virtual-circuit technique is that a route between stations is set up prior to data transfer. Note that this does not mean that this is a dedicated path, as in circuit switching. A packet is still buffered at each node, and queued for output over a line. The difference from the datagram approach is that, with virtual circuits, the node need not make a routing decision for each packet; it is made only once for all packets using that virtual circuit.

If two stations wish to exchange data over an extended period of time, there are certain advantages to virtual circuits. First, the network may provide services related to the virtual circuit, including sequencing and error control. Sequencing refers to the fact that, because all packets follow the same route, they arrive in the original order. Error control is a service that assures not only that packets arrive in proper sequence, but that all packets arrive correctly. For example, if a packet in a sequence from node 4 to node 6 fails to arrive at node 6, or arrives with an error, node 6 can request a retransmission of that packet from node 4. Another advantage is that packets should transit the network more rapidly with a virtual circuit; it is not necessary to make a routing decision for each packet at each node.

One advantage of the datagram approach is that the call setup phase is avoided. Thus, if a station wishes to send only one or a few packets, datagram delivery will be quicker. Another advantage of the datagram service is that, because it is more primitive, it is more flexible. For example, if congestion develops in one part of the network, incoming datagrams can be routed away from the congestion. With the use of virtual circuits, packets follow a predefined route, and it is thus more difficult for the network to adapt to congestion. A third advantage is that datagram delivery is inherently more reliable. With the use of virtual circuits, if a node fails, all virtual circuits that pass through that node are lost. With datagram delivery, if a node fails, subsequent packets may find an alternate route that bypasses that node.

Most currently available packet-switching networks make use of virtual circuits for their internal operation. To some degree, this reflects a historical motivation to provide a network that presents a service as reliable (in terms of sequencing) as a circuit-switching network. There are, however, several providers of private packet-switching networks that make use of datagram operation. From the user's point of view, there should be very little difference in the external behavior based on the use of datagrams or virtual circuits. If a manager is faced with a choice, other factors such as cost and performance should probably take precedence over whether the internal network operation is datagram or virtual-circuit. Finally, it should be noted that a datagram-style of operation is common in internetworks (discussed in Part IV).

## Packet Size

One important design issue is the packet size to be used in the network. There is a significant relationship between packet size and transmission time, as illustrated in

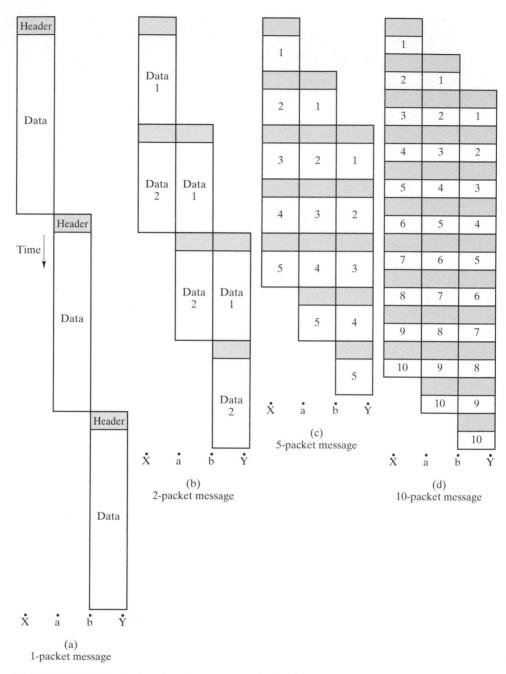

**FIGURE 9.2**   Effect of packet size on transmission time.

Figure 9.2. In this example, it is assumed that there is a virtual circuit from station *X* through nodes *a* and *b* to station *Y*. The message to be sent comprises 30 octets, and each packet contains 3 octets of control information, which is placed at the beginning of each packet and is referred to as a *header*. If the entire message is sent as a single packet of 33 octets (3 octets of header plus 30 octets of data), then the packet is first transmitted from station $X$ to node $a$ (Figure 9.2a). When the entire packet is received, it can then be transmitted from $a$ to $b$. When the entire packet is received at node $b$, it is then transferred to station $Y$. The total transmission time at the nodes is 99 octet-times (33 octets $\times$ 3 packet transmissions).

Suppose now that we break up the message into two packets, each containing 15 octets of the message and, of course, 3 octets each of header or control information. In this case, node $a$ can begin transmitting the first packet as soon as it has arrived from $X$, without waiting for the second packet. Because of this overlap in transmission, the total transmission time drops to 72 octet-times. By breaking the message up into 5 packets, each intermediate node can begin transmission even sooner and the savings in time is greater, with a total of 63 octet-times. However, this process of using more and smaller packets eventually results in increased, rather than reduced, delay as illustrated in Figure 9.2d; this is because each packet contains a fixed amount of header, and more packets means more of these headers. Furthermore, the example does not show the processing and queuing delays at each node. These delays are also greater when more packets are handled for a single message. However, we will see in Chapter 11 that an extremely small packet size (53 octets) can result in an efficient network design.

## Comparison of Circuit Switching and Packet Switching

Having looked at the internal operation of packet switching, we can now return to a comparison of this technique with circuit switching. We first look at the important issue of performance, and then examine other characteristics.

### Performance

A simple comparison of circuit switching and the two forms of packet switching are provided in Figure 9.3. The figure depicts the transmission of a message across four nodes, from a source station attached to node 1 to a destination station attached to node 4. In this figure, we are concerned with three types of delay:

- **Propagation delay.** The time it takes a signal to propagate from one node to the next. This time is generally negligible. The speed of electromagnetic signals through a wire medium, for example, is typically $2 \times 10^8$ m/s.
- **Transmission time.** The time it takes for a transmitter to send out a block of data. For example, it takes 1 s to transmit a 10,000-bit block of data onto a 10-kbps line.
- **Node delay.** The time it takes for a node to perform the necessary processing as it switches data.

For circuit switching, there is a certain amount of delay before the message can be sent. First, a call request signal is sent through the network in order to set up a connection to the destination. If the destination station is not busy, a call-accepted signal returns. Note that a processing delay is incurred at each node during the call request; this time is spent at each node setting up the route of the connection. On

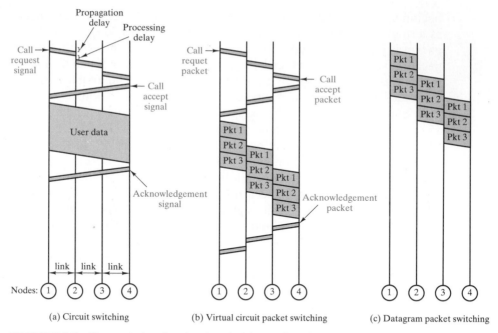

**FIGURE 9.3** Event timing for circuit switching and packet switching.

the return, this processing is not needed because the connection is already set up; once it is set up, the message is sent as a single block, with no noticeable delay at the switching nodes.

Virtual-circuit packet switching appears quite similar to circuit switching. A virtual circuit is requested using a call-request packet, which incurs a delay at each node. The virtual circuit is accepted with a call-accept packet. In contrast to the circuit-switching case, the call acceptance also experiences node delays, even though the virtual circuit route is now established; the reason is that this packet is queued at each node and must wait its turn for retransmission. Once the virtual circuit is established, the message is transmitted in packets. It should be clear that this phase of the operation can be no faster than circuit switching, for comparable networks; this is because circuit switching is an essentially transparent process, providing a constant data rate across the network. Packet switching involves some delay at each node in the path; worse, this delay is variable and will increase with increased load.

Datagram packet switching does not require a call setup. Thus, for short messages, it will be faster than virtual-circuit packet switching and perhaps circuit switching. However, because each individual datagram is routed independently, the processing for each datagram at each node may be longer than for virtual-circuit packets. Thus, for long messages, the virtual-circuit technique may be superior.

Figure 9.3 is intended only to suggest what the relative performance of the techniques might be; however, actual performance depends on a host of factors, including the size of the network, its topology, the pattern of load, and the characteristics of typical exchanges.

**TABLE 9.1**  Comparison of communication switching techniques.

| Circuit switching | Datagram packet switching | Virtual-circuit packet switching |
|---|---|---|
| Dedicated transmission path | No dedicated path | No dedicated path |
| Continuous transmission of data | Transmission of packets | Transmission of packets |
| Fast enough for interactive | Fast enough for interactive | Fast enough for interactive |
| Messages are not stored | Packets may be stored until delivered | Packets stored until delivered |
| The path is established for entire conversation | Route established for each packet | Route established for entire conversation |
| Call setup delay; negligible transmission delay | Packet transmission delay | Call setup delay; packet transmission delay |
| Busy signal if called party busy | Sender may be notified if packet not delivered | Sender notified of connection denial |
| Overload may block call setup; no delay for established calls | Overload increases packet delay | Overload may block call setup; increases packet delay |
| Electromechanical or computerized switching nodes | Small switching nodes | Small switching nodes |
| User responsible for message loss protection | Network may be responsible for individual packets | Network may be responsible for packet sequences |
| Usually no speed or code conversion | Speed and code conversion | Speed and code conversion |
| Fixed bandwidth transmission | Dynamic use of bandwidth | Dynamic use of bandwidth |
| No overhead bits after call setup | Overhead bits in each packet | Overhead bits in each packet |

## Other Characteristics

Besides performance, there are a number of other characteristics that may be considered in comparing the techniques we have been discussing. Table 9.1 summarizes the most important of these. Most of these characteristics have already been discussed. A few additional comments follow.

As was mentioned, circuit switching is essentially a transparent service. Once a connection is established, a constant data rate is provided to the connected stations; this is not the case with packet switching, which typically introduces variable delay, so that data arrive in a choppy manner. Indeed, with datagram packet switching, data may arrive in a different order than they were transmitted.

An additional consequence of transparency is that there is no overhead required to accommodate circuit switching. Once a connection is established, the analog or digital data are passed through, as is, from source to destination. For packet switching, analog data must be converted to digital before transmission; in addition, each packet includes overhead bits, such as the destination address.

### External and Internal Operation

One of the most important characteristics of a packet-switching network is whether it uses datagrams or virtual circuits. Actually, there are two dimensions of this characteristic, as illustrated in Figure 9.4. At the interface between a station and a network node, a network may provide either a connection-oriented or connectionless service. With a connection-oriented service, a station performs a call request to set up a logical connection to another station. All packets presented to the network are identified as belonging to a particular logical connection and are numbered sequentially. The network undertakes to deliver packets in sequence-number order. The logical connection is usually referred to as a virtual circuit, and the connection-oriented service is referred to as an *external virtual-circuit service*; unfortunately, this external service is distinct from the concept of *internal virtual-circuit operation*, as we shall see. An important example of an external virtual circuit service is X.25, which is examined in Section 9.4.

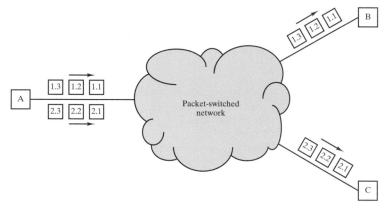

(a) External virtual circuit. A logical connection is set up between two stations. Packets are labeled with a virtual circuit number and a sequence number. Packets arrive in sequence.

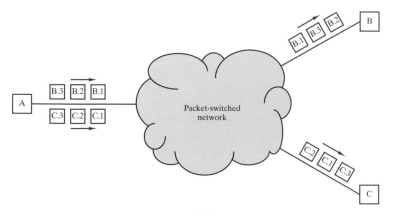

(b) External diagram. Each packet is transmitted independently. Packets are labeled with a destination address and may arrive out of sequence.

**FIGURE 9.4**   External and internal virtual circuits and datagrams. (*continued on next page*)

With connectionless service, the network only agrees to handle packets independently, and may not deliver them in order or reliably. This type of service is sometimes known as an *external datagram service*; again, this concept is distinct from that of *internal datagram operation*. Internally, the network may actually construct a fixed route between endpoints (virtual circuit), or it may not (datagram).

These internal and external design decisions need not coincide:

- **External virtual circuit, internal virtual circuit.** When the user requests a virtual circuit, a dedicated route through the network is constructed. All packets follow that same route.
- **External virtual circuit, internal datagram.** The network handles each packet separately. Thus, different packets for the same external virtual circuit may take different routes. However, the network buffers packets at the destination node, if necessary, so that they are delivered to the destination station in the proper order.
- **External datagram, internal datagram.** Each packet is treated independently from both the user's and the network's point of view.
- **External datagram, internal virtual circuit.** The external user does not see any connections, as it simply sends packets one at a time. The network, however, sets up a logical connection between stations for packet delivery and may

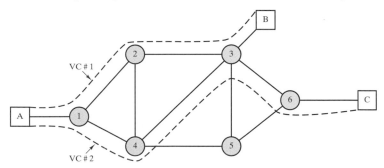

(c) Internal virtual circuit. A route for packets between two stations is defined and labeled. All packets for that virtual circuit follow the same route and arrive in sequence.

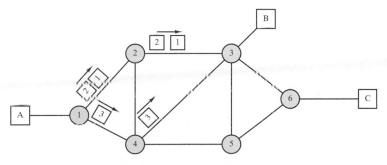

(d) Internal datagram. Each packet is treated independently by the network. Packets are labeled with a destination address and may arrive at the destination node out of sequence.

**FIGURE 9.4** (*continued*)

leave such connections in place for an extended period, so as to satisfy anticipated future needs.

The question arises as to the choice of virtual circuits or datagrams, both internally and externally. This will depend on the specific design objectives for the communication network and the cost factors that prevail.

We have already made some comments concerning the relative merits of internal datagram versus virtual-circuit operation. With respect to external service, we can make the following observations.

- The datagram service, coupled with internal datagram operation, allows for efficient use of the network; no call setup and no need to hold up packets while a packet in error is retransmitted. This latter feature is desirable in some real-time applications.
- The virtual-circuit service can provide end-to-end sequencing and error control; this service is attractive for supporting connection-oriented applications, such as file transfer and remote-terminal access.

In practice, the virtual-circuit service is much more common than the datagram service. The reliability and convenience of a connection-oriented service is seen as more attractive than the benefits of the datagram service.

## 9.2  ROUTING

One of the most complex and crucial aspects of packet-switching network design is routing. This section begins with a survey of key characteristics that can be used to classify routing strategies. Then, some specific routing strategies are discussed.

The principles described in this section are also applicable to internetwork routing, discussed in Part IV.

### Characteristics

The primary function of a packet-switching network is to accept packets from a source station and deliver them to a destination station. To accomplish this, a path or route through the network must be determined; generally, more than one route is possible. Thus, a routing function must be performed. The requirements for this function include

- Correctness
- Simplicity
- Robustness
- Stability
- Fairness
- Optimality
- Efficiency

The first two items on the list are self-explanatory. Robustness has to do with the ability of the network to deliver packets via some route in the face of localized failures and overloads. Ideally, the network can react to such contingencies without the loss of packets or the breaking of virtual circuits. The designer who seeks robustness must cope with the competing requirement for stability. Techniques that react to changing conditions have an unfortunate tendency to either react too slowly to events or to experience unstable swings from one extreme to another. For example, the network may react to congestion in one area by shifting most of the load to a second area. Now the second area is overloaded and the first is underutilized, causing a second shift. During these shifts, packets may travel in loops through the network.

A tradeoff also exists between fairness and optimality. Some performance criteria may give higher priority to the exchange of packets between nearby stations compared to an exchange between distant stations. This policy may maximize average throughput but will appear unfair to the station that primarily needs to communicate with distant stations.

Finally, any routing technique involves some processing overhead at each node and often a transmission overhead as well, both of which impair network efficiency. The penalty of such overhead needs to be less than the benefit accrued based on some reasonable metric, such as increased robustness or fairness.

With these requirements in mind, we are in a position to assess the various design elements that contribute to a routing strategy. Table 9.2 lists these elements. Some of these categories overlap or are dependent on one another. Nevertheless, an examination of this list serves to clarify and organize routing concepts.

**TABLE 9.2**  Elements of routing techniques for packet-switching networks.

| | |
|---|---|
| Performance criteria | Network information source |
| Number of hops | None |
| Cost | Local |
| Delay | Adjacent node |
| Throughput | Nodes along route |
| | All nodes |
| Decision time | |
| Packet (datagram) | Network information update timing |
| Session (virtual circuit) | Continuous |
| | Periodic |
| Decision place | Major load change |
| Each node (distributed) | Topology change |
| Central node (centralized) | |
| Originating node (source) | |

## Performance Criteria

The selection of a route is generally based on some performance criterion. The simplest criterion is to choose the minimum-hop route (one that passes through the least number of nodes) through the network; this is an easily measured criterion and should minimize the consumption of network resources. A generalization of the minimum-hop criterion is least-cost routing. In this case, a cost is associated with each link, and, for any pair of attached stations, the route through the network that accumulates the least cost is sought. For example, Figure 9.5 illustrates a net-

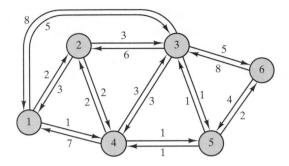

**FIGURE 9.5** Example packet-switched network.

work in which the two arrowed lines between a pair of nodes represent a link between this nodes, and the corresponding numbers represent the current link cost in each direction. The shortest path (fewest hops) from node 1 to node 6 is 1-3-6 (cost = 5 + 5 = 10), but the least-cost path is 1-4-5-6 (cost = 1 + 1 + 2 = 4). Costs are assigned to links to support one or more design objectives. For example, the cost could be inversely related to the data rate (i.e., the higher the data rate on a link, the lower the assigned cost of the link) or the current queuing delay on the link. In the first case, the least-cost route should provide the highest throughput. In the second case, the least-cost route should minimize delay.

In either the minimum-hop or least-cost approach, the algorithm for determining the optimum route for any pair of stations is relatively straightforward, and the processing time would be about the same for either computation. Because the least-cost criterion is more flexible, it is more common than the minimum-hop criterion.

Several least-cost routing algorithms are in common use. These are described in Appendix 9A.

### Decision Time and Place

Routing decisions are made on the basis of some performance criterion. Two key characteristics of the decision are the time and place that the decision is made.

Decision time is determined by whether the routing decision is made on a packet or virtual-circuit basis. When the internal operation of the network is datagram, a routing decision is made individually for each packet. For internal virtual-circuit operation, a routing decision is made at the time the virtual circuit is established. In the simplest case, all subsequent packets using that virtual circuit follow the same route. In more sophisticated network designs, the network may dynamically change the route assigned to a particular virtual circuit in response to changing conditions (e.g., overload or failure of a portion of the network).

The term *decision place* refers to which node or nodes in the network are responsible for the routing decision. Most common is distributed routing, in which each node has the responsibility of selecting an output link for routing packets as they arrive. For centralized routing, the decision is made by some designated node, such as a network control center. The danger of this latter approach is that the loss of the network control center may block operation of the network. The distributed approach is perhaps more complex, but is also more robust. A third alternative, used in some networks, is source routing. In this case, the routing decision is actually made by the source station rather than by a network node, and is then communicated to the network; this allows the user to dictate a route through the network that meets criteria local to that user.

The decision time and decision place are independent design variables. For example, in Figure 9.5, suppose that the decision place is each node and that the values depicted are the costs at a given instant in time; the costs, though, may change. If a packet is to be delivered from node 1 to node 6, it might follow the route 1-4-5-6, with each leg of the route determined locally by the transmitting node. Now let the values change such that 1-4-5-6 is no longer the optimum route. In a datagram network, the next packet may follow a different route, again determined by each node along the way, In a virtual-circuit network, each node will remember the routing decision that was made when the virtual circuit was established, and will simply pass on the packets without making a new decision.

## Network Information Source and Update Timing

Most routing strategies require that decisions be based on knowledge of the topology of the network, traffic load, and link cost. Surprisingly, some strategies use no such information and yet manage to get packets through; flooding and some random strategies (discussed below) are in this category.

With distributed routing, in which the routing decision is made by each node, the individual node may make use of only local information, such as the cost of each outgoing link. Each node might also collect information from adjacent (directly connected) nodes, such as the amount of congestion experienced at that node. Finally, there are algorithms in common use that allow the node to gain information from all nodes on any potential route of interest. In the case of centralized routing, the central node typically makes use of information obtained from all nodes.

A related concept is that of information update timing, which is a function of both the information source and the routing strategy. Clearly, if no information is used (as in flooding), there is no information to update. If only local information is used, the update is essentially continuous—that is, an individual node always knows its local conditions. For all other information source categories (adjacent nodes, all nodes), update timing depends on the routing strategy. For a fixed strategy, the information is never updated. For an adaptive strategy, information is updated from time to time to enable the routing decision to adapt to changing conditions.

As you might expect, the more information available, and the more frequently it is updated, the more likely the network is to make good routing decisions. On the other hand, the transmission of that information consumes network resources.

## Routing Strategies

A large number of routing strategies have evolved for dealing with the routing requirements of packet-switching networks; many having these strategies are also applied to internetwork routing, which we cover in Part IV. In this section, we survey four key strategies: fixed, flooding, random, and adaptive.

## Fixed Routing

For fixed routing, a route is selected for each source-destination pair of nodes in the network. Either of the least-cost routing algorithms described in Appendix 9A could be used. The routes are fixed, with the exception that they might change if there is movement in the topology of the network. Thus, the link costs used in designing routes cannot be based on any dynamic variable such as traffic. They could, however, be based on expected traffic or capacity.

Figure 9.6 suggests how fixed routing might be implemented. A central routing matrix is created, to be stored perhaps at a network control center. The matrix shows, for each source-destination pair of nodes, the identity of the next node on the route.

Note that it is not necessary to store the complete route for each possible pair of nodes. Rather, it is sufficient to know, for each pair of nodes, the identity of the first node on the route; to see this, suppose that the least-cost route from $X$ to $Y$ begins with the $X$-$A$ link. Call the remainder of the route $R_1$; this is the part from $A$

**CENTRAL ROUTING DIRECTORY**

| | | | From Node | | | | |
|---|---|---|---|---|---|---|---|
| | | 1 | 2 | 3 | 4 | 5 | 6 |
| | 1 | — | 1 | 5 | 1 | 4 | 5 |
| | 2 | 2 | — | 2 | 2 | 4 | 5 |
| **To** | 3 | 4 | 3 | — | 5 | 3 | 5 |
| **Node** | 4 | 4 | 4 | 5 | — | 4 | 5 |
| | 5 | 4 | 4 | 5 | 5 | — | 5 |
| | 6 | 4 | 4 | 5 | 5 | 6 | — |

| Node 1 Directory | | Node 2 Directory | | Node 3 Directory | |
|---|---|---|---|---|---|
| Destination | Next Node | Destination | Next Node | Destination | Next Node |
| 2 | 2 | 1 | 1 | 1 | 5 |
| 3 | 4 | 3 | 3 | 2 | 2 |
| 4 | 4 | 4 | 4 | 4 | 5 |
| 5 | 4 | 5 | 4 | 5 | 5 |
| 6 | 4 | 6 | 4 | 6 | 5 |

| Node 4 Directory | | Node 5 Directory | | Node 6 Directory | |
|---|---|---|---|---|---|
| Destination | Next Node | Destination | Next Node | Destination | Next Node |
| 1 | 1 | 1 | 4 | 1 | 5 |
| 2 | 2 | 2 | 4 | 2 | 5 |
| 3 | 5 | 3 | 3 | 3 | 5 |
| 5 | 5 | 4 | 4 | 4 | 5 |
| 6 | 5 | 6 | 6 | 5 | 5 |

**FIGURE 9.6** Fixed routing (using Figure 9.5).

to $Y$. Define $R_2$ as the least-cost route from $A$ to $Y$. Now, if the cost of $R_1$ is greater than that of $R_2$, then the $X$-$Y$ route can be improved by using $R_2$ instead. If the cost of $R_1$ is less than $R_2$, then $R_2$ is not the least-cost route from $A$ to $Y$. Therefore, $R_1 = R_2$. Thus, at each point along a route, it is only necessary to know the identity of the next node, not the entire route. In our example, the route from node 1 to node 6 begins by going through node 4. Again, consulting the matrix, the route from node 4 to node 6 goes through node 5. Finally, the route from node 5 to node 6 is a direct link to node 6. The complete route, then, from node 1 to node 6 is 1-4-5-6.

From this overall matrix, routing tables can be developed and stored at each node. From the reasoning in the preceding paragraph, it follows that each node need only store a single column of the routing directory. The node's directory shows the next node to take for each destination.

With fixed routing, there is no difference between routing for datagrams and virtual circuits. All packets from a given source to a given destination follow the same route. The advantage of fixed routing is its simplicity, and it should work well in a reliable network with a stable load. Its disadvantage is its lack of flexibility; it does not react to network congestion or failures.

A refinement to fixed routing that would accommodate link and node outages would be to supply the nodes with an alternate next node for each destination. For example, the alternate next nodes in the node 1 directory might be 4, 3, 2, 3, 3.

## Flooding

Another simple routing technique is flooding. This technique requires no network information whatsoever, and works as follows. A packet is sent by a source node to every one of its neighbors. At each node, an incoming packet is retransmitted on all outgoing links except for the link on which it arrived. For example, if node 1 in Figure 9.5 has a packet to send to node 6, it sends a copy of that packet (with a destination address of 6), to nodes 2, 3, and 4. Node 2 will send a copy to nodes 3 and 4. Node 4 will send a copy to nodes 2, 3, and 5. And so it goes. Eventually, a number of copies of the packet will arrive at node 6. The packet must have some unique identifier (e.g., source node and sequence number, or virtual-circuit number and sequence number) so that node 6 knows to discard all but the first copy.

Unless something is done to stop the incessant retransmission of packets, the number of packets in circulation just from a single source packet grows without bound; one way to prevent this is for each node to remember the identity of those packets it has already retransmitted. When duplicate copies of the packet arrive, they are discarded. A simpler technique is to include a hop count field with each packet. The count can originally be set to some maximum value, such as the diameter (length of the longest minimum-hop path through the network) of the network. Each time a node passes on a packet, it decrements the count by one. When the count reaches zero, the packet is discarded.

An example of the latter tactic is shown in Figure 9.7. A packet is to be sent from node 1 to node 6 and is assigned a hop count of 3. On the first hop, three copies of the packet are created. For the second hop of all these copies, a total of nine copies are created. One of these copies reaches node 6, which recognizes that it is the intended destination and does not retransmit. However, the other nodes generate a total of 22 new copies for their third and final hop. Note that if a node is not

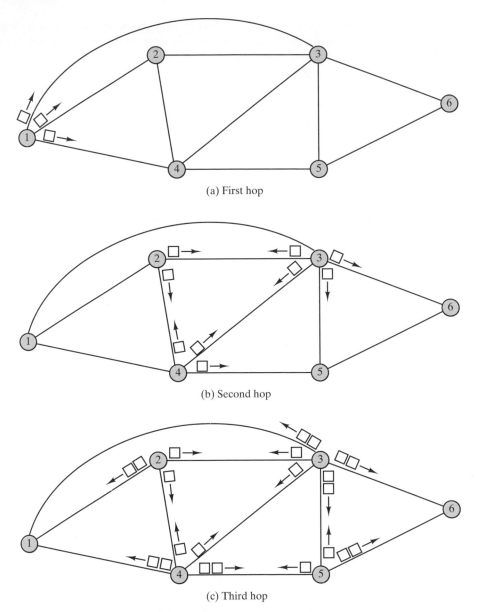

(a) First hop

(b) Second hop

(c) Third hop

**FIGURE 9.7** Flooding example (hop count = 3).

keeping track of the packet identifier, it may generate multiple copies at this third stage. All packets received from the third hop are discarded. In all, node 6 has received four additional copies of the packet.

The flooding technique has three remarkable properties:

- All possible routes between source and destination are tried. Thus, no matter what link or node outages have occurred, a packet will always get through if at least one path between source and destination exists.

- Because all routes are tried, at least one copy of the packet to arrive at the destination will have used a minimum-hop route.
- All nodes that are directly or indirectly connected to the source node are visited.

Because of the first property, the flooding technique is highly robust and could be used to send emergency messages. An example application is a military network that is subject to extensive damage. Because of the second property, flooding might be used to initially set up the route for a virtual circuit. The third property suggests that flooding can be useful for the dissemination of important information to all nodes; we will see that it is used in some schemes to disseminate routing information.

The principal disadvantage of flooding is the high traffic load that it generates, which is directly proportional to the connectivity of the network.

## Random Routing

Random routing has the simplicity and robustness of flooding with far less traffic load. With random routing, a node selects only one outgoing path for retransmission of an incoming packet. The outgoing link is chosen at random, excluding the link on which the packet arrived. If all links are equally likely to be chosen, then a node may simply utilize outgoing links in a round-robin fashion.

A refinement of this technique is to assign a probability to each outgoing link and to select the link based on that probability. The probability could be based on data rate, in which case we have

$$P_i = \frac{R_i}{\Sigma_j R_j}$$

where

$P_i$ = probability of selecting link $i$
$R_i$ = data rate on link $i$

The sum is taken over all candidate outgoing links. This scheme should provide good traffic distribution. Note that the probabilities could also be based on fixed link costs.

Like flooding, random routing requires the use of no network information. Because the route taken is random, the actual route will typically not be the least-cost route nor the minimum-hop route. Thus, the network must carry a higher than optimum traffic load, although not nearly as high as for flooding.

## Adaptive Routing

In virtually all packet-switching networks, some sort of adaptive routing technique is used. That is, the routing decisions that are made change as conditions on the network change. The principle conditions that influence routing decisions are

- **Failure.** When a node or trunk fails, it can no longer be used as part of a route.
- **Congestion.** When a particular portion of the network is heavily congested,

it is desirable to route packets around, rather than through, the area of congestion.

For adaptive routing to be possible, information about the state of the network must be exchanged among the nodes. There is a tradeoff here between the quality of the information and the amount of overhead. The more information that is exchanged, and the more frequently it is exchanged, the better will be the routing decisions that each node makes. On the other hand, this information is itself a load on the network, causing a performance degradation.

There are several drawbacks associated with the use of adaptive routing:

- The routing decision is more complex; therefore, the processing burden on network nodes increases.
- In most cases, adaptive strategies depend on status information that is collected at one place but used at another; therefore, the traffic burden on the network increases.
- An adaptive strategy may react too quickly, causing congestion-producing oscillation; if it reacts too slowly, the strategy will be irrelevant.

Despite these real dangers, adaptive routing strategies are by far the most prevalent, for two reasons:

- An adaptive routing strategy can improve performance, as seen by the network user.
- An adaptive routing strategy can aid in congestion control, as discussed later.

These benefits may or may not be realized, depending on the soundness of the design and the nature of the load. By and large, it is an extraordinarily complex task to perform properly. As demonstration of this, most major packet-switching networks, such as ARPANET and its successors, TYMNET, and those developed by IBM and DEC, have endured at least one major overhaul of their routing strategy.

A convenient way to classify adaptive routing strategies is on the basis of information source: local, adjacent nodes, all nodes. An example of an adaptive routing strategy that relies only on local information is one in which a node routes each packet to the outgoing link with the shortest queue length, $Q$. This would have the effect of balancing the load on outgoing links. However, some outgoing links may not be headed in the correct general direction. We can improve matters by also taking into account preferred direction, much as with random routing. In this case, each link emanating from the node would have a bias $B_i$, for each destination $i$. For each incoming packet headed for node $i$, the node would choose the outgoing link that minimizes $Q + B_i$. Thus, a node would tend to send packets in the right direction, with a concession made to current traffic delays.

As an example, Figure 9.8 shows the status of node 4 of Figure 9.5 at a certain point in time. Node 4 has links to four other nodes. A fair number of packets have been arriving and a backlog has built up, with a queue of packets waiting for each of the outgoing links. A packet arrives from node 1 destined for node 6. To which outgoing link should the packet be routed? Based on current queue lengths and the

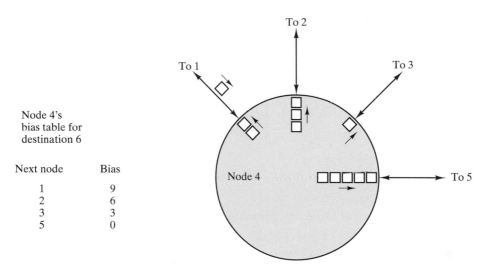

Node 4's
bias table for
destination 6

| Next node | Bias |
|-----------|------|
| 1 | 9 |
| 2 | 6 |
| 3 | 3 |
| 5 | 0 |

**FIGURE 9.8** Example of isolated adaptive routing.

values of bias $(B_6)$ for each outgoing link, the minimum value of $Q + B_6$ is 4, on the link to node 3. Thus, node 4 routes the packet through node 3.

Adaptive schemes based only on local information are rarely used because they do not exploit easily available information. Strategies based on information from adjacent nodes or all nodes are commonly found. Both take advantage of information that each node has about delays and outages that it experiences. Such adaptive strategies can be either distributed or centralized. In the distributed case, each node exchanges delay information with other nodes. Based on incoming information, a node tries to estimate the delay situation throughout the network, and applies a least-cost routing algorithm. In the centralized case, each node reports its link delay status to a central node, which designs routes based on this incoming information and sends the routing information back to the nodes.

## Examples

In this section, we look at several examples of routing strategies. All of these were initially developed for ARPANET, which is a packet-switching network that was the foundation of the present-day Internet. It is instructive to examine these strategies for several reasons. First, these strategies, and similar ones, are also used in other packet-switching networks, including those developed by DEC and IBM and including a number of networks on the Internet. Second, routing schemes based on the ARPANET work have also been used for internetwork routing the Internet and in private internetworks. And finally, the ARPANET routing scheme evolved in a way that illuminates some of the key design issues related to routing algorithms.

### First Generation

The original routing algorithm, designed in 1969, was a distributed adaptive algorithm using estimated delay as the performance criterion and a version of the

Bellman-Ford algorithm (Appendix 9A). For this algorithm, each node maintains two vectors:

$$D_i = \begin{bmatrix} d_{i1} \\ \cdot \\ \cdot \\ \cdot \\ d_{iN} \end{bmatrix} \qquad S_i = \begin{bmatrix} s_{i1} \\ \cdot \\ \cdot \\ \cdot \\ s_{iN} \end{bmatrix}$$

where

$D_i$ = delay vector for node $i$

$d_{ij}$ = current estimate of minimum delay from node $i$ to node $j$ ($d_{ii} = 0$)

$N$ = number of nodes in the network

$S_i$ = successor node vector for node $i$

$s_{ij}$ = the next node in the current minimum-delay route from $i$ to $j$

Periodically (every 128 ms), each node exchanges its delay vector with all of its neighbors. On the basis of all incoming delay vectors, a node k updates both of its vectors as follows:

$$d_{kj} = \underset{i \in A}{\text{Min}}[d_{ij} + l_{ki}]$$

$$s_{kj} = i \qquad \text{using } i \text{ that minimizes the expression above}$$

where

$A$ = set of neighbor nodes for $k$

$l_{ki}$ = current estimate of delay from $k$ to $i$

Figure 9.9 provides an example of the original ARPANET algorithm, using the network of Figure 9.10. This is the same network as that of Figure 9.5, with some of the link costs having different values (and assuming the same cost in both directions). Figure 9.9a shows the routing table for node 1 at an instant in time that reflects the link costs of Figure 9.10. For each destination, a delay is specified, as well as the next node on the route that produces that delay. At some point, the link costs change to those of Figure 9.5. Assume that node 1's neighbors (nodes 2, 3, and 4) learn of the change before node 1. Each of these nodes updates its delay vector and sends a copy to all of its neighbors, including node 1 (Figure 9.9b). Node 1 discards its current routing table and builds a new one, based solely on the incoming delay vector and its own estimate of link delay to each of its neighbors. The result is shown in Figure 9.9c.

The estimated link delay is simply the queue length for that link. Thus, in building a new routing table, the node will tend to favor outgoing links with shorter queues. This tends to balance the load on outgoing links. However, because queue lengths vary rapidly with time, the distributed perception of the shortest route could

| Desti-nation | Delay | Next node |
|---|---|---|
| 1 | 0 | – |
| 2 | 2 | 2 |
| 3 | 5 | 3 |
| 4 | 1 | 4 |
| 5 | 6 | 3 |
| 6 | 8 | 3 |

$D_1$  $S_1$

| $D_2$ | $D_3$ | $D_4$ |
|---|---|---|
| 3 | 7 | 5 |
| 0 | 4 | 2 |
| 3 | 0 | 2 |
| 2 | 2 | 0 |
| 3 | 1 | 1 |
| 5 | 3 | 3 |

| Desti-nation | Delay | Next node |
|---|---|---|
| 1 | 0 | – |
| 2 | 2 | 2 |
| 3 | 3 | 4 |
| 4 | 1 | 4 |
| 5 | 2 | 4 |
| 6 | 4 | 4 |

$1_{1,2} = 2$
$1_{1,3} = 5$
$1_{1,4} = 1$

(a) Node 1's routing table before update

(b) Delay vectors sent to node 1 from neighbor nodes

(c) Node 1's routing table after update and link costs used in update

**FIGURE 9.9**   Original ARPANET routing algorithm.

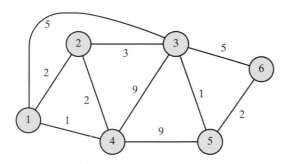

**FIGURE 9.10**   Network for example of Figure 9.9a.

change while a packet is en route; this could lead to a thrashing situation in which a packet continues to seek out areas of low congestion rather than aiming at the destination.

## Second Generation

After some years of experience and several minor modifications, the original routing algorithm was replaced by a quite different one in 1979 [MCQU80]. The major shortcomings of the old algorithm were these:

- The algorithm did not consider line speed, but merely queue length. Thus, higher-capacity links were not given the favored status they deserved.
- Queue length is, in any case, an artificial measure of delay, as some variable amount of processing time elapses between the arrival of a packet at a node and its placement in an outbound queue.
- The algorithm was not very accurate. In particular, it responded slowly to congestion and delay increases.

The new algorithm is also a distributed adaptive one, using delay as the performance criterion, but the differences are significant. Rather than using queue length as a surrogate for delay, the delay is measured directly. At a node, each incoming packet is timestamped with an arrival time. A departure time is recorded when the packet is transmitted. If a positive acknowledgment is returned, the delay for that packet is recorded as the departure time minus the arrival time plus transmission time and propagation delay. The node must therefore know link data rate and propagation time. If a negative acknowledgment comes back, the departure time is updated and the node tries again, until a measure of successful transmission delay is obtained.

Every 10 seconds, the node computes the average delay on each outgoing link. If there are any significant changes in delay, the information is sent to all other nodes using flooding. Each node maintains an estimate of delay on every network link. When new information arrives, it recomputes its routing table using Dijkstra's algorithm (Appendix 9A).

### Third Generation

Experience with this new strategy indicated that it was more responsive and stable than the old one. The overhead induced by flooding was moderate as each node does this, at most, once every 10 seconds. However, as the load on the network grew, a shortcoming in the new strategy began to appear, and the strategy was revised in 1987 [KHAN89].

The problem with the second strategy is the assumption that the measured packet delay on a link is a good predictor of the link delay encountered after all nodes reroute their traffic based on this reported delay. Thus, it is an effective routing mechanism only if there is some correlation between the reported values and those actually experienced after rerouting. This correlation tends to be rather high under light and moderate traffic loads. However, under heavy loads, there is little correlation. Therefore, immediately after all nodes have made routing updates, the routing tables are obsolete!

As an example, consider a network that consists of two regions with only two links, A and B, connecting the two regions (Figure 9.11). Each route between two nodes in different regions must pass through one of these links. Assume that a situation develops in which most of the traffic is on link A. This will cause the link delay on A to be significant, and, at the next opportunity, this delay value will be reported to all other nodes. These updates will arrive at all nodes at about the same time, and all will update their routing tables immediately. It is likely that this new delay value for link A will be high enough to make link B the preferred choice for most, if not

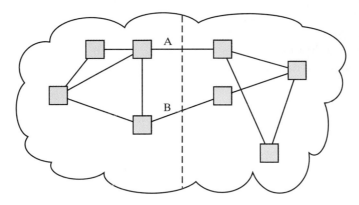

**FIGURE 9.11**   Packet-switching network subject to oscillations.

all, interregion routes. Because all nodes adjust their routes at the same time, most or all interregion traffic shifts at the same time to link B. Now, the link delay value on B will become high, and there will be a subsequent shift to link A. This oscillation will continue until the traffic volume subsides.

There are a number of reasons why this oscillation is undesirable:

1. A significant portion of available capacity is unused at just the time when it is needed most: under heavy traffic load.
2. The overutilization of some links can lead to the spread of congestion within the network. (This will be seen in the discussion of congestion in Section 9.3.)
3. The large swings in measured delay values result in the need for more frequent routing update messages; this increases the load on the network at just the time when the network is already stressed.

The ARPANET designers concluded that the essence of the problem was that every node was trying to obtain the best route for all destinations, and that these efforts conflicted. It was concluded that under heavy loads, the goal of routing should be to give the average route a good path instead of attempting to give all routes the best path.

The designers decided that it was unnecessary to change the overall routing algorithm. Rather, it was sufficient to change the function that calculates link costs. This was done in such a way as to damp routing oscillations and reduce routing overhead. The calculation begins with measuring the average delay over the last 10 seconds. This value is then transformed with the following steps:

1. Using a simple single-server queuing model, the measured delay is transformed into an estimate of link utilization. From queuing theory, utilization can be expressed as a function of delay as follows:

$$\rho = \frac{2(s - t)}{s - 2t}$$

where

$\rho$ = link utilization
$t$ = measured delay
$s$ = service time

The service time was set at the network-wide average packet size (600 bits) divided by the data rate of the link.

2. The result is then smoothed by averaging it with the previous estimate of utilization:

$$U(n + 1) = 0.5 \times \rho(n + 1) + 0.5 \times U(n)$$

where

$U(n)$ = average utilization calculated at sampling time $n$
$\rho(n)$ = link utilization measured at sampling time $n$

Averaging increases the period of routing oscillations, thus reducing routing overhead.

3. The link cost is then set as a function of average utilization that is designed to provide a reasonable estimate of cost while avoiding oscillation. Figure 9.12 indicates the way in which the estimate of utilization is converted into a cost value. The final cost value is, in effect, a transformed value of delay.

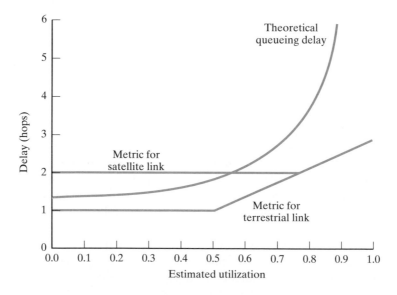

**FIGURE 9.12   ARPANET delay metrics.**

In the figure, delay is normalized to the value achieved on an idle line, which is just propagation delay plus transmission time. One curve on the figure indicates the way in which the actual delay rises as a function of utilization; the increase in delay is due to queuing delay at the node. For the revised algorithm, the cost value is kept at the minimum value until a given level of utilization is reached. This feature has the effect of reducing routing overhead at low traffic levels. Above a certain level of utilization, the cost level is allowed to rise to a maximum value that is equal to three times the minimum value. The effect of this maximum value is to dictate that traffic should not be routed around a heavily utilized line by more than two additional hops.

Note that the minimum threshold is set higher for satellite links; this encourages the use of terrestrial links under conditions of light traffic, as the terrestrial links have much lower propagation delay. Note also that the actual delay curve is much steeper than the transformation curves at high utilization levels. It is this steep rise in link cost that causes all of the traffic on a link to be shed, which in turn causes routing oscillations.

In summary, the revised cost function is keyed to utilization rather than delay. The function resembles a delay-based metric under light loads, as well as a capacity-based metric under heavy loads.

## 9.3 CONGESTION CONTROL

As with routing, the concept of traffic control in a packet-switching network is complex, and a wide variety of approaches have been proposed. The objective here is to maintain the number of packets within the network below the level at which performance falls off dramatically.

To understand the issue involved in congestion control, we need to look at some results from queuing theory. In essence, a packet-switching network is a network of queues. At each node, there is a queue of packets for each outgoing channel. If the rate at which packets arrive and queue up exceeds the rate at which packets can be transmitted, the queue size grows without bound and the delay experienced by a packet goes to infinity. Even if the packet arrival rate is less than the packet transmission rate, queue length will grow dramatically as the arrival rate approaches the transmission rate. We saw this kind of behavior in Figure 7.16. As a rule of thumb, when the line for which packets are queuing becomes more than 80% utilized, the queue length grows at an alarming rate.

Consider the queuing situation at a single packet-switching node, such as is illustrated in Figure 9.13. Any given node has a number of transmission links attached to it: one or more to other packet-switching nodes, and zero or more to host systems. On each link, packets arrive and depart. We can consider that there are two buffers at each link, one to accept arriving packets, and one to hold packets that are waiting to depart. In practice, there might be two fixed-size buffers associated with each link, or there might be a pool of memory available for all buffering activities. In the latter case, we can think of each link having two variable-size

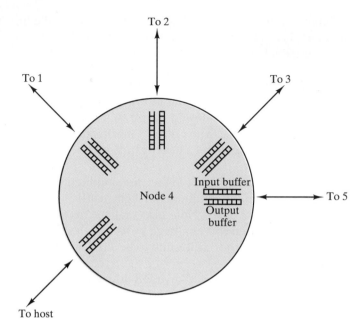

**FIGURE 9.13** Input and output queues at node 4 of Figure 9.5.

buffers associated with it, subject to the constraint that the sum of all buffer sizes is a constant.

In any case, as packets arrive, they are stored in the input buffer of the corresponding link. The node examines each incoming packet to make a routing decision, and then moves the packet to the appropriate output buffer. Packets queued up for output are transmitted as rapidly as possible; this is, in effect, statistical time-division multiplexing. Now, if packets arrive too fast for the node to process them (make routing decisions), or faster than packets can be cleared from the outgoing buffers, then, eventually, packets will arrive for which no memory is available.

When such a saturation point is reached, one of two general strategies can be adopted. The first such strategy is to simply discard any incoming packet for which there is no available buffer space. The alternative is for the node that is experiencing these problems to exercise some sort of flow control over its neighbors so that the traffic flow remains manageable. But, as Figure 9.14 illustrates, each of a node's neighbors is also managing a number of queues. If node 6 restrains the flow of packets from node 5, this causes the output buffer in node 5 for the link to node 6 to fill up. Thus, congestion at one point in the network can quickly propagate throughout a region or throughout all of the network. While flow control is indeed a powerful tool, we need to use it in such a way as to manage the traffic on the entire network.

Figure 9.15 shows the effect of congestion in general terms. Figure 9.15a plots the throughput of a network (number of packets delivered to destination stations) versus the offered load (number of packets transmitted by source stations). Both axes are normalized to the maximum capacity of the network, which can be expressed as the rate at which the network is theoretically capable of handling pack-

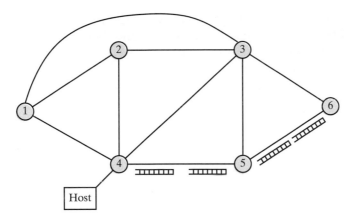

**FIGURE 9.14** The interaction of queues in a packet-switching network.

ets. In the ideal case, throughput and, hence, network utilization increase to accommodate an offered load up to the maximum capacity of the network. Utilization then remains at 100%. The ideal case, of course, requires that all stations somehow know the timing and rate of packets that can be presented to the network, which is impossible. If no congestion control is exercised, we have the curve labeled "uncontrolled." As the load increases, utilization increases for a while. Then as the queue lengths at the various nodes begin to grow, throughput actually drops because the buffers at each node are of finite size. When a node's buffers are full, it must discard packets. Thus, the source stations must retransmit the discarded packets in addition to the new packets; this only exacerbates the situation: As more and more packets are retransmitted, the load on the system grows, and more buffers become saturated. While the system is trying desperately to clear the backlog, stations are

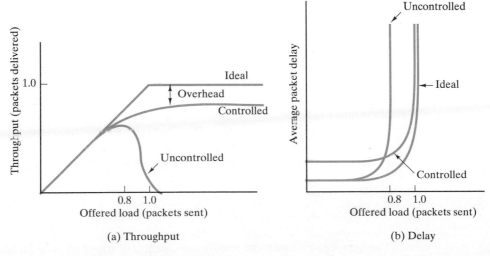

**FIGURE 9.15** The effects of congestion.

pumping old and new packets into the system. Even successfully delivered packets may be retransmitted because it takes so long to acknowledge them: The sender assumes that the packet did not go through. Under these circumstances, the effective capacity of the system is virtually zero.

It is clear that these catastrophic events must be avoided; this is the task of congestion control. The object of all congestion-control techniques is to limit queue lengths at the nodes so as to avoid throughput collapse. This control involves some unavoidable overhead. Thus, a congestion-control technique cannot perform as well as the theoretical ideal. However, a good congestion-control strategy will avoid throughput collapse and maintain a throughput that differs from the ideal by an amount roughly equal to the overhead of the control.

Figure 9.15b points out that no matter what technique is used, the average delay experienced by packets grows without bound as the load approaches the capacity of the system. Note that initially the uncontrolled policy results in less delay than a controlled policy, because of its lack of overhead. However, the uncontrolled policy will saturate at lower load.

A number of control mechanisms for congestion control in packet-switching networks have been suggested and tried. The following are examples:

1. Send a control packet from a congested node to some or all source nodes. This choke packet will have the effect of stopping or slowing the rate of transmission from sources and, hence, limit the total number of packets in the network. This approach requires additional traffic on the network during a period of congestion.

2. Rely on routing information. Routing algorithms, such as ARPANETs, provide link delay information to other nodes, which influences routing decisions. This information could also be used to influence the rate at which new packets are produced. Because these delays are being influenced by the routing decision, they may vary too rapidly to be used effectively for congestion control.

3. Make use of an end-to-end probe packet. Such a packet could be time-stamped to measure the delay between two particular endpoints. This procedure has the disadvantage of adding overhead to the network.

4. Allow packet-switching nodes to add congestion information to packets as they go by. There are two possible approaches here. A node could add such information to packets going in the direction opposite of the congestion. This information quickly reaches the source node, which can reduce the flow of packets into the network. Alternatively, a node could add such information to packets going in the same direction as the congestion. The destination either asks the source to adjust the load or returns the signal back to the source in the packets (or acknowledgments) going in the reverse direction.

## 9.4   X.25

Perhaps the best-known and most widely used protocol standard is X.25, which was originally approved in 1976 and subsequently revised in 1980, 1984, 1988, 1992, and

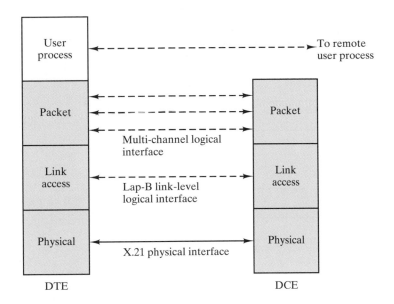

**FIGURE 9.16**   X.25 interface.

1993. The standard specifies an interface between a host system and a packet-switching network. This standard is almost universally used for interfacing to packet-switching networks and is employed for packet switching in ISDN. In this section, a brief overview of the standard is provided.

The standard specifically calls for three layers of functionality (Figure 9.16):

- Physical layer
- Link layer
- Packet layer

These three layers correspond to the lowest three layers of the OSI model (see Figure 1.10). The physical layer deals with the physical interface between an attached station (computer, terminal) and the link that attaches that station to the packet-switching node. The standard refers to user machines as data terminal equipment (DTE) and to a packet-switching node to which a DTE is attached as data circuit-terminating equipment (DCE). X.25 makes use of the physical-layer specification in a standard known as X.21, but, in many cases, other standards, such as EIA-232, are substituted. The link layer provides for the reliable transfer of data across the physical link by transmitting the data as a sequence of frames. The link-layer standard is referred to as LAPB (Link Access Protocol—Balanced). LAPB is a subset of HDLC, described in Chapter 6. The packet layer provides an external virtual-circuit service, and is described in this section.

Figure 9.17 illustrates the relationship between the levels of X.25. User data are passed down to X.25 level 3, which appends control information as a header, creating a *packet*. This control information is used in the operation of the protocol, as we shall see. The entire X.25 packet is then passed down to the LAPB entity, which appends control information at the front and back of the packet, forming an

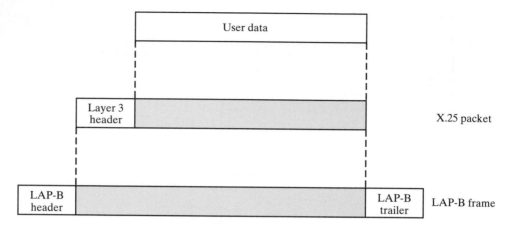

**FIGURE 9.17** User data and X.25 protocol control information.

LAPB *frame*. Again, the control information in the frame is needed for the operation of the LAPB protocol.

### Virtual Circuit Service

With the X.25 packet layer, data are transmitted in packets over external virtual circuits. The virtual-circuit service of X.25 provides for two types of virtual circuit: virtual call and permanent virtual circuit. A *virtual call* is a dynamically established virtual circuit using a call setup and call clearing procedure, explained below. A *permanent virtual circuit* is a fixed, network-assigned virtual circuit. Data transfer occurs as with virtual calls, but no call setup or clearing is required.

Figure 9.18 shows a typical sequence of events in a virtual call. The left-hand part of the figure shows the packets exchanged between user machine *A* and the packet-switching node to which it attaches; the right-hand part shows the packets exchanged between user machine *B* and its node. The routing of packets inside the network is not visible to the user.

The sequence of events is as follows:

1. *A* requests a virtual circuit to *B* by sending a Call-Request packet to *A*'s DCE. The packet includes the source and destination addresses, as well as the virtual-circuit number to be used for this new virtual circuit. Future incoming and outgoing transfers will be identified by this virtual-circuit number.
2. The network routes this call request to *B*'s DCE.
3. *B*'s DCE receives the Call Request and sends an Incoming-Call packet to *B*. This packet has the same format as the Call-Request packet but utilizes a different virtual-circuit number, selected by *B*'s DCE from the set of locally unused numbers.

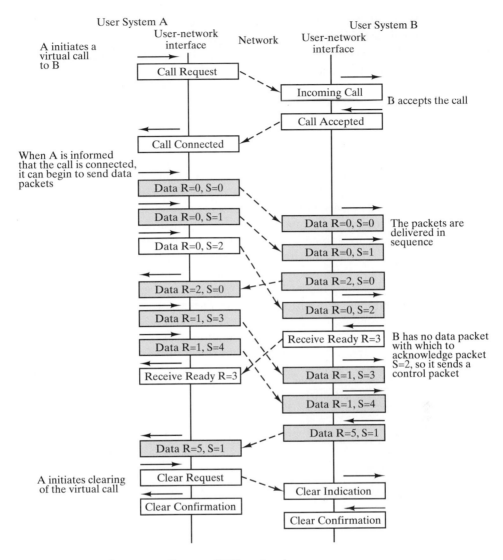

**FIGURE 9.18** Sequence of events: X.25 protocol.

4. *B* indicates acceptance of the call by sending a Call-Accepted packet specifying the same virtual circuit number as that of the Incoming-Call packet.

5. *A*'s DCE receives the Call Accepted and sends a Call-Connected packet to *A*. This packet has the same format as the Call-Accepted packet but the same virtual-circuit number as that of the original Call-Request packet.

6. *A* and *B* send data and control packets to each other using their respective virtual-circuit numbers.

7. *A* (or *B*) sends a Clear-Request packet to terminate the virtual circuit and receives a Clear-Confirmation packet.

8. *B* (or *A*) receives a Clear-Indication packet and transmits a Clear-Confirmation packet.

We now turn to some of the details of the standard.

### Packet Format

Figure 9.19 shows the basic X.25 packet formats. For user data, the data are broken up into blocks of some maximum size, and a 24-bit or 32-bit header is appended to each block to form a **data packet**. The header includes a 12-bit virtual-circuit number (expressed as a 4-bit group number and an 8-bit channel number). The P(S) and P(R) fields support the functions of flow control and error control on a virtual-circuit basis, as explained below. The M and D bits are described below. The Q bit is not defined in the standard, but allows the user to distinguish two types of data.

In addition to transmitting user data, X.25 must transmit control information related to the establishment, maintenance, and termination of virtual circuits. Control information is transmitted in a **control packet**. Each control packet includes the virtual-circuit number, the packet type, which identifies the particular control function, as well as additional control information related to that function. For example, a Call-Request packet includes the following additional fields:

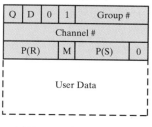

(a) Data packet with 3-bit
sequence numbers

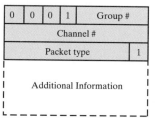

(b) Control packet for virtual calls
with 3-bit sequence numbers

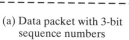

(c) RR, RNR, and REJ packets
with 3-bit sequence numbers

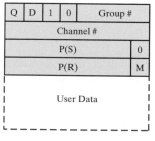

(d) Data packet with 7-bit
sequence numbers

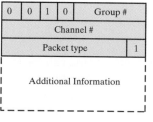

(e) Control packet for virtual calls
with 7-bit sequence numbers

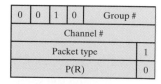

(f) RR, RNR, and REJ packets
with 7-bit sequence numbers

**FIGURE 9.19**   X.25 packet formats.

- Calling DTE address length (4 bits): length of the corresponding address field in 4-bit units.
- Called DTE address length (4 bits): length of the corresponding address field in 4-bit units.
- DTE addresses (variable): the calling and called DTE addresses.
- Facilities: a sequence of facility specifications. Each specification consists of an 8-bit facility code and zero or more parameter codes. An example of a facility is reverse charging.

Table 9.3 lists all of the X.25 packets. Most of these have already been discussed. A brief description of the remainder follow.

A DTE may send an Interrupt packet that bypasses the flow-control procedures for data packets. The interrupt packet is to be delivered to the destination DTE by the network at a higher priority than data packets in transit. An example of the use of this capability is the transmission of a terminal-break character.

The Reset packets provide a facility for recovering from an error by reinitializing a virtual circuit, meaning that the sequence numbers on both ends are set to 0. Any data or interrupt packets in transit are lost. A resct can be triggered by a number of crror conditions, including loss of a packet, sequence number error, congestion, or loss of the network's internal logical connection. In the latter case, the two DCEs must rebuild the internal logical connection to support the still-existing X.25 DTE-DTE virtual circuit.

A more serious error condition is dealt with by a Restart, which terminates all active virtual calls. An example of a condition warranting restart is temporary loss of access to the network.

The Diagnostic packet provides a means to signal certain error conditions that do not warrant reinitialization. The Registration packets are used to invoke and confirm X.25 facilities.

## Multiplexing

Perhaps the most important service provided by X.25 is multiplexing. A DTE is allowed to establish up to 4095 simultaneous virtual circuits with other DTEs over a single physical DTE-DCE link. The DTE can internally assign these circuits in any way it pleases. Individual virtual circuits could correspond to applications, processes, or terminals, for example. The DTE-DCE link provides full-duplex multiplexing; that is, at any time, a packet associated with a given virtual circuit can be transmitted in either direction.

To sort out which packets belong to which virtual circuits, each packet contains a 12-bit virtual-circuit number (expressed as a 4-bit logical group number plus an 8-bit logical channel number). The assignment of virtual-circuit numbers follows the convention depicted in Figure 9.20. Number zero is always reserved for diagnostic packets common to all virtual circuits. Then, contiguous ranges of numbers are allocated for four categories of virtual circuits. Permanent virtual circuits are assigned numbers beginning with 1. The next category is one-way, incoming virtual calls. This means that only incoming calls from the network can be assigned these

**TABLE 9.3** X.25 Packet types and parameters.

| Packet type | | Service | | Parameters |
|---|---|---|---|---|
| From DTE to DCE | From DCE to DTE | VC | PVC | |
| **Call setup and clearing** | | | | |
| Call request | Incoming call | X | | Calling DTE address, called DTE address, facilities, call user data |
| Call accepted | Call connected | X | | Calling DTE address, called DTE address, facilities, call user data |
| Clear request | Clear indication | X | | Clearing cause, diagnostic code, calling DTE address, called DTE address, facilities, clear user data |
| Clear confirmation | Clear confirmation | X | | Calling DTE address, called DTE address, facilities |
| **Data and interrupt** | | | | |
| Data | Data | X | X | — |
| Interrupt | Interrupt | X | X | Interrupt user data |
| Interrupt confirmation | Interrupt confirmation | X | X | — |
| **Flow Control and Reset** | | | | |
| RR | RR | X | X | $P(R)$ |
| RNR | RNR | X | X | $P(R)$ |
| REJ | | X | X | $P(R)$ |
| Reset request | Reset indication | X | X | Resetting cause, diagnostic code |
| Reset confirmation | Reset confirmation | X | X | — |
| **Restart** | | | | |
| Restart request | Restart indication | X | X | Restarting cause, diagnostic code |
| Restart confirmation | Restart confirmation | X | X | — |
| **Diagnostic** | | | | |
| | Diagnostic | X | X | Diagnostic code, diagnostic explanation |
| **Registration** | | | | |
| Registration request | Registration | X | X | DTE address, DCE address, registration |
| | Confirmation | X | X | Cause, diagnostic, DTE address, DCE address, registration |

numbers; the virtual circuit, however, is two-way (full duplex). When a call request comes in, the DCE selects an unused number from this category.

One-way outgoing calls are those initiated by the DTE. In this case, the DTE selects an unused number from among those allocated for these calls. This separa-

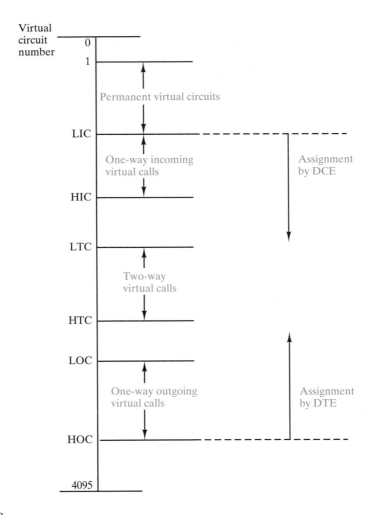

LEGEND
| | | |
|---|---|---|
| LIC = Lowest incoming channel | HTC = Highest two-way channel | Virtual circuit number = |
| HIC = Highest incoming channel | LOC = Lowest outgoing channel | logical group number and |
| LTC = Lowest two-way channel | HOC = Highest outgoing channel | logical channel number |

**FIGURE 9.20** Virtual-circuit number assignment.

tion of categories is intended to avoid the simultaneous selection of the same num ber for two different virtual circuits by the DTE and DCE.

The two-way virtual-call category provides an overflow for allocation shared by DTE and DCE, allowing for peak differences in traffic flow.

## Flow and Error Control

Flow control and error control at the X.25 packet layer are virtually identical in format and procedure to flow control used for HDLC, as described in Chapter 6.

A sliding-window protocol is used. Each data packet includes a send sequence number, P(S), and a receive sequence number, P(R). As a default, 3-bit sequence numbers are used. Optionally, a DTE may request, via the user-facility mechanism, the use of extended 7-bit sequence numbers. As Figure 9.19 indicates, for 3-bit sequence numbers, the third and fourth bits of all data and control packets are 01; for 7-bit sequence numbers, the bits are 10.

P(S) is assigned by the DTE on outgoing packets on a virtual circuit basis; that is, the P(S) of each new outgoing data packet on a virtual circuit is one more than that of the preceding packet, modulo 8 or modulo 128. P(R) contains the number of the next packet expected from the other side of a virtual circuit; this provides for piggybacked acknowledgment. If one side has no data to send, it may acknowledge incoming packets with the Receive-Ready (RR) and Receive-not-Ready (RNR) control packets, with the same meaning as for HDLC. The default window size is 2, but it may be set as high as 7 for 3-bit sequence numbers and as high as 127 for 7-bit sequence numbers.

Acknowledgment (in the form of the P(R) field in the data, RR, or RNR packet), and hence flow control, may have either local or end-to-end significance, based on the setting of the D bit. When D = 0, (the usual case), acknowledgment is exercised between the DTE and the network. This communication is used by the local DCE and/or the network to acknowledge receipt of packets and to control the flow from the DTE into the network. When D = 1, acknowledgments come from the remote DTE.

The basic form of *error control* is go-back-N ARQ. Negative acknowledgment is in the form of a Reject (REJ) control packet. If a node receives a negative acknowledgment, it will retransmit the specified packet and all subsequent packets.

## Packet Sequences

X.25 provides the capability, called a *complete packet sequence*, to identify a contiguous sequence of data packets. This feature has several uses. One important use is by internetworking protocols (described in Part IV) to allow longer blocks of data to be sent across a network with a smaller packet-size restriction without losing the integrity of the block.

To specify this mechanism, X.25 defines two types of packets: A packets and B packets. An *A packet* is one in which the M bit is set to 1, the D bit is set to 0, and the packet is full (equal to the maximum allowable packet length). A *B packet* is any packet that is not an A packet. A complete packet sequence consists of zero or more A packets followed by a B packet. The network may combine this sequence to make a larger packet. The network may also segment a B packet into smaller packets to produce a complete packet sequence.

The way in which the B packet is handled depends on the setting of the M and D bits. If D = 1, an end-to-end acknowledgment is sent by the receiving DTE to the sending DTE. This is, in effect, an acknowledgment of the entire complete packet sequence. If M = 1, there are additional complete packet sequences to follow. This enables the formation of subsequences as part of a larger sequence, so that end-to-end acknowledgment can occur before the end of the larger sequence.

Figure 9.21 shows examples of these concepts. It is the responsibility of the

EXAMPLE PACKET SEQUENCES

EXAMPLE PACKET SEQUENCE
WITH INTERMEDIATE E-E ACK

Original seq.　　　　Combined seq.

| Pkt type | M | D | | Pkt type | M | D |
|----------|---|---|---|----------|---|---|
| A | 1 | 0 ⌐ | | | | |
| A | 1 | 0 ⌐→ | A | 1 | 0 |
| A | 1 | 0 ⌐ | | | | |
| A | 1 | 0 ⌐→ | A | 1 | 0 |
| A | 1 | 0 ⌐ | | | | |
| B | 0 | 1 ⌐→ | B | 0 | 1 |

Segmented seq

| B | 0 | 0 ⌐→ | A | 1 | 0 |
| | | ⌐→ | B | 0 | 0 |

| Pkt type | M | D | |
|----------|---|---|---|
| A | 1 | 0 | |
| A | 1 | 0 | ⎫ |
| A | 1 | 0 | ⎬ * |
| B | 1 | 1 | ⎭ |
| A | 1 | 0 | ⎫ |
| A | 1 | 0 | ⎬ * |
| B | 1 | 1 | ⎭ |
| A | 1 | 0 | ⎫ |
| A | 1 | 0 | ⎬ * |
| A | 1 | 0 | ⎭ |
| B | 0 | 1 | |

end of sequence

*Groups of packets that can be combined

**FIGURE 9.21**　X.25 packet sequences.

DCEs to reconcile the changes in sequence numbering that segmentation and reassembly cause.

## 9.5 RECOMMENDED READING

The literature on packet switching is enormous. Only a few of the worthwhile references are mentioned here. Books with good treatments of this subject include [SPOH93], [BERT92] and [SPRA91]. There is also a large body of literature on performance; good summaries are to be found in [STUC85], [SCHW77], and [KLEI76].

BERT92　Bertsekas, D. and Gallager, R. *Data Networks*. Englewood Cliffs, NJ: Prentice Hall, 1992.

KLEI76　Kleinrock, L. *Queuing Systems, Volume II: Computer Applications*. New York: Wiley, 1976.

SCHW77　Schwartz, M. *Computer-Communication Network Design and Analysis*. Englewood Cliffs, NJ: Prentice Hall, 1977.

SPOH93　Spohn, D. *Data Network Design*. New York: McGraw-Hill, 1994.

SPRA91　Spragins, J., Hammond, J., and Pawlikowski, K. *Telecommunications Protocols and Design*. Reading, MA.: Addison-Wesley, 1991.

STUC85　Stuck, B. and Arthurs, E. *A Computer Communications Network Performance Analysis Primer*. Englewood Cliffs, NJ: Prentice Hall, 1985.

## 9.6 PROBLEMS

**9.1**　Explain the flaw in the following logic:
Packet switching requires control and address bits to be added to each packet. This causes considerable overhead in packet switching. In circuit switching, a transparent circuit is established. No extra bits are needed.
**a.** Therefore, there is no overhead in circuit switching.

b. Because there is no overhead in circuit switching, line utilization must be more efficient than in packet switching.

9.2 Define the following parameters for a switching network:

$N$ = number of hops between two given end systems
$L$ = message length in bits
$B$ = data rate, in bits per second (bps), on all links
$P$ = packet size
$H$ = overhead (header) bits per packet
$S$ = call setup time (circuit switching or virtual circuit) in seconds
$D$ = propagation delay per hop in seconds

a. For $N = 4$, $L = 3200$, $B = 9600$, $P = 1024$, $H = 16$, $S = 0.2$, $D = 0.001$, compute the end-to-end delay for circuit switching, virtual-circuit packet switching, and datagram packet switching. Assume that there are no acknowledgments.

b. Derive general expressions for the three techniques of part (a), taken two at a time (three expressions in all), showing the conditions under which the delays are equal.

9.3 What value of $P$, as a function of $N$, $L$, and $H$, results in minimum end-to-end delay on a datagram network? Assume that $L$ is much larger than $P$, and $D$ is zero.

9.4 Consider a packet-switching network of $N$ nodes, connected by the following topologies:

a. Star: one central node with no attached station; all other nodes attach to the central node.

b. Loop: each node connects to two other nodes to form a closed loop.

c. Fully connected: each node is directly connected to all other nodes.

For each case, give the average number of hops between stations.

9.5 Consider a binary tree topology for a packet-switching network. The root node connects to two other nodes. All intermediate nodes connect to one node in the direction toward the root, and two in the direction away from the root. At the bottom are nodes with just one link back toward the root. If there are $2^N - 1$ nodes, derive an expression for the mean number of hops per packet for large $N$, assuming that trips between all node pairs are equally likely.

9.6 Dijkstra's algorithm, for finding the least-cost path from a specified node $s$ to a specified node $t$, can be expressed in the following program:

```
for n := 1 to N do
    begin
        D[n] := ∞; final[n] := false;  {all nodes are temporarily labeled with ∞}
        pred[n] := 1
    end;
D[s] := 0; final[s] := true;          {node s is permanently labeled with 0}
recent := s;                          {the most recent node to be permanently labeled is s}
path := true;
{initialization over }

while final[t] = false do
begin
    for n := 1 to N do   {find new label}
        if (d[recent, n] <∞) AND (NOT final[n]) then
        {for every immediate successor of recent that is not permanently labeled, do }
            begin {update temporary labels}
                newlabel := D[recent] + d[recent,n];
                if newlabel <D[n] then
                    begin D[n] := newlabel; pred[n] := recent end
                    {re-label n if there is a shorter path via node recent and make
                        recent the predecessor of n on the shortest path from s}
        end;
    temp := ∞;
```

```
for x := 1 to N do {find node with smallest temporary label}
    if (NOT final[x]) AND (D[x] <temp) then
            begin y := x; temp: =D[x] end;
    if temp < ∞ then {there is a path} then
        begin final[y] := true; recent := y end
        {y, the next closest node to s gets permanently labeled}
    else begin path := false; final[t] := true end
end
```

In this program, each node is assigned a temporary label initially. As a final path to a node is determined, it is assigned a permanent label equal to the cost of the path from *s*. Write a similar program for the Bellman-Ford algorithm. Hint: The Bellman-Ford algorithm is often called a label-correcting method, in contrast to Dijkstra's label-setting method.

9.7 In the discussion of Dijkstra's algorithm in Appendix 9A, it is asserted that at each iteration, a new node is added to *M* and that the least-cost path for that new node passes only through nodes already in *M*. Demonstrate that this is true. Hint: Begin at the beginning. Show that the first node added to *M* must have a direct link to the source node. Then show that the second node to *M* must either have a direct link to the source node or a direct link to the first node added to *M*, and so on. Remember that all link costs are assumed nonnegative.

9.8 In the discussion of the Bellman-Ford algorithm in Appendix 9A, it is asserted that at the iteration for which $H = K$, if any path of length $K + 1$ is defined, the first $K$ hops of that path form a path defined in the previous iteration. Demonstrate that this is true.

9.9 In step 3 of Dijkstra's algorithm, the least-cost path values are only updated for nodes not yet in *M*. Is it not possible that a lower-cost path could be found to a node already in *M*? If so, demonstrate by example. If not, provide reasoning as to why not.

9.10 Using Dijkstra's algorithm, generate a least-cost route to all other nodes for nodes 2 through 6 of Figure 9.5. Display the results as in Table 9.4a; do the same for the Bellman-Ford algorithm.

9.11 Apply Dijkstra's routing algorithm to the networks in Figure 9.22 (next page). Provide a table similar to Table 9.4 and a figure similar to Figure 9.9.

9.12 Repeat Problem 9.11 using the Bellman-Ford algorithm.

9.13 Will Dijkstra's algorithm and the Bellman-Ford algorithm always yield the same solutions? Why or why not?

9.14 Both Dijkstra's algorithm and the Bellman-Ford algorithm find the least-cost paths from one node to all other nodes. The Floyd-Warshall algorithm finds the least-cost paths between all pairs of nodes together. Define

$N$ = set of nodes in the network
$d_{ij}$ = link cost from node *i* to node *j*; $d_{ii} = 0$; and $d_{ij} = \infty$ if the nodes are not directly connected
$D^{(n)}_{ij}$ = cost of the least-cost path from node *i* to node *j* with the constraint that only nodes 1, 2, . . . , *n* can be used as intermediate nodes on paths

The algorithm has the following steps:

1. Initialize:
$$D^{(0)}_{ij} = d_{ij}, \text{ for all } i, j, i \neq j$$

2. For $n = 0, 1, \ldots, N - 1$
$$D^{(n+1)}_{ij} = \text{Min}[D^{(n)}_{ij}, D^{(n)}_{i(n+1)} + D^{(n)}_{(n+1)i}] \text{ for all } i \neq j$$

Explain the algorithm in words. Use induction to demonstrate that the algorithm works.

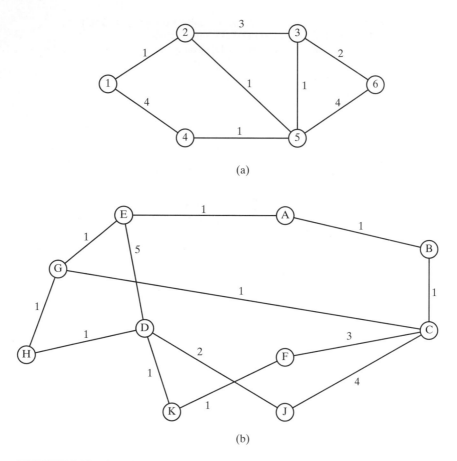

**FIGURE 9.22** Graphs for Problem 9.11.

**9.15** In Figure 9.8, node 1 sends a packet to node 6 using flooding. Counting the transmission of one packet across one link as a load of one, what is the total load generated if
   **a.** Each node discards duplicate incoming packets?
   **b.** A hop count field is used and is initially set to 5?

**9.16** It was shown that flooding can be used to determine the minimum-hop route. Can it be used to determine the minimum delay route?

**9.17** With random routing, only one copy of the packet is in existence at a time. Nevertheless, it would be wise to utilize a hop count field. Why?

**9.18** Another adaptive routing scheme is known as backward learning. As a packet is routed through the network, it carries not only the destination address, but the source address plus a running hop count that is incremented for each hop. Each node builds a routing table that gives the next node and hop count for each destination. How is the packet information used to build the table? What are the advantages and disadvantages of this technique?

**9.19** Build a centralized routing directory for the networks of Problem 9.11.

**9.20** Consider a system using flooding with a hop counter. Suppose that the hop counter is originally set to the "diameter" of the network. When the hop count reaches zero, the packet is discarded, except at its destination. Does this procedure always ensure that a packet will reach its destination if there exists at least one operable path? Why or why not?

9.21   Assuming no malfunction in any of the stations or nodes of a network, is it possible for a packet to be delivered to the wrong destination?

9.22   Flow-control mechanisms are used at both levels 2 and 3 of X.25. Are both necessary, or is this redundant? Explain.

9.23   There is no error-detection mechanism (frame check sequence) in X.25. Isn't this needed to assure that all of the packets are delivered properly?

9.24   When an X.25 DTE and the DCE to which it attaches both decide to put a call through at the same time, a call collision occurs and the incoming call is canceled. When both sides try to clear the same virtual circuit simultaneously, the clear collision is resolved without canceling either request; the virtual circuit in question is cleared. Do you think that simultaneous resets are handled like call collisions or clear collisions? Why?

9.25   In X.25, why is the virtual-circuit number used by one station of two communicating stations different from the virtual-circuit number used by the other station? After all, it is the same full-duplex virtual circuit.

> ## 9A  APPENDIX

### LEAST-COST ALGORITHMS

VIRTUALLY ALL PACKET-SWITCHED networks base their routing decision on some form of least-cost criterion. If the criterion is to minimize the number of hops, each link has a value of 1. More typically, the link value is inversely proportional to the link capacity, proportional to the current load on the link, or some combination of the two. In any case, these link or hop costs are used as input to a least-cost routing algorithm, which can be simply stated as follows:

> Given a network of nodes connected by bidirectional links, where each link has a cost associated with it in each direction, define the cost of a path between two nodes as the sum of the costs of the links traversed. For each pair of nodes, find the path with the least cost.

Note that the cost of a link may differ in its two directions; this would be true, for example, if the cost of a link equaled the length of the queue of packets awaiting transmission from each of the two nodes on the link.

Most least-cost routing algorithms in use in packet-switched networks are variations of one of two common algorithms, known as Dijkstra's algorithm and the Bellman-Ford algorithm.[1] This appendix provides a summary of these two algorithms.

### Dijkstra's Algorithm

Dijkstra's algorithm [DIJK59] can be stated as: Find the shortest paths from a given source node to all other nodes by developing the paths in order of increasing path length. The algorithm proceeds in stages. By the $k$th stage, the shortest paths to the $k$ nodes closest to (least cost away from) the source node have been determined; these nodes are in a set $M$. At stage $(k + 1)$, the node not in $M$ that has the shortest path from the source node is added to $M$. As each node is added to $M$, its path from the source is defined. The algorithm can be formally described as follows. Use the following definitions:

$N$ = set of nodes in the network

$s$ = source node

$M$ = set of nodes so far incorporated by the algorithm

$d_{ij}$ = link cost from node $i$ to node $j$; $d_{ii} = 0$; $d_{ij} = \infty$ if the two nodes are not directly connected; $d_{ij} \geq 0$ if the two nodes are directly connected

$D_n$ = cost of the least-cost path from node $s$ to node $n$ that is currently known to the algorithm

The algorithm has three steps; steps 2 and 3 are repeated until $M = N$. That is, steps 2 and 3 are repeated until final paths have been assigned to all nodes in the network:

1. Initialize:

   $M = \{s\}$         (i.e., the set of nodes so far incorporated consists of only the source node)

   $D_n = d_{sn}$ for $n \neq s$     (i.e., the initial-path costs to neighboring nodes are simply the link costs)

2. Find the neighboring node not in $M$ that has the least-cost path from node $s$ and incorporate that node into $M$: This can be expressed as

---

[1] As we shall see in Part IV, this statement is also true of routing in internetworks.

Find $w \notin M$ such that $D_w = \min_{j \notin M} D_j$
Add $w$ to $M$

3. Update least-cost paths:
$D_n = \min[D_n, D_w + d_{wn}]$ for all $n \notin M$
If the latter term is the minimum, the path from $s$ to $n$ is now the path from $s$ to $w$, concatenated with the link from $w$ to $n$.

One iteration of steps 2 and 3 adds one new node to $M$ and defines the least-cost path from $s$ to that node. That path passes only through nodes that are in $M$; to see this, consider the following line of reasoning. After $k$ iterations, there are $k$ nodes in $M$, and the least-cost path from $s$ to each of these nodes has been defined. Now consider all possible paths from $s$ to nodes not in $M$. Among those paths, there is one of least cost that passes exclusively through nodes in $M$ (see Problem 9.7), ending with a direct link from some node in $M$ to a node not in $M$. This node is added to $M$, and the associated path is defined as the least-cost path for that node.

Table 9.4a shows the result of applying this algorithm to Figure 9.5, using $s = 1$. Note that at each step, the path to each node plus the total cost of that path is generated. After the final iteration, the least-cost path to each node and the cost of that path have been developed. The same procedure can be used with node 2 as source node, and so on.

## Bellman-Ford Algorithm

The Bellman-Ford algorithm [FORD62] can be stated as follows: Find the shortest paths from a given source node subject to the constraint that the paths contain, at most, one link; then find the shortest paths with a constraint of paths of, at most, two links, and so on. This algorithm also proceeds in stages. The algorithm can be formally described as follows. Use the following definitions:

$s$ = source node

$d_{ij}$ = link cost from node $i$ to node $j$; $d_{ii} = 0$; $d_{ij} = \infty$ if the two nodes are not directly connected; $d_{ij} \geq 0$ if the two nodes are directly connected

$h$ = maximum number of links in a path at the current stage of the algorithm

$D_n^{(h)}$ = cost of the least-cost path from node $s$ to node $n$ under the constraint of no more than $h$ links

The algorithm has the following steps, step 2 of which is repeated until none of the costs change:

1. Initialize:

$$D_n^{(0)} = \infty, \text{ for all } n \neq s$$
$$D_s^{(h)} = 0, \text{ for all } h$$

2. For each successive $h \geq 0$:

$$D_n^{(h+1)} = \min_j [D_j^{(h)} + d_{jn}]$$

The path from $s$ to $i$ terminates with the link from $j$ to $i$.

For the iteration of step 2 with $h = K$, and for each destination node $n$, the algorithm compares potential paths from $s$ to $n$ of length $K + 1$ with the path that existed at the end of the previous iteration. If the previous, shorter, path has less cost, then that path is retained. Otherwise, a new path with length $K + 1$ is defined from $s$ to $n$; this path consists of a path of length $K$ from $s$ to some node $j$, plus a direct hop from node $j$ to node $n$. In this case, the path from $s$ to $j$ that is used is the $K$-hop path for $j$ defined in the previous iteration (see Problem 9.8).

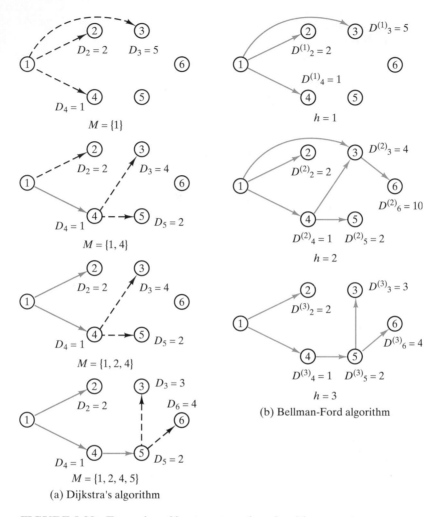

**FIGURE 9.23** Examples of least-cost routing algorithms (based on Table 9.4).

Table 9.4b shows the result of applying this algorithm to Figure 9.5, using $s = 1$. At each step, the least-cost paths with a maximum number of links equal to $h$ are found. After the final iteration, the least-cost path to each node, and the cost of that path, have been developed. The same procedure can be used with node 2 as source node, and so on. Note that the results agree with those obtained using Dijkstra's algorithm. Figure 9.23 illustrate the results of Table 9.4.

## Comparison

One interesting comparison can be made between these two algorithms, having to do with what information needs to be gathered. Consider first the Bellman-Ford algorithm. In step 2, the calculation for node $n$ involves knowledge of the link cost to all neighboring nodes to node $n$ ($d_{jn}$) plus the total path cost to each of those neighboring nodes from a particular source node $s$ ($D_j^{(h)}$). Each node can maintain a set of costs and associated paths for every other node in the network, and can exchange this information with its direct neighbors from time to time. Each node can therefore use the expression in step 2 of the Bellman-Ford algorithm, based only on information from its neighbors and knowledge of its link costs, to

**TABLE 9.4**  Example of least-cost routing algorithms (using Figure 9.5).

### (a) Dijkstra's Algorithm (s = 1)

| Iteration | M | $D_2$ | Path | $D_3$ | Path | $D_4$ | Path | $D_5$ | Path | $D_6$ | Path |
|---|---|---|---|---|---|---|---|---|---|---|---|
| 1 | {1} | 2 | 1 - 2 | 5 | 1 - 3 | 1 | 1 - 4 | ∞ | — | ∞ | — |
| 2 | {1, 4} | 2 | 1 - 2 | 4 | 1 - 4 - 3 | 1 | 1 - 4 | 2 | 1 - 4 - 5 | ∞ | — |
| 3 | {1, 2, 4} | 2 | 1 - 2 | 4 | 1 - 4 - 3 | 1 | 1 - 4 | 2 | 1 - 4 - 5 | ∞ | — |
| 4 | {1, 2, 4, 5} | 2 | 1 - 2 | 3 | 1 - 4 - 5 - 3 | 1 | 1 - 4 | 2 | 1 - 4 - 5 | 4 | 1 - 4 - 5 - 6 |
| 5 | {1, 2, 3, 4, 5} | 2 | 1 - 2 | 3 | 1 - 4 - 5 - 3 | 1 | 1 - 4 | 2 | 1 - 4 - 5 | 4 | 1 - 4 - 5 - 6 |
| 6 | {1, 2, 3, 4, 5, 6} | 2 | 1 - 2 | 3 | 1 - 4 - 5 - 3 | 1 | 1 - 4 | 2 | 1 - 4 - 5 | 4 | 1 - 4 - 5 - 6 |

### (b) Bellman-Ford Algorithm (s = 1)

| h | $D_2^{(h)}$ | Path | $D_3^{(h)}$ | Path | $D_4^{(h)}$ | Path | $D_5^{(h)}$ | Path | $D_6^{(h)}$ | Path |
|---|---|---|---|---|---|---|---|---|---|---|
| 0 | ∞ | — | ∞ | — | ∞ | — | ∞ | — | ∞ | — |
| 1 | 2 | 1 - 2 | 5 | 1 - 3 | 1 | 1 - 4 | ∞ | — | ∞ | — |
| 2 | 2 | 1 - 2 | 4 | 1 - 4 - 3 | 1 | 1 - 4 | 2 | 1 - 4 - 5 | 10 | 1 - 3 - 6 |
| 3 | 2 | 1 - 2 | 3 | 1 - 4 - 5 - 3 | 1 | 1 - 4 | 2 | 1 - 4 - 5 | 4 | 1 - 4 - 5 - 6 |
| 4 | 2 | 1 - 2 | 3 | 1 - 4 - 5 - 3 | 1 | 1 - 4 | 2 | 1 - 4 - 5 | 4 | 1 - 4 - 5 - 6 |

update its costs and paths. On the other hand, consider Dijkstra's algorithm. Step 3 appears to require that each node must have complete topological information about the network. That is, each node must know the link costs of all links in the network. Thus, for this algorithm, information must be exchanged with all other nodes.

Evaluation of the relative merits of the two algorithms should be done with respect to the processing time of the algorithm and the amount of information that must be collected from other nodes in the network. The evaluation will depend on the implementation approach and on the specific implementation.

A final point: Both algorithms are known to converge under static conditions of topology and link costs and will converge to the same solution. If the link costs change over time, the algorithm will attempt to catch up with these changes. However, if the link cost depends on traffic, which in turn depends on the routes chosen, then a feedback condition exists, and instabilities may result.

# CHAPTER 10

# FRAME RELAY

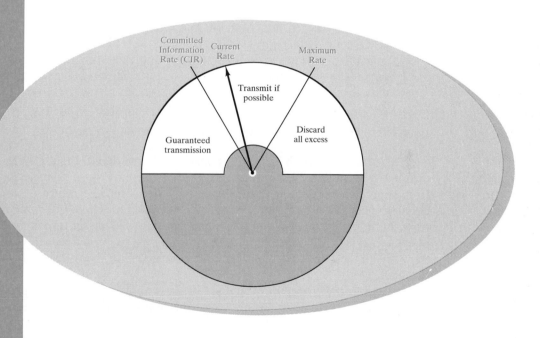

T he most important technical innovation to come out of the standardization work on ISDN is frame relay. Although designed for ISDN, frame relay now enjoys widespread use in a variety of public and private networks that do not follow the ISDN standards.

Frame relay represents a significant advance over traditional packet switching and X.25. We begin the chapter with an overview of the differences between these two approaches. Next, the details of the frame relay scheme are examined. Then, the key issue of congestion control in frame relay networks is discussed. For a discussion of ISDN, see Appendix A.

## 10.1 BACKGROUND

The traditional approach to packet switching makes use of X.25, which not only determines the user-network interface but also influences the internal design of the network. Several key features of the X.25 approach are as follows:

- Call control packets, used for setting up and clearing virtual circuits, are carried on the same channel and the same virtual circuit as data packets. In effect, inband signaling is used.
- Multiplexing of virtual circuits takes place at layer 3.
- Both layer 2 and layer 3 include flow control and error control mechanisms.

The X.25 approach results in considerable overhead. Figure 10.1a indicates the flow of data link frames required for the transmission of a single data packet from source end system to destination end system, and the return of an acknowledgment packet. At each hop through the network, the data link control protocol involves the exchange of a data frame and an acknowledgment frame. Furthermore, at each intermediate node, state tables must be maintained for each virtual circuit to deal with the call management and flow control/error control aspects of the X.25 protocol.

All of this overhead may be justified when there is a significant probability of error on any of the links in the network. This approach may not be the most appropriate for modern digital communication facilities. Today's networks employ reliable digital-transmission technology over high-quality, reliable transmission links, many of which are optical fiber. In addition, with the use of optical fiber and digital transmission, high data rates can be achieved. In this environment, the overhead of X.25 is not only unnecessary, but degrades the effective utilization of the available high data rates.

Frame relaying is designed to eliminate much of the overhead that X.25 imposes on end user systems and on the packet-switching network. The key differences between frame relaying and a conventional X.25 packet-switching service are

- Call control signaling is carried on a separate logical connection from user data. Thus, intermediate nodes need not maintain state tables or process messages relating to call control on an individual per-connection basis.

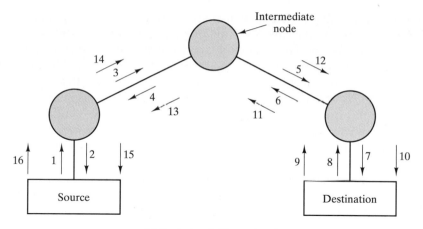

(a) Packet-switching network

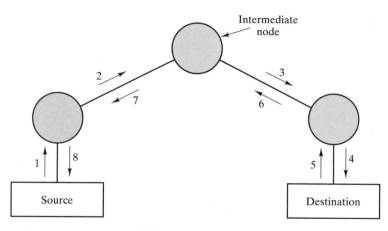

(b) Frame relay network

**FIGURE 10.1**    Packet switching versus frame relay: source sending, destination responding.

- Multiplexing and switching of logical connections take place at layer 2 instead of layer 3, eliminating one entire layer of processing.
- There is no hop-by-hop flow control and error control. End-to-end flow control and error control, if they are employed at all, are the responsibility of a higher layer.

Figure 10.1b indicates the operation of frame relay, in which a single-user data frame is sent from source to destination, and an acknowledgment, generated at a higher layer, is carried back in a frame.

Let us consider the advantages and disadvantages of this approach. The principal potential disadvantage of frame relaying, compared to X.25, is that we have lost the ability to do link-by-link flow and error control. (Although frame relay does not provide end-to-end flow and error control, this is easily provided at a higher layer.) In X.25, multiple virtual circuits are carried on a single physical link, and LAPB is available at the link level for providing reliable transmission from the source to the packet-switching network and from the packet-switching network to the destination. In addition, at each hop through the network, the link control protocol can be used for reliability. With the use of frame relaying, this hop-by-hop link control is lost. However, with the increasing reliability of transmission and switching facilities, this is not a major disadvantage.

The advantage of frame relaying is that we have streamlined the communications process. The protocol functionality required at the user-network interface is reduced, as is the internal network processing. As a result, lower delay and higher throughput can be expected. Studies indicate an improvement in throughput using frame relay, compared to X.25, of an order of magnitude or more [HARB92]. The ITU-T Recommendation I.233 indicates that frame relay is to be used at access speeds up to 2 Mbps.

The ANSI standard T1.606 lists four examples of applications that would benefit from the frame relay service used over a high-speed H channel:

1. *Block-interactive data applications*: An example of a block-interactive application would be high-resolution graphics (e.g., high-resolution videotex, CAD/CAM). The pertinent characteristics of this type of application are low delays and high throughput.

2. *File transfer*: The file transfer application is intended to cater to large file transfer requirements. Transit delay is not as critical for this application as it is, for example, in the first application. High throughput might be necessary in order to produce reasonable transfer times for large files.

3. *Multiplexed low-bit rate*: The multiplexed low-bit-rate application exploits the multiplexing capability of the frame-relaying service in order to provide an economical access arrangement for a large group of low-bit-rate applications. An example of one such low-bit-rate application is given in (4) below. The low-bit-rate sources may be multiplexed onto a channel by an NT function.

4. *Character-interactive traffic*: An example of a character-interactive traffic application is text editing. The main characteristics of this type of application are short frames, low delays, and low throughput.

## 10.2   FRAME RELAY PROTOCOL ARCHITECTURE

Figure 10.2 depicts the protocol architecture to support the frame-mode bearer service. We need to consider two separate planes of operation: a control (C) plane, which is involved in the establishment and termination of logical connections, and a user (U) plane, which is responsible for the transfer of user data between subscribers. Thus, C-plane protocols are between a subscriber and the network, while U-plane protocols provide end-to-end functionality.

### Control Plane

The control plane for frame-mode bearer services is similar to that for common-channel signaling in circuit-switching services, in that a separate logical channel is

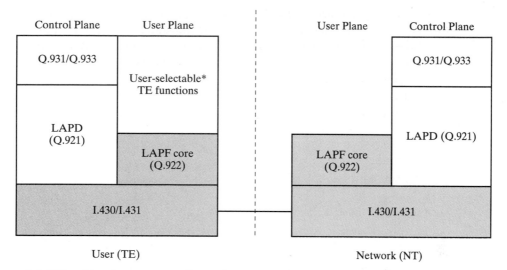

* Additional functions to support flow and error control may be provided. LAPF control is one protocol that may be used.

**FIGURE 10.2** User-network interface protocol architecture.

used for control information. In the case of ISDN, control signaling is done over the D channel, to control the establishment and termination of frame-mode virtual calls on the D, B, and H channels (see Appendix A).

At the data link layer, LAPD (Q.921) is used to provide a reliable data link control service, with error control and flow control, between user (TE) and network (NT) over the D channel. This data link service is used for the exchange of Q.933 control-signaling messages.

## User Plane

For the actual transfer of information between end users, the user-plane protocol is LAPF (Link Access Procedure for Frame-Mode Bearer Services), which is defined in Q.922. Q.922 is an enhanced version of LAPD (Q.921). Only the core functions of LAPF are used for frame relay:

- Frame delimiting, alignment, and transparency
- Frame multiplexing/demultiplexing using the address field
- Inspection of the frame to ensure that it consists of an integral number of octets prior to zero-bit insertion or following zero-bit extraction
- Inspection of the frame to ensure that it is neither too long nor too short
- Detection of transmission errors
- Congestion control functions

The last function listed above is new to LAPF, and is discussed in a later section. The remaining functions listed above are also functions of LAPD.

The core functions of LAPF in the user plane constitute a sublayer of the data link layer; this provides the bare service of transferring data link frames from one subscriber to another, with no flow control or error control. Above this, the user may choose to select additional data link or network-layer end-to-end functions. These are not part of the frame-relay service. Based on the core functions, a network offers frame relaying as a connection-oriented link layer service with the following properties:

- Preservation of the order of frame transfer from one edge of the network to the other
- A small probability of frame loss

## Comparison with X.25

As can be seen, this architecture reduces to the bare minimum the amount of work accomplished by the network. User data is transmitted in frames with virtually no processing by the intermediate network nodes, other than to check for errors and to route based on connection number. A frame in error is simply discarded, leaving error recovery to higher layers.

Figure 10.3 compares the protocol architecture of frame-mode bearer service to that of X.25. The packet-handling functions of X.25 operate at layer 3 of the OSI model. At layer 2, LAPB is used. Table 10.1 provides a functional comparison of X.25 and frame relay, and Figure 10.4 illustrates that comparison. As can be seen, the processing burden on the network for X.25 is considerably higher than for frame relay.

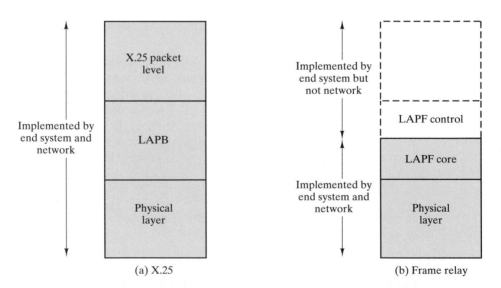

(a) X.25                    (b) Frame relay

**FIGURE 10.3** Comparison of X.25 and frame relay protocol stacks.

**TABLE 10.1**  Comparison of X.25 packet switching and frame relay.

| Function | X.25 in ISDN (X.31) | Frame Relay |
|---|---|---|
| Flag generation/recognition | X | X |
| Transparency | X | X |
| FCS generation/recognition | X | X |
| Recognize invalid frames | X | X |
| Discard incorrect frames | X | X |
| Address translation | X | X |
| Fill interframe time | X | X |
| Multiplexing of logical channels | X | X |
| Manage V(S) state variable | X | |
| Manage V(R) state variable | X | |
| Buffer packets awaiting acknowledgment | X | |
| Manage retransmission timer T1 | X | |
| Acknowledge received I-frames | X | |
| Check received N(S) against V(R) | X | |
| Generation of REJ (rejection message) | X | |
| Respond to P/F (poll/final) bit | X | |
| Keep track of number of retransmissions | X | |
| Act upon reception of REJ | X | |
| Respond to RNR (receiver not ready) | X | |
| Respond to RR (receiver ready) | X | |
| Management of D bit | X | |
| Management of M bit | X | |
| Management of Q bit | X | |
| Management of P(S) | X | |
| Management of P(R) | X | |
| Detection of out-of-sequence packets | X | |
| Management of network layer RR | X | |
| Management of network layer RNR | X | |

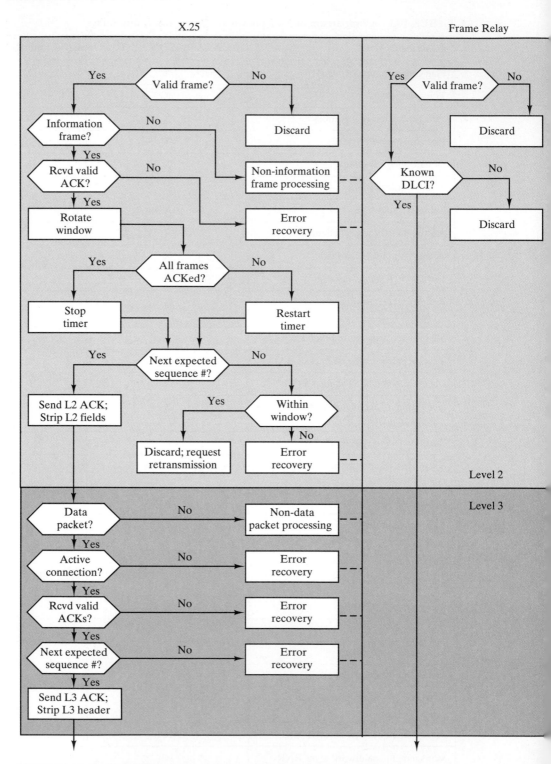

**FIGURE 10.4** Simplified model of X.25 and frame relay processing.

## 10.3  FRAME RELAY CALL CONTROL

This section examines the various approaches for setting up frame relay connections and then describes the protocol used for connection control.

### Call Control Alternatives

The call control protocol for frame relay must deal with a number of alternatives. First, let us consider two cases for the provision of frame handling services. For frame relay operation, a user is not connected directly to another user, but rather to a frame handler in the network; just as for X.25, a user is connected to a packet handler. There are two cases (Figure 10.5):

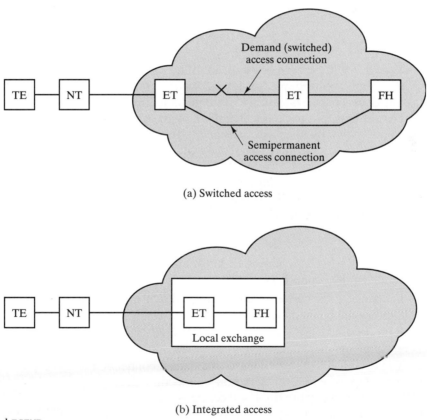

(a) Switched access

(b) Integrated access

LEGEND
TE  =  Terminal equipment
NT  =  Network equipment
ET  =  Exchange termination
FH  =  Frame handler

**FIGURE 10.5**  Frame relay access modes.

- **Switched Access.** The user is connected to a switched network, such as ISDN, and the local exchange does not provide the frame-handling capability. In this case, switched access must be provided from the user's terminal equipment (TE) to the frame handler elsewhere in the network; this can either be a demand connection (set up at the time of the call) or a semi-permanent connection (always available). In either case, the frame relay service is provided over a B or H channel.
- **Integrated Access.** The user is connected to a pure frame-relaying network or to a switched network in which the local exchange does provide the frame-handling capability. In this case, the user has direct logical access to the frame handler.

All of the above considerations have to do with the connection between the subscriber and the frame handler, which we refer to as the *access connection*. Once this connection exists, it is possible to multiplex multiple logical connections, referred to as *frame relay connections*, over this access connection. Such logical connections may be either on-demand or semipermanent.

### Frame Relay Connection

The discussion will perhaps be easier to follow if we first consider the management of frame relay connections. So, let us assume that the subscriber has somehow established an access connection to a frame handler that is part of a frame relay network. Analogous to a packet-switching network, the user is now able to exchange data frames with any other user attached to the network. For this purpose, a frame relay connection, analogous to a packet-switching virtual circuit, must first be established between two users.

As with X.25, frame relay supports multiple connections over a single link. In the case of frame relay, these are called data link connections, and each has a unique data link connection identifier (DLCI). Data transfer involves the following stages:

1. Establish a logical connection between two end points, and assign a unique DLCI to the connection.
2. Exchange information in data frames. Each frame includes a DLCI field to identify the connection.
3. Release the logical connection.

The establishment and release of a logical connection is accomplished by the exchange of messages over a logical connection dedicated to call control, with DLCI = 0. A frame with DLCI = 0 contains a call control message in the information field. At a minimum, four message types are needed: SETUP, CONNECT, RELEASE, and RELEASE COMPLETE.

Either side may request the establishment of a logical connection by sending a SETUP message. The other side, upon receiving the SETUP message, must reply with a CONNECT message if it accepts the connection; otherwise, it responds with a RELEASE COMPLETE message. The side sending the SETUP message may assign the DLCI by choosing an unused value and including this value in the SETUP message; otherwise, the DLCI value is assigned by the accepting side in the CONNECT message.

Either side may request to clear a logical connection by sending a RELEASE message. The other side, upon receipt of this message, must respond with a RELEASE COMPLETE message.

Table 10.2 shows the complete set of call control messages for frame relay. These messages are defined in ITU-T standard Q.933. They are a subset of a larger collection of messages defined in Q.931 used for common-channel signaling between a user and an ISDN.

### Access Connection

Now consider the establishment of an access connection. If the connection is semi-permanent, then no call control protocol is required. If the connection is to be set

**TABLE 10.2**  Messages for frame relay connection control.

| Message | Direction | Function |
|---------|-----------|----------|
| **Access connection establishment messages** | | |
| ALERTING | u → n | Indicates that user alerting has begun |
| CALL PROCEEDING | both | Indicates that access connection establishment has been initiated |
| CONNECT | both | Indicates access connection acceptance by called TE |
| CONNECT ACKNOWLEDGE | both | Indicates that user has been awarded the access connection |
| PROGRESS | u → n | Reports progress of an access connection in the event of interworking with a private network |
| SETUP | both | Initiates access connection establishment |
| **Access connection clearing messages** | | |
| DISCONNECT | both | Sent by user to request connection clearing; sent by network to indicate connection clearing |
| RELEASE | both | Indicates intent to release channel and call reference. |
| RELEASE COMPLETE | both | Indicates release of channel and call reference |
| **Miscellaneous messages** | | |
| STATUS | both | Sent in response to a STATUS ENQUIRY or at any time to report an error |
| STATUS ENQUIRY | both | Solicits STATUS message |

up on demand, then the user requests such a connection by means of a common-channel signaling protocol between the user and the network. In the case of ISDN, and also many other digital networks, the protocol used is Q.931.

Figure 10.6 provides an example of the types of exchanges involved for switched access to a frame handler, in this case over an ISDN. First, the calling user must establish a circuit-switched connection to a frame handler that is one of the nodes of the frame relay network; this is done with the usual SETUP, CONNECT, and CONNECT ACK messages, exchanged at the local user-network interface and at the interface between the network and a frame handler. The procedures and parameters for this exchange are carried out on the D channel, and are defined in Q.931. In the figure, it is assumed that the access connection is created for a B channel.

Once the access connection is established, an exchange takes place directly between the end user and the frame handling node for each frame mode connection that is set up. Again, the SETUP, CONNECT, and CONNECT ACK messages are

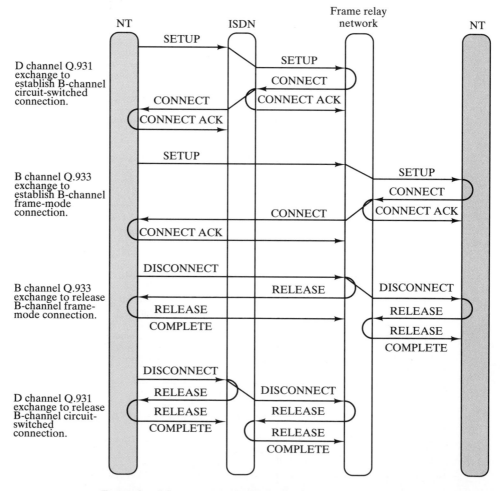

**FIGURE 10.6** Example of frame-mode control signaling.

used. In this case, the procedures and parameters for this exchange are defined in Q.933, and the exchange is carried out on the same B channel that will be used for the frame mode connection.

## 10.4 USER DATA TRANSFER

The operation of frame relay for user data transfer is best explained by beginning with the frame format, illustrated in Figure 10.7a. This is the format defined for the minimum-function LAPF protocol (known as LAPF core protocol). The format is similar to that of LAPD and LAPB with one obvious omission: There is no control field. This has the following implications:

- There is only one frame type, used for carrying user data. There are no control frames.
- It is not possible to use inband signaling; a logical connection can only carry user data.
- It is not possible to perform flow control and error control, as there are no sequence numbers.

The flag and frame check sequence (FCS) fields function as in LAPD and LAPB. The information field carries higher-layer data. If the user selects to implement additional data link control functions end-to-end, then a data link frame can

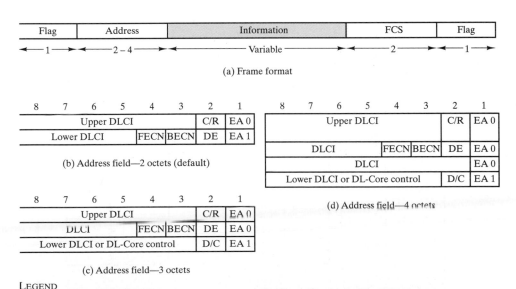

LEGEND

| | | | |
|---|---|---|---|
| EA | Address field extension bit | BECN | Backward explit congestion notification |
| C/R | Command/response bit | DLCI | Data link congestion identifier |
| FECN | Forward explicit congestion notification | D/C | DLCI or CORE control indicator |
| | | DE | Data link congestion identifier |

FIGURE 10.7 LAPF-core formats.

be carried in this field. Specifically, a common selection will be to use the full LAPF protocol (known as LAPF control protocol) in order to perform functions above the LAPF core functions. Note that the protocol implemented in this fashion is strictly between the end subscribers and is transparent to ISDN.

The address field has a default length of 2 octets and may be extended to 3 or 4 octets. It carries a data link connection identifier (DLCI) of 10, 17, or 24 bits. The DLCI serves the same function as the virtual circuit number in X.25: It allows multiple logical frame relay connections to be multiplexed over a single channel. As in X.25, the connection identifier has only local significance; each end of the logical connection assigns its own DLCI from the pool of locally unused numbers, and the network must map from one to the other. The alternative, using the same DLCI on both ends, would require some sort of global management of DLCI values.

The length of the address field, and hence of the DLCI, is determined by the address field extension (EA) bits. The C/R bit is application-specific and is not used by the standard frame relay protocol. The remaining bits in the address field have to do with congestion control, and are discussed in Section 10.6.

Figure 10.8 is another view of the protocols involved in frame relay, this time from the point of view of the individual frame relay connections. There is a common physical layer and frame relay sublayer. An optional layer-2 data link control protocol may be included above the frame relay sublayer. This selection is application-dependent and may differ for different frame relay connections (DLC-i). If frame relay call control messages are carried in frame relay frames, they are carried on DLCI 0, which provides a frame relay connection between the user and the frame handler. DLCI 8191 is dedicated to management procedures.

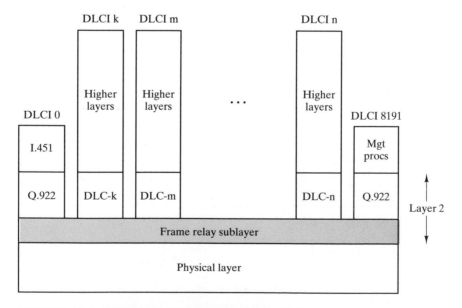

**FIGURE 10.8** Multiplexing at the frame relay sublayer.

## 10.5  NETWORK FUNCTION

The frame relaying function performed by ISDN, or any network that supports frame relaying, consists of the routing of frames with the format of Figure 10.7a, based on their DLCI values.

Figure 10.9 suggests the operation of a frame handler in a situation in which a number of users are directly connected to the same frame handler over different physical channels. The operation could just as well involve relaying a frame through two or more frame handlers. In this figure, the decision-making logic is shown conceptually as a separate module: the frame relay control point. This module is responsible for making routing decisions.

Typically, routing is controlled by entries in a connection table based on DLCI that map incoming frames from one channel to another. The frame handler switches a frame from an incoming channel to an outgoing channel, based on the appropriate entry in the connection table, and translates the DLCI in the frame before transmission. For example, incoming frames from TE B on logical connection 306 are retransmitted to TE D on logical connection 342. The figure also shows the multiplexing function: Multiple logical connections to TE D are multiplexed over the same physical channel.

Note also that all of the TEs have a logical connection to the frame relay control point with a value of DLCI = 0. These connections are reserved for in-channel call control, to be used when I.451/Q.931 on the D-channel is not used for frame relay call control.

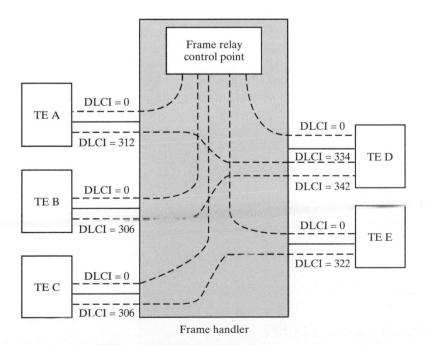

**FIGURE 10.9**  Frame handler operation.

As part of the frame relay function, the FCS of each incoming frame is checked. When an error is detected, the frame is simply discarded. It is the responsibility of the end users to institute error recovery above the frame relay protocol.

## 10.6   CONGESTION CONTROL

In Section 9.3, we discussed the potentially disastrous effects of congestion on the ability of network nodes to sustain throughput. To summarize that discussion, Figure 10.10 illustrates the effects of congestion in general terms. As the load on a network increases, a region of mild congestion is reached, where the queuing delays at the nodes results in increased end-to-end delay and reduced capability to provide desired throughput. When a point of severe congestion is reached, the classic queu-

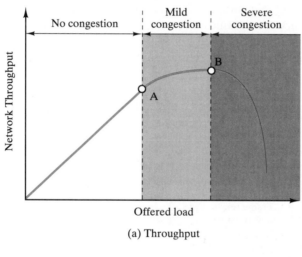

(a) Throughput

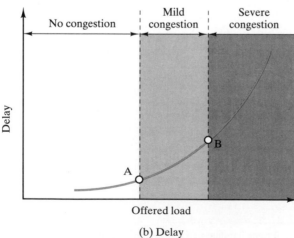

(b) Delay

**FIGURE 10.10**   The effects of congestion.

ing response results in dramatic growth in delays and a collapse in throughput.

It is clear that these catastrophic events must be avoided, which is the task of congestion control. The object of all congestion control techniques is to limit queue lengths at the frame handlers so as to avoid throughput collapse. This section provides an overview of congestion control techniques developed as part of the frame relay standardization effort.

## Approaches to Frame Relay Congestion Control

ITU-T Recommendation I.370 defines the objectives for frame relay congestion control to be the following:

- Minimize frame discard
- Maintain, with high probability and minimum variance, an agreed quality of service
- Minimize the possibility that one end user can monopolize network resources at the expense of other end users
- Be simple to implement, and place little overhead on either end user or network
- Create minimal additional network traffic
- Distribute network resources fairly among end users
- Limit spread of congestion to other networks and elements within the network
- Operate effectively regardless of the traffic flow in either direction between end users
- Have minimum interaction or impact on other systems in the frame relaying network
- Minimize the variance in quality of service delivered to individual frame relay connections during congestion (e.g., individual logical connections should not experience sudden degradation when congestion approaches or has occurred)

The challenge of congestion control is particularly acute for a frame relay network because of the limited tools available to the frame handlers. The frame relay protocol has been streamlined in order to maximize throughput and efficiency; a consequence of this is that a frame handler cannot control the flow of frames coming from a subscriber or an adjacent frame handler using the typical sliding-window flow control protocol, such as is found in LAPD.

Congestion control is the joint responsibility of the network and the end users. The network (i.e., the collection of frame handlers) is in the best position to monitor the degree of congestion, while the end users are in the best position to control congestion by limiting the flow of traffic.

Table 10.3 lists the congestion control techniques defined in the various ITU-T and ANSI documents. *Discard strategy* deals with the most fundamental response to congestion: When congestion becomes severe enough, the network is forced to discard frames; we would like to do this in a way that is fair to all users.

*Congestion a oidance* procedures are used at the onset of congestion to mini-

**TABLE 10.3** Frame relay congestion control techniques.

| Technique | Type | Function | Key elements |
|---|---|---|---|
| Discard control | Discard strategy | Provide guidance to network concerning which frames to discard. | DE bit |
| Backward explicit congestion notification | Congestion avoidance | Provides guidance to end systems about congestion in network | BECN bit |
| Forward explicit congestion notification | Congestion avoidance | Provides guidance to end systems about congestion in network | FECN bit |
| Implicit congestion notification | Congestion recovery | End system infers congestion from frame loss | Sequence numbers in higher-layer PDU |

mize the effect on the network. Thus, these procedures would be initiated at or prior to point A in Figure 10.10 to prevent congestion from progressing to point B. Near point A, there would be little evidence available to end users that congestion is increasing. Thus, there must be some *explicit signaling* mechanism from the network that will trigger the congestion avoidance.

*Congestion recovery* procedures are used to prevent network collapse in the face of severe congestion. These procedures are typically initiated when the network has begun to drop frames due to congestion. Such dropped frames will be reported by some higher layer of software (e.g., LAPF control protocol), and serve as an *implicit signaling* mechanism. Congestion recovery procedures operate around point B and within the region of severe congestion, as shown in Figure 10.10.

ITU-T and ANSI consider congestion avoidance with explicit signaling and congestion recovery with implicit signaling to be complementary forms of congestion control in the frame relaying bearer service.

## Traffic Rate Management

As a last resort, a frame relaying network must discard frames to cope with congestion. There is no getting around this fact. Because each frame handler in the network has finite memory available for queuing frames (Figure 9.9), it is possible for a queue to overflow, necessitating the discard of either the most recently arrived frame or some other frame.

The simplest way to cope with congestion is for the frame relaying network to simply discard frames arbitrarily, with no regard to the source of a particular frame. In that case, because there is no reward for restraint, the best strategy for any individual end system is to transmit frames as rapidly as possible; this, of course, exacerbates the congestion problem.

To provide for a fairer allocation of resources, the frame relaying bearer service includes the concept of a committed information rate (CIR). This is a rate, in bits per second, that the network agrees to support for a particular frame-mode connection. Any data transmitted in excess of the CIR is vulnerable to discard in the event of congestion. Despite the use of the term *committed*, there is no guarantee that even the CIR will be met. In cases of extreme congestion, the network may be forced to provide a service at less than the CIR for a given connection. However, when it comes time to discard frames, the network will choose to discard frames on connections that are exceeding their CIR before discarding frames that are within their CIR.

In theory, each frame relaying node should manage its affairs so that the aggregate of CIRs of all the connections of all the end systems attached to the node do not exceed the capacity of the node. In addition, the aggregate of the CIRs should not exceed the physical data rate across the user-network interface, known as the access rate. The limitation imposed by the access rate can be expressed as follows:

$$\sum_i \text{CIR}_{i,j} \le \text{AccessRate}_j \qquad (10.1)$$

where

$$\text{CIR}_{i,j} = \text{Committed information rate for connection } i \text{ on channel } j$$
$$\text{AccessRate}_j = \text{Data rate of user access channel } j \text{ (D, B, or H)}$$

Considerations of node capacity may result in the selection of lower values for some of the CIRs.

For permanent frame relay connections, the CIR for each connection must be established at the time the connection is made between user and network. For switched connections, the CIR parameter is negotiated; this is done in the setup phase of the call control protocol.

The CIR provides a way of discriminating among frames in determining which frames to discard in the face of congestion. Discrimination is indicated by means of the discard eligibility (DE) bit in the LAPF frame (Figure 10.7). The frame handler to which the user's station attaches performs a metering function (Figure 10.11). If the user is sending data at less than the CIR, the incoming frame handler does not alter the DE bit. If the rate exceeds the CIR, the incoming frame handler will set the DE bit on the excess frames and then forward them; such frames may get through or may be discarded if congestion is encountered. Finally, a maximum rate is defined, such that any frames above the maximum are discarded at the entry frame handler.

The CIR, by itself, does not provide much flexibility in dealing with traffic rates. In practice, a frame handler measures traffic over each logical connection for a time interval specific to that connection, and then makes a decision based on the amount of data received during that interval. Two additional parameters, assigned on permanent connections and negotiated on switched connections, are needed.

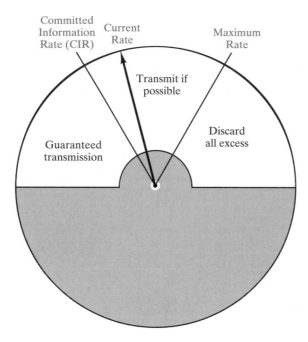

**FIGURE 10.11**   Operation of the CIR.

They are

- **Committed Burst Size ($B_c$).** The maximum amount of data that the network agrees to transfer, under normal conditions, over a measurement interval $T$. These data may or may not be contiguous (i.e., it may appear in one frame or in several frames).
- **Excess Burst Size ($B_e$).** The maximum amount of data in excess of $B_c$ that the network will attempt to transfer, under normal conditions, over a measurement interval $T$. These data are uncommitted in the sense that the network does not commit to delivery under normal conditions. Put another way, the data that represent $B_e$ are delivered with lower probability than the data within $B_c$.

The quantities $B_c$ and CIR are related. Because $B_c$ is the amount of committed data that may be transmitted by the user over a time T, and CIR is the rate at which committed data may be transmitted, we must have

$$T = \frac{B_c}{\text{CIR}} \tag{10.2}$$

Figure 10.12, based on one in ITU-T I.370, illustrates the relationship among these parameters. On each graph, the solid line plots the cumulative number of information bits transferred over a given connection since time $T_0$. The dashed line labeled Access Rate represents the data rate over the channel containing this connection. The dashed line labeled CIR represents the committed information rate

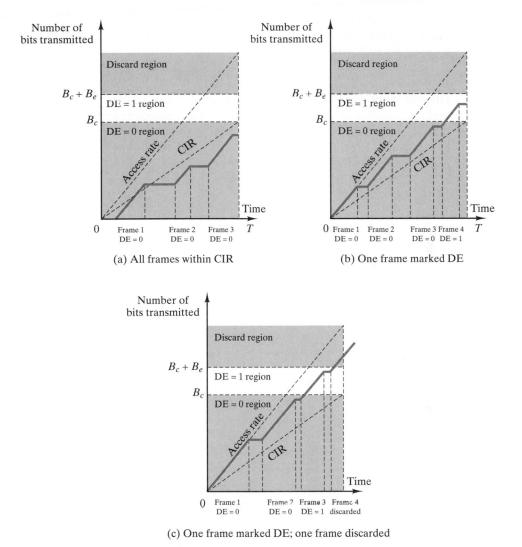

(a) All frames within CIR

(b) One frame marked DE

(c) One frame marked DE; one frame discarded

**FIGURE 10.12** Illustration of relationships among congestion parameters.

over the measurement interval T. Note that when a frame is being transmitted, the solid line is parallel to the Access Rate line; when a frame is transmitted on a channel, that channel is dedicated to the transmission of that frame. When no frame is being transmitted, the solid line is horizontal.

Part (a) of the figure shows an example in which three frames are transmitted within the measurement interval, and the total number of bits in the three frames is less than $B_c$. Note that during the transmission of the first frame, the actual transmission rate temporarily exceeds the CIR. This excess is of no consequence because the frame handler is only concerned with the cumulative number of bits transmitted over the entire interval. In part (b) of the figure, the last frame transmitted during the interval causes the cumulative number of transmitted bits to exceed $B_c$. Accordingly, that DE bit of that frame is set by the frame handler. In part (c) of the figure, the third frame exceeds $B_c$ and so is labeled for potential discard. The fourth frame exceeds $B_c + B_e$ and is discarded.

This scheme is an example of a leaky bucket algorithm, and a mechanism for implementing it is illustrated in Figure 10.13. The frame handler records the cumulative amount of data sent over a connection in a counter $C$. The counter is decremented at a rate of $B_c$ every $T$ time units. Of course, the counter is not allowed to become negative, so the actual assignment is $C \leftarrow \text{MIN}[C, B_c]$. Whenever the counter value exceeds $B_c$ but is less than $B_c + B_e$, incoming data are in excess of the committed burst size and are forwarded with the DE bit set. If the counter reaches $B_c + B_e$, all incoming frames are discarded until the counter has been decremented.

## Congestion Avoidance with Explicit Signaling

It is desirable to use as much of the available capacity in a frame relay network as possible but still react to congestion in a controlled and fair manner. This is the purpose of explicit congestion avoidance techniques. In general terms, for explicit congestion avoidance, the network alerts end systems to growing congestion within the network and the end systems take steps to reduce the offered load to the network.

As the standards for explicit congestion avoidance were being developed, two general strategies were considered [BERG91]. One group believed that congestion always occurred slowly and almost always in the network egress nodes. Another group had seen cases in which congestion grew very quickly in the internal nodes and required quick, decisive action to prevent network congestion. We will see that these two approaches are reflected in the forward and backward explicit congestion

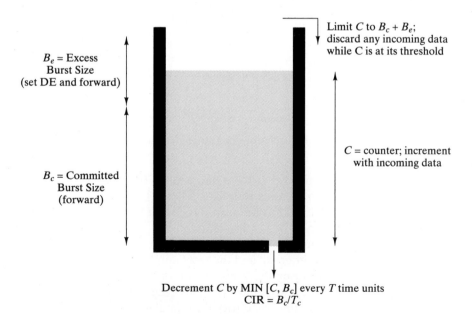

FIGURE 10.13  Leaky bucket algorithm.

avoidance techniques, respectively.

For explicit signaling, two bits in the address field of each frame are provided. Either bit may be set by any frame handler that detects congestion. If a frame handler receives a frame in which one or both of these bits are set, it must not clear the bits before forwarding the frame. Thus, the bits constitute signals from the network to the end user. The two bits are

- **Backward explicit congestion notification (BECN).** Notifies the user that congestion avoidance procedures should be initiated where applicable for traffic in the opposite direction of the received frame. The notification indicates that the frames transmitted by the user on this logical connection may encounter congested resources.
- **Forward explicit congestion notification (FECN).** Notifies the user that congestion avoidance procedures should be initiated where applicable for traffic in the same direction as the received frame. The notification indicates that this frame, on this logical connection, has encountered congested resources.

Let us consider how these bits are used by the network and the user. First, for the *network response*, it is necessary for each frame handler to monitor its queuing behavior. If queue lengths begin to grow to a dangerous level, then either FECN or BECN bits, or a combination, should be set to try to reduce the flow of frames through that frame handler. The choice of FECN or BECN may be determined by whether the end users on a given logical connection are prepared to respond to one or the other of these bits; this may be determined at configuration time. In any case, the frame handler has some choice as to which logical connections should be alerted to congestion. If congestion is becoming quite serious, all logical connections through a frame handler might be notified. In the early stages of congestion, the frame handler might just notify users for those connections that are generating the most traffic.

In an appendix to ANSI T1.618, a procedure for monitoring queue lengths is suggested. The frame handler monitors the size of each of its queues. A cycle begins when the outgoing circuit goes from idle (queue empty) to busy (non-zero queue size, including the current frame). The average queue size over the previous cycle and the current cycle is calculated. If the average size exceeds a threshold value, then the circuit is in a state of incipient congestion, and the congestion avoidance bits should be set on some or all logical connections that use that circuit. By averaging over two cycles instead of just monitoring current queue length, the system avoids reacting to temporary surges that would not necessarily produce congestion.

The average queue length may be computed by determining the area (product of queue size and time interval) over the two cycles and dividing by the time of the two cycles. This algorithm is illustrated in Figure 10.14.

The *user response* is determined by the receipt of BECN or FECN signals. The simplest procedure is the response to a BECN signal: The user simply reduces the rate at which frames are transmitted until the signal ceases. The response to an FECN is more complex, as it requires the user to notify its peer user of this connection to restrict its flow of frames. The core functions used in the frame relay pro-

$t$ = current time

$t_i$ = time of $i^{th}$ arrival or departure event

$q_i$ = number of frames in the system after the event

$T_0$ = time at the beginning of the previous cycle

$T_1$ = time at the beginning of the current cycle

The algorithm consists of three components:

1. Queue Length Update: Beginning with $q_0 := 0$
   If the $i^{th}$ event is an arrival event, $q_i := q_{i-1} + 1$
   If the $i^{th}$ event is a departure event, $q_i := q_{i-1} - 1$
2. Queue Area (integral) update:

   Area of the previous cycle $= \sum_{t_i \in [T_o, T_1)} q_{i-1}(t_i - t_{i-1})$

   Area of the current cycle $= \sum_{t_i \in [T_1, t)} q_{i-1}(t_i - t_{i-1})$

3. Average Queue Length Update
   Average queue length over the two cycles

   $$= \frac{\text{Area of the two cycles}}{\text{Time of the two cycles}} = \frac{\text{Area of the two cycles}}{t - T_0}$$

**FIGURE 10.14** Queue length averaging algorithm.

tocol do not support this notification; therefore, it must be done at a higher layer, such as the transport layer. The flow control could also be accomplished by the LAPF control protocol or some other link control protocol implemented above the frame relay sublayer (Figure 10.8). The LAPF control protocol is particularly useful because it includes an enhancement to LAPD that permits the user to adjust window size.

## Congestion Recovery with Implicit Signaling

Implicit signaling occurs when the network discards a frame, and this fact is detected by the end user at a higher, end-to-end layer, such as the LAPF control protocol. When this occurs, the end user software may deduce that congestion exists.

For example, in a data link control protocol such as the LAPF control protocol, which uses a sliding-window flow and error control technique, the protocol detects the loss of an I frame in one of two ways:

1. When a frame is dropped by the network, the following frame will generate an REJ frame from the receiving end point.
2. When a frame is dropped by the network, no acknowledgment is returned from the other end system. Eventually, the source end system will time out and transmit a command with the P bit set to 1. The subsequent response with the F bit set to 1 should indicate that the receive sequence number N(R) from the other side is less than the current send sequence number.

Once congestion is detected, the protocol uses flow control to recover from the congestion. LAPF suggests that a user that is capable of varying the flow control window size use this mechanism in response to implicit signaling. Let us assume that the layer-2 window size, $W$, can vary between the parameters $W_{min}$ and $W_{max}$, and is initially set to $W_{max}$. In general, we would like to reduce $W$, as congestion increases, to gradually throttle the transmission of frames. Three classes of adaptive window schemes based on response to one of the two conditions listed above have been suggested [CHEN89, DOSH88]:

**1.1** Set $W = \text{Max} [W - 1, W_{min}]$
**1.2** Set $W = W_{min}$
**1.3** Set $W = \text{Max} [\alpha W, W_{min}]$, where $0 < \alpha < 1$

Successful transmissions (measured by receipt of acknowledgments) may indicate that the congestion has gone away and window size should be increased. Two possible approaches are

**2.1** Set $W = \text{Min} [W + 1, W_{max}]$ after $N$ consecutive successful transmissions
**2.2** Set $W = \text{Min} [W + 1, W_{max}]$ after $W$ consecutive successful transmissions

A study reported in [CHEN89] suggests that the use of strategy 1.3 with $\alpha = 0.5$ plus strategy 2.2 provides good performance over a wide range of network parameters and traffic patterns; this is the strategy recommended in LAPF.

## 10.7 RECOMMENDED READING

[SMIT93] provides a good survey of frame relay, with an emphasis on its applications and its role in the context of other networking services; the study also provides an overview of the specifications. [BLAC94] provides a greater emphasis on the technical and protocol aspects of frame relay. Another good technical treatment is contained in [SPOH93].

BLAC94   Black, U. *Frame Relay Networks: Specifications and Implementations.* New York: McGraw-Hill, 1994.

SMIT93   Smith, P. *Frame Relay: Principles and Applications.* Reading, MA: Addison Wesley, 1993.

SPOH93   Spohn, D. *Data Network Design.* New York: McGraw-Hill, 1994.

**Recommended Web Sites**

- http://www.frforum.com: Web site of the Frame Relay Forum, which is leading the effort to expand the functionality of frame relay networks.
- http://www.mot.com/MIMS/ISG/tech/frame-relay/resources.html: Exhaustive source of information on frame relay.

## 10.8 PROBLEMS

**10.1** A proposed congestion control technique is known as isarithmic control. In this method, the total number of frames in transit is fixed by inserting a fixed number of permits into the network. These permits circulate at random through the frame relay network. Whenever a frame handler wants to relay a frame just given to it by an attached user, it must first capture and destroy a permit. When the frame is delivered to the destination user by the frame handler to which it attaches, that frame handler reissues the permit. List three potential problems with this technique.

10.2 Consider the frame relay network depicted in Figure 10.15. C is the capacity of a link in frames per second. Node $A$ presents a constant load of 0.8 frames per second destined for $A'$. Node $B$ presents a load $\lambda$ destined for $B'$. Node $S$ has a common pool of buffers that it uses for traffic both to $A'$ and $B'$. When the buffer is full, frames are discarded and are later retransmitted by the source user. S has a throughput capacity of 2. Plot the total throughput (i.e., the sum of $A$–$A'$ and $B$–$B'$ delivered traffic) as a function of $\lambda$. What fraction of the throughput is $A$–$A'$ traffic for $\lambda > 1$?

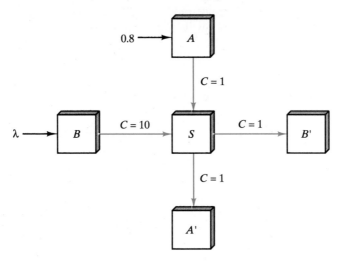

**FIGURE 10.15** Network of nodes.

# CHAPTER 11

# ASYNCHRONOUS TRANSFER MODE (ATM)

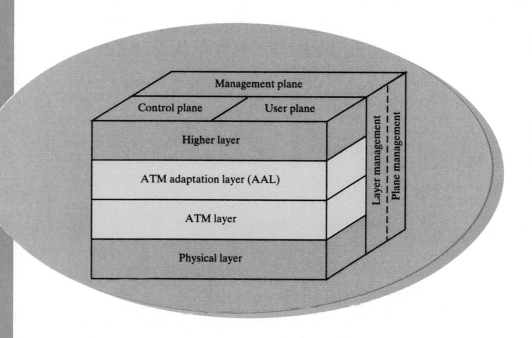

A synchronous transfer mode (ATM), also known as cell relay, is similar in concept to frame relay. Both frame relay and ATM take advantage of the reliability and fidelity of modern digital facilities to provide faster packet switching than X.25. ATM is even more streamlined than frame relay in its functionality, and can support data rates several orders of magnitude greater than frame relay.

In addition to their technical similarities, ATM and frame relay have similar histories. Frame relay was developed as part of the work of ISDN, but is now finding wide application in private networks and other non-ISDN applications, particularly in bridges and routers. ATM was developed as part of the work on broadband ISDN, but is beginning to find application in non-ISDN environments where very high data rates are required.

We begin with a discussion of the details of the ATM scheme. Then, the important concept of the ATM Adaptation Layer (AAL) is examined. Finally, the key issue of congestion control in ATM networks is discussed. For a discussion of broadband ISDN, see Appendix A.

## 11.1 PROTOCOL ARCHITECTURE

Asynchronous transfer mode (ATM), also known as cell relay, is in some ways similar to packet switching using X.25 and frame relay. Like packet switching and frame relay, ATM involves the transfer of data in discrete chunks. Also, like packet switching and frame relay, ATM allows multiple logical connections to be multiplexed over a single physical interface. In the case of ATM, the information flow on each logical connection is organized into fixed-size packets, called cells.

ATM is a streamlined protocol with minimal error and flow control capabilities; this reduces the overhead of processing ATM cells and reduces the number of overhead bits required with each cell, thus enabling ATM to operate at high data rates. Further, the use of fixed-size cells simplifies the processing required at each ATM node, again supporting the use of ATM at high data rates.

The standards issued for ATM by ITU-T are based on the protocol architecture shown in Figure 11.1, which illustrates the basic architecture for an interface between user and network. The physical layer involves the specification of a transmission medium and a signal encoding scheme. The data rates specified at the physical layer include 155.52 Mbps and 622.08 Mbps. Other data rates, both higher and lower, are possible.

Two layers of the protocol architecture relate to ATM functions. There is an ATM layer common to all services that provides packet transfer capabilities, and an ATM adaptation layer (AAL) that is service dependent. The ATM layer defines the transmission of data in fixed-size cells and also defines the use of logical connections. The use of ATM creates the need for an adaptation layer to support information transfer protocols not based on ATM. The AAL maps higher-layer information into ATM cells to be transported over an ATM network, then collects information from ATM cells for delivery to higher layers.

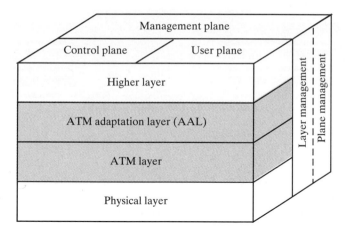

**FIGURE 11.1** ATM protocol reference model.

The protocol reference model makes reference to three separate planes:

- **User Plane.** Provides for user information transfer, along with associated controls (e.g., flow control, error control).
- **Control Plane.** Performs call control and connection control functions.
- **Management Plane.** Includes plane management, which performs management functions related to a system as a whole and provides coordination between all the planes, and layer management, which performs management functions relating to resources and parameters residing in its protocol entities.

## 11.2 ATM LOGICAL CONNECTIONS

Logical connections in ATM are referred to as virtual channel connections (VCC). A VCC is analogous to a virtual circuit in X.25 or a data link connection in frame relay; it is the basic unit of switching in an ATM network. A VCC is set up between two end users through the network and a variable-rate, full-duplex flow of fixed-size cells is exchanged over the connection. VCCs are also used for user-network exchange (control signaling) and network-network exchange (network management and routing).

For ATM, a second sublayer of processing has been introduced that deals with the concept of virtual path (Figure 11.2). A virtual path connection (VPC) is a bundle of VCCs that have the same endpoints. Thus, all of the cells flowing over all of the VCCs in a single VPC are switched together.

The virtual path concept was developed in response to a trend in high-speed networking in which the control cost of the network is becoming an increasingly higher proportion of the overall network cost. The virtual-path technique helps contain the control cost by grouping connections that share common paths through the network into a single unit. Network management actions can then be applied to a

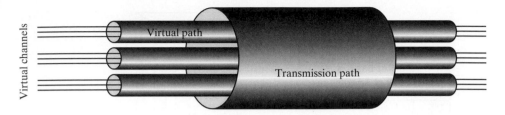

**FIGURE 11.2**  ATM connection relationships.

small number of groups of connections instead of to a large number of individual connections.

Several advantages can be listed for the use of virtual paths:

- **Simplified network architecture.** Network transport functions can be separated into those related to an individual logical connection (virtual channel) and those related to a group of logical connections (virtual path).
- **Increased network performance and reliability.** The network deals with fewer, aggregated entities.
- **Reduced processing and short connection setup time.** Much of the work is done when the virtual path is set up. By reserving capacity on a virtual path connection in anticipation of later call arrivals, new virtual channel connections can be established by executing simple control functions at the endpoints of the virtual path connection; no call processing is required at transit nodes. Thus, the addition of new virtual channels to an existing virtual path involves minimal processing.
- **Enhanced network services.** The virtual path is used internal to the network but is also visible to the end user. As a result, the user may define closed user groups or closed networks of virtual-channel bundles.

Figure 11.3 suggests in a general way the call-establishment process using virtual channels and virtual paths. The process of setting up a virtual path connection is decoupled from the process of setting up an individual virtual channel connection:

- The virtual path control mechanisms include calculating routes, allocating capacity, and storing connection state information.
- To set up a virtual channel, there must first be a virtual path connection to the required destination node with sufficient available capacity to support the virtual channel, with the appropriate quality of service. A virtual channel is set up by storing the required state information (virtual channel/virtual path mapping).

The terminology of virtual paths and virtual channels used in the standard is a bit confusing, and is summarized in Table 11.1. Whereas most of the network-layer protocols that we survey in this book relate only to the user-network interface, the concepts of virtual path and virtual channel are defined in the ITU-T Recom-

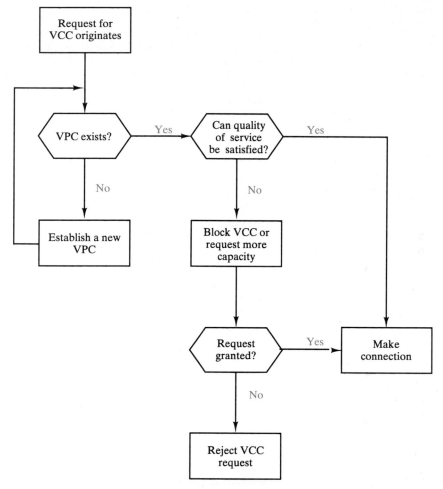

**FIGURE 11.3** Call establishment using virtual paths.

mendations with reference to both the user-network interface and the internal network operation.

## Virtual Channel Connection Uses

The endpoints of a VCC may be end users, network entities, or an end user and a network entity. In all cases, cell sequence integrity is preserved within a VCC; that is, cells are delivered in the same order in which they are sent. Let us consider examples of the three uses of a VCC:

- **Between end users.** Can be used to carry end-to-end user data; can also be used to carry control signaling between end users, as explained below. A VPC between end users provides them with an overall capacity; the VCC organization of the VPC is up to the two end users, provided the set of VCCs does not exceed the VPC capacity.

**TABLE 11.1**   Virtual path/virtual connection terminology.

| | |
|---|---|
| Virtual Channel (VC) | A generic term used to describe unidirectional transport of ATM cells associated by a common unique identifier value. |
| Virtual Channel Link | A means of unidirectional transport of ATM cells between a point where a VCI value is assigned and the point where that value is translated or terminated. |
| Virtual Channel Identifier (VCI) | Identifies a particular VC link for a given VPC. |
| Virtual Channel Connection (VCC) | A concatenation of VC links that extends between two points where the adaptation layer is accessed. VCCs are provided for the purpose of user-user, user-network, or network-network information transfer. Cell sequence integrity is preserved for cells belonging to the same VCC. |
| Virtual Path | A generic term used to describe unidirectional transport of ATM cells belonging to virtual channels that are associated by a common unique identifier value. |
| Virtual Path Link | A group of VC links, identified by a common value of VPI, between a point where a VPI value is assigned and the point where that value is translated or terminated. |
| Virtual Path Identifier (VPI) | Identifies a particular VP link. |
| Virtual Path Connection (VPC) | A concatenation of VP links that extends between the point where the VCI values are assigned and the point where those values are translated or removed, i.e., extending the length of a bundle of VC links that share the same VPI. VPCs are provided for the purpose of user-user, user-network, or network-network information transfer. |

- **Between an end user and a network entity.** Used for user-to-network control signaling, as discussed below. A user-to-network VPC can be used to aggregate traffic from an end user to a network exchange or network server.
- **Between two network entities.** Used for network traffic management and routing functions. A network-to-network VPC can be used to define a common route for the exchange of network management information.

## Virtual Path/Virtual Channel Characteristics

ITU-T Recommendation I.150 lists the following as characteristics of virtual channel connections:

- **Quality of service.** A user of a VCC is provided with a Quality of Service specified by parameters such as cell loss ratio (ratio of cells lost to cells transmitted) and cell delay variation.
- **Switched and semi-permanent virtual channel connections.** Both are switched connections, which require call-control signaling, and dedicated channels can be provided.
- **Cell sequence integrity.** The sequence of transmitted cells within a VCC is preserved.
- **Traffic parameter negotiation and usage monitoring.** Traffic parameters can be negotiated between a user and the network for each VCC. The input of

cells to the VCC is monitored by the network to ensure that the negotiated parameters are not violated.

The types of traffic parameters that can be negotiated include average rate, peak rate, burstiness, and peak duration. The network may need a number of strategies to handle congestion and to manage existing and requested VCCs. At the crudest level, the network may simply deny new requests for VCCs to prevent congestion. Additionally, cells may be discarded if negotiated parameters are violated or if congestion becomes severe. In an extreme situation, existing connections might be terminated.

I.150 also lists characteristics of VPCs. The first four characteristics listed are identical to those for VCCs. That is, quality of service, switched and semi-permanent VPCs, cell sequence integrity, and traffic parameter negotiation and usage monitoring are all also characteristics of a VPC. There are a number of reasons for this duplication. First, redundancy provides some flexibility in how the network service manages its requirements. Second, the network must be concerned with the overall requirements for a VPC, and, within a VPC, it may negotiate the establishment of virtual channels with given characteristics. Finally, once a VPC is set up, it is possible for the end users to negotiate the creation of new VCCs. The VPC characteristics impose a discipline on the choices that the end users may make.

In addition, a fifth characteristic is listed for VPCs:

- **Virtual channel identifier restriction within a VPC.** One or more virtual channel identifiers, or numbers, may not be available to the user of the VPC, but may be reserved for network use. Examples include VCCs used for network management.

## Control Signaling

In ATM, a mechanism is needed for the establishment and release of VPCs and VCCs. The exchange of information involved in this process is referred to as control signaling, and takes place on separate connections from those that are being managed.

For VCCs, I.150 specifies four methods for providing an establishment/release facility. One or a combination of these methods will be used in any particular network:

1. *Semi-permanent VCCs* may be used for user-to-user exchange. In this case, no control signaling is required.

2. If there is no pre-established call control signaling channel, then one must be set up. For that purpose, a control signaling exchange must take place between the user and the network on some channel. Hence, we need a permanent channel, probably of low data rate, that can be used to set up VCCs that can be used for call control. Such a channel is called a *meta-signaling channel*, as the channel is used to set up signaling channels.

3. The meta-signaling channel can be used to set up a VCC between the user and the network for call control signaling. This *user-to-network signaling virtual channel* can then be used to set up VCCs to carry user data.

4. The meta-signaling channel can also be used to set up a *user-to-user signaling virtual channel*. Such a channel must be set up within a pre-established VPC. It can then be used to allow the two end users, without network intervention, to establish and release user-to-user VCCs to carry user data.

For VPCs, three methods are defined in I.150:

1. A VPC can be established on a *semi-permanent* basis by prior agreement. In this case, no control signaling is required.
2. VPC establishment/release may be *customer controlled*. In this case, the customer uses a signaling VCC to request the VPC from the network.
3. VPC establishment/release may be *network controlled*. In this case, the network establishes a VPC for its own convenience. The path may be network-to-network, user-to-network, or user-to-user.

## 11.3   ATM CELLS

The asynchronous transfer mode makes use of fixed-size cells, which consist of a 5-octet header and a 48-octet information field. There are several advantages to the use of small, fixed-size cells. First, their use may reduce queuing delay for a high-priority cell, as it waits less if it arrives slightly behind a lower-priority cell that has gained access to a resource (e.g., the transmitter). Secondly, it appears that fixed-size cells can be switched more efficiently, which is important for the very high data rates of ATM. With fixed-size cells, it is easier to implement the switching mechanism in hardware.

### Header Format

Figure 11.4a shows the header format at the user-network interface. Figure 11.4b shows the cell header format internal to the network, where the generic flow control field, which performs local functions, is not retained. Instead, the virtual path identifier field is expanded from 8 to 12 bits; this allows support for an expanded number of VPCs internal to the network, to include those supporting subscribers and those required for network management.

The *generic flow control field* does not appear in the cell header internal to the network, but only at the user-network interface. Hence, it can be used for control of cell flow only at the local user-network interface. The details of its application are for further study. The field could be used to assist the customer in controlling the flow of traffic for different qualities of service. One candidate for the use of this field is a multiple-priority level indicator to control the flow of information in a service-dependent manner. In any case, the GFC mechanism is used to alleviate short-term overload conditions in the network.

The *virtual path identifier* (VPI) constitutes a routing field for the network. It is 8 bits at the user-network interface and 12 bits at the network-network interface, allowing for more virtual paths to be supported within the network. The *virtual*

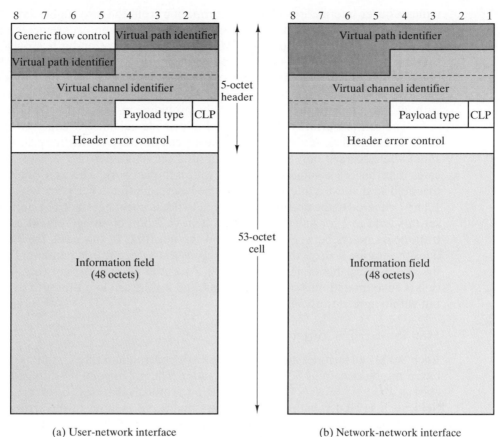

**FIGURE 11.4**    ATM cell format.

*channel identifier* (VCI) is used for routing to and from the end user. Thus, it functions much as a service access point.

The *payload-type* field indicates the type of information in the information field. Table 11.2 shows the interpretation of the PT bits. A value of 0 in the first bit

**TABLE 11.2**    Payload Type (PT) field coding.

| PT coding | Interpretation |
|---|---|
| 0 0 0 | User data cell, AAU = 0, congestion not experienced |
| 0 0 1 | User data cell, AAU = 1, congestion not experienced |
| 0 1 0 | User data cell, AAU = 0, congestion experienced |
| 0 1 1 | User data cell, AAU = 1, congestion experienced |
| 1 0 0 | OAM F5 segment associated cell |
| 1 0 1 | OAM F5 end-to-end associated cell |
| 1 1 0 | Resource management cell |
| 1 1 1 | Reserved for future function |

AAU = ATM user to ATM user indication

indicates user information—that is, information from the next higher layer. In this case, the second bit indicates whether congestion has been experienced; the third bit, known as the ATM-user-to-ATM-user (AAU) indication bit is a one-bit field that can be used to convey information between end users. A value of 1 in the first bit indicates that this cell carries network management or maintenance information. This indication allows the insertion of network-management cells into a user's VCC without impacting the user's data, thereby providing in-band control information.

The **cell-loss priority** (CLP) is used to provide guidance to the network in the event of congestion. A value of 0 indicates a cell of relatively higher priority, which should be discarded only when no other alternative is available. A value of 1 indicates that this cell is subject to discard within the network. The user might employ this field so that extra information may be inserted into the network, with a CLP of 1, and delivered to the destination if the network is not congested. The network may set this field to 1 for any data cell that is in violation of an agreement concerning traffic parameters between the user and the network. In this case, the switch that does the setting realizes that the cell exceeds the agreed traffic parameters but that the switch is capable of handling the cell. At a later point in the network, if congestion is encountered, this cell has been marked for discard in preference to cells that fall within agreed traffic limits.

### Header Error Control

Each ATM cell includes an 8-bit header error control field (HEC) that is calculated based on the remaining 32 bits of the header. The polynomial used to generate the code is $X^8 + X^2 + X + 1$. In most existing protocols that include an error control field, such as HDLC and LAPF, the data that serve as input to the error code calculation are, in general, much longer than the size of the resulting error code; this allows for error detection. In the case of ATM, the input to the calculation is only 32 bits, compared to 8 bits for the code. The fact that the input is relatively short allows the code to be used not only for error detection but, in some cases, for actual error correction; this is because there is sufficient redundancy in the code to recover from certain error patterns.

Figure 11.5 depicts the operation of the HEC algorithm at the receiver. At initialization, the receiver's error-correction algorithm is in the default mode for single-

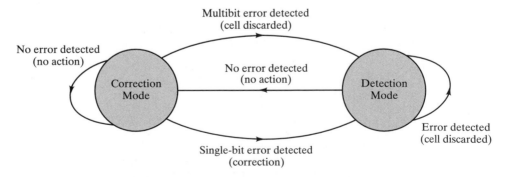

**FIGURE 11.5**  HEC operation at receiver.

bit error correction. As each cell is received, the HEC calculation and comparison is performed. As long as no errors are detected, the receiver remains in error-correction mode. When an error is detected, the receiver will correct the error if it is a single-bit error or it will detect that a multi-bit error has occurred. In either case, the receiver now moves to detection mode. In this mode, no attempt is made to correct errors. The reason for this change is a recognition that a noise burst or other event might cause a sequence of errors, a condition for which the HEC is insufficient for error correction. The receiver remains in detection mode as long as errored cells are received. When a header is examined and found not to be in error, the receiver switches back to correction mode. The flowchart of Figure 11.6 shows the consequence of errors in the cell header.

The error-protection function provides both recovery from single-bit header errors, and a low probability of the delivery of cells with errored headers under bursty error conditions. The error characteristics of fiber-based transmission sys-

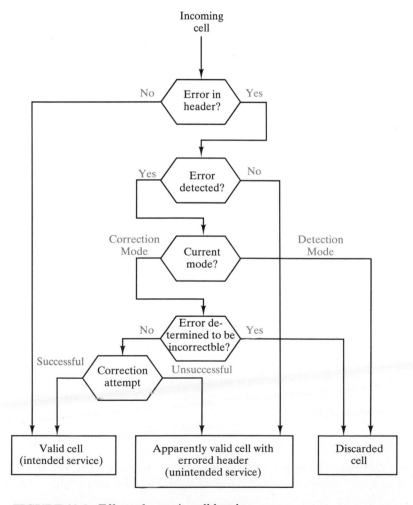

**FIGURE 11.6**  Effect of error in cell header.

tems appear to be a mix of single-bit errors and relatively large burst errors. For some transmission systems, the error-correction capability, which is more time-consuming, might not be invoked.

Figure 11.7, based on one in ITU-T I.432, indicates how random bit errors impact the probability of occurrence of discarded cells and valid cells with errored headers, when HEC is employed.

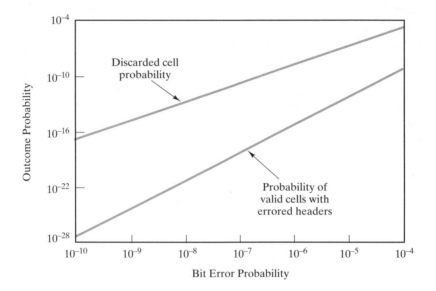

**FIGURE 11.7**   Impact of random bit errors on HEC performance.

## 11.4   TRANSMISSION OF ATM CELLS

The ITU-T Recommendations for broadband ISDN provide some detail on the data rate and synchronization techniques for ATM cell transmission across the user-network interface. The approach taken for broadband ISDN is also used in many other ATM networks.

The BISDN specifies that ATM cells are to be transmitted at a rate of 155.52 Mbps or 622.08 Mbps. As with ISDN, we need to specify the transmission structure that will be used to carry this payload. For 622.08 Mbps, the matter has been left for further study. For the 155.52-Mbps interface, two approaches are defined in I.413: a cell-based physical layer and an SDH-based physical layer. We examine each of these approaches in turn.

### Cell–Based Physical Layer

For the cell-based physical layer, no framing is imposed. The interface structure consists of a continuous stream of 53-octet cells. Because there is no external frame imposed on the cell-based approach, some form of synchronization is needed. Synchronization is achieved on the basis of the header error control (HEC) field in the cell header. The procedure is as follows (Figure 11.8):

1. In the HUNT state, a cell delineation algorithm is performed bit by bit to determine if the HEC coding law is observed (i.e., match between received HEC and calculated HEC). Once a match is achieved, it is assumed that one header has been found, and the method enters the PRESYNC state.
2. In the PRESYNC state, a cell structure is now assumed. The cell delineation algorithm is performed cell by cell until the encoding law has been confirmed consecutively $\delta$ times.
3. In the SYNC state, the HEC is used for error detection and correction (see Figure 11.5). Cell delineation is assumed to be lost if the HEC coding law is recognized as incorrect $\alpha$ times consecutively.

The values of $\alpha$ and $\delta$ are design parameters. Greater values of $\delta$ result in longer delays in establishing synchronization but in greater robustness against false delineation. Greater values of $\alpha$ result in longer delays in recognizing a misalignment but in greater robustness against false misalignment. Figures 11.9 and 11.10 show the impact of random bit errors on cell delineation performance for various values of $\alpha$ and $\delta$. The first figure shows the average amount of time that the receiver will maintain synchronization in the face of errors, with $\alpha$ as a parameter. The second figure shows the average amount of time to acquire synchronization as a function of error rate, with $\delta$ as a parameter.

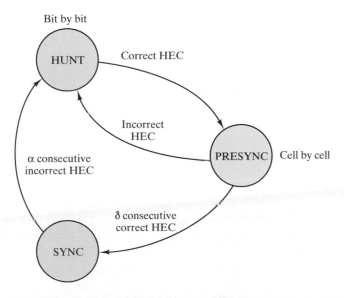

**FIGURE 11.8**   Cell delineation state diagram.

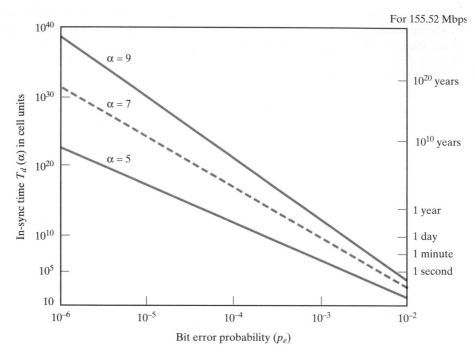

**FIGURE 11.9**   Impact of random bit errors on cell-delineation performance.

The advantage of using a cell-based transmission scheme is the simplified interface that results when both transmission- and transfer-mode functions are based on a common structure.

## SDH–Based Physical Layer

Alternatively, ATM cells can be carried over a line using SDH (synchronous digital hierarchy) or SONET. For the cell-based physical layer, framing is imposed using the STM-1 (STS-3) frame (Figure 7.12b). Figure 11.11 shows the payload portion of an STM-1 frame. This payload may be offset from the beginning of the frame, as indicated by the pointer in the section overhead of the frame. As can be seen, the payload consists of a 9-octet path overhead portion and the remainder, which contains ATM cells. Because the payload capacity (2,340 octets) is not an integer multiple of the cell length (53 octets), a cell may cross a payload boundary.

The H4 octet in the path overhead is set at the sending side to indicate the next occurrence of a cell boundary. That is, the value in the H4 field indicates the number of octets in the first cell boundary following the H4 octet. The permissible range of values is 0 to 52.

The advantages of the SDH-based approach include the following:

- It can be used to carry either ATM-based or STM-based (synchronous transfer mode) payloads, making it possible to initially deploy a high-capacity

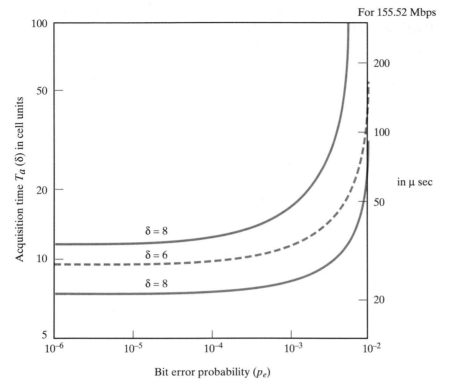

For 155.52 Mbps

**FIGURE 11.10** Acquisition time versus bit-error probability.

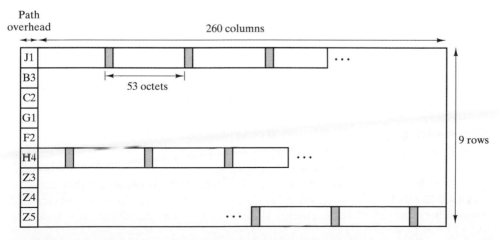

**FIGURE 11.11** STM-1 payload for SDH-based ATM cell transmission.

fiber-based transmission infrastructure for a variety of circuit-switched and dedicated applications, and then readily migrate to the support of ATM.

- Some specific connections can be circuit-switched using an SDH channel. For example, a connection carrying constant-bit-rate video traffic can be mapped into its own exclusive payload envelope of the STM-1 signal, which can be circuit switched. This procedure may be more efficient than ATM switching.

- Using SDH synchronous multiplexing techniques, several ATM streams can be combined to build interfaces with higher bit rates than those supported by the ATM layer at a particular site. For example, four separate ATM streams, each with a bit rate of 155 Mbps (STM-1), can be combined to build a 622-Mbps (STM-4) interface. This arrangement may be more cost effective than one using a single 622-Mbps ATM stream.

## 11.5 ATM ADAPTATION LAYER

The use of ATM creates the need for an adaptation layer to support information transfer protocols not based on ATM. Two examples are PCM (pulse code modulation) voice and LAPF. PCM voice is an application that produces a stream of bits from a voice signal. To employ this application over ATM, it is necessary to assemble PCM bits into cells for transmission and to read them out on reception in such a way as to produce a smooth, constant flow of bits to the receiver. LAPF is the standard data link control protocol for frame relay. In a mixed environment, in which frame relay networks interconnect with ATM networks, a convenient way of integrating the two is to map LAPF frames into ATM cells; this will usually mean segmenting one LAPF frame into a number of cells on transmission, and then reassembling the frame from cells on reception. By allowing the use of LAPF over ATM, all of the existing frame relay applications and control signaling protocols can be used on an ATM network.

### AAL Services

ITU-T I.362 lists the following general examples of services provided by AAL:

- Handling of transmission errors
- Segmentation and reassembly, to enable larger blocks of data to be carried in the information field of ATM cells
- Handling of lost and misinserted cell conditions
- Flow control and timing control

In order to minimize the number of different AAL protocols that must be specified to meet a variety of needs, ITU-T has defined four classes of service that cover a broad range of requirements (Figure 11.12). The classification is based on

|  | Class A | Class B | Class C | Class D |
|---|---|---|---|---|
| Timing relation between source and destination | Required | | Not required | |
| Bit rate | Constant | | Variable | |
| Connection mode | Connection-oriented | | | Connectionless |
| AAL Protocol | Type 1 | Type 2 | Type 3/4,Type 5 | Type 3/4 |

**FIGURE 11.12**   Service classification for AAL.

whether a timing relationship must be maintained between source and destination, whether the application requires a constant bit rate, and whether the transfer is connection-oriented or connectionless. An example of a class A service is circuit emulation. In this case, a constant bit rate, which requires the maintenance of a timing relation, is used, and the transfer is connection-oriented. An example of a class B service is variable-bit-rate video, such as might be used in a videoconference. Here, the application is connection oriented and timing is important, but the bit rate varies depending on the amount of activity in the scene. Classes C and D correspond to data-transfer applications. In both cases, the bit rate may vary and no particular timing relationship is required; differences in data rate are handled, using buffers, by the end systems. The data transfer may be either connection-oriented (class C) or connectionless (class D).

## AAL Protocols

To support these various classes of service, a set of protocols at the AAL level have been defined. The AAL layer is organized into two logical sublayers: the Convergence Sublayer (CS) and the Segmentation and Reassembly Sublayer (SAR). The convergence sublayer provides the functions needed to support specific applications using AAL. Each AAL user attaches to AAL at a service access point (SAP), which is simply the address of the application. This sublayer is, then, service dependent.

The segmentation and reassembly sublayer is responsible for packaging information received from CS into cells for transmission and unpacking the information at the other end. As we have seen, at the ATM layer, each cell consists of a 5-octet header and a 48-octet information field. Thus, SAR must pack any SAR headers and trailers, plus CS information, into 48-octet blocks.

Initially, ITU-T defined one protocol type for each class of service, named Type 1 through Type 4. Actually, each protocol type consists of two protocols, one at the CS sublayer and one at the SAR sublayer. More recently, types 3 and 4 were merged into a Type 3/4, and a new type, Type 5, was defined. Figure 11.12 shows which services are supported by which types. In all of these cases, a block of data from a higher layer is encapsulated into a protocol data unit (PDU) at the CS

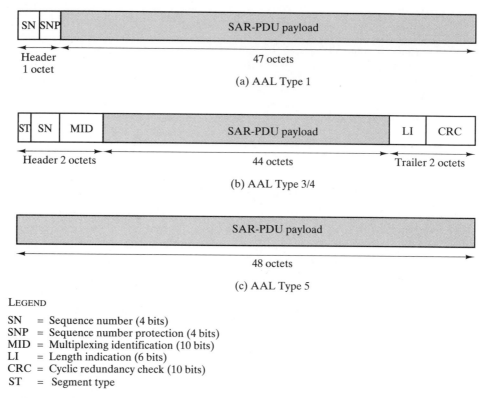

**LEGEND**

SN  = Sequence number (4 bits)
SNP = Sequence number protection (4 bits)
MID = Multiplexing identification (10 bits)
LI  = Length indication (6 bits)
CRC = Cyclic redundancy check (10 bits)
ST  = Segment type

**FIGURE 11.13**   Segmentation and reassembly (SAR) protocol data units (PDUs)

sublayer. In fact, this sublayer is referred to as the common-part convergence sublayer (CPCS), leaving open the possibility that additional, specialized functions may be performed at the CS level. The CPCS PDU is then passed to the SAR sublayer, where it is broken up into payload blocks. Each payload block can fit into an SAR-PDU, which has a total length of 48 octets. Each 48-octet SAR-PDU fits into a single ATM cell.

Figure 11.13 shows the formats of the protocol data units (PDUs) at the SAR level except for Type 2, which has not yet been defined.

In the remainder of this section, we look at AAL Type 5, which is becoming increasingly popular, especially in ATM LAN applications. This protocol was introduced to provide a streamlined transport facility for higher-layer protocols that are connection-oriented. If it is assumed that the higher layer takes care of connection management, and that the ATM layer produces minimal errors, then most of the fields in the SAR and CPCS PDUs are not necessary. For example, with connection-oriented service, the MID field is not necessary. This field is used in AAL 3/4 to multiplex different streams of data using the same virtual ATM connection (VCI/VPI). In AAL 5, it is assumed that higher-layer software takes care of such multiplexing.

Type 5 was introduced to

- Reduce protocol-processing overhead
- Reduce transmission overhead
- Ensure adaptability to existing transport protocols

To understand the operation of Type 5, let us begin with the CPCS level. The CPCS-PDU (Figure 11.14) includes a trailer with the following fields:

- **CPCS User-to-User Indication** *(1 octet)*. Used to transparently transfer user-to-user information.
- **Cyclic Redundancy Check** *(4 octets)*. Used to detect bit errors in the CPCS-PDU.
- **Common Part Indicator** *(1 octet)*. Indicates the interpretation of the remaining fields in the CPCS-PDU trailer. Currently, only one interpretation is defined.
- **Length** *(2 octets)*. Length of the CPCS-PDU payload field.

The payload from the next higher layer is padded out so that the entire CPCS-PDU is a multiple of 48 octets.

The SAR-PDU consists simply of 48 octets of payload, carrying a portion of the CPCS-PDU. The lack of protocol overhead has several implications:

1. Because there is no sequence number, the receiver must assume that all SAR-PDUs arrive in the proper order for reassembly. The CRC field in the CPCS-PDU is intended to verify such an order.
2. The lack of MID field means that it is not possible to interleave cells from different CPCS-PDUs. Therefore, each successive SAR-PDU carries a portion

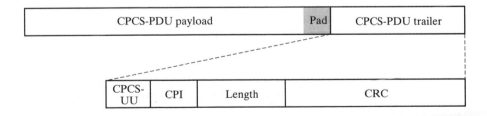

LEGEND
CPCS-UU = CPCS user-to-user indication (1 octet)
CPI = Common-part indicator (1 octet)
Length = Length of CPCS-PDU payload (2 octets)
CRC = Cyclic redundancy check (4 octets)

**FIGURE 11.14** AAL type 5 CPCS PDU.

of the current CPCS-PDU, or the first block of the next CPCS-PDU. To distinguish between these two cases, the ATM user-to-user indication (AAU) bit in the payload-type field of the ATM cell header is used (Figure 11.4). A CPCS-PDU consists of zero or more consecutive SAR-PDUs with AAU set to 0, followed immediately by an SAR-PDU with AAU set to 1.

3. The lack of an LI field means that there is no way for the SAR entity to distinguish between CPCS-PDU octets and filler in the last SAR-PDU. Therefore, there is no way for the SAR entity to find the CPCS-PDU trailer in the last SAR-PDU. To avoid this situation, it is required that the CPCS-PDU payload be padded out so that the last bit of the CPCS-trailer occurs as the last bit of the final SAR-PDU.

Figure 11.15 shows an example of AAL 5 transmission. The CPCS-PDU, including padding and trailer, is divided into 48-octet blocks. Each block is transmitted in a single ATM cell.

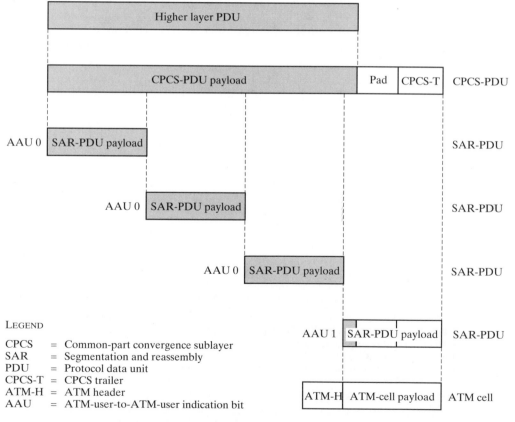

FIGURE 11.15 Example of AAL 5 transmission.

## 11.6  TRAFFIC AND CONGESTION CONTROL

As is the case with frame relay networks, traffic and congestion control techniques are vital to the successful operation of ATM-based networks. Without such techniques, traffic from user nodes can exceed the capacity of the network, causing memory buffers of ATM switches to overflow, leading to data losses.

ATM networks present difficulties in effectively controlling congestion not found in other types of networks, including frame relay networks. The complexity of the problem is compounded by the limited number of overhead bits available for exerting control over the flow of user cells. This area is currently the subject of intense research, and no consensus has emerged for a full-blown traffic- and congestion-control strategy. Accordingly, ITU-T has defined a restricted initial set of traffic- and congestion-control capabilities aiming at simple mechanisms and realistic network efficiency; these are specified in I.371.

We begin with an overview of the congestion problem and the framework adopted by ITU-T. We see that the focus of the mechanisms so far adopted is on control schemes for delay-sensitive traffic, such as voice and video. These schemes are not suited for handling bursty traffic, which is the subject of ongoing research and standardization efforts. The discussion then turns to traffic control, which refers to the set of actions taken by the network to avoid congestion. Finally, we examine congestion control, which refers to the set of actions taken by the network to minimize the intensity, spread, and duration of congestion once congestion has already occurred.

### Requirements for ATM Traffic and Congestion Control

Both the types of traffic patterns imposed on ATM network and the transmission characteristics of those network differ markedly from those of other switching networks. Most packet-switched and frame relay networks carry non-real-time data traffic. Typically, the traffic on individual virtual circuits or frame relay connections is bursty in nature, and the receiving system expects to receive incoming traffic on each connection in such a fashion. As a result,

1. The network does not need to replicate the exact timing pattern of incoming traffic at the exit node.
2. Therefore, simple statistical multiplexing can be used to accommodate multiple logical connections over the physical interface between user and network. The average data rate required by each connection is less than the burst rate for that connection, and the user-network interface (UNI) need only be designed for a capacity somewhat greater than the sum of the average data rates for all connections.

A number of tools are available for control of congestion in packet-switched and frame relay networks, as we have seen in the preceding two chapters. These types of congestion-control schemes are inadequate for ATM networks. [GERS91] cites the following reasons:

1. The majority of traffic is not amenable to flow control. For example, voice and video traffic sources cannot stop generating cells even when the network is congested.

2. Feedback is slow due to the drastically reduced cell transmission time compared to propagation delays across the network.

3. ATM networks typically support a wide range of applications requiring capacity ranging from a few kbps to several hundred Mbps. Relatively simple-minded congestion control schemes generally end up penalizing one end or the other of that spectrum.

4. Applications on ATM networks may generate very different traffic patterns (e.g., constant bit-rate versus variable bit-rate sources). Again, it is difficult for conventional congestion control techniques to handle fairly such variety.

5. Different applications on ATM networks require different network services (e.g., delay-sensitive service for voice and video, and loss-sensitive service for data).

6. The very high speeds in switching and transmission make ATM networks more volatile in terms of congestion and traffic control. A scheme that relies heavily on reacting to changing conditions will produce extreme and wasteful fluctuations in routing policy and flow control.

A key issue that relates to the above points is cell delay variation, a topic to which we now turn.

### Cell–Delay Variation

For an ATM network, voice and video signals can be digitized and transmitted as a stream of cells. A key requirement, especially for voice, is that the delay across the network be short; generally, this will be the case for ATM networks. As we have discussed, ATM is designed to minimize the processing and transmission overhead internal to the network so that very fast cell switching and routing are possible.

There is another important requirement that, to some extent, conflicts with the preceding requirement, namely that the rate of delivery of cells to the destination user must be constant. Now, it is inevitable that there will be some variability in the rate of delivery of cells, due both to effects within the network and at the source UNI; we summarize these effects presently. First, let us consider how the destination user might cope with variations in the delay of cells as they transit from source user to destination user.

A general procedure for achieving a constant bit rate (CBR) is illustrated in Figure 11.16. Let $D(i)$ represent the end-to-end delay experienced by the $i$th cell. The destination system does not know the exact amount of this delay; there is no timestamp information associated with each cell, and, even if there were, it is impossible to keep source and destination clocks perfectly synchronized. When the first cell on a connection arrives at time $t(0)$, the target user delays the cell an additional amount $V(0)$ prior to delivery to the application. $V(0)$ is an estimate of the

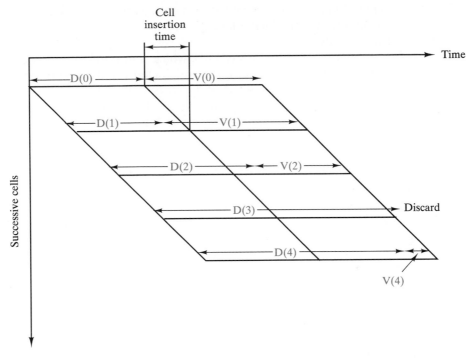

**FIGURE 11.16**   Time reassembly of CBR cells.

amount of cell delay variation that this application can tolerate and that is likely to be produced by the network.

Subsequent cells are delayed so that they are delivered to the user at a constant rate of $R$ cells per second. The time between delivery of cells to the target application is therefore $\delta = 1/R$. To achieve a constant rate, the next cell is delayed a variable amount $V(1)$ to satisfy the following:

$$t(1) + V(1) = t(0) + V(0) + \delta$$

So,

$$V(1) = V(0) - [t(1) - (t(0) + \delta)]$$

In general,

$$V(i) = V(0) - [t(i) - (t(0) + i \times \delta)]$$

which can also be expressed as

$$V(i) = V(i - 1) - [t(i) - (t(i - 1) + \delta)]$$

If the computed value of $V(i)$ is negative, then that cell is discarded. The result is that data is delivered to the higher layer at a constant bit rate, with occasional gaps due to dropped cells.

The amount of the initial delay $V(0)$, which is also the average delay applied to all incoming cells, is a function of the anticipated cell-delay variation. To minimize this delay, a subscriber will therefore request a minimal cell-delay variation from the network provider. This request leads to a trade-off; cell-delay variation can be reduced by increasing the data rate at the UNI, relative to the load, and by increasing resources within the network.

### Network Contribution to Cell-Delay Variation

One component of cell-delay variation is due to events within the network. For packet-switching networks, packet delay variation can be considerable, due to queuing effects at each of the intermediate switching nodes; to a lesser extent, this is also true of frame delay variation in frame relay networks. However, in the case of ATM networks, cell-delay variations due to network effects are likely to be minimal; the principal reasons for this are the following:

1. The ATM protocol is designed to minimize processing overhead at intermediate switching nodes. The cells are fixed-size with fixed-header formats, and there is no flow control or error control processing required.
2. To accommodate the high speeds of ATM networks, ATM switches have had to be designed to provide extremely high throughput. Thus, the processing time for an individual cell at a node is negligible.

The only factor that could lead to noticeable cell-delay variation within the network is congestion. If the network begins to become congested, either cells must be discarded or there will be a buildup of queuing delays at affected switches. Thus, it is important that the total load accepted by the network at any time not be such as to cause congestion.

### Cell-Delay Variation at the UNI

Even if an application generates data for transmission at a constant bit rate, cell-delay variation can occur at the source due to the processing that takes place at the three layers of the ATM model.

Figure 11.17 illustrates the potential causes of cell-delay variation. In this example, ATM connections A and B support user data rates of $X$ and $Y$ Mbps, respectively. At the AAL level, data is segmented into 48-octet blocks. Note that on a time diagram, the blocks appear to be of different sizes for the two connections; specifically, the time required to generate a 48-octet block of data in microseconds is

$$\text{Connection A: } \frac{48 \times 8}{X}$$

$$\text{Connection B: } \frac{48 \times 8}{Y}$$

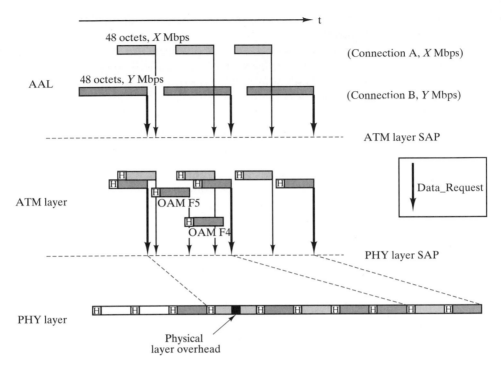

**FIGURE 11.17**  Origins of cell delay variation (I.371).

The ATM layer encapsulates each segment into a 53-octet cell. These cells must be interleaved and delivered to the physical layer to be transmitted at the data rate of the physical link. Delay is introduced into this interleaving process: If two cells from different connections arrive at the ATM layer at overlapping times, one of the cells must be delayed by the amount of the overlap. In addition, the ATM layer is generating OAM (operation and maintenance) cells that must also be interleaved with user cells.

At the physical layer, there is additional opportunity for the introduction of further cell delays. For example, if cells are transmitted in SDH frames, overhead

**TABLE 11.3**  Traffic control and congestion control functions.

| Response time | Traffic control functions | Congestion control functions |
|---|---|---|
| Long Term | • Network resource management | |
| Connection Duration | • Connection admission control | |
| Round-trip Propagation Time | • Fast resource management | • Explicit notification |
| Cell Insertion Time | • Usage parameter control<br>• Priority control | • Selective cell discarding |

bits for those frames will be inserted into the physical link, thereby delaying bits from the ATM layer.

None of the delays just listed can be predicated in any detail, and none follow any repetitive pattern. Accordingly, there is a random element to the time interval between reception of data at the ATM layer from the AAL and the transmission of that data in a cell across the UNI.

### Traffic and Congestion Control Framework

I.371 lists the following objectives of ATM layer traffic and congestion control:

- ATM layer traffic and congestion control should support a set of ATM layer Quality of Service (QOS) classes sufficient for all foreseeable network services; the specification of these QOS classes should be consistent with network performance parameters currently under study.
- ATM layer traffic and congestion control should not rely on AAL protocols that are network-service specific, nor on higher-layer protocols that are application specific. Protocol layers above the ATM layer may make use of information provided by the ATM layer to improve the utility those protocols can derive from the network.
- The design of an optimum set of ATM layer traffic controls and congestion controls should minimize network and end-system complexity while maximizing network utilization.

In order to meet these objectives, ITU-T has defined a collection of traffic and congestion control functions that operate across a spectrum of timing intervals. Table 11.3 lists these functions with respect to the response times within which they operate. Four levels of timing are considered:

- **Cell insertion time.** Functions at this level react immediately to cells as they are transmitted.
- **Round-trip propagation time.** At this level, the network responds within the lifetime of a cell in the network, and may provide feedback indications to the source.
- **Connection duration.** At this level, the network determines whether a new connection at a given QOS can be accommodated and what performance levels will be agreed to.
- **Long term.** These are controls that affect more than one ATM connection and that are established for long-term use.

The essence of the traffic-control strategy is based on (1) determining whether a given new ATM connection can be accommodated and (2) agreeing with the subscriber on the performance parameters that will be supported. In effect, the subscriber and the network enter into a traffic contract: The network agrees to support traffic at a certain level on this connection, and the subscriber agrees not to exceed performance limits. Traffic control functions are concerned with establishing these traffic parameters and enforcing them. Thus, they are concerned with congestion avoidance. If traffic control fails in certain instances, then congestion may occur. At this point, congestion-control functions are invoked to respond to and recover from the congestion.

## Traffic Control

A variety of traffic control functions have been defined to maintain the QOS of ATM connections. These include

- Network resource management
- Connection admission control
- Usage parameter control
- Priority control
- Fast resource management

We examine each of these in turn.

### Network Resource Management

The essential concept behind network resource management is to allocate network resources in such a way as to separate traffic flows according to service characteristics. So far, the only specific traffic control function based on network resource management deals with the use of virtual paths.

As discussed earlier, a virtual path connection (VPC) provides a convenient means of grouping similar virtual channel connections (VCCs). The network provides aggregate capacity and performance characteristics on the virtual path, and these are shared by the virtual connections. There are three cases to consider:

- **User-to-user application.** The VPC extends between a pair of UNIs. In this case, the network has no knowledge of the QOS of the individual VCCs within a VPC. It is the user's responsibility to assure that the aggregate demand from the VCCs can be accommodated by the VPC.
- **User-to-network application.** The VPC extends between a UNI and a network node. In this case, the network is aware of the QOS of the VCCs within the VPC and has to accommodate them.
- **Network-to-network application.** The VPC extends between two network nodes. Again, in this case, the network is aware of the QOS of the VCCs within the VPC and has to accommodate them.

The QOS parameters that are of primary concern for network resource management are cell loss ratio, cell transfer delay, and cell delay variation, all of which are affected by the number of resources devoted to the VPC by the network. If a VCC extends through multiple VPCs, then the performance on that VCC depends on the performances of the consecutive VPCs, and on how the connection is handled at any node that performs VCC-related functions. Such a node may be a switch, concentrator, or other network equipment. The performance of each VPC depends on the capacity of that VPC and the traffic characteristics of the VCCs contained within the VPC. The performance of each VCC-related function depends on the switching/processing speed at the node and on the relative priority with which various cells are handled.

Figure 11.18 gives an example. VCCs 1 and 2 experience a performance that depends on VPCs *b* and *c* and on how these VCCs are handled by the intermediate nodes; this may differ from the performance experienced by VCCs 3, 4, and 5.

There are a number of alternatives for the way in which VCCs are grouped and the type of performance they experience. If all of the VCCs within a VPC are handled similarly, then they should experience similar expected network performance, in terms of cell-loss ratio, cell-transfer delay, and cell-delay variation. Alternatively, when different VCCs within the same VPC require different QOS, the VPC performance objective agreed upon by network and subscriber should be suitably set for the most demanding VCC requirement.

In either case, with multiple VCCs within the same VPC, the network has two general options for allocating capacity to the VPC:

1. *Aggregate peak demand.* The network may set the capacity (data rate) of the VPC equal to the total of the peak data rates of all of the VCCs within the VPC. The advantage of this approach is that each VCC can be given a QOS that accommodates its peak demand. The disadvantage is that most of the time, the VPC capacity will not be fully utilized, and, therefore, the network will have underutilized resources.

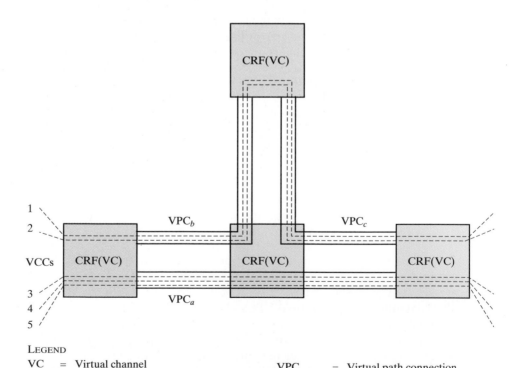

LEGEND

| | | | | | |
|---|---|---|---|---|---|
| VC | = | Virtual channel | VPC | = | Virtual path connection |
| VCC | = | Virtual channel connection | CRF(VC) | = | VCC-related functions |

**FIGURE 11.18** Configuration of VCCs and VPCs (I.371).

2. *Statistical multiplexing.* If the network sets the capacity of the VPC to be greater than or equal to the average data rates of all the VCCs but less than the aggregate peak demand, then a statistical multiplexing service is supplied. With statistical multiplexing, VCCs experience greater cell-delay variation and greater cell-transfer delay. Depending on the size of buffers used to queue cells for transmission, VCCs may also experience greater cell-loss ratio. This approach has the advantage of more efficient utilization of capacity, and is attractive if the VCCs can tolerate the lower QOS.

When statistical multiplexing is used, it is preferable to group VCCs into VPCs on the basis of similar traffic characteristics and similar QOS requirements. If dissimilar VCCs share the same VPC and statistical multiplexing is used, it is difficult to provide fair access to both high-demand and low-demand traffic streams.

### Connection Admission Control

Connection admission control is the first line of defense for the network in protecting itself from excessive loads. In essence, when a user requests a new VPC or VCC, the user must specify (implicitly or explicitly) the traffic characteristics in both directions for that connection. The user selects traffic characteristics by selecting a QOS from among the QOS classes that the network provides. The network accepts the connection only if it can commit the resources necessary to support that traffic level while at the same time maintaining the agreed-upon QOS of existing connections. By accepting the connection, the network forms a *traffic contract* with the user. Once the connection is accepted, the network continues to provide the agreed-upon QOS as long as the user complies with the traffic contract.

For the current specification, the traffic contract consists of the four parameters defined in Table 11.4: peak cell rate (PCR), cell-delay variation (CDV), sustainable

**TABLE 11.4** Traffic parameters used in defining VCC/VPC quality of service.

| Parameter | Description | Traffic type |
|---|---|---|
| Peak Cell Rate (PCR) | An upper bound on the traffic that can be submitted on an ATM connection. | CBR, VBR |
| Cell Delay Variation (CDV) | An upper bound on the variability in the pattern of cell arrivals observed at a single measurement point with reference to the peak cell rate. | CBR, VBR |
| Sustainable Cell Rate (SCR) | An upper bound on the average rate of an ATM connection, calculated over the duration of the connection. | VBR |
| Burst Tolerance | An upper bound on the variability in the pattern of cell arrivals observed at a single measurement point with reference to the sustainable cell rate. | VBR |

CBR = constant bit rate
VBR = variable bit rate

cell rate (SCR), and burst tolerance. Only the first two parameters are relevant for a constant bit rate (CBR) source; all four parameters may be used for variable bit rate (VBR) sources.

As the name suggests, the peak cell rate is the maximum rate at which cells are generated by the source on this connection. However, we need to take into account the cell-delay variation. Although a source may be generating cells at a constant peak rate, cell-delay variations introduced by various factors (see Figure 11.17) will affect the timing, causing cells to clump up and gaps to occur. Thus, a source may temporarily exceed the peak cell rate due to clumping. For the network to properly allocate resources to this connection, it must know not only the peak cell rate but also the CDV.

The exact relationship between peak cell rate and CDV depends on the operational definitions of these two terms. The standards provide these definitions in terms of a cell rate algorithm. Because this algorithm can be used for usage parameter control, we defer a discussion until the next subsection.

The PCR and CDV must be specified for every connection. As an option for variable-bit rate sources, the user may also specify a sustainable cell rate and burst tolerance. These parameters are analogous to PCR and CDV, respectively, but apply to an average rate of cell generation rather than to a peak rate. The user can describe the future flow of cells in greater detail by using the SCR and burst tolerance as well as the PCR and CDV. With this additional information, the network may be able to more efficiently utilize the network resources. For example, if a number of VCCs are statistically multiplexed over a VPC, knowledge of both average and peak cell rates enables the network to allocate buffers of sufficient size to handle the traffic efficiently without cell loss.

For a given connection (VPC or VCC), the four traffic parameters may be specified in several ways, as illustrated in Table 11.5. Parameter values may be implicitly defined by default rules set by the network operator. In this case, all connections are assigned the same values or all connections of a given class are assigned

**TABLE 11.5**  Procedures used to set values of traffic contract parameters.

|  | Explicitly specified parameters | | Implicitly specified parameters |
|---|---|---|---|
|  | Parameter values set at connection-setup time | Parameter values specified at subscription time | Parameter values set using default rules |
|  | Requested by user/NMS | assigned by network operator | |
| SVC | signaling | by subscription | network-operator default rules |
| PVC | NMS | by subscription | network-operator default rules |

SVC = switched virtual connection
PVC = permanent virtual connection
NMS = network management system

the same values for that class. The network operator may also associate parameter values with a given subscriber and assign these at the time of subscription. Finally, parameter values tailored to a particular connection may be assigned at connection time. In the case of a permanent virtual connection, these values are assigned by the network when the connection is set up. For a switched virtual connection, the parameters are negotiated between the user and the network via a signaling protocol.

Another aspect of quality of service that may be requested or assigned for a connection is cell-loss priority. A user may request two levels of cell-loss priority for an ATM connection; the priority of an individual cell is indicated by the user through the CLP bit in the cell header (see Figure 11.4). When two priority levels are used, the traffic parameters for both cell flows must be specified; typically, this is done by specifying a set of traffic parameters for high-priority traffic (CLP = 0) and a set of traffic parameters for all traffic (CLP = 0 or 1). Based on this breakdown, the network may be able to allocate resources more efficiently.

## Usage Parameter Control

Once a connection has been accepted by the Connection Admission Control function, the Usage Parameter Control (UPC) function of the network monitors the connection to determine whether the traffic conforms to the traffic contract. The main purpose of Usage Parameter Control is to protect network resources from an overload on one connection that would adversely affect the QOS on other connections by detecting violations of assigned parameters and taking appropriate actions.

Usage parameter control can be done at both the virtual path and virtual channel levels. Of these, the more important is VPC-level control, as network resources are, in general, initially allocated on the basis of virtual paths, with the virtual path capacity shared among the member virtual channels.

There are two separate functions encompassed by usage parameter control:

- Control of peak cell rate and the associated cell-delay variation (CDV)
- Control of sustainable cell rate and the associated burst tolerance

Let us first consider the peak cell rate and the associated cell-delay variation. In simple terms, a traffic flow is compliant if the peak rate of cell transmission does not exceed the agreed-upon peak cell rate, subject to the possibility of cell-delay variation within the agreed-upon bound. I.371 defines an algorithm, the peak cell-rate algorithm, that monitors compliance. The algorithm operates on the basis of two parameters: a peak cell-rate $R$ and a CDV tolerance limit of $\tau$. Then, $T = 1/R$ is the interarrival time between cells if there were no CDV. With CDV, $T$ is the average interarrival time at the peak rate. The algorithm uses a form of leaky-bucket mechanism to monitor the rate at which cells arrive in order to assure that the interarrival time is not too short to cause the flow to exceed the peak cell rate by an amount greater than the tolerance limit.

The same algorithm, with different parameters can be used to monitor the sustainable cell rate and the associated burst tolerance. In this case, the parameters are the sustainable cell-rate $R_s$ and a burst tolerance $\tau_s$.

The cell-rate algorithm is rather complex; details can be found in [STAL95a]. The cell-rate algorithm simply defines a way to monitor compliance with the traffic contract. To perform usage parameter control, the network must act on the results of the algorithm. The simplest strategy passes along compliant cells and discards noncompliant cells at the point of the UPC function.

At the network's option, cell tagging may also be used for noncompliant cells. In this case, a noncompliant cell may be tagged with CLP = 1 (low priority) and passed. Such cells are then subject to discard at a later point in the network.

If the user has negotiated two levels of cell-loss priority for a network, then the situation is more complex. Recall that the user may negotiate a traffic contract for high-priority traffic (CLP = 0) and a separate contract for aggregate traffic (CLP 0 or 1). The following rules apply:

1. A cell with CLP = 0 that conforms to the traffic contract for CLP = 0 passes.
2. A cell with CLP = 0 that is noncompliant for (CLP = 0) traffic but compliant for (CLP 0 or 1) traffic is tagged and passed.
3. A cell with CLP = 0 that is noncompliant for (CLP = 0) traffic and noncompliant for (CLP 0 or 1) traffic is discarded.
4. A cell with CLP = 1 that is compliant for (CLP = 1) traffic is passed.
5. A cell with CLP = 1 that is noncompliant for (CLP 0 or 1) traffic is discarded.

### Priority Control

Priority control comes into play when the network, at some point beyond the UPC function, discards (CLP = 1) cells. The objective is to discard lower priority cells in order to protect the performance for higher-priority cells. Note that the network has no way to discriminate between cells that were labeled as lower-priority by the source and cells that were tagged by the UPC function.

### Fast Resource Management

Fast resource management functions operate on the time scale of the round-trip propagation delay of the ATM connection. The current version of I.371 lists fast-resource management as a potential tool for traffic control that is for further study. One example of such a function that is given in the Recommendation is the ability of the network to respond to a request by a user to send a burst. That is, the user would like to temporarily exceed the current traffic contract to send a relatively large amount of data. If the network determines that the resources exist along the route for this VCC or VPC for such a burst, then the network reserves those resources and grants permission. Following the burst, the normal traffic control is enforced.

### Congestion Control

ATM congestion control refers to the set of actions taken by the network to minimize the intensity, spread, and duration of congestion. These actions are triggered by congestion in one or more network elements. The following two functions have been defined:

- Selective cell discarding
- Explicit forward congestion indication

## Selective Cell Discarding

Selective cell discarding is similar to priority control. In the priority control function (CLP = 1), cells are discarded to avoid congestion. However, only "excess" cells are discarded. That is, cells are limited so that the performance objectives for the (CLP = 0) and (CLP = 1) flows are still met. Once congestion actually occurs, the network is no longer bound to meet all performance objectives. To recover from a congested condition, the network is free to discard any (CLP = 1) cell and may even discard (CLP = 0) cells on ATM connections that are not complying with their traffic contract.

## Explicit Forward Congestion Indication

Explicit forward congestion notification for ATM network works in essentially the same manner as for frame relay networks. Any ATM network node that is experiencing congestion may set an explicit forward congestion indication in the payload type field of the cell header of cells on connections passing through the node (Figure 11.4). The indication notifies the user that congestion avoidance procedures should be initiated for traffic in the same direction as the received cell. It indicates that this cell on this ATM connection has encountered congested resources. The user may then invoke actions in higher-layer protocols to adaptively lower the cell rate of the connection.

The network issues the indication by setting the first two bits of the payload type field in the cell header to 01 (Table 11.2). Once this value is set by any node, it may not be altered by other network nodes along the path to the destination user.

Note that the generic flow control (GFC) field is not involved. The GFC field has only local significance and cannot be communicated across the network.

## 11.7  RECOMMENDED READING

[GORA95], [MCDY95], [HAND94], and [PRYC93] provide in-depth coverage of ATM. An interesting overview of ATM is [BOUD92]. The virtual path/virtual channel approach of ATM is examined in [SATO90], [SATO91], and [BURG91].

[ARMI93] and [SUZU94] discuss AAL and compare Types 3/4 and 5.

[ONVU94] is devoted to issues related to the performance of ATM networks, including traffic and congestion control. The following special issues are devoted to the topics of this chapter: April 1991 issue of IEEE Journal on Selected Areas in Communications; October 1991 issue of IEEE Communications Magazine; and September 1992 issue of IEEE Network.

ARMI93  Armitage, G. and Adams, K. "Packet Reassembly During Cell Loss." *IEEE Network*, September 1993.

**BOUD92** Boudec, J. "The Asynchronous Transfer Mode: A Tutorial." *Computer Networks and ISDN Systems*, May 1992.

**BURG91** Burg, J. and Dorman, D. "Broadband ISDN Resource Management: The Role of Virtual Paths." *IEEE Communications Magazine*, September 1991.

**GORA95** Goralski, W. *Introduction to ATM Networking.* New York: McGraw-Hill, 1995.

**HAND94** Handel, R., Huber, N., and Schroder, S. ATM Networks: *Concepts, Protocols, Applications.* Reading, MA: Addison-Wesley, 1994.

**MCDY95** McDysan, D. and Spohn, D. *ATM: Theory and Application.* New York: McGraw-Hill, 1995.

**ONVU94** Onvural, R. *Asynchronous Transfer Mode Networks: Performance Issues.* Boston: Artech House, 1994.

**PRYC93** Prycker, M. *Asynchronous Transfer Mode: Solutions for Broadband ISDN.* New York: Ellis Horwood, 1993.

**SATO90** Sato, K., Ohta, S., and Tokizawa, I. "Broad-band ATM Network Architecture Based on Virtual Paths." *IEEE Transactions on Communications*, August 1990.

**SATO91** Sato, K., Ueda, H., and Yoshikai, M. "The Role of Virtual Path Crossconnection." *IEEE LTS*, August 1991.

**SUZU94** Suzuki, T. "ATM Adaptation Layer Protocol." *IEEE Communications Magazine*, April 1994.

## Recommended Web Sites

- http://www.atmforum.com: The web site of the ATM forum, which is leading the effort to expand the funtionality of ATM networks.
- http://www.atm25.com/ATM_Reference.html: Links to dozens of ATM reference sites on the Internet.

## 11.8 PROBLEMS

**11.1** One method of transmitting ATM cells is as a continuous stream of cells, with no framing imposed; therefore, the transmission is simply a stream of bits, with all bits being part of cells. Because there is no external frame, some other form of synchronization is needed, and can be achieved using the HEC function. The requirement is to assure that the receiver knows the beginning and ending cell boundaries and does not drift with respect to the sender. Draw a state diagram for the use of the HEC to achieve cell synchronization, and then explain its functionality.

**11.2** Although ATM does not include any end-to-end error detection and control functions on the user data, it is provided with an HEC field to detect and correct header errors. Let us consider the value of this feature. Suppose that the bit error rate of the transmission system is $B$. If errors are uniformly distributed, then the probability of an error in the header is

$$\frac{h}{h + i} \times B$$

and the probability of an error in the data field is

$$\frac{i}{h + i} \times B$$

where $h$ is the number of bits in the header and $i$ is the number of bits in the data field.

**a.** Suppose that errors in the header are not detected and not corrected. In this case, a header error may result in a misrouting of the cell to the wrong destination; therefore, $i$ bits will arrive at an incorrect destination, and $i$ bits will not arrive at the correct destination. What is the overall bit error rate $B1$? Find an expression for the multiplication effect on the bit error rate $M1 = B1/B$.

**b.** Now suppose that header errors are detected but not corrected. In that case, $i$ bits will not arrive at the correct destination. What is the overall bit error rate $B2$? Find an expression for the multiplication effect on the bit error rate: $M2 = B2/B$.

**c.** Now suppose that header errors are detected and corrected. What is the overall bit error rate $B3$? Find an expression for the multiplication effect on the bit rate error $M3 = B3/B$.

**d.** Plot $M1$, $M2$, and $M3$ as a function of header length, for $i = 48 \times 8 = 384$ bits. Comment on the results.

**11.3**   One key design decision for ATM was whether to use fixed or variable length cells. Let us consider this decision from the point of view of efficiency. We can define transmission efficiency as

$$N = \frac{\text{Number of information octets}}{\text{Number of information octets} + \text{Number of overhead octets}}$$

**a.** Consider the use of fixed-length packets. In this case, the overhead consists of the header octets. Define the following:

$L$ = Data-field size of the cell in octets
$H$ = Header size of the cell in octets
$X$ = Number of information octets to be transmitted as a single message

Derive an expression for N. Hint, the expression will need to use the operator $\lceil \cdot \rceil$, where

$\lceil Y \rceil$ = the smallest integer greater than or equal to $Y$.

**b.** If cells have variable length, then overhead is determined by the header, plus the flags to delimit the cells or an additional length field in the header. Let $Hv$ = additional overhead octets required to enable the use of variable-length cells. Derive an expression for $N$ in terms of $X$, $H$, and $Hv$.

**c.** Let $L = 48$, $H = 5$, and $Hv = 2$. Plot $N$ versus message size for fixed- and variable-length cells. Comment on the results.

**11.4**   Another key design decision for ATM is the size of the data field for fixed-size cells. Let us consider this decision from the point of view of efficiency and delay.

**a.** Assume that an extended transmission takes place, so that all cells are completely filled. Derive an expression for the efficiency $N$ as a function of $H$ and $L$.

**b.** Packetization delay is the delay introduced into a transmission stream by the need to buffer bits until an entire packet is filled before transmission. Derive an expression for this delay as a function of $L$ and the data rate $R$ of the source.

**c.** Common data rates for voice coding are 32 kbps and 64 kbps. Plot packetization delay as a function of $L$ for these two data rates; use a left-hand $y$ axis with a maximum value of 2 ms. On the same graph, plot transmission efficiency as a function of $L$; use a right hand $y$ axis with a maximum value of 100%. Comment on the results.

**11.5**   Suppose that AAL 5 is being used and that the receiver is in an idle state (no incoming cells). Then, a block of user data is transmitted as a sequence of SAR-PDUs.

**a.** Suppose that a single bit error in one of the SAR-PDUs occurs. What happens at the receiving end?

**b.** Suppose that one of the cells with AAU = 0 is lost. What happens at the receiving end?

**c.** Suppose that one of the cells with AAU = 1 is lost. What happens at the receiving end?

**11.6** Compare Sustainable Cell Rate and Burst Tolerance, as used in ATM networks, with Committed Information Rate and Excess Burst Size, as used in frame relay networks. Do the respective terms represent the same concepts?

# PART THREE

# Local Area Networks

## CHAPTER 12

# LAN TECHNOLOGY

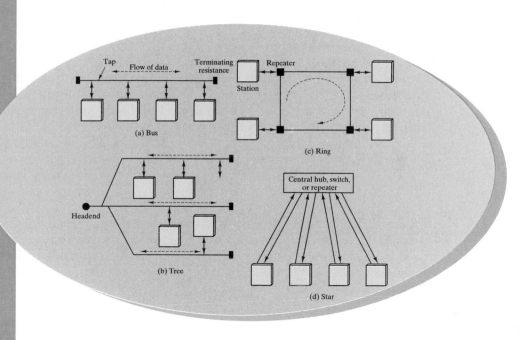

I n this part, we examine local area networks (LANs) and metropolitan area networks (MANs). These networks share the characteristic of being packet broadcasting networks. With a broadcast communications network, each station is attached to a transmission medium shared by other stations. In its simplest form, a transmission from any one station is broadcast to and received by all other stations. As with packet-switched networks, transmission on a packet broadcasting network is in the form of packets. Table 12.1 provides useful definitions of LANs and MANs, taken from one of the IEEE 802 standards documents.

This chapter begins our discussion of LANs[1] with a description of the protocol architecture that is in common use for implementing LANs. This architecture is also the basis of standardization efforts. Our overview covers the physical, medium access control (MAC), and logical link control (LLC) levels.

Following this overview, the chapter focuses on aspects of LAN technology. The key technology ingredients that determine the nature of a LAN or MAN are

- Topology
- Transmission medium
- Medium access control technique

This chapter surveys the topologies and transmission media that are most commonly used for LANs and MANs. The issue of access control is briefly raised, but is covered in more detail in Chapter 13. The concept of a bridge, which plays a critical role in extending LAN coverage, is discussed in Chapter 14.

## 12.1 LAN ARCHITECTURE

The architecture of a LAN is best described in terms of a layering of protocols that organize the basic functions of a LAN. This section opens with a description of the standardized protocol architecture for LANs, which encompasses physical, medium access control, and logical link control layers. Each of these layers is then examined in turn.

### Protocol Architecture

Protocols defined specifically for LAN and MAN transmission address issues relating to the transmission of blocks of data over the network. In OSI terms, higher-layer protocols (layer 3 or 4 and above) are independent of network architecture and are applicable to LANs, MANs, and WANs. Thus, a discussion of LAN protocols is concerned principally with lower layers of the OSI model.

Figure 12.1 relates the LAN protocols to the OSI architecture (first introduced in Figure 1.10). This architecture was developed by the IEEE 802 committee and has been adopted by all organizations working on the specification of LAN standards. It is generally referred to as the IEEE 802 reference model.

---

[1] For the sake of brevity, the book often uses LAN when referring to LAN and MAN concerns. The context should clarify when only LAN or both LAN and MAN is meant.

**TABLE 12.1**    Definitions of LANs and MANs.*

The LANs described herein are distinguished from other types of data networks in that they are optimized for a moderate size geographic area such as a single office building, a warehouse, or a campus. The IEEE 802 LAN is a shared medium peer-to-peer communications network that broadcasts information for all stations to receive. As a consequence, it does not inherently provide privacy. The LAN enables stations to communicate directly using a common physical medium on a point-to-point basis without any intermediate switching node being required. There is always need for an access sublayer in order to arbitrate the access to the shared medium. The network is generally owned, used, and operated by a single organization. This is in contrast to Wide Area Networks (WANs) that interconnect communication facilities in different parts of a country or are used as a public utility. These LANs are also different from networks, such as backplane buses, that are optimized for the interconnection of devices on a desk top or components within a single piece of equipment.

A MAN is optimized for a larger geographical area than a LAN, ranging from several blocks of buildings to entire cities. As with local networks, MANs can also depend on communications channels of moderate-to-high data rates. Error rates and delay may be slightly higher than might be obtained on a LAN. A MAN might be owned and operated by a single organization, but usually will be used by many individuals and organizations. MANs might also be owned and operated as public utilities. They will often provide means for internetworking of local networks. Although not a requirement for all LANs, the capability to perform local networking of integrated voice and data (IVD) devices is considered an optional function for a LAN. Likewise, such capabilities in a network covering a metropolitan area are optional functions of a MAN.

* From IEEE 802 Standard, *Local and Metropolitan Area Networks: Overview and Architecture*, 1990.

Working from the bottom up, the lowest layer of the IEEE 802 reference model corresponds to the *physical layer* of the OSI model, and includes such functions as

- Encoding/decoding of signals
- Preamble generation/removal (for synchronization)
- Bit transmission/reception

In addition, the physical layer of the 802 model includes a specification of the transmission medium and the topology. Generally, this is considered *below* the lowest layer of the OSI model. However, the choice of transmission medium and topology is critical in LAN design, and so a specification of the medium is included.

Above the physical layer are the functions associated with providing service to LAN users. These include

- On transmission, assemble data into a frame with address and error-detection fields.
- On reception, disassemble frame, perform address recognition and error detection.
- Govern access to the LAN transmission medium.
- Provide an interface to higher layers and perform flow and error control.

These are functions typically associated with OSI layer 2. The set of functions in the last bulleted item are grouped into a *logical link control* (LLC) layer. The

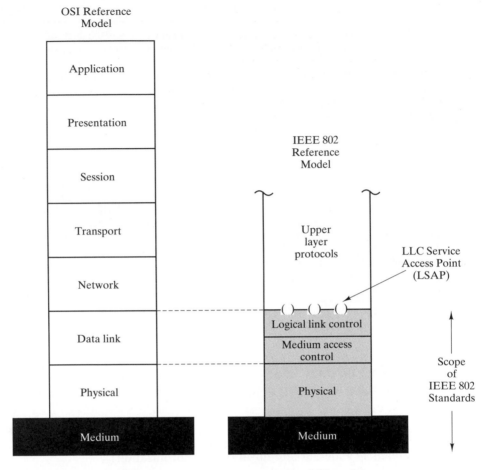

**FIGURE 12.1** IEEE 802 protocol layers compared to OSI model.

functions in the first three bullet items are treated as a separate layer, called *medium access control* (MAC). The separation is done for the following reasons:

- The logic required to manage access to a shared-access medium is not found in traditional layer-2 data link control.
- For the same LLC, several MAC options may be provided.

The standards that have been issued are illustrated in Figure 12.2. Most of the standards were developed by a committee known as IEEE 802, sponsored by the Institute for Electrical and Electronics Engineers. All of these standards have subsequently been adopted as international standards by the International Organization for Standardization (ISO).

Figure 12.3 illustrates the relationship between the levels of the architecture (compare Figure 9.17). User data are passed down to LLC, which appends control

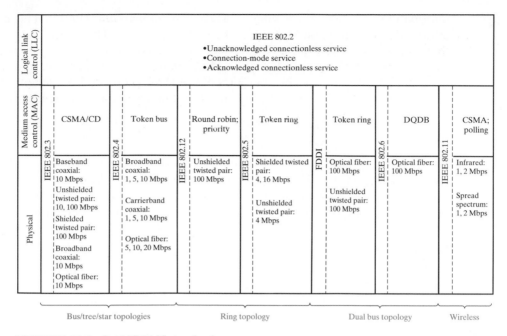

**FIGURE 12.2**  LAN/MAN standards.

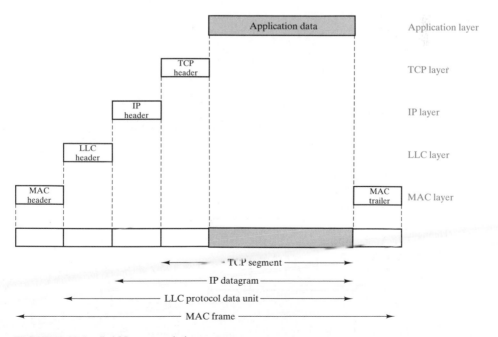

**FIGURE 12.3**  LAN protocols in context.

information as a header, creating an LLC *protocol data unit* (PDU). This control information is used in the operation of the LLC protocol. The entire LLC PDU is then passed down to the MAC layer, which appends control information at the front and back of the packet, forming a MAC *frame*. Again, the control information in the frame is needed for the operation of the MAC protocol. For context, the figure also shows the use of TCP/IP and an application layer above the LAN protocols.

## Topologies

For the physical layer, we confine our discussion for now to an introduction of the basic LAN topologies. The common topologies for LANs are bus, tree, ring, and star (Figure 12.4). The bus is a special case of the tree, with only one trunk and no branches; we shall use the term **bus/tree** when the distinction is unimportant.

### Bus and Tree Topologies

Both bus and tree topologies are characterized by the use of a multipoint medium. For the bus, all stations attach, through appropriate hardware interfacing known as a tap, directly to a linear transmission medium, or bus. Full-duplex operation between the station and the tap allows data to be transmitted onto the bus and received from the bus. A transmission from any station propagates the length of the medium in both directions and can be received by all other stations. At each end of the bus is a terminator, which absorbs any signal, removing it from the bus.

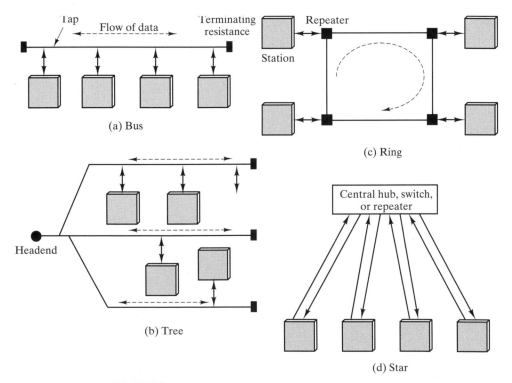

FIGURE 12.4  LAN/MAN topologies.

The tree topology is a generalization of the bus topology. The transmission medium is a branching cable with no closed loops. The tree layout begins at a point known as the *headend*, where one or more cables start, and each of these may have branches. The branches in turn may have additional branches to allow quite complex layouts. Again, a transmission from any station propagates throughout the medium and can be received by all other stations.

Two problems present themselves in this arrangement. First, because a transmission from any one station can be received by all other stations, there needs to be some way of indicating for whom the transmission is intended. Second, a mechanism is needed to regulate transmission. To see the reason for this, consider that if two stations on the bus attempt to transmit at the same time, their signals will overlap and become garbled. Or, consider that one station decides to transmit continuously for a long period of time.

To solve these problems, stations transmit data in small blocks, known as frames. Each frame consists of a portion of the data that a station wishes to transmit, plus a frame header that contains control information. Each station on the bus is assigned a unique address, or identifier, and the destination address for a frame is included in its header.

Figure 12.5 illustrates the scheme. In this example, station C wishes to transmit a frame of data to A. The frame header includes A's address. As the frame propagates along the bus, it passes B, which observes the address and ignores the frame. A, on the other hand, sees that the frame is addressed to itself and therefore copies the data from the frame as it goes by.

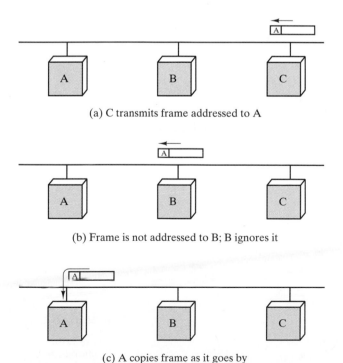

(a) C transmits frame addressed to A

(b) Frame is not addressed to B; B ignores it

(c) A copies frame as it goes by

**FIGURE 12.5**  Frame transmission on a bus LAN.

So the frame structure solves the first problem mentioned above: It provides a mechanism for indicating the intended recipient of data. It also provides the basic tool for solving the second problem, the regulation of access. In particular, the stations take turns sending frames in some cooperative fashion; this involves putting additional control information into the frame header.

With the bus or tree, no special action needs to be taken to remove frames from the medium. When a signal reaches the end of the medium, it is absorbed by the terminator.

### Ring Topology

In the ring topology, the network consists of a set of *repeaters* joined by point-to-point links in a closed loop. The repeater is a comparatively simple device, capable of receiving data on one link and transmitting them, bit by bit, on the other link as fast as they are received, with no buffering at the repeater. The links are unidirectional; that is, data are transmitted in one direction only and all are oriented in the same way. Thus, data circulate around the ring in one direction (clockwise or counterclockwise).

Each station attaches to the network at a repeater and can transmit data onto the network through that repeater.

As with the bus and tree, data are transmitted in frames. As a frame circulates past all the other stations, the destination station recognizes its address and copies the frame into a local buffer as it goes by. The frame continues to circulate until it returns to the source station, where it is removed (Figure 12.6).

Because multiple stations share the ring, medium access control is needed to determine at what time each station may insert frames.

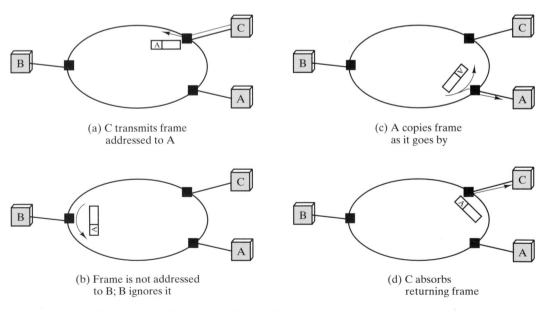

(a) C transmits frame
addressed to A

(c) A copies frame
as it goes by

(b) Frame is not addressed
to B; B ignores it

(d) C absorbs
returning frame

**FIGURE 12.6**   Frame transmission on a ring LAN.

### Star Topology

In the star LAN topology, each station is directly connected to a common central node. Typically, each station attaches to a central node, referred to as the star coupler, via two point-to-point links, one for transmission and one for reception.

In general, there are two alternatives for the operation of the central node. One approach is for the central node to operate in a broadcast fashion. A transmission of a frame from one station to the node is retransmitted on all of the outgoing links. In this case, although the arrangement is physically a star, it is logically a bus; a transmission from any station is received by all other stations, and only one station at a time may successfully transmit.

Another approach is for the central node to act as a frame switching device. An incoming frame is buffered in the node and then retransmitted on an outgoing link to the destination station.

## Medium Access Control

All LANs and MANs consist of collections of devices that must share the network's transmission capacity. Some means of controlling access to the transmission medium is needed to provide for an orderly and efficient use of that capacity. This is the function of a medium access control (MAC) protocol.

The key parameters in any medium access control technique are where and how. *Where* refers to whether control is exercised in a centralized or distributed fashion. In a centralized scheme, a controller is designated that has the authority to grant access to the network. A station wishing to transmit must wait until it receives permission from the controller. In a decentralized network, the stations collectively perform a medium access control function to dynamically determine the order in which stations transmit. A centralized scheme has certain advantages, such as the following:

- It may afford greater control over access for providing such things as priorities, overrides, and guaranteed capacity.
- It enables the use of relatively simple access logic at each station.
- It avoids problems of distributed coordination among peer entities.

The principal disadvantages of centralized schemes are

- It creates a single point of failure; that is, there is a point in the network that, if it fails, causes the entire network to fail.
- It may act as a bottleneck, reducing performance.

The pros and cons of distributed schemes are mirror images of the points made above.

The second parameter, *how*, is constrained by the topology and is a trade-off among competing factors, including cost, performance, and complexity. In general, we can categorize access control techniques as being either synchronous or asynchronous. With synchronous techniques, a specific capacity is dedicated to a connection; this is the same approach used in circuit switching, frequency-division multiplexing (FDM), and synchronous time-division multiplexing (TDM). Such techniques are generally not optimal in LANs and MANs because the needs of the stations are unpredictable. It is preferable to be able to allocate capacity in an asynchronous (dynamic) fashion, more or less in response to immediate demand. The asynchronous approach can be further subdivided into three categories: *round robin, reservation, and contention.*

### Round Robin

With round robin, each station in turn is given the opportunity to transmit. During that opportunity, the station may decline to transmit or may transmit subject to a specified upper bound, usually expressed as a maximum amount of data transmitted or time for this opportunity. In any case, the station, when it is finished, relinquishes its turn, and the right to transmit passes to the next station in logical sequence. Control of sequence may be centralized or distributed. Polling is an example of a centralized technique.

When many stations have data to transmit over an extended period of time, round robin techniques can be very efficient. If only a few stations have data to transmit over an extended period of time, then there is a considerable overhead in passing the turn from station to station, as most of the stations will not transmit but simply pass their turns. Under such circumstances, other techniques may be preferable, largely depending on whether the data traffic has a stream or bursty characteristic. Stream traffic is characterized by lengthy and fairly continuous transmissions; examples are voice communication, telemetry, and bulk file transfer. Bursty traffic is characterized by short, sporadic transmissions; interactive terminal-host traffic fits this description.

### Reservation

For stream traffic, reservation techniques are well suited. In general, for these techniques, time on the medium is divided into slots, much as with synchronous TDM. A station wishing to transmit reserves future slots for an extended or even an indefinite period. Again, reservations may be made in a centralized or distributed fashion.

### Contention

For bursty traffic, contention techniques are usually appropriate. With these techniques, no control is exercised to determine whose turn it is; all stations contend for time in a way that can be, as we shall see, rather rough and tumble. These techniques are, of necessity, distributed by nature. Their principal advantage is that they are simple to implement and, under light to moderate load, efficient. For some of these techniques, however, performance tends to collapse under heavy load.

Although both centralized and distributed reservation techniques have been implemented in some LAN products, round robin and contention techniques are the most common.

The discussion above has been somewhat abstract and should become clearer as specific techniques are discussed in Chapter 13. For future reference, Table 12.2 lists the MAC protocols that are defined in LAN and MAN standards.

**TABLE 12.2** Standardized medium access control techniques.

|  | Bus topology | Ring topology | Switched topology |
|---|---|---|---|
| **Round robin** | Token Bus (IEEE 802.4)<br><br>Polling (IEEE 802.11) | Token Ring (IEEE 802.5; FDDI) | Request/priority (IEEE 802.12) |
| **Reservation** | DQDB (IEEE 802.6) |  |  |
| **Contention** | CSMA/CD (IEEE 802.3)<br>CSMA (IEEE 802.11) |  | CSMA/CD (IEEE 802.3) |

## MAC Frame Format

The MAC layer receives a block of data from the LLC layer and is responsible for performing functions related to medium access and for transmitting the data. As with other protocol layers, MAC implements these functions, making use of a protocol data unit at its layer; in this case, the PDU is referred to as a MAC frame.

The exact format of the MAC frame differs somewhat for the various MAC protocols in use. In general, all of the MAC frames have a format similar to that of Figure 12.7. The fields of this frame are

- **MAC control.** This field contains any protocol control information needed for the functioning of the MAC protocol. For example, a priority level could be indicated here.
- **Destination MAC address.** The destination physical attachment point on the LAN for this frame.
- **Source MAC address.** The source physical attachment point on the LAN for this frame.

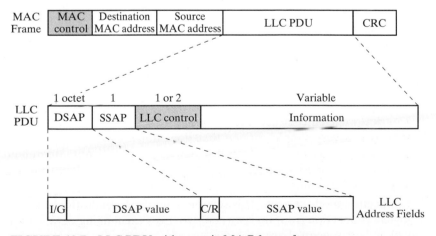

**FIGURE 12.7** LLC PDU with generic MAC frame format.

- **LLC.** The LLC data from the next higher layer.
- **CRC.** The cyclic redundancy check field (also known as the frame check sequence, FCS, field). This is an error-detecting code, as we have seen in HDLC and other data link control protocols (Chapter 6).

In most data link control protocols, the data link protocol entity is responsible not only for detecting errors using the CRC, but for recovering from those errors by retransmitting damaged frames. In the LAN protocol architecture, these two functions are split between the MAC and LLC layers. The MAC layer is responsible for detecting errors and discarding any frames that are in error. The LLC layer optionally keeps track of which frames have been successfully received and retransmits unsuccessful frames.

## Logical Link Control

The LLC layer for LANs is similar in many respects to other link layers in common use. Like all link layers, LLC is concerned with the transmission of a link-level protocol data unit (PDU) between two stations, without the necessity of an intermediate switching node. LLC has two characteristics not shared by most other link control protocols:

1. It must support the multi-access, shared-medium nature of the link. (This differs from a multidrop line in that there is no primary node.)
2. It is relieved of some details of link access by the MAC layer.

Addressing in LLC involves specifying the source and destination LLC users. Typically, a user is a higher-layer protocol or a network management function in the station. These LLC user addresses are referred to as *service access points* (SAPs), in keeping with OSI terminology for the user of a protocol layer.

We look first at the services that LLC provides to a higher-level user, then at the LLC protocol.

### LLC Services

LLC specifies the mechanisms for addressing stations across the medium and for controlling the exchange of data between two users. The operation and format of this standard is based on HDLC. Three services are provided as alternatives for attached devices using LLC:

- **Unacknowledged connectionless service.** This service is a datagram-style service. It is a very simple service that does not involve any of the flow- and error-control mechanisms. Thus, the delivery of data is not guaranteed. However, in most devices, there will be some higher layer of software that deals with reliability issues.
- **Connection-mode service.** This service is similar to that offered by HDLC. A logical connection is set up between two users exchanging data, and flow control and error control are provided.

- **Acknowledged connectionless service.** This is a cross between the previous two services. It provides that datagrams are to be acknowledged, but no prior logical connection is set up.

Typically, a vendor will provide these services as options that the customer can select when purchasing the equipment. Alternatively, the customer can purchase equipment that provides two or all three services and select a specific service based on application.

The *unacknowledged connectionless service* requires minimum logic and is useful in two contexts. First, it will often be the case that higher layers of software will provide the necessary reliability and flow-control mechanism, and it is efficient to avoid duplicating them. For example, either TCP or the ISO transport protocol standard would provide the mechanisms needed to ensure that data are delivered reliably. Second, there are instances in which the overhead of connection establishment and maintenance is unjustified or even counterproductive: for example, data collection activities that involve the periodic sampling of data sources, such as sensors and automatic self-test reports from security equipment or network components. In a monitoring application, the loss of an occasional data unit would not cause distress, as the next report should arrive shortly. Thus, in most cases, the unacknowledged connectionless service is the preferred option.

The *connection-mode service* could be used in very simple devices, such as terminal controllers, that have little software operating above this level. In these cases, it would provide the flow control and reliability mechanisms normally implemented at higher layers of the communications software.

The *acknowledged connectionless service* is useful in several contexts. With the connection-mode service, the logical link control software must maintain some sort of table for each active connection, so as to keep track of the status of that connection. If the user needs guaranteed delivery, but there are a large number of destinations for data, then the connection-mode service may be impractical because of the large number of tables required; an example is a process-control or automated factory environment where a central site may need to communicate with a large number of processors and programmable controllers; another use is the handling of important and time-critical alarm or emergency control signals in a factory. Because of their importance, an acknowledgment is needed so that the sender can be assured that the signal got through. Because of the urgency of the signal, the user might not want to take the time to first establish a logical connection and then send the data.

## LLC Protocol

The basic LLC protocol is modeled after HDLC, and has similar functions and formats. The differences between the two protocols can be summarized as follows:

1. LLC makes use of the asynchronous, balanced mode of operation of HDLC in order to support connection-mode LLC service; this is referred to as type 2 operation. The other HDLC modes are not employed.
2. LLC supports a connectionless service using the unnumbered information PDU; this is known as type 1 operation.

3. LLC supports an acknowledged connectionless service by using two new unnumbered PDUs; this is known as type 3 operation.

4. LLC permits multiplexing by the use of LLC service access points (LSAPs).

All three LLC protocols employ the same PDU format (Figure 12.7), which consists of four fields. The DSAP and SSAP fields each contain 7-bit addresses, which specify the destination and source users of LLC. One bit of the DSAP indicates whether the DSAP is an individual or group address. One bit of the SSAP indicates whether the PDU is a command or response PDU. The format of the LLC control field is identical to that of HDLC (Figure 6.10), using extended (7-bit) sequence numbers.

For *type 1 operation*, which supports the unacknowledged connectionless service, the unnumbered information (UI) PDU is used to transfer user data. There is no acknowledgment, flow control, or error control. However, there is error detection and discard at the MAC level.

Two other PDUs are used to support management functions associated with all three types of operation. Both PDUs are used in the following fashion. An LLC entity may issue a command (C/R bit = 0) XID or TEST. The receiving LLC entity issues a corresponding XID or TEST in response. The XID PDU is used to exchange two types of information: types of operation supported and window size. The TEST PDU is used to conduct a loop-back test of the transmission path between two LLC entities. Upon receipt of a TEST command PDU, the addressed LLC entity issues a TEST response PDU as soon as possible.

With *type 2 operation*, a data link connection is established between two LLC SAPs prior to data exchange. Connection establishment is attempted by the type 2 protocol in response to a request from a user. The LLC entity issues a SABME PDU[2] to request a logical connection with the other LLC entity. If the connection is accepted by the LLC user designated by the DSAP, then the destination LLC entity returns an unnumbered acknowledgment (UA) PDU. The connection is henceforth uniquely identified by the pair of user SAPs. If the destination LLC user rejects the connection request, its LLC entity returns a disconnected mode (DM) PDU.

Once the connection is established, data are exchanged using information PDUs, as in HDLC. The information PDUs include send and receive sequence numbers, for sequencing and flow control. The supervisory PDUs are used, as in HDLC, for flow control and error control. Either LLC entity can terminate a logical LLC connection by issuing a disconnect (DISC) PDU.

With *type 3 operation*, each transmitted PDU is acknowledged. A new (not found in HDLC) unnumbered PDU, the Acknowledged Connectionless (AC) Information PDU is defined. User data are sent in AC command PDUs and must be acknowledged using an AC response PDU. To guard against lost PDUs, a 1-bit sequence number is used. The sender alternates the use of 0 and 1 in its AC com-

---

[2] This stands for Set Asynchronous Balanced Mode Extended. It is used in HDLC to choose ABM and to select extended sequence numbers of seven bits. Both ABM and 7-bit sequence numbers are mandatory in type 2 operation.

mand PDU, and the receiver responds with an AC PDU with the opposite number of the corresponding command. Only one PDU in each direction may be outstanding at any time.

## 12.2  BUS/TREE LANs

This section provides some technical details on bus/tree topology LANs and MANs. The section begins with an overview of the general characteristics of this topology. The remainder of the section examines the use of coaxial cable and optical fiber for implementing this topology.

### Characteristics of the Bus/Tree Topology

The bus/tree topology is a multipoint configuration. That is, there are more than two devices connected to the medium and capable of transmitting on the medium. This situation gives rise to several design issues, the first of which is the need for a medium access control technique.

Another design issue has to do with signal balancing. When two stations exchange data over a link, the signal strength of the transmitter must be adjusted to be within certain limits. The signal must be strong enough so that, after attenuation across the medium, it meets the receiver's minimum signal-strength requirements. It must also be strong enough to maintain an adequate signal-to-noise ratio. On the other hand, the signal must not be so strong that it overloads the circuitry of the transmitter, as the signal would become distorted. Although easily accomplished for a point-to-point link, signal balancing is no easy task for a multipoint line. If any station can transmit to any other station, then the signal balancing must be performed for all permutations of stations taken two at a time. For $n$ stations, that works out to $n \times (n-1)$ permutations. So, for a 200-station network (not a particularly large system), 39,800 signal-strength constraints must be satisfied simultaneously; with interdevice distances ranging from tens to thousands of meters, this would be an extremely difficult task for any but small networks. In systems that use radio-frequency (RF) signals, the problem is compounded because of the possibility of RF signal interference across frequencies. A common solution is to divide the medium into smaller segments within which pairwise balancing is possible, using amplifiers or repeaters between segments.

### Baseband Coaxial Cable

For bus/tree LANs, the most popular medium is coaxial cable. The two common transmission techniques that are used on coaxial cable are baseband and broadband, which are compared in Table 12.3. This subsection is devoted to baseband systems, while the next section discusses broadband LANs.

A baseband LAN or MAN is defined as one that uses digital signaling; that is, the binary data to be transmitted are inserted onto the cable as a sequence of voltage pulses, usually using Manchester or Differential Manchester encoding (see

**TABLE 12.3** Transmission techniques for coaxial cable bus/tree LANs.

| Baseband | Broadband |
|---|---|
| Digital signaling | Analog signaling (requires RF modem) |
| Entire bandwidth consumed by signal—no frequency division multiplexing (FDM) | FDM possible—multiple channels for data, video, audio |
| Bidirectional | Unidirectional |
| Bus topology | Bus or tree topology |
| Distance: up to a few kilometers | Distance: up to tens of kilometers |

Figure 4.2). The nature of digital signals is such that the entire frequency spectrum of the cable is consumed. Hence, it is not possible to have multiple channels (frequency-division multiplexing) on the cable. Transmission is bidirectional. That is, a signal inserted at any point on the medium propagates in both directions to the ends, where it is absorbed (Figure 12.8a). The digital signaling requires a bus topology; unlike analog signals, digital signals cannot easily be propagated through the branching points required for a tree topology. Baseband bus systems can extend only a few kilometers, at most; this is because the attenuation of the signal, which is most pronounced at higher frequencies, causes a blurring of the pulses and a weakening of the signal to the extent that communication over larger distances is impractical.

The original use of baseband coaxial cable for a bus LAN was the Ethernet system, which operates at 10 Mbps. Ethernet became the basis of the IEEE 802.3 standard.

Most baseband coaxial cable systems use a special 50-ohm cable rather than the standard CATV 75-ohm cable. These values refer to the impedance of the cable. Roughly speaking, impedance is a measure of how much voltage must be applied to the cable to achieve a given signal strength. For digital signals, the 50-ohm cable suffers less intense reflections from the insertion capacitance of the taps and provides better immunity against low-frequency electromagnetic noise, compared to 75-ohm cable.

As with any transmission system, there are engineering trade-offs involving data rate, cable length, number of taps, and the electrical characteristics of the cable and the transmit/receive components. For example, the lower the data rate, the longer the cable can be. That statement is true for the following reason: When a signal is propagated along a transmission medium, the integrity of the signal suffers due to attenuation, noise, and other impairments. The longer the length of propagation, the greater the effect, thereby increasing the probability of error. However, at a lower data rate, the individual pulses of a digital signal last longer and can be recovered in the presence of impairments more easily than higher-rate, shorter pulses.

Here is one example that illustrates some of the trade-offs. The Ethernet specification and the original IEEE 802.3 standard specified the use of 50-ohm cable with a 0.4-inch diameter, and a data rate of 10 Mbps. With these parameters, the maximum length of the cable is set at 500 meters. Stations attach to the cable by

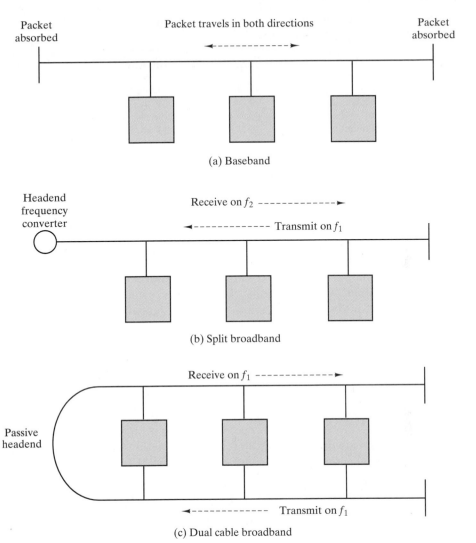

**FIGURE 12.8**   Baseband and broadband transmission techniques.

means of a tap, with the distance between any two taps being a multiple of 2.5 m; this is to ensure that reflections from adjacent taps do not add in phase [YEN83]. A maximum of 100 taps is allowed. In IEEE jargon, this system is referred to as 10BASE5 (10 Mbps, baseband, 500-m cable length).

To provide a lower-cost system for personal computer LANs, IEEE 802.3 later added a 10BASE2 specification. Table 12.4 compares this scheme, dubbed Cheapernet, with 10BASE5. The key change is the use of a thinner (0.25 in) cable of the type employed in products such as public address systems. The thinner cable is more flexible; thus, it is easier to bend around corners and bring to a workstation rather than installing a cable in the wall and having to provide a drop cable between the main cable and the workstation. The cable is easier to install and uses cheaper electronics than the thicker cable. On the other hand, the thinner cable suffers

**TABLE 12.4** IEEE 802.3 specifications for 10-Mbps baseband coaxial cable bus LANs.

|  | 10BASE5 | 10BASE2 |
|---|---|---|
| Data rate | 10 Mbps | 10 Mbps |
| Maximum Segment Length | 500 m | 185 m |
| Network Span | 2500 m | 1000 m |
| Nodes per Segment | 100 | 30 |
| Node Spacing | 2.5 m | 0.5 m |
| Cable Diameter | 0.4 in | 0.25 in |

greater attenuation and lower noise resistance than the thicker cable; as a result, it supports fewer taps over a shorter distance.

To extend the length of the network, a repeater may be used. This device works in a somewhat different fashion than the repeater on the ring. The bus repeater is not used as a device attachment point and is capable of transmitting in both directions. A repeater joins two segments of cable and passes digital signals in both directions between the two segments. A repeater is transparent to the rest of the system; as it does no buffering, it does not logically isolate one segment from another. So, for example, if two stations on different segments attempt to transmit at the same time, their packets will interfere with each other (collide). To avoid multipath interference, only one path of segments and repeaters is allowed between any two stations. Figure 12.9 illustrates a multiple-segment baseband bus LAN.

## Broadband Coaxial Cable

In the local network context, the term broadband refers to coaxial cable on which analog signaling is used. Table 12.3 summarizes the key characteristics of broad-

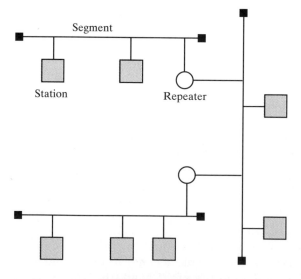

**FIGURE 12.9** Baseband configuration.

band systems. As mentioned, broadband implies the use of analog signaling. FDM is possible, as the frequency spectrum of the cable can be divided into channels or sections of bandwidth. Separate channels can support data traffic, video, and radio signals. Broadband components allow splitting and joining operations; hence, both bus and tree topologies are possible. Much greater distances—tens of kilometers— are possible with broadband compared to baseband because the analog signals that carry the digital data can propagate greater distances before the noise and attenuation damage the data.

### Dual and Split Configurations

As with baseband, stations on a broadband LAN attach to the cable by means of a tap. Unlike baseband, however, broadband is inherently a unidirectional medium; the taps that are used allow signals inserted onto the medium to propagate in only one direction. The primary reason for this is that it is unfeasible to build amplifiers that will pass signals of one frequency in both directions. This unidimensional property means that only those stations "downstream" from a transmitting station can receive its signals. How, then, to achieve full connectivity?

Clearly, two data paths are needed. These paths are joined at a point on the network known as the *headend*. For a bus topology, the headend is simply one end of the bus. For a tree topology, the headend is the root of the branching tree. All stations transmit on one path toward the headend (inbound). Signals arriving at the headend are then propagated along a second data path away from the headend (outbound). All stations receive on the outbound path.

Physically, two different configurations are used to implement the inbound and outbound paths (Figure 12.8b and c). On a *dual-cable* configuration, the inbound and outbound paths are separate cables, with the headend simply a passive connector between the two. Stations send and receive on the same frequency.

By contrast, on a *split* configuration, the inbound and outbound paths are different frequency bands on the same cable. Bidirectional amplifiers[3] pass lower frequencies inbound, and higher frequencies outbound. Between the inbound and outbound frequency bands is a guardband, which carries no signals and serves merely as a separator. The headend contains a device for converting inbound frequencies to outbound frequencies.

The frequency-conversion device at the headend can be either an analog or digital device. An analog device, known as a *frequency translator*, converts a block of frequencies from one range to another. A digital device, known as a *remodulator*, recovers the digital data from the inbound analog signal and then retransmits the data on the outbound frequency. Thus, a remodulator provides better signal quality by removing all of the accumulated noise and attenuation and transmitting a cleaned-up signal.

Split systems are categorized by the frequency allocation of the two paths, as shown in Table 12.5. Subsplit, commonly used by the cable television industry, was designed for metropolitan area television distribution, with limited subscriber-to-central-office communication. It provides the easiest way to upgrade existing

---

[3] Unfortunately, this terminology is confusing, as we have said that broadband is inherently a unidirectional medium. At a given frequency, broadband is unidirectional. However, there is no difficulty in having signals in nonoverlapping frequency bands traveling in opposite directions on the cable.

**TABLE 12.5**   Common broadband cable frequency splits.

| Format | Inbound Frequency Band | Outbound Frequency Band | Maximum Two-way Bandwidth |
|---|---|---|---|
| Subsplit | 5 to 30 MHz | 54 to 400 MHz | 25 Mhz |
| Midsplit | 5 to 116 MHz | 168 to 400 MHz | 111 Mhz |
| Highsplit | 5 to 174 MHz | 232 to 400 MHz | 168 Mhz |
| Dual Cable | 40 to 400 MHz | 40 to 400 MHz | 360 Mhz |

one-way cable systems to two-way operation. Subsplit has limited usefulness for local area networking because a bandwidth of only 25 MHz is available for two-way communication. Midsplit is more suitable for LANs, because it provides a more equitable distribution of bandwidth. However, midsplit was developed at a time when the practical spectrum of a cable-TV cable was 300 MHz, whereas a spectrum of 400 to 450 MHz is now available. Accordingly, a highsplit specification has been developed to provide greater two-way bandwidth for a split cable system.

The differences between split and dual configurations are minor. The split system is useful when a single cable plant is already installed in a building. If a large amount of bandwidth is needed, or the need is anticipated, then a dual cable system is indicated. Beyond these considerations, it is a matter of a trade-off between cost and size. The single-cable system has the fixed cost of the headend remodulator or frequency translator. The dual cable system makes use of more cable, taps, splitters, and amplifiers. Thus, dual cable is cheaper for smaller systems, where the fixed cost of the headend is noticeable, and single cable is cheaper for larger systems, where incremental costs dominate.

## Carrierband

There is another application of analog signaling on a LAN, known as carrierband, or single-channel broadband. In this case, the entire spectrum of the cable is devoted to a single transmission path for the analog signals; no frequency-division multiplexing is possible.

Typically, a carrierband LAN has the following characteristics. Bidirectional transmission, using a bus topology, is employed. Hence, there can be no amplifiers, and there is no need for a headend. Although the entire spectrum is used, most of the signal energy is concentrated at relatively low frequencies, which is an advantage, because attenuation is less at lower frequencies.

Because the cable is dedicated to a single task, it is not necessary to take care that the modem output be confined to a narrow bandwidth. Energy can spread over the entire spectrum. As a result, the electronics are simple and relatively inexpensive. Typically, some form of frequency-shift keying (FSK) is used. Carrierband would appear to give comparable performance, at a comparable price, to baseband.

## Optical Fiber Bus

Several approaches can be taken in the design of a fiber bus topology LAN or MAN. The differences have to do with the nature of the taps into the bus and the detailed topology.

### Optical Fiber Taps

With an optical fiber bus, either an active or passive tap can be used. In the case of an active tap (Figure 12.10a), the following steps occur:

1. Optical signal energy enters the tap from the bus.
2. Clocking information is recovered from the signal, and the signal is converted to an electrical signal.
3. The converted signal is presented to the node and perhaps modified by the latter.
4. The optical output (a light beam) is modulated according to the electrical signal and launched into the bus.

In effect, the bus consists of a chain of point-to-point links, and each node acts as a repeater. Each tap actually consists of two of these active couplers and requires two fibers; this is because of the inherently unidirectional nature of the device of Figure 12.10a.

In the case of a passive tap (Figure 12.10b), the tap extracts a portion of the optical energy from the bus for reception and it injects optical energy directly into the medium for transmission. Thus, there is a single run of cable rather than a chain

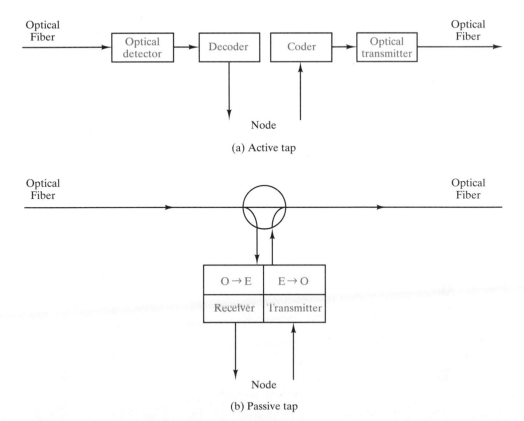

**FIGURE 12.10** Optical fiber bus taps.

of point-to-point links. This passive approach is equivalent to the type of taps typically used for twisted pair and coaxial cable. Each tap must connect to the bus twice: once for transmit and once for receive.

The electronic complexity and interface cost are drawbacks for the implementation of the active tap. Also, each tap will add some increment of delay, just as in the case of a ring. For passive taps, the lossy nature of pure optical taps limits the number of devices and the length of the medium. However, the performance of such taps has improved sufficiently in recent years so to make fiber bus networks practical.

### Optical Fiber Bus Configurations

A variety of configurations for the optical fiber bus have been proposed, all of which fall into two categories: those that use a single bus and those that use two buses.

Figure 12.11a shows a typical single-bus configuration, referred to as a loop bus. The operation of this bus is essentially the same as that of the dual-bus broadband coaxial system described earlier. Each station transmits on the bus in the direction toward the headend, and receives on the bus in the direction away from the headend. In addition to the two connections shown, some MAC protocols require that each station have an additional **sense tap** on the inbound (toward the headend) portion of the bus. The sense tap is able to sense the presence or absence of light on the fiber, but it is not able to recover data.

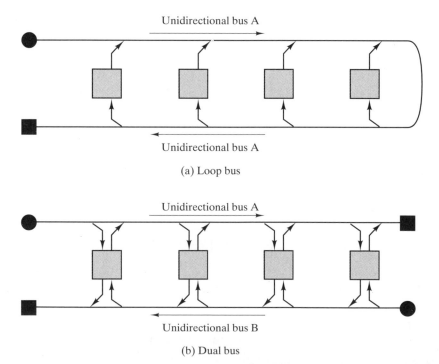

(a) Loop bus

(b) Dual bus

**FIGURE 12.11**  Optical fiber bus configurations.

Figure 12.11b shows the two-bus configuration. Each station attaches to both buses and has both transmit and receive taps on both buses. On each bus, a station may transmit only to those stations downstream from it. By using both buses, a station may transmit to, and receive from, all other stations. A given node, however, must know which bus to use to transmit to another node; if such information were unavailable, all data would have to be sent out on both buses; this is the configuration used in the IEEE 802.6 MAN, and is described in Chapter 13.

## 12.3 RING LANs

### Characteristics of Ring LANs

A ring consists of a number of repeaters, each connected to two others by unidirectional transmission links to form a single closed path. Data are transferred sequentially, bit by bit, around the ring from one repeater to the next. Each repeater regenerates and retransmits each bit.

For a ring to operate as a communication network, three functions are required: data insertion, data reception, and data removal. These functions are provided by the repeaters. Each repeater, in addition to serving as an active element on the ring, serves as a device attachment point. Data insertion is accomplished by the repeater. Data are transmitted in packets, each of which contains a destination address field. As a packet circulates past a repeater, the address field is copied. If the attached station recognizes the address, the remainder of the packet is copied.

Repeaters perform the data insertion and reception functions in a manner not unlike that of taps, which serve as device attachment points on a bus or tree. Data removal, however, is more difficult on a ring. For a bus or tree, signals inserted onto the line propagate to the endpoints and are absorbed by terminators. Hence, shortly after transmission ceases, the bus or tree is clean of data. However, because the ring is a closed loop, a packet will circulate indefinitely unless it is removed. A packet may by removed by the addressed repeater. Alternatively, each packet could be removed by the transmitting repeater after it has made one trip around the loop. This latter approach is more desirable because (1) it permits automatic acknowledgment and (2) it permits multicast addressing: one packet sent simultaneously to multiple stations.

A variety of strategies can be used for determining how and when packets are inserted onto the ring. These strategies are, in effect, medium access control protocols, and are discussed in Chapter 13.

The repeater, then, can be seen to have two main purposes: (1) to contribute to the proper functioning of the ring by passing on all the data that come its way, and (2) to provide an access point for attached stations to send and receive data. Corresponding to these two purposes are two states (Figure 12.12): the listen state and the transmit state.

In the listen state, each received bit is retransmitted with a small delay, required to allow the repeater to perform required functions. Ideally, the delay should be on the order of one bit time (the time it takes for a repeater to transmit one complete bit onto the outgoing line). These functions are

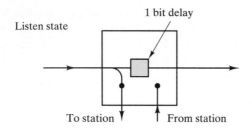

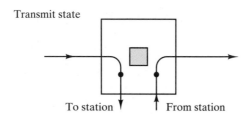

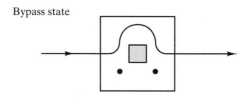

**FIGURE 12.12** Ring repeater states.

- Scan passing bit stream for pertinent patterns. Chief among these is the address or addresses of attached stations. Another pattern, used in the token control strategy explained later, indicates permission to transmit. Note that to perform the scanning function, the repeater must have some knowledge of packet format.
- Copy each incoming bit and send it to the attached station, while continuing to retransmit each bit. This will be done for each bit of each packet addressed to this station.
- Modify a bit as it passes by. In certain control strategies, bits may be modified, for example, to indicate that the packet has been copied; this would serve as an acknowledgment.

When a repeater's station has data to send, and when the repeater, based on the control strategy, has permission to send, the repeater enters the transmit state. In this state, the repeater receives bits from the station and retransmits them on its outgoing link. During the period of transmission, bits may appear on the incoming ring link. There are two possibilities, and they are treated differently:

- The bits could be from the same packet that the repeater is still in the process of sending. This will occur if the bit length of the ring is shorter than the packet. In this case, the repeater passes the bits back to the station, which can check them as a form of acknowledgment.
- For some control strategies, more than one packet could be on the ring at the same time. If the repeater, while transmitting, receives bits from a packet it did not originate, it must buffer them to be transmitted later.

These two states, listen and transmit, are sufficient for proper ring operation. A third state, the bypass state, is also useful. In this state, a bypass relay can be activated so that signals propagate past the repeater with no delay other than from medium propagation. The bypass relay affords two benefits: (1) it provides a partial solution to the reliability problem, discussed later, and (2) it improves performance by eliminating repeater delay for those stations that are not active on the network.

Twisted pair, baseband coax, and fiber optic cable can all be used to provide the repeater-to-repeater links. Broadband coax, however, could not easily be used. Each repeater would have to be capable, asynchronously, of receiving and transmitting data on multiple channels.

### Timing Jitter

On a ring transmission medium, some form of clocking is included with the signal, as for example with the use of Differential Manchester encoding (Section 4.1). As data circulate around the ring, each repeater receives the data, and recovers the clocking for two purposes: first, to know when to sample the incoming signal to recover the bits of data, and second, to use the clocking for transmitting the signal to the next repeater. This clock recovery will deviate in a random fashion from the mid-bit transitions of the received signal for several reasons, including noise during transmission and imperfections in the receiver circuitry; the predominant reason, however, is delay distortion (described in Section 2.3). The deviation of clock recovery is known as timing jitter.

As each repeater receives incoming data, it issues a clean signal with no distortion. However, the timing error is not eliminated. Thus, the digital pulse width will expand and contract in a random fashion as the signal travels around the ring and the timing jitter accumulates. The cumulative effect of the jitter is to cause the bit latency, or bit length, of the ring to vary. However, unless the latency of the ring remains constant, bits will be dropped (not retransmitted) as the latency of the ring decreases, or they will be added as the latency increases.

This timing jitter places a limitation on the number of repeaters in a ring. Although this limitation cannot be entirely overcome, several measures can be taken to improve matters. In essence, two approaches are used in combination. First, each repeater can include a phase-lock loop. This is a device that uses feedback to minimize the deviation from one bit time to the next. Second, a buffer can be used at one or more repeaters. The buffer is initialized to hold a certain number of bits, and expands and contracts to keep the bit length of the ring constant. The combination of phase-locked loops and a buffer significantly increases maximum feasible ring size.

## Potential Ring Problems

There are a number of potential problems with the ring topology: A break in any link or the failure of a repeater disables the entire network; installation of a new repeater to support new devices requires the identification of two nearby, topologically adjacent repeaters; timing jitter must be dealt with; and finally, because the ring is closed, a means is needed to remove circulating packets, with backup techniques to guard against error.

The last problem is a protocol issue and will be discussed later. The remaining problems can be handled by a refinement of the ring topology and will be discussed next.

## The Star–Ring Architecture

Two observations can be made about the basic ring architecture described above. First, there is a practical limit to the number of repeaters on a ring. This limit is suggested by the jitter, reliability, and maintenance problems just cited, and by the accumulating delay of a large number of repeaters. A limit of a few hundred repeaters seems reasonable. Second, the functioning of the ring does not depend on the actual routing of the cables that link the repeaters.

These observations have led to the development of a refined ring architecture, the star-ring, which overcomes some of the problems of the ring and allows the construction of larger local networks.

As a first step, consider the rearrangement of a ring into a star. This is achieved by having the interrepeater links all thread through a single site. This ring wiring concentrator has a number of advantages. Because there is centralized access to the signal on every link, it is a simple matter to isolate a fault. A message can be launched into the ring and tracked to see how far it gets without mishap. A faulty segment can be disconnected and repaired at a later time. New repeaters can easily be added to the ring: Simply run two cables from the new repeater to the site of the ring wiring concentration and splice into the ring.

The bypass relay associated with each repeater can be moved into the ring wiring concentrator. The relay can automatically bypass its repeater and two links in the event of any malfunction. A nice effect of this feature is that the transmission path from one working repeater to the next is approximately constant; thus, the range of signal levels to which the transmission system must automatically adapt is much smaller.

The ring wiring concentrator permits rapid recovery from a cable or repeater failure. Nevertheless, a single failure could, at least temporarily, disable the entire network. Furthermore, throughput and jitter considerations still place a practical upper limit on the number of stations in a ring, as each repeater adds an increment of delay. Finally, in a spread-out network, a single wire concentration site dictates a great deal of cable.

To attack these remaining problems, a LAN consisting of multiple rings connected by bridges can be constructed. We explore the use of bridges in Chapter 14.

### Bus Versus Ring

For the user with a large number of devices and high-capacity requirements, the bus or tree broadband LAN seems the best suited to the requirements. For more moderate requirements, however, the choice between a baseband bus LAN and a ring LAN is not at all clear-cut.

The baseband bus is the simpler system. Passive taps rather than active repeaters are used. There is no need for the complexity of bridges and ring wiring concentrators.

The most important benefit of the ring is that it uses point-to-point communication links, and here there are a number of implications. First, because the transmitted signal is regenerated at each node, transmission errors are minimized and greater distances can be covered than with baseband bus. Broadband bus/tree can cover a similar range, but cascaded amplifiers can result in loss of data integrity at high data rates. Second, the ring can accommodate optical fiber links, which provide very high data rates and excellent electromagnetic interference (EMI) characteristics. Finally, the electronics and maintenance of point-to-point lines are simpler than for multipoint lines.

## 12.4 STAR LANs

### Twisted Pair Star LANs

In recent years, there has been increasing interest in the use of twisted pair as a transmission medium for LANs. From the earliest days of commercial LAN availability, twisted pair bus LANs have been popular. However, such LANs suffer in comparison with a coaxial cable LAN. First of all, the apparent cost advantage of twisted pair is not as great as it might seem, at least when a linear bus layout is used. True, twisted pair cable is less expensive than coaxial cable. On the other hand, much of the cost of LAN wiring is in the labor cost of installing the cable, which is no greater for coaxial cable than for twisted pair. Secondly, coaxial cable provides superior signal quality, and therefore can support more devices over longer distances at higher data rates than twisted pair.

The renewed interest in twisted pair, at least in the context of bus/tree type LANs, is in the use of unshielded twisted pair in a star-wiring arrangement. The reason for the interest is that unshielded twisted pair is simply telephone wire, and virtually all office buildings are equipped with spare twisted pairs running from wiring closets to each office. This yields several benefits when deploying a LAN:

1. There is essentially no installation cost with unshielded twisted pair, as the wire is already there. Coaxial cable has to be pulled. In older buildings, this may be difficult because existing conduits may be crowded.

2. In most office buildings, it is impossible to anticipate all the locations where network access will be needed. Because it is extravagantly expensive to run coaxial cable to every office, a coaxial cable-based LAN will typically cover only a portion of a building. If equipment subsequently has to be moved to an

office not covered by the LAN, significant expense is involved in extending the LAN coverage. With telephone wire, this problem does not arise, as all offices are covered.

The most popular approach to the use of unshielded twisted pair for a LAN is therefore a star-wiring approach. The products on the market use a scheme suggested by Figure 12.13, in which the central element of the star is an active element, referred to as the *hub*. Each station is connected to the hub by two twisted pairs (transmit and receive). The hub acts as a repeater: When a single station transmits, the hub repeats the signal on the outgoing line to each station.

Note that although this scheme is physically a star, it is logically a bus: A transmission from any one station is received by all other stations, and, if two stations transmit at the same time, there will be a collision.

Multiple levels of hubs can be cascaded in a hierarchical configuration. Figure 12.14 illustrates a two-level configuration. There is one *header hub* (HHUB) and one or more *intermediate hubs* (IHUB). Each hub may have a mixture of stations and other hubs attached to it from below. This layout fits well with building wiring practices. Typically, there is a wiring closet on each floor of an office building, and a hub can be placed in each one. Each hub could service the stations on its floor.

Figure 12.15 shows an abstract representation of the intermediate and header hubs. The header hub performs all the functions described previously for a single-hub configuration. In the case of an intermediate hub, any incoming signal from below is repeated upward to the next higher level. Any signal from above is repeated on all lower-level outgoing lines. Thus, the logical bus characteristic is retained: A transmission from any one station is received by all other stations, and, if two stations transmit at the same time, there will be a collision.

### Optical Fiber Star

One of the first commercially available approaches for fiber LANs was the passive star coupler. The passive star coupler is fabricated by fusing together a number of

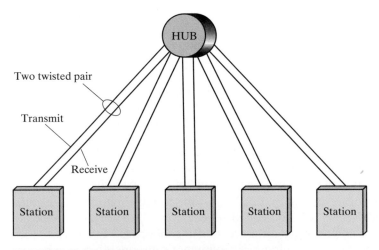

**FIGURE 12.13**  Twisted-pair star topology.

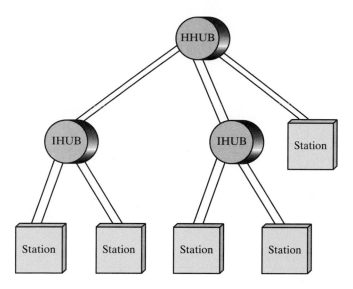

**FIGURE 12.14**   Two-level twisted-pair star topology.

optical fibers. Light that is input to one of the fibers on one side of the coupler is equally divided among, and output through, all the fibers on the other side. To form a network, each device is connected to the coupler with two fibers, one for transmit and one for receive (Figure 12.16). All of the transmit fibers enter the coupler on one side, and all of the receive fibers exit on the other side. Thus, although the arrangement is physically a star, it acts like a bus: A transmission from any one device is received by all other devices, and if two devices transmit at the same time, there will be a collision.

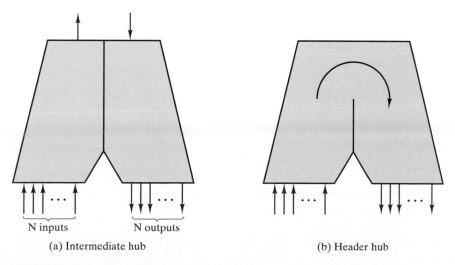

(a) Intermediate hub                    (b) Header hub

**FIGURE 12.15**   Intermediate and header hubs.

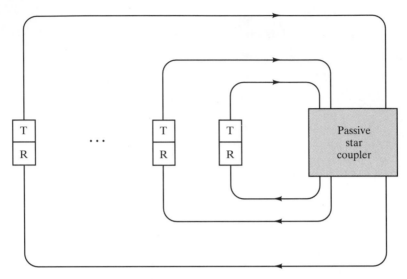

**FIGURE 12.16** Optical fiber passive star configuration.

Two methods of fabrication of the star coupler have been pursued: the biconic fused coupler and the mixing rod coupler. In the biconic fused coupler, the fibers are bundled together and heated with an oxyhydrogen flame before being pulled into a biconical tapered shape. That is, the rods come together into a fused mass that tapers into a conical shape and then expands back out again. (The mixing rod approach begins in the same fashion.) Then, the biconical taper is cut at the waist and a cylindrical rod is inserted between the tapers and fused to the two cut ends. This latter technique allows the use of a less-narrow waist, and it is easier to fabricate.

Commercially available passive star couplers can support a few tens of stations at a radial distance of up to a kilometer or more. The limitations on number of stations and distances are imposed by the losses in the network. The attenuation that will occur in the network consists of the following components:

- **Optical connector losses.** Connectors are used to splice together cable segments for increased length. Typical connector losses are 1.0 to 1.5 dB per connector. A typical passive star network will have from 0 to 4 connectors in a path from transmitter to receiver, for a total maximum attenuation of 4 to 6 dB.
- **Optical cable attenuation.** Typical cable attenuation for the cable that has been used in these systems ranges from 3 to 6 dB per kilometer.
- **Optical power division in the coupler.** The coupler divides the optical power from one transmission path equally among all reception paths. Expressed in decibels, the loss seen by any node is 10 log $N$, where $N$ is the number of nodes. For example, the effective loss in a 16-port coupler is about 12 dB.

## 12.5 WIRELESS LANs

In just the past few years, wireless LANs have come to occupy a significant niche in the local area network market. Increasingly, organizations are finding that wireless LANs are an indispensable adjunct to traditional wired LANs, as they satisfy requirements for mobility, relocation, ad hoc networking, and coverage of locations difficult to wire.

As the name suggests, a wireless LAN is one that makes use of a wireless transmission medium. Until relatively recently, wireless LANs were little used; the reasons for this included high prices, low data rates, occupational safety concerns, and licensing requirements. As these problems have been addressed, the popularity of wireless LANs has grown rapidly.

In this section, we first look at the requirements for and advantages of wireless LANs, and then preview the key approaches to wireless LAN implementation.

### Wireless LANs Applications

[PAHL95a] lists four application areas for wireless LANs: LAN extension, cross-building interconnect, nomadic access, and ad hoc networks. Let us consider each of these in turn.

### LAN Extension

Early wireless LAN products, introduced in the late 1980s, were marketed as substitutes for traditional wired LANs. A wireless LAN saves the cost of the installation of LAN cabling and eases the task of relocation and other modifications to network structure. However, this motivation for wireless LANs was overtaken by events. First, as awareness of the need for LAN became greater, architects designed new buildings to include extensive prewiring for data applications. Second, with advances in data transmission technology, there has been an increasing reliance on twisted pair cabling for LANs and, in particular, Category 3 unshielded twisted pair. Most older building are already wired with an abundance of Category 3 cable. Thus, the use of a wireless LAN to replace wired LANs has not happened to any great extent.

However, in a number of environments, there is a role for the wireless LAN as an alternative to a wired LAN. Examples include buildings with large open areas, such as manufacturing plants, stock exchange trading floors, and warehouses; historical buildings with insufficient twisted pair and in which drilling holes for new wiring is prohibited; and small offices where installation and maintenance of wired LANs is not economical. In all of these cases, a wireless LAN provides an effective and more attractive alternative. In most of these cases, an organization will also have a wired LAN to support servers and some stationary workstations. For example, a manufacturing facility typically has an office area that is separate from the factory floor but which must be linked to it for networking purposes. Therefore, typically, a wireless LAN will be linked into a wired LAN on the same premises. Thus, this application area is referred to as LAN extension.

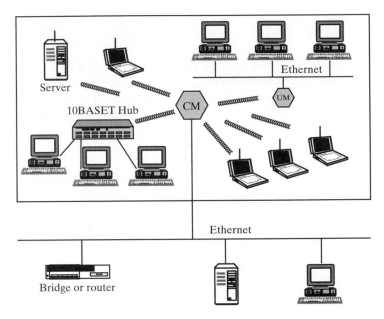

**FIGURE 12.17**  Example single-cell wireless LAN configuration.

Figure 12.17 indicates a simple wireless LAN configuration that is typical of many environments. There is a backbone wired LAN, such as Ethernet, that supports servers, workstations, and one or more bridges or routers to link with other networks. In addition there is a control module (CM) that acts as an interface to a wireless LAN. The control module includes either bridge or router functionality to link the wireless LAN to the backbone. In addition, it includes some sort of access control logic, such as a polling or token-passing scheme, to regulate the access from the end systems. Note that some of the end systems are standalone devices, such as a workstation or a server. In addition, hubs or other user modules (UM) that control a number of stations off a wired LAN may also be part of the wireless LAN configuration.

The configuration of Figure 12.17 can be referred to as a single-cell wireless LAN; all of the wireless end systems are within range of a single control module. Another common configuration, suggested by Figure 12.18, is a multiple-cell wireless LAN. In this case, there are multiple control modules interconnected by a wired LAN. Each control module supports a number of wireless end systems within its transmission range. For example, with an infrared LAN, transmission is limited to a single room; therefore, one cell is needed for each room in an office building that requires wireless support.

## Cross-Building Interconnect

Another use of wireless LAN technology is to connect LANs in nearby buildings, be they wired or wireless LANs. In this case, a point-to-point wireless link is used between two buildings. The devices so connected are typically bridges or routers. This single point-to-point link is not a LAN per se, but it is usual to include this application under the heading of wireless LAN.

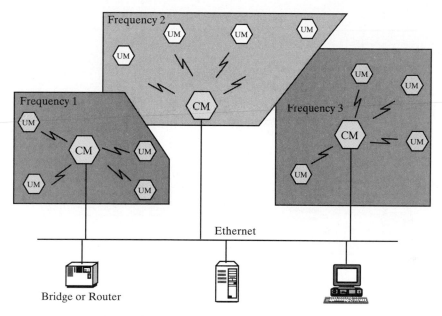

**FIGURE 12.18**  Example multiple-cell wireless LAN configuration.

## Nomadic Access

Nomadic access provides a wireless link between a LAN hub and a mobile data terminal equipped with an antenna, such as a laptop computer or notepad computer. One example of the utility of such a connection is to enable an employee returning from a trip to transfer data from a personal portable computer to a server in the office. Nomadic access is also useful in an extended environment such as a campus or a business operating out of a cluster of buildings. In both of these cases, users may move around with their portable computers and may wish access to the servers on a wired LAN from various locations.

## Ad Hoc Networking

An ad hoc network is a peer-to-peer network (no centralized server) set up temporarily to meet some immediate need. For example, a group of employees, each with a laptop or palmtop computer, may convene in a conference room for a business or classroom meeting. The employees link their computers in a temporary network just for the duration of the meeting.

Figure 12.19 suggests the differences between an ad hoc wireless LAN and a wireless LAN that supports LAN extension and nomadic access requirements. In the former case, the wireless LAN forms a stationary infrastructure consisting of one or more cells with a control module for each cell. Within a cell, there may be a number of stationary end systems. Nomadic stations can move from one cell to another. In contrast, there is no infrastructure for an ad hoc network. Rather, a peer collection of stations within range of each other may dynamically configure themselves into a temporary network.

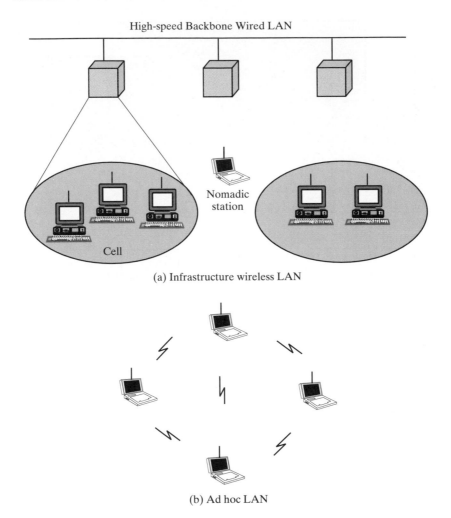

(a) Infrastructure wireless LAN

(b) Ad hoc LAN

**FIGURE 12.19** Wireless LAN configurations.

## Wireless LAN Requirements

A wireless LAN must meet the same sort of requirements typical of any LAN, including high capacity, ability to cover short distances, full connectivity among attached stations, and broadcast capability. In addition, there are a number of requirements specific to the wireless LAN environment. The following are among the most important requirements for wireless LANs:

- **Throughput.** The medium access control protocol should make as efficient use as possible of the wireless medium to maximize capacity.
- **Number of nodes.** Wireless LANs may need to support hundreds of nodes across multiple cells.
- **Connection to backbone LAN.** In most cases, interconnection with stations on a wired backbone LAN is required. For infrastructure wireless LANs, this is easily accomplished through the use of control modules that connect to both

types of LANs. There may also need to be accommodation for mobile users and ad hoc wireless networks.

- **Service area.** A typical coverage area for a wireless LAN may be up to a 300 to 1000 foot diameter.
- **Battery power consumption.** Mobile workers use battery-powered workstations that need to have a long battery life when used with wireless adapters. This suggests that a MAC protocol that requires mobile nodes to constantly monitor access points or to engage in frequent handshakes with a base station is inappropriate.
- **Transmission robustness and security.** Unless properly designed, a wireless LAN may be interference-prone and easily eavesdropped upon. The design of a wireless LAN must permit reliable transmission even in a noisy environment and should provide some level of security from eavesdropping.
- **Collocated network operation.** As wireless LANs become more popular, it is quite likely for two of them to operate in the same area or in some area where interference between the LANs is possible. Such interference may thwart the normal operation of a MAC algorithm and may allow unauthorized access to a particular LAN.
- **License-free operation.** Users would prefer to buy and operate wireless LAN products without having to secure a license for the frequency band used by the LAN.
- **Handoff/roaming.** The MAC protocol used in the wireless LAN should enable mobile stations to move from one cell to another.
- **Dynamic configuration.** The MAC addressing and network management aspects of the LAN should permit dynamic and automated addition, deletion, and relocation of end systems without disruption to other users.

## Wireless LAN Technology

Wireless LANs are generally categorized according to the transmission technique that is used. All current wireless LAN products fall into one of the following categories:

- **Infrared (IR) LANs.** An individual cell of an IR LAN is limited to a single room, as infrared light does not penetrate opaque walls.
- **Spread Spectrum LANs.** This type of LAN makes use of spread spectrum transmission technology. In most cases, these LANs operate in the ISM (Industrial, Scientific, and Medical) bands, so that no FCC licensing is required for their use in the U.S.
- **Narrowband Microwave.** These LANs operate at microwave frequencies but do not use spread spectrum. Some of these products operate at frequencies that require FCC licensing, while others use one of the unlicensed ISM bands.

Table 12.6 summarizes some of the key characteristics of these three technologies.

**TABLE 12.6** Comparison of wireless LAN technologies.

| | Infrared | | Spread Spectrum | | Radio |
|---|---|---|---|---|---|
| | Diffused Infrared | Directed Beam Infrared | Frequency Hopping | Direct Sequence | Narrowband Microwave |
| **Data rate (Mbps)** | 1–4 | 1–10 | 1–3 | 2–20 | 5–10 |
| **Mobility** | Stationary/mobile | Stationary with LOS | Mobile | Stationary/mobile | |
| **Range (ft)** | 50–200 | 80 | 100–300 | 100–800 | 40–130 |
| **Detectability** | Negligible | | Little | | Some |
| **Wavelength/frequency** | λ: 800 – 900 nm | | ISM bands: 902 – 928 MHz 2.4 – 2.4835 GHz 5.725 – 5.85 GHz | | 18.825 – 19.205 GHz or ISM band |
| **Modulation technique** | OOK | | GFSK | QPSK | FS/QPSK |
| **Radiated power** | N/A | | <1W | | 25 mW |
| **Access method** | CSMA | Token Ring, CSMA | CSMA | | Reservation ALOHA, CSMA |
| **License required** | No | | No | | Yes unless ISM |

## 12.6  RECOMMENDED READING

The literature on LANs and MANs is vast. The material in this chapter is covered in much more depth in [STAL97].

[MART94] and [MADR94] are book-length treatments of LANs. [SADI95] and [KESS92] cover MANs.

[PAHL95a] and [BANT94] are excellent survey articles on wireless LANs. Two book-length treatments are noteworthy: [SANT94] focuses on the technology of wireless LAN components and on signal encoding techniques; [DAVI95] addresses applications for wireless LANs as well as configuration and management issues.

**BANT94**  Bantz, D. and Bauchot, F. "Wireless LAN Design Alternatives." *IEEE Network*, March/April, 1994.

**DAVI95**  Davis, P. and McGuffin, C. *Wireless Local Area Networks*. New York: McGraw-Hill, 1995.

**KESS92**  Kessler, G. and Train, D. *Metropolitan Area Networks: Concepts, Standards, and Services*. New York: McGraw-Hill, 1992.

**MADR94**  Madron, T. *Local Area Networks: New Technologies, Emerging Standards*. New York: Wiley, 1994.

**MART94**  Martin, J., Chapman, K., and Leben, J. *Local Area Networks: Architectures and Implementations*. Englewood Cliffs, NJ: Prentice-Hall, 1994.

**PAHL95a**  Pahlavan, K., Probert, T., and Chase, M. "Trends in Local Wireless Networks." *IEEE Communications Magazine*, March 1995.

**SADI95**  Sadiku, M. *Metropolitan Area Networks*. Boca Raton, FL: CRC Press, 1995.

**SANT94**  Santamaria, A. and Lopez-Hernandez, F. (*editors*). *Wireless LAN Systems*. Boston MA: Artech House, 1994.

**STAL97**  Stallings, W. *Local and Metropolitan Area Networks, Fifth Edition*. Upper Saddle River, NJ: Prentice Hall, 1997.

### Recommended Web Site

- http://web.syr.edu/~jmwobus/lans: This site has links to most important sources of LAN information on the Internet, including all of the related FAQs.

## 12.7  PROBLEMS

**12.1**  Could HDLC be used as a data link control protocol for a LAN? If not, what is missing?

**12.2**  An asynchronous device, such as a teletype, transmits characters one at a time with unpredictable delays between characters. What problems, if any, do you foresee if such a device is connected to a local network and allowed to transmit at will (subject to gaining access to the medium)? How might such problems be resolved?

**12.3**  Consider the transfer of a file containing one million characters from one station to another. What is the total elapsed time and effective throughput for the following cases:

**a.** A circuit-switched, star topology local network. Call setup time is negligible, and the data rate on the medium is 64 kbps.

**b.** A bus topology local network with two stations a distance $D$ apart, a data rate of $B$ bps, and a packet size $P$ with 80 bits of overhead. Each packet is acknowledged with an 88-bit packet before the next is sent. The propagation speed on the bus is 200 m/μs. Solve for

(1) $D = 1$ km, $\quad B = 1$ Mbps, $\quad\quad P = 256$ bits
(2) $D = 1$ km, $\quad B = 10$ Mbps, $\quad\quad P = 256$ bits
(3) $D = 10$ km, $\quad B = 1$ Mbps, $\quad\quad P = 256$ bits
(4) $D = 1$ km, $\quad B = 50$ Mbps, $\quad\quad P = 10,000$ bits

c. A ring topology with a total circular length of $2D$, with the two stations a distance $D$ apart. Acknowledgment is achieved by allowing a packet to circulate past the destination station, back to the source station. There are $N$ repeaters on the ring, each of which introduces a delay of one bit time. Repeat the calculation for each of b(1) through b(4) for $N = 10$; 100; 1000.

**12.4** Consider a baseband bus with a number of equally spaced stations with a data rate of 10 Mbps and a bus length of 1 km.
a. What is the average time to send a frame of 1000 bits to another station, measured from the beginning of transmission to the end of reception? Assume a propagation speed of 200 m/μs.
b. If two stations begin to transmit at exactly the same time, their packets will interfere with each other. If each transmitting station monitors the bus during transmission, how long before it notices an interference, in seconds? In bit times?

**12.5** Repeat Problem 12.4 for a data rate of 1 Mbps.

**12.6** Repeat Problems 12.4 and 12.5 for
a. Broadband bus
b. Broadband tree consisting of 10 cables each of length 100 m emanating from a headend.

**12.7** At a propagation speed of 200 m/μs, what is the effective length added to a ring by a bit delay at each repeater:
a. At 1 Mbps?
b. At 40 Mbps?

**12.8** A tree-topology local network is to be provided that spans two buildings. If permission can be obtained to string cable between the two buildings, one continuous tree layout will be used. Otherwise, each building will have an independent tree-topology network, and a point-to-point link will connect a special communications station on one network with a communications station on the other network. What functions must the communications stations perform? Repeat for ring and star.

**12.9** System A consists of a single ring with 300 stations, one per repeater. System B consists of three 100-station rings linked by a bridge. If the probability of a link failure is $P_1$, a repeater failure is $P_r$, and a bridge failure is $P_b$, derive an expression for parts (a) through (d):
a. Probability of failure of system A.
b. Probability of complete failure of system B.
c. Probability that a particular station will find the network unavailable, for systems A and B.
d. Probability that any two stations, selected at random, will be unable to communicate, for systems A and B
e. Compute values for parts (a) through (d) for $P_1, = P_b = P_r = 10^{-2}$.

# CHAPTER **13**

## LAN Systems

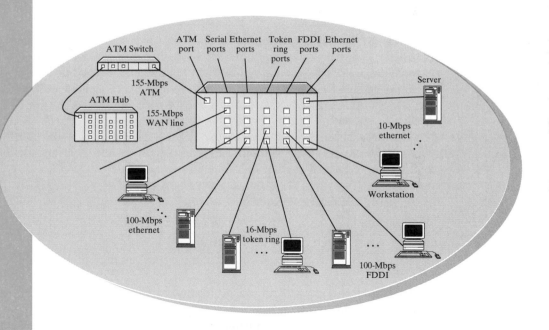

W e now move to a consideration of specific LAN systems. As was mentioned in Chapter 12, the medium access control technique and topology are key characteristics used in the classification of LANs and in the development of standards. The following systems are discussed in this chapter:[1]

- Ethernet and Fast Ethernet (CSMA/CD)
- Token Ring/FDDI
- 100VG-AnyLAN
- ATM LANs
- Fibre Channel
- Wireless LANs

## 13.1 ETHERNET AND FAST ETHERNET (CSMA/CD)

The most commonly used medium access control technique for bus/tree and star topologies is carrier-sense multiple access with collision detection (CSMA/CD). The original baseband version of this technique was developed by Xerox as part of the Ethernet LAN. The original broadband version was developed by MITRE as part of its MITREnet LAN. All of this work formed the basis for the IEEE 802.3 standard.

In this section, we will focus on the IEEE 802.3 standard. As with other LAN standards, there is both a medium access control layer and a physical layer, which are considered in turn in what follows.

### IEEE 802.3 Medium Access Control

It is easier to understand the operation of CSMA/CD if we look first at some earlier schemes from which CSMA/CD evolved.

#### Precursors

CSMA/CD and its precursors can be termed random access, or contention, techniques. They are random access in the sense that there is no predictable or scheduled time for any station to transmit; station transmissions are ordered randomly. They exhibit contention in the sense that stations contend for time on the medium.

The earliest of these techniques, known as ALOHA, was developed for packet radio networks. However, it is applicable to any shared transmission medium. ALOHA, or pure ALOHA as it is sometimes called, is a true free-for-all. Whenever a station has a frame to send, it does so. The station then listens for an amount of time equal to the maximum possible round-trip propagation delay on the network (twice the time it takes to send a frame between the two most widely separated stations) plus a small fixed time increment. If the station hears an acknowl-

---

[1] Two other systems illustrated in Figure 12.2, DQDB MANs and Token Bus, are not discussed in this chapter due to space constraints. These systems are not as widely used as the others covered in this chapter.

edgment during that time, fine; otherwise, it resends the frame. If the station fails to receive an acknowledgment after repeated transmissions, it gives up. A receiving station determines the correctness of an incoming frame by examining a frame-check-sequence field, as in HDLC. If the frame is valid and if the destination address in the frame header matches the receiver's address, the station immediately sends an acknowledgment. The frame may be invalid due to noise on the channel or because another station transmitted a frame at about the same time. In the latter case, the two frames may interfere with each other at the receiver so that neither gets through; this is known as a *collision*. If a received frame is determined to be invalid, the receiving station simply ignores the frame.

ALOHA is as simple as can be, and pays a penalty for it. Because the number of collisions rise rapidly with increased load, the maximum utilization of the channel is only about 18% (see [STAL97]).

To improve efficiency, a modification of ALOHA, known as slotted ALOHA, was developed. In this scheme, time on the channel is organized into uniform slots whose size equals the frame transmission time. Some central clock or other technique is needed to synchronize all stations. Transmission is permitted to begin only at a slot boundary. Thus, frames that do overlap will do so totally. This increases the maximum utilization of the system to about 37%.

Both ALOHA and slotted ALOHA exhibit poor utilization. Both fail to take advantage of one of the key properties of both packet radio and LANs, which is that propagation delay between stations is usually very small compared to frame transmission time. Consider the following observations. If the station-to-station propagation time is large compared to the frame transmission time, then, after a station launches a frame, it will be a long time before other stations know about it. During that time, one of the other stations may transmit a frame; the two frames may interfere with each other and neither gets through. Indeed, if the distances are great enough, many stations may begin transmitting, one after the other, and none of their frames get through unscathed. Suppose, however, that the propagation time is small compared to frame transmission time. In that case, when a station launches a frame, all the other stations know it almost immediately. So, if they had any sense, they would not try transmitting until the first station was done. Collisions would be rare because they would occur only when two stations began to transmit almost simultaneously. Another way to look at it is that a short delay time provides the stations with better feedback about the state of the network; this information can be used to improve efficiency.

The foregoing observations led to the development of carrier-sense multiple access (CSMA). With CSMA, a station wishing to transmit first listens to the medium to determine if another transmission is in progress (carrier sense). If the medium is in use, the station must wait. If the medium is idle, the station may transmit. It may happen that two or more stations attempt to transmit at about the same time. If this happens, there will be a collision; the data from both transmissions will be garbled and not received successfully. To account for this, a station waits a reasonable amount of time, after transmitting, for an acknowledgment, taking into account the maximum round-trip propagation delay, and the fact that the acknowledging station must also contend for the channel in order to respond. If there is no acknowledgment, the station assumes that a collision has occurred and retransmits.

One can see how this strategy would be effective for networks in which the average frame transmission time is much longer than the propagation time. Collisions can occur only when more than one user begins transmitting within a short time (the period of the propagation delay). If a station begins to transmit a frame, and there are no collisions during the time it takes for the leading edge of the packet to propagate to the farthest station, then there will be no collision for this frame because all other stations are now aware of the transmission.

The maximum utilization achievable using CSMA can far exceed that of ALOHA or slotted ALOHA. The maximum utilization depends on the length of the frame and on the propagation time; the longer the frames or the shorter the propagation time, the higher the utilization. This subject is explored in Appendix 13A.

With CSMA, an algorithm is needed to specify what a station should do if the medium is found busy. The most common approach, and the one used in IEEE 802.3, is the *1-persistent technique*. A station wishing to transmit listens to the medium and obeys the following rules:

1. If the medium is idle, transmit; otherwise, go to step 2.
2. If the medium is busy, continue to listen until the channel is sensed idle; then transmit immediately.

If two or more stations are waiting to transmit, a collision is guaranteed. Things get sorted out only after the collision.

## Description of CSMA/CD

CSMA, although more efficient than ALOHA or slotted ALOHA, still has one glaring inefficiency: When two frames collide, the medium remains unusable for the duration of transmission of both damaged frames. For long frames, compared to propagation time, the amount of wasted capacity can be considerable. This waste can be reduced if a station continues to listen to the medium while transmitting. This leads to the following rules for CSMA/CD:

1. If the medium is idle, transmit; otherwise, go to step 2.
2. If the medium is busy, continue to listen until the channel is idle, then transmit immediately.
3. If a collision is detected during transmission, transmit a brief jamming signal to assure that all stations know that there has been a collision and then cease transmission.
4. After transmitting the jamming signal, wait a random amount of time, then attempt to transmit again. (Repeat from step 1.)

Figure 13.1 illustrates the technique for a baseband bus. At time $t_0$, station A begins transmitting a packet addressed to D. At $t_1$, both B and C are ready to transmit. B senses a transmission and so defers. C, however, is still unaware of A's transmission and begins its own transmission. When A's transmission reaches C, at $t_2$, C detects the collision and ceases transmission. The effect of the collision propagates

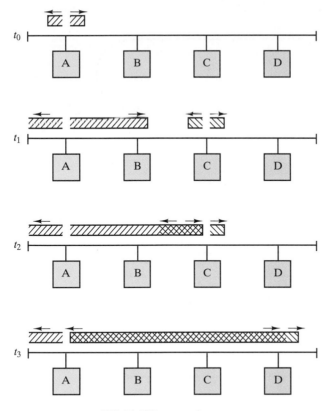

**FIGURE 13.1**   CSMA/CD operation.

back to A, where it is detected some time later, $t_3$, at which time A ceases transmission.

With CSMA/CD, the amount of wasted capacity is reduced to the time it takes to detect a collision. Question: how long does that take? Let us consider first the case of a baseband bus and consider two stations as far apart as possible. For example, in Figure 13.1, suppose that station A begins a transmission and that just before that transmission reaches D, D is ready to transmit. Because D is not yet aware of A's transmission, it begins to transmit. A collision occurs almost immediately and is recognized by D. However, the collision must propagate all the way back to A before A is aware of the collision. By this line of reasoning, we conclude that the amount of time that it takes to detect a collision is no greater than twice the end-to-end propagation delay. For a broadband bus, the delay is even longer. Figure 13.2 shows a dual-cable system. This time, the worst case occurs for two stations as close together as possible and as far as possible from the headend. In this case, the maximum time to detect a collision is four times the propagation delay from an end of the cable to the headend.

An important rule followed in most CSMA/CD systems, including the IEEE standard, is that frames should be long enough to allow collision detection prior to the end of transmission. If shorter frames are used, then collision detection does not

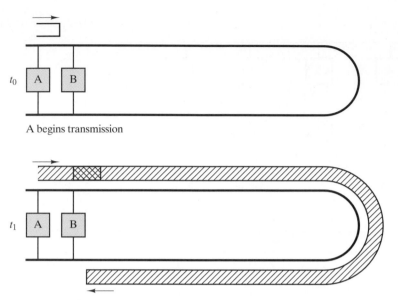

A begins transmission

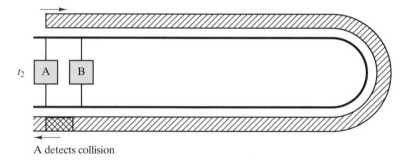

B begins transmission just before leading edge of A's packet arrives at B's receiver;
B almost immediately detects A's transmission and ceases its own transmission.

A detects collision

**FIGURE 13.2** Broadband collision detection timing.

occur, and CSMA/CD exhibits the same performance as the less efficient CSMA protocol.

Although the implementation of CSMA/CD is substantially the same for baseband and broadband, there are differences. One is the means for performing carrier sense; for baseband systems, this is done by detecting a voltage pulse train. For broadband, the RF carrier is detected.

Collision detection also differs for the two systems. For baseband, a collision should produce substantially higher voltage swings than those produced by a single transmitter. Accordingly, the IEEE standard dictates that the transmitter will detect a collision if the signal on the cable at the transmitter tap point exceeds the maximum that could be produced by the transmitter alone. Because a transmitted signal attenuates as it propagates, there is a potential problem: If two stations far apart are transmitting, each station will receive a greatly attenuated signal from the other. The signal strength could be so small that when it is added to the transmitted signal at the transmitter tap point, the combined signal does not exceed the CD threshold. For this reason, among others, the IEEE standard restricts the maximum length of coaxial cable to 500 m for 10BASE5 and to 200 m for 10BASE2.

A much simpler collision detection scheme is possible with the twisted pair star-topology approach (Figure 12.13). In this case, collision detection is based on logic rather than on sensing voltage magnitudes. For any hub, if there is activity (signal) on more than one input, a collision is assumed. A special signal called the collision presence signal is generated. This signal is generated and sent out as long as activity is sensed on any of the input lines. This signal is interpreted by every node as an occurrence of a collision.

There are several possible approaches to collision detection in broadband systems. The most common of these is to perform a bit-by-bit comparison between transmitted and received data. When a station transmits on the inbound channel, it begins to receive its own transmission on the outbound channel after a propagation delay to the headend and back. Note the similarity to a satellite link. Another approach, for split systems, is for the headend to perform detection based on garbled data.

## MAC Frame

Figure 13.3 depicts the frame format for the 802.3 protocol; it consists of the following fields:

- **Preamble.** A 7-octet pattern of alternating 0s and 1s used by the receiver to establish bit synchronization.
- **Start frame delimiter.** The sequence 10101011, which indicates the actual start of the frame and which enables the receiver to locate the first bit of the rest of the frame.
- **Destination address (DA).** Specifies the station(s) for which the frame is intended. It may be a unique physical address, a group address, or a global address. The choice of a 16- or 48-bit address length is an implementation decision, and must be the same for all stations on a particular LAN.
- **Source address (SA).** Specifies the station that sent the frame.
- **Length.** Length of the LLC data field.
- **LLC data.** Data unit supplied by LLC.
- **Pad.** Octets added to ensure that the frame is long enough for proper CD operation.

| Octets | 7 | 1 | 2 or 6 | 2 or 6 | 2 | ≥ 0 | ≥ 0 | 4 |
|--------|---|---|--------|--------|---|-----|-----|---|
| | Preamble | SFD | DA | SA | Length | LLC data | Pad | FCS |

LEGEND

SFD = Start-frame delimiter  
DA = Destination address  

SA = Source address  
FCS = Frame-check sequence  

**FIGURE 13.3**   IEEE 802.3 frame format.

- **Frame check sequence (FCS).** A 32-bit cyclic redundancy check, based on all fields except the preamble, the SFD, and the FCS.

## IEEE 802.3 10-Mbps Specifications (Ethernet)

The IEEE 802.3 committee has been the most active in defining alternative physical configurations; this is both good and bad. On the good side, the standard has been responsive to evolving technology. On the bad side, the customer, not to mention the potential vendor, is faced with a bewildering array of options. However, the committee has been at pains to ensure that the various options can be easily integrated into a configuration that satisfies a variety of needs. Thus, the user that has a complex set of requirements may find the flexibility and variety of the 802.3 standard to be an asset.

To distinguish among the various implementations that are available, the committee has developed a concise notation:

<data rate in Mbps><signaling method><maximum segment length in hundreds of meters>

The defined alternatives are:[2]

- 10BASE5
- 10BASE2
- 10BASE-T
- 10BROAD36
- 10BASE-F

Note that 10BASE-T and 10-BASE-F do not quite follow the notation; "T" stands for twisted pair, and "F" stands for optical fiber. Table 13.1 summarizes these options. All of the alternatives listed in the table specify a data rate of 10 Mbps. In addition to these alternatives, there are several versions that operate at 100 Mbps; these are covered later in this section.

### 10BASE5 Medium Specification

10BASE5 is the original 802.3 medium specification and is based on directly on Ethernet. 10BASE5 specifies the use of 50-ohm coaxial cable and uses Manchester digital signaling.[3] The maximum length of a cable segment is set at 500 meters. The length of the network can be extended by the use of repeaters, which are transparent to the MAC level; as they do no buffering, they do not isolate one segment from another. So, for example, if two stations on different segments attempt to transmit at the same time, their transmissions will collide. To avoid looping, only one path of segments and repeaters is allowed between any two stations. The standard allows a

---

[2] There is also a 1BASE-T alternative that defines a 1-Mbps twisted pair system using a star topology; this is considered obsolete although it is contained in the most recent version of the standard.

[3] See Section 4.1.

**TABLE 13.1**   IEEE 802.3 10-Mbps physical layer medium alternatives.

|                               | 10BASE5                      | 10BASE2                      | 10BASE-T                     | 10BROAD36                    | 10BASE-FP                    |
| ----------------------------- | ---------------------------- | ---------------------------- | ---------------------------- | ---------------------------- | ---------------------------- |
| Transmission medium           | Coaxial Cable (50 ohm)       | Coaxial Cable (50 ohm)       | Unshielded twisted pair      | Coaxial Cable (75 ohm)       | 850-nm optical fiber pair    |
| Signaling technique           | Baseband (Manchester)        | Baseband (Manchester)        | Baseband (Manchester)        | Broadband (DPSK)             | Manchester/ On-off           |
| Topology                      | Bus                          | Bus                          | Star                         | Bus/Tree                     | Star                         |
| Maximum segment length (m)    | 500                          | 185                          | 100                          | 1800                         | 500                          |
| Nodes per segment             | 100                          | 30                           | —                            | —                            | 33                           |
| Cable diameter (mm)           | 10                           | 5                            | 0.4–0.6                      | 10–25                        | 62.5/125 μm                  |

maximum of four repeaters in the path between any two stations, thereby extending the effective length of the medium to 2.5 kilometers.

## 10BASE2 Medium Specification

To provide a lower-cost system than 10BASE5 for personal computer LANs, 10BASE2 was added. As with 10BASE5, this specification uses 50-ohm coaxial cable and Manchester signaling. The key difference is that 10BASE2 uses a thinner cable, which supports fewer taps over a shorter distance than the 10BASE5 cable.

Because they have the same data rate, it is possible to combine 10BASE5 and 10BASE2 segments in the same network, by using a repeater that conforms to 10BASE5 on one side and 10BASE2 on the other side. The only restriction is that a 10BASE2 segment should not be used to bridge two 10BASE5 segments, because a "backbone" segment should be as resistant to noise as the segments it connects.

## 10BASE-T Medium Specification

By sacrificing some distance, it is possible to develop a 10-Mbps LAN using the unshielded twisted pair medium. Such wire is often found prewired in office buildings as excess telephone cable, and can be used for LANs. Such an approach is specified in the 10BASE-T specification. The 10BASE-T specification defines a star-shaped topology. A simple system consists of a number of stations connected to a central point, referred to as a multiport repeater, via two twisted pairs. The central point accepts input on any one line and repeats it on all of the other lines.

Stations attach to the multiport repeater via a point-to-point link. Ordinarily, the link consists of two unshielded twisted pairs. Because of the high data rate and the poor transmission qualities of unshielded twisted pair, the length of a link is limited to 100 meters. As an alternative, an optical fiber link may be used. In this case, the maximum length is 500 m.

### 10BROAD36 Medium Specification

The 10BROAD36 specification is the only 802.3 specification for broadband. The medium employed is the standard 75-ohm CATV coaxial cable. Either a dual-cable or split-cable configuration is allowed. The maximum length of an individual segment, emanating from the headend, is 1800 meters; this results in a maximum end-to-end span of 3600 meters.

The signaling on the cable is differential phase-shift keying (DPSK). In ordinary PSK, a binary zero is represented by a carrier with a particular phase, and a binary one is represent by a carrier with the opposite phase (180-degree difference). DPSK makes use of differential encoding, in which a change of phase occurs when a zero occurs, and there is no change of phase when a one occurs. The advantage of differential encoding is that it is easier for the receiver to detect a change in phase than to determine the phase itself.

The characteristics of the modulation process are specified so that the resulting 10 Mbps signal fits into a 14 MHz bandwidth.

### 10BASE-F Medium Specification

The 10BASE-F specification enables users to take advantage of the distance and transmission characteristics available with the use of optical fiber. The standard actually contains three specifications:

- **10-BASE-FP (passive).** A passive-star topology for interconnecting stations and repeaters with up to 1 km per segment.
- **10-BASE-FL (link).** Defines a point-to-point link that can be used to connect stations or repeaters at up to 2 km.
- **10-BASE-FB (backbone).** Defines a point-to-point link that can be used to connect repeaters at up to 2 km.

All three of these specifications make use of a pair of optical fibers for each transmission link, one for transmission in each direction. In all cases, the signaling scheme involves the use of Manchester encoding. Each Manchester signal element is then converted to an optical signal element, with the presence of light corresponding to high and the absence of light corresponding to low. Thus, a 10-Mbps Manchester bit stream actually requires 20 Mbps on the fiber.

The 10-BASE-FP defines a passive star system that can support up to 33 stations attached to a central passive star, of the type described in Chapter 3. 10-BASE-FL and 10-BASE-FB define point-to-point connections that can be used to extend the length of a network; the key difference between the two is that 10-BASE-FB makes use of synchronous retransmission. With synchronous signaling, an optical signal coming into a repeater is retimed with a local clock and retransmitted. With conventional asynchronous signaling, used with 10-BASE-FL, no such retiming takes place, so that any timing distortions are propagated through a series of repeaters. As a result, 10BASE-FB can be used to cascade up to 15 repeaters in sequence to achieve greater length.

### IEEE 802.3 100–Mbps Specifications (Fast Ethernet)

Fast Ethernet refers to a set of specifications developed by the IEEE 802.3 committee to provide a low-cost, Ethernet-compatible LAN operating at 100 Mbps. The blanket designation for these standards is 100BASE-T. The committee defined a number of alternatives to be used with different transmission media.

Figure 13.4 shows the terminology used in labeling the specifications and indicates the media used. All of the 100BASE-T options use the IEEE 802.3 MAC protocol and frame format. 100BASE-X refers to a set of options that use the physical medium specifications originally defined for Fiber Distributed Data Interface (FDDI; covered in the next section). All of the 100BASE-X schemes use two physical links between nodes: one for transmission and one for reception. 100BASE-TX makes use of shielded twisted pair (STP) or high-quality (Category 5) unshielded twisted pair (UTP). 100BASE-FX uses optical fiber.

In many buildings, each of the 100BASE-X options requires the installation of new cable. For such cases, 100BASE-T4 defines a lower-cost alternative that can use Category-3, voice grade UTP in addition to the higher-quality Category 5 UTP.[4] To achieve the 100-Mbps data rate over lower-quality cable, 100BASE-T4 dictates the use of four twisted pair lines between nodes, with the data transmission making use of three pairs in one direction at a time.

For all of the 100BASE-T options, the topology is similar to that of 10BASE-T, namely a star-wire topology.

Table 13.2 summarizes key characteristics of the 100BASE-T options.

### 100BASE-X

For all of the transmission media specified under 100BASE-X, a unidirectional data rate of 100 Mbps is achieved by transmitting over a single link (single twisted pair, single optical fiber). For all of these media, an efficient and effective signal

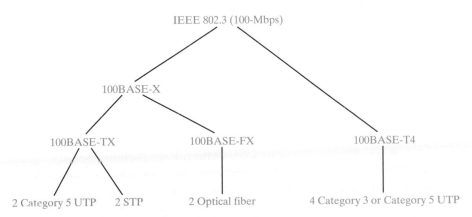

**FIGURE 13.4**   IEEE 802.3 100BASE-T options.

---

[4] See Chapter 3 for a discussion of Category 3 and Category 5 cable.

**TABLE 13.2** IEEE 802.3 100BASE-T physical layer medium alternatives.

|  | 100BASE-TX | | 100BASE-FX | 100BASE-T4 |
|---|---|---|---|---|
| Transmission medium | 2 pair, STP | 2 pair, Category 5 UTP | 2 optical fibers | 4 pair, Category 3, 4, or 5 UTP |
| Signaling technique | MLT-3 | MLT-3 | 4B5B, NRZI | 8B6T, NRZ |
| Data rate | 100 Mbps | 100 Mbps | 100 Mbps | 100 Mbps |
| Maximum segment length | 100 m | 100 m | 100 m | 100 m |
| Network span | 200 m | 200 m | 400 m | 200 m |

encoding scheme is required. The one chosen was originally defined for FDDI, and can be referred to as 4B/5B-NRZI. See Appendix 13A for a description.

The 100BASE-X designation includes two physical-medium specifications, one for twisted pair, known as 100BASE-TX, and one for optical fiber, known as 100-BASE-FX.

100BASE-TX makes use of two pairs of twisted pair cable, one pair used for transmission and one for reception. Both STP and Category 5 UTP are allowed. The MTL-3 signaling scheme is used (described in Appendix 13A).

100BASE-FX makes use of two optical fiber cables, one for transmission and one for reception. With 100BASE-FX, a means is needed to convert the 4B/5B-NRZI code groups stream into optical signals. The technique used is known as intensity modulation. A binary 1 is represented by a burst or pulse of light; a binary 0 is represented by either the absence of a light pulse or by a light pulse at very low intensity.

## 100BASE-T4

100BASE-T4 is designed to produce a 100-Mbps data rate over lower-quality Category 3 cable, thus taking advantage of the large installed base of Category 3 cable in office buildings. The specification also indicates that the use of Category 5 cable is optional. 100BASE-T4 does not transmit a continuous signal between packets, which makes it useful in battery-powered applications.

For 100BASE-T4 using voice-grade Category 3 cable, it is not reasonable to expect to achieve 100 Mbps on a single twisted pair. Instead, 100BASE-T4 specifies that the data stream to be transmitted is split up into three separate data streams, each with an effective data rate of $33\frac{1}{3}$ Mbps. Four twisted pairs are used. Data are transmitted using three pairs and received using three pairs. Thus, two of the pairs must be configured for bidirectional transmission.

As with 100BASE-X, a simple NRZ encoding scheme is not used for 100BASE-T4; this would require a signaling rate of 33 Mbps on each twisted pair and does not provide synchronization. Instead, a ternary signaling scheme known as 8B6T is used (described in Appendix 13A).

## 13.2   TOKEN RING AND FDDI

Token ring is the most commonly used MAC protocol for ring-topology LANs. In this section, we examine two standard LANs that use token ring: IEEE 802.5 and FDDI.

### IEEE 802.5 Medium Access Control

#### MAC Protocol

The token ring technique is based on the use of a small frame, called a *token*, that circulates when all stations are idle. A station wishing to transmit must wait until it detects a token passing by. It then seizes the token by changing one bit in the token, which transforms it from a token into a start-of-frame sequence for a data frame. The station then appends and transmits the remainder of the fields needed to construct a data frame.

When a station seizes a token and begins to transmit a data frame, there is no token on the ring, so other stations wishing to transmit must wait. The frame on the ring will make a round trip and be absorbed by the transmitting station. The transmitting station will insert a new token on the ring when both of the following conditions have been met:

* The station has completed transmission of its frame.
* The leading edge of the transmitted frame has returned (after a complete circulation of the ring) to the station.

If the bit length of the ring is less than the frame length, the first condition implies the second; if not, a station could release a free token after it has finished transmitting but before it begins to receive its own transmission. The second condition is not strictly necessary, and is relaxed under certain circumstances. The advantage of imposing the second condition is that it ensures that only one data frame at a time may be on the ring and that only one station at a time may be transmitting, thereby simplifying error-recovery procedures.

Once the new token has been inserted on the ring, the next station downstream with data to send will be able to seize the token and transmit. Figure 13.5 illustrates the technique. In the example, A sends a packet to C, which receives it and then sends its own packets to A and D.

Note that under lightly loaded conditions, there is some inefficiency with token ring because a station must wait for the token to come around before transmitting. However, under heavy loads, which is when it matters, the ring functions in a round-robin fashion, which is both efficient and fair. To see this, consider the configuration in Figure 13.5. After station A transmits, it releases a token. The first station with an opportunity to transmit is D. If D transmits, it then releases a token and C has the next opportunity, and so on.

The principal advantage of token ring is the flexible control over access that it

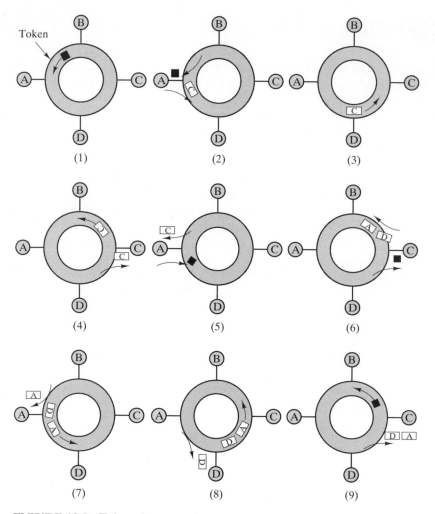

**FIGURE 13.5**   Token ring operation.

provides. In the simple scheme just described, the access if fair. As we shall see, schemes can be used to regulate access to provide for priority and for guaranteed bandwidth services.

The principal disadvantage of token ring is the requirement for token maintenance. Loss of the token prevents further utilization of the ring. Duplication of the token can also disrupt ring operation. One station must be selected as a monitor to ensure that exactly one token is on the ring and to ensure that a free token is reinserted, if necessary.

### MAC Frame

Figure 13.6 depicts the frame format for the 802.5 protocol. It consists of the following fields:

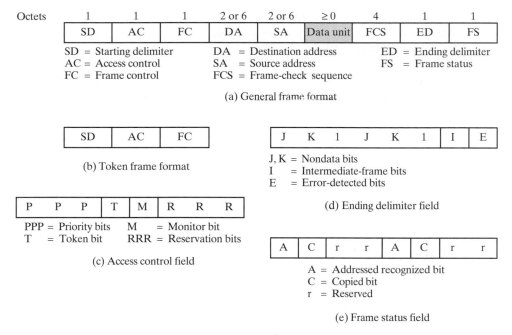

Octets

| 1 | 1 | 1 | 2 or 6 | 2 or 6 | ≥ 0 | 4 | 1 | 1 |
|----|----|----|----|----|----|----|----|----|
| SD | AC | FC | DA | SA | Data unit | FCS | ED | FS |

SD = Starting delimiter      DA = Destination address      ED = Ending delimiter
AC = Access control          SA = Source address           FS = Frame status
FC = Frame control           FCS = Frame-check sequence

(a) General frame format

| SD | AC | FC |
|----|----|----|

(b) Token frame format

| P | P | P | T | M | R | R | R |
|---|---|---|---|---|---|---|---|

PPP = Priority bits    M   = Monitor bit
T   = Token bit        RRR = Reservation bits

(c) Access control field

| J | K | 1 | J | K | 1 | I | E |
|---|---|---|---|---|---|---|---|

J, K = Nondata bits
I    = Intermediate-frame bits
E    = Error-detected bits

(d) Ending delimiter field

| A | C | r | r | A | C | r | r |
|---|---|---|---|---|---|---|---|

A = Addressed recognized bit
C = Copied bit
r = Reserved

(e) Frame status field

**FIGURE 13.6**   IEEE 802.5 frame format.

- **Starting delimiter (SD).** Indicates start of frame. The SD consists of signaling patterns that are distinguishable from data. It is coded as follows: JK0JK000, where J and K are nondata symbols. The actual form of a nondata symbol depends on the signal encoding on the medium.
- **Access control (AC).** Has the format PPPTMRRR, where PPP and RRR are 3-bit priority and reservation variables, and $M$ is the monitor bit; their use is explained below. T indicates whether this is a token or data frame. In the case of a token frame, the only remaining field is ED.
- **Frame control (FC).** Indicates whether this is an LLC data frame. If not, bits in this field control operation of the token ring MAC protocol.
- **Destination address (DA).** As with 802.3.
- **Source address (SA).** As with 802.3.
- **Data unit.** Contains LLC data unit.
- **Frame check sequence (FCS).** As with 802.3.
- **End delimiter (ED).** Contains the error-detection bit (E), which is set if any repeater detects an error, and the intermediate bit (I), which is used to indicate that this is a frame other than the final one of a multiple-frame transmission.
- **Frame status (FS).** Contains the address recognized (A) and frame-copied (C) bits, whose use is explained below. Because the A and C bits are outside the scope of the FCS, they are duplicated to provide a redundancy check to detect erroneous settings.

We can now restate the token ring algorithm for the case when a single priority is used. In this case, the priority and reservation bits are set to 0. A station wishing to transmit waits until a token goes by, as indicated by a token bit of 0 in the AC field. The station seizes the token by setting the token bit to 1. The SD and AC fields of the received token now function as the first two fields of the outgoing frame. The station transmits one or more frames, continuing until either its supply of frames is exhausted or a token-holding timer expires. When the AC field of the last transmitted frame returns, the station sets the token bit to 0 and appends an ED field, resulting in the insertion of a new token on the ring.

Stations in the receive mode listen to the ring. Each station can check passing frames for errors and can set the $E$ bit to 1 if an error is detected. If a station detects its own MAC address, it sets the $A$ bit to 1; it may also copy the frame, setting the $C$ bit to 1. This allows the originating station to differentiate three results of a frame transmission:

- Destination station nonexistent or not active ($A = 0$, $C = 0$)
- Destination station exists but frame not copied ($A = 1$, $C = 0$)
- Frame received ($A = 1$, $C = 1$)

## Token Ring Priority

The 802.5 standard includes a specification for an optional priority mechanism. Eight levels of priority are supported by providing two 3-bit fields in each data frame and token: a priority field and a reservation field. To explain the algorithm, let us define the following variables:

$P_f$ = priority of frame to be transmitted by station

$P_s$ = service priority: priority of current token

$P_r$ = value of $P_s$ as contained in the last token received by this station

$R_s$ = reservation value in current token

$R_r$ = highest reservation value in the frames received by this station during the last token rotation

The scheme works as follows:

1. A station wishing to transmit must wait for a token with $P_s \leq P_f$.
2. While waiting, a station may reserve a future token at its priority level ($P_f$). If a data frame goes by, and if the reservation field is less than its priority ($R_s < P_f$), then the station may set the reservation field of the frame to its priority ($R_s \leftarrow P_f$). If a token frame goes by, and if ($R_s < P_f$ AND $P_f < P_s$), then the station sets the reservation field of the frame to its priority ($R_s \leftarrow P_f$). This setting has the effect of preempting any lower-priority reservation.
3. When a station seizes a token, it sets the token bit to 1 to start a data frame, sets the reservation field of the data frame to 0, and leaves the priority field unchanged (the same as that of the incoming token frame).
4. Following transmission of one or more data frames, a station issues a new

**TABLE 13.3**  Actions performed by the token holder to implement the priority scheme [based on VALE92].

| Conditions | Actions |
|---|---|
| Frame available AND $P_s \leq P_f$ | Send frame |
| (Frame not available OR THT expired) AND $P_r \geq$ MAX $[R_r, P_f]$ | Send token with: $P_s \leftarrow P_f$ $R_s \leftarrow$ MAX $[R_r, P_f]$ |
| (Frame not available OR THT expired) AND $P_r <$ MAX $[R_r, P_f]$ AND $P_r > S_x$ | Send token with: $P_s \leftarrow$ MAX $[R_r, P_f]$ $R_s \leftarrow 0$ Push $S_r \leftarrow P_r$ Push $S_x \leftarrow P_s$ |
| (Frame not available OR THT expired) AND $P_r <$ MAX $[R_r, P_f]$ AND $P_r = S_x$ | Send token with: $P_s \leftarrow$ MAX $[R_r, P_f]$ $R_s \leftarrow 0$ Pop $S_x$ Push $S_x \leftarrow P_s$ |
| (Frame not available OR (Frame available and $P_f < S_x$)) AND $P_s = S_x$ AND $R_r > S_r$ | Send token with: $P_s \leftarrow R_r$ $R_s \leftarrow 0$ Pop $S_x$ Push $S_x \leftarrow P_s$ |
| (Frame not available OR (Frame available and $P_f < S_x$)) AND $P_s = S_x$ AND $R_r \leq S_r$ | Send token with: $P_s \leftarrow R_r$ $R_s \leftarrow 0$ Pop $S_r$ Pop $S_x$ |

token with the priority and reservation fields set as indicated in Table 13.3.

The effect of the above steps is to sort the competing claims and to allow the waiting transmission of highest priority to seize the token as soon as possible. A moment's reflection reveals that, as stated, the algorithm has a ratchet effect on priority, driving it to the highest used level and keeping it there. To avoid this, a station that raises the priority (issues a token that has a higher priority than the token that it received) has the responsibility of later lowering the priority to its previous level. Therefore, a station that raises priority must remember both the old and the new priorities and must downgrade the priority of the token at the appropriate time. In essence, each station is responsible for assuring that no token circulates indefinitely because its priority is too high. By remembering the priority of earlier transmissions, a station can detect this condition and downgrade the priority to a previous, lower priority or reservation.

To implement the downgrading mechanism, two stacks are maintained by each station, one for reservations and one for priorities:

$S_x$ = stack used to store new values of token priority
$S_r$ = stack used to store old values of token priority

The reason that stacks rather than scalar variables are required is that the priority can be raised a number of times by one or more stations. The successive raises must be unwound in the reverse order.

To summarize, a station having a higher priority frame to transmit than the current frame can reserve the next token for its priority level as the frame passes by. When the next token is issued, it will be at the reserved priority level. Stations of lower priority cannot seize the token, so it passes to the reserving station or an intermediate station with data to send of equal or higher priority level than the reserved priority level. The station that upgraded the priority level is responsible for downgrading it to its former level when all higher-priority stations are finished. When that station sees a token at the higher priority after it has transmitted, it can assume that there is no more higher-priority traffic waiting, and it downgrades the token before passing it on.

Figure 13.7 is an example. The following events occur:

1. A is transmitting a data frame to B at priority 0. When the frame has completed a circuit of the ring and returns to A, A will issue a token frame. However, as the data frame passes D, D makes a reservation at priority 3 by setting the reservation field to 3.
2. A issues a token with the priority field set to 3.
3. If neither B nor C has data of priority 3 or greater to send, they cannot seize the token. The token circulates to D, which seizes the token and issues a data frame.
4. After D's data frame returns to D, D issues a new token at the same priority as the token that it received: priority 3.
5. A sees a token at the priority level that it used to last issue a token; it therefore seizes the token even if it has no data to send.
6. A issues a token at the previous priority level: priority 0.

Note that, after A has issued a priority 3 token, any station with data of priority 3 or greater may seize the token. Suppose that at this point station C now has priority 4 data to send. C will seize the token, transmit its data frame, and reissue a priority 3 token, which is then seized by D. By the time that a priority 3 token arrives at A, all intervening stations with data of priority 3 or greater to send will have had the opportunity. It is now appropriate, therefore, for A to downgrade the token.

## Early Token Release

When a station issues a frame, if the bit length of the ring is less than that of the frame, the leading edge of the transmitted frame will return to the transmitting sta-

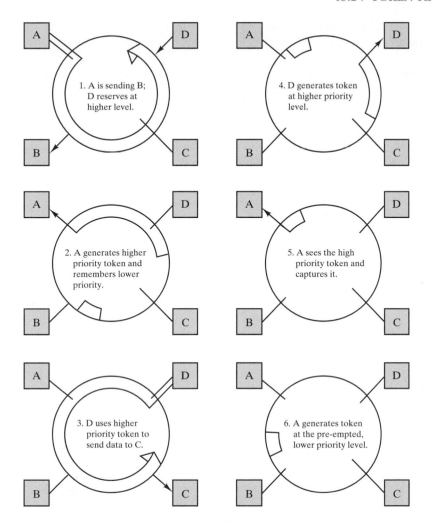

**FIGURE 13.7**   IEEE token ring priority scheme.

tion before it has completed transmission; in this case, the station may issue a token as soon as it has finished frame transmission. If the frame is shorter than the bit length of the ring, then after a station has completed transmission of a frame, it must wait until the leading edge of the frame returns before issuing a token. In this latter case, some of the potential capacity of the ring is unused.

To allow for more efficient ring utilization, an early token release (ETR) option has been added to the 802.5 standard. ETR allows a transmitting station to release a token as soon as it completes frame transmission, whether or not the frame header has returned to the station. The priority used for a token released prior to receipt of the previous frame header is the priority of the most recently received frame.

One effect of ETR is that access delay for priority traffic may increase when the ring is heavily loaded with short frames. Because a station must issue a token before it can read the reservation bits of the frame it just transmitted, the station will not respond to reservations. Thus, the priority mechanism is at least partially disabled.

Stations that implement ETR are compatible and interoperable with those that do not complete such implementation.

## IEEE 802.5 Physical Layer Specification

The 802.5 standard (Table 13.4) specifies the use of shielded twisted pair with data rates of 4 and 16 Mbps using Differential Manchester encoding. An earlier specification of a 1-Mbps system has been dropped from the most recent edition of the

**TABLE 13.4** IEEE 802.5 physical layer medium alternatives.

| Transmission medium | Shielded twisted pair | Unshielded twisted pair |
|---|---|---|
| Data rate (Mbps) | 4 or 16 | 4 |
| Signaling technique | Differential Manchester | Differential Manchester |
| Maximum number of repeaters | 250 | 72 |
| Maximum length between repeaters | Not specified | Not specified |

standard.

A recent addition to the standard is the use of unshielded twisted pair at 4 Mbps.

## FDDI Medium Access Control

FDDI is a token ring scheme, similar to the IEEE 802.5 specification, that is designed for both LAN and MAN applications. There are several differences that are designed to accommodate the higher data rate (100 Mbps) of FDDI.

| Bits | 64 | 8 | 8 | 16 or 48 | 16 or 48 | ≥ 0 | 32 | 4 | 12 |
|---|---|---|---|---|---|---|---|---|---|
| | Preamble | SD | FC | DA | SA | Info | FCS | ED | FS |

(a) General frame format

| | Preamble | SD | FC | ED |
|---|---|---|---|---|

(b) Token frame format

LEGEND

SD = Start-frame delimiter  SA = Source address  ED = Ending delimiter
FC = Frame control  FCS = Frame-check sequence  FS = Frame status
DA = Destination address

**FIGURE 13.8** FDDI frame formats.

## MAC Frame

Figure 13.8 depicts the frame format for the FDDI protocol. The standard defines the contents of this format in terms of symbols, with each data symbol corresponding to 4 data bits. Symbols are used because, at the physical layer, data are encoded in 4-bit chunks. However, MAC entities, in fact, must deal with individual bits, so the discussion that follows sometimes refers to 4-bit symbols and sometime to bits. A frame other than a token frame consists of the following fields:

- **Preamble.** Synchronizes the frame with each station's clock. The originator of the frame uses a field of 16 idle symbols (64 bits); subsequent repeating stations may change the length of the field, as consistent with clocking requirements. The idle symbol is a nondata fill pattern. The actual form of a nondata symbol depends on the signal encoding on the medium.
- **Starting delimiter (SD).** Indicates start of frame. It is coded as JK, where J and K are nondata symbols.
- **Frame control (FC).** Has the bit format CLFFZZZZ, where C indicates whether this is a synchronous or asynchronous frame (explained below); L indicates the use of 16- or 48-bit addresses; FF indicates whether this is an LLC, MAC control, or reserved frame. For a control frame, the remaining 4 bits indicate the type of control frame.
- **Destination address (DA).** Specifies the station(s) for which the frame is intended. It may be a unique physical address, a multicast-group address, or a broadcast address. The ring may contain a mixture of 16- and 48-bit address lengths.
- **Source address (SA).** Specifies the station that sent the frame.
- **Information**. Contains an LLC data unit or information related to a control operation.
- **Frame check sequence (FCS).** A 32-bit cyclic redundancy check, based on the FC, DA, SA, and information fields.
- **Ending delimiter (ED).** Contains a nondata symbol (T) and marks the end of the frame, except for the FS field.
- **Frame Status (FS).** Contains the error detected (E), address recognized (A), and frame copied (F) indicators. Each indicator is represented by a symbol, which is R for "reset" or "false" and S for "set" or "true."

A token frame consists of the following fields:

- **Preamble.** As above.
- **Starting delimiter.** As above.
- **Frame control (FC).** Has the bit format 10000000 or 11000000 to indicate that this is a token.
- **Ending delimiter (ED).** Contains a pair of nondata symbols (T) that terminate the token frame.

A comparison with the 802.5 frame (Figure 13.6) shows that the two are quite similar. The FDDI frame includes a preamble to aid in clocking, which is more demanding at the higher data rate. Both 16- and 48-bit addresses are allowed in the same network with FDDI; this is more flexible than the scheme used on all the 802 standards. Finally, there are some differences in the control bits. For example, FDDI does not include priority and reservation bits; capacity allocation is handled in a different way, as described below.

## MAC Protocol

The basic (without capacity allocation) FDDI MAC protocol is fundamentally the same as IEEE 802.5. There are two key differences:

1. In FDDI, a station waiting for a token seizes the token by aborting (failing to repeat) the token transmission as soon as the token frame is recognized. After the captured token is completely received, the station begins transmitting one or more data frames. The 802.5 technique of flipping a bit to convert a token to the start of a data frame was considered impractical because of the high data rate of FDDI.
2. In FDDI, a station that has been transmitting data frames releases a new token as soon as it completes data frame transmission, even if it has not begun to receive its own transmission. This is the same technique as the early token release option of 802.5. Again, because of the high data rate, it would be too inefficient to require the station to wait for its frame to return, as in normal 802.5 operation.

Figure 13.9 gives an example of ring operation. After station A has seized the token, it transmits frame F1, and immediately transmits a new token. F1 is addressed to station C, which copies it as it circulates past. The frame eventually returns to A, which absorbs it. Meanwhile, B seizes the token issued by A and transmits F2 followed by a token. This action could be repeated any number of times, so that, at any one time, there may be multiple frames circulating the ring. Each station is responsible for absorbing its own frames based on the source address field.

A further word should be said about the frame status (FS) field. Each station can check passing bits for errors and can set the E indicator if an error is detected. If a station detects its own address, it sets the A indicator; it may also copy the frame, setting the C indicator; this allows the originating station, when it absorbs a frame that it previously transmitted, to differentiate among three conditions:

- Station nonexistent/nonactive
- Station active but frame not copied
- Frame copied

When a frame is absorbed, the status indicators (E, A, C) in the FS field may be examined to determine the result of the transmission. However, if an error or failure to receive condition is discovered, the MAC protocol entity does not attempt to retransmit the frame, but reports the condition to LLC. It is the responsibility of LLC or some higher-layer protocol to take corrective action.

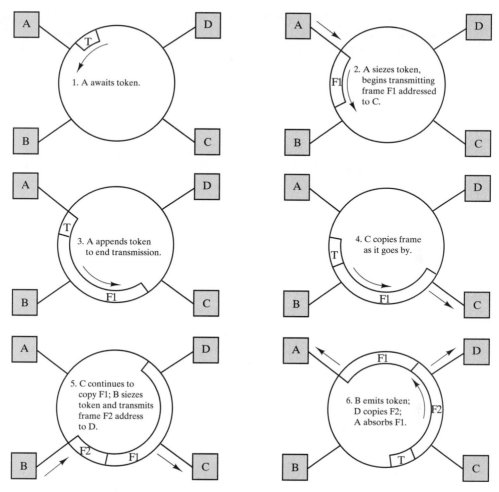

**FIGURE 13.9**   Example of FDDI token ring operation.

## Capacity Allocation

The priority scheme used in 802.5 will not work in FDDI, as a station will often issue a token before its own transmitted frame returns. Hence, the use of a reservation field is not effective. Furthermore, the FDDI standard is intended to provide for greater control over the capacity of the network than 802.5 to meet the requirements for a high-speed LAN. Specifically, the FDDI capacity-allocation scheme seeks to accommodate a mixture of stream and bursty traffic,

To accommodate this requirement, FDDI defines two types of traffic: synchronous and asynchronous. Each station is allocated a portion of the total capacity (the portion may be zero); the frames that it transmits during this time are referred to as synchronous frames. Any capacity that is not allocated or that is allocated but not used is available for the transmission of additional frames, referred to as asynchronous frames.

The scheme works as follows. A *target token-rotation time* (TTRT) is defined; each station stores the same value for TTRT. Some or all stations may be provided a *synchronous allocation* (SA$_i$), which may vary among stations. The allocations must be such that

$$\text{DMax} + \text{FMax} + \text{Token Time} + \Sigma \, \text{SA}_i \leq \text{TTRT}$$

where

$$\text{SA}_i = \text{synchronous allocation for station } i$$
$$\text{DMax} = \text{propagation time for one complete circuit of the ring}$$
$$\text{FMAX} = \text{time required to transmit a maximum-length frame (4500 octets)}$$
$$\text{TokenTime} = \text{time required to transmit a token}$$

The assignment of values for SA$_i$ is by means of a station management protocol involving the exchange of station management frames. The protocol assures that the above equation is satisfied. Initially, each station has a zero allocation, and it must request a change in the allocation. Support for synchronous allocation is optional; a station that does not support synchronous allocation may only transmit asynchronous traffic.

All stations have the same value of TTRT and a separately assigned value of SA$_i$. In addition, several variables that are required for the operation of the capacity-allocation algorithm are maintained at each station:

- Token-rotation timer (TRT)
- Token-holding timer (THT)
- Late counter (LC)

Each station is initialized with TRT set equal to TTRT and LC set to zero.[5] When the timer is enabled, TRT begins to count down. If a token is received before TRT expires, TRT is reset to TTRT. If TRT counts down to 0 before a token is received, then LC is incremented to 1 and TRT is reset to TTRT and again begins to count down. IF TRT expires a second time before receiving a token, LC is incremented to 2, the token is considered lost, and a Claim process (described below) is initiated. Thus, LC records the number of times, if any, that TRT has expired since the token was last received at that station. The token is considered to have arrived early if TRT has not expired since the station received the token—that is, if LC = 0.

When a station receives the token, its actions will depend on whether the token is early or late. If the token is early, the station saves the remaining time from TRT in THT, resets TRT, and enables TRT:

$$\text{THT} \leftarrow \text{TRT}$$

---

[5] Note: All timer values in the standard are negative numbers with counters counting up to zero. For clarity, the discussion uses positive numbers.

$$TRT \leftarrow TTRT$$

enable TRT

The station can then transmit according to the following rules:

1. It may transmit synchronous frames for a time $SA_i$.
2. After transmitting synchronous frames, or if there were no synchronous frames to transmit, THT is enabled. The station may begin transmission of asynchronous frames as long as THT > 0.

If a station receives a token and the token is late, then LC is set to zero and TRT continues to run. The station can then transmit synchronous frames for a time $SA_i$. The station may not transmit any asynchronous frames.

This scheme is designed to assure that the time between successive sightings of a token is on the order of TTRT or less. Of this time, a given amount is always available for synchronous traffic, and any excess capacity is available for asynchronous traffic. Because of random fluctuations in traffic, the actual token-circulation time may exceed TTRT, as demonstrated below.

Figure 13.10 provides a simplified example of a 4-station ring. The following assumptions are made:

1. Traffic consists of fixed-length frames.
2. TTRT = 100 frame times.
3. $SA_i$ = 20 frame times for each station.
4. Each station is always prepared to send its full synchronous allocation as many asynchronous frames as possible.
5. The total overhead during one complete token circulation is 4 frame times (one frame time per station).

One row of the table corresponds to one circulation of the token. For each station, the token arrival time is shown, followed by the value of TRT at the time of arrival, followed by the number of synchronous and asynchronous frames transmitted while the station holds the token.

The example begins after a period during which no data frames have been sent, so that the token has been circulating as rapidly as possible (4 frame times). Thus, when Station 1 receives the token at time 4, it measures a circulation time of 4 (its TRT = 96). It is therefore able to send not only its 20 synchronous frames but also 96 asynchronous frames; recall that THT is not enabled until after the station has sent its synchronous frames. Station 2 experiences a circulation time of 120 (20 frames + 96 frames + 4 overhead frames), but is nevertheless entitled to transmit its 20 synchronous frames. Note that if each station continues to transmit its maximum allowable synchronous frames, then the circulation time surges to 180 (at time 184), but soon stabilizes at approximately 100. With a total synchronous utilization of 80 and an overhead of 4 frame times, there is an average capacity of 16 frame times available for asynchronous transmission. Note that if all stations always have a full backlog of asynchronous traffic, the opportunity to transmit asynchro-

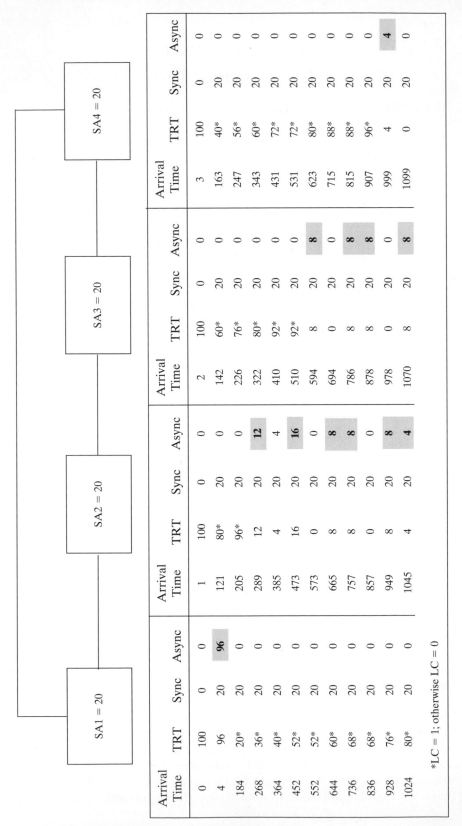

**FIGURE 13.10** Operation of FDDI capaciaty allocation scheme.

TABLE 13.5    FDDI physical layer medium alternatives.

| Transmission medium | Optical fiber | Twisted pair |
|---|---|---|
| Data rate (Mbps) | 100 | 100 |
| Signaling technique | 4B/5B/NRZI | MLT-3 |
| Maximum number of repeaters | 100 | 100 |
| Maximum length between repeaters | 2 km | 100 m |

nous frames is distributed among them.

## FDDI Physical Layer Specification

The FDDI standard specifies a ring topology operating at 100 Mbps. Two media are included (Table 13.5). The optical fiber medium uses 4B/5B-NRZI encoding. Two twisted pair media are specified: 100-ohm Category 5 unshielded twisted pair[6] and 150-ohm shielded twisted pair. For both twisted pair media, MLT-3 encoding is used. See Appendix 13A for a discussion of these encoding schemes.

## 13.3    100VG-ANYLAN

Like 100BASE-T, 100VG-AnyLAN[7] is intended to be a 100-Mbps extension to the 10-Mbps Ethernet and to support IEEE 802.3 frame types. It also provides compatibility with IEEE 802.5 token ring frames. 100VG-AnyLAN uses a new MAC scheme known as *demand priority* to determine the order in which nodes share the network. Because this specification does not use CSMA/CD, it has been standardized under a new working group, IEEE 802.12, rather than allowed to remain in the 802.3 working group.

### Topology

The topology for a 100VG-AnyLAN network is hierarchical star. The simplest configuration consists of a single central hub and a number of attached devices. More complex arrangements are possible, in which there is a single root hub, with one or more subordinate level-2 hubs; a level-2 hub can have additional subordinate hubs at level 3, and so on to an arbitrary depth.

### Medium Access Control

The MAC algorithm for 802.12 is a round-robin scheme with two priority levels. We first describe the algorithm for a single-hub network and then discuss the general

---

[6] See Chapter 3 for a discussion of Category 5 unshielded twisted pair.

[7] VG = voice grade. AnyLAN = support for multiple LAN frame types.

case.

### Single-Hub Network

When a station wishes to transmit a frame, it first issues a request to the central hub and then awaits permission from the hub to transmit. A station must designate each request as normal-priority or high-priority.

The central hub continually scans all of its ports for a request in round-robin fashion. Thus, an $n$-port hub looks for a request first on port 1, then on port 2, and so on up to port $n$. The scanning process then begins again at port 1. The hub maintains two pointers: a high-priority pointer and a normal-priority pointer. During one complete cycle, the hub grants each high-priority request in the order in which the requests are encountered. If at any time there are no pending high-priority requests, the hub will grant any normal-priority requests that it encounters.

Figure 13.11 gives an example. The sequence of events is as follows:

1. The hub sets both pointers to port 1 and begins scanning. The first request encountered is a low-priority request from port 2. The hub grants this request and updates the low-priority pointer to port 3.

2. Port 2 transmits a low-priority frame. The hub receives this frame and retransmits it. During this period, two high-priority requests are generated.

3. Once the frame from port 2 is transmitted, the hub begins granting high-priority requests in round-robin order, beginning with port 1 and followed by port 5. The high-priority pointer is set to port 6.

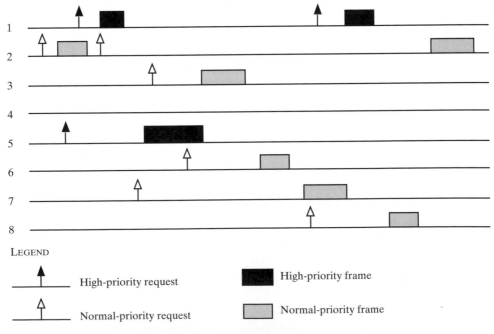

LEGEND

|  | High-priority request |  | High-priority frame |
|---|---|---|---|
|  | Normal-priority request |  | Normal-priority frame |

**FIGURE 13.11** Example frame sequence in a single-repeater network.

4. After the high-priority frame from port 5 completes, there are no outstanding high-priority requests and the hub turns to the normal-priority requests. Four requests have arrived since the last low-priority frame was transmitted: from ports 2, 7, 3, and 6. Because the normal-priority pointer is set to port 3, these requests will be granted in the order 3, 6, 7, and 2 if no other requests intervene.

5. The frames from ports 3, 6, and 7 are transmitted in turn. During the transmission of frame 7, a high-priority request arrives from port 1 and a normal priority request arrives from port 8. The hub sets the normal-priority pointer to port 8.

6. Because high-priority requests take precedence, port 1 is granted access next.

7. After the frame from port 1 is transmitted, the hub has two outstanding normal-priority requests. The request from port 2 has been waiting the longest; however, port 8 is next in round-robin order to be satisfied and so its request is granted, followed by that of port 2.

## Hierarchical Network

In a hierarchical network, all of the end-system ports on all hubs are treated as a single set of ports for purposes of the round-robin algorithm. The hubs are configured to cooperate in scanning the ports in the proper order. Put another way, the set of hubs is treated logically as a single hub.

Figure 13.12 indicates port ordering in a hierarchical network. The order is generated by traversing a tree representation of the network, in which the branches

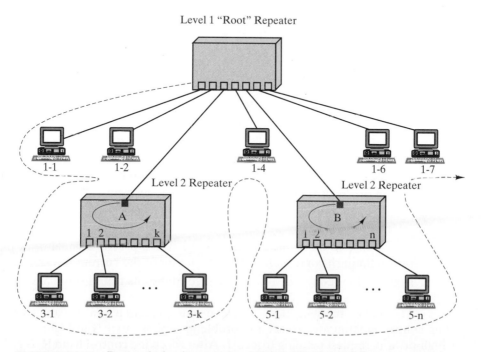

**FIGURE 13.12** Port ordering in a two-level IEEE 802.12 network.

under each node in the tree are arranged in increasing order from left to right. With this convention, the port order is generated by traversing the tree in what is referred to as preorder traversal, which is defined recursively as follows:

1. Visit the root.
2. Traverse the subtrees from left to right.

This method of traversal is also known as a depth-first search of the tree.

Let us now consider the mechanics of medium access and frame transmission in a hierarchical network. There are a number of contingencies to consider. First, consider the behavior of the root hub. This hub performs the high-priority and normal-priority round-robin algorithms for all directly attached devices. Thus, if there are one or more pending high-priority requests, the hub grants these requests in round-robin fashion. If there are no pending high-priority requests, the hub grants any normal-priority requests in round-robin fashion. When a request is granted by the root hub to a directly-attached end system, that system may immediately transmit a frame. When a request is granted by the root hub to a directly-attached level-2 hub, then control passes to the level-2 hub, which then proceeds to execute its own round-robin algorithms.

Any end system that is ready to transmit sends a request signal to the hub to which it attaches. If the end system is attached directly to the root hub, then the request is conveyed directly to the root hub. If the end system is attached to a lower-level hub, then the request is transmitted directly to that hub. If that hub does not currently have control of the round-robin algorithm, then it passes the request up to the next higher-level hub. Eventually, all requests that are not granted at a lower level are passed up to the root hub.

The scheme described so far does enforce a round-robin discipline among all attached stations, but two refinements are needed. First, a preemption mechanism is needed. This is best explained by an example. Consider the following sequence of events:

1. Suppose that the root hub (R) in Figure 13.12 is in control and that there are no high-priority requests pending anywhere in the network. However, stations 5-1, 5-2, and 5-3 have all issued normal-priority requests, causing hub B to issue a normal-priority request to R.
2. R will eventually grant this request, passing control to B.
3. B then proceeds to honor its outstanding requests one at a time.
4. While B is honoring its first normal-priority request, station 1-6 issues a high-priority request.
5. In response to the request from 1-6, R issues a preempt signal to B; this tells B to relinquish control after the completion of the current transmission.
6. R grants the request of 1-6 and then continues its round-robin algorithm.

The second refinement is a mechanism to prevent a nonroot hub from retaining control indefinitely. To see the problem, suppose that B in Figure 13.12 has a high-priority request pending from 5-1. After receiving control from R, B grants the request to 5-1. Meanwhile, other stations subordinate to B issue high-priority requests. B could continue in round-robin fashion to honor all of these requests. If additional requests arrive from other subordinates of B during these other transmissions, then B would be able to continue granting requests indefinitely, even though there are other high-priority requests pending elsewhere in the network. To prevent this kind of lockup, a subordinate hub may only retain control for a single round-robin cycle through all of its ports.

The IEEE 802.12 MAC algorithm is quite effective. When multiple stations offer high loads, the protocol behaves much like a token ring protocol, with network access rotating among all high-priority requesters, followed by low-priority requesters when there are no outstanding high-priority requests. At low load, the protocol behaves in a similar fashion to CSMA/CD under low load: A single requester gains medium access almost immediately.

## 100VG-AnyLANPhysical Layer Specification

The current version of IEEE 801.12 calls for the use of 4-pair unshielded twisted pair (UTP) using Category 3, 4, or 5 cable. Future versions will also support 2-pair Category-5 UTP, shielded twisted pair, and fiber optic cabling. In all cases, the data rate is 100 Mbps.

### Signal Encoding

A key objective of the 100VG-AnyLAN effort is to be able to achieve 100 Mbps over short distances using ordinary voice-grade (Category 3) cabling. The advantage of this is that in many existing buildings, there is an abundance of voice-grade cabling and very little else. Thus, if this cabling can be used, installation costs are minimized.

With present technology, a data rate of 100 Mbps over one or two Category 3 pairs is impractical. To meet the objective, 100VG-AnyLAN specifies a novel encoding scheme that involves using four pair to transmit data in a half-duplex mode. Thus, to achieve a data rate of 100 Mbps, a data rate of only 25 Mbps is needed on each channel. An encoding scheme known as 5B6B is used. (See Appendix 13A for a description.)

Data from the MAC layer can be viewed as a stream of bits. The bits from this stream are taken five at a time to form a stream of quintets that are then passed down to the four transmission channels in round-robin fashion. Next, each quintet passes through a simple scrambling algorithm to increase the number of transitions between 0 and 1 and to improve the signal spectrum. At this point, it might be possible to simply transmit the data using NRZ. However, even with the scrambling, the further step of 5B6B encoding is used to ensure synchronization and also to maintain dc balance.

Because the MAC frame is being divided among four channels, the beginning and ending of a MAC frame must be delimited on each of the channels, which is the purpose of the delimiter generators. Finally, NRZ transmission is used on each channel.

## 13.4 ATM LANs

A document on customer premises networks jointly prepared by Apple, Bellcore, Sun, and Xerox [ABSX92] identifies three generations of LANs:

- **First Generation.** Typified by the CSMA/CD and Token Ring LANs. The first generation provided terminal-to-host connectivity and supported client/server architectures at moderate data rates.
- **Second Generation.** Typified by FDDI. The second generation responds to the need for backbone LANs and for support of high-performance workstations.
- **Third Generation.** Typified by ATM LANs. The third generation is designed to provide the aggregate throughputs and real-time transport guarantees that are needed for multimedia applications.

Typical requirements for a third generation LAN include the following:

1. Support multiple, guaranteed classes of service. A live video application, for example, may require a guaranteed 2-Mbps connection for acceptable performance, while a file transfer program can utilize a *background* class of service.
2. Provide scalable throughput that is capable of growing in both per-host capacity (to enable applications that require large volumes of data in and out of a single host) and in aggregate capacity (to enable installations to grow from a few to several hundred high-performance hosts).
3. Facilitate the interworking between LAN and WAN technology.

ATM is ideally suited to these requirements. Using virtual paths and virtual channels, multiple classes of service are easily accommodated, either in a preconfigured fashion (permanent connections) or on demand (switched connections). ATM is easily scalable by adding more ATM switching nodes and using higher (or lower) data rates for attached devices. Finally, with the increasing acceptance of cell-based transport for wide-area networking, the use of ATM for a premises network enables seamless integration of LANs and WANs.

The term ATM LAN has been used by vendors and researchers to apply to a variety of configurations. At the very least, an ATM LAN implies the use of ATM as a data transport protocol somewhere within the local premises. Among the possible types of ATM LANs:

- **Gateway to ATM WAN.** An ATM switch acts as a router and traffic concentrator for linking a premises network complex to an ATM WAN.
- **Backbone ATM switch.** Either a single ATM switch or a local network of ATM switches interconnect other LANs.
- **Workgroup ATM.** High-performance multimedia workstations and other end systems connect directly to an ATM switch.

These are all "pure" configurations. In practice, a mixture of two or all three of these types of networks is used to create an ATM LAN.

Figure 13.13 shows an example of a backbone ATM LAN that includes links

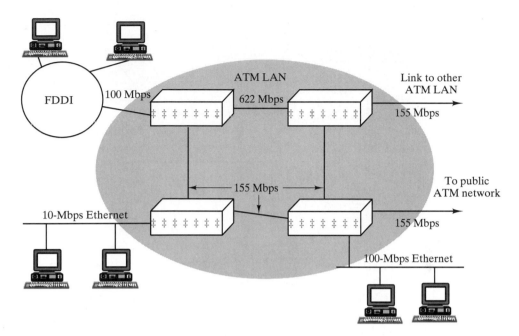

**FIGURE 13.13**    Example ATM LAN configuration.

to the outside world. In this example, the local ATM network consists of four switches interconnected with high-speed, point-to-point links running at the standardized ATM rates of 155 and 622 Mbps. On the premises, there are three other LANs, each of which has a direct connection to one of the ATM switches. The data rate from an ATM switch to an attached LAN conforms to the native data rate of that LAN. For example, the connection to the FDDI network is at 100 Mbps. Thus, the switch must include some buffering and speed conversion capability to map the data rate from the attached LAN to an ATM data rate. The ATM switch must also perform some sort of protocol conversion from the MAC protocol used on the attached LAN to the ATM cell stream used on the ATM network. A simple approach is for each ATM switch that attaches to a LAN to function as a bridge or router.[8]

An ATM LAN configuration such as that shown in Figure 13.13 provides a relatively painless method for inserting a high-speed backbone into a local environment. As the on-site demand rises, it is a simple matter to increase the capacity of the backbone by adding more switches, increasing the throughput of each switch, and increasing the data rate of the trunks between switches. With this strategy, the load on individual LANs within the premises can be increased, and the number of LANs can grow.

However, this simple backbone ATM LAN does not address all of the needs for local communications. In particular, in the simple backbone configuration, the end systems (workstations, servers, etc.) remain attached to shared-media LANs with the limitations on data rate imposed by the shared medium.

---

[8] The functionality of bridges and routers is examined in depth in Chapters 14 and 16.

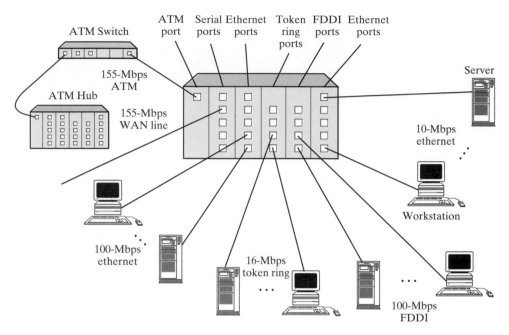

**FIGURE 13.14**   ATM LAN hub configuration.

A more advanced, and more powerful approach, is to use ATM technology in a hub. Figure 13.14 suggests the capabilities that can be provided with this approach. Each ATM hub includes a number of ports that operate at different data rates and that use different protocols. Typically, such a hub consists of a number of rack-mounted modules, with each module containing ports of a given data rate and protocol.

The key difference between the ATM hub shown in Figure 13.14 and the ATM nodes depicted in Figure 13.13 is the way in which individual end systems are handled. Notice that in the ATM hub, each end system has a dedicated point-to-point link to the hub. Each end system includes the communications hardware and software to interface to a particular type of LAN, but in each case, the LAN contains only two devices: the end system and the hub! For example, each device attached to a 10-Mbps Ethernet port operates using the CSMA/CD protocol at 10 Mbps. However, because each end system has its own dedicated line, the effect is that each system has its own dedicated 10-Mbps Ethernet. Therefore, each end system can operate at close to the maximum 10-Mbps data rate.

The use of a configuration such as that of either Figure 13.13 or 13.14 has the advantage that existing LAN installations and LAN hardware—so-called legacy LANs—can continue to be used while ATM technology is introduced. The disadvantage is that the use of such a mixed-protocol environment requires the implementation of some sort of protocol conversion capability, a topic that is explored in Section 14.3. A simpler approach, but one that requires that end systems be equipped with ATM capability, is to implement a "pure" ATM LAN.

One issue that was not addressed in our discussion so far has to do with the interoperability of end systems on a variety of interconnected LANs. End systems attached directly to one of the legacy LANs implement the MAC layer appropriate to that type of LAN. End systems attached directly to an ATM network implement the ATM and AAL protocols. As a result, there are three areas of compatibility to consider:

1. Interaction between an end system on an ATM network and an end system on a legacy LAN.
2. Interaction between an end system on a legacy LAN and an end system on another legacy LAN of the same type (e.g., two IEEE 802.3 networks).
3. Interaction between an end system on a legacy LAN and an end system on another legacy LAN of a different type (e.g., an IEEE 802.3 network and an IEEE 802.5 network).

A discussion of approaches to satisfying these requirement involves consideration of bridge logic. Accordingly, we defer this discussion until Chapter 14.

## 13.5 FIBRE CHANNEL

As the speed and memory capacity of personal computers, workstations, and servers have grown, and as applications have become ever more complex with greater reliance on graphics and video, the requirement for greater speed in delivering data to the processor has grown. This requirement affects two methods of data communications with the processor: I/O channel and network communications.

An I/O channel is a direct point-to-point or multipoint communications link, predominantly hardware-based and designed for high speed over very short distances. The I/O channel transfers data between a buffer at the source device and a buffer at the destination device, moving only the user contents from one device to another, without regard for the format or meaning of the data. The logic associated with the channel typically provides the minimum control necessary to manage the transfer plus hardware error detection. I/O channels typically manage transfers between processors and peripheral devices, such as disks, graphics equipment, CD-ROMs, and video I/O devices.

A network is a collection of interconnected access points with a software protocol structure that enables communication. The network typically allows many different types of data transfer, using software to implement the networking protocols and to provide flow control, error detection, and error recovery. As we have discussed in this book, networks typically manage transfers between end systems over local, metropolitan, or wide-area distances.

Fibre Channel is designed to combine the best features of both technologies—the simplicity and speed of channel communications with the flexibility and interconnectivity that characterize protocol-based network communications. This fusion of approaches allows system designers to combine traditional peripheral connection, host-to-host internetworking, loosely-coupled processor clustering, and multimedia applications in a single multi-protocol interface. The types of channel-oriented facilities incorporated into the Fibre Channel protocol architecture include

- Data-type qualifiers for routing frame payload into particular interface buffers
- Link-level constructs associated with individual I/O operations
- Protocol interface specifications to allow support of existing I/O channel architectures, such as the Small Computer System Interface (SCSI)

The types of network-oriented facilities incorporated into the Fibre Channel protocol architecture include

- Full multiplexing of traffic between multiple destinations
- Peer-to-peer connectivity between any pair of ports on a Fiber Channel network
- Capabilities for internetworking to other connection technologies

Depending on the needs of the application, either channel or networking approaches can be used for any data transfer. The Fibre Channel Association, which is the industry consortium promoting Fibre Channel, lists the following ambitious requirements that Fibre Channel is intended to satisfy [FCA94]:

- Full duplex links with two fibers per link
- Performance from 100 Mbps to 800 Mbps on a single link (200 Mbps to 1600 Mbps per link)
- Support for distances up to 10 km
- Small connectors
- High-capacity utilization with distance insensitivity
- Greater connectivity than existing multidrop channels
- Broad availability (i.e., standard components)
- Support for multiple cost/performance levels, from small systems to super-computers
- Ability to carry multiple existing interface command sets for existing channel and network protocols

The solution was to develop a simple generic transport mechanism based on point-to-point links and a switching network. This underlying infrastructure supports a simple encoding and framing scheme that in turn supports a variety of channel and network protocols.

### Fibre Channel Elements

The key elements of a Fibre Channel network are the end systems, called *nodes*, and the network itself, which consists of one or more switching elements. The collection of switching elements is referred to as a *fabric*. These elements are interconnected by point-to-point links between ports on the individual nodes and

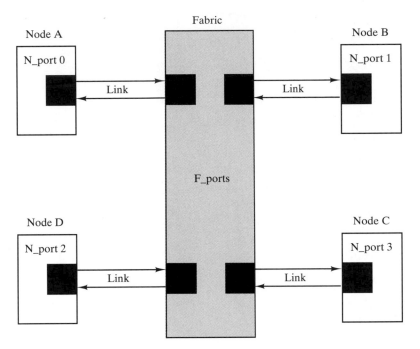

**FIGURE 13.15**   Fibre channel port types.

switches. Communication consists of the transmission of frames across the point-to-point links.

Figure 13.15 illustrates these basic elements. Each node includes three or more ports, called N_ports, for interconnection. Similarly, each fabric-switching element includes one or more ports, called F_ports. Interconnection is by means of bidirectional links between ports. Any node can communicate with any other node connected to the same fabric using the services of the fabric. All routing of frames between N_ports is done by the fabric. Frames may be buffered within the fabric, making it possible for different nodes to connect to the fabric at different data rates.

A fabric can be implemented as a single fabric element, as depicted in Figure 13.15, or as a more general network of fabric elements, as shown in Figure 13.16. In either case, the fabric is responsible for buffering and for routing frames between source and destination nodes.

The Fibre Channel network is quite different from the other LANs that we have examined so far. Fibre Channel is more like a traditional circuit-switched or packet-switched network, in contrast to the typical shared-medium LAN. Thus, Fibre Channel need not be concerned with medium access control issues. Because it is based on a switching network, the Fibre Channel scales easily in terms of N_ports, data rate, and distance covered. This approach provides great flexibility. Fibre Channel can readily accommodate new transmission media and data rates by adding new switches and F_ports to an existing fabric. Thus, an existing investment is not lost with an upgrade to new technologies and equipment. Further, as we shall see, the layered protocol architecture accommodates existing I/O interface and networking protocols, preserving the pre-existing investment.

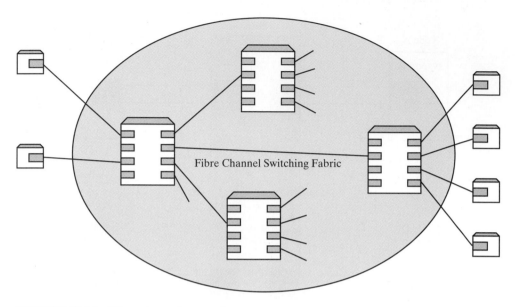

**FIGURE 13.16** Fibre channel network.

## Fibre Channel Protocol Architecture

The Fibre Channel standard is organized into five levels. These are illustrated in Figure 13.17, with brief definitions in Table 13.6. Each level defines a function or set of related functions. The standard does not dictate a correspondence between levels and actual implementations, with a specific interface between adjacent levels. Rather, the standard refers to the level as a "document artifice" used to group related functions.

Levels FC-0 through FC-2 of the Fibre Channel hierarchy are currently defined in a standard referred to as Fiber Channel Physical and Signaling Interface (FC-PH). Currently, there is no final standard for FC-3. At level FC-4, individual

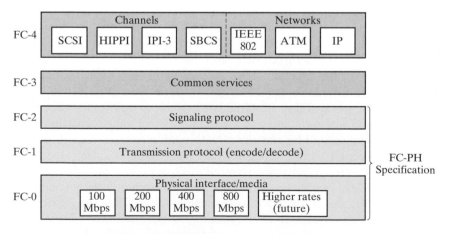

**FIGURE 13.17** Fibre channel levels.

**TABLE 13.6**   Fibre channel levels.

---

FC-O physical media
- Optical cable with laser or LED transmitters for long distance transmissions
- Copper coaxial cable for highest speeds over short distances
- Shielded twisted pair for lower speeds over short distances

---

FC-1 byte synchronization and encoding
- 8B/10B encoding/decoding scheme provides balance, is simple to implement, and provides useful error-detection capability
- Special code character maintains byte and word alignment

---

FC-2 actual transport mechanism
- Framing protocol and flow control between N_ports
- Three classes of service between ports

---

FC-3 common services layer
- Port-related services
- Services across two or more ports in a node

---

FC-4 upper layer protocols
- Supports a variety of channel and network protocols

---

standards have been produced for mapping a variety of channel and network protocols onto lower levels.

We briefly examine each of these levels in turn in the remainder of this section.

## Physical Interface and Media

Fibre Channel level FC-0 allows a variety of physical media and data rates; this is one of the strengths of the specification. Currently, data rates ranging from 100 Mbps to 800 Mbps per fiber are defined. The physical media are optical fiber, coaxial cable, and shielded twisted pair. Depending on the data rate and medium involved, maximum distances for individual point-to-point links range from 50 meters to 10 km.

## Transmission Protocol

FC-1, the transmission protocol level, defines the signal encoding technique used for transmission and for synchronization across the point-to-point link. The encoding scheme used is 8B/10B, in which each 8 bits of data from level FC-2 is converted into 10 bits for transmission. See Appendix 13A for a description.

## Framing Protocol

Level FC-2, referred to as the Framing Protocol level, deals with the transmission of data between N_ports in the form of frames. Among the concepts defined at this level are

- Node and N_port and their identifiers

- Topologies
- Classes of service provided by the fabric
- Segmentation of data into frames and reassembly
- Grouping of frames into logical entities called sequences and exchanges
- Sequencing, flow control, and error control

## Common Services

FC-3 provides a set of services that are common across multiple N_Ports of a node. The functions so-far defined in the draft FC-3 documents include

- **Striping.** Makes use of multiple N_Ports in parallel to transmit a single information unit across multiple links simultaneously; this achieves higher aggregate throughput. A likely use is for transferring large data sets in real time, as in video-imaging applications.
- **Hunt Groups.** A hunt group is a set of associated N_Ports at a single node. This set is assigned an alias identifier that allows any frame sent to this alias to be routed to any available N_Port within the set. This may decrease latency by decreasing the chance of waiting for a busy N_Port.
- **Multicast.** Delivers a transmission to multiple destinations. This includes sending to all N_Ports on a fabric (broadcast) or to a subset of the N_Ports on a fabric.

## Mapping

FC-4 defines the mapping of various channel and network protocols to FC-PH. I/O channel interfaces include

- **Small Computer System Interface (SCSI).** A widely used high-speed interface typically implemented on personal computers, workstations, and servers.[9] SCSI is used to support high-capacity and high-data-rate devices, such as disks and graphics and video equipment.
- **High-Performance Parallel Interface (HIPPI).** A high-speed channel standard primarily used for mainframe/supercomputer environments. At one time, HIPPI and extensions to HIPPI were viewed as a possible general-purpose high-speed LAN solution, but HIPPI has been superseded by Fibre Channel.

Network interfaces include

- **IEEE 802.** IEEE 802 MAC frames map onto Fibre Channel frames.
- **Asynchronous Transfer Mode**
- **Internet Protocol (IP).** This protocol is described in Chapter 16.

The FC-4 mapping protocols make use of the FC-PH capabilities to transfer upper-layer protocol (ULP) information. Each FC-4 specification defines the for-

---

[9] See [STAL96] for a detailed discussion of SCSI.

mats and procedures for ULP.

## Fibre Channel Physical Media and Topologies

One of the major strengths of the Fibre Channel standard is that it provides a range of options for the physical medium, the data rate on that medium, and the topology of the network.

### Transmission Media

Table 13.7 summarizes the options that are available under Fibre Channel for physical transmission medium and data rate. Each entry specifies the maximum point-to-point link distance (between ports) that is defined for a given transmission medium at a given data rate. These media may be mixed in an overall configuration. For example, a single-mode optical link could be used to connect switches in different buildings, with multimode optical links used for vertical distribution inside, and shielded twisted pair or coaxial cable links to individual workstations.

### Topologies

The most general topology supported by Fibre Channel is referred to as a fabric or switched topology. This is an arbitrary topology that includes at least one switch to interconnect a number of N_ports, as shown in Figure 13.18a. The fabric topology may also consist of a number of switches forming a switched network, with some or all of these switches also supporting end nodes (Figure 13.16).

Routing in the fabric topology is transparent to the nodes. Each port in the configuration has a unique address. When data from a node are transmitted into the fabric, the edge switch to which the node is attached uses the destination port address in the incoming data frame to determine the destination port location. The switch then either delivers the frame to another node attached to the same switch or transfers the frame to an adjacent switch to begin the routing of the frame to a remote destination.

The fabric topology provides scalability of capacity: As additional ports are added, the aggregate capacity of the network increases, thus minimizing congestion and contention, and increasing throughput. The fabric is protocol-independent and largely distance-insensitive. The technology of the switch itself and of the transmis-

**TABLE 13.7**  Maximum distance for Fibre Channel media types.

|  | 800 Mbps | 400 Mbps | 200 Mbps | 100 Mbps |
|---|---|---|---|---|
| Single mode fiber | 10 km | 10 km | 10 km | — |
| 50-μm multimode fiber | 0.5 km | 1 km | 2 km | 10 km |
| 62.5-μm multimode fiber | 175 m | 350 m | 1500 m | 1500 m |
| Video coaxial cable | 25 m | 50 m | 75 m | 100 m |
| Miniature coaxial cable | 10 m | 15 m | 25 m | 35 m |
| Shielded twisted pair | — | — | 50 m | 100 m |

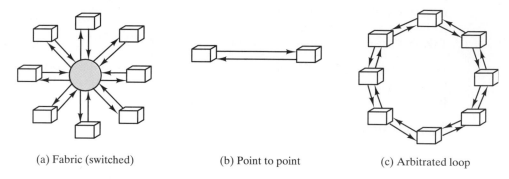

(a) Fabric (switched)          (b) Point to point          (c) Arbitrated loop

**FIGURE 13.18**    Basic Fibre Channel topologies.

sion links connecting the switch to nodes may be changed without affecting the overall configuration. Another advantage of the fabric topology is that the burden on nodes is minimized. An individual Fibre Channel node (end systems) is only responsible for managing a simple point-to-point connection between itself and the fabric; the fabric is responsible for routing between N_ports and error detection.

In addition to the fabric topology, the Fibre Channel standard defines two other topologies. With the point-to-point topology (Figure 13.18b) there are only two N_ports, and these are directly connected, with no intervening fabric switches. In this case, there is no routing.

Finally, the arbitrated loop topology (Figure 13.18c) is a simple, low-cost topology for connecting up to 126 nodes in a loop. The ports on an arbitrated loop must contain the functions of both N_ports and F_ports; these are called NL_ports. The arbitrated loop operates in a manner roughly equivalent to the token ring protocols that we have seen. Each port sees all frames and passes and ignores those not addressed to itself. There is a token acquisition protocol to control access to the loop.

The fabric and arbitrated loop topologies may be combined in one configuration to optimize the cost of the configuration. In this case, one of the nodes on the arbitrated loop must be a fabric-loop (FL_port) node so that it participates in routing with the other switches in the fabric configuration.

The type of topology need not be configured manually by a network manager. Rather, the type of topology is discovered early in the link initialization process.

## 13.6 WIRELESS LANS

A set of wireless LAN standards has been developed by the IEEE 802.11 committee. The terminology and some of the specific features of 802.11 are unique to this standard and are not reflected in all commercial products. However, it is useful to be familiar with the standard as its features are representative of required wireless LAN capabilities.

Figure 13.19 indicates the model developed by the 802.11 working group. The

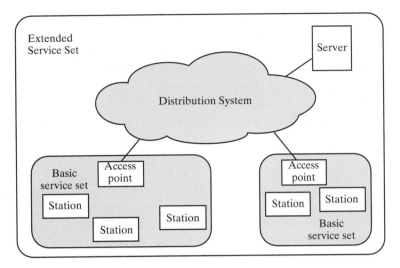

**FIGURE 13.19** IEEE 802.11 architecture.

smallest building block of a wireless LAN is a basic service set (BSS), which consists of some number of stations executing the same MAC protocol and competing for access to the same shared medium. A basic service set may be isolated, or it may connect to a backbone distribution system through an access point. The access point functions as a bridge. The MAC protocol may be fully distributed or controlled by a central coordination function housed in the access point. The basic service set generally corresponds to what is referred to as a cell in the literature.

An extended service set (ESS) consists of two or more basic service sets interconnected by a distribution system. Typically, the distribution system is a wired backbone LAN. The extended service set appears as a single logical LAN to the logical link control (LLC) level.

The standard defines three types of stations, based on mobility:

- **No-transition.** A station of this type is either stationary or moves only within the direct communication range of the communicating stations of a single BSS.
- **BSS-transition.** This is defined as a station movement from one BSS to another BSS within the same ESS. In this case, delivery of data to the station requires that the addressing capability be able to recognize the new location of the station.
- **ESS-transition.** This is defined as a station movement from a BSS in one ESS to a BSS within another ESS. This case is supported only in the sense that the station can move. Maintenance of upper-layer connections supported by 802.11 cannot be guaranteed. In fact, disruption of service is likely to occur.

## Physical Medium Specification

Three physical media are defined in the current 802.11 standard:

- Infrared at 1 Mbps and 2 Mbps operating at a wavelength between 850 and 950 nm.
- Direct-sequence spread spectrum operating in the 2.4-GHz ISM band. Up to 7 channels, each with a data rate of 1 Mbps or 2 Mbps, can be used.
- Frequency-hopping spread spectrum operating in the 2.4-GHz ISM band. The details of this option are for further study.

### Medium Access Control

The 802.11 working group considered two types of proposals for a MAC algorithm: distributed-access protocols which, like CSMA/CD, distributed the decision to transmit over all the nodes using a carrier-sense mechanism; and centralized access protocols, which involve regulation of transmission by a centralized decision maker. A distributed access protocol makes sense of an ad hoc network of peer workstations and may also be attractive in other wireless LAN configurations that consist primarily of bursty traffic. A centralized access protocol is natural for configurations in which a number of wireless stations are interconnected with each other and with some sort of base station that attaches to a backbone wired LAN; it is especially useful if some of the data is time-sensitive or high priority.

The end result of the 802.11 is a MAC algorithm called DFWMAC (distributed foundation wireless MAC) that provides a distributed access-control mechanism with an optional centralized control built on top of that. Figure 13.20 illustrates the architecture. The lower sublayer of the MAC layer is the distributed coordination function (DCF). DCF uses a contention algorithm to provide access to all traffic. Ordinary asynchronous traffic directly uses DCF. The point coordination function (PCF) is a centralized MAC algorithm used to provide contention-free service.

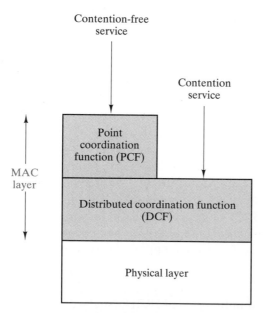

**FIGURE 13.20** IEEE 802.11 protocol architecture.

PCF is built on top of DCF and exploits features of DCF to assure access for its users. Let us consider these two sublayers in turn.

### Distributed Coordination Function

The DCF sublayer makes use of a simple CSMA algorithm. If a station has a MAC frame to transmit, it listens to the medium. If the medium is idle, the station may transmit; otherwise, the station must wait until the current transmission is complete before transmitting. The DCF does not include a collision-detection function (i.e., CSMA/CD) because collision detection is not practical on a wireless network. The dynamic range of the signals on the medium is very large, so that a transmitting station cannot effectively distinguish incoming weak signals from noise and the effects of its own transmission.

To ensure the smooth and fair functioning of this algorithm, DCF includes a set of delays that amounts to a priority scheme. Let us start by considering a single delay known as an interframe space (IFS). In fact, there are three different IFS values, but the algorithm is best explained by initially ignoring this detail. Using an IFS, the rules for CSMA access are as follows:

1. A station with a frame to transmit senses the medium. If the medium is idle, the station waits to see if the medium remains idle for a time equal to IFS, and, if this is so, the station may immediately transmit.
2. If the medium is busy (either because the station initially finds the medium busy or because the medium becomes busy during the IFS idle time), the station defers transmission and continues to monitor the medium until the current transmission is over.
3. Once the current transmission is over, the station delays another IFS. If the medium remains idle for this period, then the station backs off using a binary exponential backoff scheme and again senses the medium. If the medium is still idle, the station may transmit.

As with Ethernet, the binary exponential backoff provides a means of handling a heavy load. If a station attempts to transmit and finds the medium busy, it backs off a certain amount and tries again. Repeated failed attempts to transmit result in longer and longer backoff times.

The above scheme is refined for DCF to provide priority-based access by the simple expedient of using three values for IFS:

- **SIFS (short IFS).** The shortest IFS, used for all immediate response actions, as explained below.
- **PIFS (point coordination function IFS).** A mid-length IFS, used by the centralized controller in the PCF scheme when issuing polls.
- **DIFS (distributed coordination function IFS).** The longest IFS, used as a minimum delay for asynchronous frames contending for access.

Figure 13.21a illustrates the use of these time values. Consider first the SIFS. Any station using SIFS to determine transmission opportunity has, in effect, the

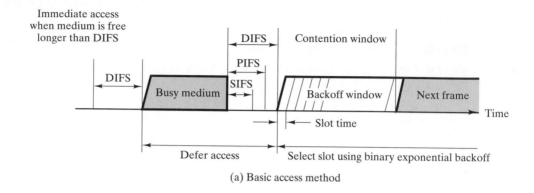

(a) Basic access method

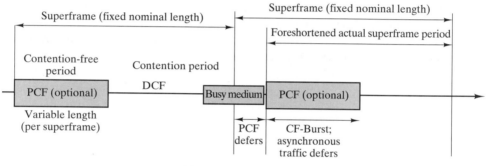

(b) PCF superframe construction

**FIGURE 13.21** IEEE 802.11 MAC timing.

highest priority, because it will always gain access in preference to a station waiting an amount of time equal to PIFS or DIFS. The SIFS is used in the following circumstances:

- **Acknowledgment (ACK).** When a station receives a frame addressed only to itself (not multicast or broadcast) it responds with an ACK frame after waiting only for an SIFS gap; this has two desirable effects. First, because collision detection is not used, the likelihood of collisions is greater than with CSMA/CD, and the MAC-level ACK provides for efficient collision recovery. Second, the SIFS can be used to provide efficient delivery of an LLC protocol data unit (PDU) that requires multiple MAC frames. In this case, the following scenario occurs. A station with a multiframe LLC PDU to transmit sends out the MAC frames one at a time. Each frame is acknowledged by the recipient after SIFS. When the source receives an ACK, it immediately (after SIFS) sends the next frame in the sequence. The result is that once a station has contended for the channel, it will maintain control of the channel until it has sent all of the fragments of an LLC PDU.
- **Clear to Send (CTS).** A station can ensure that its data frame will get through by first issuing a small Request to Send (RTS) frame. The station to which this frame is addressed should immediately respond with a CTS frame if it is ready

to receive. All other stations receive the RTS and defer using the medium until they see a corresponding CTS, or until a timeout occurs.

**Poll response.** This is explained in the discussion of PCF, below.

The next longest IFS interval is the PIFS; this is used by the centralized controller in issuing polls and takes precedence over normal-contention traffic. However, those frames transmitted using SIFS have precedence over a PCF poll.

Finally, the DIFS interval is used for all ordinary asynchronous traffic.

### Point Coordination Function

PCF is an alternative access method implemented on top of the DCF. The operation consists of polling with the centralized polling master (point coordinator). The point coordinator makes use of PIFS when issuing polls. Because PIFS is smaller than DIFS, the point coordinator can seize the medium and lock out all asynchronous traffic while it issues polls and receives responses.

As an extreme, consider the following possible scenario. A wireless network is configured so that a number of stations with time-sensitive traffic are controlled by the point coordinator while remaining traffic, using CSMA, contends for access. The point coordinator could issue polls in a round-robin fashion to all stations configured for polling. When a poll is issued, the polled station may respond using SIFS. If the point coordinator receives a response, it issues another poll using PIFS. If no response is received during the expected turnaround time, the coordinator issues a poll.

If the discipline of the preceding paragraph were implemented, the point coordinator would lock out all asynchronous traffic by repeatedly issuing polls. To prevent this situation, an interval known as the superframe is defined. During the first part of this interval, the point coordinator issues polls in a round-robin fashion to all stations configured for polling. The point coordinator then idles for the remainder of the superframe, allowing a contention period for asynchronous access.

Figure 13.21b illustrates the use of the superframe. At the beginning of a superframe, the point coordinator may optionally seize control and issue polls for a give period of time. This interval varies because of the variable frame size issued by responding stations. The remainder of the superframe is available for contention-based access. At the end of the superframe interval, the point coordinator contends for access to the medium using PIFS. If the medium is idle, the point coordinator gains immediate access, and a full superframe period follows. However, the medium may be busy at the end of a superframe. In this case, the point coordinator must wait until the medium is idle to gain access; this results in a foreshortened superframe period for the next cycle.

## 13.7  RECOMMENDED READING

[STAL97] covers, in greater detail, all of the LAN systems discussed in this chapter
[HEGE93] and [BIRD94] cover CSMA/CD and token ring LANs, respectively, in some depth. Two detailed accounts of FDDI are [MILL95] and [SHAH94]; the former pro-

vides more detail on physical-layer issues, while the latter has more coverage of the MAC protocol. [SPUR95] contains a concise summary of the specifications for 100BASE-T, including configuration guidelines for a single segment of each media type, as well as guidelines for building multi-segment Ethernets using a variety of media types. [WATS95] provides good technical summaries of 100VG-AnyLAN. [KAVA95] and [NEWM94] are good survey articles on LAN ATM architecture and configurations. The most comprehensive description of Fiber Channel is [STEP95]. This book provides a detailed technical treatment of each layer of the Fibre Channel architecture. A shorter but worthwhile treatment is [FCA94], which is a 50-page book from the Fiber Channel Association, an industry consortium formed to promote the Fiber Channel.

Books with rigorous treatments of LAN/MAN performance include [STUC85], [HAMM86], [SPRA91], and [BERT92].

BERT92    Bertsekas, D. and Gallager, R. *Data Networks*. Englewood Cliffs, NJ: Prentice Hall, 1992.

BIRD94    Bird, D. *Token Ring Network Design*. Reading, MA: Addison-Wesley, 1994.

FCA94    Fibre Channel Association. *Fibre Channel: Connection to the Future*. Austin, TX: Fibre Channel Association, 1994.

HAMM86    Hammond, J. and O'Reilly, P. *Performance Analysis of Local Computer Networks*. Reading, MA: Addison-Wesley, 1986.

HEGE93    Hegering, H. and Lapple, A. *Ethernet: Building a Communications Infrastructure*. Reading, MA: Addison-Wesley, 1993.

KAVA95    Kavak, N. "Data Communication in ATM Networks." *IEEE Network*, May/June 1995.

MILL95    Mills, A. *Understanding FDDI*. Englewood Cliffs, NJ: Prentice-Hall, 1995.

NEWM94    Newman, P. "ATM Local Area Networks." *IEEE Communications Magazine*, March 1994.

SHAH94    Shah, A. and Ramakrishnan, G. FDDI: *A High-Speed Network*. Englewood Cliffs, NJ: Prentice Hall, 1994.

SPRA91    Apragins, J. Hammond, J. and Pawlikowski, K. *Telecommunications Protocols and Design*. Reading, MA: Addison-Wesley, 1991.

SPUR95    Spurgeon, C. *Quick Reference Guide to Ethernet*. Austin, TX: Harris Park Press, 1995.

STAL97    Stallings, W. *Local and Metropolitan Area Networks*, Fifth Edition. Upper Saddle River, NJ: 1997.

STEP95    Stephens, G. and Dedek, J. *Fiber Channel*. Menlo Park, CA: Ancot Corporation, 1995.

STUC85    Stuck, B. and Arthurs, E. A *Computer Communications Network Performance Analysis Primer*. Englewood Cliffs, NJ: Prentice Hall, 1985.

WATS95    Watson, G., et al. "The Demand Priority MAC Protocol." *IEEE Network*, January/February 1995.

## Recommended Web Sites

- http://wwwhost.ots.utexas.edu/ethernet: Provides general Ethernet information, technical specifications, an Ethernet reading list, and an image of inventor Robert Metcalf's original 1976 Ethernet drawing.

- http://www.astral.org: Site of the Alliance for Strategic Token Ring Advancement and Leadership, a vendor organization.

- http://www.amdahl.com/ext/CARP/FCA/FCA.html: Web site of the Fibre Channel Association.

- http://www.iol.unh.edu: University of New Hampshire (equipment testing for ATM, FDDI, Fast Ethernet, FDSE, Ethernet, OSPF, Network Management (SNMP), Token Ring, and VG-AnyLAN).

## 13.8  PROBLEMS

**13.1**  A disadvantage of the contention approach for LANs is the capacity wasted due to multiple stations attempting to access the channel at the same time. Suppose that time is divided into discrete slots with each of $N$ stations attempting to transmit with probability $p$ during each slot. What fraction of slots is wasted due to multiple simultaneous transmission attempts?

**13.2**  A simple medium access control protocol would be to use a fixed assignment time-division multiplexing (TDM) scheme, as described in section 2.1. Each station is assigned one time slot per cycle for transmission. For the bus and tree, the length of each slot is the time to transmit 100 bits plus the end-to-end propagation delay. For the ring, assume a delay of one bit time per station, and assume that a round-robin assignment is used. Stations monitor all time slots for reception. Assume a propagation time of $2 \times 10^8$ m/sec. What are the limitations, in terms of number of stations and throughput per station, for

  **a.** A 1-km, 10-Mbps baseband bus?
  **b.** A 1-km (headend to farthest point), 10-Mbps broadband bus?
  **c.** A 10-Mbps broadband tree consisting of a 0.5-km trunk emanating from the headend and five 0.1-km branches from the trunk at the following points: 0.05 km, 0.15 km, 0.25 km, 0.35 km, 0.45 km?
  **d.** A 10-Mbps ring with a total length of 1 km?
  **e.** A 10-Mbps ring with a length of 0.1 km between repeaters?
  **f.** Compute throughput for all of the above for 10 and 100 stations.

**13.3**  Consider two stations on a baseband bus at a distance of 1 km from each other. Let the data rate be 1 Mbps, the frame length be 100 bits, and the propagation velocity be $2 \times 10^8$ m/s. Assume that each station generates frames at an average rate of 1000 frames per second. For the ALOHA protocol, if one station begins to transmit a frame at time $t$, what is the probability of collision? Repeat for slotted ALOHA. Repeat for ALOHA and slotted-ALOHA at 10 Mbps.

**13.4**  Repeat Problem 13.3 for a broadband bus. Assume that the two stations are 1 km apart and that one is very near the headend.

**13.5**  The binary exponential backoff algorithm is defined by IEEE 802 as follows:

> The delay is an integral multiple of slot time. The number of slot times to delay before the $n$th retransmission attempt is chosen as a uniformly distributed random integer $r$ in the range $0 < r < 2^K$, where $K = \min(n, 10)$.

Slot time is, roughly, twice the round-trip propagation delay. Assume that two stations always have a frame to send. After a collision, what is the mean number of retransmission attempts before one station successfully retransmits? What is the answer if three stations always have frames to send?

**13.6**  Consider the 100VG-AnyLAN network shown in Figure 13.12 and suppose that requests are issued in the following order:

1-2(N), 3-8(N), 1-1(H), 1-2(N), 5-1(N), 3-6(H), 1-4(N), 5-2(N), 1-1(H)

Generate a timing diagram similar to that of Figure 13.11 that shows the transmission sequence of the above requests. Assume all frames are of equal length and that requests arrive at a uniform rate of one per 0.5 frame times.

**13.7**  For a token ring LAN, suppose that the destination station removes the data frame and immediately sends a short acknowledgment frame to the sender, rather than letting the original frame return to sender. How will this procedure affect performance?

**13.8**  Another medium access control technique for rings is the slotted ring. A number of fixed-length slots circulate continuously on the ring. Each slot contains a leading bit to designate the slot as empty or full. A station wishing to transmit waits until an empty slot arrives, marks the slot full, and inserts a frame of data as the slot goes by. The full slot makes a complete round trip, to be marked empty again by the station that marked it full. In what sense are the slotted ring and token ring protocols the complement of each other?

13.9 Consider a slotted ring of length 10 km with a data rate of 10 Mbps and 500 repeaters, each of which introduces a 1-bit delay. Each slot contains room for one source-address byte, one destination-address byte, two data bytes, and five control bits for a total length of 37 bits. How many slots are on the ring?

13.10 Compare the capacity allocation schemes for IEEE 802.5 token ring and FDDI. What are the relative pros and cons?

13.11 Rework the example of Figure 13.10 using a TTRT of 12 frames and assume that no station ever has more than 8 asynchronous frames to send.

13.12 With 8B6T coding, the effective data rate on a single channel is 33 Mbps with a signaling rate of 25 Mbaud. If a pure ternary scheme were used, what would be the effective data rate for a signaling rate of 25 Mbaud?

13.13 With 8B6T coding, the DC algorithm sometimes negates all of the ternary symbols in a code group. How does the receiver recognize this condition? How does the receiver discriminate between a negated code group and one that has not been negated? For example, the code group for data byte 00 is +–00+– and the code group for data byte 38 is the negation of that, namely –+00–+.

13.14 Draw the MLT decoder state diagram that corresponds to the encoder state diagram of Figure 13.2.

13.15 For the bit stream 0101110, sketch the waveforms for NRZ, NRZI, Manchester, and Differential Manchester, and MLT-3.

13.16 Fill in all the values for the 5B6B decoding table, whose outline is shown below.

| Received Sextet | Mode 2 Output Quintet | Mode 4 Output Quintet |
|---|---|---|
| 000000 | | |
| • • • | | |
| 111111 | | |

### DIGITAL SIGNAL ENCODING FOR LANS

IN CHAPTER 4, we looked at some of the common techniques for encoding digital data for transmission, including Manchester and Differential Manchester, which are used in some of the LAN standards. In this appendix, we examine some additional encoding schemes referred to in this chapter.

#### 4B/5B–NRZI

This scheme, which is actually a combination of two encoding algorithms, is used both for 100BASE-X and FDDI. To understand the significance of this choice, first consider the simple alternative of an NRZ (non-return to zero) coding scheme. With NRZ, one signal state represents binary one, and one signal state represents binary zero. The disadvantage of this approach is its lack of synchronization. Because transitions on the medium are unpredictable, there is no way for the receiver to synchronize its clock to the transmitter. A solution to this problem is to encode the binary data to guarantee the presence of transitions. For example, the data could first be encoded using Manchester encoding. The disadvantage of this approach is that the efficiency is only 50%. That is, because there can be as many as two transitions per bit time, a signaling rate of 200 million signal elements per second (200 Mbaud) is needed to achieve a data rate of 100 Mbps; this represents an unnecessary cost and technical burden.

Greater efficiency can be achieved using the 4B/5B code. In this scheme, encoding is done four bits at a time; each four bits of data are encoded into a symbol with five *code bits*, such that each code bit contains a single signal element. The block of five code bits is called a code group. In effect, each set of 4 bits is encoded as 5 bits. The efficiency is thus raised to 80%; 100 Mbps is achieved with 125 Mbaud.

To ensure synchronization, there is a second stage of encoding: each code bit of the 4B/5B stream is treated as a binary value and encoded using Nonreturn to Zero Inverted (NRZI) (see Figure 4.2). In this code, a binary 1 is represented with a transition at the beginning of the bit interval, and a binary 0 is represented with no transition at the beginning of the bit interval; there are no other transitions. The advantage of NRZI is that it employs differential encoding. Recall from Chapter 4 that in differential encoding, the signal is decoded by comparing the polarity of adjacent signal elements rather than the absolute value of a signal element. A benefit of this scheme is that it is generally more reliable in detecting a transition in the presence of noise and distortion than in comparing a value to a threshold.

Now we are in a position to describe the 4B/5B code and to understand the selections that were made. Table 13.8 shows the symbol encoding. Each 5-bit code group pattern is shown, together with its NRZI realization. Because we are encoding four bits with a 5-bit pattern, only 16 of the 32 possible patterns are needed for data encoding. The codes selected to represent the 16 4-bit data blocks are such that a transition is present at least twice for each 5-code group code. No more than three zeros in a row are allowed across one or more code groups.

The encoding scheme can be summarized as follows:

1. A simple NRZ encoding is rejected because it does not provide synchronization; a string of 1s or 0s will have no transitions.
2. The data to be transmitted must first be encoded to assure transitions. The 4B/5B code is chosen over Manchester because it is more efficient.
3. The 4B/5B code is further encoded using NRZI so that the resulting differential signal will improve reception reliability.
4. The specific 5-bit patterns for the encoding of the 16 4-bit data patterns are chosen to guarantee no more than three zeros in a row, to provide for adequate synchronization.

**TABLE 13.8**  4B/5B code groups.

| Data input (4 bits) | Code group (5 bits) | NRZI pattern | Interpretation |
|---|---|---|---|
| 0000 | 11110 | | Data 0 |
| 0001 | 01001 | | Data 1 |
| 0010 | 10100 | | Data 2 |
| 0011 | 10101 | | Data 3 |
| 0100 | 01010 | | Data 4 |
| 0101 | 01011 | | Data 5 |
| 0110 | 01110 | | Data 6 |
| 0111 | 01111 | | Data 7 |
| 1000 | 10010 | | Data 8 |
| 1001 | 10011 | | Data 9 |
| 1010 | 10110 | | Data A |
| 1011 | 10111 | | Data B |
| 1100 | 11010 | | Data C |
| 1101 | 11011 | | Data D |
| 1110 | 11100 | | Data E |
| 1111 | 11101 | | Data F |
| | 11111 | | Idle |
| | 11000 | | Start of stream delimiter, part 1 |
| | 10001 | | Start of stream delimiter, part 2 |
| | 01101 | | End of stream delimiter, part 1 |
| | 00111 | | End of stream delimiter, part 2 |
| | 00100 | | Transmit error |
| | other | | Invalid codes |

Those code groups not used to represent data are either declared invalid or are assigned special meaning as control symbols. These assignments are listed in Table 13.8. The nondata symbols fall into the following categories:

- **Idle.** The idle code group is transmitted between data transmission sequences. It consists of a constant flow of binary ones, which in NRZI comes out as a continuous alternation between the two signal levels. This continuous fill pattern establishes and maintains synchronization and is used in the CSMA/CD protocol to indicate that the shared medium is idle.
- **Start-of-stream delimiter.** Used to delineate the starting boundary of a data transmission sequence; it consists of two different code groups.
- **End-of-stream delimiter.** Used to terminate normal data transmission sequences; it consists of two different code groups.
- **Transmit error.** This code group is interpreted as a signaling error. The normal use of this indicator is for repeaters to propagate received errors.

## MLT-3

Although 4B/5B-NRZI is effective over optical fiber, it is not suitable, as is, for use over twisted pair. The reason is that the signal energy is concentrated in such a way as to produce undesirable radiated emissions from the wire. MLT-3, which is used on both 100BASE-TX and the twisted pair version of FDDI, is designed to overcome this problem.

The following steps are involved:

1. *NRZI to NRZ conversion*: The 4B/5B NRZI signal of the basic 100BASE-X is converted back to NRZ.
2. *Scrambling*: The bit stream is scrambled to produce a more uniform spectrum distribution for the next stage.
3. *Encoder*: The scrambled bit stream is encoded using a scheme known as MLT-3.
4. *Driver*: The resulting encoding is transmitted.

The effect of the MLT-3 scheme is to concentrate most of the energy in the transmitted signal below 30 MHz, which reduces radiated emissions; this, in turn, reduces problems due to interference.

The MLT-3 encoding produces an output that has a transition for every binary one that uses three levels: a positive voltage ($+V$), a negative voltage ($-V$) and no voltage ($0$). The encoding rules are best explained with reference to the encoder state diagram shown in Figure 13.22:

1. If the next input bit is zero, then the next output value is the same as the preceding value.
2. If the next input bit is one, then the next output value involves a transition:
   a. If the preceding output value was either $+V$ or $-V$, then the next output value is $0$.
   b. If the preceding output value was $0$, then the next output value is nonzero, and that output is of the opposite sign to the last nonzero output.

Figure 13.23 provides an example. Every time there is an input of 1, there is a transition. The occurrences of $+V$ and $-V$ alternate.

## 8B6T

The 8B6T encoding algorithm uses ternary signaling. With this method, each signal element can take on one of three values (positive voltage, negative voltage, zero voltage). A pure ternary code is one in which the full information-carrying capacity of the ternary signal is exploited. However, pure ternary is not attractive for the same reasons that a pure binary

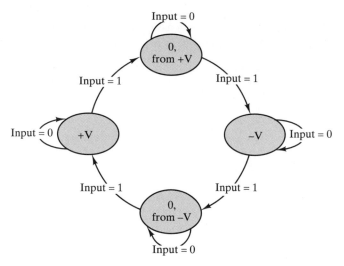

**FIGURE 13.22** MLT-3 encoder state diagram.

(NRZ) code is rejected: lack of synchronization. However, there are schemes referred to as **block-coding methods** that approach the efficiency of ternary and overcome this disadvantage. A new block coding scheme known as 8B6T is used for 100BASE-T4.

With 8B6T, the data to be transmitted are handled in 8-bit blocks. Each block of 8 bits is mapped into a code group of six ternary symbols. The stream of code groups is then transmitted in round-robin fashion across the three output channels (Figure 13.24). Thus, the ternary transmission rate on each output channel is

$$\frac{6}{8} \times 33\frac{1}{3} = 25\text{Mbaud}$$

Table 13.9 shows a portion of the 8B6T code table; the full table maps all possible 8-bit patterns into a unique code group of six ternary symbols. The mapping was chosen with two requirements in mind: synchronization and DC balance. For synchronization, the codes were chosen so as to maximize the average number of transitions per code group. The second requirement is to maintain DC balance, so that the average voltage on the line is zero; for this purpose, all of the selected code groups have either an equal number of positive and negative symbols or an excess of one positive symbol. To maintain balance, a DC balancing algorithm is used. In essence, this algorithm monitors the cumulative weight of all code groups transmitted on a single pair. Each code group has a weight of 0 or 1. To maintain balance, the algorithm may negate a transmitted code group (change all + symbols to – symbols

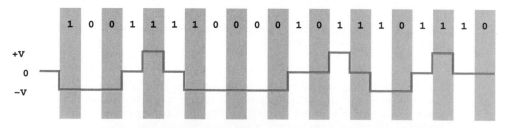

**FIGURE 13.23** Example of MLT-3 encoding.

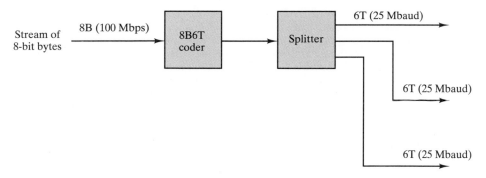

**FIGURE 13.24**   8B6T transmission scheme.

and all – symbols to + symbols), so that the cumulative weight at the conclusion of each code group is always either 0 or 1.

### 5B6B

The 5B6B encoding is used in the 100VG-AnyLAN specification in the following way: A MAC frame is divided into 5-bit chunks (quintets), and each successive chunk is transmitted over a different channel in round-robin fashion. Thus, to achieve a data rate of 100 Mbps, a data rate of only 25 Mbps is needed on each channel.

To ensure adequate transitions on each line for synchronization, an encoding scheme known as 5B6B is used. The 5B6B scheme is based on the same strategy as the 4B/5B scheme described earlier. In this case, each group of 5 input bits is mapped into a set of 6 output bits. Thus, for an effective data rate of 25 Mbps, a signaling rate of 30 Mbaud is required.

With the 5B6B scheme, there are 32 possible 5-bit inputs. Ideally, we would like to assign to each 5-bit input a 6-bit code that has an equal number of ones and zeros; this would maintain a dc balance of zero. However, there are only twenty 6-bit code words that have three ones and zeros. These codes are assigned to 20 of the input patterns. For the remaining 12 input patterns, two code words are assigned, one with four zeros and two ones (mode

**TABLE 13.9**   Portion of 8B6T code table.

| Data octet | 6T code group | Data octet | 6T code group | Data octet | 6T code group | Data octet | 6T code group |
|---|---|---|---|---|---|---|---|
| 00 | +−00+− | 10 | +0+−−0 | 20 | 00−++− | 30 | +−00−+ |
| 01 | 0+−+−0 | 11 | ++0−0− | 21 | −−+00+ | 31 | 0+−−+0 |
| 02 | +−0+−0 | 12 | +0+−0− | 22 | ++−0+− | 32 | +−0−+0 |
| 03 | −0++−0 | 13 | 0++−0− | 23 | ++−0−+ | 33 | −0+−+0 |
| 04 | −0+0+− | 14 | 0++−−0 | 24 | 00+0−+ | 34 | −0+0−+ |
| 05 | 0+−−0+ | 15 | ++00−− | 25 | 00+0+− | 35 | 0+−+0− |
| 06 | +−0−0+ | 16 | +0+0−− | 26 | 00−00+ | 36 | +−0+0− |
| 07 | −0+−0+ | 17 | 0++0−− | 27 | −−+++− | 37 | −0++0− |
| 08 | −+00+− | 18 | 0+−0+− | 28 | −0−++0 | 38 | −+00−+ |
| 09 | 0−++−0 | 19 | 0+−0−+ | 29 | −−0+0+ | 39 | 0−+−+0 |
| 0A | −+0+−0 | 1A | 0+−++− | 2A | −0−+0+ | 3A | −+0−+0 |
| 0B | +0−+−0 | 1B | 0+−00+ | 2B | 0−−+0+ | 3B | +0−−+0 |
| 0C | +0−0+− | 1C | 0−+00+ | 2C | 0−−++0 | 3C | +0−0−+ |
| 0D | 0−+−0+ | 1D | 0−+++− | 2D | −−00++ | 3D | 0−++0− |
| 0E | −+0−0+ | 1E | 0−+0−+ | 2E | −0−0++ | 3E | −+0+0− |
| 0F | +0−−0+ | 1F | 0−+0+− | 2F | 0−−0++ | 3F | +0−+0− |

2) and one with two zeros and four ones (mode 4). Successive instances of any of these 24 unbalanced code words must alternate between mode 2 and mode 4 output to maintain balance. If, during reception, a station or repeater receives two of the same type of unbalanced words in a row (with any number of intervening balanced words), the receiver knows that a transmission error has occurred and will ask for a retransmission of the data.

Table 13.10 shows the complete 5B6B encoding scheme. There is a unique output code word for 20 of the input patterns; for the rest, the transmitter keeps track of whether the last unbalanced transmitted word was mode 2 or mode 4 and transmits the appropriate output code word to maintain balance.

## 8B/10B

The encoding scheme used for Fibre Channel is 8B/10B, in which each 8 bits of data is converted into 10 bits for transmission. This scheme has a similar philosophy to the 4B/5B scheme used for FDDI, as discussed earlier. The 8B/10B scheme was developed and patented by IBM for use in its 200-megabaud ESCON interconnect system [WIDM83]. The 8B/10B scheme is more powerful than 4B/5B in terms of transmission characteristics and error detection capability.

The developers of this code list the following advantages:

- It can be implemented with relatively simple and reliable transceivers at low cost.
- It is well-balanced, with minimal deviation from the occurrence of an equal number of 1 and 0 bits across any sequence.
- It provides good transition density for easier clock recovery.
- It provides useful error-detection capability.

The 8B/10B code is an example of the more general $mBnB$ code, in which $m$ binary source bits are mapped into $n$ binary bits for transmission. Redundancy is built into the code to provide the desired transmission features by making $n > m$.

Figure 13.25 illustrates the operation of this code. The code actually combines two other codes, a 5B/6B code and a 3B/4B code. The use of these two codes is simply an artifact that simplifies the definition of the mapping and the implementation; the mapping could have been defined directly as an 8B/10B code. In any case, a mapping is defined that maps

**TABLE 13.10**   5B6B encoding table.

| Input Quintet | Mode 2 Output | Mode 4 Output | Input Quintet | Mode 2 Output | Mode 4 Output |
| --- | --- | --- | --- | --- | --- |
| 00000 | 001100 | 110011 | 10000 | 000101 | 111010 |
| 00001 | 101100 | 101100 | 10001 | 100101 | 100101 |
| 00010 | 100010 | 101110 | 10010 | 001001 | 110110 |
| 00011 | 001101 | 001101 | 10011 | 010110 | 010110 |
| 00100 | 001010 | 110101 | 10100 | 111000 | 111000 |
| 00101 | 010101 | 010101 | 10101 | 011000 | 100111 |
| 00110 | 001110 | 001110 | 10110 | 011001 | 011001 |
| 00111 | 001011 | 001011 | 10111 | 100001 | 011110 |
| 01000 | 000111 | 000111 | 11000 | 110001 | 110001 |
| 01001 | 100011 | 100011 | 11001 | 101010 | 101010 |
| 01010 | 100110 | 100110 | 11010 | 010100 | 101011 |
| 01011 | 000110 | 111001 | 11011 | 110100 | 110100 |
| 01100 | 101000 | 010111 | 11100 | 011100 | 011100 |
| 01101 | 011010 | 011010 | 11101 | 010011 | 010011 |
| 01110 | 100100 | 011011 | 11110 | 010010 | 101101 |
| 01111 | 101001 | 101001 | 11111 | 110010 | 110010 |

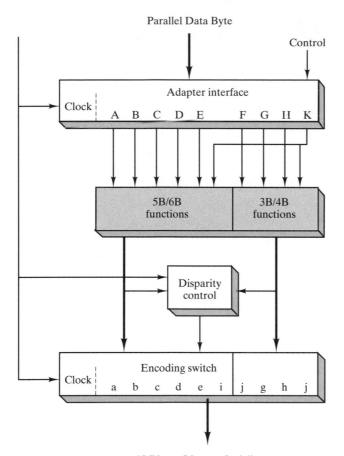

**FIGURE 13.25**  8B/10B encoding.

each of the possible 8-bit source blocks into a 10-bit code block. There is also a function called *disparity control*. In essence, this function keeps track of the excess of zeros over ones or ones over zeros. An excess in either direction is referred to as a disparity. If there is a disparity, and if the current code block would add to that disparity, then the disparity control block complements the 10-bit code block. This has the effect of either eliminating the disparity or at least moving it in the opposite direction of the current disparity.

The encoding mechanism also includes a control line input, K, which indicates whether the lines A through H are data or control bits. In the latter case, a special nondata 10-bit block is generated. A total of 12 of these nondata blocks is defined as valid in the standard; these are used for synchronization and for other control purposes.

## PERFORMANCE ISSUES

THE CHOICE OF a LAN or MAN architecture is based on many factors, but one of the most important is performance. Of particular concern is the behavior (throughput, response time) of the network under heavy load. Here, we provide an introduction to this topic. A more detailed discussion can be found in [STAL97].

### The Effect of Propagation Delay and Transmission Rate

In Chapter 6, we introduced the parameter $a$, defined as

$$a = \frac{\text{Propagation time}}{\text{Transmission time}}$$

In that context, we were concerned with a point-to-point link, with a given propagation time between the two endpoints and a transmission time for either a fixed or an average frame size. It was shown that $a$ could be expressed as

$$a = \frac{\text{Length of data link in bits}}{\text{Length of frame in bits}}$$

This parameter is also important in the context of LANs and MANs, and, in fact, determines an upper bound on utilization. Consider a perfectly efficient access mechanism that allows only one transmission at a time. As soon as one transmission is over, another station begins transmitting. Furthermore, the transmission is pure data; there are no overhead bits. What is the maximum possible utilization of the network? It can be expressed as the ratio of total throughput of the network to its capacity:

$$U = \frac{\text{Throughput}}{\text{Data Rate}} \tag{13.1}$$

Now define, as in Chapter 6,

$R$ = data rate of the channel
$d$ = maximum distance between any two stations
$V$ = velocity of signal propagation
$L$ = average or fixed frame length

The throughput is just the number of bits transmitted per unit time. A frame contains $L$ bits, and the amount of time devoted to that frame is the actual transmission time ($L/R$) plus the propagation delay ($d/V$). Thus,

$$\text{Throughput} = \frac{L}{d/V + L/R} \tag{13.2}$$

But by our definition of $a$, above

$$a = \frac{d/V}{L/R} = \frac{Rd}{LV} \tag{13.3}$$

Substituting (13.2) and (13.3) into (13.1)

$$U = \frac{1}{1 + a} \tag{13.4}$$

Note that the above differs from Equation (6.2), because the latter assumed a half-duplex protocol (no piggybacked acknowledgments).

So, utilization varies with $a$; this can be grasped intuitively by studying Figure 13.26, which shows a baseband bus with two stations as far apart as possible (worst case) that take turns sending frames. If we normalize time such that frame transmission time = 1, then the propagation time = $a$. For $a < 1$, the sequence of events is as follows:

1. A station begins transmitting at $t_0$.
2. Reception begins at $t_0 + a$.
3. Transmission is completed at $t_0 + 1$.
4. Reception ends at $t_0 + 1 + a$.
5. The other station begins transmitting.

For $a > 1$, events 2 and 3 are interchanged. In both cases, the total time for one "turn" is $1 + a$, but the transmission time is only 1 for a utilization of $1/(1 + a)$.

The same effect as above can be seen to apply to a ring network in Figure 13.27. Here we assume that one station transmits and then waits to receive its own transmission before any other station transmits. The identical sequence of events outlined above applies.

Typical values of $a$ range from about 0.01 to 0.1 for LANs and 0.1 to well over 1.0 for MANs. Table 13.11 gives some representative values for a bus topology. As can be seen, for larger and/or higher-speed networks, utilization suffers. For this reason, the restriction of only one frame at a time is lifted for LANs such as FDDI.

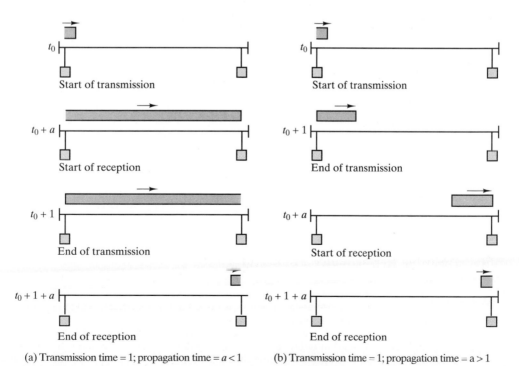

(a) Transmission time = 1; propagation time = $a < 1$    (b) Transmission time = 1; propagation time = $a > 1$

**FIGURE 13.26** The effect of $a$ on utilization for baseband bus.

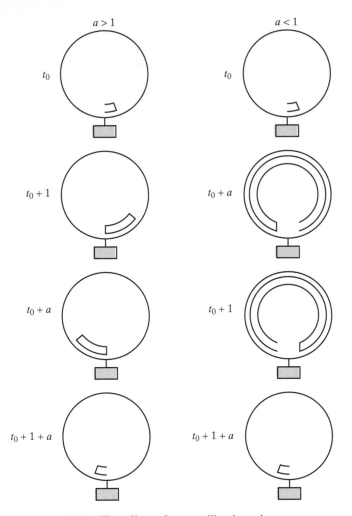

**FIGURE 13.27**   The effect of $a$ on utilization: ring.

Finally, the analysis above assumes a "perfect" protocol, for which a new frame can be transmitted as soon as an old frame is received. In practice, the MAC protocol adds overhead that makes utilization worse. This is demonstrated in the next subsection for token-passing and for CSMA/CD.

### Simple Performance Models of Token Passing and CSMA/CD

The purpose of this section is to give the reader some insight into the relative performance of the most important LAN protocols—CSMA/CD, token bus, and token ring—by developing two simple performance models. It is hoped that this exercise will aid in delineating the results of more rigorous analyses.

For these models, we assume a local network with $N$ active stations, and a maximum normalized propagation delay of $a$. To simplify the analysis, we assume that each station is always prepared to transmit a frame; this allows us to develop an expression for maximum achievable utilization ($U$). Although this should not be construed to be the sole figure of

**TABLE 13.11** Representative values of $a$.

| Data rate (Mbps) | Frame size (bits) | Network length (km) | $a$ | $\frac{1}{1+a}$ |
|---|---|---|---|---|
| 1 | 100 | 1 | 0.05 | 0.95 |
| 1 | 1,000 | 10 | 0.05 | 0.95 |
| 1 | 100 | 10 | 0.5 | 0.67 |
| 10 | 100 | 1 | 0.5 | 0.67 |
| 10 | 1,000 | 1 | 0.05 | 0.95 |
| 10 | 1,000 | 10 | 0.5 | 0.67 |
| 10 | 10,000 | 10 | 0.05 | 0.95 |
| 100 | 35,000 | 200 | 2.8 | 0.26 |
| 100 | 1,000 | 50 | 25 | 0.04 |

merit for a local network, it is the single most analyzed figure of merit, and does permit useful performance comparisons.

First, let us consider token ring. Time on the ring will alternate between data frame transmission and token passing. Refer to a single instance of a data frame followed by a token as a cycle and define the following:

$C$ = average time for one cycle
$T_1$ = average time to transmit a data frame
$T_2$ = average time to pass a token

It should be clear that the average cycle rate is just $1/C = 1/(T_1 + T_2)$. Intuitively,

$$U = \frac{T_1}{T_1 + T_2} \tag{13.5}$$

That is, the throughput, normalized to system capacity, is just the fraction of time that is spent transmitting data.

Refer now to Figure 13.26; time is normalized such that frame transmission time equals 1 and propagation time equals $a$. Note that the propagation time must include repeater delays. For the case of $a < 1$, a station transmits a frame at time $t_0$, receives the leading edge of its own frame at $t_0 + a$, and completes transmission at $t_0 + 1$. The station then emits a token, which takes an average time $a/N$ to reach the next station. Thus, one cycle takes $1 + a/N$ and the transmission time is 1. So $U = 1/(1 + a/N)$.

For $a > 1$, the reasoning is slightly different. A station transmits at $t_0$, completes transmission at $t_0 + 1$, and receives the leading edge of its frame at $t_0 + a$. At that point, it is free to emit a token, which takes an average time $a/N$ to reach the next station. The cycle time is, therefore, $a + a/N$ and $U = 1/(a (1 + 1/N))$.

Summarizing,

$$\text{Token:} \qquad U = \begin{cases} \dfrac{1}{1 + a/N} & a < 1 \\[4mm] \dfrac{1}{a(1 + 1/N)} & a > 1 \end{cases} \tag{13.6}$$

The reasoning above applies equally well to token bus, where we assume that the logical ordering is the same as the physical ordering and that token-passing time is, therefore, $a/N$.

For CSMA/CD, consider time on the medium to be organized into slots whose length is twice the end-to-end propagation delay. This is a convenient way to view the activity on the medium; the slot time is the maximum time, from the start of transmission, required to detect a collision. Again, assume that there are $N$ active stations. Clearly, if each station always has a frame to transmit, and does so, there will be nothing but collisions on the line. As a result, we assume that each station restrains itself to transmitting during an available slot with probability $P$.

Time on the medium consists of two types of intervals: first is a transmission interval, which lasts $1/2a$ slots; second is a contention interval, which is a sequence of slots with either a collision or no transmission in each slot. The throughput is just the amount of time spent in transmission intervals (similar to the reasoning for Equation (13.5)).

To determine the average length of a contention interval, we begin by computing $A$, the probability that exactly one station attempts a transmission in a slot and, therefore, acquires the medium. This is just the binomial probability that any one station attempts to transmit and the others do not:

$$A = \binom{N}{1}p^1(1-P)^{N-1}$$
$$= NP(1-P)^{N-1}$$

This function takes on a maximum over $P$ when $P = 1/N$:

$$A = (1 - 1/N)^{N-1}$$

We are interested in the maximum because we want to calculate the maximum throughput of the medium; it should be clear that maximum throughput will be achieved if we maximize the probability of successful seizure of the medium. Therefore, the following rule should be enforced: During periods of heavy usage, a station should restrain its offered load to $1/N$. (This assumes that each station knows the value of $N$. In order to derive an expression for maximum possible throughput, we live with this assumption.) On the other hand, during periods of light usage, maximum utilization cannot be achieved because the load is too low; this region is not of interest here.

Now we can estimate the mean length of a contention interval, $w$, in slots:

$$\mathrm{E}[w] = \sum_{i=1}^{\infty} i \times \mathrm{Pr}\left[\begin{array}{l} i \text{ slots in a row with a collision or no} \\ \text{transmission followed by a slot with one} \\ \text{transmission} \end{array}\right]$$

$$= \sum_{i=1}^{\infty} i(1 - A)^i A$$

The summation converges to

$$\mathrm{E}[w] = \frac{1 - A}{A}$$

We can now determine the maximum utilization, which is just the length of a transmission interval as a proportion of a cycle consisting of a transmission and a contention interval:

$$\text{CSMA / CD:} \qquad U = \frac{1/2a}{1/2a + (1 - A)/A} = \frac{1}{1 + 2a(1 - A)/A} \qquad (13.7)$$

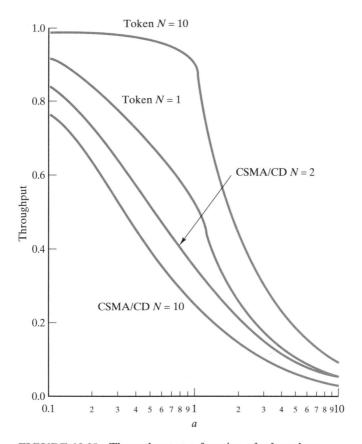

**FIGURE 13.28**   Throughput as a function of $a$ for token passing and CSMA/CD.

Figure 13.28 shows normalized throughput as a function of various values of $N$ and for both token passing and CSMA/CD. For both protocols, throughput declines as $a$ increases; this is to be expected. The dramatic difference, though, between the two protocols is seen in Figure 13.29, which shows throughput as a function of $N$. Token-passing performance actually improves as a function of $N$, because less time is spent in token passing. Conversely, the performance of CSMA/CD decreases because of the increased likelihood of collision or no transmission.

It is interesting to note the asymptotic value of $U$ as $N$ increases. For token passing,

Token:  $$\lim_{N \to \infty} U = \begin{cases} 1 & a < 1 \\ 1/a & a > 1 \end{cases} \qquad (13.8)$$

For CSMA/CD, we need to know that $\lim_{N \to \infty} (1 - 1/N)^{N-1} = 1/e$. Then we have

CSMA/CD:  $$\lim_{N \to \infty} U = \frac{1}{1 + 3.44a} \qquad (13.9)$$

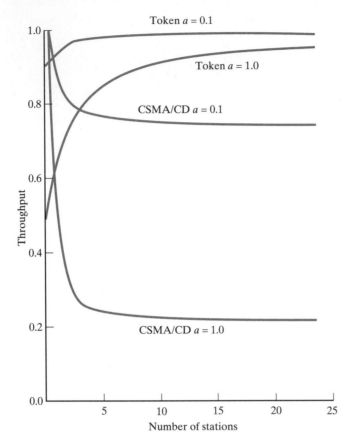

**FIGURE 13.29** Throughput as a function of $N$ for token pasing and CSMA/CD.

# CHAPTER 14

# BRIDGES

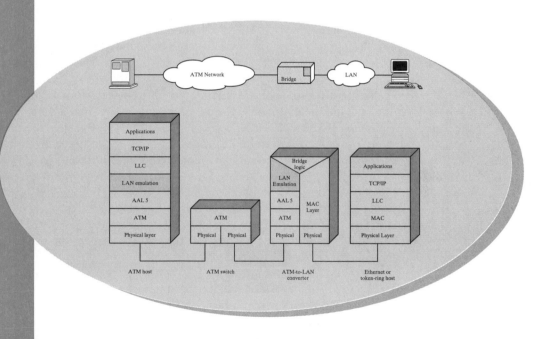

In most cases, a LAN or MAN is not an isolated entity. An organization may have more than one type of LAN at a given site to satisfy a spectrum of needs. An organization may have multiple LANs of the same type at a given site to accommodate performance or security requirements. Furthermore, an organization may have LANs and possibly MANs at various sites and may need them to be interconnected for central control of distributed information exchange.

The simplest approach to extending the range of LAN coverage is the use of bridges to interconnect a number of individual LANs. A more general solution, which allows the interconnection of local and wide area networks, is the use of an internetworking protocol and routers. This latter area is discussed in Chapter 16. Here, we concentrate on the bridge.

The chapter begins with a discussion of the basic operation of bridges. Then, we look at the most complex design issues associated with bridges, which is routing. Finally, we will return to the topic of ATM LANs, introduced in Chapter 13, and examine the concept of ATM LAN emulation.

## 14.1   BRIDGE OPERATION

The early designs for bridges were intended for use between local area networks (LANs) that use identical protocols for the physical and medium access layers (e.g., all conforming to IEEE 802.3 or all conforming to FDDI). Because the devices all use the same protocols, the amount of processing required at the bridge is minimal. In recent years, bridges that operate between LANs with different MAC protocols have been developed. However, the bridge remains a much simpler device than the router, which is discussed in Chapter 16.

Because the bridge is used in a situation in which all of the LANs have the same characteristics, the reader may ask why one does not simply use one large LAN. Depending on circumstance, there are several reasons for the use of multiple LANs connected by bridges:

- **Reliability.** The danger in connecting all data processing devices in an organization to one network is that a fault on the network may disable communication for all devices. By using bridges, the network can be partitioned into self-contained units.
- **Performance.** In general, performance on a LAN or MAN declines with an increase in the number of devices or with the length of the medium. A number of smaller LANs will often give improved performance if devices can be clustered so that *intra*-network traffic significantly exceeds *inter*-network traffic.
- **Security.** The establishment of multiple LANs may improve security of communications. It is desirable to keep different types of traffic (e.g., accounting, personnel, strategic planning) that have different security needs on physically separate media. At the same time, the different types of users with different levels of security need to communicate through controlled and monitored mechanisms.

- **Geography.** Clearly, two separate LANs are needed to support devices clustered in two geographically distant locations. Even in the case of two buildings separated by a highway, it may be far easier to use a microwave bridge link than to attempt to string coaxial cable between the two buildings. In the case of widely separated networks, two *half bridges* are needed (see Figure 14.3, below).

### Functions of a Bridge

Figure 14.1 illustrates the operation of a bridge between two LANs, A and B. The bridge performs the following functions:

- Reads all frames transmitted on A, and accepts those addressed to stations on B.
- Using the medium access control protocol for B, retransmits the frames onto B.
- Does the same for B-to-A traffic.

Several design aspects of a bridge are worth highlighting:

1. The bridge makes no modification to the content or format of the frames it receives, nor does it encapsulate them with an additional header. Each frame to be transferred is simply copied from one LAN and repeated with exactly the same bit pattern as the other LAN. Because the two LANs use the same LAN protocols, it is permissible to do this.

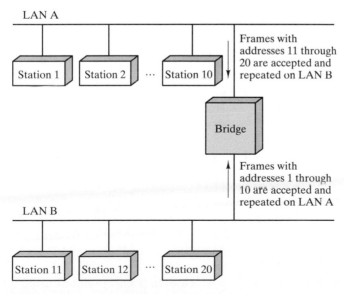

**FIGURE 14.1** Bridge operation.

2. The bridge should contain enough buffer space to meet peak demands. Over a short period of time, frames may arrive faster than they can be retransmitted.

3. The bridge must contain addressing and routing intelligence. At a minimum, the bridge must know which addresses are on each network in order to know which frames to pass. Further, there  may be more than two LANs interconnected by a number of bridges. In that case, a frame may have to be routed through several bridges in its journey from source to destination.

4. A bridge may connect more than two LANs.

The bridge provides an extension to the LAN that requires no modification to the communications software in the stations attached to the LANs. It appears to all stations on the two (or more) LANs that there is a single LAN on which each station has a unique address. The station uses that unique address and need not explicitly discriminate between stations on the same LAN and stations on other LANs; the bridge takes care of that.

The description above has applied to the simplest sort of bridge. More sophisticated bridges can be used in more complex collections of LANs. These constructions would include additional functions, such as,

- Each bridge can maintain status information on other bridges, together with the cost and number of bridge-to-bridge hops required to reach each network. This information may be updated by periodic exchanges of information among bridges; this allows the bridges to perform a dynamic routing function.

- A control mechanism can manage frame buffers in each bridge to overcome congestion. Under saturation conditions, the bridge can give precedence to en route packets over new packets just entering the internet from an attached LAN, thus preserving the investment in line bandwidth and processing time already made in the en route frame.

### Bridge Protocol Architecture

The IEEE 802.1D specification defines the protocol architecture for MAC bridges. In addition, the standard suggests formats for a globally administered set of MAC station addresses across multiple homogeneous LANs. In this subsection, we examine the protocol architecture of these bridges.

Within the 802 architecture, the endpoint or station address is designated at the MAC level. Thus, it is at the MAC level that a bridge can function. Figure 14.2 shows the simplest case, which consists of two LANs connected by a single bridge. The LANs employ the same MAC and LLC protocols. The bridge operates as previously described. A MAC frame whose destination is not on the immediate LAN is captured by the bridge, buffered briefly, and then transmitted on the other LAN. As far as the LLC layer is concerned, there is a dialogue between peer LLC entities in the two endpoint stations. The bridge need not contain an LLC layer, as it is merely serving to relay the MAC frames.

Figure 14.2b indicates the way in which data is encapsulated using a bridge. Data are provided by some user to LLC. The LLC entity appends a header and

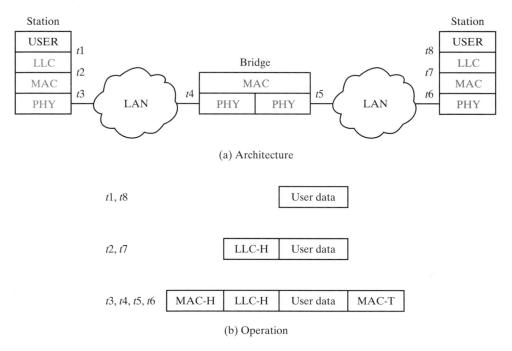

(a) Architecture

(b) Operation

**FIGURE 14.2**   Connection of two LANs by a bridge.

passes the resulting data unit to the MAC entity, which appends a header and a trailer to form a MAC frame. On the basis of the destination MAC address in the frame, it is captured by the bridge. The bridge does not strip off the MAC fields; its function is to relay the MAC frame intact to the destination LAN. Thus, the frame is deposited on the destination LAN and captured by the destination station.

The concept of a MAC relay bridge is not limited to the use of a single bridge to connect two nearby LANs. If the LANs are some distance apart, then they can be connected by two bridges that are in turn connected by a communications facility. For example, Figure 14.3 shows the case of two bridges connected by a point-to-point link. In this case, when a bridge captures a MAC frame, it appends a link layer (e.g., HDLC) header and trailer to transmit the MAC frame across the link to the other bridge. The target bridge strips off these link fields and transmits the original, unmodified MAC frame to the destination station.

The intervening communications facility can be a network, such as a wide-area–packet-switching network, as illustrated in Figure 14.4. In this case, the bridge is somewhat more complicated, although it performs the same function of relaying MAC frames. The connection between bridges is via an X.25 virtual circuit. Again, the two  LLC entities in the end systems have a direct logical relationship with no intervening LLC entities. Thus, in this situation, the X.25 packet layer is operating below an 802 LLC layer. As before, a MAC frame is passed intact between the end-points. When the bridge on the source LAN receives the frame, it appends an X.25 packet-layer header and an X.25 link-layer header and trailer and sends the data to the DCE (packet-switching node) to which it attaches. The DCE strips off the link-layer fields and sends the X.25 packet through the network to another DCE. The

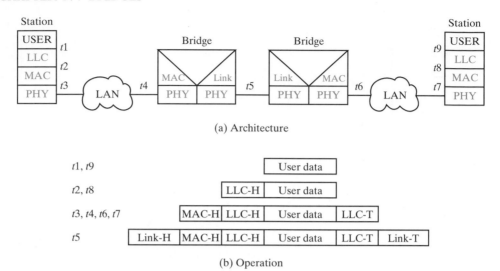

(a) Architecture

| | | | | | |
|---|---|---|---|---|---|
| t1, t9 | | | User data | | |
| t2, t8 | | LLC-H | User data | | |
| t3, t4, t6, t7 | | MAC-H LLC-H | User data | LLC-T | |
| t5 | Link-H | MAC-H LLC-H | User data | LLC-T | Link-T |

(b) Operation

**FIGURE 14.3** Bridge over a point-to-point link.

target DCE appends the link-layer field and sends this to the target bridge. The target bridge strips off all the X.25 fields and transmits the original unmodified MAC frame to the destination endpoint.

## 14.2 ROUTING WITH BRIDGES

In the configuration of Figure 14.1, the bridge makes the decision to relay a frame on the basis of destination MAC address. In a more complex configuration, the bridge must also make a routing decision. Consider the configuration of Figure 14.5. Suppose that station 1 transmits a frame on LAN A intended for station 5. The frame will be read by both bridge 101 and bridge 102. For each bridge, the addressed station is not on a LAN to which the bridge is attached. Therefore, each bridge must make a decision of whether or not to retransmit the frame on its other LAN, in order to move it closer to its intended destination. In this case, bridge 101 should repeat the frame on LAN B, whereas bridge 102 should refrain from retransmitting the frame. Once the frame has been transmitted on LAN B, it will be picked up by both bridges 103 and 104. Again, each must decide whether or not to forward the frame. In this case, bridge 104 should retransmit the frame on LAN E, where it will be received by the destination, station 5.

Thus, we see that, in the general case, the bridge must be equipped with a routing capability. When a bridge receives a frame, it must decide whether or not to forward it. If the bridge is attached to two or more networks, then it must decide whether or not to forward the frame and, if so, on which LAN the frame should be transmitted.

The routing decision may not always be a simple one. In Figure 14.6, bridge 107 is added to the previous configuration, directly linking LAN A and LAN E. Such an addition may be made to provide for higher overall internet availability. In this case, if Station 1 transmits a frame on LAN A intended for station 5 on LAN

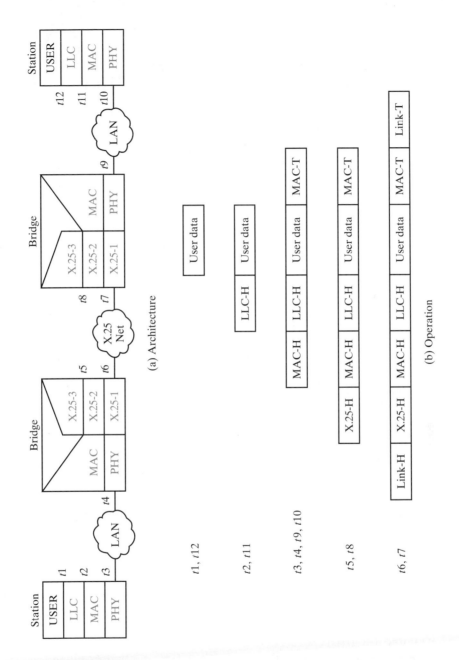

**FIGURE 14.4** Bridge over an X.25 network.

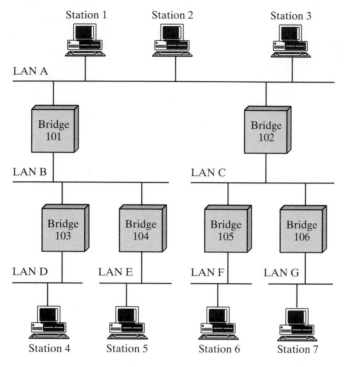

**FIGURE 14.5** Configuration of bridges and LANs.

E, then either bridge 101 or bridge 107 could forward the frame. It would appear preferable for bridge 107 to forward the frame, as it will involve only one *hop*, whereas if the frame travels through bridge 101, it must suffer two hops. Another consideration is that there may be changes in the configuration. For example, bridge 107 may fail, in which case subsequent frames from station 1 to station 5 should go through bridge 101. We can say, then, that the routing capability must take into account the topology of the internet configuration and may need to be dynamically altered.

Figure 14.6 suggests that a bridge knows the identity of each station on each LAN. In a large configuration, such an arrangement is unwieldy. Furthermore, as stations are added to and dropped from LANs, all directories of station location must be updated. It would facilitate the development of a routing capability if all MAC-level addresses were in the form of a network part and a station part. For example, the IEEE 802.5 standard suggests that 16-bit MAC addresses consist of a 7-bit LAN number and an 8-bit station number, and that 48-bit addresses consist of a 14-bit LAN number and a 32-bit station number.[1] In the remainder of this discussion, we assume that all MAC addresses include a LAN number and that routing is based on the use of that portion of the address only.

---

[1] The remaining bit in the 16-bit format is used to indicate whether this is a group or individual address. Of the two remaining bits in the 48-bit format, one is used to indicate whether this is a group or individual address, and the other is used to indicate whether this is a locally administered or globally administered address.

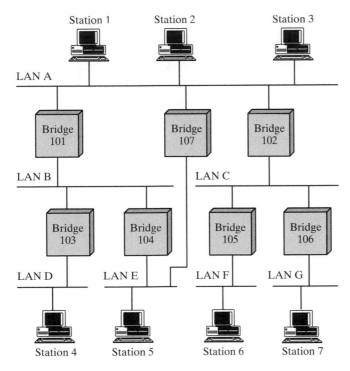

**FIGURE 14.6** Configuration of bridges and LANs, with alternate routes.

A variety of routing strategies have been proposed and implemented in recent years. The simplest and most common strategy is *fixed routing*. This strategy is suitable for small LAN collections and for interconnections that are relatively stable. More recently, two groups within the IEEE 802 committee have developed specifications for routing strategies. The IEEE 802.1 group has issued a standard for routing based on the use of a *spanning tree* algorithm. The token ring committee, IEEE 802.5, has issued its own specification, referred to as *source routing*. We examine these three strategies in turn.

## Fixed Routing

Fixed routing was introduced in our discussion of routing for packet-switching networks. For fixed routing with bridges, a route is selected for each source-destination pair of LANs in the internet. If alternate routes are available between two LANs, then typically the route with the least number of hops is selected. The routes are fixed, or at least only change when there is a change in the topology of the internet.

Figure 14.7 shows a fixed-routing design for the configuration of Figure 14.6. A central routing matrix shows, for each source-destination pair of LANs, the identity of the first bridge on the route. So, for example, the route from LAN E to LAN F begins by going through bridge 107 to LAN A. Again, consulting the matrix, the route from LAN A to LAN F goes through bridge 102 to LAN C. Finally, the route from LAN C to LAN F is directly through bridge 105. Thus, the

## CENTRAL ROUTING DIRECTORY

| | | A | B | C | D | E | F | G |
|---|---|---|---|---|---|---|---|---|
| | | | | | Source LAN | | | |
| | A | — | 101 | 102 | 103 | 107 | 105 | 106 |
| | B | 101 | — | 102 | 103 | 104 | 105 | 106 |
| | C | 102 | 101 | — | 103 | 107 | 105 | 106 |
| Destination LAN | D | 101 | 103 | 102 | — | 104 | 105 | 106 |
| | E | 107 | 104 | 102 | 103 | — | 105 | 106 |
| | F | 102 | 101 | 105 | 103 | 107 | — | 106 |
| | G | 102 | 101 | 106 | 103 | 107 | 105 | — |

**Bridge 101 Table**

| from LAN A | | from LAN B | |
|---|---|---|---|
| Dest | Next | Dest | Next |
| B | B | A | A |
| C | — | C | A |
| D | B | D | — |
| E | — | E | — |
| F | — | F | A |
| G | — | G | A |

**Bridge 102 Table**

| from LAN A | | from LAN C | |
|---|---|---|---|
| Dest | Next | Dest | Next |
| B | — | A | A |
| C | C | B | A |
| D | — | D | A |
| E | — | E | A |
| F | C | F | — |
| G | C | G | — |

**Bridge 103 Table**

| from LAN B | | from LAN D | |
|---|---|---|---|
| Dest | Next | Dest | Next |
| A | — | A | B |
| C | — | B | B |
| D | D | C | B |
| E | — | E | B |
| F | — | F | B |
| G | — | G | B |

**Bridge 104 Table**

| from LAN B | | from LAN E | |
|---|---|---|---|
| Dest | Next | Dest | Next |
| A | — | A | — |
| C | — | B | B |
| D | — | C | — |
| E | E | D | B |
| F | — | F | — |
| G | — | G | — |

**Bridge 105 Table**

| from LAN C | | from LAN F | |
|---|---|---|---|
| Dest | Next | Dest | Next |
| A | — | A | C |
| B | — | B | C |
| D | — | C | C |
| E | — | D | C |
| F | F | E | C |
| G | — | G | C |

**Bridge 106 Table**

| from LAN C | | from LAN G | |
|---|---|---|---|
| Dest | Next | Dest | Next |
| A | — | A | C |
| B | — | B | C |
| D | — | C | C |
| E | — | D | C |
| F | — | E | C |
| G | G | F | C |

**Bridge 107 Table**

| from LAN A | | from LAN E | |
|---|---|---|---|
| Dest | Next | Dest | Next |
| B | — | A | A |
| C | — | B | — |
| D | — | C | A |
| E | E | D | — |
| F | — | F | A |
| G | — | G | A |

**FIGURE 14.7    Fixed routing (using Figure 14.6).**

complete route from LAN E to LAN F is bridge 107, LAN A, bridge 102, LAN C, bridge 105.

Only one column of this matrix is needed in each bridge for each LAN to which it attaches. For example, bridge 105 has two tables, one for frames arriving from LAN C and one for frames arriving from LAN F. The table shows, for each possible destination MAC address, the identity of the LAN to which the bridge should forward the frame. The table labeled "From LAN C" is derived from the column labeled C in the routing matrix. Every entry in that column that contains bridge number 105 results in an entry in the corresponding table in bridge 105.

Once the directories have been established, routing is a simple matter. A bridge copies each incoming frame on each of its LANs. If the destination MAC address corresponds to an entry in its routing table, the frame is retransmitted on the appropriate LAN.

The fixed routing strategy is widely used in commercially available products; it has the advantage of simplicity and minimal processing requirements. However, in a complex internet, in which bridges may be dynamically added and in which failures must be allowed for, this strategy is too limited. In the next two subsections, we cover more powerful alternatives.

## Spanning Tree Routing

The spanning tree approach is a mechanism in which bridges automatically develop a routing table and update that table in response to changing topology. The algorithm consists of three mechanisms: frame forwarding, address learning, and loop resolution.

### Frame Forwarding

In this scheme, a bridge maintains a *filtering database*, which is based on MAC address. Each entry consists of a MAC individual or group address, a port number, and an aging time (described below); we can interpret this in the following fashion. A station is listed with a given port number if it is on the *same side* of the bridge as the port. For example, for bridge 102 of Figure 14.5, stations on LANs C, F, and G are on the same side of the bridge as the LAN C port; and stations on LANs A, B, D, and E are on the same side of the bridge as the LAN A port. When a frame is received on any port, the bridge must decide whether that frame is to be forwarded through the bridge and out through one of the bridge's other ports. Suppose that a bridge receives a MAC frame on port $x$. The following rules are applied (Figure 14.8):

1. Search the forwarding database to determine if the MAC address is listed for any port except port $x$.
2. If the destination MAC address is not found, flood the frame by sending it out on all ports except the port by which it arrived.
3. If the destination address is in the forwarding database for some port $y \neq x$, then determine whether port $y$ is in a blocking or a forwarding state. For reasons explained below, a port may sometimes be blocked, which prevents it from receiving or transmitting frames.

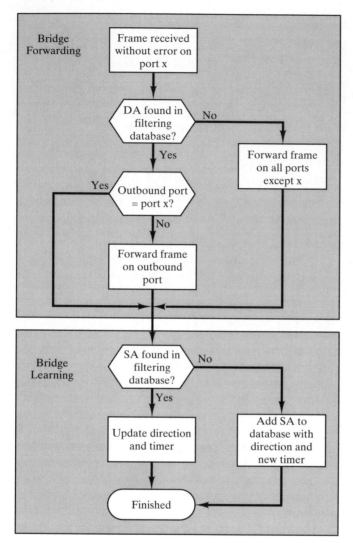

**FIGURE 14.8**   Bridge forwarding and learning.

4. If port *y* is not blocked, transmit the frame through port *y* onto the LAN to which that port attaches.

Rule (2) is needed because of the dynamic nature of the filtering database. When a bridge is initialized, the database is empty. Because the bridge does not know where to send the frame, it floods the frame onto all of its LANs except the LAN on which the frame arrives. As the bridge gains information, the flooding activity subsides.

## Address Learning

The above scheme is based on the use of a filtering database that indicates the direction, from the bridge, of each destination station. This information can be preloaded into the bridge, as in static routing. However, an effective automatic mechanism for learning the direction of each station is desirable. A simple scheme for acquiring this information is based on the use of the source address field in each MAC frame (Figure 14.8).

When a frame arrives on a particular port, it clearly has come from the direction of the incoming LAN. The source address field of the frame indicates the source station. Thus, a bridge can update its filtering database for that MAC address. To allow for changes in topology, each entry in the database is equipped with an aging timer. When a new entry is added to the database, its timer is set; the recommended default value is 300 seconds. If the timer expires, then the entry is eliminated from the database, as the corresponding direction information may no longer be valid. Each time a frame is received, its source address is checked against the database. If the entry is already in the database, the entry is updated (the direction may have changed) and the timer is reset. If the entry is not in the database, a new entry is created, with its own timer.

The above discussion indicated that the individual entries in the database are station addresses. If a two-level address structure (LAN number, station number) is used, then only LAN addresses need to be entered in the database. Both schemes work the same. The only difference is that the use of station addresses requires a much larger database than the use of LAN addresses.

Note from Figure 14.8 that the bridge learning process is applied to all frames, not just those that are forwarded.

## Spanning Tree Algorithm

The address learning mechanism described above is effective if the topology of the internet is a tree; that is, if there are no alternate routes in the network. The existence of alternate routes means that there is a closed loop. For example in Figure 14.6, the following is a closed loop: LAN A, bridge 101, LAN B, bridge 104, LAN E, bridge 107, LAN A.

To see the problem created by a closed loop, consider Figure 14.9. At time $t_0$, station A transmits a frame addressed to station B. The frame is captured by both bridges. Each bridge updates its database to indicate that station A is in the direction of LAN X, and retransmits the frame on LAN Y. Say that bridge $\alpha$ retransmits at time $t_1$ and bridge $\beta$ a short time later, $t_2$. Thus, B will receive two copies of the frame. Furthermore, each bridge will receive the other's transmission on LAN Y. Note that each transmission is a MAC frame with a source address of A and a destination address of B. Each bridge, then, will update its database to indicate that station A is in the direction of LAN Y. Neither bridge is capable now of forwarding a frame addressed to station A.

But the problem is potentially more serious. Assume that the two bridges do not yet know of the existence of station B. In this case, we have the following scenario. A transmits a frame addressed to B. Each bridge captures the frame. Then, each bridge, because it does not have information about B, automatically retransmits a copy of the frame on LAN Y. The frame transmitted by bridge $\alpha$ is captured by station B *and* by bridge $\beta$. Because bridge $\beta$ does not know where B is, it takes this frame and retransmits it on LAN X. Similarly, bridge $\alpha$ receives bridge $\beta$'s transmission on LAN Y and retransmits the frame on LAN X. There are now two

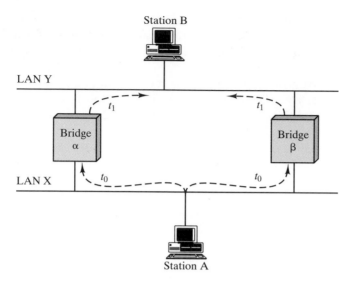

**FIGURE 14.9**  Loop of bridges.

frames on LAN X that will be picked up for retransmission on LAN Y. This process repeats indefinitely.

To overcome the above problem, a simple result from graph theory is used: For any connected graph, consisting of nodes and edges connecting pairs of nodes, there is a spanning tree of edges that maintains the connectivity of the graph but contains no closed loops. In terms of internets, each LAN corresponds to a graph node, and each bridge corresponds to a graph edge. Thus, in Figure 14.6, the removal of one (and only one) of bridges 107, 101, or 104, results in a spanning tree. What is desired is to develop a simple algorithm by which the bridges of the internet can exchange sufficient information to automatically (without user intervention) derive a spanning tree. The algorithm must be dynamic. That is, when a topology change occurs, the bridges must be able to discover this fact and automatically derive a new spanning tree.

The algorithm is based on the use of the following:

1. Each bridge is assigned a unique identifier; in essence, the identifier consists of a MAC address for the bridge plus a priority level.
2. There is a special group MAC address that means "all bridges on this LAN." When a MAC frame is transmitted with the group address in the destination address field, all of the bridges on the LAN will capture that frame and interpret it as a frame addressed to itself.
3. Each port of a bridge is uniquely identified within the bridge, with a *port identifier*.

With this information established, the bridges are able to exchange routing information in order to determine a spanning tree of the internet. We will explain the operation of the algorithm using Figures 14.10 and 14.11 as an example. The following concepts are needed in the creation of the spanning tree:

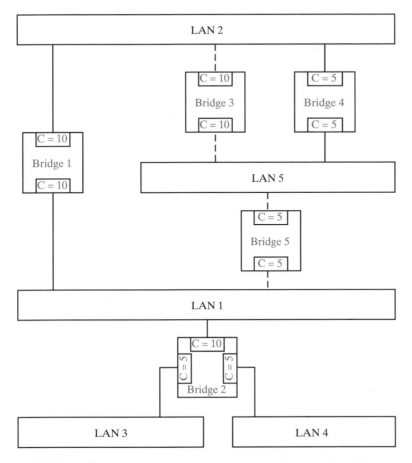

**FIGURE 14.10**  Example configuration for spanning tree algorithm.

- **Root bridge.** The bridge with the lowest value of bridge identifier is chosen to be the root of the spanning tree.
- **Path cost.** Associated with each port on each bridge is a path cost, which is the cost of transmitting a frame onto a LAN through that port. A path between two stations will pass through 0 or more bridges. At each bridge, the cost of transmission is added to give a total cost for a particular path. In the simplest case, all path costs would be assigned a value of 1; thus, the cost of a path would simply be a count of the number of bridges along the path. Alternatively, costs could be assigned in inverse proportion to the data rate of the corresponding LAN, or any other criterion chosen by the network manager.
- **Root port.** Each bridge discovers the first hop on the minimum-cost path to the root bridge. The port used for that hop is labeled the root port. When the cost is equal for two ports, the lower port number is selected so that a unique spanning tree is constructed.

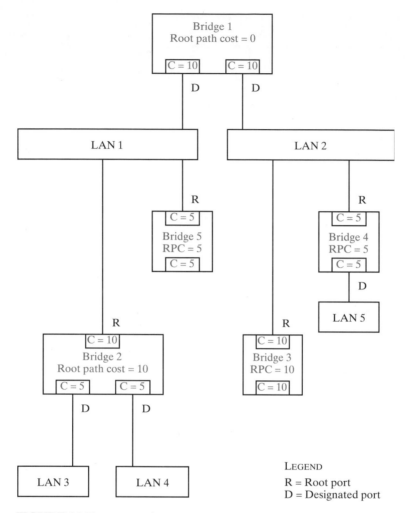

**FIGURE 14.11**   Spanning tree for configuration of Figure 14.10.

- **Root path cost.** For each bridge, the cost of the path to the root bridge with minimum cost (the path that starts at the root port) is the root path cost for that bridge.
- **Designated bridge, designated port.** On each LAN, one bridge is chosen to be the designated bridge. This is the bridge on that LAN that provides the minimum cost path to the root bridge. This is the only bridge allowed to forward frames from the LAN for which it is the designated bridge toward the root bridge. The port of the designated bridge that attaches the bridge to the LAN is the designated port. For all LANs to which the root bridge is attached, the root bridge is the designated bridge. All internet traffic to and from the LAN passes through the designated port.

In general terms, the spanning tree is constructed in the following fashion:

1. Determine the root bridge.
2. Determine the root port on all other bridges.
3. Determine the designated port on each LAN. This will be the port with the minimum root path cost. In the case of two or more bridges with the same root path cost, the highest-priority bridge is chosen as the designated bridge. If the designated bridge has two or more ports attached to this LAN, then the port with the lowest value of port identifier is chosen.

By this process, when two LANs are directly connected by more than one bridge, all of the bridges but one are eliminated. This cuts any loops that involve two LANs. It can be demonstrated that this process also eliminates all loops involving more than two LANs and that connectivity is preserved. Thus, this process discovers a spanning tree for the given internet. In our example, the solid lines indicate the bridge ports that participate in the spanning tree.

The steps outlined above require that the bridges exchange information. The information is exchanged in the form of bridge protocol data units (BPDUs). A BPDU transmitted by one bridge is addressed to and received by all of the other bridges on the same LAN. Each BPDU contains the following information:

- The identifier of this bridge and the port on this bridge
- The identifier of the bridge that this bridge considers to be the root
- The root path cost for this bridge

To begin, all bridges consider themselves to be the root bridge. Each bridge will broadcast a BPDU on each of its LANs that asserts this fact. On any given LAN, only one claimant will have the lowest-valued identifier and will maintain its belief. Over time, as BPDUs propagate, the identity of the lowest-valued bridge identifier throughout the internet will be known to all bridges. The root bridge will regularly broadcast the fact that it is the root bridge on all of the LANs to which it is attached; this allows the bridges on those LANs to determine their root port and the fact that they are directly connected to the root bridge. Each of these bridges in turn broadcasts a BPDU on the other LANs to which it is attached (all LANs except the one on its root port), indicating that it is one hop away from the root bridge. This activity is propagated throughout the internet. Every time that a bridge receives a BPDU, it transmits BPDUs, indicating the identity of the root bridge and the number of hops to reach the root bridge. On any LAN, the bridge claiming to be the one that is closest to the root becomes the designated bridge.

We can trace some of this activity with the configuration in Figure 14.10. At startup time, bridges 1, 3, and 4 all transmit BPDUs on LAN 2, each claiming to be the root bridge. When bridge 3 receives the transmission from bridge 1, it recognizes a superior claimant and defers. Bridge 3 has also received a claiming BPDU from bridge 5 via LAN 5. Bridge 3 recognizes that bridge 1 has a superior claim to be the root bridge; it therefore assigns its LAN 2 port to be its root port, and sets the root path cost to 10. By similar actions, bridge 4 ends up with a root path cost of 5 via LAN 2; bridge 5 has a root path cost of 5 via LAN 1; and bridge 2 has a root path cost of 10 via LAN 1.

Now consider the assignment of designated bridges. On LAN 5, all three bridges transmit BPDUs, attempting to assert a claim to be designated bridge. Bridge 3 defers because it receives BPDUs from the other bridges that have a lower root path cost. Bridges 4 and 5 have the same root path cost, but bridge 4 has the higher priority and therefore becomes the designated bridge.

The results of all this activity are shown in Figure 14.11. Only the designated bridge on each LAN is allowed to forward frames. All of the ports on all of the other bridges are placed in a blocking state. After the spanning tree is established, bridges continue to periodically exchange BPDUs to be able to react to any change in topology, cost assignments, or priority assignment. Anytime that a bridge receives a BPDU on a port, it makes two assessments:

1. If the BPDU arrives on a port that is considered the designated port, does the transmitting port have a better claim to be the designated port?
2. Should this port be my root port?

## Source Routing

The IEEE 802.5 committee has developed a bridge routing approach referred to as source routing. With this approach, the sending station determines the route that the frame will follow and includes the routing information with the frame; bridges read the routing information to determine if they should forward the frame.

### Basic Operation

The basic operation of the algorithm can be described by making reference to the configuration in Figure 14.12. A frame from station X can reach station Z by either of the following routes:

- LAN 1, bridge B1, LAN 3, bridge B3, LAN 2
- LAN 1, bridge B2, LAN 4, bridge B4, LAN 2

Station X may choose one of these two routes and place the information, in the form of a sequence of LAN and bridge identifiers, in the frame to be transmitted. When a bridge receives a frame, it will forward that frame if the bridge is on the designated route; all other frames are discarded. In this case, if the first route above is specified, bridges B1 and B3 will forward the frame; if the second route is specified, bridges B2 and B4 will forward the frame.

Note that with this scheme, bridges need not maintain routing tables. The bridge makes the decision whether or not to forward a frame solely on the basis of the routing information contained in that frame. All that is required is that the bridge know its own unique identifier and the identifier of each LAN to which it is attached. The responsibility for designing the route falls to the source station.

For this scheme to work, there must be a mechanism by which a station can determine a route to any destination station. Before addressing this issue, we need to discuss various types of routing directives.

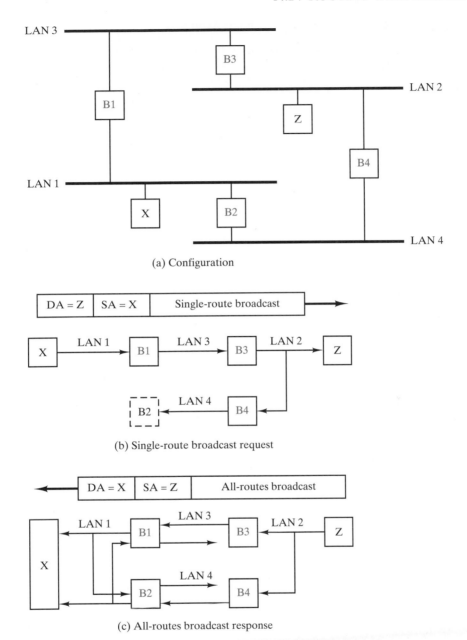

(a) Configuration

(b) Single-route broadcast request

(c) All-routes broadcast response

**FIGURE 14.12**   Route discovery example.

## Routing Directives and Addressing Modes

The source routing scheme developed by the IEEE 802.5 committee includes four different types of routing directives. Each frame that is transmitted includes an indicator of the type of routing desired. The four directive types are

- **Null.** No routing is desired. In this case, the frame can only be delivered to stations on the same LAN as the source station.
- **Nonbroadcast.** The frame includes a route, consisting of a sequence of LAN numbers and bridge numbers, that defines a unique route from the source station to the destination station. Only bridges on that route forward the frame, and only a single copy of the frame is delivered to the destination station.
- **All-routes broadcast.** The frame will reach each LAN of the internet by all possible routes. Thus, each bridge will forward each frame once to each of its ports in a direction away from the source node, and multiple copies of the frame may appear on a LAN. The destination station will receive one copy of the frame for each possible route through the network.
- **Single-route broadcast.** Regardless of the destination address of the frame, the frame will appear once, and only once, on each LAN in the internet. For this effect to be achieved, the frame is forwarded by all bridges that are on a spanning tree (with the source node as the root) of the internet. The destination station receives a single copy of the frame.

Let us first examine the potential application of each of these four types of routing, and then examine the mechanisms that may be employed to achieve these procedures. First, consider null routing. In this case the bridges that share the LAN with the source station are told not to forward the frame; this will be done if the intended destination is on the same LAN as the source station. Nonbroadcast routing is used when the two stations are not on the same LAN and the source station knows a route that can be used to reach the destination station. Only the bridges on that route will forward the frame.

The remaining two types of routing can be used by the source to discover a route to the destination. For example, the source station can use all-routes broadcasting to send a request frame to the intended destination. The destination returns a response frame on each of the routes, using nonbroadcast routing, followed by the incoming request frame. The source station can pick one of these routes and send future frames on that route. Alternatively, the source station could use single-route broadcasting to send a single request frame to the destination station. The destination station could send its response frame via all-routes broadcasting. The incoming frames would reveal all of the possible routes to the destination station, and the source station could pick one of these for future transmissions. Finally, single-route broadcasting could be used for group addressing, as discussed below.

Now consider the mechanisms for implementing these various routing directives. Each frame must include an indicator of which of the four types of routing is required. For null routing, the frame is ignored by the bridge. For nonbroadcast routing, the frame includes an ordered list of LAN numbers and bridge numbers. When a bridge receives a nonbroadcast frame, it forwards the frame only if the routing information contains the sequence LAN $i$, Bridge $x$, LAN $j$, where

LAN $i$ = LAN from which the frame arrived

Bridge $x$ = this bridge

LAN $j$ = another LAN to which this bridge is attached

For all-routes broadcasting, the source station marks the frame, but includes no routing information. Each bridge that forwards the frame will add its bridge number and the outgoing LAN number to the frame's routing information field. Thus, when the frame reaches its destination, it will include a sequenced list of all LANs and bridges visited. To prevent the endless repetition and looping of frames, a bridge obeys the following rule. When an all-routes broadcast frame is received, the bridge examines the routing information field. If the field contains the number of a LAN to which the bridge is attached, the bridge will refrain from forwarding the frame on that LAN. Put the other way, the bridge will only forward the frame to a LAN that the frame has not already visited.

Finally, for single-route broadcasting, a spanning tree of the internet must be developed. This can either be done automatically, as in the 802.1 specification, or manually. In either case, as with the 802.1 strategy, one bridge on each LAN is the designated bridge for that LAN, and is the only one that forwards single-route frames.

It is worth noting the relationship between addressing mode and routing directive. There are three types of MAC addresses:

- **Individual.** The address specifies a unique destination station.
- **Group.** The address specifies a group of destination addresses; this is also referred to as *multicast*.
- **All-stations.** The address specifies all stations that are capable of receiving this frame; this is also referred to as *broadcast*. We will refrain from using this latter term as it is also used in the source routing terminology.

In the case of a single, isolated LAN, group and all-stations addresses refer to stations on the same LAN as the source station. In an internet, it may be desirable to transmit a frame to multiple stations on multiple LANs. Indeed, because a set of LANs interconnected by bridges should appear to the user as a single LAN, the ability to do group and all-stations addressing across the entire internet is mandatory.

Table 14.1 summarizes the relationship between routing specification and addressing mode. If no routing is specified, then all addresses refer only to the immediate LAN. If nonbroadcast routing is specified, then addresses may refer to any station on any LAN visited on the nonbroadcast route. From an addressing point of view, this combination is not generally useful for group and all-stations addressing. If either the all-routes or single-route specification is included in a frame, then all stations on the internet can be addressed. Thus, the total internet acts as a single network from the point of view of MAC addresses. Because less traffic is generated by the single-route specification, this single-network characteristic is to be preferred for group and all-stations addressing. Note also that the single-route mechanism in source routing is equivalent to the 802.1 spanning tree

**TABLE 14.1** Effects of various combinations of addressing and source routing.

| Addressing mode | Routing specification | | | |
|---|---|---|---|---|
| | No routing | Nonbroadcast | All-routes | Single-route |
| *Individual* | Received by station if it is on the same LAN | Received by station if it is on one of the LANs on the route | Received by station if it is on any LAN | Received by station if it is on any LAN |
| *Group* | Received by all group members on the same LAN | Received by all group members on all LANs visited on this route | Received by all group members on all LANs | Received by all group members on all LANs |
| *All-Stations* | Received by all stations on the same LAN | Received by all stations on all LANs visited on this route | Received by all stations on all LANs | Received by all stations on all LANs |

approach. Thus, the spanning tree approach supports both group and all-stations addressing.

### Route Discovery and Selection

With source routing, bridges are relieved of the burden of storing and using routing information. Thus, the burden falls on the stations that wish to transmit frames. Clearly, some mechanism is needed by which the source stations can know the route by which frames are to be sent. Three strategies suggest themselves:

1. Manually load the information into each station. This is simple and effective but has several drawbacks. First, anytime that the configuration is changed, the routing information at all stations must be updated. Secondly, this approach does not provide for automatic adjustment in the face of the failure of a bridge or LAN.
2. One station on a LAN can query other stations on the same LAN for routing information about distant stations. This approach may reduce the overall amount of routing messages that must be transmitted, compared to options 3 or 4, below. However, at least one station on each LAN must have the needed routing information, so this is not a complete solution.
3. When a station needs to learn the route to a destination station, it engages in a dynamic route discovery procedure.

Option 3 is the most flexible and the one that is specified by IEEE 802.5; as was mentioned earlier, two approaches are possible. The source station can transmit an all-routes request frame to the destination. Thus, all possible routes to the destination are discovered. The destination station can then send back a nonbroadcast response on each of the discovered routes, allowing the source to choose which route to follow in subsequently transmitting the frame. This approach generates quite a bit of both forward and backward traffic, and requires the destination station to receive and transmit a number of frames. An alternative is for the source station to transmit a single-route request frame. Only one copy of this frame will reach the destination. The destination responds with an all-routes response frame, which generates all possible routes back to the source. Again, the source can choose among these alternative routes.

Figure 14.12 illustrates the latter approach. Assume that the spanning tree that has been chosen for this internet consists of bridges B1, B3, and B4. In this example, station X wishes to discover a route to station Z. Station X issues a single-route request frame. Bridge B2 is not on the spanning tree and so does not forward the frame. The other bridges do forward the frame, and it reaches station Z. Note that bridge B4 forwards the frame to LAN 4, although this is not necessary; it is simply an effect of the spanning tree mechanism. When Z receives this frame, it responds with an all-routes frame. Two messages reach X: one on the path LAN 2, B3, LAN 3, B1, LAN 1, and the other on the path LAN 2, B4, LAN 4, B2, LAN 1. Note that a frame that arrived by the latter route is received by bridge B1 and forwarded onto LAN 3. However, when bridge B3 receives this frame, it sees in the routing information field that the frame has already visited LAN 2; therefore, it does not forward the frame. A similar fate occurs for the frame that follows the first route and is forwarded by bridge B2.

Once a collection of routes has been discovered, the source station needs to select one of the routes. The obvious criterion would be to select the minimum-hop route. Alternatively, a minimum-cost route could be selected, where the cost of a network is inversely proportional to its data rate. In either case, if two or more routes are equivalent by the chosen criterion, then there are two alternatives:

1. Choose the route corresponding to the response message that arrives first. One may assume that that particular route is less congested than the others as the frame on that route arrived earliest.
2. Choose randomly. This should have the effect, over time, of leveling the load among the various bridges.

Another point to consider is how often to update a route. Routes should certainly be changed in response to network failures and should perhaps be changed in response to network congestion. If connection-oriented logical link control is used (see Chapter 6), then one possibility is to rediscover the route with each new connection. Another alternative, which works with either connection-oriented or connectionless service, is to associate a timer with each selected route, and to rediscover the route when its time expires.

## 14.3 ATM LAN EMULATION

One issue that was not addressed in our discussion of ATM LANs in Section 13.4 has to do with the interoperability of end systems on a variety of interconnected LANs. End systems attached directly to one of the legacy LANs implement the

MAC layer appropriate to that type of LAN. End systems attached directly to an ATM network implement the ATM and AAL protocols. As a result, there are three areas of compatibility to consider:

1. Interaction between an end system on an ATM network and an end system on a legacy LAN.
2. Interaction between an end system on a legacy LAN and an end system on another legacy LAN of the same type (e.g., two IEEE 802.3 networks).
3. Interaction between an end system on a legacy LAN and an end system on another legacy LAN of a different type (e.g., an IEEE 802.3 network and an IEEE 802.5 network).

The most general solution to this problem is the router, which is explored in Chapter 16. In essence, the router operates at the level of the Internet Protocol (IP). All of the end systems implement IP, and all networks are interconnected with routers. If data are to travel beyond the scope of an individual LAN, they are directed to the local router. There, the LLC and MAC layers are stripped off, and the IP PDU is routed across one or more other networks to the destination LAN, where the appropriate LLC and MAC layers are invoked. Similarly, if one or both of the end systems are directly attached to an ATM network, the AAL and ATM layers are stripped off or added to an IP PDU.

While this approach is effective, it introduces a certain amount of processing overhead and delay at each router. In very large internetworks, these delays can become substantial. Networks of 1000 routers are increasingly common, and networks of as many as 10,000 routers have been installed [LANG95]. A technique that exploits the efficiency of ATM and that reduces the number of required routers is desired.

Another way to approach the problem is to convert all end systems such that they operate directly on ATM. In this case, there is a seamless technology used throughout any network, including local and wide area components. However, with millions of Ethernet and token ring nodes installed on today's shared-media LANs, most organizations simply can't afford a one-shot upgrade of all systems to ATM. In addition, although the cost of ATM interface cards is dropping, Ethernet and token ring interfaces remain cheaper for the time being.

In response to this need, the ATM Forum[2] has created a specification for the coexistence of legacy LANs and ATM LANs, known as ATM LAN emulation [ATM95]. The objective on ATM LAN emulation is to enable existing shared-

---

[2] The ATM Forum is a nonprofit international industry consortium, which is playing a crucial role in the development of ATM standards. In the ITU and the constituent member bodies from the participating countries, the process of developing standards is characterized by wide participation on the part of government, users, and industry representatives, and by consensus decision-making. This process can be quite time-consuming. While ITU-T has streamlined its efforts, the delays involved in developing standards is particularly significant in the area of ATM technology. Because of the strong level of interest in ATM, the ATM Forum was created with the goal of accelerating the development of ATM standards. The ATM Forum has seen more active participation from computing vendors than has been the case in ITU-T. Because the forum works on the basis of majority rule rather than consensus, it has been able to move rapidly to define some of the needed details for the implementation of ATM. This effort, in turn, has fed into the ITU-T standardization effort.

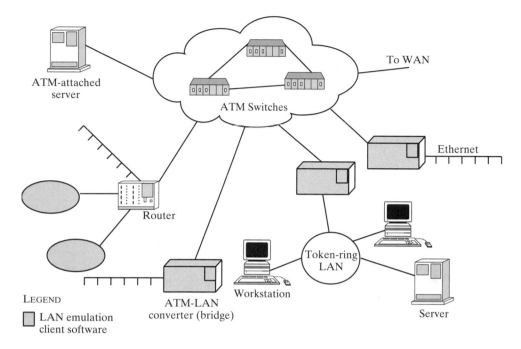

**FIGURE 14.13** Example ATM LAN emulation configuration.

media LAN nodes to interoperate across an ATM network and to interoperate with devices that connect directly to ATM switches.

Figure 14.13 illustrates the type of configuration that can be constructed using ATM LAN emulation. In its present form, the ATM specification satisfies two of the three requirements listed earlier; namely, ATM LAN emulation defines the following:

1. The way in which end systems on two separate LANs of the same type (same MAC layer) can exchange MAC frames across the ATM network.
2. The way in which an end system on a LAN can interoperate with an end system emulating the same LAN type and attached directly to an ATM switch.

The specification does not as yet address interoperability between end systems on different LANs with different MAC protocols.

## Protocol Architecture

Figure 14.14 indicates the protocol architecture involved in ATM LAN emulation. In this case, we are looking at the interaction of an ATM-attached system with an end system attached to a legacy LAN. Note that the end system attached to a legacy LAN is unaffected; it is able to use the ordinary repertoire of protocols, including the MAC protocol specific to this LAN and LLC running on top of the MAC. Thus, the end system runs TCP/IP over LLC, and various application-level protocols on top of that; the various application-level protocols are unaware that there is an

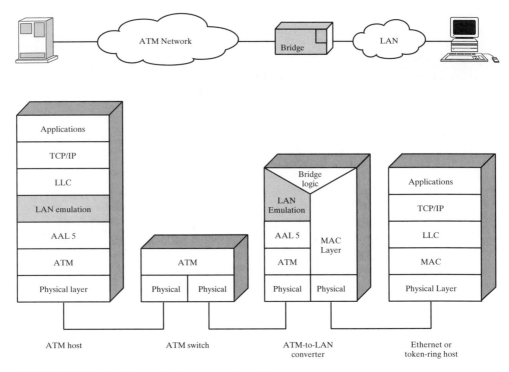

**FIGURE 14.14** LAN emulation protocol architecture.

ATM network underneath. The key to this diagram is the use of a bridge device known as an ATM-to-LAN converter.

In Figure 14.14, the bridge logic must be augmented by the capability of converting MAC frames to and from ATM cells. This is one of the key functions of the LAN emulation module. The ATM Forum specification calls for making use of AAL 5 to segment MAC frames into ATM cells and to reassemble incoming ATM cells into MAC frames. For outgoing ATM cells, the ATM-to-LAN converter connects in the usual fashion to an ATM switch as part of an ATM network.

Figure 14.14 shows the case in which a host on a legacy LAN is exchanging data with a host attached directly to an ATM network. To accommodate this exchange, the ATM host must include a LAN emulation module that accepts MAC frames from AAL and must pass up the contents to an LLC layer. Thus, the host is indeed emulating a LAN because it can receive and transmit MAC frames in the same format as the distant legacy LAN. From the point of view of end systems on the legacy LAN, the ATM host is just another end system with a MAC address. The entire LAN emulation process is transparent to existing systems implementing LLC and MAC.

## Emulated LANs

With the protocol architecture just described, it is possible to set up a number of logically independent, *emulated LANs*. An emulated LAN supports a single

MAC protocol, of which two types are currently defined: Ethernet/IEEE 802.3 and IEEE 802.5 (token ring). An emulated LAN consists of some combination of the following:

- End systems on one or more legacy LANs
- End systems attached directly to an ATM switch

Each end system on an emulated LAN must have a unique MAC address. Data interchange between end systems on the same emulated LAN involves the use of the MAC protocol and is transparent to the upper layers. That is, it appears to LLC that all of the end systems on an emulated LAN are on the same shared-medium LAN. Communication between end systems on different emulated LANs is possible only through routers or bridges. Note that the bridges or routers have to reassemble the cells into packets and then chop them up into cells to send them to another emulated LAN.

## LAN Emulation Clients and Servers

The discussion so far leaves out a number of issues that must be addressed, including the following:

1. Devices attached directly to ATM switches and to ATM-to-LAN converter systems have ATM-based addresses. How are translations made between these addresses and MAC addresses?
2. ATM makes use of a connection-oriented protocol involving virtual channels and virtual paths. How can the connectionless LAN MAC protocol be supported over this connection-oriented framework?
3. Multicasting and broadcasting on a shared-medium LAN is easily achieved. How is this capability carried over into the ATM environment?

To address these issues, the ATM Forum developed a capability based on a client/server approach, which is discussed next.

ATM LAN emulation requires two types of components: clients and servers. Clients operate on behalf of devices that are attached to legacy LANs and that use MAC addresses. A client is responsible for adding its MAC entities into the overall configuration and for dealing with the tasks associated with translating between MAC addresses and ATM addresses. Typically, a client would be provided in a router, in an ATM-attached server (see Figure 14.13), or perhaps in an ATM switch that directly connects to one of the above (referred to as an *edge switch*). Servers are responsible for integrating MAC entities into the overall configuration and for managing all of the associated tasks, such as finding addresses and emulating broadcasting. Servers may be implemented in separate components or in ATM switches. Each emulated LAN consists of one or more clients and a single LAN emulation service.

The LAN emulation service in fact comprises three types of servers, which perform separate tasks: the LAN Emulation Configuration Server (LECS), the LAN Emulation Server (LES), and the Broadcast and Unknown Server (BUS). The reason for breaking the server up into three modules is that a manager may decide to have more of one kind of server than another, for efficient operation, and may decide to distribute the servers physically to minimize the communications burden. Table 14.2 provides a brief definition of the three types of servers and of the client.

**TABLE 14.2** LAN emulation client and servers.

| Entity | Description |
|---|---|
| LAN Emulation Client (LEC) | Sets up control connections to LAN emulation servers; sets up data connections to other clients; maps MAC addresses to ATM addresses. |
| LAN Emulation Configuration Server (LECS) | Assists client in selecting an LES. |
| LAN Emulation Server (LES) | Performs initial address mapping; accepts clients. |
| Broadcast and Unknown Server (BUS) | Performs multicasting. |

Figure 14.15 indicates the way in which clients and the three types of servers interact. The client can establish virtual channel connections, called control connections, to the LECS and the LES. The link to the LECS is used by an LEC to gain

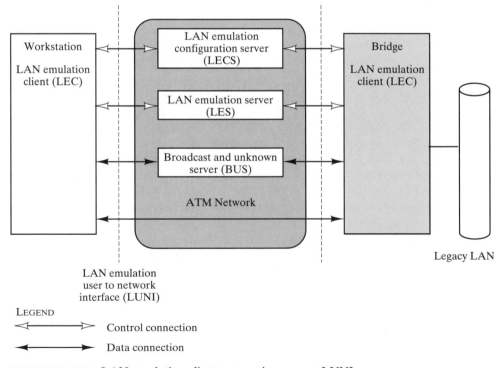

**FIGURE 14.15** LAN emulation client connections across LUNI.

entrance to an emulated LAN and to locate an LES. The LES is responsible for registering new clients and their MAC addresses into an emulated LAN, as well as for mapping between MAC addresses and ATM addresses.

Once a client and its end systems have joined an emulated LAN, most of the work is done across virtual channel connections called data connections. MAC frames, segmented into ATM cells, are transmitted via data connections between end systems on the same emulated LAN. For a unicast transmission, a virtual channel connection is set up between two clients; this is the protocol setup illustrated in Figure 14.14. Finally, the data connection between a client and a BUS carries transmissions intended for broadcast or multicast, and it also is used to handle transmissions in which the sending client does not know the address of the receiving client.

## LAN Emulation Scenario

To clarify the concepts involved in LAN emulation, let us follow a typical sequence of events.

### Initialization

To join an emulated LAN, a client must begin by obtaining the ATM address of the LAN emulation server (LES) for that emulated LAN. Typically, the way in which this is done is that the client establishes a virtual channel connection to the LAN emulation configuration server (LECS).

There are three possible techniques by which the client can discover the LECS ATM address so that it can perform initialization:

1. The client can use a network management procedure defined as part of the ATM Forum's Interim Local Management Interface (ILMI). This procedure takes place between the client and ILMI software in the associated ATM switch. If the ILMI software has the LECS address for the requested emulated LAN, it provides that address to the client. The client then establishes a virtual channel connection to the LECS.

2. If the ILMI procedure fails, the client tries a predefined address listed in the specification, called the *well-known address*. This address is supposed to correspond to an LECS on any ATM network that conforms to the ATM Forum specification. The client uses this address to establish a virtual channel connection to the LECS.

3. If the well-known address fails, the client tries the well-known *virtual path identifier/virtual channel identifier* defined in the ATM Forum specification. When the ATM network is configured, the network manager can establish this permanent virtual path/virtual channel.

### Configuration

Once a connection is established between the client and the LECS, the client can engage in a dialogue with the LECS. Based upon its own policies, configuration database, and information provided by the client, the LECS assigns the client to a particular emulated LAN service by giving the client the LES's ATM address. The LECS returns information to the client about the emulated LAN, including MAC protocol, maximum frame size, and the name of the emulated LAN. The name may be something defined by the configuration manager to be meaningful in defining logical workgroups (e.g., finance, personnel).

### Joining

The client now has the information it needs to join an emulated LAN. It proceeds by setting up a control connection to the LES. The client then issues a JOIN REQUEST to the LES, which includes the client's ATM address, its MAC address, LAN type, maximum frame size, a client identifier, and a proxy indication. This latter parameter indicates whether this client corresponds to an end system attached directly to an ATM switch or is a LAN-to-ATM converter supporting end systems on a legacy LAN.

If the LES is prepared to accept this client, it sends back a JOIN RESPONSE, indicating acceptance. Otherwise, it sends back a JOIN RESPONSE indicating rejection.

### Registration and BUS Initialization

Once a client has joined an emulated LAN, it goes through a registration procedure. If the client is a proxy for a number of end systems on a legacy LAN, it sends a list of all MAC addresses on the legacy LAN that are to be part of this emulated LAN to the LES.

Next, the client sends a request to the LES for the ATM address of the BUS. This address functions as the broadcast address for the emulated LAN and is used when a MAC frame is to be broadcast to all stations on the emulated LAN. The client then sets up a data connection to the BUS.

### Data Transfer

Once a client is registered, it is able to send and receive MAC frames. First, consider the sending of MAC frames. In the case of an end system attached to an ATM switch, the end system generates its own MAC frames for transmission to one or more other end systems on the emulated LAN. In the case of a proxy client, it functions as a bridge that receives MAC frames from end systems on its legacy LAN and then transmits those MAC frames. In both cases, an outgoing MAC frame must be segmented into ATM cells and transmitted over a virtual channel. There are three cases to consider:

- Unicast MAC frame, ATM address known
- Unicast MAC frame, address unknown
- Multicast or broadcast MAC frame

If the client knows the ATM address of the unicast frame, it checks whether it has a virtual data connection already established to the destination client. If so, it sends the frame over that connection (as a series of ATM cells); otherwise, it uses ATM signaling to set up the connection and then sends the frame.

If the address is unknown, the sending client performs two actions. First, the client sends the frame to the BUS over the data connection that it maintains with the BUS. The BUS, in turn, either transmits the frame to the intended MAC destination or else broadcasts the frame to all MAC destinations on the emulated LAN. In the latter case, the intended destination will recognize its MAC address and accept the frame. Second, the client attempts to learn the ATM address for this MAC for future reference. It does this by sending an LE_ARP_REQUEST (LAN Emulation Address Resolution Protocol Request) command to the LES; the command includes the MAC address for which an ATM address is desired. If the LES knows the ATM address, it returns the address to the client in an LE_ARP_RESPONSE. Otherwise, the LES holds the request while it attempts to learn the ATM address. The LES sends out its own LE_ARP_REQUEST to all clients on the emulated LAN. The client that represents the MAC address in question will return its ATM address to the LES, which can then send that address back to the original requesting client.

Finally, if the MAC frame is a multicast or broadcast frame, the sending client transmits the frame to the BUS over the virtual data connection it has to the BUS. The bus then replicates that frame and sends it over virtual data connections to all of the clients on the emulated LAN.

## 14.4 RECOMMENDED READING

The definitive study of bridges is [PERL92]. [BERT92] and [SPRA91] examine the performance implications of transparent bridging and source routing.

LAN emulation is explained in [TRUO95] and [JEFF94].

BERT92   Bertsekas, D. and Gallager, R. *Data Networks*. Englewood Cliffs, NJ: Prentice Hall, 1992.

JEFF94   Jeffries, R. "ATM LAN Emulation: The Inside Story." *Data Communications*, September 21, 1994.

PERL92   Perlman, R. *Interconnections: Bridges and Routers*. Reading, MA: Addison Wesley, 1992.

SPRA91   Spragins, J., Hammond, J., and Pawlikowski, K. *Telecommunications Protocols and Design*. Reading, MA: Addison-Wesley, 1991.

TRUO95   Truong, H. et al. "LAN Emulation on an ATM Network." *IEEE Communications Magazine*, May 1995.

## 14.5 PROBLEMS

14.1   The token ring MAC protocol specifies that the A and C bits may be set by a station on the ring to indicate address recognized and frame copied, respectively. This information is then available to the source station when the frame returns after circulating around the ring. If a bridge captures a frame and forwards it, should it set the A and C bits or not? Make a case for each policy.

14.2 Draw a figure similar to Figure 14.14 that shows the protocol architecture for the interconnection of two end systems on separate LANs (with the same MAC protocol) across an ATM switch.

# Communications Architecture and Protocols

## CHAPTER 15

# PROTOCOLS AND ARCHITECTURE

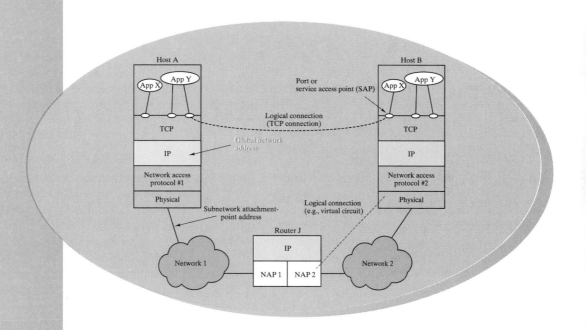

The purpose of this chapter is to serve as an overview and necessary background to the detailed material that follows in the remainder of Part Four. It will also serve to show how the concepts of Parts One through Three fit into the broader area of computer networks and computer communications.

We begin with an exposition of the concept of a communications protocol. It is shown that protocols are fundamental to all data communications. Next, we look at a way of systematically describing and implementing the communications function by viewing the communications task in terms of a column of layers, each of which contains protocols; this is the view of the now-famous Open Systems Interconnection (OSI) model.

Although the OSI model is almost universally accepted as the framework for discourse in this area, there is another model, known as the TCP/IP protocol architecture, which has gained commercial dominance at the expense of OSI. Most of the specific protocols described in Part Four are part of the TCP/IP suite of protocols. In this chapter, we provide an overview.

## 15.1 PROTOCOLS

We begin with an overview of characteristics of protocols. The reader should review the concepts of OSI and TCP/IP presented in Chapter 1 before proceeding. Following this overview, we look in more detail at OSI and TCP/IP.

### Characteristics

The concepts of distributed processing and computer networking imply that entities in different systems need to communicate. We use the terms *entity* and *system* in a very general sense. Examples of entities are user application programs, file transfer packages, data base management systems, electronic mail facilities, and terminals. Examples of systems are computers, terminals, and remote sensors. Note that in some cases the entity and the system in which it resides are coextensive (e.g., terminals). In general, an entity is anything capable of sending or receiving information, and a system is a physically distinct object that contains one or more entities.

For two entities to successfully communicate, they must "speak the same language." What is communicated, how it is communicated, and when it is communicated must conform to some mutually acceptable set of conventions between the entities involved. The set of conventions is referred to as a protocol, which may be defined as a set of rules governing the exchange of data between two entities. The key elements of a protocol are

- **Syntax.** Includes such things as data format, coding, and signal levels.
- **Semantics.** Includes control information for coordination and error handling.
- **Timing.** Includes speed matching and sequencing.

HDLC is an example of a protocol. The data to be exchanged must be sent in frames of a specific format (syntax). The control field provides a variety of regulatory functions, such as setting a mode and establishing a connection (semantics). Provisions are also included for flow control (timing). Most of Part Four will be devoted to discussing other examples of protocols.

Some important characteristics of a protocol are

- Direct/indirect
- Monolithic/structured
- Symmetric/asymmetric
- Standard/nonstandard

Communication between two entities may be direct or indirect. Figure 15.1 depicts possible situations. If two systems share a point-to-point link, the entities in these systems may communicate directly; that is, data and control information pass directly between entities with no intervening active agent. The same may be said of

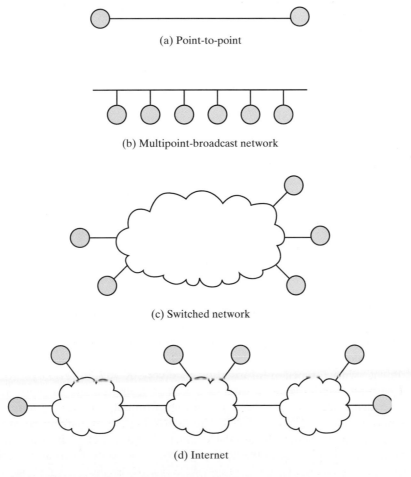

(a) Point-to-point

(b) Multipoint-broadcast network

(c) Switched network

(d) Internet

**FIGURE 15.1** Means of connection of communicating systems.

a multipoint configuration, although here the entities must be concerned with the issue of access control, making the protocol more complex. If systems connect through a switched communication network, a direct protocol is no longer possible. The two entities must depend on the functioning of other entities to exchange data. A more extreme case is a situation in which two entities do not even share the same switched network, but are indirectly connected through two or more networks. A set of such interconnected networks is termed an internet.

A protocol is either monolithic or structured. It should become clear as Part Four proceeds that the task of communication between entities on different systems is too complex to be handled as a unit. For example, consider an electronic mail package running on two computers connected by a synchronous HDLC link. To be truly monolithic, the package would need to include all of the HDLC logic. If the connection were over a packet-switched network, the package would still need the HDLC logic (or some equivalent) to attach to the network. It would also need logic for breaking up mail into packet-sized chunks, logic for requesting a virtual circuit, and so forth. Mail should only be sent when the destination system and entity are active and ready to receive; logic is needed for that kind of coordination, and, as we shall see, the list goes on. A change in any aspect means that this huge package must be modified, with the risk of introducing difficult-to-find bugs.

An alternative is to use structured design and implementation techniques. Instead of a single protocol, there is a set of protocols that exhibit a hierarchical or layered structure. Primitive functions are implemented in lower-level entities that provide services to higher-level entities. For example, there could be an HDLC module (entity) that is invoked by an electronic mail facility when needed, which is just another form of indirection; higher-level entities rely on lower-level entities to exchange data.

When structured protocol design is used, we refer to the hardware and software that implements the communications function as a communications architecture; the remainder of this chapter, after this section, is devoted to this concept.

A protocol may be either symmetric or asymmetric. Most of the protocols that we shall study are symmetric; that is, they involve communication between peer entities. Asymmetry may be dictated by the logic of an exchange (e.g., a client and a server process), or by the desire to keep one of the entities or systems as simple as possible. An example of the latter situation is the normal response mode of HDLC. Typically, this involves a computer that polls and selects a number of terminals. The logic on the terminal end is quite straightforward.

Finally, a protocol may be either standard or nonstandard. A nonstandard protocol is one built for a specific communications situation or, at most, a particular model of a computer. Thus, if $K$ different kinds of information sources have to communicate with $L$ types of information receivers, $K \times L$ different protocols are needed without standards and a total of $2 \times K \times L$ implementations are required (Figure 15.2a). If all systems shared a common protocol, only $K + L$ implementations would be needed (Figure 15.2b). The increasing use of distributed processing and the decreasing inclination of customers to remain locked into a single vendor dictate that all vendors implement protocols that conform to an agreed-upon standard.

Sources      Destinations     Sources      Destinations

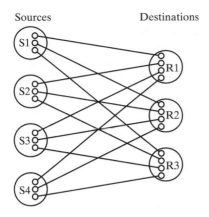
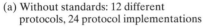
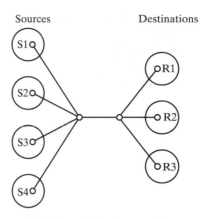

(a) Without standards: 12 different     (b) With standards: 1 protocol,
  protocols, 24 protocol implementations     7 implementations

**FIGURE 15.2** The use of standard protocols.

## Functions

Before turning to a discussion of communications architecture and the various levels of protocols, let us consider a rather small set of functions that form the basis of all protocols. Not all protocols have all functions; this would involve a significant duplication of effort. There are, nevertheless, many instances of the same type of function being present in protocols at different levels.

This discussion will, of necessity, be rather abstract; it does, however, provide an integrated overview of the characteristics and functions of communications protocols. The concept of protocol is fundamental to all of the remainder of Part Four, and, as we proceed, specific examples of all these functions will be seen.

We can group protocol functions into the following categories:

- Segmentation and reassembly
- Encapsulation
- Connection control
- Ordered delivery
- Flow control
- Error control
- Addressing
- Multiplexing
- Transmission services

### Segmentation and Reassembly[1]

A protocol is concerned with exchanging streams of data between two entities. Usually, the transfer can be characterized as consisting of a sequence of blocks of data

---

[1] In most protocol specifications related to the TCP/IP protocol suite, the term fragmentation rather than segmentation is used. The meaning is the same.

of some bounded size. At the application level, we refer to a logical unit of data transfer as a message. Now, whether the application entity sends data in messages or in a continuous stream, lower-level protocols may need to break the data up into blocks of some smaller bounded size; this process is called segmentation. For convenience, we shall refer to a block of data exchanged between two entities via a protocol as a protocol data unit (PDU).

There are a number of motivations for segmentation, depending on the context. Among the typical reasons for segmentation are

- The communications network may only accept blocks of data up to a certain size. For example, an ATM network is limited to blocks of 53 octets; Ethernet imposes a maximum size of 1526 octets.
- Error control may be more efficient with a smaller PDU size. For example, fewer bits need to be retransmitted using smaller blocks with the selective repeat technique.
- More equitable access to shared transmission facilities, with shorter delay, can be provided. For example, without a maximum block size, one station could monopolize a multipoint medium.
- A smaller PDU size may mean that receiving entities can allocate smaller buffers.
- An entity may require that data transfer comes to some sort of closure from time to time, for checkpoint and restart/recovery operations.

There are several disadvantages to segmentation that argue for making blocks as large as possible:

- Each PDU, as we shall see, contains a fixed minimum amount of control information. Hence, the smaller the block, the greater the percentage overhead.
- PDU arrival may generate an interrupt that must be serviced. Smaller blocks result in more interrupts.
- More time is spent processing smaller, more numerous PDUs.

All of these factors must be taken into account by the protocol designer in determining minimum and maximum PDU size.

The counterpart of segmentation is reassembly. Eventually, the segmented data must be reassembled into messages appropriate to the application level. If PDUs arrive out of order, the task is complicated.

The process of segmentation was illustrated in Figure 1.7.

## Encapsulation

Each PDU contains not only data but control information. Indeed, some PDUs consist solely of control information and no data. The control information falls into three general categories:

- **Address.** The address of the sender and/or receiver may be indicated.
- **Error-detecting code.** Some sort of frame check sequence is often included for error detection.

- **Protocol control.** Additional information is included to implement the protocol functions listed in the remainder of this section.

The addition of control information to data is referred to as encapsulation. Data are accepted or generated by an entity and encapsulated into a PDU containing that data plus control information (See Figures 1.7 and 1.8). An example of this is the HDLC frame (Figure 6.10).

## Connection Control

An entity may transmit data to another entity in such a way that each PDU is treated independently of all prior PDUs. This process is known as connectionless data transfer; an example is the use of the datagram. While this mode is useful, an equally important technique is connection-oriented data transfer, of which the virtual circuit is an example.

Connection-oriented data transfer is to be preferred (even required) if stations anticipate a lengthy exchange of data and/or certain details of their protocol must be worked out dynamically. A logical association, or connection, is established between the entities. Three phases occur (Figure 15.3):

- Connection establishment
- Data transfer
- Connection termination

With more sophisticated protocols, there may also be connection interrupt and recovery phases to cope with errors and other sorts of interruptions.

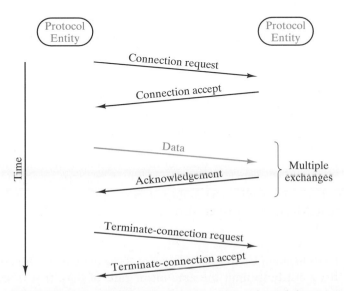

**FIGURE 15.3**   The phases of a connection-oriented data transfer.

During the connection establishment phase, two entities agree to exchange data. Typically, one station will issue a connection request (in connectionless fashion!) to the other. A central authority may or may not be involved. In simpler protocols, the receiving entity either accepts or rejects the request and, in the former case, away they go. In more complex proposals, this phase includes a negotiation concerning the syntax, semantics, and timing of the protocol. Both entities must, of course, be using the same protocol. But the protocol may allow certain optional features, and these must be agreed upon by means of negotiation. For example, the protocol may specify a PDU size of up to 8000 octets; one station may wish to restrict this to 1000 octets.

Following connection establishment, the data transfer phase is entered; here, both data and control information (e.g., flow control, error control) are exchanged. The figure shows a situation in which all of the data flows in one direction, with acknowledgments returned in the other direction. More typically, data and acknowledgments flow in both directions. Finally, one side or the other wishes to terminate the connection and does so by sending a termination request. Alternatively, a central authority might forcibly terminate a connection.

The key characteristic of connection-oriented data transfer is that sequencing is used. Each side sequentially numbers the PDUs that it sends to the other side. Because each side remembers that it is engaged in a logical connection, it can keep track of both outgoing numbers, which it generates, and incoming numbers, which are generated by the other side. Indeed, one can essentially define a connection-oriented data transfer as one in which both sides number PDUs and keep track of the incoming and outgoing numbers. Sequencing supports three main functions: ordered deliver, flow control, and error control.

## Ordered Delivery

If two communicating entities are in different hosts connected by a network, there is a risk that PDUs will not arrive in the order in which they were sent, because they may traverse different paths through the network. In connection-oriented protocols, it is generally required that PDU order be maintained. For example, if a file is transferred between two systems, we would like to be assured that the records of the received file are in the same order as those of the transmitted file, and not shuffled. If each PDU is given a unique number, and numbers are assigned sequentially, then it is a logically simple task for the receiving entity to reorder received PDUs on the basis of sequence number. A problem with this scheme is that, with a finite sequence number field, sequence numbers repeat (modulo some maximum number). Evidently, the maximum sequence number must be greater than the maximum number of PDUs that could be outstanding at any time. In fact, the maximum number may need to be twice the maximum number of PDUs that could be outstanding (e.g., selective-repeat ARQ; see Chapter 6).

## Flow Control

Flow control was introduced in Chapter 6. In essence, flow control is a function performed by a receiving entity to limit the amount or rate of data that is sent by a transmitting entity.

The simplest form of flow control is a stop-and-wait procedure, in which each PDU must be acknowledged before the next can be sent. More efficient protocols involve some form of credit provided to the transmitter, which is the amount of data that can be sent without an acknowledgment. The sliding-window technique is an example of this mechanism.

Flow control is a good example of a function that must be implemented in several protocols. Consider again Figure 1.6. The network will need to exercise flow control over station 1's network services module via the network access protocol, in order to enforce network traffic control. At the same time, station 2's network services module has only limited buffer space and needs to exercise flow control over station 1's network services module via the process-to-process protocol. Finally, even though station 2's network service module can control its data flow, station 2's application may be vulnerable to overflow. For example, the application could be hung up waiting for disk access. Thus, flow control is also needed over the application-oriented protocol.

## Error Control

Another previously introduced function is error control. Techniques are needed to guard against loss or damage of data and control information. Most techniques involve error detection, based on a frame check sequence, and PDU retransmission. Retransmission is often activated by a timer. If a sending entity fails to receive an acknowledgment to a PDU within a specified period of time, it will retransmit.

As with flow control, error control is a function that must be performed at various levels of protocol. Consider again Figure 1.6. The network access protocol should include error control to assure that data are successfully exchanged between station and network. However, a packet of data may be lost inside the network, and the process-to-process protocol should be able to recover from this loss.

## Addressing

The concept of addressing in a communications architecture is a complex one and covers a number of issues. At least four separate issues need to be discussed:

- Addressing level
- Addressing scope
- Connection identifiers
- Addressing mode

During the discussion, we illustrate the concepts using Figure 15.4, which shows a configuration using the TCP/IP protocol architecture. The concepts are essentially the same for the OSI architecture or any other communications architecture.

*Addressing level* refers to the level in the communications architecture at which an entity is named. Typically, a unique address is associated with each end system (e.g., host or terminal) and each intermediate system (e.g., router) in a configuration. Such an address is, in general, a network-level address. In the case of the TCP/IP architecture, this is referred to as an IP address, or simply an internet

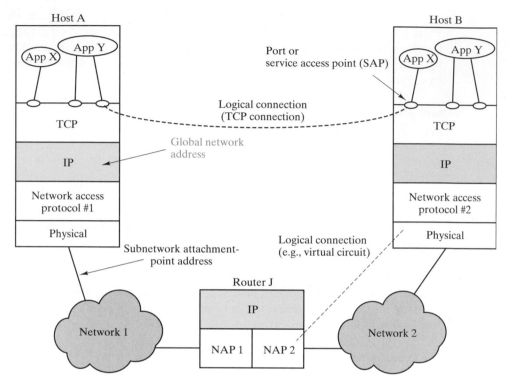

**FIGURE 15.4** Addressing concepts.

address. In the case of the OSI architecture, this is referred to as a network service access point (NSAP). The network-level address is used to route a PDU through a network or networks to a system indicated by a network-level address in the PDU.

Once data arrives at a destination system, it must be routed to some process or application in the system. Typically, a system will support multiple applications, and an application may support multiple users. Each application and, perhaps, each concurrent user of an application, is assigned a unique identifier, referred to as a port in the TCP/IP architecture, and as a service access point (SAP) in the OSI architecture. For example, a host system might support both an electronic mail application and a file transfer application. At minimum, each application would have a port number or SAP that is unique within that system. Further, the file transfer application might support multiple simultaneous transfers, in which case, each transfer is dynamically assigned a unique port number or SAP.

Figure 15.4 illustrates two levels of addressing within a system; this is typically the case for the TCP/IP architecture. However, there can be addressing at each level of an architecture. For example, a unique SAP can be assigned to each level of the OSI architecture.

Another issue that relates to the address of an end system or intermediate system is *addressing scope*. The internet address or NSAP address referred to above is a global address. The key characteristics of a global address are

- **Global nonambiguity.** A global address identifies a unique system. Synonyms are permitted. That is, a system may have more than one global address.
- **Global applicability.** It is possible at any global address to identify any other global address, in any system, by means of the global address of the other system.

Because a global address is unique and globally applicable, it enables an internet to route data from any system attached to any network to any other system attached to any other network.

Figure 15.4 illustrates that another level of addressing may be required. Each subnetwork must maintain a unique address for each device interface on the subnetwork. Examples are a MAC address on an IEEE 802 network and an X.25 DTE address, both of which enable the subnetwork to route data units (e.g., MAC frames, X.25 packets) through the subnetwork and deliver them to the intended attached system. We can refer to such an address as a *subnetwork attachment-point address*.

The issue of addressing scope is generally only relevant for network-level addresses. A port or SAP above the network level is unique within a given system but need not be globally unique. For example, in Figure 15.4, there can be a port 1 in system A and a port 1 in system B. The full designation of these two ports could be expressed as A.1 and B.1, which are unique designations.

The concept of *connection identifiers* comes into play when we consider connection-oriented data transfer (e.g., virtual circuit) rather than connectionless data transfer (e.g., datagram). For connectionless data transfer, a global name is used with each data transmission. For connection-oriented transfer, it is sometimes desirable to use only a connection name during the data transfer phase. The scenario is this: Entity 1 on system A requests a connection to entity 2 on system B, perhaps using the global address B.2. When B.2 accepts the connection, a connection name (usually a number) is provided and is used by both entities for future transmissions. The use of a connection name has several advantages:

- **Reduced overhead.** Connection names are generally shorter than global names. For example, in the X.25 protocol (discussed in Chapter 9) used over packet-switched networks, connection-request packets contain both source and destination address fields, each with a system-defined length that may be a number of octets. After a virtual circuit is established, data packets contain just a 12-bit virtual circuit number.
- **Routing.** In setting up a connection, a fixed route may be defined. The connection name serves to identify the route to intermediate systems, such as packet-switching nodes, for handling future PDUs.
- **Multiplexing.** We address this function in more general terms below. Here we note that an entity may wish to enjoy more than one connection simultaneously. Thus, incoming PDUs must be identified by connection name.
- **Use of state information.** Once a connection is established, the end systems can maintain state information relating to the connection; this enables such functions as flow control and error control using sequence numbers, as we saw with HDLC (Chapter 6) and X.25 (Chapter 9).

Figure 15.4 shows several examples of connections. The logical connection between router J and host B is at the network level. For example, if network 2 is a packet-switching network using X.25, then this logical connection would be a virtual circuit. At a higher level, many transport-level protocols, such as TCP, support logical connections between users of the transport service. Thus, TCP can maintain a connection between two ports on different systems.

Another addressing concept is that of *addressing mode*. Most commonly, an address refers to a single system or port; in this case, it is referred to as an individual or *unicast address*. It is also possible for an address to refer to more than one entity or port. Such an address identifies multiple simultaneous recipients for data. For example, a user might wish to send a memo to a number of individuals. The network control center may wish to notify all users that the network is going down. An address for multiple recipients may be *broadcast*—intended for all entities within a domain—or *multicast*—intended for a specific subset of entities. Table 15.1 illustrates the possibilities.

## Multiplexing

Related to the concept of addressing is that of multiplexing. One form of multiplexing is supported by means of multiple connections into a single system. For example, with X.25, there can be multiple virtual circuits terminating in a single end system; we can say that these virtual circuits are multiplexed over the single physical interface between the end system and the network. Multiplexing can also be accomplished via port names, which also permit multiple simultaneous connections. For example, there can be multiple TCP connections terminating in a given system, each connection supporting a different pair of ports.

Multiplexing is used in another context as well, namely the mapping of connections from one level to another. Consider again Figure 15.4. Network A might provide a virtual circuit service. For each process-to-process connection established at the network services level, a virtual circuit could be created at the network access level. This is a one-to-one relationship, but need not be so. Multiplexing can be used in one of two directions (Figure 15.5). Upward multiplexing occurs when multiple higher-level connections are multiplexed on, or share, a single lower-level connec-

TABLE 15.1   Addressing modes.

| Destination | Network address | System address | Port/SAP address |
|---|---|---|---|
| Unicast | Individual | Individual | Individual |
| Multicast | Individual<br>Individual<br>All | Individual<br>All<br>All | Group<br>Group<br>Group |
| Broadcast | Individual<br>Individual<br>All | Individual<br>All<br>All | All<br>All<br>All |

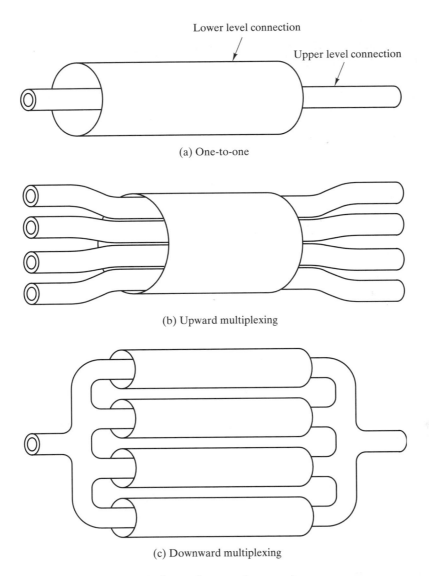

(a) One-to-one

(b) Upward multiplexing

(c) Downward multiplexing

**FIGURE 15.5** Multiplexing and protocol connections.

tion in order to make more efficient use of the lower-level service or to provide several higher-level connections in an environment where only a single lower-level connection exists. Figure 15.5 shows an example of upward multiplexing. Downward multiplexing, or splitting, means that a single higher-level connection is built on top of multiple lower-level connections, the traffic on the higher connection being divided among the various lower connections. This technique may be used to provide reliability, performance, or efficiency.

### Transmission Services

A protocol may provide a variety of additional services to the entities that use it. We mention here three common examples:

- **Priority.** Certain messages, such as control messages, may need to get through to the destination entity with minimum delay. An example would be a close-connection request. Thus, priority could be assigned on a per-message basis. Additionally, priority could be assigned on a per-connection basis.
- **Grade of service.** Certain classes of data may require a minimum throughput or a maximum delay threshold.
- **Security.** Security mechanisms, restricting access, may be invoked.

All of these services depend on the underlying transmission system and on any intervening lower-level entities. If it is possible for these services to be provided from below, the protocol can be used by the two entities to exercise such services.

## 15.2 OSI

As discussed in Chapter 1, standards are needed to promote interoperability among vendor equipment and to encourage economies of scale. Because of the complexity of the communications task, no single standard will suffice. Rather, the functions should be broken down into more manageable parts and organized as a communications architecture, which would then form the framework for standardization.

This line of reasoning led ISO in 1977 to establish a subcommittee to develop such an architecture. The result was the Open Systems Interconnection (OSI) reference model. Although the essential elements of the model were put into place quickly, the final ISO standard, ISO 7498, was not published until 1984. A technically compatible version was issued by CCITT as X.200 (now ITU-T).

### The Model

A widely accepted structuring technique, and the one chosen by ISO, is layering. The communications functions are partitioned into a hierarchical set of layers. Each layer performs a related subset of the functions required to communicate with another system, relying on the next-lower layer to perform more primitive functions, and to conceal the details of those functions, as it provides services to the next-higher layer. Ideally, the layers should be defined so that changes in one layer do not require changes in the other layers. Thus, we have decomposed one problem into a number of more manageable subproblems.

The task of ISO was to define a set of layers and to delineate the services performed by each layer. The partitioning should group functions logically, and should have enough layers to make each one manageably small, but should not have so many layers that the processing overhead imposed by their collection is burdensome. The principles that guided the design effort are summarized in Table 15.2. The resulting reference model has seven layers, which are listed with a brief defin-

**TABLE 15.2**   Principles used in defining the OSI layers (ISO 7498).

1. Do not create so many layers as to make the system engineering task of describing and integrating the layers more difficult than necessary.
2. Create a boundary at a point where the description of services can be small and the number of interactions across the boundary are minimized.
3. Create separate layers to handle functions that are manifestly different in the process performed or the technology involved.
4. Collect similar functions into the same layer.
5. Select boundaries at a point which past experience has demonstrated to be succesful.
6. Create a layer of easily localized functions so that the layer could be totally redesigned and its protocols changed in a major way to take advantage of new advances in architecture, hardware or software technology without changing the services expected from and provided to the adjacent layers.
7. Create a boundary where it may be useful at some point in time to have the corresponding interface standardized.[1,2]
8. Create a layer where there is a need for a different level of abstraction in the handling of data, for example morphology, syntax, semantic.
9. Allow changes of functions or protocols to be made within a layer without affecting other layers.
10. Create for each layer boundaries with its upper and lower layer only.

   Similar principles have been applied to sublayering:

11. Create further subgrouping and organization of functions to form sublayers within a layer in cases where distinct communication services need it.
12. Create, where needed, two or more sublayers with a common, and therefore minimal functionality to allow interface operation with adjacent layers.
13. Allow by-passing of sublayers.

---

[1] Advantages and drawbacks of standardizing internal interfaces within open systems are not considered in this International Standard. In particular, mention of, or references to principle (7) should not be taken to imply usefulness of standards for such internal interfaces.

[2] It is important to note that OSI *per se* does not require interfaces within open systems to be standardized. Moreover, whenever standards for such interfaces are defined, adherence to such internal interface standards can in no way be considered as a condition of openness.

ition in Figure 1.10. Table 15.3 provides ISO's justification for the selection of these layers.

Figure 15.6 illustrates the OSI architecture. Each system contains the seven layers. Communication is between applications in the two computers, labeled application X and application Y in the figure. If application X wishes to send a message to application Y, it invokes the application layer (layer 7). Layer 7 establishes a peer relationship with layer 7 of the target computer, using a layer-7 protocol (application protocol). This protocol requires services from layer 6, so the two layer-6 entities use a protocol of their own, and so on down to the physical layer, which actually transmits bits over a transmission medium.

Note that there is no direct communication between peer layers except at the physical layer. That is, above the physical layer, each protocol entity sends data down to the next-lower layer to get the data across to its peer entity. Even at the physical layer, the OSI model does not stipulate that two systems be directly connected. For example, a packet-switched or circuit-switched network may be used to provide the communication link.

**TABLE 15.3** Justification of the OSI layers (ISO 7498).

1. It is essential that the architecture permits usage of a realistic variety of physical media for interconnection with different control procedures (for example V.24, V.25, etc . . .). Application of principles 3, 5, and 8 (Table 15.2) leads to identification of a **Physical Layer** as the lowest layer in the architecture.
2. Some physical communication media (for example telephone line) require specific techniques to be used in order to transmit data between systems despite a relatively high error rate (i.e., an error rate not acceptable for the great majority of applications). These specific techniques are used in data-link control procedures which have been studied and standardized for a number of years. It must also be recognized that new physical communication media (for example fiber optics) will require different data-link control procedures. Application of principles 3, 5, and 8 leads to identification of a **Data Link Layer** on top of the Physical Layer in the architecture.
3. In the open systems architecture, some open systems will act as the final destination of data. Some open systems may act only as intermediate nodes (forwarding data to other systems). Application of principles 3, 5, and 7 leads to identification of a **Network Layer** on top of the data link layer. Network oriented protocols such as routing, for example, will be grouped in this layer. Thus, the Network Layer will provide a connection path (network-connection) between a pair of transport entities; including the case where intermediate nodes are involved.
4. Control of data transportation from source end open system to destination end open system (which is not performed in intermediate nodes) is the last function to be performed in order to provide the totality of the transport service. Thus, the upper layer in the transport service part of the architecture is the **Transport Layer**, on top of the Network Layer. This Transport Layer relieves higher layer entities from any concern with the transportation of data between them.
5. There is a need to organize and synchronize dialogue, and to manage the exchange of data. Application of principles 3 and 4 leads to the identification of a **Session Layer** on top of the Transport Layer.
6. The remaining set of general interests functions are those related to representation and manipulation of structured data for the benefit of application programs. Application of principles 3 and 4 leads to the identification of a **Presentation Layer** on top of the Session Layer.
7. Finally, there are applications consisting of application processes which perform information processing. An aspect of these application processes and the protocols by which they communicate comprise the **Application Layer** as the highest layer of the architecture.

Figure 15.6 also highlights the use of protocol data units (PDUs) within the OSI architecture. First, consider the most common way in which protocols are realized. When application X has a message to send to application Y, it transfers those data to an application entity in the application layer. A header is appended to the data that contains the required information for the peer–layer-7 protocol (encapsulation). The original data, plus the header, are now passed as a unit to layer 6. The presentation entity treats the whole unit as data and appends its own header (a second encapsulation). This process continues down through layer 2, which generally adds both a header and a trailer (e.g., HDLC). This layer-2 unit, called a *frame*, is then passed by the physical layer onto the transmission medium. When the frame is received by the target system, the reverse process occurs. As the data ascend, each layer strips off the outermost header, acts on the protocol information contained therein, and passes the remainder up to the next layer.

At each stage of the process, a layer may fragment the data unit it receives from the next-higher layer into several parts, in order to accommodate its own requirements. These data units must then be reassembled by the corresponding peer layer before being passed up.

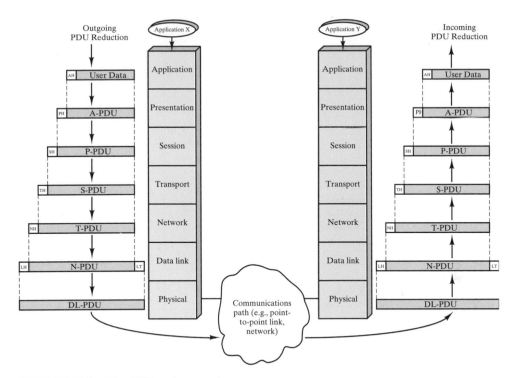

FIGURE 15.6    The OSI environment.

## Standardization Within the OSI Framework

The principal motivation for the development of the OSI model was to provide a framework for standardization. Within the model, one or more protocol standards can be developed at each layer. The model defines, in general terms, the functions to be performed at that layer and facilitates the standards-making process in two ways:

- Because the functions of each layer are well-defined, standards can be developed independently and simultaneously for each layer, thereby speeding up the standards-making process.
- Because the boundaries between layers are well defined, changes in standards in one layer need not affect already existing software in another layer; this makes it easier to introduce new standards.

Figure 15.7 illustrates the use of the OSI model as such a framework. The overall communications function is decomposed into seven distinct layers, using the principles outlined in Table 15.2. These principles essentially amount to the use of modular design. That is, the overall function is broken up into a number of modules, making the interfaces between modules as simple as possible. In addition, the design principle of information-hiding is used: Lower layers are concerned with greater levels of detail; upper layers are independent of these details. Within each

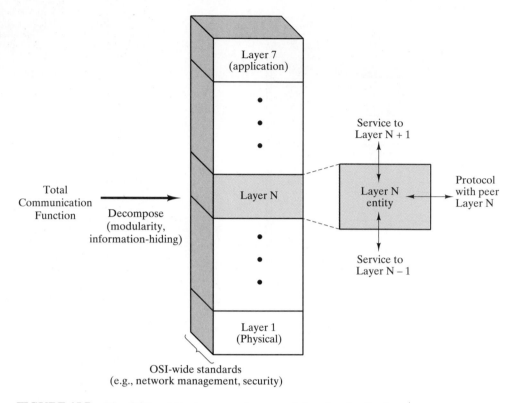

**FIGURE 15.7** The OSI architecture as a framework for standardization.

layer, there exist both the service provided to the next higher layer and the protocol to the peer layer in other systems.

Figure 15.8 shows more specifically the nature of the standardization required at each layer. Three elements are key:

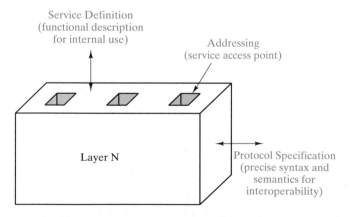

**FIGURE 15.8** Layer-specific standards.

- **Protocol specification.** Two entities at the same layer in different systems cooperate and interact by means of a protocol. Because two different open systems are involved, the protocol must be specified precisely; this includes the format of the protocol data units exchanged, the semantics of all fields, and the allowable sequence of PDUs.
- **Service definition.** In addition to the protocol or protocols that operate at a given layer, standards are needed for the services that each layer provides to the next-higher layer. Typically, the definition of services is equivalent to a functional description that defines *what* services are provided, but not *how* the services are to be provided.
- **Addressing.** Each layer provides services to entities at the next-higher layer. These entities are referenced by means of a service access point (SAP). Thus, a network service access point (NSAP) indicates a transport entity that is a user of the network service.

The need to provide a precise protocol specification for open systems is self-evident. The other two items listed above warrant further comment. With respect to service definitions, the motivation for providing only a functional definition is as follows. First, the interaction between two adjacent layers takes places within the confines of a single open system and is not the concern of any other open system. Thus, as long as peer layers in different systems provide the same services to their next-higher layers, the details of how the services are provided may differ from one system to another without loss of interoperability. Second, it will usually be the case that adjacent layers are implemented on the same processor. In that case, we would like to leave the system programmer free to exploit the hardware and operating system to provide an interface that is as efficient as possible.

### Service Primitives and Parameters

The services between adjacent layers in the OSI architecture are expressed in terms of *primitives* and *parameters*. A primitive specifies the function to be performed, and a parameter is used to pass data and control information. The actual form of a primitive is implementation-dependent; an example is a procedure call.

Four types of primitives are used in standards to define the interaction between adjacent layers in the architecture (X.210). These are defined in Table 15.4. The layout of Figure 15.9a suggests the time ordering of these events. For

**TABLE 15.4**  Service primitive types.

| | |
|---|---|
| REQUEST | A primitive issued by a service user to invoke some service and to pass the parameters needed to fully specify the requested service. |
| INDICATION | A primitive issued by a service provider to either<br>    1. indicate that a procedure has been invoked by the peer service user on the connection and to provide the associated parameters, or<br>    2. notify the service user of a provider-initiated action. |
| RESPONSE | A primitive issued by a service user to acknowledge or complete some procedure previously invoked by an indication to that user. |
| CONFIRM | A primitive issued by a service provider to acknowledge or complete some procedure previously invoked by a request by the service user. |

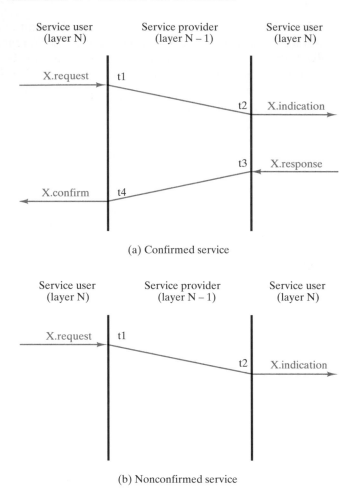

**FIGURE 15.9**   Time sequence diagrams for service primitives.

example, consider the transfer of data from an (N) entity to a peer (N) entity in another system. The following steps occur:

1. The source (N) entity invokes its (N–1) entity with a DATA.request primitive. Associated with the primitive are the needed parameters, such as the data to be transmitted and the destination address.

2. The source (N–1) entity prepares an (N–1) PDU to be sent to its peer (N–1) entity.

3. The destination (N–1) entity delivers the data to the appropriate destination (N) entity via a DATA.indication, which includes the data and source address as parameters.

4. If an acknowledgment is called for, the destination (N) entity issues a DATA.response to its (N–1) entity.

5. The (N–1) entity conveys the acknowledgment in an (N–1) PDU.
6. The acknowledgment is delivered to the (N) entity as a DATA.confirm.

This sequence of events is referred to as a *confirmed service*, as the initiator receives confirmation that the requested service has had the desired effect at the other end. If only request and indication primitives are involved (corresponding to steps 1 through 3), then the service dialogue is a *nonconfirmed service*; the initiator receives no confirmation that the requested action has taken place (Figure 15.9b).

## The OSI Layers

In this section, we discuss briefly each of the layers and, where appropriate, give examples of standards for protocols at those layers.

### Physical Layer

The physical layer covers the physical interface between devices and the rules by which bits are passed from one to another. The physical layer has four important characteristics:

- **Mechanical.** Relates to the physical properties of the interface to a transmission medium. Typically, the specification is of a pluggable connector that joins one or more signal conductors, called *circuits*.
- **Electrical.** Relates to the representation of bits (e.g., in terms of voltage levels) and the data transmission rate of bits.
- **Functional.** Specifies the functions performed by individual circuits of the physical interface between a system and the transmission medium.
- **Procedural.** Specifies the sequence of events by which bit streams are exchanged across the physical medium.

We have already covered physical layer protocols in some detail in Section 5.3. Examples of standards at this layer are EIA-232-E, as well as portions of ISDN and LAN standards.

### Data Link Layer

Whereas the physical layer provides only a raw bit-stream service, the data link layer attempts to make the physical link reliable while providing the means to activate, maintain, and deactivate the link. The principal service provided by the data link layer to higher layers is that of error detection and control. Thus, with a fully functional data-link-layer protocol, the next higher layer may assume error-free transmission over the link. However, if communication is between two systems that are not directly connected, the connection will comprise a number of data links in tandem, each functioning independently. Thus, the higher layers are not relieved of any error control responsibility.

Chapter 6 was devoted to data link protocols; examples of standards at this layer are HDLC, LAPB, LLC, and LAPD.

## Network Layer

The network layer provides for the transfer of information between end systems across some sort of communications network. It relieves higher layers of the need to know anything about the underlying data transmission and switching technologies used to connect systems. At this layer, the computer system engages in a dialogue with the network to specify the destination address and to request certain network facilities, such as priority.

There is a spectrum of possibilities for intervening communications facilities to be managed by the network layer. At one extreme, there is a direct point-to-point link between stations. In this case, there may be no need for a network layer because the data link layer can perform the necessary function of managing the link.

Next, the systems could be connected across a single network, such as a circuit-switching or packet-switching network. As an example, the packet level of the X.25 standard is a network layer standard for this situation. Figure 15.10 shows how the presence of a network is accommodated by the OSI architecture. The lower three layers are concerned with attaching to and communicating with the network. The packets created by the end system pass through one or more network nodes

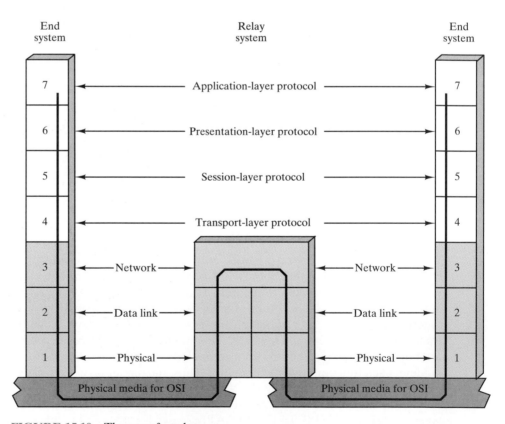

**FIGURE 15.10** The use of a relay.

that act as relays between the two end systems. The network nodes implement layers 1–3 of the architecture. In the figure, two end systems are connected through a single network node. Layer 3 in the node performs a switching and routing function. Within the node, there are two data link layers and two physical layers, corresponding to the links to the two end systems. Each data link (and physical) layer operates independently to provide service to the network layer over its respective link. The upper four layers are *end-to-end* protocols between the attached end systems.

At the other extreme, two end systems might wish to communicate but are not even connected to the same network. Rather, they are connected to networks that, directly or indirectly, are connected to each other. This case requires the use of some sort of internetworking technique; we explore this approach in Chapter 16.

## Transport Layer

The transport layer provides a mechanism for the exchange of data between end systems. The connection-oriented transport service ensures that data are delivered error-free, in sequence, with no losses or duplications. The transport layer may also be concerned with optimizing the use of network services and with providing a requested quality of service to session entities. For example, the session entity may specify acceptable error rates, maximum delay, priority, and security.

The size and complexity of a transport protocol depend on how reliable or unreliable the underlying network and network layer services are. Accordingly, ISO has developed a family of five transport protocol standards, each oriented toward a different underlying service. In the TCP/IP protocol suite, there are two common transport-layer protocols: the connection-oriented TCP (transmission control protocol) and the connectionless UDP (user datagram protocol).

## Session Layer

The lowest four layers of the OSI model provide the means for the reliable exchange of data and provide an expedited data service. For many applications, this basic service is insufficient. For example, a remote terminal access application might require a half-duplex dialogue. A transaction-processing application might require checkpoints in the data-transfer stream to permit backup and recovery. A message-processing application might require the ability to interrupt a dialogue in order to prepare a new portion of a message and later to resume the dialogue where it was left off.

All these capabilities could be embedded in specific applications at layer 7. However, because these types of dialogue-structuring tools have widespread applicability, it makes sense to organize them into a separate layer: the session layer.

The session layer provides the mechanism for controlling the dialogue between applications in end systems. In many cases, there will be little or no need for session-layer services, but for some applications, such services are used. The key services provided by the session layer include

- **Dialogue discipline.** This can be two-way simultaneous (full duplex) or two-way alternate (half duplex).

- **Grouping.** The flow of data can be marked to define groups of data. For example, if a retail store is transmitting sales data to a regional office, the data can be marked to indicate the end of the sales data for each department; this would signal the host computer to finalize running totals for that department and start new running counts for the next department.
- **Recovery.** The session layer can provide a checkpointing mechanism, so that if a failure of some sort occurs between checkpoints, the session entity can retransmit all data since the last checkpoint.

ISO has issued a standard for the session layer that includes, as options, services such as those just described.

### Presentation Layer

The presentation layer defines the format of the data to be exchanged between applications and offers application programs a set of data transformation services. The presentation layer also defines the syntax used between application entities and provides for the selection and subsequent modification of the representation used. Examples of specific services that may be performed at this layer include data compression and encryption.

### Application Layer

The application layer provides a means for application programs to access the OSI environment. This layer contains management functions and generally useful mechanisms that support distributed applications. In addition, general-purpose applications such as file transfer, electronic mail, and terminal access to remote computers are considered to reside at this layer.

## 15.3  TCP/IP PROTOCOL SUITE

For many years, the technical literature on protocol architectures was dominated by discussions related to OSI and to the development of protocols and services at each layer. Throughout the 1980s, the belief was widespread that OSI would come to dominate commercially, both over architectures such as IBM's SNA, as well as over competing multivendor schemes such as TCP/IP; this promise was never realized. In the 1990s, TCP/IP has become firmly established as the dominant commercial architecture and as the protocol suite upon which the bulk of new protocol development is to be done.

There are a number of reasons for the success of the TCP/IP protocols over OSI:

1. TCP/IP protocols were specified, and enjoyed extensive use, prior to ISO standardization of alternative protocols. Thus, organizations in the 1980s with an immediate need were faced with the choice of waiting for the always-

promised, never-delivered complete OSI package, and the up-and-running, plug-and-play TCP/IP suite. Once the obvious choice of TCP/IP was made, the cost and technical risks of migrating from an installed base inhibited OSI acceptance.

2. The TCP/IP protocols were initially developed as a U.S. military research effort funded by the Department of Defense (DOD). Although DOD, like the rest of the U.S. government, was committed to international standards, DOD had immediate operational needs that could not be met during the 1980s and early 1990s by off-the-shelf OSI-based products. Accordingly, DOD mandated the use of TCP/IP protocols for virtually all software purchases. Because DOD is the largest consumer of software products in the world, this policy created an enormous market, encouraging vendors to develop TCP/IP-based products.

3. The Internet is built on the foundation of the TCP/IP suite. The dramatic growth of the Internet, and especially the World Wide Web, has cemented the victory of TCP/IP over OSI.

## The TCP/IP Approach

The TCP/IP protocol suite recognizes that the task of communications is too complex and too diverse to be accomplished by a single unit. Accordingly, the task is broken up into modules or entities that may communicate with peer entities in another system. One entity within a system provides services to other entities and, in turn, uses the services of other entities. Good software-design practice dictates that these entities be arranged in a modular and hierarchical fashion.

The OSI model is based on this system of communication, but takes it one step further, recognizing that, in many respects, protocols at the same level of the hierarchy have certain features in common. This thinking yields the concept of rows or layers, as well as the attempt to describe in an abstract fashion what features are held in common by the protocols within a given row.

As an explanatory tool, a layered model has significant value and, indeed, the OSI model is used for precisely that purpose in many books on data communications and telecommunications. The objection sometimes raised by the designers of the TCP/IP protocol suite and its protocols is that the OSI model is prescriptive rather than descriptive. It dictates that protocols within a given layer perform certain functions, which may not be always desirable. It is possible to define more than one protocol at a given layer, and the functionality of those protocols may not be the same or even similar. Rather, what is common about a set of protocols at the same layer is that they share the same set of support protocols at the next lower layer.

Furthermore, there is the implication in the OSI model that, because interfaces between layers are well-defined, a new protocol can be substituted for an old one at a given layer with no impact on adjacent layers (see principle 6, Table 15.2); this is not always desirable or even possible. For example, a LAN lends itself easily to multicast and broadcast addressing at the link level. If the IEEE 802 link level were inserted below a network protocol entity that did not support multicasting and broadcasting, that service would be denied to upper layers of the hierarchy. To get around some of these problems, OSI proponents talk of null layers and sublayers. It sometimes seems that these artifacts save the model at the expense of good protocol design.

In the TCP/IP model, as we shall see, the strict use of all layers is not mandated. For example, there are application-level protocols that operate directly on top of IP.

## TCP/IP Protocol Architecture

The TCP/IP protocol suite was introduced in Chapter 1. As we pointed out, there is no official TCP/IP protocol model. However, it is useful to characterize the protocol suite as involving five layers. To summarize from Chapter 1, these layers are

- **Application layer.** Provides communication between processes or applications on separate hosts.
- **Host-to-host, or transport layer.** Provides end-to-end, data-transfer service. This layer may include reliability mechanisms. It hides the details of the underlying network or networks from the application layer.
- **Internet layer.** Concerned with routing data from source to destination host through one or more networks connected by routers.
- **Network access layer.** Concerned with the logical interface between an end system and a subnetwork.
- **Physical layer.** Defines characteristics of the transmission medium, signaling rate, and signal encoding scheme.

## Operation of TCP and IP

Figure 15.4 indicates how the TCP/IP protocols are configured for communications. To make clear that the total communications facility may consist of multiple networks, the constituent networks are usually referred to as subnetworks. Some sort of network access protocol, such as token ring, is used to connect a computer to a subnetwork. This protocol enables the host to send data across the subnetwork to another host or, in the case of a host on another subnetwork, to a router. IP is implemented in all of the end systems and the routers, acting as a relay to move a block of data from one host, through one or more routers, to another host. TCP is implemented only in the end systems; it keeps track of the blocks of data to assure that all are delivered reliably to the appropriate application.

For successful communication, every entity in the overall system must have a unique address. Actually, two levels of addressing are needed. Each host on a subnetwork must have a unique global internet address; this allows the data to be delivered to the proper host. Each process with a host must have an address that is unique within the host; this allows the host-to-host protocol (TCP) to deliver data to the proper process. These latter addresses are known as *ports*.

Let us trace a simple operation. Suppose that a process, associated with port 1 at host A, wishes to send a message to another process, associated with port 2 at host B. The process at A hands the message down to TCP with instructions to send it to host B, port 2. TCP hands the message down to IP with instructions to send it to host B. Note that IP need not be told the identity of the destination port. All that

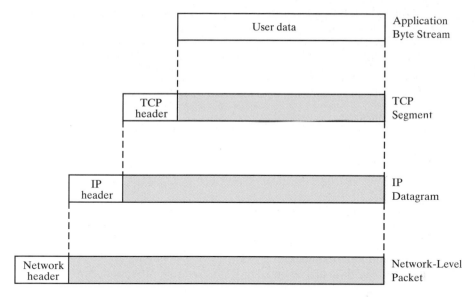

**FIGURE 15.11** Protocol data units in the TCP/IP architecture.

it needs to know is that the data are intended for host B. Next, IP hands the message down to the network access layer (e.g., Ethernet logic) with instructions to send it to router X (the first hop on the way to B).

To control this operation, control information as well as user data must be transmitted, as suggested in Figure 15.11. Let us say that the sending process generates a block of data and passes this to TCP. TCP may break this block into smaller pieces to make it more manageable. To each of these pieces, TCP appends control information known as the TCP header, thereby forming a TCP segment. The control information is to be used by the peer TCP protocol entity at host B. Examples of items that are included in this header are

- **Destination port.** When the TCP entity at B receives the segment, it must know to whom the data are to be delivered.
- **Sequence number.** TCP numbers the segments that it sends to a particular destination port sequentially, so that if they arrive out of order, the TCP entity at B can reorder them.
- **Checksum.** The sending TCP includes a code that is a function of the contents of the remainder of the segment. The receiving TCP performs the same calculation and compares the result with the incoming code. A discrepancy results if there has been some error in transmission.

Next, TCP hands each segment over to IP, with instructions to transmit it to B. These segments must be transmitted across one or more subnetworks and relayed through one or more intermediate routers. This operation, too, requires the use of control information. Thus, IP appends a header of control information to each segment to form an IP datagram. An example of an item stored in the IP header is the destination host address (in this example, B).

Finally, each IP datagram is presented to the network access layer for transmission across the first subnetwork in its journey to the destination. The network access layer appends its own header, creating a packet, or frame. The packet is transmitted across the subnetwork to router J. The packet header contains the information that the subnetwork needs to transfer the data across the subnetwork. Examples of items that may be contained in this header include

- **Destination subnetwork address.** The subnetwork must know to which attached device the packet is to be delivered.
- **Facilities requests.** The network access protocol might request the use of certain subnetwork facilities, such as priority.

At router X, the packet header is stripped off and the IP header examined. On the basis of the destination-address information in the IP header, the IP module in the router directs the datagram out across subnetwork 2 to B; to do this, the datagram is again augmented with a network access header.

When the data are received at B, the reverse process occurs. At each layer, the corresponding header is removed, and the remainder is passed on to the next higher layer until the original user data are delivered to the destination process.

## Protocol Interfaces

Each layer in the TCP/IP protocol suite interacts with its immediate adjacent layers. At the source, the process layer makes use of the services of the host-to-host layer and provides data down to that layer. A similar relationship exists at the interface of the host-to-host and internet layers and at the interface of the internet and network access layers. At the destination, each layer delivers data up to the next-higher layer.

This use of each individual layer is not required by the architecture. As Figure 15.12 suggests, it is possible to develop applications that directly invoke the services of any one of the layers. Most applications require a reliable end-to-end protocol and thus make use of TCP; some special-purpose applications, however, do not need such services, for example, the simple network management protocol (SNMP) that uses an alternative host-to-host protocol known as the *user datagram protocol* (UDP); others may make use of IP directly. Applications that do not involve internetworking and that do not need TCP have been developed to invoke the network access layer directly.

## The Applications

Figure 15.12 shows the position of some of the key protocols commonly implemented as part of the TCP/IP protocol suite. Most of these protocols are discussed in the remainder of Part Four. In this section, we briefly highlight three protocols that have traditionally been considered mandatory elements of TCP/IP, and which were designated as military standards, along with TCP and IP, by DOD.

The *simple mail transfer protocol* (SMTP) provides a basic electronic mail facility. It provides a mechanism for transferring messages among separate hosts. Features of SMTP include mailing lists, return receipts, and forwarding. The SMTP

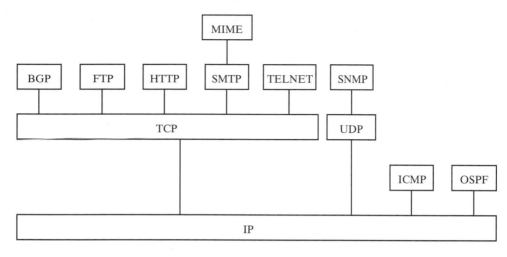

LEGEND

BGP   = Border Gateway Protocol
FTP   = File Transfer Protocol
HTTP  = Hyptertext Transfer Protocol
ICMP  = Internet Control Message Protocol
IP    = Internet Protocol
OSPF  = Open Shortest Path First

MIME  = Multi-Purpose Internet Mail Extension
SMTP  = Simple Mail Transfer Protocol
SNMP  = Simple Network Management Protocol
TCP   = Transmission Control Protocol
UDP   = User Datagram Protocol

**FIGURE 15.12**   Some protocols in the TCP/IP protocol suite.

protocol does not specify the way in which messages are to be created; some local editing or native electronic mail facility is required. Once a message is created, SMTP accepts the message and makes use of TCP to send it to an SMTP module on another host. The target SMTP module will make use of a local electronic mail package to store the incoming message in a user's mailbox.

The *file transfer protocol* (FTP) is used to send files from one system to another under user command. Both text and binary files are accommodated, and the protocol provides features for controlling user access. When a user requests a file transfer, FTP sets up a TCP connection to the target system for the exchange of control messages; these allow user ID and password to be transmitted and allow the user to specify the file and file actions desired. Once a file transfer is approved, a second TCP connection is set up for the data transfer. The file is transferred over the data connection, without the overhead of any headers or control information at the application level. When the transfer is complete, the control connection is used to signal the completion and to accept new file transfer commands.

*TELNET* provides a remote log-on capability, which enables a user at a terminal or personal computer to log on to a remote computer and function as if directly connected to that computer. The protocol was designed to work with simple scroll-mode terminals. TELNET is actually implemented in two modules. User TELNET interacts with the terminal I/O module to communicate with a local terminal; it converts the characteristics of real terminals to the network standard and vice versa. Server TELNET interacts with an application, acting as a surrogate terminal handler so that remote terminals appear as local to the application. Terminal traffic between User and Server TELNET is carried on a TCP connection.

## 15.4  RECOMMENDED READING

For the reader interested in greater detail on TCP/IP, there are two three-volume works that are more than adequate. The works by Comer and Stevens have become classics and are considered definitive [COME95, COME94a, COME94b]. The works by Stevens and Wright are equally worthwhile [STEV94, STEV96, WRIG95]. A more compact and very useful reference work is [MURP95], which covers the spectrum of TCP/IP related protocols in a technically concise but thorough fashion, including coverage of some protocols not found in the other two works.

One of the best treatments of OSI and OSI-related protocols is [JAIN93]. [HALS96] also provides good coverage.

COME94a  Comer, D. and Stevens, D. *Internetworking with TCP/IP, Volume II: Design Implementation, and Internals*. Englewood Cliffs, NJ: Prentice Hall, 1994.

COME94b  Comer, D. and Stevens, D. *Internetworking with TCP/IP, Volume III: Client-Server Programming and Applications*. Englewood Cliffs, NJ: Prentice Hall, 1994.

COME95  Comer, D. *Internetworking with TCP/IP, Volume I: Principles, Protocols, and Architecture*. Upper Saddle River, NJ: Prentice Hall, 1995.

HALS96  Halsall, F. *Data Communications, Computer Networks, and Open Systems*. Reading, MA: Addison-Wesley, 1996.

JAIN93  Jain, B. and Agrawala, A. *Open Systems Interconnection*. New York: McGraw-Hill, 1993.

MURP95  Murphy, E., Hayes, S., and Enders, M. *TCP/IP: Tutorial and Technical Overview*. Upper Saddle River: NJ: Prentice Hall, 1995.

STEV94  Stevens, W. *TCP/IP Illustrated, Volume 1: The Protocols*. Reading, MA: Addison-Wesley, 1994.

STEV96  Stevens, W. *TCP/IP Illustrated, Volume 3: TCP for Transactions, HTTP, NNTP, and the UNIX(R) Domain Protocol*. Reading, MA: Addison-Wesley, 1996.

WRIG95  Wright, G. and Stevens, W. *TCP/IP Illustrated, Volume 2: The Implementation*. Reading, MA: Addison-Wesley, 1995.

## 15.4  PROBLEMS

**15.1**  List the major disadvantages with the layered approach to protocols.

**15.2**  Based on the principles enunciated in Table 15.2, design an architecture with eight layers and make a case for it. Design one with six layers and make a case for that.

**15.3**  Two blue armies are each poised on opposite hills preparing to attack a single red army in the valley. The red army can defeat either of the blue armies separately but will fail to defeat both blue armies if they attack simultaneously. The blue armies communicate via an unreliable communications system (a foot soldier). The commander, with one of the blue armies, would like to attack at noon. His problem is this: If he sends a message ordering the attack, he cannot be sure it will get through. He could ask for acknowledgment but that might not get through. Is there a protocol that the two blue armies can use to avoid defeat?

**15.4**  Discuss the need or lack of need for a network layer (OSI layer 3) in a broadcast network.

# CHAPTER 16

# INTERNETWORKING

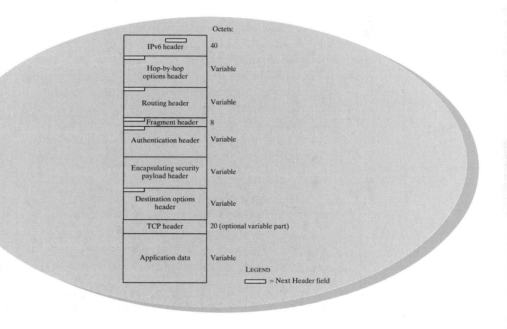

**P**acket-switched and packet broadcasting networks grew out of a need to allow the computer user to have access to resources beyond those available in a single system. In a similar fashion, the resources of a single network are often inadequate to meet users' needs. Because the networks that might be of interest exhibit so many differences, it is impractical to consider merging them into a single network. Rather, what is needed is the ability to interconnect various networks so that any two stations on any of the constituent networks can communicate.

Table 16.1 lists some commonly used terms relating to the interconnection of networks, or internetworking. An interconnected set of networks, from a user's point of view, may appear simply as a larger network. However, if each of the constituent networks retains its identity, and special mechanisms are needed for communicating across multiple networks, then the entire configuration is often referred to as an **internet**, and each of the constituent networks as a **subnetwork**.

Each constituent subnetwork in an internet supports communication among the devices attached to that subnetwork; these devices are referred to as **end systems** (ESs). In addition, subnetworks are connected by devices referred to in the ISO documents as **intermediate systems** (ISs). ISs provide a communications path and perform the necessary relaying and routing functions so that data can be exchanged between devices attached to different subnetworks in the internet.

Two types of ISs of particular interest are bridges and routers. The differences between them have to do with the types of protocols used for the internetworking logic. In essence, a **bridge** operates at layer 2 of the open systems interconnection (OSI) 7-layer architecture and acts as a relay of frames between like networks. (Bridges were examined in detail in Chapter 14.) A **router** operates at layer 3 of the OSI architecture and routes packets between potentially different networks.

**TABLE 16.1**  Internetworking terms.

Communication Network
  A facility that provides a data transfer service among stations attached to the network.
Internet
  A collection of communication networks interconnected by bridges and/or routers.
Subnetwork
  Refers to a constituent network of an internet. This avoids ambiguity since the entire internet, from a user's point of view, is a single network.
End System (ES)
  A device attached to one of the subnetworks of an internet that is used to support end-user applications or services.
Intermediate System (IS)
  A device used to connect two subnetworks and permit communication between end systems attached to different subnetworks.
Bridge
  An IS used to connect two LANs that use identical LAN protocols. The bridge acts as an address filter, picking up packets from one LAN that are intended for a destination on another LAN and passing those packets on. The bridge does not modify the contents of the packets and does not add anything to the packet. The bridge operates at layer 2 of the OSI model.
Router
  An IS used to connect two networks that may or may not be similar. The router employs an internet protocol present in each router and each host of the network. The router operates at layer 3 of the OSI model.

Both the bridge and the router assume that the same upper-layer protocols are in use.

We begin our examination with a discussion of the principles underlying various approaches to internetworking. We then examine the most important architectural approach to internetworking: the connectionless router. As an example, we describe the most widely used internetworking protocol, called simply the Internet Protocol (IP). These three approaches are explored in some detail. The chapter then turns to the issue of internetwork routing algorithms. Finally, we look at the newest standardized internetworking protocol, known as IPv6.

Figure 16.1 highlights the position of the protocols discussed in this chapter within the TCP/IP protocol.

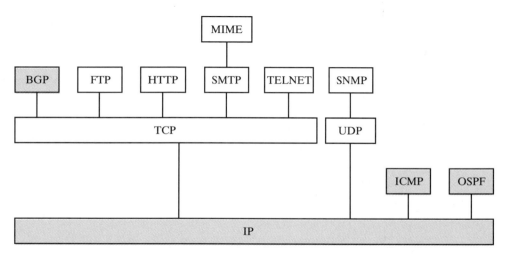

**FIGURE 16.1**   Internetworking protocols in context.

## 16.1  PRINCIPLES OF INTERNETWORKING

### Requirements

Although a variety of approaches have been taken to provide internetwork service, the overall requirements on the internetworking facility can be stated in general; these include

1. Providing a link between networks. At minimum, a physical and link control connection is needed.
2. Providing for the routing and delivery of data between processes on different networks.
3. Providing an accounting service that keeps track of the use of the various networks and routers and that maintains status information.

4. Providing the services listed above in such a way as not to require modifications to the networking architecture of any of the constituent networks; this means that the internetworking facility must accommodate a number of differences among networks, including

   a) **Different addressing schemes.** The networks may use different endpoint names and addresses and directory maintenance schemes. Some form of global network-addressing must be provided, as well as a directory service.

   b) **Different maximum packet size.** Packets from one network may have to be broken up into smaller pieces for another. This process is referred to as segmentation, or fragmentation.

   c) **Different network-access mechanisms.** The network-access mechanism between station and network may be different for stations on different networks.

   d) **Different timeouts.** Typically, a connection-oriented transport service will await an acknowledgment until a timeout expires, at which time it will retransmit its block of data. In general, longer times are required for successful delivery across multiple networks. Internetwork timing procedures must allow for successful transmission that avoids unnecessary retransmissions.

   e) **Error recovery.** Intranetwork procedures may provide anything from no error recovery up to reliable end-to-end (within the network) service. The internetwork service should not depend on, nor be interfered with, by the nature of the individual network's error recovery capability.

   f) **Status reporting.** Different networks report status and performance differently. Yet it must be possible for the internetworking facility to provide such information on internetworking activity to interested and authorized processes.

   g) **Routing techniques.** Intranetwork routing may depend on fault detection and congestion control techniques peculiar to each network; the internetworking facility must be able to coordinate these to adaptively route data between stations on different networks.

   h) **User-access control.** Each network will have its own user-access control technique (authorization for use of the network) that must be invoked by the internetwork facility as needed. Further, a separate internetwork access control technique may be required.

   i) **Connection, connectionless.** Individual networks may provide connection-oriented (e.g., virtual circuit) or connectionless (datagram) service. It may be desirable for the internetwork service not to depend on the nature of the connection service of the individual networks.

These points are worthy of further comment but are best pursued in the context of specific architectural approaches. We outline these approaches next, and then turn to a more detailed discussion of the router-based connectionless approach.

## Architectural Approaches

In describing the interworking function, two dimensions are important:

- The mode of operation (connection-mode or connectionless)
- The protocol architecture

The mode of operation determines the protocol architecture. There are two general approaches, depicted in Figure 16.2.

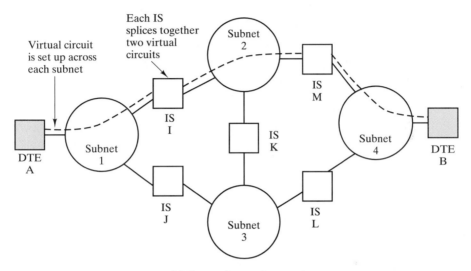

(a) Connection-mode operation

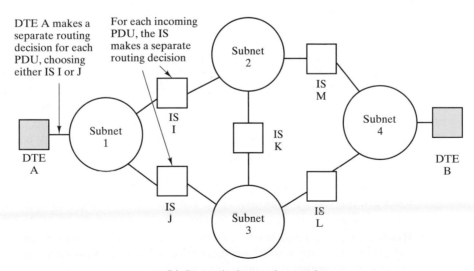

(b) Connectionless-mode operation

**FIGURE 16.2**  Internetworking approaches.

## Connection-Mode Operation

In the connection-mode operation, it is assumed that each subnetwork provides a connection-mode form of service. That is, it is possible to establish a logical network connection (e.g., virtual circuit) between any two DTEs attached to the same subnetwork. With this in mind, we can summarize the connection-mode approach as follows:

1. ISs are used to connect two or more subnetworks; each IS appears as a DTE to each of the subnetworks to which it is attached.
2. When DTE A wishes to exchange data with DTE B, a logical connection is set up between them. This logical connection consists of the concatenation of a sequence of logical connections across subnetworks. The sequence is such that it forms a path from DTE A to DTE B.
3. The individual subnetwork logical connections are spliced together by ISs. For example, there is a logical connection from DTE A to IS I across subnetwork 1 and another logical connection from IS I to IS M across subnetwork 2. Any traffic arriving at IS I on the first logical connection is retransmitted on the second logical connection, and vice versa.

Several additional points can be made about this form of operation. First, this approach is suited to providing support for a connection-mode network service. From the point of view of network users in DTEs A and B, a logical network connection is established between them that provides all of the features of a logical connection across a single network.

The second point to be made is that this approach assumes that there is a connection-mode service available from each subnetwork and that these services are equivalent; clearly, this may not always be the case. For example, an IEEE 802 or FDDI local area network provides a service defined by the logical link control (LLC). Two of the options with LLC provide only connectionless service. Therefore, in this case, the subnetwork service must be enhanced. An example of how this would be done is for the ISs to implement X.25 on top of LLC across the LAN.

Figure 16.3a illustrates the protocol architecture for connection-mode operation. Access to all subnetworks, either inherently or by enhancement, is by means of the same network layer protocol. The interworking units operate at layer 3. As was mentioned, layer 3 ISs are commonly referred to as routers. A connection-oriented router performs the following key functions:

- **Relaying.** Data units arriving from one subnetwork via the network layer protocol are relayed (retransmitted) on another subnetwork. Traffic is over logical connections that are spliced together at the routers.
- **Routing.** When an end-to-end logical connection, consisting of a sequence of logical connections, is to be set up, each router in the sequence must make a routing decision that determines the next hop in the sequence.

Thus, at layer 3, a relaying operation is performed. It is assumed that all of the end systems share common protocols at layer 4 (transport), and above, for successful end-to-end communication.

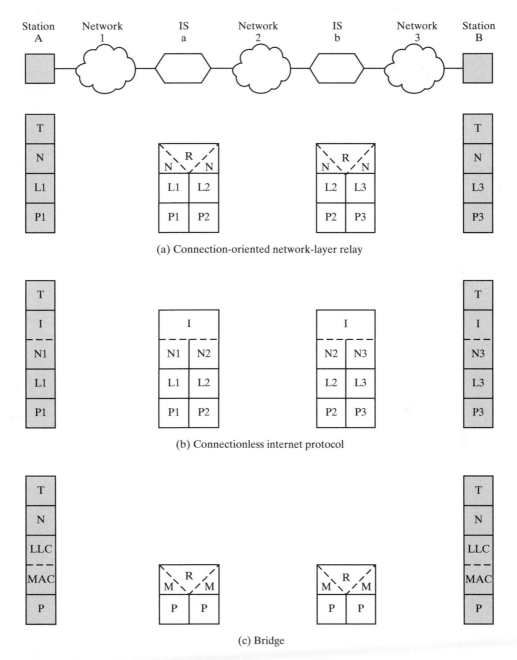

FIGURE 16.3 Internetwork architectures.

## Connectionless-Mode Operation

Figure 16.3b illustrates the connectionless mode of operation. Whereas connection-mode operation corresponds to the virtual circuit mechanism of a packet-switching network (Figure 9.4c), connectionless-mode operation corresponds to the datagram mechanism of a packet-switching network (Figure 9.4d). Each network protocol data unit is treated independently and routed from source DTE to destination DTE through a series of routers and networks. For each data unit transmitted by A, A makes a decision as to which router should receive the data unit. The data unit hops across the internet from one router to the next until it reaches the destination subnetwork. At each router, a routing decision is made (independently for each data unit) concerning the next hop. Thus, different data units may travel different routes between source and destination DTE.

Figure 16.3b illustrates the protocol architecture for connectionless-mode operation. All DTEs and all routers share a common network layer protocol known generically as the internet protocol (IP). An internet protocol was initially developed for the DARPA internet project and published as RFC 791, and has become an Internet Standard. The ISO standard, ISO 8473, provides similar functionality. Below this internet protocol, a protocol is needed to access the particular subnetwork. Thus, there are typically two protocols operating in each DTE and router at the network layer: an upper sublayer that provides the internetworking function, and a lower sublayer that provides subnetwork access.

### Bridge Approach

A third approach that is quite common is the use of a bridge. The bridge, also known as a MAC-level relay, uses a connectionless mode of operation (Figure 16.2b), but does so at a lower level than a router.

The protocol architecture for a bridge is illustrated in Figure 16.3c. In this case, the end systems share common transport and network protocols. In addition, it is assumed that all of the networks use the same protocols at the link layer. In the case of IEEE 802 and FDDI LANs, this means that all of the LANs share a common LLC protocol and a common MAC protocol. For example, all of the LANs are IEEE 802.3 using the unacknowledged connectionless form of LLC. In this case, MAC frames are relayed through bridges between the LANs.

The bridge approach is examined in Chapter 14.

## 16.2   CONNECTIONLESS INTERNETWORKING

The internet protocol (IP) was developed as part of the DARPA internet project. Somewhat later, when the international standards community recognized the need for a connectionless approach to internetworking, the ISO connectionless network protocol (CLNP) was standardized. The functionality of IP and CLNP is very similar; they differ in the formats used and in some minor functional features. In this section, we examine the essential functions of an internetworking protocol, which apply to both CLNP and IP. For convenience, we refer to IP, but it should be understood that the narrative in this section applies to both IP and CLNP.

### Operation of a Connectionless Internetworking Scheme

IP provides a connectionless, or datagram, service between end systems. There are a number of advantages to this connectionless approach:

- A connectionless internet facility is flexible. It can deal with a variety of networks, some of which are themselves connectionless. In essence, IP requires very little from the constituent networks.

- A connectionless internet service can be made highly robust. This is basically the same argument made for a datagram network service versus a virtual circuit service. For a further discussion, the reader is referred to Section 9.1.

- A connectionless internet service is best for connectionless transport protocols.

Figure 16.4 depicts a typical example of IP, in which two LANs are interconnected by an X.25 packet-switched WAN. The figure depicts the operation of the internet protocol for data exchange between host A on one LAN (subnetwork 1) and host B on another departmental LAN (subnetwork 2) through the WAN. The figure shows the format of the data unit at each stage. The end systems and routers must all share a common internet protocol. In addition, the end systems must share the same protocols above IP. The intermediate routers need only implement up through IP.

The IP at A receives blocks of data to be sent to B from the higher layers of software in A. IP attaches a header specifying, among other things, the global internet address of B. That address is logically in two parts: network identifier and end system identifier. The result is called an internet-protocol data unit, or simply a datagram. The datagram is then encapsulated with the LAN protocol and sent to the router, which strips off the LAN fields to read the IP header. The router then encapsulates the datagram with the X.25 protocol fields and transmits it across the WAN to another router. This router strips off the X.25 fields and recovers the datagram, which it then wraps in LAN fields appropriate to LAN 2 and sends it to B.

Let us now look at this example in more detail. End system A has a datagram to transmit to end system B; the datagram includes the internet address of B. The IP module in A recognizes that the destination (B) is on another subnetwork. So, the first step is to send the data to a router, in this case router X. To do this, IP passes the datagram down to the next lower layer (in this case LLC) with instructions to send it to router X. LLC in turn passes this information down to the MAC layer, which inserts the MAC-level address of router X into the MAC header. Thus, the block of data transmitted onto LAN 1 includes data from a layer or layers above TCP, plus a TCP header, an IP header, and LLC header, and a MAC header and trailer.

Next, the packet travels through subnetwork 1 to router X. The router removes MAC and LLC fields and analyzes the IP header to determine the ultimate destination of the data, in this case B. The router must now make a routing decision. There are three possibilities:

1. The destination station Y is connected directly to one of the subnetworks to which the router is attached. In this case, the router sends the datagram directly to the destination.

2. To reach the destination, one or more additional routers must be traversed. In this case, a routing decision must be made: To which router should the datagram be sent? In both cases, the IP module in the router sends the datagram

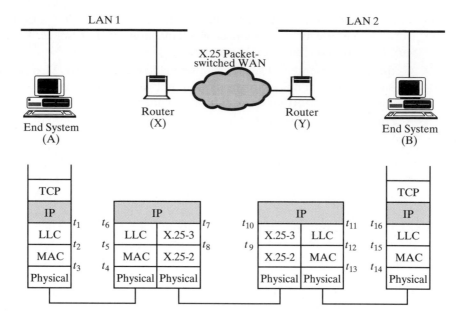

**FIGURE 16.4** Internet protocol operation.

down to the next lower layer with the destination subnetwork address. Please note that we are speaking here of a lower-layer address that refers to this network.

3. The router does not know the destination address. In this case, the router returns an error message to the source of the datagram.

In this example, the data must pass through router Y before reaching the destination. Router X, then, constructs a new packet by appending an X.25 header, containing the address of router Y, to the IP data unit. When this packet arrives at router Y, the packet header is stripped off. The router determines that this IP data unit is destined for B, which is connected directly to a network to which this router is attached. The router therefore creates a frame with a destination address of B and sends it out onto LAN 2. The data finally arrive at B, where the LAN and IP headers can be stripped off.

At each router, before the data can be forwarded, the router may need to segment the data unit to accommodate a smaller maximum packet-size limitation on the outgoing network. The data unit is split into two or more segments, each of which becomes an independent IP data unit. Each new data unit is wrapped in a lower-layer packet and queued for transmission. The router may also limit the length of its queue for each network to which it attaches so as to avoid having a slow network penalize a faster one. Once the queue limit is reached, additional data units are simply dropped.

The process described above continues through as many routers as it takes for the data unit to reach its destination. As with a router, the destination end system recovers the IP data unit from its network wrapping. If segmentation has occurred, the IP module in the destination end system buffers the incoming data until the entire original data field can be reassembled. This block of data is then passed to a higher layer in the end system.

This service offered by the internet protocol is an unreliable one. That is, the internet protocol does not guarantee that all data will be delivered or that the data that are delivered will arrive in the proper order. It is the responsibility of the next higher layer (e.g., TCP) to recover from any errors that occur. This approach provides for a great deal of flexibility.

With the internet protocol approach, each unit of data is passed from router to router in an attempt to get from source to destination. Because delivery is not guaranteed, there is no particular reliability requirement on any of the subnetworks; thus, the protocol will work with any combination of subnetwork types. And, since the sequence of delivery is not guaranteed, successive data units can follow different paths through the internet; this allows the protocol to react to both congestion and failure in the internet by changing routes.

## Design Issues

With that brief sketch of the operation of an IP-controlled internet, we can now go back and examine some design issues in greater detail:

- Routing
- Datagram lifetime
- Segmentation and reassembly
- Error control
- Flow control

As we proceed with this discussion, the reader will note many similarities between the design issues and techniques relevant to packet-switched networks. To

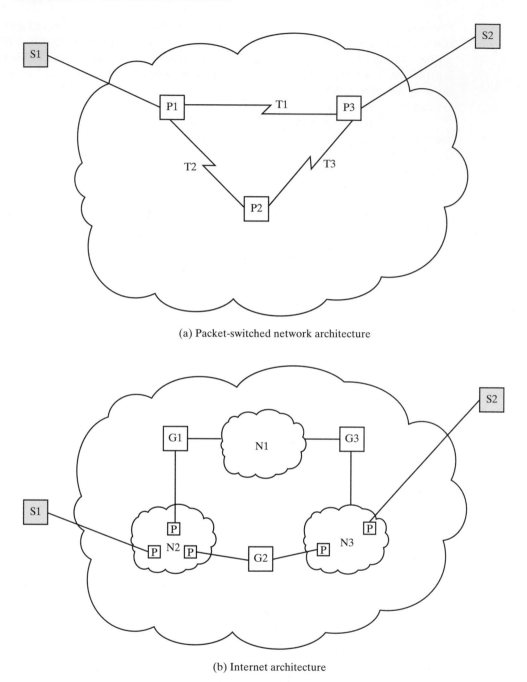

(a) Packet-switched network architecture

(b) Internet architecture

**FIGURE 16.5**   The internet as a network (based on HIND831).

see the reason for these parallels, consider Figure 16.5, which compares an internet architecture with a packet-switched network architecture. The routers (G1, G2, G3) in the internet correspond to the packet-switched nodes (P1, P2, P3) in the network, and the networks (N1, N2, N3) in the internet correspond to the transmission links

(T1, T2, T3) in the networks. The routers perform essentially the same functions as packet-switched nodes, and use the intervening networks in a manner analogous to transmission links.

## Routing

Routing is generally accomplished by maintaining a routing table in each end system and router that gives, for each possible destination network, the next router to which the internet datagram should be sent.

The routing table may be static or dynamic. A static table, however, could contain alternate routes if a router is unavailable. A dynamic table is more flexible in responding to both error and congestion conditions. In the Internet, for example, when a router goes down, all of its neighbors will send out a status report, allowing other routers and stations to update their routing tables. A similar scheme can be used to control congestion; this is a particularly important function because of the mismatch in capacity between local and wide-area networks. Section 16.4 discusses routing protocols.

Routing tables may also be used to support other internetworking services, such as those governing security and priority. For example, individual networks might be classified to handle data up to a given security classification. The routing mechanism must assure that data of a given security level are not allowed to pass through networks not cleared to handle such data.

Another routing technique is source routing. The source station specifies the route by including a sequential list of routers in the datagram. This, again, could be useful for security or priority requirements.

Finally, we mention a service related to routing: route recording. To record a route, each router appends its internet address to a list of addresses in the datagram. This feature is useful for testing and debugging purposes.

## Datagram Lifetime

If dynamic or alternate routing is used, the potential exists for a datagram to loop indefinitely through the internet. This is undesirable for two reasons. First, an endlessly circulating datagram consumes resources. Second, we will see in Chapter 17 that a transport protocol may depend on there being an upper bound on datagram lifetime. To avoid these problems, each datagram can be marked with a lifetime. Once the lifetime expires, the datagram is discarded.

A simple way to implement lifetime is to use a hop count. Each time that a datagram passes through a router, the count is decremented. Alternatively, the lifetime could be a true measure of time; this requires that the routers must somehow know how long it has been since the datagram or fragment last crossed a router, in order to know by how much to decrement the lifetime field. This would seem to require some global clocking mechanism. The advantage of using a true time measure is that it can be used in the reassembly algorithm, described next.

## Segmentation and Reassembly

Individual subnetworks within an internet may specify different maximum packet sizes. It would be inefficient and unwieldy to try to dictate uniform packet size across networks. Thus, routers may need to segment incoming datagrams into smaller pieces, called fragments, before transmitting on to the next subnetwork.

If datagrams can be segmented (perhaps more than once) in the course of their travels, the question arises as to where they should be reassembled. The easiest solution is to have reassembly performed at the destination only. The principal disadvantage of this approach is that fragments can only get smaller as data move through the internet; this may impair the efficiency of some networks. However, if intermediate router reassembly is allowed, the following disadvantages result:

1. Large buffers are required at routers, and there is the risk that all of the buffer space will be used up in the storing partial datagrams.
2. All fragments of a datagram must pass through the same router, thereby inhibiting the use of dynamic routing.

In IP, datagram fragments are reassembled at the destination end system. The IP segmentation technique uses the following fields in the IP header:

- Data Unit Identifier (ID)
- Data Length
- Offset
- More-flag

The ID is a means of uniquely identifying an end-system-originated datagram. In IP, it consists of the source and destination addresses, an identifier of the protocol layer that generated the data (e.g., TCP), and a sequence number supplied by that protocol layer. Data length indicates the length of the user data field in octets, and the offset is the position of a fragment of user data in the data field of the original datagram, in multiples of 64 bits.

The source end system creates a datagram with a data length equal to the entire length of the data field, with Offset = 0, and a more-flag set to 0 (false). To segment a long datagram, an IP module in a router performs the following tasks:

1. Create two new datagrams and copy the header fields of the incoming datagram into both.
2. Divide the incoming user data field into two approximately equal portions along a 64-bit boundary, placing one portion in each new datagram. The first portion must be a multiple of 64 bits.
3. Set the Data Length of the first new datagram to the length of the inserted data, and set more-flag to 1 (true). The Offset field is unchanged.
4. Set the data length of the second new datagram to the length of the inserted data, and add the length of the first data portion divided by 8 to the Offset field. The more-flag remains the same.

Table 16.2 gives an example. The procedure can easily be generalized to an *n*-way split.

To reassemble a datagram, there must be sufficient buffer space at the reassembly point. As fragments with the same ID arrive, their data fields are inserted in the proper position in the buffer until the entire data field is reassem-

TABLE 16.2  Segmentation example.

| Original datagram | First segment | Second segment |
|---|---|---|
| Data Length = 472<br>Segment Offset = 0<br>More = 0 | Data Length = 240<br>Segment Offset = 0<br>More = 1 | Data Length = 232<br>Segment Offset = 30<br>More = 0 |

bled, which is achieved when a contiguous set of data exists, starting with an offset of zero and ending with data from a fragment with a false more-flag.

One eventuality that must be dealt with is that one or more of the fragments may not get through; the IP service does not guarantee delivery. Some means is needed to decide whether to abandon a reassembly effort to free up buffer space. Two approaches are commonly used. First, one can assign a reassembly lifetime to the first fragment to arrive. This is a local, real-time clock assigned by the reassembly function and decremented while the fragments of the original datagram are being buffered. If the time expires prior to complete reassembly, the received fragments are discarded. A second approach is to make use of the datagram lifetime, which is part of the header of each incoming fragment. The lifetime field continues to be decremented by the reassembly function; as with the first approach, if the lifetime expires prior to complete reassembly, the received fragments are discarded.

### Error Control

The internetwork facility does not guarantee successful delivery of every datagram. When a datagram is discarded by a router, the router should attempt to return some information to the source, if possible. The source internet protocol entity may use this information to modify its transmission strategy, and it may notify higher layers. To report that a specific datagram has been discarded, some means of datagram identification is needed.

Datagrams may be discarded for a number of reasons, including lifetime expiration, congestion, and FCS error. In the latter case, notification is not possible, as the source address field may have been damaged.

### Flow Control

Internet flow control allows routers and/or receiving stations to limit the rate at which they receive data. For the connectionless type of service we are describing, flow control mechanisms are limited. The best approach would seem to be to send flow control packets, requesting reduced data flow, to other routers and source stations.

## 16.3  THE INTERNET PROTOCOL

The Internet Protocol (IP) is part of the TCP/IP protocol suite, and is the most widely-used internetworking protocol. It is functionally similar to the ISO standard connectionless network protocol (CLNP). As with any protocol standard, IP is specified in two parts:

- The interface with a higher layer (e.g., TCP), specifying the services that IP provides
- The actual protocol format and mechanisms

In this section, we first examine IP services and then the IP protocol. This is followed by a discussion of IP address formats. Finally, the Internet Control Message Protocol (ICMP), which is an integral part of IP, is described.

## IP Services

IP provides two service primitives at the interface to the next-higher layer (Figure 16.6). The Send primitive is used to request transmission of a data unit. The Deliver primitive is used by IP to notify a user of the arrival of a data unit. The parameters associated with the two primitives are

- **Source address.** Internetwork address of sending IP entity.
- **Destination address.** Internetwork address of destination IP entity.
- **Protocol.** Recipient protocol entity (an IP user).
- **Type of service indicators.** Used to specify the treatment of the data unit in its transmission through component networks.
- **Identifier.** Used in combination with the source and destination addresses and user protocol to identify the data unit uniquely. This parameter is needed for reassembly and error reporting.
- **Don't-fragment identifier.** Indicates whether IP can segment (called fragment in the standard) data to accomplish delivery.
- **Time to live.** Measured in network hops.
- **Data length.** Length of data being transmitted.
- **Option data.** Options requested by the IP user.
- **Data.** User data to be transmitted.

```
Send (                              Deliver (
      Source address                      Source address
      Destination address                 Destination address
      Protocol                            Protocol
      Type of service indicators          Type of service indicators
      Identifier
      Don't-fragment identifier
      Time to live
      Data length                         Data length
      Option data                         Option data
      Data                                Data
      )                                   )
```

FIGURE 16.6    IP service primitives and parameters.

Note that the *identifier, don't-fragment identifier*, and *time-to-live* parameters are present in the Send primitive but not in the Deliver primitive. These three parameters provide instructions to IP that are not of concern to the recipient IP user.

The sending IP user includes the *type-of-service* parameter to request a particular quality of service. The user may specify one or more of the services listed in Table 16.3. This parameter can be used to guide routing decisions. For example, if a router has several alternative choices for the next hop in routing a datagram, it may choose a network of a higher data rate if the high throughput option has been selected. This parameter, if possible, is also passed down to the network access protocol for use over individual networks. For example, if a precedence level is selected, and if the subnetwork supports precedence or priority levels, the precedence level will be mapped onto the network level for this hop.

The options parameter allows for future extensibility and for inclusion of parameters that are usually not invoked. The currently defined options are

- **Security.** Allows a security label to be attached to a datagram.
- **Source routing.** A sequenced list of router addresses that specifies the route to be followed. Routing may be strict (only identified routers may be visited) or loose (other intermediate routers may be visited).
- **Route recording.** A field is allocated to record the sequence of routers visited by the datagram.
- **Stream identification.** Names reserved resources used for stream service. This service provides special handling for volatile periodic traffic (e.g., voice).
- **Timestamping.** The source IP entity and some or all intermediate routers add a timestamp (precision to milliseconds) to the data unit as it goes by.

## IP Protocol

The protocol between IP entities is best described with reference to the IP datagram format, shown in Figure 16.7. The fields are

- **Version (4 bits).** Indicates the version number, to allow evolution of the protocol.
- **Internet header length (IHL) (4 bits).** Length of header in 32-bit words. The minimum value is five, for a minimum header length of 20 octets.

TABLE 16.3   IP Service quality options.

| | |
|---|---|
| Precedence | A measure of a datagram's relative importance. Eight levels of precedence are used. IP will attempt to provide preferential treatment for higher precedence datagrams. |
| Reliability | One of two levels may be specified: normal or high. A high value indicates a request that attempts be made to minimize the likelihood that this datagram will be lost or damaged. |
| Delay | One of two levels may be specified: normal or low. A low value indicates a request to minimize the delay that this datagram will experience. |
| Throughput | One of two levels may be specified: normal or high. A high value indicates a request to maximize the throughput for this datagram. |

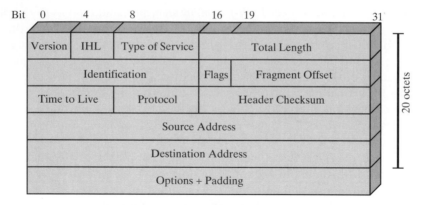

**FIGURE 16.7** IP header.

- **Type of service (8 bits).** Specifies reliability, precedence, delay, and throughput parameters.
- **Total length (16 bits).** Total datagram length, in octets.
- **Identifier (16 bits).** A sequence number that, together with the source address, destination address, and user protocol, is intended to uniquely identify a datagram. Thus, the identifier should be unique for the datagram's source address, destination address, and user protocol for the time during which the datagram will remain in the internet.
- **Flags (3 bits).** Only two of the bits are currently defined. The More bit is used for segmentation (fragmentation) and reassembly, as previously explained. The Don't-Fragment bit prohibits fragmentation when set. This bit may be useful if it is known that the destination does not have the capability to reassemble fragments. However, if this bit is set, the datagram will be discarded if it exceeds the maximum size of an en route subnetwork. Therefore, if the bit is set, it may be advisable to use source routing to avoid subnetworks with small maximum packet size.
- **Fragment offset (13 bits).** Indicates where in the original datagram this fragment belongs, measured in 64-bit units, implying that fragments other than the last fragment must contain a data field that is a multiple of 64 bits.
- **Time to live (8 bits).** Measured in router hops.
- **Protocol (8 bits).** Indicates the next higher level protocol that is to receive the data field at the destination.
- **Header checksum (16 bits).** An error-detecting code applied to the header only. Because some header fields may change during transit (e.g., time to live, segmentation-related fields), this is reverified and recomputed at each router. The checksum field is the 16-bit one's complement addition of all 16-bit words in the header. For purposes of computation, the checksum field is itself initialized to a value of zero.
- **Source address (32 bits).** Coded to allow a variable allocation of bits to specify the network and the end system attached to the specified network (7 and 24 bits, 14 and 16 bits, or 21 and 8 bits).

- **Destination address (32 bits).** As above.
- **Options (variable).** Encodes the options requested by the sending user.
- **Padding (variable).** Used to ensure that the datagram header is a multiple of 32 bits.
- **Data (variable).** The data field must be an integer multiple of 8 bits. The maximum length of the datagram (data field plus header) is 65,535 octets.

It should be clear how the IP services specified in the Send and Deliver primitives map into the fields of the IP datagram.

## IP Addresses

The source and destination address fields in the IP header each contain a 32-bit global internet address, generally consisting of a network identifier and a host identifier. The address is coded to allow a variable allocation of bits to specify network and host, as depicted in Figure 16.8. This encoding provides flexibility in assigning addresses to hosts and allows a mix of network sizes on an internet. In particular, the three network classes are best suited to the following conditions:

- **Class A.** Few networks, each with many hosts.
- **Class B.** Medium number of networks, each with a medium number of hosts.
- **Class C.** Many networks, each with a few hosts.

In a particular environment, it may be best to use addresses all from one class. For example, a corporate internetwork that consists of a large number of departmental local area networks may need to use class C addresses exclusively. However, the format of the addresses is such that it is possible to mix all three classes of

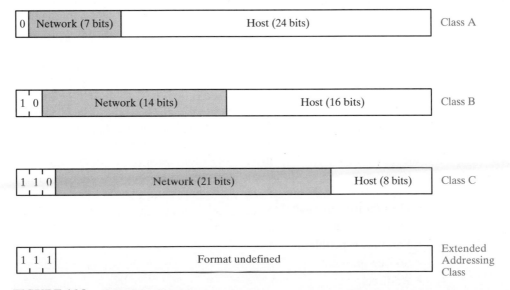

**FIGURE 16.8**  IP address formats.

addresses on the same internetwork; this is what is done in the case of the Internet itself. A mixture of classes is appropriate for an internetwork consisting of a few large networks, many small networks, plus some medium-sized networks.

### The Internet Control Message Protocol (ICMP)

The IP standard specifies that a compliant implementation must also implement ICMP (RFC 792). ICMP provides a means for transferring messages from routers and other hosts to a host. In essence, ICMP provides feedback about problems in the communication environment. Examples of its use are: When a datagram cannot reach its destination, when the router does not have the buffering capacity to forward a datagram, and when the router can direct the station to send traffic on a shorter route. In most cases, an ICMP message is sent in response to a datagram, either by a router along the datagram's path, or by the intended destination host.

Although ICMP is, in effect, at the same level as IP in the TCP/IP architecture, it is a user of IP. An ICMP message is constructed and then passed down to IP, which encapsulates the message with an IP header and then transmits the resulting datagram in the usual fashion. Because ICMP messages are transmitted in IP datagrams, their delivery is not guaranteed and their use cannot be considered reliable.

Figure 16.9 shows the format of the various ICMP message types. All ICMP message start with a 64-bit header consisting of the following:

- **Type (8 bits).** Specifies the type of ICMP message.
- **Code (8 bits).** Used to specify parameters of the message that can be encoded in one or a few bits.
- **Checksum (16 bits).** Checksum of the entire ICMP message. This is the same checksum algorithm used for IP.
- **Parameters (32 bits).** Used to specify more lengthy parameters.

These fields are generally followed by additional information fields that further specify the content of the message.

In those cases in which the ICMP message refers to a prior datagram, the information field includes the entire IP header plus the first 64 bits of the data field of the original datagram. This enables the source host to match the incoming ICMP message with the prior datagram. The reason for including the first 64 bits of the data field is that this will enable the IP module in the host to determine which upper-level protocol or protocols were involved. In particular, the first 64 bits would include a portion of the TCP header or other transport-level header.

ICMP messages include the following:

- Destination unreachable
- Time exceeded
- Parameter problem
- Source quench
- Redirect

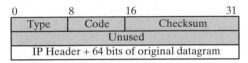

| 0 | 8 | 16 | 31 |
|---|---|---|---|
| Type | Code | Checksum | |
| Unused | | | |
| IP Header + 64 bits of original datagram | | | |

(a) Destination unreachable;
time exceeded; source quench

| 0 | 8 | 16 | 31 |
|---|---|---|---|
| Type | Code | Checksum | |
| Identifier | | Sequence number | |
| Originate timestamp | | | |

(e) Timestamp

| 0 | 8 | 16 | 31 |
|---|---|---|---|
| Type | Code | Checksum | |
| Pointer | Unused | | |
| IP Header + 64 bits of original datagram | | | |

(b) Parameter problem

| 0 | 8 | 16 | 31 |
|---|---|---|---|
| Type | Code | Checksum | |
| Identifier | | Sequence number | |
| Originate timestamp | | | |
| Receive timestamp | | | |
| Transmit timestamp | | | |

(e) Timestamp reply

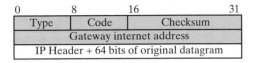

| 0 | 8 | 16 | 31 |
|---|---|---|---|
| Type | Code | Checksum | |
| Gateway internet address | | | |
| IP Header + 64 bits of original datagram | | | |

(c) Redirect

| 0 | 8 | 16 | 31 |
|---|---|---|---|
| Type | Code | Checksum | |
| Identifier | | Sequence number | |

(g) Address mask request

| 0 | 8 | 16 | 31 |
|---|---|---|---|
| Type | Code | Checksum | |
| Identifier | | Sequence number | |
| IP Header + 64 bits of original datagram | | | |

(d) Echo, echo reply

| 0 | 8 | 16 | 31 |
|---|---|---|---|
| Type | Code | Checksum | |
| Identifier | | Sequence Number | |
| Address mask | | | |

(h) Address mask reply

**FIGURE 16.9** ICMP message formats.

- Echo
- Echo reply
- Timestamp
- Timestamp reply
- Address mask request
- Address mask reply

The **destination-unreachable** message covers a number of contingencies. A router may return this message if it does not know how to reach the destination network. In some networks, an attached router may be able to determine if a particular host is unreachable, and then return the message. The destination host itself may return this message if the user protocol or some higher-level service access point is unreachable. This could happen if the corresponding field in the IP header was set incorrectly. If the datagram specifies a source route that is unusable, a message is returned. Finally, if a router must fragment a datagram but the Don't-Fragment flag is set, a message is returned.

A router will return a **time-exceeded** message if the lifetime of the datagram expires. A host will send this message if it cannot complete reassembly within a time limit.

A syntactic or semantic error in an IP header will cause a *parameter-problem* message to be returned by a router or host. For example, an incorrect argument may be provided with an option. The parameter field contains a pointer to the octet in the original header where the error was detected.

The *source-quench* message provides a rudimentary form of flow control. Either a router or a destination host may send this message to a source host, requesting that it reduce the rate at which it is sending traffic to the internet destination. On receipt of a source-quench message, the source host should cut back the rate at which it is sending traffic to the specified destination until it no longer receives source-quench messages; this message can be used by a router or host that must discard datagrams because of a full buffer. In this case, the router or host will issue a source-quench message for every datagram that it discards. In addition, a system may anticipate congestion and issue such messages when its buffers approach capacity. In that case, the datagram referred to in the source-quench message may well be delivered. Thus, receipt of the message does not imply delivery or nondelivery of the corresponding datagram.

A router sends a *redirect* message to a host on a directly connected router to advise the host of a better route to a particular destination; the following is an example of its use. A router, R1, receives a datagram from a host on a network to which the router is attached. The router, R1, checks its routing table and obtains the address for the next router, R2, on the route to the datagram's internet destination network, X. If R2 and the host identified by the internet source address of the datagram are on the same network, a redirect message is sent to the host. The redirect message advises the host to send its traffic for network X directly to router R2, as this is a shorter path to the destination. The router forwards the original datagram to its internet destination (via R2). The address of R2 is contained in the parameter field of the redirect message.

The *echo* and *echo-reply* messages provide a mechanism for testing that communication is possible between entities. The recipient of an echo message is obligated to return the message in an echo-reply message. An identifier and sequence number are associated with the echo message to be matched in the echo-reply message. The identifier might be used like a service access point to identify a particular session, and the sequence number might be incremented on each echo request sent.

The *timestamp* and *timestamp-reply* messages provide a mechanism for sampling the delay characteristics of the internet. The sender of a timestamp message may include an identifier and sequence number in the parameters field and include the time that the message is sent (originate timestamp). The receiver records the time it received the message and the time that it transmits the reply message in the timestamp-reply message. If the timestamp message is sent using strict source routing, then the delay characteristics of a particular route can be measured.

The *address-mask-request* and *address-mask-reply* messages are useful in an environment that includes what are referred to as subnets. The concept of the subnet was introduced to address the following requirement. Consider an internet that includes one or more WANs and a number of sites, each of which has a number of LANs. We would like to allow arbitrary complexity of interconnected LAN structures within an organization, while insulating the overall internet against explosive growth in network numbers and routing complexity. One approach to this problem is to assign a single network number to all of the LANs at a site. From the point of view of the rest of the internet, there is a single network at that site, which simplifies addressing and routing. To allow the routers within the site to function properly, each LAN is assigned a subnet number. The host portion of the internet address is partitioned into a subnet number and a host number to accommodate this new level of addressing.

Within the subnetted network, the local routers must route on the basis of an extended network number consisting of the network portion of the IP address and the subnet number. The bit positions containing this extended network number are indicated by the address mask. The address-mask request and reply messages allow a host to learn the address mask for the LAN to which it connects. The host broadcasts an address-mask request message on the LAN. The router on the LAN responds with an address-mask reply message that contains the address mask. The use of the address mask allows the host to determine whether an outgoing datagram is destined for a host on the same LAN (send directly) or another LAN (send datagram to router). It is assumed that some other means (e.g., manual configuration) is used to create address masks and to make them known to the local routers.

## 16.4 ROUTING PROTOCOLS

The routers in an internet are responsible for receiving and forwarding packets through the interconnected set of subnetworks. Each router makes routing decisions based on knowledge of the topology and on the conditions of the internet. In a simple internet, a fixed routing scheme is possible. In more complex internets, a degree of dynamic cooperation is needed among the routers. In particular, the router must avoid portions of the network that have failed and should avoid portions of the network that are congested. In order to make such dynamic routing decisions, routers exchange routing information using a special routing protocol for that purpose. Information is needed about the status of the internet, in terms of which networks can be reached by which routes, and in terms of the delay characteristics of various routes.

In considering the routing function of routers, it is important to distinguish two concepts:

- **Routing information.** Information about the topology and delays of the internet.
- **Routing algorithm.** The algorithm used to make a routing decision for a particular datagram, based on current routing information.

There is another way to partition the problem that is useful from two points of view: allocating routing functions properly and effective standardization; this is to partition the routing function into

- Routing between end systems (ESs) and routers
- Routing between routers

The reason for the partition is that there are fundamental differences between what an ES must know to route a packet and what a router must know. In the case of an ES, the router must first know whether the destination ES is on the same subnet. If the answer is yes, then data can be delivered directly using the subnetwork access protocol; otherwise, the ES must forward the data to a router attached to the same subnetwork. If there is more than one such router, it is simply a matter of choosing one. The router forwards datagrams on behalf of other systems and needs to have some idea of the overall topology of the network in order to make a global routing decision.

In this section, we look at an example of an ES-to-router and router-to-router protocol.

## Autonomous Systems

In order to proceed in our discussion of router-router protocols, we need to introduce the concept of an *autonomous system*. An autonomous system is an internet connected by homogeneous routers; generally, the routers are under the administrative control of a single entity. An *interior router protocol* (IRP) passes routing information between routers within an autonomous system. The protocol used within the autonomous system does not need to be implemented outside of the system. This flexibility allows IRPs to be custom-tailored to specific applications and requirements.

It may happen, however, that an internet will be constructed of more than one autonomous system. For example, all of the LANs at a site, such as an office complex or campus, could be linked by routers to form an autonomous system. This system might be linked through a wide-area network to other autonomous systems. The situation is illustrated in Figure 16.10. In this case, the routing algorithms and routing tables used by routers in different autonomous systems may differ themselves. Nevertheless, the routers in one autonomous system need at least a minimal level of information concerning networks that can be reached outside the system. The protocol used to pass routing information between routers in different autonomous systems is referred to as an *exterior router protocol* (ERP).

We can expect that an ERP will need to pass less information and be simpler than an IRP, for the following reason. If a datagram is to be transferred from a host in one autonomous system to a host in another autonomous system, a router in the first system need only determine the target autonomous system and devise a route to get into that system. Once the datagram enters the target autonomous system, the routers there can cooperate to finally deliver the datagram.

In the remainder of this section, we look at what are perhaps the most important examples of these two types of routing protocols.

## Border Gateway Protocol

The Border Gateway Protocol (BGP) was developed for use in conjunction with internets that employ the TCP/IP protocol suite, although the concepts are applicable to any internet. BGP has become the standardized exterior router protocol for the Internet.

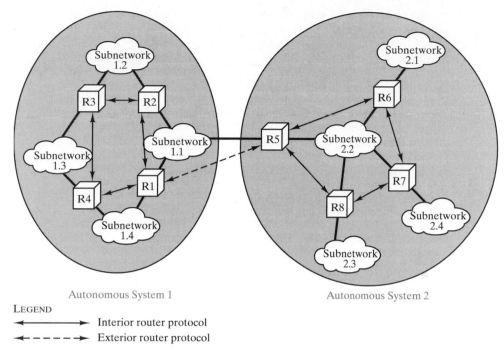

LEGEND

⟵————————⟶  Interior router protocol

⟵— — — —⟶  Exterior router protocol

**FIGURE 16.10**    Application of exterior and interior routing protocols.

## Functions

BGP was designed to allow routers, called gateways in the standard, in different autonomous systems (ASs) to cooperate in the exchange of routing information. The protocol operates in terms of messages, which are sent over TCP connections. The repertoire of messages is summarized in Table 16.4.

**TABLE 16.4**    BGP-4 messages.

| | |
|---|---|
| Open | Used to open a neighbor relationship with another router. |
| Update | Used to (1) transmit information about a single route and/or (2) to list multiple routes to be withdrawn. |
| Keepalive | Used to (1) acknowledge an Open message and (2) periodically confirm the neighbor relationship. |
| Notification | Send when an error condition is detected. |

Three functional procedures are involved in BGP.

- Neighbor acquisition
- Neighbor reachability
- Network reachability

Two routers are considered to be neighbors if they are attached to the same subnetwork. If the two routers are in different autonomous systems, they may wish to exchange routing information. For this purpose, it is necessary to first perform *neighbor acquisition.* The term "neighbor" refers to two routers that share the same subnetwork. In essence, neighbor acquisition occurs when two neighboring routers in different autonomous systems agree to regularly exchange routing information. A formal acquisition procedure is needed because one of the routers may not wish to participate. For example, the router may be overburdened and does not want to be responsible for traffic coming in from outside the system. In the neighbor-acquisition process, one router sends a request message to the other, which may either accept or refuse the offer. The protocol does not address the issue of how one router knows the address, or even the existence of, another router, nor how it decides that it needs to exchange routing information with that particular router. These issues must be addressed at configuration time or by active intervention of a network manager.

To perform neighbor acquisition, one router sends an Open message to another. If the target router accepts the request, it returns a Keepalive message in response.

Once a neighbor relationship is established, the **neighbor-reachability** procedure is used to maintain the relationship. Each partner needs to be assured that the other partner still exists and is still engaged in the neighbor relationship. For this purpose, the two routers periodically issue Keepalive messages to each other.

The final procedure specified by BGP is **network reachability**. Each router maintains a database of the subnetworks that it can reach and the preferred route for reaching that subnetwork. Whenever a change is made to this database, the router issues an Update message that is broadcast to all other routers implementing BGP. By the broadcasting of these Update message, all of the BGP routers can build up and maintain routing information.

### BGP Messages

Figure 16.11 illustrates the formats of all of the BGP messages. Each message begins with a 19-octet header containing three fields, as indicated by the shaded portion of each message in the figure:

- **Marker.** Reserved for authentication. The sender may insert a value in this field that would be used as part of an authentication mechanism to enable the recipient to verify the identity of the sender.
- **Length.** Length of message in octets.
- **Type.** Type of message: Open, Update, Notification, Keepalive.

To acquire a neighbor, a router first opens a TCP connection to the neighbor router of interest. It then sends an Open message. This message identifies the AS to which the sender belongs and provides the IP address of the router. It also includes a Hold Time parameter, which indicates the number of seconds that the sender proposes for the value of the Hold Timer. If the recipient is prepared to open a neighbor relationship, it calculates a value of Hold Timer that is the minimum of its Hold Time and the Hold Time in the Open message. This calculated value is the maximum number of seconds that may elapse between the receipt of successive Keepalive and/or Update messages by the sender.

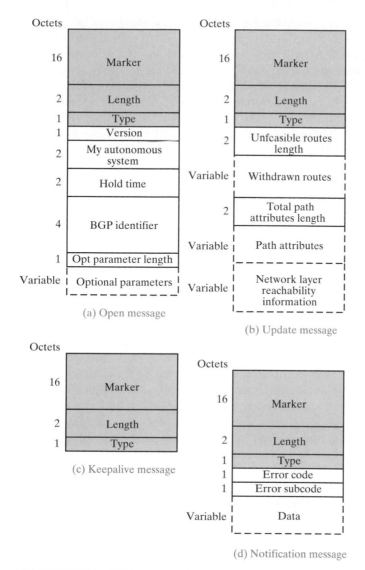

FIGURE 16.11    BGP message formats.

The Keepalive message consists simply of the header. Each router issues these messages to each of its peers often enough to prevent the Hold Time from expiring.
The Update message communicates two types of information:

1. Information about a single route through the internet. This information is available to be added to the database of any recipient router.

2. A list of routes previously advertised by this router that are being withdrawn.

An Update message may contain one or both types of information. Let us consider the first type of information first. Information about a single route through the network involves three fields: the Network Layer Reachability Information (NLRI) field, the Total Path Attributes Length field, and the Path Attributes field. The NLRI field consists of a list of identifiers of subnetworks that can be reached by this route. Each subnetwork is identified by its IP address, which is actually a portion of a full IP address. Recall that an IP address is a 32-bit quantity of the form {network, end system}. The left-hand, or prefix portion of this quantity, identifies a particular subnetwork.

The Path Attributes field contains a list of attributes that apply to this particular route. The following are the defined attributes:

- **Origin.** Indicates whether this information was generated by an interior router protocol (e.g., OSPF) or an exterior router protocol (in particular, BGP).
- **AS_Path.** A list of the ASs that are traversed for this route.
- **Next_Hop.** The IP address of the border router that should be used as the next hop to the destinations listed in the NLRI field.
- **Multi_Exit_Disc.** Used to communicate some information about routes internal to an AS. This is described later in this section.
- **Local_Pref.** Used by a router to inform other routers within the same AS of its degree of preference for a particular route. It has no significance to routers in other ASs.
- **Atomic_Aggregate, Aggregator.** These two fields implement the concept of route aggregation. In essence, an internet and its corresponding address space can be organized hierarchically, or as a tree. In this case, subnetwork addresses are structured in two or more parts. All of the subnetworks of a given subtree share a common partial internet address. Using this common partial address, the amount of information that must be communicated in NLRI can be significantly reduced.

The AS_Path attribute actually serves two purposes. Because it lists the ASs that a datagram must traverse if it follows this route, the AS_Path information enables a router to perform policy routing. That is, a router may decide to avoid a particular path in order to avoid transiting a particular AS. For example, information that is confidential may be limited to certain kinds of ASs. Or, a router may have information about the performance or quality of the portion of the internet that is included in an AS that leads the router to avoid that AS. Examples of performance or quality metrics include link speed, capacity, tendency to become congested, and overall quality of operation. Another criterion that could be used is minimizing the number of transit ASs.

The reader may wonder about the purpose of the Next_Hop attribute. The requesting router will necessarily want to know which networks are reachable via the responding router, but why provide information about other routers? This is best explained with reference to Figure 16.10. In this example, router R1 in autonomous system 1, and router R5 in autonomous system 2, implement BGP and acquire a neighbor relationship. R1 issues Update messages to R5 indicating which networks it could reach and the distances (network hops) involved. R1 also provides the same information on behalf of R2. That is, R1 tells R5 what networks are reachable via R2. In this example, R2 does not implement BGP. Typically, most of the routers in an autonomous system will not implement BGP; only a few will be assigned responsibility for communicating with routers in other autonomous systems. A final point: R1 is in possession of the necessary information about R2, as R1 and R2 share an interior router protocol (IRP).

The second type of update information is the withdrawal of one or more routes. In each case, the route is identified by the IP address of the destination subnetwork.

Finally, the notification message is sent when an error condition is detected. The following errors may be reported:

- **Message header error.** Includes authentication and syntax errors.
- **Open message error.** Includes syntax errors and options not recognized in an Open message. This message can also be used to indicate that a proposed Hold Time in an Open message is unacceptable.
- **Update message error.** Includes syntax and validity errors in an Update message.
- **Hold timer expired.** If the sending router has not received successive Keepalive and/or Update and/or Notification messages within the Hold Time period, then this error is communicated and the connection is closed.
- **Finite state machine error.** Includes any procedural error.
- **Cease.** Used by a router to close a connection with another router in the absence of any other error.

## BGP Routing Information Exchange

The essence of BGP is the exchange of routing information among participating routers in multiple ASs. This process can be quite complex. In what follows, we provide a simplified overview.

Let us consider router R1 in autonomous system 1 (AS1), in Figure 16.10. To begin, a router that implements BGP will also implement an internal routing protocol, such as OSPF. Using OSPF, R1 can exchange routing information with other routers within AS1 and build up a picture of the topology of the subnetworks and routers in AS1 and construct a routing table. Next, R1 can issue an Update message to R5 in AS2. The Update message could include the following:

- AS_Path: the identity of AS1
- Next_Hop: the IP address of R1
- NLRI: a list of all of the subnetworks in AS1

This message informs R5 that all of the subnetworks listed in NLRI are reachable via R1 and that the only autonomous system traversed is AS1.

Suppose now that R5 also has a neighbor relationship with another router in another autonomous system, say R9 in AS3. R5 will forward the information just received from R1 to R9 in a new Update message. This message includes the following:

- AS_Path: the list of identifiers {AS2, AS1}
- Next_Hop: the IP address of R5
- NLRI: a list of all of the subnetworks in AS1

This message informs R9 that all of the subnetworks listed in NLRI are reachable via R5 and that the autonomous systems traversed are AS2 and AS1. R9 must now decide if this is its preferred route to the subnetworks listed. It may have knowledge of an alternate route to some or all of these subnetworks that it prefers for reasons of performance or some other policy metric. If R9 decides that the route provided in R5's update message is preferable, then R9 incorporates that routing information into its routing database and forwards this new routing information to other neighbors. This new message will include an AS_Path field of {AS1, AS2, AS3}.

In the above fashion, routing update information is propagated through the larger internet consisting of a number of interconnected autonomous systems. The AS_Path field is used to assure that such messages do not circulate indefinitely: If an Update message is received by a router in an AS that is included in the AS_Path field, that router will not forward the update information to other routers, thereby preventing looping of messages.

The preceding discussion leaves out several details that are briefly summarized here. Routers within the same AS, called internal neighbors, may exchange BGP information. In this case, the sending router does not add the identifier of the common AS to the AS_Path field. When a router has selected a preferred route to an external destination, it transmits this route to all of its internal neighbors. Each of these routers then decides if the new route is preferred; if so, the new route is added to its database and a new Update message goes out.

When there are multiple entry points into an AS that are available to a border router in another AS, the Multi_Exit_Disc attribute may be used to choose among them. This attribute contains a number that reflects some internal metric for reaching destinations within an AS. For example, suppose in Figure 16.10 that both R1 and R2 implemented BGP and that both had a neighbor relationship with R5. Each provides an Update message to R5 for subnetwork 1.3 that includes a routing metric used internally to AS1, such as a routing metric associated with the OSPF internal router protocol. R5 could then use these two metrics as the basis for choosing between the two routes.

## Open Shortest Path First (OSPF) Protocol

The history of interior routing protocols on the Internet mirrors that of packet-switching protocols on ARPANET. Recall that ARPANET began with a protocol based on the Bellman-Ford algorithm. The resulting protocol required each node to exchange path-delay information with its neighbors. Information about a change in network conditions would gradually ripple through the network. A second generation protocol was based on Dijkstra's algorithm and required each node to exchange link-delay information with all other nodes using flooding. It was found that this latter technique was more effective.

Similarly, the initial interior routing protocol on the DARPA internet was the Routing Information Protocol (RIP), which is essentially the same protocol as the first-generation ARPANET protocol. This protocol requires each router to transmit its entire routing table. Although the algorithm is simple and easy to implement, as the internet expands, routing updates grow larger and consume significantly more network bandwidth. Accordingly, OSPF operates in a fashion similar to the revised ARPANET routing algorithm. OSPF uses what is known as a link-state routing algorithm. Each router maintains descriptions of the state of its local links to subnetworks, and from time to time transmits updated state information to all of the routers of which it is aware. Every router receiving an update packet must acknowledge it to the sender. Such updates produce a minimum of routing traffic because the link descriptions are small and rarely need to be sent.

The OSPF protocol (RFC 1583) is now widely used as the interior router protocol in TCP/IP networks. OSPF computes a route through the internet that incurs the least cost based on a user-configurable metric of cost. The user can configure the cost to express a function of delay, data rate, dollar cost, or other factors. OSPF is able to equalize loads over multiple equal-cost paths.

Each router maintains a database that reflects the known topology of the autonomous system of which it is a part. The topology is expressed as a directed graph. The graph consists of

- Vertices, or nodes, of two types:
  1. router
  2. network, which is, in turn, of two types:
     a) transit, if it can carry data that neither originates nor terminates on an end system attached to this network.
     b) stub, if it is not a transit network.
- Edges of two types:
  1. graph edges that connect two router vertices when the corresponding routers are connected to each other by a direct point-to-point link.
  2. graph edges that connect a router vertex to a network vertex when the router is directly connected to the network.

Figure 16.12 shows an example of an autonomous system, and Figure 16.13 is the resulting directed graph. The mapping is straightforward:

- Two routers joined by a point-to-point link are represented in the graph as being directly connected by a pair of edges, one in each direction (e.g., routers 6 and 10).
- When multiple routers are attached to a network (such as a LAN or packet-switching network), the directed graph shows all routers bidirectionally connected to the network vertex (e.g., routers 1, 2, 3, and 4 all connect to network 3).
- If a single router is attached to a network, the network will appear in the graph as a stub connection (e.g., network 7).

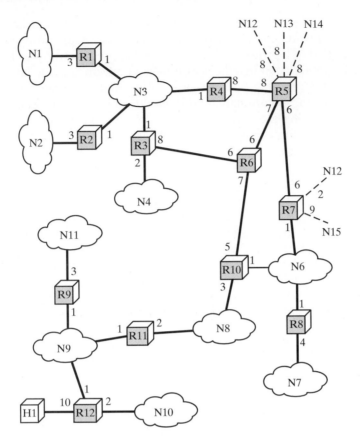

**FIGURE 16.12**   A sample autonomous system.

- An end system, called a host, can be directly connected to a router; such a case is depicted in the corresponding graph (e.g., host 1).
- If a router is connected to other autonomous systems, then the path cost to each network in the other system must be obtained by some exterior routing protocol (ERP). Each such network is represented on the graph by a stub and an edge to the router with the known path cost (e.g., networks 12 through 15).

A cost is associated with the output side of each router interface. This cost is configurable by the system administrator. Arcs on the graph are labeled with the cost of the corresponding router-output interface. Arcs having no labeled cost have a cost of 0. Note that arcs leading from networks to routers always have a cost of 0.

A database corresponding to the directed graph is maintained by each router. It is pieced together from link-state messages from other routers in the internet. Using Dijkstra's algorithm (see Appendix 9A), a router calculates the least-cost path to all destination networks. The result for router 6 of Figure 16.12 is shown as a tree in Figure 16.14, with R6 as the root of the tree. The tree gives the entire route to any destination network or host. However, only the next hop to the destination is used in the forwarding process. The resulting routing table for router 6 is shown in Table 16.5. The table includes entries for routers advertising external routes

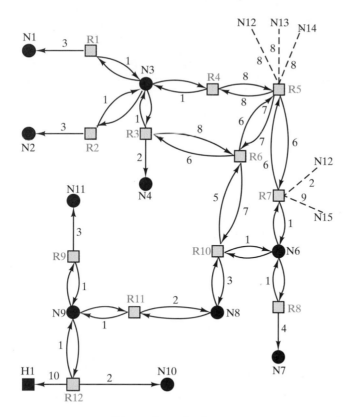

**FIGURE 16.13**   Directed graph of autonomous system of Figure 16.12.

**TABLE 16.5**   Routing Table for RT6.

| Destination | Next hop | Distance |
|:-----------:|:--------:|:--------:|
| N1  | RT3  | 10 |
| N2  | RT3  | 10 |
| N3  | RT3  | 7  |
| N4  | RT3  | 8  |
| N6  | RT10 | 8  |
| N7  | RT10 | 12 |
| N8  | RT10 | 10 |
| N9  | RT10 | 11 |
| N10 | RT10 | 13 |
| N11 | RT10 | 14 |
| H1  | RT10 | 21 |
| RT5 | RT5  | 6  |
| RT7 | RT10 | 8  |
| N12 | RT10 | 10 |
| N13 | RT5  | 14 |
| N14 | RT5  | 14 |
| N15 | RT10 | 17 |

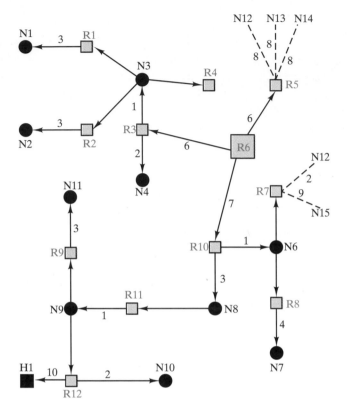

**FIGURE 16.14**  The SPF tree for router R6.

(routers 5 and 7). For external networks whose identity is known, entries are also provided.

## 16.5  IPv6 (IPNG)

The Internet Protocol (IP) has been the foundation of the Internet and of virtually all multivendor private internetworks. This protocol is reaching the end of its useful life, and a new protocol, known as IPv6 (IP version 6), has been defined to ultimately replace IP.[1]

We first look at the motivation for developing a new version of IP, and then examine some of its details.

---

[1] You may think a few versions in this narrative have been skipped. The currently deployed version of IP is actually IP version 4; previous versions of IP (1 through 3) were successively defined and replaced to reach IPv4. Version 5 was the number assigned to the Stream Protocol, a connection-oriented internet-level protocol—hence the use of the label, version 6.

## IP Next Generation

The driving motivation for the adoption of a new version of IP was the limitation imposed by the 32-bit address field in IPv4. With a 32-bit address field, it is, in principle, possible to assign $2^{32}$ different addresses, which represents over 4 billion possibilities. One might think that this number of addresses was more than adequate to meet addressing needs on the Internet. However, in the late 1980s, it was perceived that there would be a problem, and this problem began to manifest itself in the early 1990s. Some of the reasons for the inadequacy of 32-bit addresses include

- The two-level structure of the IP address (network number, host number) is convenient but wasteful of the address space. Once a network number is assigned to a network, all of the host-number addresses for that network number are assigned to that network. The address space for that network may be sparsely used, but as far as the effective IP address space is concerned, if a network number is used, then all addresses within the network are used.
- The IP addressing model generally requires that a unique network number be assigned to each IP network whether or not it is actually connected to the Internet.
- Networks are proliferating rapidly. Most organizations boast multiple LANs, not just a single LAN system; wireless networks have rapidly assumed a major role; and the Internet itself has grown explosively for years.
- Growth of TCP/IP usage into new areas will result in a rapid growth in the demand for unique IP addresses. Examples include using TCP/IP for the interconnection of electronic point-of-sale terminals and for cable television receivers.
- Typically, a single IP address is assigned to each host. A more flexible arrangement is to allow multiple IP addresses per host; this, of course, increases the demand for IP addresses.

So, the need for an increased address space dictated that a new version of IP was needed. In addition, IP is a very old protocol, and new requirements in the areas of security, routing flexibility, and traffic support had been defined.

In response to these needs, the Internet Engineering Task Force (IETF) issued a call for proposals for a next generation IP (IPng) in July of 1992. A number of proposals were received, and by 1994, the final design for IPng emerged. A major milestone was reached with the publication of RFC 1752, "The Recommendation for the IP Next Generation Protocol," issued in January 1995. RFC 1752 outlines the requirements for IPng, specifies the PDU formats, and highlights the IPng approach in the areas of addressing, routing, and security. A number of other Internet documents defined details of the protocol, now officially called IPv6; these include an overall specification of IPv6 (RFC 1883), an RFC discussing the Flow Label in the IPv6 header (RFC 1809), and several RFCs dealing with addressing aspects of IPv6 (RFC 1884, RFC 1886, RFC 1887).

IPv6 includes the following enhancements over IPv4:

- **Expanded Address Space.** IPv6 uses 128-bit addresses instead of the 32-bit addresses of IPv4. This is an increase of address space by a factor of $2^{96}$! It has been pointed out [HIND95] that this allows on the order of $6 \times 10^{23}$ unique addresses per square meter of the surface of the earth! Even if addresses are very inefficiently allocated, this address space seems secure.
- **Improved Option Mechanism.** IPv6 options are placed in separate optional headers that are located between the IPv6 header and the transport-layer header. Most of these optional headers are not examined or processed by any router on the packet's path; this simplifies and speeds up router processing of IPv6 packets, as compared to IPv4 datagrams.[2] It also makes it easier to add additional options.
- **Address Autoconfiguration.** This capability provides for dynamic assignment of IPv6 addresses.
- **Increased Addressing Flexibility.** IPv6 includes the concept of an anycast address, for which a packet is delivered to just one of a set of nodes. The scalability of multicast routing is improved by adding a scope field to multicast addresses.
- **Support for Resource Allocation.** Instead of the type-of-service field in IPv4, IPv6 enables the labeling of packets belonging to a particular traffic flow for which the sender requests special handling; this aids in the support of specialized traffic, such as real-time video.
- **Security Capabilities.** IPv6 includes features that support authentication and privacy.

All of these features are explored in the remainder of this section, except for the security features, which are discussed in Chapter 18.

### IPv6 Structure

An IPv6 protocol data unit (known as a packet) has the following general form:

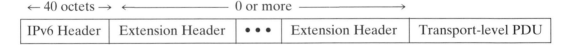

The only header that is required is referred to simply as the IPv6 header. This is of fixed size with a length of 40 octets, compared to 20 octets for the mandatory portion of the IPv4 header (Figure 16.7). The following extension headers have been defined:

- **Hop-by-Hop Options Header.** Defines special options that require hop-by-hop processing.

---

[2] The protocol data unit for IPv6 is referred to as a packet rather than as a datagram, which is the term used for IPv4 PDUs.

- **Routing Header.** Provides extended routing, similar to IPv4 source routing.
- **Fragment Header.** Contains fragmentation and reassembly information.
- **Authentication Header.** Provides packet integrity and authentication.
- **Encapsulating Security Payload Header.** Provides privacy.
- **Destination Options Header.** Contains optional information to be examined by the destination node.

The IPv6 standard recommends that, when multiple extension headers are used, the IPv6 headers appear in the following order:

1. IPv6 header: Mandatory, must always appear first.
2. Hop-by-Hop Options header.
3. Destination Options header: For options to be processed by the first destination that appears in the IPv6 Destination Address field plus subsequent destinations listed in the Routing header.
4. Routing Header.
5. Fragment Header.
6. Authentication Header.
7. Encapsulating Security Payload header.
8. Destination Options header: For options to be processed only by the final destination of the packet.

Figure 16.15 shows an example of an IPv6 packet that includes an instance of each header. Note that the IPv6 header and each extension header include a Next Header field. This field identifies the type of the immediately following header. If the next header is an extension header, then this field contains the type identifier of that header; otherwise, this field contains the protocol identifier of the upper-layer protocol using IPv6 (typically a transport-level protocol), using the same values as the IPv4 Protocol field. In the figure, the upper-layer protocol is TCP, so that the upper-layer data carried by the IPv6 packet consists of a TCP header followed by a block of application data.

We first look at the main IPv6 header, and then examine each of the extensions in turn.

### IPv6 Header

The IPv6 header has a fixed length of 40 octets, consisting of the following fields (Figure 16.16):

- **Version (4 bits).** Internet Protocol version number; the value is 6.
- **Priority (4 bits).** Priority value, discussed below.
- **Flow Label (24 bits).** May be used by a host to label those packets for which it is requesting special handling by routers within a network; discussed below.
- **Payload Length (16 bits).** Length of the remainder of the IPv6 packet following the header, in octets. In other words, this is the total length of all of the extension headers plus the transport-level PDU.

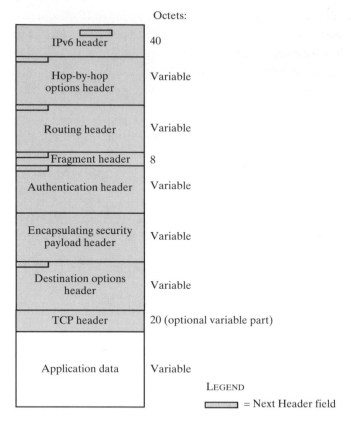

**FIGURE 16.15** IPv6 packet with all extension headers.

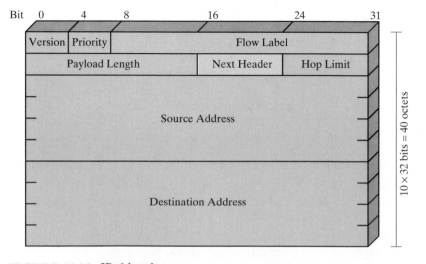

**FIGURE 16.16** IPv6 header.

- **Next Header (8 bits).** Identifies the type of header immediately following the IPv6 header.
- **Hop Limit (8 bits).** The remaining number of allowable hops for this packet. The hop limit is set to some desired maximum value by the source, and decremented by 1 by each node that forwards the packet. The packet is discarded if Hop Limit is decremented to zero; this is simpler than the processing required for the time-to-live field of IPv4. The consensus was that the extra effort in accounting for time intervals in IPv4 added no significant value to the protocol.
- **Source Address (128 bits).** The address of the originator of the packet.
- **Destination Address (128 bits).** The address of the intended recipient of the packet. This may not in fact be the intended ultimate destination if a Routing header is present, as explained below.

Although the IPv6 header is longer than the mandatory portion of the IPv4 header (40 octets versus 20 octets), it contains fewer fields (8 versus 12). Thus, routers have less processing to do per header, which should speed up routing.

## Priority Field

The 4-bit priority field enables a source to identify the desired transmit and delivery priority of each packet relative to other packets from the same source. In fact, the field enables the source to specify separate priority-related characteristics for each packet. First, packets are classified as being part of either traffic for which the source is providing congestion control or traffic for which the source is not providing congestion control; and second, packets are assigned one of eight levels of relative priority within each classification. Figure 16.17 illustrates the interpretation of priority-field values.

*Congestion-controlled traffic* refers to traffic for which the source "backs off" in response to congestion; an example is TCP. Let us consider what this means. If there is congestion in the network, TCP segments will take longer to arrive at the destination, and, hence, acknowledgments from the destination back to the source will take longer. As congestion increases, it becomes necessary for segments to be discarded en route. The discarding could be done by a router when that router experiences buffer overflow, or it could be done by an individual network along the

| | Congestion-controlled traffic | | Non-congestion-controlled traffic | |
|---|---|---|---|---|
| | 0 | uncharacterized traffic | 8 | Most willing to discard |
| | 1 | "Filler" traffic (e.g., netnews) | | (e.g., high-fidelity video) |
| | 2 | Unattended data transfer (e.g., mail) | | • |
| Increasing priority | 3 | (Reserved) | | • |
| | 4 | Attended bulk transfer (e.g., FTP, HTTP) | | • |
| | 5 | (Reserved) | | • |
| | 6 | Interactive Traffic (e.g., TELNET, X) | | • |
| | 7 | Internet control traffic (e.g., routing protocols, SNMP) | 15 | Least willing to discard (e.g., low-fidelity audio) |

*Increasing priority* (left arrow) — *Increasing priority* (right arrow)

**FIGURE 16.17**  IPv6 priorities.

route, when a switching node within the network becomes congested. Whether it is a data segment or an acknowledgment segment, the effect is that TCP does not receive an acknowledgment to its transmitted data segment. TCP responds by retransmitting the segment and by reducing the flow of segments that it generates.

The nature of congestion-controlled traffic is that it is acceptable for there to be a variable amount of delay in the delivery of packets and even for packets to arrive out of order. IPv6 defines the following categories of congestion-controlled traffic, in order of decreasing priority:

- **Internet Control Traffic.** This is the most important traffic to deliver, especially during times of high congestion. For example, routing protocols, such as OSPF and BGP, need to receive updates concerning traffic conditions so that they can adjust routes to try to relieve congestion. Management protocols, such as SNMP, need to be able to report congestion to network-management applications, as well as to be able to perform dynamic reconfiguration and to alter performance-related parameters to cope with congestion.
- **Interactive Traffic.** After Internet-control traffic, the most important traffic to support is interactive traffic, such as on-line user-to-host connections. User efficiency is critically dependent on rapid response time during interactive sessions, so delay must be minimized.
- **Attended Bulk Transfer.** These are applications that may involve the transfer of a large amount of data and for which the user is generally waiting for the transfer to complete. This category differs from interactive traffic in the sense that the user is prepared to accept a longer delay for the bulk transfer than experienced during an interactive dialogue; a good example of this is FTP. Another example is hypertext transfer protocol (HTTP), which supports web browser-server interaction (discussed in Chapter 19).[3]
- **Unattended Data Transfer.** These are applications that are initiated by a user but which are not expected to be delivered instantly. Generally, the user will not wait for the transfer to be complete, but will go on to other tasks. The best example of this category is electronic mail.
- **Filler Traffic.** This is traffic that is expected to be handled in the background, when other forms of traffic have been delivered. USENET messages are good examples.
- **Uncharacterized Traffic.** If the upper-layer application gives IPv6 no guidance about priority, then the traffic is assigned this lowest-priority value.

**Non-congestion-control traffic** is traffic for which a constant data rate and a constant delivery delay are desirable; examples are real-time video and audio. In these cases, it makes no sense to retransmit discarded packets, and, further, it is important to maintain a smooth delivery flow. Eight levels of priority are allocated for this type of traffic from the lowest priority 8 (most willing to discard) to the high-

---

[3] In the case of HTTP, the duration of the underlying connection may be too brief for the sender to receive feedback and therefore HTTP may not do congestion control.

est priority 15 (least willing to discard). In general, the criterion is how much the quality of the received traffic will deteriorate in the face of some dropped packets. For example, low-fidelity audio, such as a telephone voice conversation, would typically be assigned a high priority. The reason is that the loss of a few packets of audio is readily apparent as clicks and buzzes on the line. On the other hand, a high-fidelity video signal contains a fair amount of redundancy, and the loss of a few packets will probably not be noticeable; therefore, this traffic is assigned a relatively low priority.

Please note that there is no priority relationship implied between the congestion-controlled priorities on the one hand and the non–congestion-controlled priorities on the other hand. Priorities are relative only within each category.

## Flow Label

The IPv6 standard defines a flow as a sequence of packets sent from a particular source to a particular (unicast or multicast) destination, for which the source desires special handling by the intervening routers. A flow is uniquely identified by the combination of a source address and a nonzero 24-bit flow label. Thus, all packets that are to be part of the same flow are assigned the same flow label by the source.

From the source's point of view, a flow, typically, will be a sequence of packets that are generated from a single application instance at the source and that have the same transfer service requirements. A flow may comprise a single TCP connection or even multiple TCP connections; an example of the latter is a file transfer application, which could have one control connection and multiple data connections. A single application may generate a single flow or multiple flows; an example of the latter is multimedia conferencing, which might have one flow for audio and one for graphic windows, each with different transfer requirements in terms of data rate, delay, and delay variation.

From the router's point of view, a flow is a sequence of packets that share attributes that affect how those pockets are handled by the router; these include path, resource allocation, discard requirements, accounting, and security attributes. The router may treat packets from different flows differently in a number of ways, including allocating different buffer sizes, giving different precedence in terms of forwarding, and requesting different qualities of service from subnetworks.

There is no special significance to any particular flow label; instead, the special handling to be provided for a packet flow must be declared in some other way. For example, a source might negotiate or request special handling ahead of time, from routers by means of a control protocol, or at transmission time, by information in one of the extension headers in the packet, such as the Hop-by-Hop Options header. Examples of special handling that might be requested are some non-default quality of service and a form of real-time service.

In principle, all of a user's requirements for a particular flow could be defined in an extension header and included with each packet. If we wish to leave the concept of flow open to include a wide variety of requirements, this design approach could result in very large packet headers. The alternative, adopted for IPv6, is the flow label, in which the flow requirements are defined prior to flow commencement and in which a unique flow label is assigned to the flow. In this case, the router must save flow-requirement information about each flow.

The following rules apply to the flow label:

1. Hosts or routers that do not support the Flow Label field must set the field to zero when originating a packet, pass the field unchanged when forwarding a packet, and ignore the field when receiving a packet.

2. All packets originating from a given source with the same non-zero Flow Label must have the same Destination Address, Source Address, Hop-by-Hop Options header contents (if this header is present), and Routing header contents (if this header is present). The intent is that a router can decide how to route and process the packet by simply looking up the flow label in a table, without having to examine the rest of the header.

3. The source assigns a flow label to a flow. New flow labels must be chosen (pseudo-) randomly and uniformly in the range 1 to $2^{24}-1$, subject to the restriction that a source must not re-use a flow label for a new flow within the lifetime of the existing flow. The zero flow label is reserved to indicate that no flow label is being used.

This last point requires some elaboration. The router must maintain information about the characteristics of each active flow that may pass through it, presumably in some sort of table. In order to be able to forward packets efficiently and rapidly, table lookup must be efficient. One alternative is to have a table with $2^{24}$ (about 16 million) entries, one for each possible flow label; this imposes an unnecessary memory burden on the router. Another alternative is to have one entry in the table per active flow, include the flow label with each entry, and require the router to search the entire table each time a packet is encountered; this imposes an unnecessary processing burden on the router. Instead, most router designs are likely to use some sort of hash-table approach. With this approach, a moderate-sized table is used, and each flow entry is mapped into the table using a hashing function on the flow label. The hashing function might simply be the low-order few bits (say 10 or 12) of the flow label or some simple calculation on the 24 bits of the flow label. In any case, the efficiency of the hash approach typically depends on the flow labels being uniformly distributed over their possible range—hence requirement number 3 listed above.

## IPv6 Addresses

IPv6 addresses are 128 bits in length. Addresses are assigned to individual interfaces on nodes, not to the nodes themselves.[4] A single interface may have multiple unique unicast addresses. Any of the unicast addresses associated with a node's interface may be used to uniquely identify that node.

The combination of long addresses and multiple addresses per interface enables improved routing efficiency over IPv4. In IPv4, addresses generally do not have a structure that assists routing, and, therefore, a router may need to maintain huge tables of routing paths. Longer internet addresses allow for aggregating addresses by hierarchies of network, access provider, geography, corporation, and so on. Such aggregation should make for smaller routing tables and faster table

---

[4] In IPv6, a node is any device that implements IPv6; this includes hosts and routers.

look-ups. The allowance for multiple addresses per interface would allow a subscriber that uses multiple access providers across the same interface to have separate addresses aggregated under each provider's address space.

The first field of any IPv6 address is the variable-length Format Prefix, which identifies various categories of addresses. Table 16.6 indicates the current allocation of addresses based on the Format Prefix, and Figure 16.18 shows some IPv6 address formats.

**TABLE 16.6**  Address allocation.

| Allocation space | Prefix (binary) | Fraction of address space |
|---|---|---|
| Reserved | 0000 0000 | 1/256 |
| Unassigned | 0000 0001 | 1/256 |
| Reserved for NSAP Allocation | 0000 001 | 1/128 |
| Reserved for IPX Allocation | 0000 010 | 1/128 |
| Unassigned | 0000 011 | 1/128 |
| Unassigned | 0000 1 | 1/32 |
| Unassigned | 0001 | 1/16 |
| Unassigned | 001 | 1/8 |
| Provider-Based Unicast Address | 010 | 1/8 |
| Unassigned | 011 | 1/8 |
| Reserved for Geographic-Based Unicast Addresses | 100 | 1/8 |
| Unassigned | 101 | 1/8 |
| Unassigned | 110 | 1/8 |
| Unassigned | 1110 | 1/16 |
| Unassigned | 1111 0 | 1/32 |
| Unassigned | 1111 10 | 1/64 |
| Unassigned | 1111 110 | 1/128 |
| Unassigned | 1111 1110 0 | 1/512 |
| Link Local Use Addresses | 1111 1110 10 | 1/1024 |
| Site Local Use Addresses | 1111 1110 11 | 1/1024 |
| Multicast Addresses | 1111 1111 | 1/256 |

IPv6 allows three types of addresses:

- **Unicast.** An identifier for a single interface. A packet sent to a unicast address is delivered to the interface identified by that address.
- **Anycast.** An identifier for a set of interfaces (typically belonging to different nodes). A packet sent to an anycast address is delivered to one of the interfaces identified by that address (the "nearest" one, according to the routing protocols' measure of distance).
- **Multicast.** An identifier for a set of interfaces (typically belonging to different nodes). A packet sent to a multicast address is delivered to all interfaces identified by that address.

## Unicast Addresses

Unicast addresses may be structured in a number of ways. The following have been identified:

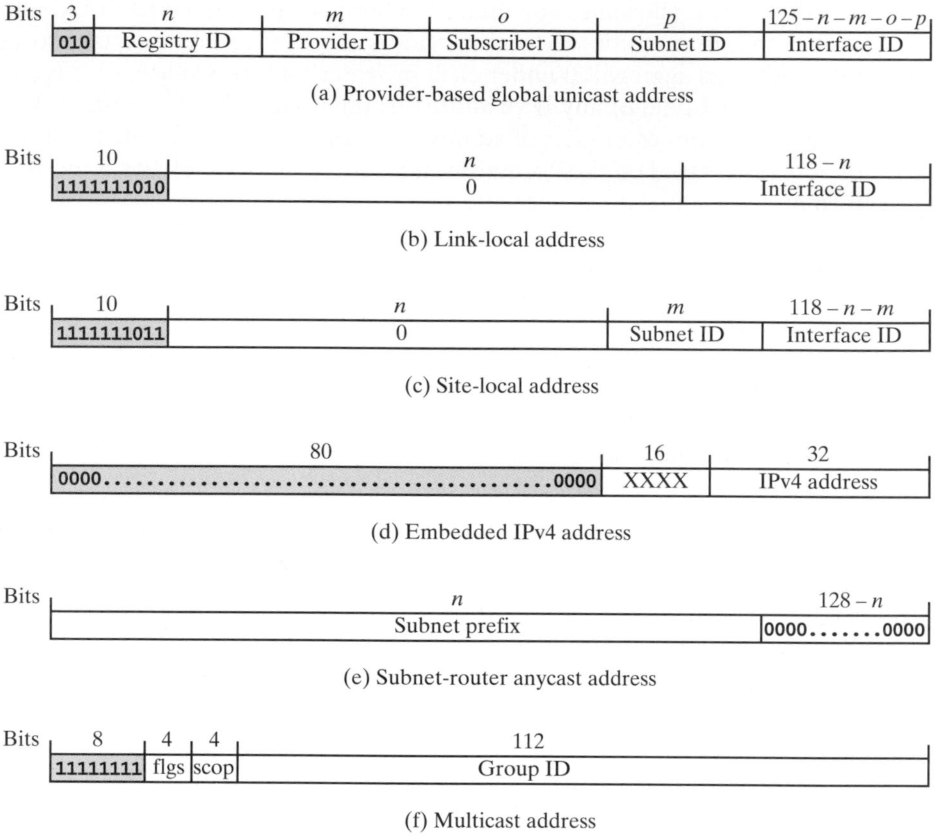

| Bits | 3 | $n$ | $m$ | $o$ | $p$ | $125-n-m-o-p$ |
|---|---|---|---|---|---|---|
| | 010 | Registry ID | Provider ID | Subscriber ID | Subnet ID | Interface ID |

(a) Provider-based global unicast address

| Bits | 10 | $n$ | $118-n$ |
|---|---|---|---|
| | 1111111010 | 0 | Interface ID |

(b) Link-local address

| Bits | 10 | $n$ | $m$ | $118-n-m$ |
|---|---|---|---|---|
| | 1111111011 | 0 | Subnet ID | Interface ID |

(c) Site-local address

| Bits | 80 | 16 | 32 |
|---|---|---|---|
| | 0000.........................................0000 | XXXX | IPv4 address |

(d) Embedded IPv4 address

| Bits | $n$ | $128-n$ |
|---|---|---|
| | Subnet prefix | 0000.......0000 |

(e) Subnet-router anycast address

| Bits | 8 | 4 | 4 | 112 |
|---|---|---|---|---|
| | 11111111 | flgs | scop | Group ID |

(f) Multicast address

**FIGURE 16.18** IPv6 address formats.

- Provider-Based Global
- Link-Local
- Site-Local
- Embedded IPv4
- Loopback

A **provider-based global unicast address** provides for global addressing across the entire universe of connected hosts. The address has five fields after the Format Prefix (Figure 16.18a):

- **Registry ID.** Identifies the registration authority, which assigns the provider portion of the address.
- **Provider ID.** A specific internet service provider, which assigns the subscriber portion of the address.
- **Subscriber ID.** Distinguishes among multiple subscribers attached to the provider portion of the address.

- **Subnet ID.** A topologically connected group of nodes within the subscriber network.
- **Node ID.** Identifies a single node interface among the group of interfaces identified by the subnet prefix.

At present, there is no fixed length assigned to any of these fields. However, from the point of view of a network manager or network designer responsible for a subscriber's installation, the Subnet ID and Node ID are the principal concern. The subscriber can deal with these fields in a number of ways. One possibility for a LAN-based installation is to use a 48-bit node field and use the IEEE 802 medium access control (MAC) address for that field. The remainder of the available bits would then be the Subnet ID field, identifying a particular LAN at that subscriber site.

IPv6 accommodates local-use unicast addresses. Packets with such addresses can only be routed locally—that is, within a subnetwork or set of subnetworks of a given subscriber.

Two types of local-use addresses have been defined: link-local and site-local.

*Link-local addresses* are to be used for addressing on a single link or subnetwork (Figure 16.18b). They cannot be integrated into the global addressing scheme. Examples of their use include auto-address configuration, discussed presently, and neighbor discovery.

*Site-local addresses* are designed for local use but formatted in such a way that they can later be integrated into the global address scheme. The advantage of such addresses is that they can be used immediately by an organization that expects to transition to the use of global addresses. The structure of these addresses (Figure 16.18c) is such that the meaningful portion of the address is confined to the low-order bits not used for global addresses. The remaining bits consist of a local-use Format Prefix (1111 1101 10 or 1111 1101 11), followed by a zero field. When an organization is ready for global connection, these remaining bits can be replaced with a global prefix (e.g., 010 + Registry ID + Provider ID + Subscriber ID + ID).

A key issue in deploying IPv6 is the transition from IPv4 to IPv6. It is not practical to simply replace all IPv4 routers in the Internet or a private internet with IPv6 routers and then replace all IPv4 addresses with IPv6 addresses. Instead, there will be a lengthy transition period when IPv6 and IPv4 must coexist, and, therefore, IPv6 addresses and IPv4 addresses must coexist. *Embedded IPv4 addresses* accommodate this coexistence period. An embedded IPv4 address consists of a 32-bit IPv4 address in the lower-order 32 bits prefixed by either 96 zeroes or prefixed by 80 zeros followed by 16 ones (Figure 16.18d). The first form is known as an IPv4-compatible IPv6 address, and the latter as an IPv4-mapped IPv6 address.

During the transition, the following types of devices will be supported:

- Dual-use routers: These are capable of routing both IPv6 and IPv4 packets.
- Dual-use hosts: These implement both IPv6 and IPv4 and have both IPv6 and IPv4 addresses; the IPv6 address is an *IPv4-compatible IPv6 address.*
- IPv4-only routers: Can only recognize and route IPv4 packets and only know about hosts with IPv4 addresses.

- IPv4-only hosts: Implement only IPv4 and have only an IPv4 address. This address can be represented in the IPv6 realm using an *IPv4-mapped IPv6 address.*

With this configuration, full interoperability is maintained. The details of this interoperability are rather complex (see [GILL95] for a discussion). However, the following general principles apply:

1. Traffic generated by IPv4-only hosts. If the traffic passes through an IPv6 portion of the Internet, a dual-use router must convert the IPv4 destination address to an embedded IPv4 address of the appropriate type and then construct the IPv6 header.
2. Traffic generated by a dual-use host. A technique known as tunneling may be employed to forward such traffic through IPv4 routing topologies. In essence, an IPv6 packet is encapsulated in an IPv4 datagram.

Full coexistence can be maintained so long as all IPv6 nodes employ an IPv4-compatible address. Once more general IPv6 addresses come into use, coexistence will be more difficult to maintain.

The unicast address 0:0:0:0:0:0:0:1 is called the *loopback address.*[5] It may be used by a node to send an IPv6 packet to itself; such packets are not to be sent outside a single node.

### Anycast Addresses

An anycast address enables a source to specify that it wants to contact any one node from a group of nodes via a single address. A packet with such an address will be routed to the nearest interface in the group, according to the router's measure of distance. A possible use of an anycast address might be found within a routing header to specify an intermediate address along a route. The anycast address could refer to the group of routers associated with a particular provider or particular subnet, thus dictating that the packet be routed through that provider or internet in the most efficient manner.

Anycast addresses are allocated from the same address space as unicast addresses. Thus, members of an anycast group must be configured to recognize that addresses and routers must be configured to be able to map an anycast address to a group of unicast interface addresses.

One particular form of anycast address, the *subnet-router anycast address,* is predefined (Figure 16.18e). The subnet prefix field identifies a specific subnetwork. For example, in a provider-based global address space, the subnet prefix is of the form (010 + Registry ID + Provider ID + Subscriber ID + Subnet ID). Thus, the anycast address is identical to a unicast address for an interface on this subnetwork, with the interface ID portion set to zero. Any packet sent to this address will be

---

[5] The preferred form for representing IPv6 addresses as text strings is x:x:x:x:x:x:x:x, where each x is the hexadecimal value of a 16-bit portion of the address; it is not necessary to show leading zeros, but each position must have at least one digit.

delivered to one router on the subnetwork; all that is required is to insert the correct interface ID into the anycast address to form the unicast destination address.

## Multicast Addresses

IPv6 includes the capability of addressing a predefined group of interfaces with a single multicast address. A packet with a multicast address is to be delivered to all members of the group; this address consists of an 8-bit format prefix of all ones, a 4-bit flags field, a 4-bit scope field, and a 112-bit group ID.

At present, the flags field consists of 3 zero bits followed by a T bit with

- $T = 0$: Indicates a permanently-assigned, or well-known, multicast address, assigned by the global-internet numbering authority.
- $T = 1$: Indicates a non-permanently-assigned, or transient, multicast address.

The scope value is used to limit the scope of the multicast group. The values are

| | | | | | | | |
|---|---|---|---|---|---|---|---|
| 0 | reserved | 4 | unassigned | 8 | organization-local | 12 | unassigned |
| 1 | node-local | 5 | site-local | 9 | unassigned | 13 | unassigned |
| 2 | link-local | 6 | unassigned | 10 | unassigned | 14 | global |
| 3 | unassigned | 7 | unassigned | 11 | unassigned | 15 | reserved |

The group ID identifies a multicast group, either permanent or transient, within the given scope. In the case of a permanent multicast address, the address itself is independent of the scope field, but that field limits the scope of addressing for a particular packet. For example, if the "NTP servers group" is assigned a permanent multicast address with a group ID of 43 (hex), then

FF05:0:0:0:0:0:0:43 means all NTP servers at the same site as the sender.
FF0E:0:0:0:0:0:0:43 means all NTP servers in the internet.

Non-permanently-assigned multicast addresses are only meaningful within a given scope, thereby enabling the same group ID to be reused, with different interpretations, at different sites.

Multicasting is a useful capability in a number of contexts. For example, it allows hosts and routers to send neighbor discovery messages only to those machines that have registered to receive them, removing the necessity for all other machines to examine and discard irrelevant packets. Another example is that most LANs provide a natural broadcast capability. Therefore, a multicast address can be assigned that has a scope of link-local and with a group ID that is configured on all nodes on the LAN to be a subnet broadcast address.

## Address Autoconfiguration

Typically, in an IPv4 environment, users or network managers must manually configure IPv4 addresses on nodes. This is a task that is error-prone if done by individual users and time-consuming if done by network managers. It also requires that every node be manually reconfigured in order to change network addresses. Address autoconfiguration is a feature defined as part of the IPv6 specification that enables a host to configure automatically one or more addresses per interface. The aim of this feature is to support a "plug-and-play" capability, which will allow a user to attach a host to a subnetwork and have IPv6 addresses automatically assigned to its interfaces, with no user intervention.

Three models of address assignment have been defined: local scope, stateless server, and stateful server. The **local scope model** is designed for use on a network without routers, isolated from other networks. In this case, the IPv6 address could simply be the MAC address (FE:[MAC]), or it could be an address assigned by some simple dynamic address assignment capability; this would be a link-local address (Figure 16.18b) that is not useful for later integration into the global environment.

With the **stateless server model**, a new device sends a request packet to a local well-known multicast address. This request includes something to identify the device, such as its MAC address or some other key value. An address server receives this request, constructs an IPv6 address for the device based on its knowledge of the network, and sends the address back to the device in a response packet. The address server need not retain any memory of the transaction. This is a very simple configuration mechanism and requires minimal system administration support.

The **stateful server model** supports greater administrative system control by retaining information about address-assignment transactions. In this case, the MAC address or other key value received in a request packet is used to look up information in a database and create a new IPv6 address. This new address is given a lifetime value, after which the host must request again. The result is that subnetwork-wide address reconfiguration is more easily supported.

## Hop-by-Hop Options Header

The hop-by-hop options header carries optional information that, if present, must be examined by every router along the path. This header consists of (Figure 16.19a):

- **Next Header (8 bits).** Identifies the type of header immediately following this header.
- **Header Extension Length (8 bits).** Length of this header in 64-bit units, not including the first 64 bits.
- **Options.** A variable-length field consisting of one or more option definitions. Each definition is in the form of three subfields: *option type* (8 bits), which identifies the option; *length* (8 bits), which specifies the length of the *option data* field in octets; and *option data*, which is a variable-length specification of the option.

It is actually the lowest-order five bits of the option type field that are used to specify a particular option. The high-order two bits indicate the particular action to be taken by a node that does not recognize this option type, as follows:

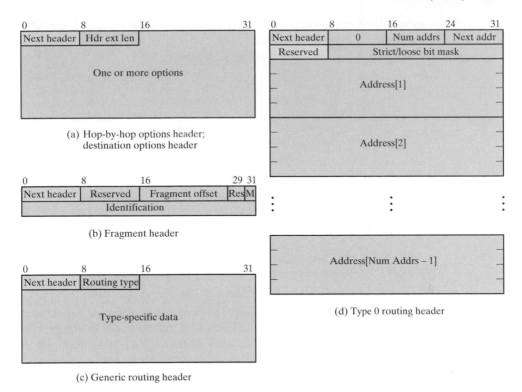

FIGURE 16.19   IPv6 extension headers.

**00**   Skip over this option and continue processing the header.

**01**   Discard the packet.

**10**   Discard the packet and send an ICMP parameter problem, code 2, message to the packet's source address, pointing to the unrecognized option type.

**11**   Discard the packet and, only if the packet's Destination Address is not a multicast address, send an ICMP parameter problem, code 2, message to the packet's source address, pointing to the unrecognized option type.

The third highest-order bit specifies whether the Option Data field does not change (0) or may change (1) en route from source to destination. Data that may change must be excluded from authentication calculations, as discussed in Section 18.4.

These conventions for the option type field also apply to the destination options header.

In the IPv6 standard, only one option is so far specified: the *jumbo payload* option, used to send IPv6 packets with payloads longer than $2^{16} = 65,536$ octets. The option data field of this option is 32 bits long and gives the length of the packet in octets, excluding the IPv6 header. For such packets, the payload length field in the IPv6 header must be set to zero, and there must be no fragment header. With this option, IPv6 supports packet sizes up to more than 4 billion octets; this facilitates the transmission of large video packets and enables IPv6 to make the best use of available capacity over any transmission medium.

### Fragment Header

In IPv6, fragmentation may only be performed by source nodes, not by routers along a packet's delivery path. To take full advantage of the internetworking environment, a node must perform a path-discovery algorithm that enables it to learn the smallest maximum transmission unit (MTU) supported by any subnetwork on the path. With this knowledge, the source node will fragment, as required, for each given destination address. Otherwise the source must limit all packets to 576 octets, which is the minimum MTU that must be supported by each subnetwork.

The fragment header consists of (Figure 16.19b) the following:

- **Next Header (8 bits).** Identifies the type of header immediately following this header.
- **Reserved (8 bits).** For future use.
- **Fragment Offset (13 bits).** Indicates where in the original packet the payload of this fragment belongs. It is measured in 64-bit units; this implies that fragments (other than the last fragment) must contain a data field that is a multiple of 64 bits.
- **Res (2 bits).** Reserved for future use.
- **M Flag (1 bit).** 1 = more fragments; 0 = last fragment.
- **Identification (32 bits).** Intended to uniquely identify the original packet. The identifier must be unique for the packet's source address and destination address, for the time during which the packet will remain in the internet.

The fragmentation algorithm is the same as that described in Section 16.1.

### Routing Header

The routing header contains a list of one or more intermediate nodes to be visited on the way to a packet's destination. All routing headers start with an 8-bit next-header field and an 8-bit routing-type field, followed by routing data specific to a given routing type (Figure 16.19c). If a router does not recognize the routing-type value, it must discard the packet. Type-0 routing has been defined and has the following fields (Figure 16.19d):

- **Next Header (8 bits).** Identifies the type of header immediately following this header.
- **Routing Type (8 bits).** Set to zero.
- **Num Addrs (8 bits).** Number of addresses in the routing header; the maximum value is 23.
- **Next Addr (8 bits).** Index of the next address to be processed; initialized to zero by the originating node.

- **Reserved (8 bits).** For future use.
- **Strict/Loose Bit Mask (24 bits)**. Numbered from left to right (bit 0 through bit 23), with each bit corresponding to one of the addresses. Each bit indicates whether the corresponding next destination address must be a neighbor of the preceding address (1 = strict, must be a neighbor; 0 = loose, need not be a neighbor).

When using the routing header, the source node does not place the ultimate destination address in the IPv6 header. Instead, that address is the last one listed in the routing header (Address[Num Addr - a] in Figure 16.19d), and the IPv6 header contains the destination address of the first desired router on the path. The routing header will not be examined until the packet reaches the node identified in the IPv6 header. At that point, the packet IPv6 and routing header contents are updated, and the packet is forwarded.

IPv6 requires an IPv6 node to reverse routes in a packet it receives containing a routing header, in order to return a packet to the sender; with this in mind, let us consider a set of examples from [HIND95], which illustrate the power and flexibility of the routing header feature. Figure 16.20 shows a configuration in which two hosts are connected by two providers, and the two providers are in turn connected by a wireless network. In the scenarios to follow, address sequences are shown in the following format:

$$\text{SRC}, I_1, I_2, \ldots I_n, \text{DST}$$

where SRC is the source address listed in the IPv6 header, $I_i$ is the $i$th intermediate address, and DST is the ultimate destination. If there is no routing header, DST appears in the IPv6 header; otherwise, it is the last address in the routing header. Now consider three scenarios in which H1 sends a packet to H2.

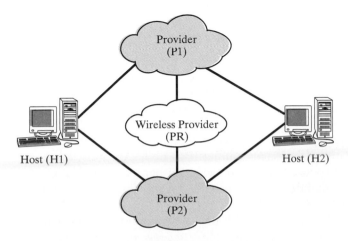

**FIGURE 16.20**  Example routing configuration.

1. No routing header is used. H1 sends a packet to H2 containing the sequence (H1, H2). H2 replies with a packet containing (H2, H1). In this case, either provider could be used on each transfer.

2. H1 wants to enforce a policy that all traffic between itself and H2 can only use P1. It constructs a packet with the sequence (H1, P1, H2) and dictates strict routing; this ensures that when H2 replies to H1, it will use the sequence (H2, P1, H1) with strict routing, thus enforcing H1's policy of using P1.

3. H1 becomes mobile and moves to provider PR. It could maintain communication (not breaking any TCP connections) with H2 by sending packets with (H1, PR, P1, H2); this would ensure that H2 would enforce the policy of using P1 by replying with (H2, PR, P1, H1).

These examples show the ability in IPv6 to select a particular provider, to maintain connections while mobile, and to route packets to new addresses dynamically.

### Destination Options Header

The *destination options* header carries optional information that, if present, is examined only by the packet's destination node. The format of this header is the same as that of the hop-by-hop options header (Figure 16.19a).

## 16.6  ICMPv6

As with IPv4, IPv6 requires the use of ICMP, the original version of which does not meet all of the needs for IPv6. Hence, a new version, known as ICMPv6, has been specified (RFC 1885). Key features of ICMPv6 are as follows:

- ICMPv6 uses a new protocol number to distinguish it from the ICMP that works with IPv4.
- Both protocols use the same header format.
- Some little-used ICMP messages have been omitted from ICMPv6.
- The maximum size of ICMPv6 messages is larger (576 octets, including IPv6 headers) so as to exploit the increased size of packets that IPv6 guarantees will be transmitted without fragmentation.

As with ICMP for IPv4, ICMPv6 provides a means for transferring error messages and informational messages among IPv6 nodes. In most cases, an ICMPv6 message is sent in response to an IPv6 packet, either by a router along the packet's path or by the intended destination node. ICMPv6 messages are carried encapsulated in an IPv6 packet.

All ICMPv6 messages begin with the same common header fields:

- **Type (8 bits).** Identifies the type of ICMPv6 message. Currently, there are four types of error messages and five types of informational messages.

- **Code (8 bits).** Used to specify parameters of the message that can be encoded in a few bits.
- **Checksum (16 bits).** The 16-bit one's complement of the one's complement sum of the entire ICMPv6 message, plus a pseudo-header, described next.
- **Parameters (32 bits).** Used to specify more lengthy parameters.

The checksum field applies to the entire ICMPv6 message, plus a pseudo-header prefixed to the header at the time of calculation (at both transmission and reception). The pseudo-header includes the following fields from the IPv6 header: source and destination addresses, payload length, and the next-header field (Figure 16.21). By including the pseudo-header, ICMPv6 protects itself from misdelivery by IP. That is, if IP delivers a message to the wrong host, even if the message contains no bit errors, the receiving ICMPv6 entity will detect the delivery error.

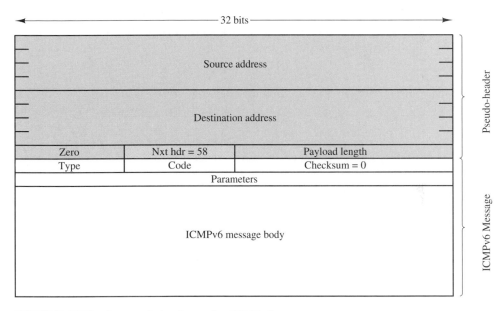

**FIGURE 16.21**    Scope of checksum for ICMPv6.

## Error Messages

ICMPv6 includes four error messages:

- Destination unreachable
- Packet too big
- Time exceeded
- Parameter problem

Each of these messages refers to a prior IPv6 packet and is sent to the originator of the message. The message body includes as much of the original packet as possible, up to a limit on the size of the IPv6 packet carrying this message of 576 octets (Figure 16.22a to c); this enables the source node to match the incoming ICMPv6 message with the prior datagram.

The *destination unreachable* message covers a number of contingencies, which are indicated by the code field value:

- **No route to destination (0).** Router does not know how to reach the destination subnetwork.
- **Communication with destination administratively prohibited (1).** Delivery prevented by a firewall of other administrative policy.
- **Not a neighbor (2).** The router field of the packet identifies the next node on the path with the strict bit set, but that node is not a neighbor.
- **Address unreachable (3).** Unable to resolve the IPv6 destination address into a link address, or a link-specific problem of some kind.
- **Port unreachable (4).** The destination transport protocol (e.g., UDP) is not listening on that port, and that transport protocol has no other means to inform the sender.

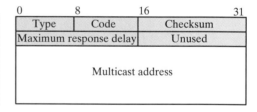

FIGURE 16.22   ICMPv6 message formats.

The *packet-too-big* message is sent by a router in response to a packet whose size exceeds the MTU of the outgoing link. The MTU field in this message (Figure 16.22b) is the MTU of the next-hop link or subnetwork. This message can be used as part of a path MTU discovery process, by which a source node learns of the MTU along various paths.

The *time exceeded* message is sent by a router if it receives a packet with a hop limit of zero, or if it decrements the hop limit to zero. The code is set to 0. This message may also be sent by a destination node, with a code of 1, if reassembly timeout occurs. For IPv6, it is expected that each node will set a local reassembly timeout value for the reassembly process.

A syntactic or semantic error in an IPv6 header will cause a *parameter problem* message to be returned by a router or host. Three kinds of error conditions are identified by the code field: erroneous header field (0), unrecognized next-header type (1), and unrecognized IPv6 option (2). The pointer field contains a pointer to the octet in the original header where the error was detected.

## Informational Messages

ICMPv6 includes three informational messages (Figure 16.22d and e):

- Echo request
- Echo reply
- Group membership

The *echo request* and *echo reply* messages provide a mechanism for testing that communication is possible between entities. The recipient of an echo request message is obligated to return the message body in an echo reply message. An identifier and sequence number are associated with the echo request message to be matched in the echo reply message. The identifier might be used like a service access point to identify a particular session, and the sequence number might be incremented on each echo request sent.

The *group-management* message implements the procedures of the Internet Group Management Protocol (IGMP), defined in RFC 1112. IGMP is an extension of ICMP that provides a mechanism for deciding whether a router should forward a multicast IPv4 datagram. In ICMPv6, there are actually three different messages with different type values:

- Group-membership query (type = 130)
- Group-membership report (type = 131)
- Group-membership termination (type = 132)

A host may join a multicast group by sending a group-membership report on a subnetwork with the multicast address in the body of the message; the IPv6 packet containing this message is addressed to that same multicast address. Routers on the subnetwork receive the report and store the information that at least one node on that subnetwork is a member of the group. A host may terminate its membership by sending a group-membership termination message.

At regular intervals, routers send out group-membership query messages. The IPv6 destination address can be a specific multicast address, or it can be the link-local–all-nodes multicast address. The maximum response delay value is the maximum time that a responding report message may be delayed, in milliseconds. Each host which still wishes to be a member of the group or groups replies for each appropriate group with a group-membership report.

## 16.7 RECOMMENDED READING

Good coverage of internetworking and IP can be found in [COME95]. Detailed coverage of OSPF and other routing algorithms is provided by [HUIT95]; these topics are also treated in [STEE95] and [PERL92].

[BRAD96] is the most thorough treatment of IPv6-related issues. However, the actual technical treatment of IPv6 is limited to less than is covered in this book; instead, the book provides a relatively nontechnical discussion of the requirements for IPv6 and of the history of the IPv6 development. [GILL95] provides a detailed description of the IPv4-to-IPv6 transition, with emphasis on tunneling mechanisms; [MURP95] also contains a useful discussion of the topic.

BRAD96   Bradner, S. and Mankin, A. *IPng: Internet Protocol Next Generation*. Reading, MA: Addison-Wesley, 1996.

COME95   Comer, D. *Internetworking with TCP/IP, Volume I: Principles, Protocols, and Architecture*. Englewood Cliffs, NJ: Prentice Hall, 1995.

GILL95   Gilligan, R. and Callon, R. "IPv6 Transition Mechanisms Overview." *Connexions*, October, 1995.

HUIT95   Huitema, C. *Routing in the Internet*. Englewood Cliffs, NJ: Prentice Hall, 1995.

MURP95   Murphy, E. Hayes, S. and Enders, M. *TCP/IP: Tutorial and Technical Overview*. Upper Saddle River, NJ: Prentice Hall, 1995.

PERL92   Perlman, R. *Interconnections: Bridges and Routers*. Reading, MA: Addison-Wesley, 1992.

STEE95   Steenstrup, M. *Routing in Communications Networks*. Englewood Cliffs, NJ: Prentice Hall, 1995.

**Recommended Web Site**

- http://playground.sun.com/pub/ipng/html/ipng-main.html: Contains information about IPv6 and related topics.

## 16.8 PROBLEMS

16.1   In the discussion of IP, it was mentioned that the *identifier, don't-fragment identifier*, and *time to live* parameters are present in the Send primitive but not in the Deliver primitive because they are only of concern to IP. For each of these primitives, indicate whether it is of concern to the IP entity in the source, to the IP entities in any intermediate routers, and to the IP entity in the destination end systems. Justify your answer.

16.2   What are the pros and cons of intermediate reassembly of an internet segmented datagram versus reassembly at the final destination?

16.3   What is the header overhead in the IP protocol?

16.4   Describe some circumstances where it might be desirable to use source routing rather than let the routers make the routing decision.

16.5   Because of segmentation, an IP datagram can arrive in several pieces, not necessarily in the correct order. The IP entity at the receiving-end system must accumulate these segments until the original datagram is reconstituted.

    a.   Consider that the IP entity creates a buffer for assembling the data field in the original datagram. As assembly proceeds, the buffer will contain blocks of data and "holes" between the data blocks. Describe an algorithm for reassembly based on this concept.

    b.   For the algorithm in part (a), it is necessary to keep track of the holes; describe a simple mechanism for doing this.

16.6   The IP checksum needs to be recalculated at routers because of changes to the IP header, such as the lifetime field. It is possible to recalculate the checksum from scratch. Suggest a procedure that involves less calculation. Hint: Suppose that the value in octet $k$ is changed by $Z = $ new_value–old_value; consider the effect of this change on the checksum.

16.7   An IP datagram is to be segmented. Which options in the option field need to be copied into the header of each segment, and which need only be retained in the first segment? Justify the handling of each option.

16.8   A transport layer message consisting of 1500 bits of data and 160 bits of header is sent to an internet layer which appends another 160 bits of header; this is then transmitted through two networks, each of which uses a 24-bit packet header. The destination network has a maximum packet size of 800 bits. How many bits, including headers, are delivered to the network layer protocol at the destination?

16.9   The ICMP format includes the first 64 bits of the datagram data field. What might be the purpose of including these bits?

16.10   The architecture suggested by Figure 16.4 is to be used. What functions could be added to the routers to alleviate some of the problems caused by the mismatched local and long-haul networks?

16.11   Would the spanning tree approach be good for an internet including routers?

16.12   Should internetworking be concerned with a network's internal routing? Why or why not?

16.13   Compare the individual fields of the IPv4 header with the IPv6 header. Account for the functionality provided by each IPv4 field by showing how the same functionality is provided in IPv6.

16.14   Justify the recommended order in which IPv6 extension headers appear (i.e., why is the hop-by-hop options header first, why is the routing header before the fragment header, and so on).

16.15   The IPv6 standard states that if a packet with a non-zero flow label arrives at a router, and the router has no information for that flow label, the router should ignore the flow label and forward the packet.

    a.   What are the disadvantages of treating this event as an error, discarding the packet and sending an ICMP message?

    b.   Are there situations in which routing the packet as if its flow label were zero will cause the wrong result? Explain.

16.16   The IPv6 flow mechanism assumes that the state associated with a given flow label is stored in routers, so they know how to handle packets that carry that flow label. A design requirement is to flush flow labels that are no longer being used (stale flow label) from routers.

    a. Assume that a source always sends a control message to all affected routers deleting a flow label when the source finishes with that flow. In that case, how could a stale flow label persist?

    b. Suggest router and source mechanisms to overcome the problem of stale flow labels.

16.17  The question arises as to which packets generated by a source should carry non-zero IPv6 flow labels. For some applications, the answer is obvious. Small exchanges of data should have a zero flow label because it is not worth creating a flow for a few packets. Real-time flows should have a flow label; such flows are a primary reason flow labels were created. A more difficult issue is what to do with peers sending large amounts of best-effort traffic (e.g., TCP connections). Make a case for assigning a unique flow label to each long-term TCP connection. Make a case for not doing this.

16.18  The original IPv6 specifications combined the priority and flow label fields into a single 28-bit flow label field. This allowed flows to redefine the interpretation of different values of priority. Suggest reasons why the final specification includes the Priority field as a distinct field.

16.19  Based on Table 16.6, what percentage of the total address space has already been assigned?

16.20  For Type 0 IPv6 routing, specify the algorithm for updating the IPv6 and routing headers by intermediate nodes.

# CHAPTER 17

# TRANSPORT PROTOCOLS

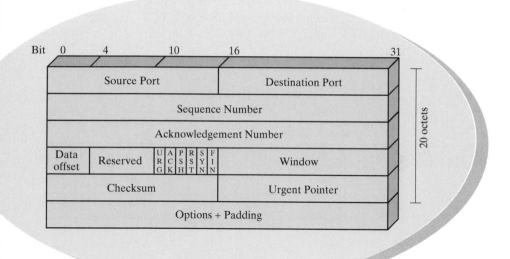

The transport protocol is the keystone of the whole concept of a computer-communications architecture. Lower-layer protocols are needed, to be sure, but they are less important for 1) pedagogical purposes, and 2) designing purposes. For one thing, lower-level protocols are better understood and, on the whole, less complex than transport protocols. Also, standards have settled out quite well for most kinds of layer 1 to 3 transmission facilities, and there is a large body of experience behind their use.

Viewed from the other side, upper-level protocols depend heavily on the transport protocol. The transport protocol provides the basic end-to-end service of transferring data between users and relieves applications and other upper-layer protocols from the need to deal with the characteristics of intervening communications networks and services.

We begin by looking at the services that one might expect from a transport protocol. Next, we examine the protocol mechanisms required to provide these services. We find that most of the complexity relates to connection-oriented services. As might be expected, the less the network service provides, the more the transport protocol must do. The remainder of the chapter looks at two widely used transport protocols: transmission control protocol (TCP) and user datagram protocol (UDP). Figure 17.1 highlights the position of these protocols within the TCP/IP protocol suite.

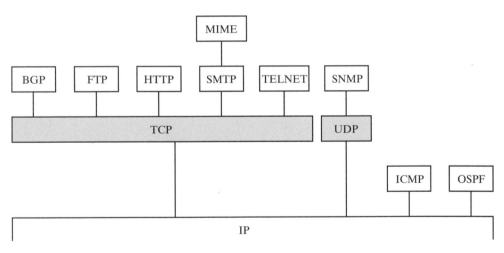

**FIGURE 17.1**   Transport-level protocols in context.

## 17.1  TRANSPORT SERVICES

We begin by looking at the kinds of services that a transport protocol can or should provide to higher-level protocols. Figure 17.2 places the concept of transport services in context. In a system, there is a transport entity that provides services to TS

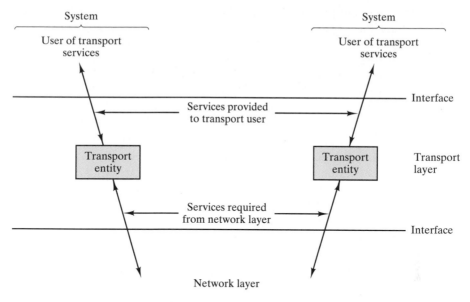

**FIGURE 17.2**  Transport entity context.

users,[1] which might be an application process or a session-protocol entity. This local transport entity communicates with some remote-transport entity, using the services of some lower layer, such as the network layer.

We have already mentioned that the general service provided by a transport protocol is the end-to-end transport of data in a way that shields the TS user from the details of the underlying communications systems. To be more specific, we must consider the specific services that a transport protocol can provide. The following categories of service are useful for describing the transport service:

- Type of service
- Quality of service
- Data transfer
- User interface
- Connection management
- Expedited delivery
- Status reporting
- Security

## Type of Service

Two basic types of service are possible: connection-oriented and connectionless, or datagram service. A connection-oriented service provides for the establishment,

---
[1] For brevity, we will refer to the user of a transport service as a TS user; this term is used in ISO documents.

maintenance, and termination of a logical connection between TS users. This has, so far, been the most common type of protocol service available and has a wide variety of applications. The connection-oriented service generally implies that the service is reliable.

The strengths of the connection-oriented approach are clear. It allows for connection-related features such as flow control, error control, and sequenced delivery. Connectionless service, however, is more appropriate in some contexts. At lower layers (internet, network), connectionless service is more robust (e.g., see discussion in Section 9.1). In addition, it represents a "least common denominator" of service to be expected at higher layers. Further, even at transport and above, there is justification for a connectionless service. There are instances in which the overhead of connection establishment and maintenance is unjustified or even counterproductive. Some examples follow:

- **Inward data collection.** Involves the periodic active or passive sampling of data sources, such as sensors, and automatic self-test reports from security equipment or network components. In a real-time monitoring situation, the loss of an occasional data unit would not cause distress, as the next report should arrive shortly.
- **Outward data dissemination.** Includes broadcast messages to network users, the announcement of a new node or the change of address of a service, and the distribution of real-time clock values.
- **Request-response.** Applications in which a transaction service is provided by a common server to a number of distributed TS users, and for which a single request-response sequence is typical. Use of the service is regulated at the application level, and lower-level connections are often unnecessary and cumbersome.
- **Real-time applications.** Such as voice and telemetry, involving a degree of redundancy and/or a real-time transmission requirement; these must not have connection-oriented functions, such as retransmission.

Thus, there is a place at the transport level for both a connection-oriented and a connectionless type of service.

## Quality of Service

The transport protocol entity should allow the TS user to specify the quality of transmission service to be provided. The transport entity will attempt to optimize the use of the underlying link, network, and internet resources to the best of its ability, so as to provide the collective requested services.

Examples of services that might be requested are

- Acceptable error and loss levels
- Desired average and maximum delay
- Desired average and minimum throughput
- Priority levels

Of course, the transport entity is limited to the inherent capabilities of the underlying service. For example, IP does provide a quality-of-service parameter. It allows for specification of eight levels of precedence or priority as well as a binary specification for normal or low delay, normal or high throughput, and normal or high reliability. Thus, the transport entity can "pass the buck" to the internetwork entity. However, the internet protocol entity is itself limited; routers have some freedom to schedule items preferentially from buffers, but beyond that are still dependent on the underlying transmission facilities. Here is another example: X.25 provides for throughput class negotiation as an optional user facility. The network may alter flow control parameters and the amount of network resources allocated on a virtual circuit to achieve desired throughput.

The transport layer may also resort to other mechanisms to try to satisfy TS user requests, such as splitting one transport connection among multiple virtual circuits to enhance throughput.

The TS user of the quality-of-service feature needs to recognize that

- Depending on the nature of the transmission facility, the transport entity will have varying degrees of success in providing a requested grade of service.
- There is bound to be a trade-off among reliability, delay, throughput, and cost of services.

Nevertheless, certain applications would benefit from, or even require, certain qualities of service and, in a hierarchical or layered architecture, the easiest way for an application to extract this quality of service from a transmission facility is to pass the request down to the transport protocol.

Examples of applications that might request particular qualities of service are as follows:

- A file transfer protocol might require high throughput. It may also require high reliability to avoid retransmissions at the file transfer level.
- A transaction protocol (e.g., web browser–web server) may require low delay.
- An electronic mail protocol may require multiple priority levels.

One approach to providing a variety of qualities of service is to include a quality-of-service facility within the protocol; we have seen this with IP and will see that transport protocols typically follow the same approach. An alternative is to provide a different transport protocol for different classes of traffic; this is to some extent the approach taken by the ISO-standard family of transport protocols.

## Data Transfer

The whole purpose, of course, of a transport protocol is to transfer data between two transport entities. Both user data and control data must be transferred, either on the same channel or separate channels. Full-duplex service must be provided. Half-duplex and simplex modes may also be offered to support peculiarities of particular TS users.

## User Interface

It is not clear that the exact mechanism of the user interface to the transport protocol should be standardized. Rather, it should be optimized to the station environment. As examples, a transport entity's services could be invoked by

- Procedure calls.
- Passing of data and parameters to a process through a mailbox.
- Use of direct memory access (DMA) between a host user and a front-end processor containing the transport entity.

A few characteristics of the interface may be specified, however. For example, a mechanism is needed to prevent the TS user from swamping the transport entity with data. A similar mechanism is needed to prevent the transport entity from swamping a TS user with data. Another aspect of the interface has to do with the timing and significance of confirmations. Consider the following: A TS user passes data to a transport entity to be delivered to a remote TS user. The local transport entity can acknowledge receipt of the data immediately, or it can wait until the remote transport entity reports that the data have made it through to the other end. Perhaps the most useful interface is one that allows immediate acceptance or rejection of requests, with later confirmation of the end-to-end significance.

## Connection Management

When connection-oriented service is provided, the transport entity is responsible for establishing and terminating connections. A symmetric connection-establishment procedure should be provided, which allows either TS user to initiate connection establishment. An asymmetric procedure may also be provided to support simplex connections.

Connection termination can be either *abrupt* or *graceful*. With an abrupt termination, data in transit may be lost. A graceful termination prevents either side from shutting down until all data have been delivered.

## Expedited Delivery

A service similar to that provided by priority classes is the expedited delivery of data. Some data submitted to the transport service may supersede data submitted previously. The transport entity will endeavor to have the transmission facility transfer the data as rapidly as possible. At the receiving end, the transport entity will interrupt the TS user to notify it of the receipt of urgent data. Thus, the expedited data service is in the nature of an interrupt mechanism, and is used to transfer occasional urgent data, such as a break character from a terminal or an alarm condition. In contrast, a priority service might dedicate resources and adjust parameters such that, on average, higher priority data are delivered more quickly.

## Status Reporting

A status reporting service allows the TS user to obtain or be notified of information concerning the condition or attributes of the transport entity or a transport connection. Examples of status information are

- Performance characteristics of a connection (e.g., throughput, mean delay)
- Addresses (network, transport)
- Class of protocol in use
- Current timer values
- State of protocol "machine" supporting a connection
- Degradation in requested quality of service

## Security

The transport entity may provide a variety of security services. Access control may be provided in the form of local verification of sender and remote verification of receiver. The transport service may also include encryption/decryption of data on demand. Finally, the transport entity may be capable of routing through secure links or nodes if such a service is available from the transmission facility.

## 17.2   PROTOCOL MECHANISMS

It is the purpose of this section to make good on our claim that a transport protocol may need to be very complex. For purposes of clarity, we present the transport protocol mechanisms in an evolutionary fashion. We begin with a network service that makes life easy for the transport protocol, by guaranteeing the delivery of all transport data units in order, as well as defining the required mechanisms. Then we will look at the transport protocol mechanisms required to cope with an unreliable network service.

### Reliable Sequencing Network Service

In this case, we assume that the network service will accept messages of arbitrary length and will, with virtually 100% reliability, deliver them in sequence to the destination. Examples of such networks follow:

- A highly reliable packet-switching network with an X.25 interface
- A frame relay network using the LAPF control protocol
- An IEEE 802.3 LAN using the connection-oriented LLC service

The assumption of a reliable sequencing networking services allows the use of a quite simple transport protocol. Four issues need to be addressed:

- Addressing
- Multiplexing
- Flow control
- Connection establishment/termination

### Addressing

The issue concerned with addressing is simply this: A user of a given transport entity wishes to either establish a connection with or make a connectionless data transfer to a user of some other transport entity. The target user needs to be specified by all of the following:

- User identification
- Transport entity identification
- Station address
- Network number

The transport protocol must be able to derive the information listed above from the TS user address. Typically, the user address is specified as *station* or *port*. The *port* variable represents a particular TS user at the specified station; in OSI, this is called a transport service access point (TSAP). Generally, there will be a single transport entity at each station, so a transport entity identification is not needed. If more than one transport entity is present, there is usually only one of each type. In this latter case, the address should include a designation of the type of transport protocol (e.g., TCP, UDP). In the case of a single network, *station* identifies an attached network device. In the case of an internet, station is a global internet address. In TCP, the combination of port and station is referred to as a socket.

Because routing is not a concern of the transport layer, it simply passes the station portion of the address down to the network service. Port is included in a transport header, to be used at the destination by the destination transport protocol.

One question remains to be addressed: How does the initiating TS user know the address of the destination TS user? Two static and two dynamic strategies suggest themselves:

1. The TS user must know the address it wishes to use ahead of time; this is basically a system configuration function. For example, a process may be running that is only of concern to a limited number of TS users, such as a process that collects statistics on performance. From time to time, a central network management routine connects to the process to obtain the statistics. These processes generally are not, and should not be, well-known and accessible to all.

2. Some commonly used services are assigned "well-known addresses" (for example, time sharing and word processing).

3. A name server is provided. The TS user requests a service by some generic or global name. The request is sent to the name server, which does a directory lookup and returns an address. The transport entity then proceeds with the connection. This service is useful for commonly used applications that change location from time to time. For example, a data entry process may be moved from one station to another on a local network in order to balance load.

4. In some cases, the target user is to be a process that is spawned at request time. The initiating user can send a process request to a well-known address. The user at that address is a privileged system process that will spawn the new process and return an address. For example, a programmer has developed a private application (e.g., a simulation program) that will execute on a remote

mainframe but be invoked from a local minicomputer. An RJE-type request can be issued to a remote job-management process that spawns the simulation process.

## Multiplexing

We now turn to the concept of multiplexing, which was discussed in general terms in Section 15.1. With respect to the interface between the transport protocol and higher-level protocols, the transport protocol performs a multiplexing/demultiplexing function. That is, multiple users employ the same transport protocol, and are distinguished by either port numbers or service access points.

The transport entity may also perform a multiplexing function with respect to the network services that it uses. Recall that we defined upward multiplexing as the multiplexing of multiple connections on a single lower-level connection, and downward multiplexing as the splitting of a single connection among multiple lower-level connections.

Consider, for example, a transport entity making use of an X.25 service. Why should the transport entity employ upward multiplexing? There are, after all, 4095 virtual circuits available. In the typical case, this is more than enough to handle all active TS users. However, most X.25 networks base part of their charge on virtual-circuit connect time, as each virtual circuit consumes some node buffer resources. Thus, if a single virtual circuit provides sufficient throughput for multiple TS users, upward multiplexing is indicated.

On the other hand, downward multiplexing or splitting might be used to improve throughput. For example, each X.25 virtual circuit is restricted to a 3-bit or 7-bit sequence number. A larger sequence space might be needed for high-speed, high-delay networks. Of course, throughput can only be increased so far. If there is a single station-node link over which all virtual circuits are multiplexed, the throughput of a transport connection cannot exceed the data rate of that link.

## Flow Control

Whereas flow control is a relatively simple mechanism at the link layer, it is a rather complex mechanism at the transport layer, for two main reasons:

- Flow control at the transport level involves the interaction of TS users, transport entities, and the network service.
- The transmission delay between transport entities is generally long compared to actual transmission time, and, what is worse, it is variable.

Figure 17.3 illustrates the first point. TS user A wishes to send data to TS user B over a transport connection. We can view the situation as involving four queues. A generates data and queues it up to send. A must wait to send that data until

- It has permission from B (peer flow control).
- It has permission from its own transport entity (interface flow control).

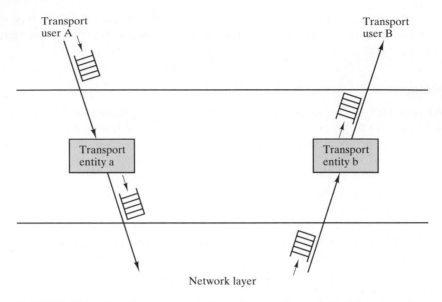

**FIGURE 17.3** Queuing representation of connection-oriented data transfer.

As data flow down from A to transport entity a, a queues the data until it has permission to send it on from b and the network service. The data are then handed to the network layer for delivery to b. The network service must queue the data until it receives permission from b to pass them on. Finally, b must await B's permission before delivering the data to their destination.

To see the effects of delay, consider the possible interactions depicted in Figure 17.4. When a TS user wishes to transmit data, it sends these data to its transport

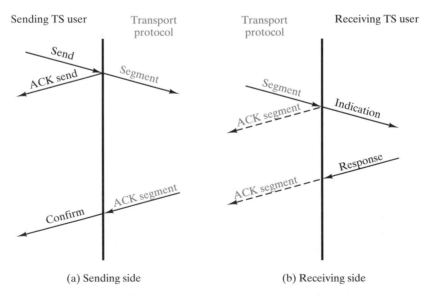

**FIGURE 17.4** Interaction between transport service user and transport protocol.

entity (e.g., using a Send call); this triggers two events. The transport entity generates one or more transport-level protocol data units, which we will call segments,[2] and passes these on to the network service. It also in some way acknowledges to the TS user that it has accepted the data for transmission. At this point, the transport entity can exercise flow control across the user-transport interface by simply withholding its acknowledgment. The transport entity is most likely to do this if the entity itself is being held up by a flow control exercised by either the network service or the target transport entity.

In any case, once the transport entity has accepted the data, it sends out a segment. Some time later, it receives an acknowledgment that the data have been received at the remote end. It then sends a confirmation to the sender.

At the receiving end, a segment arrives at the transport entity, which unwraps the data and sends them on (e.g., by an Indication primitive) to the destination TS user. When the TS user accepts the data, it issues an acknowledgment (e.g., in the form of a Response primitive). The TS user can exercise flow control over the transport entity by withholding its response.

The target transport entity has two choices regarding acknowledgment. Either it can issue an acknowledgment as soon as it has correctly received the segment (the usual practice), or it can wait until it knows that the TS user has correctly received the data before acknowledging; the latter course is the safer, where the confirmation is in fact a confirmation that the destination TS user received the data. In the former case, the entity merely confirms that the data made it through to the remote transport entity.

With the discussion above in mind, we can cite two reasons why one transport entity would want to restrain the rate of segment transmission over a connection from another transport entity:

- The user of the receiving transport entity cannot keep up with the flow of data.
- The receiving transport entity itself cannot keep up with the flow of segments.

How do such problems manifest themselves? Well, presumably a transport entity has a certain amount of buffer space, to which incoming segments are added. Each buffered segment is processed (i.e., the transport header is examined) and the data are sent to the TS user. Either of the two problems mentioned above will cause the buffer to fill up. Thus, the transport entity needs to take steps to stop or slow the flow of segments so as to prevent buffer overflow. This requirement is not so easy to fulfill, because of the annoying time gap between sender and receiver. We return to this point in a moment. First, we present four ways of coping with the flow control requirement. The receiving transport entity can

1. Do nothing.
2. Refuse to accept further segments from the network service.
3. Use a fixed sliding-window protocol.
4. Use a credit scheme.

---

[2] In this chapter, we use the terminology of TCP for convenience. ISO standards simply refer to this object as a transport PDU, or TPDU.

Alternative 1 means that the segments that overflow the buffer are discarded. The sending transport entity, failing to get an acknowledgment, will retransmit. This is a shame, as the advantage of a reliable network is that one never has to retransmit. Furthermore, the effect of this maneuver is to exacerbate the problem! The sender has increased its output to include new segments, plus retransmitted old segments.

The second alternative is a backpressure mechanism that relies on the network service to do the work. When a buffer of a transport entity is full, it refuses additional data from the network service. This triggers flow control procedures within the network that throttle the network service at the sending end. This service, in turn, refuses additional segments from its transport entity. It should be clear that this mechanism is clumsy and coarse-grained. For example, if multiple transport connections are multiplexed on a single network connection (virtual circuit), flow control is exercised only on the aggregate of all transport connections.

The third alternative is already familiar to you from our discussions of link layer protocols. The key ingredients, recall, are

- The use of sequence numbers on data units.
- The use of a window of fixed size.
- The use of acknowledgments to advance the window.

With a reliable network service, the sliding window technique would actually work quite well. For example, consider a protocol with a window size of 7. Whenever the sender receives an acknowledgment to a particular segment, it is automatically authorized to send the succeeding seven segments. (Of course, some may already have been sent.) Now, when the receiver's buffer capacity gets down to seven segments, it can withhold acknowledgment of incoming segments to avoid overflow. The sending transport entity can send, at most, seven additional segments and then must stop. Because the underlying network service is reliable, the sender will not time-out and retransmit. Thus, at some point, a sending transport entity may have a number of segments outstanding, for which no acknowledgment has been received. Because we are dealing with a reliable network, the sending transport entity can assume that the segments will get through and that the lack of acknowledgment is a flow control tactic. Such a strategy would not work well in an unreliable network, as the sending transport entity would not know whether the lack of acknowledgment is due to flow control or a lost segment.

The fourth alternative, a credit scheme, provides the receiver with a greater degree of control over data flow. Although it is not strictly necessary with a reliable network service, a credit scheme should result in a smoother traffic flow; further, it is a more effective scheme with an unreliable network service, as we shall see.

The credit scheme decouples acknowledgment from flow control. In fixed sliding-window protocols, such as X.25 and HDLC, the two are synonymous. In a credit scheme, a segment may be acknowledged without granting new credit, and vice versa. Figure 17.5 illustrates the protocol (compare Figure 6.4). For simplicity, we show a data flow in one direction only. In this example, data segments are numbered sequentially modulo 8 (e.g., SN 0 = segment with sequence number 0). Initially, through the connection-establishment process, the sending and receiving

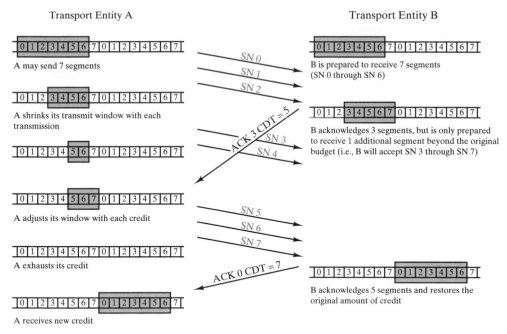

Transport Entity A

Transport Entity B

A may send 7 segments

B is prepared to receive 7 segments
(SN 0 through SN 6)

A shrinks its transmit window with each
transmission

B acknowledges 3 segments, but is only prepared
to receive 1 additional segment beyond the original
budget (i.e., B will accept SN 3 through SN 7)

A adjusts its window with each credit

A exhausts its credit

B acknowledges 5 segments and restores the
original amount of credit

A receives new credit

**FIGURE 17.5** Example of credit allocation mechanism.

sequence numbers are synchronized, and A is granted a credit allocation of 7. A advances the trailing edge of its window each time that it transmits, and advances the leading edge only when it is granted credit.

Figure 17.6 shows the view of this mechanism from the sending and receiving sides; of course, both sides take both views because data may be exchanged in both directions. From the sending point of view, sequence numbers fall into four regions:

- **Data sent and acknowledged.** Beginning with the initial sequence number used on this connection through the last acknowledged number.
- **Data sent but not yet acknowledged.** Represents data that have already been transmitted, with the sender now awaiting acknowledgment.
- **Permitted data transmission.** The window of allowable transmissions, based on unused credit allocated from the other side.
- **Unused and unusable numbers.** Numbers above the window.

From the receiving point of view, the concern is for received data and for the window of credit that has been allocated. Note that the receiver is not required to immediately acknowledge incoming segments, but may wait and issue a cumulative acknowledgment for a number of segments; this is true for both TCP and the ISO transport protocol.

In both the credit allocation scheme and the sliding window scheme, the receiver needs to adopt some policy concerning the amount of data it permits the sender to transmit. The conservative approach is to only allow new segments up to the limit of available buffer space. If this policy were in effect in Figure 17.5, the first

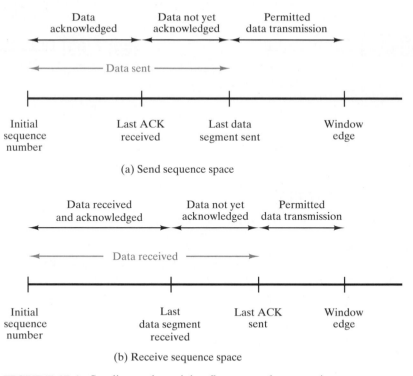

**FIGURE 17.6**   Sending and receiving flow control perspectives.

credit message implies that B has five free buffer slots, and the second message that B has seven free slots.

A conservative flow control scheme may limit the throughput of the transport connection in long-delay situations. The receiver could potentially increase throughput by optimistically granting credit for space it does not have. For example, if a receiver's buffer is full but it anticipates that it can release space for two segments within a round-trip propagation time, it could immediately send a credit of 2. If the receiver can keep up with the sender, this scheme may increase throughput and can do no harm. If the sender is faster than the receiver, however, some segments may be discarded, necessitating a retransmission. Because retransmissions are not otherwise necessary with a reliable network service, an optimistic flow control scheme will complicate the protocol.

## Connection Establishment and Termination

Even with a reliable network service, there is a need for connection establishment and termination procedures to support connection-oriented service. Connection establishment serves three main purposes:

- It allows each end to assure that the other exists.
- It allows negotiation of optional parameters (e.g., maximum segment size, maximum window size, quality of service).

- It triggers allocation of transport entity resources (e.g., buffer space, entry in connection table).

Connection establishment is by mutual agreement and can be accomplished by a simple set of user commands and control segments, as shown in the state diagram of Figure 17.7. To begin, a TS user is in an CLOSED state (i.e., it has no open transport connection). The TS user can signal that it will passively wait for a request with a Passive Open command. A server program, such as time sharing or a file transfer application, might do this. The TS user may change its mind by sending a Close command. After the Passive Open command is issued, the transport entity creates a connection object of some sort (i.e., a table entry) that is in the LISTEN state.

From the CLOSED state, the TS user may open a connection by issuing an Active Open command, which instructs the transport entity to attempt connection establishment with a designated user, which then triggers the transport entity to send an SYN (for synchronize) segment. This segment is carried to the receiving transport entity and interpreted as a request for connection to a particular port. If the destination transport entity is in the LISTEN state for that port, then a connection is established through the following actions by the receiving transport entity:

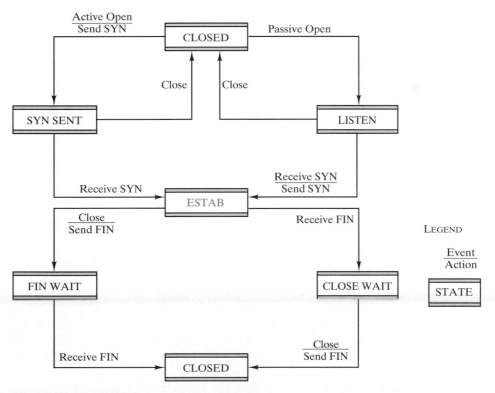

**FIGURE 17.7**  Simple connection state diagram.

- Signal the TS user that a connection is open.
- Send an SYN as confirmation to the remote transport entity.
- Put the connection object in an ESTAB (established) state.

When the responding SYN is received by the initiating transport entity, it too can move the connection to an ESTAB state. The connection is prematurely aborted if either TS user issues a Close command.

Figure 17.8 shows the robustness of this protocol. Either side can initiate a connection. Further, if both sides initiate the connection at about the same time, it is established without confusion; this is because the SYN segment functions both as a connection request and a connection acknowledgment.

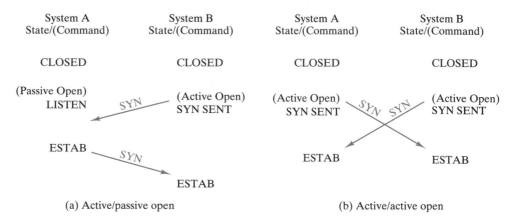

(a) Active/passive open          (b) Active/active open

**FIGURE 17.8**  Connection establishment scenarios.

The reader may ask what happens if an SYN comes in while the requested TS user is idle (not listening). Three courses may be followed:

- The transport entity can reject the request by sending an RST (reset) segment back to the other transport entity.
- The request can be queued until a matching Open is issued by the TS user.
- The transport entity can interrupt or otherwise signal the TS user to notify it of a pending request.

Note that if the latter mechanism is used, a Passive Open command is not strictly necessary, but may be replaced by an Accept command, which is a signal from the user to the transport entity that it accepts the request for connection.

Connection termination is handled similarly. Either side, or both sides, may initiate a close. The connection is closed by mutual agreement. This strategy allows for either abrupt or graceful termination. To achieve the latter, a connection in the CLOSE WAIT state must continue to accept data segments until a FIN (finish) segment is received.

Similarly, the diagram defines the procedure for graceful termination. First, consider the side that initiates the termination procedure:

1. In response to a TS user's Close primitive, a FIN segment is sent to the other side of the connection, requesting termination.
2. Having sent the FIN, the transport entity places the connection in the FIN WAIT state. In this state, the transport entity must continue to accept data from the other side and deliver that data to its user.
3. When a FIN is received in response, the transport entity informs its user and closes the connection.

From the point of view of the side that does not initiate a termination,

1. When a FIN segment is received, the transport entity informs its user of the termination request and places the connection in the CLOSE WAIT state. In this state, the transport entity must continue to accept data from its user and transmit it in data segments to the other side.
2. When the user issues a Close primitive, the transport entity sends a responding FIN segment to the other side and closes the connection.

This procedure ensures that both sides have received all outstanding data and that both sides agree to connection termination before actual termination.

### Unreliable Network Service

The most difficult case for a transport protocol is that of an unreliable network service. Examples of such networks are

- An internetwork using IP
- A frame relay network using only the LAPF core protocol
- An IEEE 802.3 LAN using the unacknowledged connectionless LLC service

The problem is not just that segments are occasionally lost, but that segments may arrive out of sequence due to variable transit delays. As we shall see, elaborate machinery is required to cope with these two interrelated network deficiencies. We shall also see that a discouraging pattern emerges. The combination of unreliability and nonsequencing creates problems with every mechanism we have discussed so far. Generally, the solution to each problem raises new problems, and although there are problems to be overcome for protocols at all levels, it seems that there are more difficulties with a reliable connection-oriented transport protocol than any other sort of protocol.

Seven issues need to be addressed:

- Ordered delivery
- Retransmission strategy
- Duplicate detection
- Flow control
- Connection establishment
- Connection termination
- Crash recovery

## Ordered Delivery

With an unreliable network service, it is possible that segments, even if they are all delivered, may arrive out of order. The required solution to this problem is to number segments sequentially. We have seen that for data link control protocols, such as HDLC, and for X.25, that each data unit (frame, packet) is numbered sequentially with each successive sequence number being one more than the previous sequence number; this scheme is used in some transport protocols, such as the ISO transport protocols. However, TCP uses a somewhat different scheme in which each data octet that is transmitted is implicitly numbered. Thus, the first segment may have a sequence number of 0. If that segment has 1000 octets of data, then the second segment would have the sequence number 1000, and so on. For simplicity in the discussions of this section, we will assume that each successive segment's sequence number is one more than that of the previous segment.

## Retransmission Strategy

Two events necessitate the retransmission of a segment. First, the segment may be damaged in transit but, nevertheless, could arrive at its destination. If a frame check sequence is included with the segment, the receiving transport entity can detect the error and discard the segment. The second contingency is that a segment fails to arrive. In either case, the sending transport entity does not know that the segment transmission was unsuccessful. To cover this contingency, we require that a positive acknowledgment (ACK) scheme be used: The receiver must acknowledge each successfully received segment. For efficiency, we do not require one ACK per segment. Rather, a cumulative acknowledgment can be used, as we have seen many times in this book. Thus, the receiver may receive segments numbered 1, 2, and 3, but only send ACK 4 back. The sender must interpret ACK 4 to mean that number 3 and all previous segments have been successfully received.

If a segment does not arrive successfully, no ACK will be issued and a retransmission becomes necessary. To cope with this situation, there must be a timer associated with each segment as it is sent. If the timer expires before the segment is acknowledged, the sender must retransmit.

So, the addition of a timer solves this first problem. Next, at what value should the timer be set? If the value is too small, there will be many unnecessary retransmissions, thereby wasting network capacity. If the value is too large, the protocol will be sluggish in responding to a lost segment. The timer should be set at a value a bit longer than the round trip delay (send segment, receive ACK). Of course this delay is variable even under constant network load. Worse, the statistics of the delay will vary with changing network conditions.

Two strategies suggest themselves. A fixed timer value could be used, based on an understanding of the network's typical behavior; this suffers from an inability to respond to changing network conditions. If the value is set too high, the service will always be sluggish. If it is set too low, a positive feedback condition can develop, in which network congestion leads to more retransmissions, which increase congestion.

An adaptive scheme has its own problems. Suppose that the transport entity keeps track of the time taken to acknowledge data segments and sets its retransmission timer based on the average of the observed delays. This value cannot be trusted for three reasons:

- The peer entity may not acknowledge a segment immediately; recall that we gave it the privilege of cumulative acknowledgments.
- If a segment has been retransmitted, the sender cannot know whether the received ACK is a response to the initial transmission or the retransmission.
- Network conditions may change suddenly.

Each of these problems is a cause for some further tweaking of the transport algorithm, but the problem admits of no complete solution. There will always be some uncertainty concerning the best value for the retransmission timer.

Incidentally, the retransmission timer is only one of a number of timers needed for proper functioning of a transport protocol; these are listed in Table 17.1, together with a brief explanation. Further discussion will be found in what follows.

## Duplicate Detection

If a segment is lost and then retransmitted, no confusion will result. If, however, an ACK is lost, one or more segments will be retransmitted and, if they arrive successfully, will be duplicates of previously received segments. Thus, the receiver must be able to recognize duplicates. The fact that each segment carries a sequence number helps but, nevertheless, duplicate detection and handling is no easy thing. There are two cases:

- A duplicate is received prior to the close of the connection.
- A duplicate is received after the close of the connection.

Notice that we say "a" duplicate rather than "the" duplicate. From the sender's point of view, the retransmitted segment is the duplicate. However, the retransmitted segment may arrive before the original segment, in which case the receiver views the original segment as the duplicate. In any case, two tactics are needed to cope with a duplicate received prior to the close of a connection:

- The receiver must assume that its acknowledgment was lost and therefore must acknowledge the duplicate. Consequently, the sender must not get confused if it receives multiple ACKs to the same segment.

**TABLE 17.1**  Transport protocol timers.

| | |
|---|---|
| Retransmission timer | Retransmit an unacknowledged segment |
| Reconnection timer | Minimum time between closing one connection and opening another with the same destination address |
| Window timer | Maximum time between ACK/CREDIT segments |
| Retransmit-SYN timer | Time between attempts to open a connection |
| Persistence timer | Abort connection when no segments are acknowledged |
| Inactivity timer | Abort connection when no segments are received |

- The sequence number space must be long enough so as not to "cycle" in less than the maximum possible segment lifetime.

Figure 17.9 illustrates the reason for the latter requirement. In this example, the sequence space is of length 8. For simplicity, we assume a sliding-window protocol with a window size of 3. Suppose that A has transmitted data segments 0, 1, and 2 and receives no acknowledgments. Eventually, it times-out and retransmits segment 0. B has received 1 and 2, but 0 is delayed in transit. Thus, B does not send any ACKs. When the duplicate segment 0 arrives, B acknowledges 0, 1, and 2. Meanwhile, A has timed-out again and retransmits 1, which B acknowledges with another ACK 3. Things now seem to have sorted themselves out, and data transfer continues. When the sequence space is exhausted, A cycles back to sequence number 0 and continues. Alas, the old segment 0 makes a belated appearance and is accepted by B before the new segment 0 arrives.

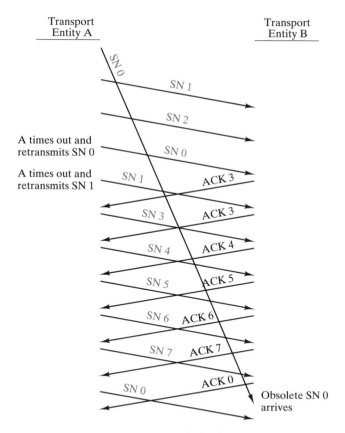

**FIGURE 17.9** Example of incorrect duplicate detection.

It should be clear that the untimely emergence of the old segment would have caused no difficulty if the sequence numbers had not yet wrapped around. The problem is: How big must the sequence space be? This depends on, among other things, whether the network enforces a maximum packet lifetime, as well as the rate at which segments are being transmitted. Fortunately, each addition of a single bit to the sequence number field doubles the sequence space, so it is rather easy to select a safe size. As we shall see, the standard transport protocols allow stupendous sequence spaces.

## Flow Control

The credit-allocation flow control mechanism described earlier is quite robust in the face of an unreliable network service and requires little enhancement. We assume that the credit allocation scheme is tied to acknowledgments in the following way: To both acknowledge segments and grant credit, a transport entity sends a control segment of the form (ACK $N$, CREDIT $M$), where ACK $N$ acknowledges all data segments through number $N - 1$, and CREDIT $M$ allows segments number $N$ though $N + M + 1$ to be transmitted. This mechanism is quite powerful. Consider that the last control segment issued by B was (ACK $N$, CREDIT $M$). Then,

- To increase or decrease credit to $X$ when no additional segments have arrived, B can issue (ACK $N$, CREDIT $X$).
- To acknowledge a new segment without increasing credit, B can issue (ACK $N + 1$, CREDIT $M - 1$).

If an ACK/CREDIT segment is lost, little harm is done. Future acknowledgments will resynchronize the protocol. Further, if no new acknowledgments are forthcoming, the sender times-out and retransmits a data segment, which triggers a new acknowledgment. However, it is still possible for deadlock to occur. Consider a situation in which B sends (ACK $N$, CREDIT 0), temporarily closing the window. Subsequently, B sends (ACK $N$, CREDIT $M$), but this segment is lost. A is awaiting the opportunity to send data, and B thinks that it has granted that opportunity. To overcome this problem, a window timer can be used. This timer is reset with each outgoing ACK/CREDIT segment. If the timer ever expires, the protocol entity is required to send an ACK/CREDIT segment, even if it duplicates a previous one. This breaks the deadlock and also assures the other end that the protocol entity is still alive.

An alternative or supplemental mechanism is to provide for acknowledgments to the ACK/CREDIT segment. With this mechanism in place, the window timer can have quite a large value without causing much difficulty.

## Connection Establishment

As with other protocol mechanisms, connection establishment must take into account the unreliability of a network service. Recall that a connection establishment calls for the exchange of SYNs, a procedure sometimes referred to as a two-way handshake. Suppose that A issues an SYN to B. It expects to get an SYN back, confirming the connection. Two things can go wrong: A's SYN can be lost or B's answering SYN can be lost. Both cases can be handled by use of a retransmit-SYN timer. After A issues an SYN, it will reissue the SYN when the timer expires.

This situation gives rise, potentially, to duplicate SYNs. If A's initial SYN was lost, there are no duplicates. If B's response was lost, then B may receive two SYNs from A. Further, if B's response was not lost, but simply delayed, A may get two responding SYNs; all of this means that A and B must simply ignore duplicate SYNs once a connection is established.

There are other problems with which to contend. Just as a delayed SYN or lost response can give rise to a duplicate SYN, a delayed data segment or lost acknowledgment can give rise to duplicate data segments, as we have seen in Figure 17.9). Such a delayed or duplicated data segment can interfere with connection establishment, as illustrated in Figure 17.10. Assume that with each new connection, each transport protocol entity begins numbering its data segments with sequence number 0. In the figure, a duplicate copy of segment 2 from an old connection arrives during the lifetime of a new connection and is delivered to B before delivery of the legitimate data segment number 2. One way of attacking this problem is to start each new connection with a different sequence number, far removed from the last sequence number of the most recent connection. For this purpose, the connection request is of the form SYN i, where i is the sequence number of the first data segment that will be sent on this connection.

Now, consider that a duplicate SYN i may survive past the termination of the connection. Figure 17.11 depicts the problem that may arise. An old SYN i arrives at B after the connection is terminated. B assumes that this is a fresh request and responds with SYN j. Meanwhile, A has decided to open a new connection with B and sends SYN k; B discards this as a duplicate. Now, both sides have transmitted and subsequently received a SYN segment, and therefore think that a valid con-

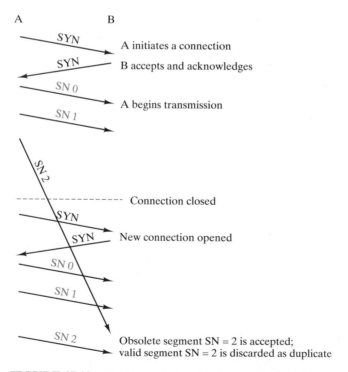

**FIGURE 17.10**  The two-way handshake: problem with obsolete data segment.

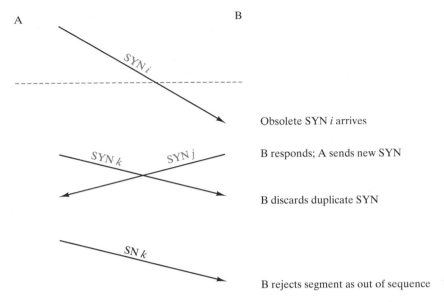

A

B

SYN $i$

Obsolete SYN $i$ arrives

SYN $k$    SYN $j$

B responds; A sends new SYN

B discards duplicate SYN

SN $k$

B rejects segment as out of sequence

**FIGURE 17.11**   The two-way handshake: problem with obsolete SYN segments.

nection exists. However, when A initiates data transfer with a segment numbered $k$, B rejects the segment as being out of sequence.

The way out of this problem is for each side to acknowledge explicitly the other's SYN and sequence number. The procedure is known as a three-way handshake. The revised connection state diagram, which is the one employed by TCP, is shown in the upper part of Figure 17.12. A new state (SYN RECEIVED) is added, in which the transport entity hesitates during connection opening to assure that the SYN segments sent by the two sides have both been acknowledged before the connection is declared established. In addition to the new state, there is a control segment (RST) to reset the other side when a duplicate SYN is detected.

Figure 17.13 illustrates typical three-way handshake operations. Transport entity A initiates the connection; a SYN includes the sending sequence number, $i$. The responding SYN acknowledges that number and includes the sequence number for the other side. A acknowledges the SYN/ACK in its first data segment. Next is shown a situation in which an old SYN $X$ arrives at B after the close of the relevant connection. B assumes that this is a fresh request and responds with SYN $j$, ACK $i$. When A receives this message, it realizes that it has not requested a connection and therefore sends an RST, ACK $j$. Note that the ACK $j$ portion of the RST message is essential so that an old duplicate RST does not abort a legitimate connection establishment. The final example shows a case in which an old SYN, ACK arrives in the middle of a new connection establishment. Because of the use of sequence numbers in the acknowledgments, this event causes no mischief.

The upper part of Figure 17.12 does not include transitions in which RST is sent. This was done for simplicity. The basic rule is to send an RST if the connection state is not yet OPEN and an invalid ACK (one that does not reference something that was sent) is received. The reader should try various combinations of

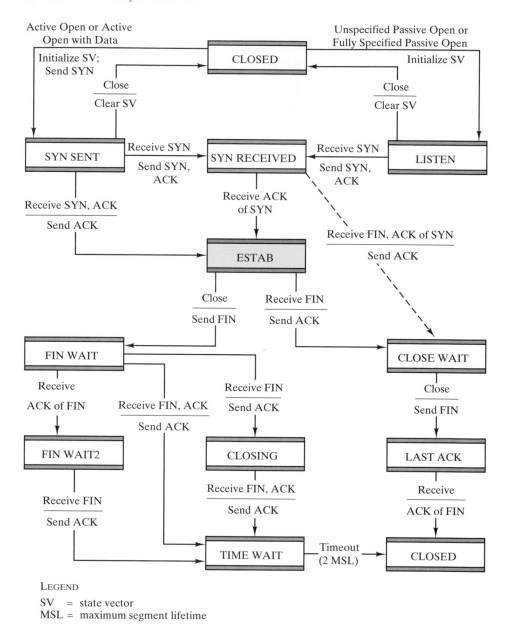

**FIGURE 17.12** TCP entity state diagram.

events to see that this connection establishment procedure works in spite of any combination of old and lost segments.

## Connection Termination

The state diagram of Figure 17.7 defines the use of a simple two-way handshake for connection establishment, which was found to be unsatisfactory in the face of an unreliable network service. Similarly, the two-way handshake defined in that dia-

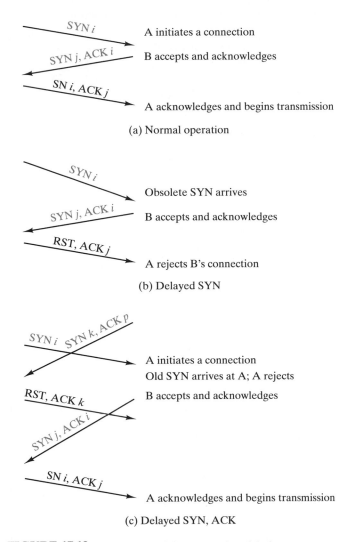

**FIGURE 17.13**    Examples of three-way handshake.

gram for connection termination is inadequate for an unreliable network service. The following scenario could be caused by a misordering of segments. A transport entity in the CLOSE WAIT state sends its last data segment, followed by a FIN segment, but the FIN segment arrives at the other side before the last data segment. The receiving transport entity will accept that FIN, close the connection, and lose the last segment of data. To avoid this problem, a sequence number can be associated with the FIN, which can be assigned the next sequence number after the last octet of transmitted data. With this refinement, the receiving transport entity, upon receiving a FIN, will wait if necessary for the late-arriving data before closing the connection.

A more serious problem is the potential loss of segments and the potential presence of obsolete segments. Figure 17.12 shows that the termination procedure adopts a similar solution to that used for connection establishment. Each side must explicitly acknowledge the FIN of the other, using an ACK with the sequence number of the FIN to be acknowledged. For a graceful close, a transport entity requires the following:

- It must send a FIN $i$ and receive an ACK $i$.
- It must receive a FIN $j$ and send an ACK $j$.
- It must wait an interval equal to twice the maximum-expected segment lifetime

### Crash Recovery

When the system upon which a transport entity is running fails and subsequently restarts, the state information of all active connections is lost. The affected connections become *half-open*, as the side that did not fail does not yet realize the problem.

The still active side of a half-open connection can close the connection using a give-up timer. This timer measures the time the transport machine will continue to await an acknowledgment (or other appropriate reply) of a transmitted segment after the segment has been retransmitted the maximum number of times. When the timer expires, the transport entity assumes that either the other transport entity or the intervening network has failed. As a result, the timer closes the connection, and signals an abnormal close to the TS user.

In the event that a transport entity fails and quickly restarts, half-open connections can be terminated more quickly by the use of the RST segment. The failed side returns an RST $i$ to every segment $i$ that it receives. When the RST $i$ reaches the other side, it must be checked for validity based on the sequence number $i$, as the RST could be in response to an old segment. If the reset is valid, the transport entity performs an abnormal termination.

These measures clean up the situation at the transport level. The decision as to whether to reopen the connection is up to the TS users. The problem is one of synchronization. At the time of failure, there may have been one or more outstanding segments in either direction. The TS user on the side that did not fail knows how much data it has received, but the other user may not if state information were lost. Thus, there is the danger that some user data will be lost or duplicated.

## 17.3   TCP

The TCP/IP protocol suite includes two transport-level protocols: the Transmission Control Protocol (TCP), which is connection-oriented, and the User Datagram Protocol (UDP), which is connectionless. In this section, we look at TCP (specified in RFC 793)—first at the service it provides to the TS user, and then at the internal protocol details.

## TCP Services

TCP is designed to provide reliable communication between pairs of processes (TCP users) across a variety of reliable and unreliable networks and internets. Functionally, it is equivalent to Class 4 ISO Transport. In contrast to the ISO model, TCP is stream oriented. That is, TCP users exchange streams of data. The data are placed in allocated buffers and transmitted by TCP in segments. TCP supports security and precedence labeling. In addition, TCP provides two useful facilities for labeling data, *push* and *urgent*:

- **Data stream push.** Ordinarily, TCP decides when sufficient data have accumulated to form a segment for transmission. The TCP user can require TCP to transmit all outstanding data up to and including those labeled with a push flag. On the receiving end, TCP will deliver these data to the user in the same manner; a user might request this if it has come to a logical break in the data.
- **Urgent data signaling.** This provides a means of informing the destination TCP user that significant or "urgent" data is in the upcoming data stream. It is up to the destination user to determine appropriate action.

As with IP, the services provided by TCP are defined in terms of primitives and parameters. The services provided by TCP are considerably richer than those provided by IP, and, hence, the set of primitives and parameters is more complex. Table 17.2 lists TCP service request primitives, which are issued by a TCP user to TCP, and Table 17.3 lists TCP service response primitives, which are issued by TCP to a local TCP user. Table 17.4 provides a brief definition of the parameters involved. Several comments are in order.

The two Passive Open commands signal the TCP user's willingness to accept a connection request. The Active Open with Data allows the user to begin transmitting data with the opening of the connection.

## TCP Header Format

TCP uses only a single type of protocol data unit, called a TCP segment. The header is shown in Figure 17.14. Because one header must serve to perform all protocol mechanisms, it is rather large, with a minimum length of 20 octets. The fields are

- **Source port (16 bits).** Source service access point.
- **Destination port (16 bits).** Destination service access point.
- **Sequence number (32 bits).** Sequence number of the first data octet in this segment except when SYN flag is set. If SYN is set, it is the initial sequence number (ISN), and the first data octet is ISN + 1.
- **Acknowledgment number (32 bits).** A piggybacked acknowledgment. Contains the sequence number of the next data octet that the TCP entity expects to receive.
- **Data offset (4 bits).** Number of 32-bit words in the header.

**TABLE 17.2**   TCP service request primitives.

| Primitive | Parameters | Description |
|---|---|---|
| Unspecified Passive Open | source-port, [timeout], [timeout-action], [precedence], [security-range] | Listen for connection attempt at specified security and precedence from any remote destination. |
| Fully Specified Passive Open | source-port, destination-port, destination-address, [timeout], [timeout-action], [precedence], [security-range] | Listen for connection attempt at specified security and precedence from specified destination. |
| Active Open | source-port, destination-port, destination-address, [timeout], [timeout-action], [precedence], [security] | Request connection at a particular security and precedence to a specified destination. |
| Active Open with Data | source-port, destination-port, destination-address, [timeout], [timeout-action], [precedence], [security], data, data-length, PUSH-flag, URGENT-flag | Request connection at a particular security and precedence to a specified destination and transmit data with the request |
| Send | local-connection-name, data, data-length, PUSH-flat, URGENT-flag, [timeout], [timeout-action] | Transfer data across named connection |
| Allocate | local-connection-name, data-length | Issue incremental allocation for receive data to TCP |
| Close | local-connection-name | Close connection gracefully |
| Abort | local-connection-name | Close connection abruptly |
| Status | local-connection-name | Query connection status |

Note: Square brackets indicate optional parameters.

- **Reserved (6 bits).** Reserved for future use.
- **Flags (6 bits).**
  - URG: Urgent pointer field significant.
  - ACK: Acknowledgment field significant.
  - PSH: Push function.
  - RST: Reset the connection.
  - SYN: Synchronize the sequence numbers.
  - FIN: No more data from sender.
- **Window (16 bits).** Flow control credit allocation, in octets. Contains the number of data octets beginning with the one indicated in the acknowledgment field that the sender is willing to accept.
- **Checksum (16 bits).** The one's complement of the sum modulo $2^{16}-1$ of all the 16-bit words in the segment, plus a pseudo-header. The situation is described below.
- **Urgent Pointer (16 bits).** Points to the last octet in a sequence of urgent data; this allows the receiver to know how much urgent data is coming.
- **Options (Variable).** At present, only one option is defined, which specifies the maximum segment size that will be accepted.

**TABLE 17.3** TCP service response primitives.

| Primitive | Parameters | Description |
|---|---|---|
| Open ID | local-connection-name, source-port, destination-port*, destination-address*, | Informs TCP user of connection name assigned to pending connection requested in an Open primitive |
| Open Failure | local-connection-name | Reports failure of an Active Open request |
| Open Success | local-connection-name | Reports completion of pending Open request |
| Deliver | local-connection-name, data, data-length, URGENT-flag | Reports arrival of data |
| Closing | local-connection-name | Reports that remote TCP user has issued a Close and that all data sent by remote user have been delivered |
| Terminate | local-connection-name, description | Reports that the connection has been terminated; a description of the reason for termination is provided |
| Status Response | local-connection-name, source-port, source-address, destination-port, destination-address, connection-state, receive-window, send-window, amount-awaiting-ACK, amount-awaiting-receipt, urgent-state, precedence, security, timeout | Reports current status of connection |
| Error | local-connection-name, description | Reports service-request or internal error |

\* = Not used for Unspecified Passive Open.

Several of the fields in the TCP header warrant further elaboration. The *source port* and *destination port* specify the sending and receiving users of TCP. As with IP, there are a number of common users of TCP that have been assigned numbers; these numbers should be reserved for that purpose in any implementation. Other port numbers must be arranged by agreement between communicating parties.

The *sequence number* and *acknowledgment number* are bound to octets rather than to entire segments. For example, if a segment contains sequence number 1000 and includes 600 octets of data, the sequence number refers to the first octet in the data field; the next segment in logical order will have sequence number 1600. Thus, TCP is logically stream-oriented: It accepts a stream of octets from the user, groups them into segments as it sees fit, and numbers each octet in the stream.

The *checksum* field applies to the entire segment, plus a pseudo-header prefixed to the header at the time of calculation (at both transmission and reception). The pseudo-header includes the following fields from the IP header: source and destination internet address and protocol, plus a segment length field (Figure 17.15). By including the pseudo-header, TCP protects itself from misdelivery by IP. That is, if IP delivers a segment to the wrong host, even if the segment contains no bit errors, the receiving TCP entity will detect the delivery error. If TCP is used over IPv6, then the pseudo-header is different, and is depicted in Figure 16.21.

The reader may feel that some items are missing from the TCP header, and that is indeed the case. TCP is designed specifically to work with IP. Hence, some

**TABLE 17.4** TCP Service parameters.

| | |
|---|---|
| Source Port | Local TCP user. |
| Timeout | Longest delay allowed for data delivery before automatic connection termination or error report; user specified. |
| Timeout-action | Indicates whether the connection is terminated or an error is reported to the TCP user in the event of a timeout. |
| Precedence | Precedence level for a connection. Takes on values zero (lowest) through seven (highest); same parameter as defined for IP |
| Security-range | Allowed ranges in compartment, handling restriction, transmission control codes, and security levels. |
| Destination Port | Remote TCP user. |
| Destination Address | Internet address of remote host. |
| Security | Security information for a connection, including security level, compartment, handling restriction, and transmission control code; same parameter as defined for IP. |
| Data | Block of data sent by TCP user or delivered to a TCP user. |
| Data Length | Length of block of data sent or delivered. |
| PUSH flag | If set, indicates that the associated data are to be provided with the urgent data stream push service. |
| URGENT flag | If set, indicates that the associated data are to be provided with the urgent data signaling service. |
| Local Connection Name | Identifier of a connection defined by a (local socket, remote socket) pair; provided by TCP. |
| Description | Supplementary information in a Terminate or Error primitive. |
| Source Address | Internet address of the local host. |
| Connection State | State of referenced connection (CLOSED, ACTIVE OPEN, PASSIVE OPEN, ESTABLISHED, CLOSING). |
| Receive Window | Amount of data in octets the local TCP entity is willing to receive. |
| Send Window | Amount of data in octets permitted to be sent to remote TCP entity. |
| Amount Awaiting ACK | Amount of previously transmitted data awaiting acknowledgment. |
| Amount Awaiting Receipt | Amount of data in octets buffered at local TCP entity pending receipt by local TCP user. |
| Urgent State | Indicates to the receiving TCP user whether there are urgent data available or whether all urgent data, if any, have been delivered to the user. |

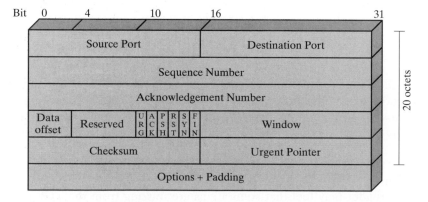

**FIGURE 17.14** TCP header.

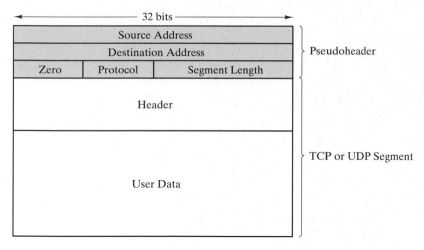

**FIGURE 17.15**    Scope of checksum for TCP and UDP.

user parameters are passed down by TCP to IP for inclusion in the IP header. The relevant ones are

- Precedence: a 3-bit field
- Normal-delay/low-delay
- Normal-throughput/high-throughput
- Normal-reliability/high-reliability
- Security: an 11-bit field

It is worth observing that this TCP/IP linkage means that the required minimum overhead for every data unit is actually 40 octets.

## TCP Mechanisms

### Connection Establishment

Connection establishment in TCP always uses a three-way handshake. When the SYN flag is set, the segment is essentially a request for connection (RFC), and thus functions as explained in Section 17.2. To initiate a connection, an entity sends an RFC $X$, where $X$ is the initial sequence number. The receiver responds with RFC $Y$, ACK $X$ by setting both the SYN and ACK flags. Finally, the initiator responds with ACK $Y$. If both sides issue crossing RFCs, no problem results; both sides respond with ACKs.

A connection is uniquely determined by the source and destination ports. Thus, at any one time, there can only be a single TCP connection between a unique pair of ports. However, a given port can support multiple connections, each with a different partner port.

### Data Transfer

Although data are transferred in segments over a transport connection, data transfer is viewed logically as consisting of a stream of octets. Hence, every octet is numbered, modulo $2^{32}$. Each segment contains the sequence number of the first octet in the data field. Flow control is exercised using a credit allocation scheme in which the credit is a number of octets rather than a number of segments.

As was mentioned, data are buffered by the transport entity on both transmission and reception. TCP normally exercises its own discretion as to when to construct a segment for transmission and when to release received data to the user. The PUSH flag is used to force the data so-far accumulated to be sent by the transmitter and passed on by the receiver. This serves an end-of-letter function.

The user may specify a block of data as urgent. TCP will designate the end of that block with an urgent pointer and send it out in the ordinary data stream. The receiving user is alerted that urgent data are being received.

If, during data exchange, a segment arrives that is apparently not meant for the current connection, the RST flag is set on an outgoing segment. Examples of this situation are delayed duplicate SYNs and an acknowledgment of data not yet sent.

### Connection Termination

The normal means of terminating a connection consists of a graceful close. Each TCP user must issue a CLOSE primitive. The transport entity sets the FIN bit on the last segment that it sends out, which also contains the last of the data to be sent on this connection.

An abrupt termination occurs if the user issues an ABORT primitive. In this case, the entity abandons all attempts to send or receive data and discards data in its transmission and reception buffers. An RST segment is sent to the other side.

## TCP Implementation Policy Options

The TCP standard provides a precise specification of the protocol to be used between TCP entities. However, certain aspects of the protocol admit several possible implementation options. Although two implementations that choose alternative options will be interoperable, there may be performance implications. The design-area options are the following:

- Send policy
- Deliver policy
- Accept policy
- Retransmit policy
- Acknowledge policy

### Send Policy

In the absence of pushed data and a closed transmission window (see Figure 17.6a), a sending TCP entity is free to transmit data at its own convenience. As data are issued by the user, they are buffered in the transmit buffer. TCP may construct a segment for each batch of data provided by its user, or it may wait until a certain amount of data accumulates before constructing and sending a segment. The actual policy will depend on performance considerations. If transmissions are infrequent and large, there is low overhead in terms of segment generation and processing. On the other hand, if transmissions are frequent and small, then the system is providing quick response.

One danger of frequent, small transmissions is known as the silly window syndrome, which is discussed in Problem 17.19.

### Deliver Policy

In the absence of a push, a receiving TCP entity is free to deliver data to the user at its own convenience. It may deliver data as each in-order segment is received, or it may buffer data from a number of segments in the receive buffer before delivery. The actual policy will depend on performance considerations. If deliveries are infrequent and large, the user is not receiving data as promptly as may be desirable. On the other hand, if deliveries are frequent and small, there may be unnecessary processing both in TCP and in the user software, as well as an unnecessary number of operating-system interrupts.

### Accept Policy

When all data segments arrive in order over a TCP connection, TCP places the data in a receive buffer for delivery to the user. It is possible, however, for segments to arrive out of order. In this case, the receiving TCP entity has two options:

- **In-order.** Accept only segments that arrive in order; any segment that arrives out of order is discarded.
- **In-window.** Accept all segments that are within the receive window (see Figure 17.6b).

The in-order policy makes for a simple implementation but places a burden on the networking facility, as the sending TCP must time-out and retransmit segments that were successfully received but discarded because of misordering. Furthermore, if a single segment is lost in transit, then all subsequent segments must be retransmitted once the sending TCP times out on the lost segment.

The in-window policy may reduce transmissions but requires a more complex acceptance test and a more sophisticated data storage scheme to buffer and keep track of data accepted out of order.

For class 4 ISO transport (TP4), the in-window policy is mandatory.

### Retransmit Policy

TCP maintains a queue of segments that have been sent but not yet acknowledged. The TCP specification states that TCP will retransmit a segment if it fails to receive an acknowledgment within a given time. A TCP implementation may employ one of three retransmission strategies:

- **First-only.** Maintain one retransmission timer for the entire queue. If an acknowledgment is received, remove the appropriate segment or segments from the queue and reset the timer. If the timer expires, retransmit the segment at the front of the queue and reset the timer.

- **Batch.** Maintain one retransmission timer for the entire queue. If an acknowledgment is received, remove the appropriate segment or segments from the queue and reset the timer. If the timer expires, retransmit all segments in the queue and reset the timer.
- **Individual.** Maintain one timer for each segment in the queue. If an acknowledgment is received, remove the appropriate segment or segments from the queue and destroy the corresponding timer or timers. If any timer expires, retransmit the corresponding segment individually and reset its timer.

The first-only policy is efficient in terms of traffic generated, as only lost segments (or segments whose ACK was lost) are retransmitted. Because the timer for the second segment in the queue is not set until the first segment is acknowledged, however, there can be considerable delays; the individual policy solves this problem at the expense of a more complex implementation. The batch policy also reduces the likelihood of long delays but may result in unnecessary retransmissions.

The actual effectiveness of the retransmit policy depends in part on the accept policy of the receiver. If the receiver is using an in-order accept policy, then it will discard segments received after a lost segment; this fits best with batch retransmission. If the receiver is using an in-window accept policy, then a first-only or individual retransmission policy is best. Of course, in a mixed network of computers, both accept policies may be in use.

The ISO TP4 specification outlines essentially the same options for a retransmit policy without mandating a particular one.

### Acknowledge Policy

When a data segment arrives that is in sequence, the receiving TCP entity has two options concerning the timing of acknowledgment:

- **Immediate.** When data are accepted, immediately transmit an empty (no data) segment containing the appropriate acknowledgment number.
- **Cumulative.** When data are accepted, record the need for acknowledgment, but wait for an outbound segment with data on which to piggyback the acknowledgment. To avoid a long delay, set a window timer (see Table 17.1); if the timer expires before an acknowledgment is sent, transmit an empty segment containing the appropriate acknowledgment number.

The immediate policy is simple and keeps the sending TCP entity fully informed, which limits unnecessary retransmissions. However, this policy results in extra segment transmissions, namely, empty segments used only to ACK. Furthermore, the policy can cause a further load on the network. Consider that a TCP entity receives a segment and immediately sends an ACK; then the data in the segment are released to the application, which expands the receive window, triggering another empty TCP segment to provide additional credit to the sending TCP entity.

Because of the potential overhead of the immediate policy, the cumulative policy is typically used. Recognize, however, that the use of this policy requires more processing at the receiving end and complicates the task of estimating round-trip delay by the sending TCP entity.

The ISO TP4 specification outlines essentially the same options for an acknowledge policy without mandating a particular one.

## 17.4 UDP

In addition to TCP, there is one other transport-level protocol that is in common use as part of the TCP/IP protocol suite: the user datagram protocol (UDP), specified in RFC 768.

UDP provides a connectionless service for application-level procedures. Thus, UDP is basically an unreliable service; delivery and duplicate protection are not guaranteed. However, the overhead of the protocol is low, which may be adequate in many cases. An example of the use of UDP is in the context of network management, as described in Chapter 19.

UDP sits on top of IP. Because it is connectionless, UDP has very little to do. Essentially, it adds a port addressing capability to IP, best seen by examining the UDP header, shown in Figure 17.16. The header includes a source port and a destination port. The length field contains the length of the entire UDP segment, including header and data. The checksum is the same algorithm used for TCP and IP. For UDP, the checksum applies to the entire UDP segment plus a pseudo-header prefixed to the UDP header at the time of calculation and is the same one used for TCP (Figure 17.15). If an error is detected, the segment is discarded and no further action is taken.

The checksum field in UDP is optional. If it is not used, it is set to zero. However, it should be pointed out that the IP checksum applies only to the IP header and not to the data field, which in this case consists of the UDP header and the user data. Thus, if no checksum calculation is performed by UDP, then no check is made on the user data.

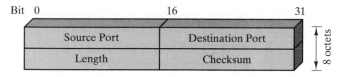

**FIGURE 17.16**   UDP header.

## 17.5 RECOMMENDED READING

[PART88] contains reprints of a number of key papers dealing with specific transport protocol design issues. Good accounts of transport protocols can be found in [SPRA91] and [HALS96].

HALS96   Halsall, F. *Data Communications, Computer Networks, and Open Systems*. Reading, MA: Addison-Wesley, 1996.

PART88   Partridge, C. *Innovations in Internetworking*. Norwood, MA: Artech House, 1988.

SPRA91   Spragins, J., Hammond, J., and Pawlikowski, K. *Telecommunications Protocols and Design*. Reading, MA: Addison-Wesley, 1991.

## 17.6 PROBLEMS

**17.1** It is common practice in most transport protocols (indeed, most protocols at all levels) for control and data to be multiplexed over the same logical channel on a per–user-connection basis. An alternative is to establish a single control transport connection between each pair of communicating transport entities. This connection would be used to carry control signals relating to all user transport connections between the two entities. Discuss the implications of this strategy.

**17.2** The discussion of flow control with a reliable network service referred to a back-pressure mechanism utilizing a lower-level flow control protocol. Discuss the disadvantages of this strategy.

**17.3** Two transport entities communicate across a reliable network. Let the normalized time to transmit a segment equal 1. Assume that the end-to-end propagation delay is 3, and that it takes a time 2 to deliver data from a received segment to the transport user. The sender initially granted a credit of seven segments. The receiver uses a conservative flow control policy and updates its credit allocation at every opportunity. What is the maximum achievable throughput?

**17.4** Draw diagrams similar to Figure 17.8 for the following. (Assume a reliable sequenced network service.)
  a. Connection termination: active/passive.
  b. Connection termination: active/active.
  c. Connection rejection.
  d. Connection abortion: User issues an OPEN to a listening user, and then issues a CLOSE before any data are exchanged.

**17.5** With a reliable sequencing network service, are segment sequence numbers strictly necessary? What, if any, capability is lost without them?

**17.6** Consider a connection-oriented network service that suffers a reset. How could this problem be dealt with by a transport protocol that assumes that the network service is reliable except for resets?

**17.7** The discussion of retransmission strategy made reference to three problems associated with dynamic timer calculation. What modifications to the strategy would help to alleviate those problems?

**17.8** Consider a transport protocol that uses a connection-oriented network service. Suppose that the transport protocol uses a credit-allocation flow control scheme, and the network protocol uses a sliding window scheme. What relationship, if any, should there be between the dynamic window of the transport protocol and the fixed window of the network protocol?

**17.9** In a network that has a maximum packet size of 128 bytes, a maximum packet lifetime of 30 s, and an 8-bit packet sequence number, what is the maximum data rate per connection?

**17.10** Is a deadlock possible using only a two-way handshake instead of a three-way handshake? Give an example or prove otherwise.

**17.11** Why is UDP needed? Why can't a user program directly access IP?

**17.12** Listed below are four strategies that can be used to provide a transport user with the address of the destination transport user. For each one, describe an analogy with the Postal Service user.
  a. Know the address ahead of time.
  b. Make use of a "well-known address."
  c. Use a name server.
  d. Addressee is spawned at request time.

**17.13** In a credit flow control scheme, what provision can be made for credit allocations that are lost or misordered in transit?

**17.14** What happens in Figure 17.7 if an SYN comes in while the requested user is in CLOSED? Is there any way to get the attention of the user when it is not listening?

**17.15** In Section 17.2, it was pointed out that an adaptive, or dynamic, calculation of the retransmission timer may be desirable. One approach would be to simply take the average of observed round-trip times over a number of segments, and then set the retransmission timer equal to a value slightly greater then the average. If the average accurately predicts future round-trip delays, then the resulting retransmission timer will yield good performance. The simple averaging method can be expressed as follows:

$$ARTT(K + 1) = \frac{1}{K + 1} \sum_{i=1}^{K+1} RTT(i)$$

where $RTT(K)$ is the round-trip time observed for the $K$th transmitted segment, and $ARTT(K)$ is the average round-trip time for the first $K$ segments. This expression can be rewritten as follows:

$$ARTT(K + 1) = \frac{K}{K + 1} ARTT(K) + \frac{1}{K + 1} RTT(K + 1)$$

a. The TCP standard recommends the following formulas for estimating round-trip time and setting the retransmission timer:

$$SRTT(K + 1) = \alpha \times SRTT(K) + (1 - \alpha) \times RTT(K + 1)$$
$$RXT(K + 1) = MIN(UBOUND, MAX(LBOUND, \beta \times SRTT(K + 1)))$$

where $SRTT$ is referred to as the smoothed round-trip time, $RXT(K)$ is the retransmission timer value assigned after the first $K$ segments, UBOUND and LBOUND are pre-chosen fixed upper and lower bounds on the timer value, and $\alpha$ and $\beta$ are constants. The recommended initial values for a new connection are $RTT = 0$ seconds, and $RXT = 3$ seconds.

Now, consider that the observed round-trip times for the first 20 segments on a connection have the following values: 1, 2, 3, 4, 5, 6, 7, 8, 9, 10, 10, 10, 10, 10, 10, 10, 10, 10, 10, 10. Show the values for $ARRT(K)$, $SRTT(K)$, and $RXT(K)$ for this sequence. For the latter two parameters, include results for $\alpha = 0.25$, 0.75, and 0.875, and $\beta = 1.0$ and 1.25.

b. Repeat part (a) for the sequence 20, 19, 18, 17, 16, 15, 14, 13, 12, 11, 10, 10, 10, 10, 10, 10, 10, 10, 10, 10.

c. What function do $\alpha$ and $\beta$ perform, and what is the effect of higher and lower values of each? Compare $SRTT$ with $ARTT$.

**17.16** The technique specified in the TCP standard, and described in the previous problem, enables a TCP entity to adapt to changes in round-trip time. However, it does not cope well with a situation in which the round-trip time exhibits a relatively high variance. To cope with this, Von Jacobsen proposed a refinement to the standard algorithm that has now been officially adopted for use with TCP. The algorithm can be summarized as follows:

$$SRTT(K + 1) = (1-\gamma) \times SRTT(K) + \gamma \times RTT(K + 1)$$
$$ERR(K + 1) = RTT(K + 1) - SRTT(K)$$
$$SDEV(K + 1) = SDEV(K) + \gamma \times (|ERR(K + 1)| - SDEV(K))$$
$$= (1-\gamma) \times SDEV(K) + \gamma \times |ERR(K + 1)|$$
$$RXT(K + 1) = SRTT(K + 1) + 2 \times SDEV(K + 1)$$

where $SDEV$ is the smoothed estimate of deviation of round-trip time, and $ERR$ is the difference between the predicted and observed values of round-trip time.

a. Show the values of $SRTT(K)$ and $RXT(K)$ for the same sequences used in parts (a) and (b) of the preceding problem, for $\gamma = 0.75$, 0.25, and 0.125.

**b.** Compare Von Jacobsen's algorithm with the original TCP algorithm. What does the Von Jacobsen algorithm do? How is it superior to the original algorithm?

**17.17** The Von Jacobsen algorithm is quite effective in tracking the round-trip time until there is a period in which the variability of round-trip times is high or until there is a need to retransmit segments due to timer expiration.

**a.** What problem does retransmission cause in estimating round-trip time?

**b.** Suggest and justify a way to compensate for retransmissions. Hint: The approach mandated for TCP, known as Karn's algorithm, is as follows: Follow the Von Jacobsen algorithm until a timer expires, necessitating retransmission. Then use a different strategy until an acknowledgment arrives before a timer expires. Now all you need to do is come up with this alternative strategy.

**17.18** The primary objective of developing a dynamic retransmission timer algorithm is to coordinate the needs of sender and receiver so that the sender is not delivering data either too quickly or too slowly for the receiver. A dynamic retransmission timer has the side effect of helping to cope with network congestion. As network congestion increases, retransmission timers will lengthen, thereby reducing the total network load. However, dynamic timers alone are insufficient to fully cope with severe network congestion. Because the details of the network level are hidden from TCP, it is difficult for TCP to shape its behavior to respond to congestion. However, the fact that retransmission timers are lengthening gives the TCP entity some feel for the degree of congestion.

**a.** TCP mandates the use of a congestion window, whose size is altered to respond to congestion. At any time, TCP acts as if its window size is

$$\text{allowed\_window} = \text{MIN [received\_credit, congestion\_window]}.$$

During periods of normal traffic, the congestion window is the same as the actual window. Suggest a strategy for altering the congestion window during periods of congestion. Hint: Review the binary-exponential backoff technique used for CSMA/CD LANs.

**b.** When a period of congestion appears to be over, we would like to restore transmission to the use of the actual window. However, it is best to avoid an abrupt transition to the full window, as this might reawaken congestion. Suggest a conservative approach.

**17.19** A poor implementation of TCP's sliding-window scheme can lead to extremely poor performance. There is a phenomenon known as the Silly Window Syndrome (SWS), which can easily cause degradation in performance by several factors of ten. As an example of SWS, consider an application that is engaged in a lengthy file transfer, and that TCP is transferring this file in 200-octet segments. The receiver initially provides a credit of 1000. The sender uses up this window with five segments of 200 octets. Now suppose that the receiver returns an acknowledgment to each segment and provides an additional credit of 200 octets for every received segment. From the receiver's point of view, this opens the window back up to 1000 octets. However, from the sender's point of view, if the first acknowledgment arrives after five segments have been sent, a window of only 200 octets becomes available. Assume that at some point, the receiver calculates a window of 200 octets but has only 50 octets to send until it reaches a "push" point. It therefore sends 50 octets in one segment, followed by 150 octets in the next segment, and then resumes transmission of 200-octet segments. What might now happen to cause a performance problem? State the SWS in more general terms.

**17.20** TCP mandates that both the receiver and the sender should incorporate mechanisms to cope with SWS.

**a.** Suggest a strategy for the receiver. Hint: Let the receiver "lie" about how much buffer space is available under certain circumstances; state a reasonable rule of thumb for this approach.

**b.** Suggest a strategy for the sender. Hint: Consider the relationship between the maximum possible send window and what is currently available to send.

# CHAPTER **18**

# NETWORK SECURITY

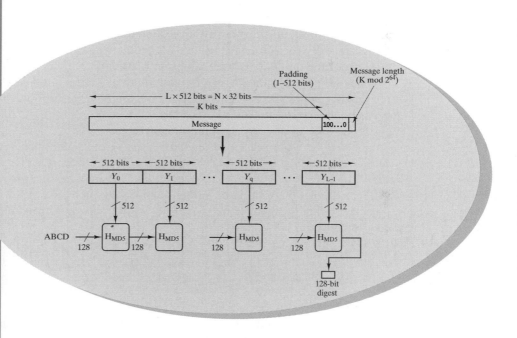

T he requirements of **information security** within an organization have undergone two major changes in the last several decades. Before the widespread use of data processing equipment, the security of information felt to be valuable to an organization was provided primarily by physical and administrative means; an example of the former is the use of rugged filing cabinets with a combination lock for storing sensitive documents; an example of the latter is personnel screening procedures used during the hiring process.

With the introduction of the computer, the need for automated tools for protecting files and other information stored on the computer became evident; this is especially the case for a shared system, such as a time-sharing system, and the need is even more acute for systems that can be accessed over a public telephone or data network. The generic name for the collection of tools designed to protect data and to thwart hackers is **computer security**. Although this is an important topic, it is beyond the scope of this book and will be dealt with only briefly.

The second major change that affected security is the introduction of distributed systems and the use of networks and communications facilities for carrying data between terminal user and computer and between computer and computer. **Network security** measures are needed to protect data during their transmission, and to guarantee that data transmissions are authentic.

The essential technology underlying virtually all automated network and computer security applications is encryption. Two fundamental approaches are in use: conventional encryption, also known as symmetric encryption, and public-key encryption, also known as asymmetric encryption. As we look at the various approaches to network security, these two types of encryption will be explored.

The chapter begins with an overview of the requirements for network security. Next, we look at conventional encryption and its use in providing privacy; this is followed by a discussion of message authentication. We then look at the use of public-key encryption and digital signatures. The chapter closes with an examination of security features in IPv4 and IPv6.

## 18.1   SECURITY REQUIREMENTS AND ATTACKS

In order to be able to understand the types of threats that exist to security, we need to have a definition of security requirements. Computer and network security address three requirements:

- **Secrecy.** Requires that the information in a computer system only be accessible for reading by authorized parties. This type of access includes printing, displaying, and other forms of disclosure, including simply revealing the existence of an object.
- **Integrity.** Requires that computer system assets can be modified only by authorized parties. Modification includes writing, changing, changing status, deleting, and creating.
- **Availability.** Requires that computer system assets are available to authorized parties.

The types of attacks on the security of a computer system or network are best characterized by viewing the function of the computer system as providing information. In general, there is a flow of information from a source, such as a file or a region of main memory, to a destination, such as another file or a user. This normal flow is depicted in Figure 18.1a. The remaining parts of the figure show the following four general categories of attack:

- **Interruption.** An asset of the system is destroyed or becomes unavailable or unusable. This is an attack on **availability**. Examples include destruction of a piece of hardware, such as a hard disk, the cutting of a communication line, or the disabling of the file management system.
- **Interception.** An unauthorized party gains access to an asset. This is an attack on **confidentiality**. The unauthorized party could be a person, a program, or a computer. Examples include wiretapping to capture data in a network, and the illicit copying of files or programs.
- **Modification.** An unauthorized party not only gains access to but tampers with an asset. This is an attack on **integrity**. Examples include changing values in a data file, altering a program so that it performs differently, and modifying the content of messages being transmitted in a network.
- **Fabrication.** An unauthorized party inserts counterfeit objects into the system. This is an attack on **authenticity**. Examples include the insertion of spurious messages in a network or the addition of records to a file.

A useful categorization of these attacks is in terms of passive attacks and active attacks (Figure 18.2).

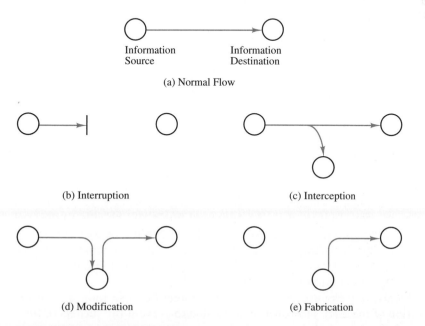

(a) Normal Flow

(b) Interruption

(c) Interception

(d) Modification

(e) Fabrication

**FIGURE 18.1**   Security threats.

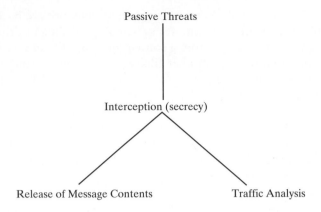

**FIGURE 18.2**   Active and passive network security threats.

## Passive Attacks

Passive attacks mean the eavesdropping on, or monitoring of, transmissions. The goal of the opponent is to obtain information that is being transmitted. Two types of attacks are involved here: release-of-message contents and traffic analysis.

The *release-of-message contents* is easily understood. A telephone conversation, an electronic mail message, a transferred file may contain sensitive or confidential information. We would like to prevent the opponent from learning the contents of these transmissions.

The second passive attack, *traffic analysis,* is more subtle. Suppose that we had a way of masking the contents of messages or other information traffic so that opponents, even if they captured the message, could not extract the information from the message. The common technique for masking contents is encryption. If we had encryption protection in place, an opponent might still be able to observe the pattern of these messages. The opponent could determine the location and identity of communicating hosts and could observe the frequency and length of messages being exchanged. This information might be useful in guessing the nature of the communication that was taking place.

Passive attacks are very difficult to detect because they do not involve any alteration of the data. However, it is feasible to prevent the success of these attacks.

Thus, the emphasis in dealing with passive attacks is on prevention rather than detection.

### Active Attacks

The second major category of attack is *active attacks*. These attacks involve some modification of the data stream or the creation of a false stream and can be subdivided into four categories: masquerade, replay, modification of messages, and denial of service.

A *masquerade* takes place when one entity pretends to be a different entity. A masquerade attack usually includes one of the other forms of active attack. For example, authentication sequences can be captured and replayed after a valid authentication sequence has taken place, thus enabling an authorized entity with few privileges to obtain extra privileges by impersonating an entity that has those privileges.

*Replay* involves the passive capture of a data unit and its subsequent retransmission to produce an unauthorized effect.

*Modification of messages* simply means that some portion of a legitimate message is altered, or that messages are delayed or reordered, to produce an unauthorized effect. For example, a message meaning "Allow John Smith to read confidential file *accounts*" is modified to mean "Allow Fred Brown to read confidential file *accounts*."

The *denial of service* prevents or inhibits the normal use or management of communications facilities. This attack may have a specific target; for example, an entity may suppress all messages directed to a particular destination (e.g., the security audit service). Another form of service denial is the disruption of an entire network, either by disabling the network or by overloading it with messages so as to degrade performance.

Active attacks present the opposite characteristics of passive attacks. Whereas passive attacks are difficult to detect, measures are available to prevent their success. On the other hand, it is quite difficult to prevent active attacks absolutely, as to do so would require physical protection of all communications facilities and paths at all times. Instead, the goal is to detect them and to recover from any disruption or delays caused by them. Because the detection has a deterrent effect, it may also contribute to prevention.

## 18.2 PRIVACY WITH CONVENTIONAL ENCRYPTION

The universal technique for providing privacy for transmitted data is conventional encryption. This section looks first at the basic concept of conventional encryption, followed by a discussion of the two most popular conventional encryption techniques: DES and triple DES. We then examine the application of these techniques to achieve privacy.

### Conventional Encryption

Figure 18.3 illustrates the conventional encryption process. The original intelligible message, referred to as *plaintext*, is converted into apparently random nonsense, referred to as *ciphertext*. The encryption process consists of an algorithm and a key. The key is a value independent of the plaintext that controls the algorithm. The algorithm will produce a different output depending on the specific key being used at the time. Changing the key changes the output of the algorithm.

Once the ciphertext is produced, it is transmitted. Upon reception, the ciphertext can be transformed back to the original plaintext by using a decryption algorithm and the same key that was used for encryption.

The security of conventional encryption depends on several factors. First, the encryption algorithm must be powerful enough so that it is impractical to decrypt a message on the basis of the ciphertext alone. Beyond that, the security of conventional encryption depends on the secrecy of the key, not on the secrecy of the algorithm. That is, it is assumed that it is impractical to decrypt a message on the basis of the ciphertext *plus* knowledge of the encryption/decryption algorithm. In other words, we don't need to keep the algorithm secret; we only need to keep the key secret.

This feature of conventional encryption is what makes it feasible for widespread use. The fact that the algorithm need not be kept secret means that manufacturers can and have developed low-cost chip implementations of data encryption algorithms. These chips are widely available and incorporated into a number of products. With the use of conventional encryption, the principal security problem is maintaining the secrecy of the key.

Let us take a closer look at the essential elements of a conventional encryption scheme, again using Figure 18.3. There is some source for a message, which

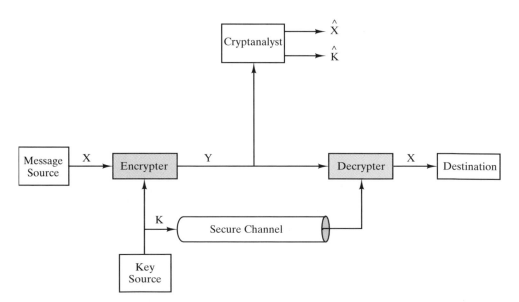

**FIGURE 18.3**   Model of conventional cryptosystem.

produces the following message in plaintext: $X = [X_1, X_2, \ldots, X_M]$. The $M$ elements of $X$ are letters in some finite alphabet. Traditionally, the alphabet usually consisted of the 26 capital letters. Nowadays, the binary alphabet {0, 1} is typically used. For encryption, a key of the form $K = [K_1, K_2, \ldots, K_J]$ is generated. If the key is generated at the message source, then it must also be provided to the destination by means of some secure channel. Alternatively, a third party could generate the key and securely deliver it to both source and destination.

With the message $X$ and the encryption key $K$ as input, the encryption algorithm, or encrypter, forms the ciphertext $Y = [Y_1, Y_2, \ldots, Y_N]$. We can write this as

$$Y = \mathrm{E}_K(X)$$

This notation indicates that $Y$ is produced by using encryption algorithm E as a function of the plaintext $X$, with the specific function determined by the value of the key $K$.

The intended receiver, in possession of the key, is able to invert the transformation:

$$X = \mathrm{D}_K(Y)$$

An opponent, observing $Y$ but not having access to $K$ or $X$, must attempt to recover $X$ or $K$ or both $X$ and $K$. It is assumed that the opponent does have knowledge of the encryption (E) and decryption (D) algorithms. If the opponent is interested in only this particular message, then the focus of the effort is to recover $X$ by generating a plaintext estimate $\hat{X}$. Often, however, the opponent is interested in being able to read future messages as well, in which case an attempt is made to recover $K$ by generating a plaintext estimate $\hat{K}$.

## Encryption Algorithms

The most commonly used conventional encryption algorithms are block ciphers. A block cipher processes the plaintext input in fixed-size blocks, and produces a block of ciphertext of equal size for each plaintext block. The two most important conventional algorithms, both of which are block ciphers, are DES and Triple DES.

### The Data Encryption Standard (DES)

The most widely used encryption scheme is defined in the data encryption standard (DES) adopted in 1977 by the National Bureau of Standards, now the National Institute of Standards and Technology (NIST), as Federal Information Processing Standard 46 (FIPS PUB 46). In 1994, NIST "reaffirmed" DES for federal use for another five years [NIST94]; NIST recommends the use of DES for applications other than the protection of classified information.

The overall scheme for DES encryption is illustrated in Figure 18.4. As with any encryption scheme, there are two inputs to the encryption function: the plaintext to be encrypted and the key. In this case, the plaintext must be 64 bits in length, and the key is 56 bits in length.

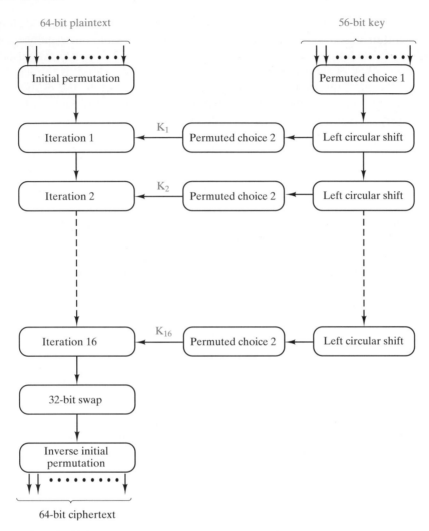

**FIGURE 18.4** General depiction of DES algorithm.

The processing of the plaintext proceeds in three phases. First, the 64-bit plaintext passes through an initial permutation (IP) that rearranges the bits to produce the *permuted input*. This IP is followed by a phase consisting of 16 iterations of the same function. The output of the last (16th) iteration consists of 64 bits that are a function of the plaintext input and the key. The left and right halves of the output are swapped to produce the *preoutput*. Finally, the preoutput is passed through a permutation (IP$^{-1}$) that is the inverse of the initial permutation function, in order to produce the 64-bit ciphertext.

The right-hand portion of Figure 18.4 shows the way in which the 56-bit key is used. Initially, the key is passed through a permutation function. Then, for each of the 16 iterations, a *subkey* (K$_i$) is produced by the combination of a left circular shift and a permutation. The permutation function is the same for each iteration, but a different subkey is produced because of the repeated shifting of the key bits.

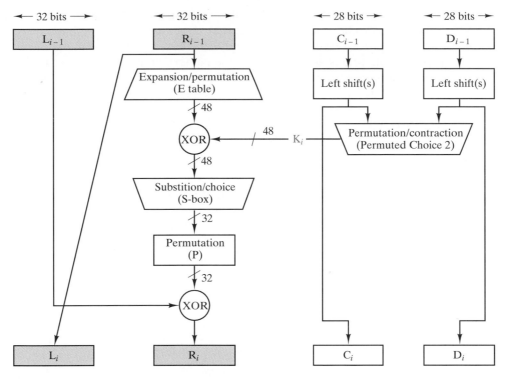

**FIGURE 18.5**   Single iteration of DES algorithm.

Figure 18.5 examines more closely the algorithm for a single iteration. The 64-bit permuted input passes through 16 iterations, producing an intermediate 64-bit value at the conclusion of each iteration. The left- and right-half of each 64-bit intermediate value are treated as separate 32-bit quantities, labeled L (left) and R (right). The overall processing at each iteration can be summarized in the following formulas:

$$L_i = R_{i-1}$$
$$R_i = L_{i-1} \oplus f(R_{i-1}, K_i)$$

where $\oplus$ denotes the bitwise XOR function.

Thus, the left-hand output of an iteration ($L_i$) is simply equal to the right-hand input to that iteration ($R_{i-1}$). The right-hand output ($R_i$) is the exclusive-or of $L_{i-1}$ and a complex function f of $R_{i-1}$ and $K_i$. This complex function involves both permutation and substitution operations. The substitution operation, represented as tables called "S-boxes," simply maps each combination of 48 input bits into a particular 32-bit pattern.

Returning to Figure 18.4, we see that the 56-bit key used as input to the algorithm is first subjected to a permutation. The resulting 56-bit key is then treated as two 28-bit quantities, labeled $C_0$ and $D_0$. At each iteration, C and D are separately subjected to a circular left shift, or rotation, of 1 or 2 bits. These shifted values serve as input to the next iteration. They also serve as input to another permutation function, which produces a 48-bit output that serves as input to the function $f(R_{i-1}, K_i)$.

The process of decryption with DES is essentially the same as the encryption process. The rule is as follows: Use the ciphertext as input to the DES algorithm, but use the keys $K_i$ in reverse order. That is, use $K_{16}$ on the first iteration, $K_{15}$ on the second iteration, and so on until $K_1$ is used on the 16th and last iteration.

## The Strength of DES

Since its adoption as a federal standard, there have been lingering concerns about the level of security provided by DES. These concerns, by and large, fall into two areas: the nature of the algorithm and key size.

For many years, the more important concern was the possibility of exploiting the characteristics of the DES algorithm to perform cryptanalysis. The focus of concern has been on the eight substitution tables, or S-boxes, that are used in each iteration. Because the design criteria for these boxes, and indeed for the entire algorithm, have never been made public, there is a suspicion that the boxes were constructed in such a way that cryptanalysis is possible for an opponent who knows the weaknesses in the S-boxes. This assertion is tantalizing, and over the years a number of regularities and unexpected behaviors of the S-boxes have been discovered. Despite this problem, no one has so far succeeded in discovering the supposed fatal weaknesses in the *S*-boxes. Indeed, as advances in cryptanalytic techniques have occurred, the underlying strength of the DES algorithm has become more apparent. As of this writing, no practical attack method for DES has been published. Given that the algorithm has survived years of intensive scrutiny unscathed, it is probably safe to say that DES is one of the strongest encryption algorithms ever devised.

The more serious concern, today, is the key size. With a key length of 56 bits, there are $2^{56}$ possible keys, which is approximately $7.6 \times 10^{16}$ keys. Thus, on the face of it, a brute-force attack appears impractical. Assuming that on average half the key space has to be searched, a single machine performing one DES encryption per microsecond would take more than a thousand years to break the cipher.

However, the assumption of one encryption per microsecond is overly conservative. As far back as 1977, Diffie and Hellman, the inventors of public-key encryption, postulated that the technology existed to build a parallel machine with 1 million encryption devices, each of which could perform one encryption per microsecond. The authors estimated that the cost would be about $20 million in 1977 dollars.

The most rigorous recent analysis of the problem was done by Wiener [WIEN93] and is based on a known plaintext attack. That is, it is assumed that the attacker has at least one (plaintext, ciphertext) pair. Wiener takes care to provide the details of his design. To quote his paper,

> There have been numerous unverifiable claims about how fast the DES key space can be searched. To avoid adding to this list of questionable claims, a great deal of detail in the design of a key search machine is included in the appendices. This detailed work was done to obtain an accurate assessment of the cost of the machine and the time required to find a DES key. There are no plans to actually build such a machine.

Wiener reports on the design of a chip that uses pipelined techniques to achieve a key search rate of 50 million keys per second. Using 1993 costs, he designed a module that costs $100,000 and contains 5,760 key search chips. With this design, the following results are obtained:

| Key Search Machine Unit Cost | Expected Search Time |
|---|---|
| $100,000 | 35 hours |
| $1,000,000 | 3.5 hours |
| $10,000,000 | 21 minutes |

In addition, Wiener estimates a one-time development cost of about $500,000.

The Wiener design represents the culmination of years of concern about the security of DES and may in retrospect have been a turning point. As of the time of this writing, it still seems reasonable to rely on DES for personal and commercial applications. But the time has come to investigate alternatives for conventional encryption. One of the most promising and widely used candidates for replacing DES is triple DES.

## Triple DES

Triple DES was first proposed by Tuchman [TUCH79], and first standardized for use in financial applications [ANSI85]. Triple DES uses two keys and three executions of the DES algorithm (Figure 18.6). The function follows an encrypt-decrypt-encrypt (EDE) sequence:

$$C = E_{K_1} [ D_{K_2} [ E_{K_1} [P] ] ]$$

There is no cryptographic significance to the use of decryption for the second stage. Its only advantage is that it allows users of triple DES to decrypt data encrypted by users of the older, single DES:

$$C = E_{K_1} [ D_{K_1} [ E_{K_1} [P] ] ] = E_{K_1} [P]$$

Although only two keys are used, three instances of the DES algorithm are required. It turns out that there is a simple technique, known as a meet-in-the-

FIGURE 18.6 Triple DES.

middle attack, that would reduce a double DES system with two keys to the relative strength of ordinary single DES. With three iterations of the DES function, the effective key length is 112 bits.

### Location of Encryption Devices

The most powerful, and most common, approach to countering the threats to network security is encryption. In using encryption we need to decide what to encrypt and where the encryption gear should be located. As Figure 18.7 indicates, there are two fundamental alternatives: link encryption and end-to-end encryption.

With link encryption, each vulnerable communications link is equipped on both ends with an encryption device. Thus, all traffic over all communications links is secured. Although this requires many encryption devices in a large network, the value of this approach is clear. However, one disadvantage of this approach is that the message must be decrypted each time it enters a packet switch; this is necessary because the switch must read the address (virtual circuit number) in the packet header in order to route the packet. Thus, the message is vulnerable at each switch. If this is a public packet-switching network, the user has no control over the security of the nodes.

With end-to-end encryption, the encryption process is carried out at the two end systems. The source host, or terminal, encrypts the data, which, in encrypted form, is then transmitted unaltered across the network to the destination terminal or host. The destination shares a key with the source and so is able to decrypt the

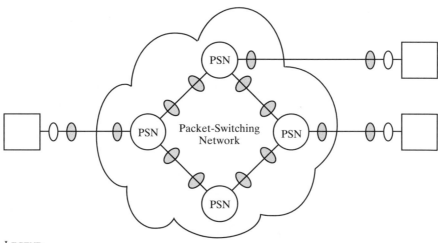

LEGEND

◯ = End-to-end encryption device

◯ = Link encryption device

PSN = Link encryption device

**FIGURE 18.7**   Encryption across a packet-switching network.

data. This approach would seem to secure the transmission against attacks on the network links or switches. There is, however, still a weak spot.

Consider the following situation. A host connects to an X.25 packet-switching network, sets up a virtual circuit to another host, and is prepared to transfer data to that other host using end-to-end encryption. Data are transmitted over such a network in the form of packets, consisting of a header and some user data. What part of each packet will the host encrypt? Suppose that the host encrypts the entire packet, including the header. This will not work because, remember, only the other host can perform the decryption. The packet-switching node will receive an encrypted packet and be unable to read the header. Therefore, it will not be able to route the packet! It follows that the host may only encrypt the user data portion of the packet and must leave the header in the clear, so that it can be read by the network.

Thus, with end-to-end encryption, the user data are secure; however, the traffic pattern is not, as packet headers are transmitted in the clear. To achieve greater security, both link and end-to-end encryption are needed, as is shown in Figure 18.7.

To summarize, when both forms are employed, the host encrypts the user data portion of a packet using an end-to-end encryption key. The entire packet is then encrypted using a link-encryption key. As the packet traverses the network, each switch decrypts the packet using a link-encryption key in order to read the header and then encrypts the entire packet again so as to send it out on the next link. Now the entire packet is secure, except for the time that the packet is actually in the memory of a packet switch, at which time the packet header is in the clear.

## Key Distribution

For conventional encryption to work, the two parties in an exchange must have the same key, and that key must be protected from access by others. Furthermore, frequent key changes are usually desirable to limit the amount of data compromised if an attacker learns the key. Therefore, the strength of any cryptographic system rests with the key distribution technique, a term that refers to the means of delivering a key to two parties who wish to exchange data without allowing others to see the key. Key distribution can be achieved in a number of ways. For two parties $A$ and $B$

1. A key could be selected by $A$ and physically delivered to $B$.
2. A third party could select the key and physically deliver it to $A$ and $B$.
3. If $A$ and $B$ have previously and recently used a key, one party could transmit the new key to the other, encrypted using the old key.
4. If $A$ and $B$ each have an encrypted connection to a third party $C$, $C$ could deliver a key on the encrypted links to $A$ and $B$.

Options 1 and 2 call for manual delivery of a key; for link encryption, this is a reasonable requirement, as each link encryption device is only going to be exchanging data with its partner on the other end of the link. However, for end-to-end encryption, manual delivery is awkward. In a distributed system, any given host or terminal may need to engage in exchanges with many other hosts and terminals over time. Thus, each device needs a number of keys, supplied dynamically. The problem is especially difficult in a wide-area distributed system.

Option 3 is a possibility for either link encryption or end-to-end encryption, but if an attacker ever succeeds in gaining access to one key, then all subsequent keys are revealed. Even if frequent changes are made to the link-encryption keys, these should be done manually. To provide keys for end-to-end encryption, option 4 is preferable.

Figure 18.8 illustrates an implementation that satisfies option 4 for end-to-end encryption. In the figure, link encryption is ignored. This can be added, or not, as required. For this scheme, two kinds of keys are identified:

- **Session key.** When two end systems (hosts, terminals, etc.) wish to communicate, they establish a logical connection (e.g., virtual circuit). For the duration of that logical connection, all user data are encrypted with a one-time session key. At the conclusion of the session, or connection, the session key is destroyed.
- **Permanent key.** A permanent key is one used between entities for the purpose of distributing session keys.

The configuration consists of the following elements:

- **Key distribution center.** The key distribution center determines which systems are allowed to communicate with each other. When permission is granted for two systems to establish a connection, the key distribution center provides a one-time session key for that connection.
- **Front-end processor.** The front-end processor performs end-to-end encryption and obtains session keys on behalf of its host or terminal.

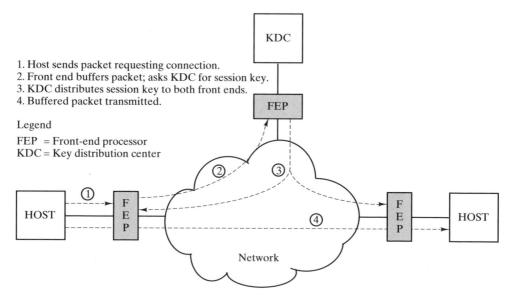

1. Host sends packet requesting connection.
2. Front end buffers packet; asks KDC for session key.
3. KDC distributes session key to both front ends.
4. Buffered packet transmitted.

Legend

FEP = Front-end processor
KDC = Key distribution center

**FIGURE 18.8** Automatic key distribution for connection-oriented protocol.

The steps involved in establishing a connection are shown in the figure. When one host wishes to set up a connection to another host, it transmits a connection-request packet (step 1). The front-end processor saves that packet and applies to the KDC for permission to establish the connection (step 2). The communication between the FEP and the KDC is encrypted using a master key shared only by the FEP and the KDC. If the KDC approves the connection request, it generates the session key and delivers it to the two appropriate front-end processors, using a unique permanent key for each front end (step 3). The requesting front-end processor can now release the connection-request packet, and a connection is set up between the two end systems (step 4). All user data exchanged between the two end systems are encrypted by their respective front-end processors using the one-time session key.

The automated key distribution approach provides the flexibility and dynamic characteristics needed both to allow a number of terminal users to access a number of hosts and for the hosts to exchange data with each other.

Of course, another approach to key distribution uses public-key encryption, which is discussed in Section 18.4.

## Traffic Padding

We mentioned that, in some cases, users are concerned about security from traffic analysis. With the use of link encryption, packet headers are encrypted, reducing the opportunity for traffic analysis. However, it is still possible in those circumstances for an attacker to assess the amount of traffic on a network and to observe the amount of traffic entering and leaving each end system. An effective countermeasure to this attack is traffic padding, illustrated in Figure 18.9.

Traffic padding is a function that produces ciphertext output continuously, even in the absence of plaintext. A continuous random data stream is generated.

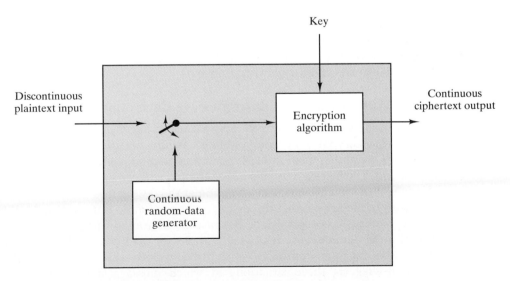

**FIGURE 18.9**   Traffic-padding encryption device.

When plaintext is available, it is encrypted and transmitted. When input plaintext is not present, the random data are encrypted and transmitted. This makes it impossible for an attacker to distinguish between true data flow and noise, and it is therefore impossible for the intruder to deduce the amount of traffic.

## 18.3   MESSAGE AUTHENTICATION AND HASH FUNCTIONS

Encryption protects against passive attack (eavesdropping). A different requirement is to protect against active attack (falsification of data and transactions). Protection against such attacks is known as message authentication.

### Approaches to Message Authentication

A message, file, document, or other collection of data is said to be authentic when it is genuine and actually coming from its alleged source. Message authentication is a procedure that allows communicating parties to verify that received messages are authentic. The two important aspects are to verify that the contents of the message have not been altered and that the source is authentic. We may also wish to verify a message's timeliness (it has not been artificially delayed and replayed) and sequence, relative to other messages flowing between two parties.

#### Authentication Using Conventional Encryption

It is possible to perform authentication simply by the use of conventional encryption. If we assume that only the sender and receiver share a key (which is as it should be), then only the genuine sender would be able to successfully encrypt a message for the other participant. Furthermore, if the message includes an error-detection code and a sequence number, the receiver is assured that no alterations have been made and that sequencing is proper. If the message also includes a time-stamp, the receiver is assured that the message has not been delayed beyond that time normally expected for network transit.

#### Message Authentication Without Message Encryption

In this section, we examine several approaches to message authentication that do not rely on encryption but on a related family of functions. In all of these approaches, an authentication tag is generated and appended to each message for transmission. The message itself is not encrypted and can be read at the destination independent of the authentication function at the destination.

Because the approaches discussed in this section do not encrypt the message, message secrecy is not provided. Because conventional encryption will provide authentication, and because it is widely used with readily available products, why not simply use such an approach, which provides both secrecy and authentication? [DAVI90] suggests three situations in which message authentication without secrecy is preferable:

1. There are a number of applications in which the same message is broadcast to a number of destinations—for example, notification to users that the network is now unavailable or an alarm signal in a control center. It is cheaper and more reliable to have only one destination responsible for monitoring authenticity. Thus, the message must be broadcast in plaintext with an associated message authentication tag. The responsible system performs authentication. If a violation occurs, the other destination systems are alerted by a general alarm.

2. Another possible scenario is an exchange in which one side has a heavy load and cannot afford the time to decrypt all incoming messages. Authentication is carried out on a selective basis, with the messages being chosen at random for checking.

3. Authentication of a computer program in plaintext is an attractive service. The computer program can be executed without having to decrypt it every time, which would be wasteful of processor resources. However, if a message authentication tag were attached to the program, it could be checked whenever assurance is required of the integrity of the program.

Thus, there is a place for both authentication and encryption in meeting security requirements.

## Message Authentication Code

One authentication technique involves the use of a secret key to generate a small block of data, known as a message authentication code, that is appended to the message. This technique assumes that two communicating parties, say A and B, share a common secret key $K_{AB}$. When A has a message to send to B, it calculates the message authentication code as a function of the message and the key: $MAC_M = F(K_{AB}, M)$. The message plus code are transmitted to the intended recipient. The recipient performs the same calculation on the received message, using the same secret key, to generate a new message authentication code. The received code is compared to the calculated code (Figure 18.10). If we assume that only the receiver and the sender know the identity of the secret key, and if the received code matches the calculated code, then,

1. The receiver is assured that the message has not been altered. If an attacker alters the message but does not alter the code, then the receiver's calculation of the code will differ from the received code. Because the attacker is assumed not to know the secret key, the attacker cannot alter the code to correspond to the alterations in the message.

2. The receiver is assured that the message is from the alleged sender. Because no one else knows the secret key, no one else could prepare a message with a proper code.

3. If the message includes a sequence number (such as is used with X.25, HDLC, TCP, and the ISO transport protocol), then the receiver can be assured of the proper sequence, as an attacker cannot successfully alter the sequence number.

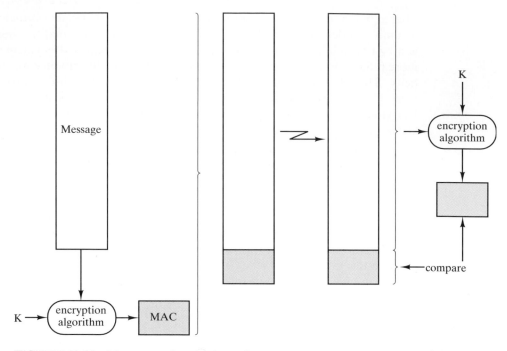

**FIGURE 18.10**    Message authentication using a message authentication code (MAC).

A number of algorithms could be used to generate the code. The National Bureau of Standards, in its publication *DES Modes of Operation*, recommends the use of the DES algorithm. The DES algorithm is used to generate an encrypted version of the message, and the last number of bits of ciphertext are used as the code. A 16- or 32-bit code is typical.

The process just described is similar to encryption. One difference is that the authentication algorithm need not be reversible, as it must for decryption. It turns out that because of the mathematical properties of the authentication function, it is less vulnerable to being broken than is encryption.

### One-Way Hash Function.

A variation on the message authentication code that has received much attention recently is the one-way hash function. As with the message authentication code, a hash function accepts a variable-size message M as input and produces a fixed-size tag H(M), sometimes called a message digest, as output. To authenticate a message, the message digest is sent with the message in such a way that the message digest is authentic.

Figure 18.11 illustrates three ways in which the message digest can be authenticated. The message digest can be encrypted using conventional encryption (part (a)); if it is assumed that only the sender and receiver share the encryption key, then authenticity is assured. The message can also be encrypted using public-key encryption (part (b)). The public-key approach has two advantages: It provides a digital

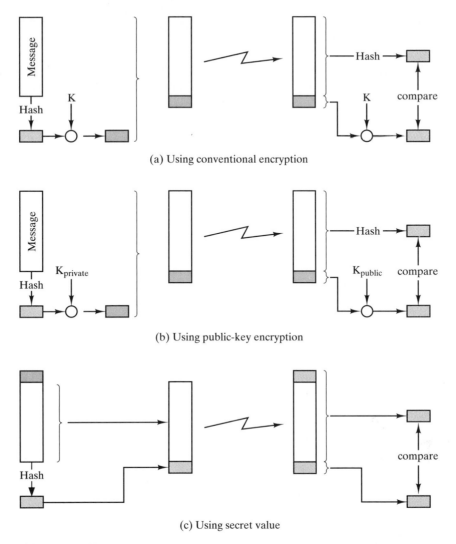

(a) Using conventional encryption

(b) Using public-key encryption

(c) Using secret value

**FIGURE 18.11**  Message authentication using a one-way hash function.

signature as well as message authentication; and it does not require the distribution of keys to communicating parties.

These two approaches have an advantage over approaches that encrypt the entire message, in that less computation is required. Nevertheless, there has been an interest in developing a technique that avoids encryption altogether. Several reasons for this interest are pointed out in [TSUD92]:

- Encryption software is quite slow. Even though the amount of data to be encrypted per message is small, there may be a steady stream of messages into and out of a system.

- Encryption hardware costs are non-negligible. Low-cost chip implementations of DES are available, but the cost adds up if all nodes in a network must have this capability.
- Encryption hardware is optimized toward large data sizes. For small blocks of data, a high proportion of the time is spent in initialization/invocation overhead.
- Encryption algorithms may be covered by patents. Some encryption algorithms, such as the RSA public-key algorithm, are patented and must be licensed, adding a cost.
- Encryption algorithms may be subject to export control. This is true of DES.

Figure 18.11c shows a technique that uses a hash function but no encryption for message authentication. This technique assumes that two communicating parties, say A and B, share a common secret value $S_{AB}$. When A has a message to send to B, it calculates the hash function over the concatenation of the secret value and the message: $MD_M = H(S_{AB}\|M)$.[1] It then sends $[M\|MD_M]$ to B. Because B possesses $S_{AB}$, it can recompute $H(S_{AB}\|M)$ and verify $MD_M$, and, because the secret value itself is not sent, it is not possible for an attacker to modify an intercepted message. As long as the secret value remains secret, it is also not possible for an attacker to generate a false message.

This third technique, using a shared secret value, is the one adopted for IP security (described in Chapter 19); it has also been tentatively specified for SNMPv2.[2]

### Secure Hash Functions

The one-way hash function, or secure hash function, is important not only in message authentication but in digital signatures. In this section, we begin with a discussion of requirements for a secure hash function. Then we look at two very simple hash functions that are not secure, to gain an appreciation of the structure of such functions. Finally, we examine one of the most important hash functions, MD5.

### Hash Function Requirements

The purpose of a hash function is to produce a "fingerprint" of a file, message, or other block of data. To be useful for message authentication, a hash function H must have the following properties, adapted from a list in [NECH91]:

1. H can be applied to a block of data of any size.
2. H produces a fixed-length output.
3. $H(x)$ is relatively easy to compute for any given $x$, making both hardware and software implementations practical.

---

[1] $\|$ denotes concatenation.

[2] When SNMPv2 was first issued in 1993 as a set of proposed Internet standards, it included a security function that used the technique just discussed. SNMPv2 was reissued as draft Internet standards in 1996 without the security function because of lack of agreement on all the details. However, the final security standard for SNMP is likely to include the technique just discussed.

4. For any given code $m$, it is computationally infeasible to find $x$ such that $H(x) = m$.

5. For any given block $x$, it is computationally infeasible to find $y \neq x$ with $H(y) = H(x)$.

6. It is computationally infeasible to find any pair $(x, y)$ such that $H(x) = H(y)$.

The first three properties are requirements for the practical application of a hash function to message authentication.

The fourth property is the *one-way* property: It is easy to generate a code given a message, but virtually impossible to generate a message given a code. This property is important if the authentication technique involves the use of a secret value (Figure 18.11c), which is not itself sent; however, if the hash function is not one-way, an attacker can easily discover the secret value: If the attacker can observe or intercept a transmission, he or she obtains the message M and the hash code $MD_M = H(S_{AB}||M)$. The attacker then inverts the hash function to obtain $S_{AB}||M = H^{-1}(MD_M)$. Because the attacker now has both M and $S_{AB}||M$, it is a trivial matter to recover $S_{AB}$.

The fifth property guarantees that an alternative message hashing to the same value as a given message cannot be found; this prevents forgery when an encrypted hash code is used (Figure 18.11b and c). If this property were not true, an attacker would be capable of the following sequence: First, observe or intercept a message plus its encrypted hash code; second, generate an unencrypted hash code from the message; third, generate an alternate message with the same hash code.

A hash function that satisfies the first five properties in the preceding list is referred to as a weak hash function. If the sixth property is also satisfied, then it is referred to as a strong hash function. The sixth property protects against a sophisticated class of attack known as the birthday attack.[3]

In addition to providing authentication, a message digest also provides data integrity. It performs the same function as a frame check sequence: If any bits in the message are accidentally altered in transit, the message digest will be in error.

## Simple Hash Functions

All hash functions operate using the following general principles. The input (message, file, etc.) is viewed as a sequence of $n$-bit blocks. The input is processed one block at a time in an iterative fashion to produce an $n$-bit hash function.

One of the simplest hash functions is to take the bit-by-bit–exclusive-or (XOR) of every block; this can be expressed as follows:

$$C_i = b_{i1} \oplus b_{i2} \oplus \ldots \oplus b_{im}$$

where

$C_i = i$th bit of the hash code, $1 \leq i \leq n$

$m = $ number of $n$-bit blocks in the input

$b_{ij} = i$th bit in $j$th block

$\oplus = $ XOR operation

---

[3] See [STAL95b] for a discussion of birthday attacks.

| | bit 1 | bit 2 | • • • | bit n |
|---|---|---|---|---|
| **block 1** | $b_{11}$ | $b_{21}$ | | $b_{n1}$ |
| **block 2** | $b_{12}$ | $b_{22}$ | | $b_{n2}$ |
| | • • • | • • • | • • • | • • • |
| **block m** | $b_{1m}$ | $b_{2m}$ | | $b_{nm}$ |
| **hash code** | $C_1$ | $C_2$ | | $C_n$ |

**FIGURE 18.12**  Simple hash function using bitwise XOR.

```
main (int argc, char*argv[]) {
        unsigned long hash [4] = (0, 0, 0, 0), data [4] ;
        FILE *fp;
        int i;
        if ((fp = = fopen (argv [1], "rb")) != NULL) {
            while ((fread (data, 4,,4, fp) != NULL)
                for (i=0; i<4; i++)
                    hash [i] ^=data [i];
            fclose (fp);
            for (i=0; i<4; i++)
                printf ("%081x", hash [i]);
            printf ("\n") ;
        }   }
```

**(a) XOR of every 128-bit block**

```
main (int argc, char *argv []) {
        unsigned long hash [4] = (0, 0, 0, 0), data [4] ;
        FILE *fp;
        int i;
        if ((fp = = fopen (argv [1], "rb")) !=NULL) {
            while ((fread (data, 4,,4, fp) !=NULL)
                for (i=0; i<4; i++)   {
                    hash [i] ^=data [i];
                    hash [i] = hash [i] >>1 ^ hash [i] <<31 ;
                    }
            fclose (fp);
            for (i=0; i<4; i++)
                printf ("%081x", hash [i]) ;
            printf ("\n") ;
        }   }
```

**(b) Rolling each longword 1 bit to the right**

**FIGURE 18.13**  Simple hash functions (based on [SCHN91]).

Figure 18.12 illustrates this operation. Figure 18.13a is a C program that produces a 128-bit hash code. This type of code produces a simple parity for each bit position and is known as a longitudinal redundancy check. It is reasonably effective for random data as a data integrity check. Each 128-bit hash value is equally likely. Thus, the probability that a data error will result in an unchanged hash value is $2^{-128}$. With more predictably formatted data, the function is less effective. For example, in most normal text files, the high-order bit of each octet is always zero. Therefore, 16 bits in the hash will always be zero, and the effectiveness is reduced to $2^{-112}$.

A simple way to improve matters is to perform a one-bit circular shift, or rotation on the hash value after each block is processed, as defined in Figure 18.13b. This has the effect of "randomizing" the input more completely and overcoming any regularities that appear in the input.

Although the second program provides a good measure of data integrity, it is virtually useless for data security. Consider the following task of a potential attacker: Given a hash code, produce a message that yields that hash code. The attacker would simply need to prepare the desired message and then append a 128-bit block that forces the new message, plus block, to yield the desired hash code.

Thus, we need a hash algorithm that is a much more complex function of the input bits.

## MD5 Algorithm Description

The MD5 message-digest algorithm, specified in RFC 1321, was developed by Ron Rivest at MIT (the "R" in the RSA [Rivest-Shamir-Adelman] public-key encryption algorithm). The algorithm takes as input a message of arbitrary length and produces as output a 128-bit message digest. The input is processed in 512-bit blocks.

Figure 18.14 depicts the overall processing of a message to produce a digest. The processing consists of the following steps:

- **Step 1: Append Padding Bits**

The message is padded so that its length in bits is congruent to 448 modulo 512 (length = 448 mod 512). That is, the length of the padded message is 64 bits less than an integer multiple of 512 bits. Padding is always added, even if the message is already of the desired length. For example, if the message is 448 bits long, it is padded by 512 bits to a length of 960 bits. Thus, the number of padding bits is in the range of 1 to 512.

The padding consists of a single 1-bit followed by the necessary number of 0-bits.

- **Step 2: Append Length**

A 64-bit representation of the length in bits of the original message (before the padding) is appended to the result of step 1. If the original length is greater than $2^{64}$, then only the low-order 64 bits of the length are used. Thus, the field contains the length of the original message, modulo $2^{64}$. The inclusion of a length value at the end of the message makes more difficult a type of attack known as a padding attack [TSUD92].

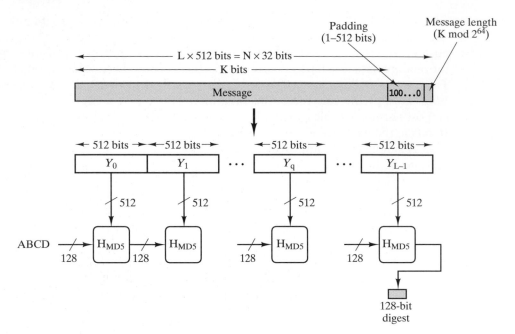

**FIGURE 18.14** Message digest generation using MD5.

The outcome of the first two steps yields a message that is an integer multiple of 512 bits in length. In the figure, the expanded message is represented as the sequence of 512-bit blocks $Y_0, Y_1, \ldots, Y_{L-1}$, so that the total length of the expanded message is $L \times 512$ bits. Equivalently, the result is a multiple of sixteen 32-bit words. Let M[0 $\ldots$ N $-$ 1] denote the words of the resulting message, with N an integer multiple of 16. Thus, $N = L \times 16$.

- **Step 3: Initialize MD Buffer**

A 128-bit buffer is used to hold intermediate and final results of the hash function. The buffer can be represented as four 32-bit registers (A, B, C, D), which are initialized to the following hexadecimal values (low-order octets first):

    A = 01234567
    B = 89ABCDEF
    C = FEDCBA98
    D = 76543210

- **Step 4: Process Message in 512-Bit (16-Word) Blocks**

The heart of the algorithm is a module that consists of four "rounds" of processing; this module is labeled $H_{MD5}$ in Figure 18.14, and its logic is illustrated in Figure 18.15. The four rounds have a similar structure, but each uses a different primitive logical function, referred to as F, G, H, and I in the specification. In the figure,

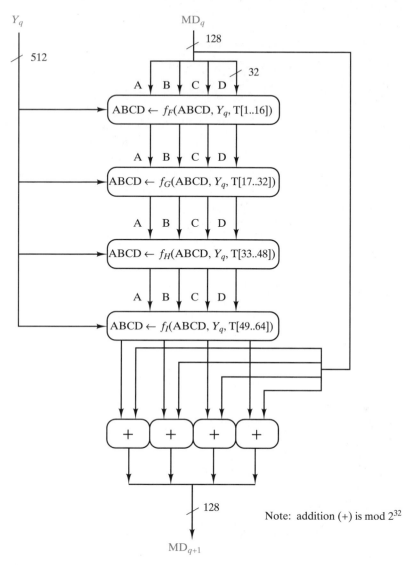

**FIGURE 18.15** MD5 processing of a single 512-bit block ($H_{MD5}$).

the four rounds are labeled $f_F$, $f_G$, $f_H$, $f_I$, to indicate that each round has the same general functional structure, f, but depends on a different primitive function (F, G, H, I).

Each primitive function takes three 32-bit words as input and produces a 32-bit word output. Each function performs a set of bitwise logical operations; that is, the $n$th bit of the output is a function of the $n$th bit of the three inputs. The functions are

$$F(X,Y,Z) = (X \cdot Y) + (X' \cdot Z)$$

$$G(X,Y,Z) = (X \cdot Z) + (Y \cdot Z')$$

$$H(X,Y,Z) = X \oplus Y \oplus Z$$

$$I(X,Y,Z) = Y \oplus (X + Z')$$

where the logical operators (AND, OR, NOT, XOR) are represented by the symbols $(\cdot, +, ', \oplus)$. Function F is a conditional function: If X then Y else Z. Function H produces a parity bit. Table 18.1 is a truth table of the four functions.

Note that each round takes as input the current 512-bit block being processed ($Yq$) and the 128-bit buffer value ABCD and updates the contents of the buffer. Each round also makes use of one-fourth of a 64-element table T[1 . . . 64], constructed from the sine function. The $i$th element of T, denoted T[$i$], has a value equal to the integer part of $2^{32} \times$ abs[(sin($i$)], where $i$ is in radians. Because abs[(sin($i$)] is a number between 0 and 1, each element of T is an integer that can be represented in 32 bits. The table provides a "randomized" set of 32-bit patterns, which should eliminate any regularities in the input data.

Overall, for block $Y_q$, the algorithm takes $Y_q$ and an intermediate digest value $MD_q$ as inputs. $MD_q$ is placed into buffer ABCD. The output of the fourth round is added to $MD_q$ to produce $MD_{q+1}$. The addition is done independently for each of the four words in the buffer with each of the corresponding words in $MD_q$, using addition modulo $2^{32}$.

**TABLE 18.1** Truth table of logical functions for MD5.

| X | Y | Z | F | G | H | I |
|---|---|---|---|---|---|---|
| 0 | 0 | 0 | 0 | 0 | 0 | 1 |
| 0 | 0 | 1 | 1 | 0 | 1 | 0 |
| 0 | 1 | 0 | 0 | 1 | 1 | 0 |
| 0 | 1 | 1 | 1 | 0 | 0 | 1 |
| 1 | 0 | 0 | 0 | 0 | 1 | 1 |
| 1 | 0 | 1 | 0 | 1 | 0 | 1 |
| 1 | 1 | 0 | 1 | 1 | 0 | 0 |
| 1 | 1 | 1 | 1 | 1 | 1 | 0 |

• **Step 5: Output**

After all $L$ 512-bit blocks have been processed, the output from the $L$th stage is the 128-bit message digest.

The MD5 algorithm has the property that every bit of the hash code is a function of every bit in the input. The complex repetition of the basic functions (F, G, H, I) produces results that are well mixed; that is, it is unlikely that two messages chosen at random, even if they exhibit similar regularities, will have the same hash code. Rivest conjectures in the RFC that MD5 is as strong as possible for a 128-bit hash code; namely, the difficulty of coming up with two messages having the same message digest is on the order of $2^{64}$ operations, whereas the difficulty of finding a message with a given digest is on the order of $2^{128}$ operations. As of this writing, no analysis has been done to disprove these conjectures.

## 18.4 PUBLIC-KEY ENCRYPTION AND DIGITAL SIGNATURES

Of equal importance to conventional encryption is public-key encryption, which finds use in message authentication and key distribution. This section looks first at the basic concept of public-key encryption, followed by a discussion of the most widely used public-key algorithm: RSA. We then look at the problem of key distribution.

### Public-Key Encryption

Public-key encryption, first publicly proposed by Diffie and Hellman in 1976 [DIFF76], is the first truly revolutionary advance in encryption in literally thousands of years. For one thing, public-key algorithms are based on mathematical functions rather than on substitution and permutation. But more importantly, public-key cryptography is asymmetric, involving the use of two separate keys, in contrast to the conventional symmetric encryption, which uses only one key. The use of two keys has profound consequences in the areas of confidentiality, key distribution, and authentication.

Before proceeding, we should mention several common misconceptions concerning public-key encryption. One such misconception is that public-key encryption is more secure from cryptanalysis than conventional encryption. In fact, the security of any encryption scheme depends on the length of the key and the computational work involved in breaking a cipher. There is nothing in principle about either conventional or public-key encryption that makes one superior to another from the point of view of resisting cryptanalysis. A second misconception is that public-key encryption is a general-purpose technique that has made conventional encryption obsolete. On the contrary, because of the computational overhead of current public-key encryption schemes, there seems no foreseeable likelihood that conventional encryption will be abandoned. Finally, there is a feeling that key distribution is trivial when using public-key encryption, compared to the rather cumbersome handshaking involved with key distribution centers for conventional encryption. In fact, some form of protocol is needed, often involving a central agent, and the procedures involved are no simpler nor any more efficient than those required for conventional encryption.

A public-key cryptographic algorithm relies on one key for encryption and a different but related key for decryption. Furthermore, these algorithms have the following important characteristic:

- It is computationally infeasible to determine the decryption key given only knowledge of the cryptographic algorithm and the encryption key.

In addition, some algorithms, such as RSA, also exhibit the following characteristic:

- Either of the two related keys can be used for encryption, with the other used for decryption.

The essential steps are the following:

1. Each end system in a network generates a pair of keys to be used for encryption and decryption of messages that it will receive.
2. Each system publishes its encryption key by placing it in a public register or file. This is the public key. The companion key is kept private.
3. If A wishes to send a message to B, it encrypts the message using B's public key.
4. When *B* receives the message, it decrypts it using B's private key. No other recipient can decrypt the message because only B knows B's private key.

With this approach, all participants have access to public keys, and private keys are generated locally by each participant and therefore need never be distributed. As long as a system controls its private key, its incoming communication is secure. At any time, a system can change its private key and publish the companion public key to replace its old public key.

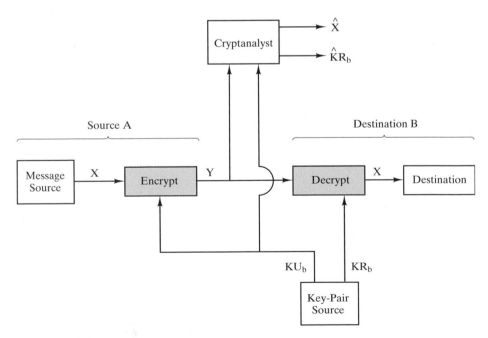

**FIGURE 18.16**  Public-key cryptosystem: secrecy.

Figure 18.16 illustrates the process (compare Figure 18.3). There is some source A for a message, which produces a message in plaintext, $X = [X_1, X_2, \ldots, X_M]$. The $M$ elements of X are letters in some finite alphabet. The message is intended for destination B, which generates a related pair of keys: a public key $KU_b$, and a private key, $KR_b$. $KR_b$ is secret, known only to B, whereas $KU_b$ is publicly available, and therefore accessible by A.

With the message X and the encryption key $KU_b$ as input, A forms the ciphertext $Y = [Y_1, Y_2, \ldots, Y_N]$:

$$Y = E_{KUb}(X)$$

The intended receiver, in possession of the matching private key, is able to invert the transformation:

$$X = D_{KRb}(Y)$$

An opponent, observing Y and having access to $KU_b$, but not having access to $KR_b$ or X, must attempt to recover X and/or $KR_b$. It is assumed that the opponent does have knowledge of the encryption (E) and decryption (D) algorithms.

We mentioned earlier that either of the two related keys can be used for encryption, with the other being used for decryption. This enables a rather different cryptographic scheme to be implemented. Whereas the scheme illustrated in Figure 18.16 provides privacy, Figure 18.17 shows the use of public-key encryption to provide authentication:

$$Y = E_{KRa}(X)$$
$$X = D_{KUa}(Y)$$

In this case, A prepares a message to B and encrypts it using A's private key before transmitting it. B can decrypt the message using A's public key. Because the message was encrypted using A's private key, only A could have prepared the message. Therefore, the entire encrypted message serves as a **digital signature**. In addition, it is impossible to alter the message without access to A's private key, so the message is authenticated both in terms of source and in terms of data integrity.

In the preceding scheme, the entire message is encrypted, and, although it validates both author and contents, the encryption requires a great deal of storage; each document must be kept in plaintext to be used for practical purposes, and a copy also must be stored in ciphertext so that the origin and contents can be verified in case of a dispute. A more efficient way of achieving the same results is to encrypt a small block of bits that is a function of the document. Such a block, called an authenticator, must have the property that it is infeasible to change the document without changing the authenticator. If the authenticator is encrypted with the sender's private key, it serves as a signature that verifies origin, content, and sequencing. A secure hash code can serve this function.

It is important to emphasize that the encryption process just described does not provide confidentiality. That is, the message being sent is safe from alteration but not safe from eavesdropping. This is obvious in the case of a signature based on a portion of the message, as the rest of the message is transmitted in the clear. Even

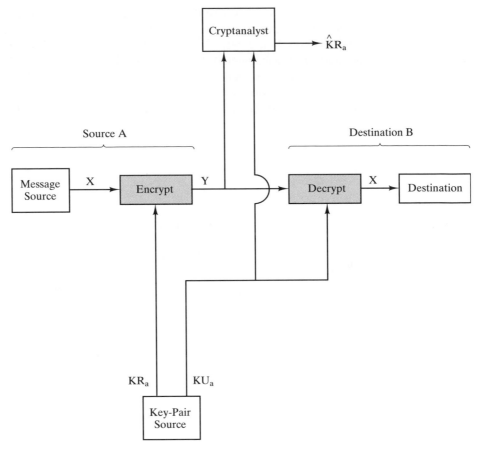

**FIGURE 18.17** Public-key cryptosystem: authentication.

in the case of complete encryption, there is no protection of confidentiality because any observer can decrypt the message by using the sender's public key.

## The RSA Public-Key Encryption Algorithm

One of the first public-key schemes was developed in 1977 by Ron Rivest, Adi Shamir, and Len Adleman at MIT, and first published in 1978 [RIVE78]. The RSA scheme has since reigned supreme as the only widely accepted and implemented approach to public-key encryption. RSA is a block cipher in which the plaintext and ciphertext are integers between 0 and $n-1$ for some $n$.

Encryption and decryption are of the following form, for some plaintext block M and ciphertext block C:

$$C = M^e \bmod n$$
$$M = C^d \bmod n = (M^e)^d \bmod n = M^{ed} \bmod n$$

Both sender and receiver must know the value of $n$. The sender knows the value of $e$, and only the receiver knows the value of $d$. Thus, this is a public-key encryption algorithm with a public key of KU = $\{e, n\}$ and a private key of KR = $\{d, n\}$. For this algorithm to be satisfactory for public-key encryption, the following requirements must be met:

1. Is it possible to find values of $e$, $d$, and $n$ such that $M^{ed} = M$ mod $n$ for all $M < n$?
2. Is it relatively easy to calculate $M^e$ and $C^d$ for all values of M $< n$?
3. Is it infeasible to determine $d$ given $e$ and $n$?

The answer to the first two questions is yes. The answer to the third question is yes, for large values of $e$ and $n$.

Figure 18.18 summarizes the RSA algorithm. Begin by selecting two prime numbers, $p$ and $q$, and calculating their product $n$, which is the modulus for encryption and decryption. Next, we need the quantity $\phi(n)$, which is referred to as the Euler totient of $n$, which is the number of positive integers less than $n$ and relatively prime to $n$. Then select an integer $d$ that is relatively prime to $\phi(n)$, (i.e., the greatest common divisor of $d$ and $\phi(n)$ is 1). Finally, calculate $e$ as the multiplicative inverse of $d$, modulo $\phi(n)$. It can be shown that $d$ and $e$ have the desired properties.

The private key consists of $\{d, n\}$, and the public key consists of $\{e, n\}$. Suppose that user A has published its public key and that user B wishes to send the message M to A. Then, B calculates C = $M^e$ (mod $n$) and transmits C. On receipt of this ciphertext, user A decrypts by calculating M = $C^d$ (mod $n$).

---

**Key Generation**

| | |
|---|---|
| Select $p, q$ | $p$ and $q$ both prime |
| Calculate n $= p \times q$ | |
| Select integer $d$ | $gcd(\phi(n), d) = 1; 1 < d < \phi(n)$ |
| Calculate $e$ | $e = d^{-1}$ mod $\phi(n)$ |
| Public key | KU = $\{e, n\}$ |
| Private key | KR = $\{d, n\}$ |

---

**Encryption**

Plaintext: M $< n$
Ciphertext: C = $M^e$ (mod $n$)

---

**Decryption**

Ciphertext: C
Plaintext: M = $C^d$ (mod $n$)

---

FIGURE 18.18  The RSA algorithm.

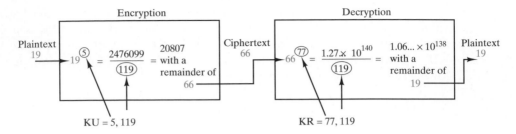

**FIGURE 18.19** Example of RSA algorithm.

An example is shown in Figure 18.19. For this example, the keys were generated as follows:

1. Select two prime numbers, $p = 7$ and $q = 17$.
2. Calculate $n = pq = 7 \times 17 = 119$.
3. Calculate $\phi(n) = (p-1)(q-1) = 96$.
4. Select $e$ such that $e$ is relatively prime to $\phi(n) = 96$ and less than $\phi(n)$; in this case, $e = 5$.
5. Determine $d$ such that $de = 1 \bmod 96$ and $d < 96$. The correct value is $d = 77$, because $77 \times 5 = 385 = 4 \times 96 + 1$.

The resulting keys are public key $KU = \{5, 119\}$ and private key $KR = \{77, 119\}$. The example shows the use of these keys for a plaintext input of $M = 19$. For encryption, 19 is raised to the 5th power, yielding 2476099. Upon division by 119, the remainder is determined to be 66. Hence, $19^5 \equiv 66 \bmod 119$, and the ciphertext is 66. For decryption, it is determined that $66^{77} \equiv 19 \bmod 119$.

There are two possible approaches to defeating the RSA algorithm. The first is the brute force approach: Try all possible private keys. Thus, the larger the number of bits in $e$ and $d$, the more secure the algorithm. However, because the calculations involved, both in key generation and in encryption/decryption, are complex, the larger the size of the key, the slower the system will run.

Most discussions of the cryptanalysis of RSA have focused on the task of factoring $n$ into its two prime factors. Until recently, this was felt to be infeasible for numbers in the range of 100 decimal digits or so, which is about 300 or more bits. To demonstrate the strength of RSA, its three developers issued a challenge to decrypt a message that was encrypted using a 129-decimal-digit number as their public modulus. The authors predicted that it would take 40 quadrillion years with current technology to crack the code. Recently the code was cracked by a worldwide team cooperating over the Internet and using over 1600 computers after only eight months of work [LEUT94]. This result does not invalidate the use of RSA; it simply means that larger key sizes must be used. Currently, a 1024-bit key size (about 300 decimal digits) is considered strong enough for virtually all applications.

### Key Management

With conventional encryption, a fundamental requirement for two parties to communicate securely is that they share a secret key. Suppose Bob wants to create a messaging application that will enable him to exchange e-mail securely with anyone who has access either to the Internet or to some other network that the two of them share (e.g., an on-line service such as Compuserve). Suppose Bob wants to do this using only conventional encryption. With conventional encryption, Bob and his correspondent, say, Alice, must come up with a way to share a unique secret key that no one else knows. How are they going to do that? If Alice is in the next room from Bob, Bob could generate a key and write it down on a piece of paper or store it on a diskette and hand it to Alice. But if Alice is on the other side of the continent, or maybe the world, what can Bob do? Well, he could encrypt this key using conventional encryption and e-mail it to Alice, but this means that Bob and Alice must share a secret key in order to encrypt this new secret key. Furthermore, Bob and everyone else who use this new e-mail package face the same problem with every potential correspondent: Each pair of correspondents must share a unique secret key.

How to distribute secret keys securely is the most difficult problem for conventional encryption. This problem is wiped away with public-key encryption by the simple fact that the private key is never distributed. If Bob wants to correspond with Alice and other people, he generates a single pair of keys, one private and one public. He keeps the private key secure and broadcasts the public key to all and sundry; if Alice does the same, then Bob has Alice's public key, Alice has Bob's public key, and they can now communicate securely. When Bob wishes to communicate with Alice, Bob can do the following:

1. Prepare a message.
2. Encrypt that message using conventional encryption with a one-time conventional session key.
3. Encrypt the session key using public-key encryption with Alice's public key.
4. Attach the encrypted session key to the message and send it to Alice.

Only Alice is capable of decrypting the session key and therefore recovering the original message.

It is only fair to point out, however, that we have replaced one problem with another. Bob's private key is secure as he need never reveal it; however, Alice must be sure that the public key with Bob's name written all over it is in fact Bob's public key. Someone else could have broadcast a public key and said it was Bob's. The common way to overcome this problem is ingenious: Use public-key encryption to authenticate the public key. This encryption assumes the existence of some trusted signing authority or individual, and works as follows:

1. A public key is generated by Bob and submitted to Agency X for certification.
2. X determines by some procedure, such as a face-to-face meeting, that this is, authentically, Bob's public key.

3. X appends a timestamp to the public key, generates the hash code of the result, and encrypts that result with its private key forming the signature.
4. The signature is attached to the public key.

Anyone equipped with a copy of X's public key can now verify that Bob's public key is authentic.

## 18.5  IPv4 AND IPv6 SECURITY

In August 1995, the IETF published five security-related Proposed Standards that define a security capability at the internet level. The documents are

- RFC 1825: An overview of a security architecture
- RFC 1826: Description of a packet authentication extension to IP
- RFC 1828: A specific authentication mechanism
- RFC 1827: Description of a packet encryption extension to IP
- RFC 1829: A specific encryption mechanism

Support for these features is mandatory for IPv6 and optional for IPv4. In both cases, the security features are implemented as extension headers that follow the main IP header. The extension header for authentication is known as the Authentication header; the one designated for privacy is known as the Encapsulating Security Payload (ESP) header.

### Security Associations

A key concept that appears in both the authentication and privacy mechanisms for IP is the security association. An association is a one-way relationship between a sender and a receiver. If a peer relationship is needed, for two-way secure exchange, then two security associations are required.

A security association is uniquely identified by an internet address and a security parameter index (SPI). Hence, in any IP packet,[4] the security association is uniquely identified by the Destination Address in the IPv4 or IPv6 header and the SPI in the enclosed extension header (Authentication header or Encapsulating Security Payload header).

A security association is normally defined by the following parameters:

- Authentication algorithm and algorithm mode being used with the IP Authentication Header (required for AH implementations).
- Key(s) used with the authentication algorithm in use with the Authentication Header (required for AH implementations).

---

[4] In the remainder of this section, the term IP packet refers to either an IPv4 datagram or an IPv6 packet.

- Encryption algorithm, algorithm mode, and transform being used with the IP Encapsulating Security Payload (required for ESP implementations).
- Key(s) used with the encryption algorithm in use with the Encapsulating Security Payload (required for ESP implementations).
- Presence/absence and size of a cryptographic synchronization or initialization vector field for the encryption algorithm (required for ESP implementations).
- Authentication algorithm and mode used with the ESP transform, if any is in use (recommended for ESP implementations).
- Authentication key(s) used with the authentication algorithm that is part of the ESP transform, if any (recommended for ESP implementations).
- Lifetime of the key or time when key change should occur (recommended for all implementations).
- Lifetime of this Security Association (recommended for all implementations).
- Source Address(es) of the Security Association, might be a wildcard address if more than one sending system shares the same Security Association with the destination (recommended for all implementations).
- Sensitivity level (for example, Secret or Unclassified) of the protected data (required for all systems claiming to provide multi-level security, recommended for all other systems).

The key management mechanism that is used to distribute keys is coupled to the authentication and privacy mechanisms only by way of the Security Parameters Index. Hence, authentication and privacy have been specified independently of any specific key-management mechanism.

## Authentication

The Authentication header provides support for data integrity and authentication of IP packets. The Authentication Header consists of the following fields (Figure 18.20):

- **Next Header (8 bits).** Identifies the type of header immediately following this header.

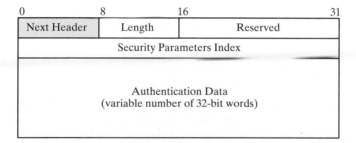

**FIGURE 18.20**   Authentication header.

- **Length (8 bits).** Length of Authentication Data field in 32-bit words.
- **Reserved (16 bits).** For future use.
- **Security Parameters Index (32 bits).** Identifies a security association.
- **Authentication Data (variable).** An integral number of 32-bit words.

The authentication data field contents will depend on the authentication algorithm specified. In any case, the authentication data is calculated over the entire IP packet, excluding any fields that may change in transit. Such fields are set to zero for purposes of calculation at both source and destination. The authentication calculation is performed prior to fragmentation at the source and after reassembly at the destination. Hence, fragmentation-related fields can be included in the calculation.

For IPv4, the Time-to-Live and Header Checksum fields are subject to change and are therefore set to zero for the authentication calculation. IPv4 options must be handled in accordance with the rule that any option whose value might change during transit must not be included in the calculation.

For IPv6, the Hop Limit field is the only field in the base IPv6 header subject to change; it is therefore set to zero for the calculation. For the Hop-by-Hop Options and Destination Options headers, the Option Type field for each option contains a bit that indicates whether the Option Data field for this option may change during transit; if so, this option is excluded from the authentication calculation.

### Authentication Using Keyed MD5

RFC 1828 specifies the use of MD5 for authentication. The MD5 algorithm is performed over the IP packet plus a secret key by the source and then inserted into the IP packet. At the destination, the same calculation is performed on the IP packet plus the secret key and compared to the received value. This procedure provides both authentication and data integrity.

Specifically, the MD5 calculation is performed over the following sequence:

$$\text{key, keyfill, IP packet, key, MD5fill}$$

where

$$
\begin{aligned}
\text{key} &= \text{the secret key for this security association} \\
\text{keyfill} &= \text{padding so that key + keyfill is an integer multiple of 512 bits} \\
\text{IP packet} &= \text{with the appropriate fields set to zero} \\
\text{MD5fill} &= \text{padding supplied by MD5 so that the entire block is an integer} \\
&\quad\;\; \text{multiple of 512 bits}
\end{aligned}
$$

Figure 18.21 shows two ways in which the IP authentication service can be used. In one case, authentication is provided directly between a server and client workstations; the workstation can be either on the same network as the server or on an external network. So long as the workstation and the server share a protected

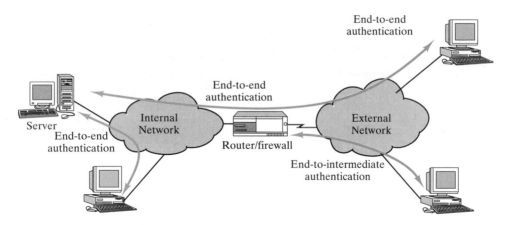

**FIGURE 18.21**    End-to-end versus end-to-intermediate authentication [DOTY95].

secret key, the authentication process is secure. In the other case, a remote work-station authenticates itself to the corporate firewall, either for access to the entire internal network or because the requested server does not support the authentication feature.

### Encapsulating Security Payload

The use of the Encapsulating Security Payload provides support for privacy and data integrity for IP packets. Depending on the user's requirements, this mechanism can be used to encrypt either a transport-layer segment (e.g., TCP, UDP, ICMP), known as transport-mode ESP, or an entire IP packet, known as tunnel-mode ESP.

The ESP header begins with a 32-bit Security Parameters Index (SPI), which identifies a security association. The remainder of the header, if any, may contain parameters dependent on the encryption algorithm being used. In general, the first part of the header, including the SPI and possibly some parameters, is transmitted in unencrypted (plaintext) form, while the remainder of the header, if any, is transmitted in encrypted (ciphertext) form.

### Transport-Mode ESP

Transport-mode ESP is used to encrypt the data carried by IP. Typically, these data are a transport-layer segment, such as a TCP or UDP segment, which in turn contains application-level data. For this mode, the ESP header is inserted into the IP packet immediately prior to the transport-layer header (e.g., TCP, UDP, ICMP). In the case of IPv6, if a Destination Options header is present, the ESP header is inserted immediately prior to that header (see Figure 16.16).

Transport-mode operation may be summarized as follows:

1. At the source, the block of data consisting of a trailing portion of the ESP header, plus the entire transport-layer segment, is encrypted, and the plaintext

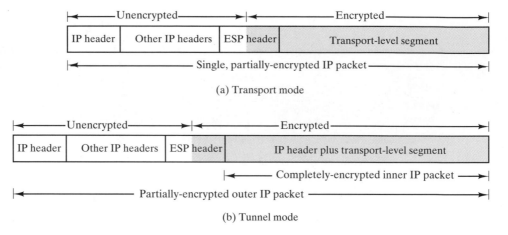

FIGURE 18.22 Secure IPv4 datagram or IPv6 packet.

of this block is replaced with its ciphertext to form the IP packet for transmission (Figure 18.22a).

2. This IP packet is then routed to the destination. Each intermediate router needs to examine and process the IP header plus any plaintext IP extension headers, but does not need to examine the ciphertext.

3. The destination node examines and processes the IP header plus any plaintext IP extension headers. Then, on the basis of the SPI in the ESP header, the destination node decrypts the remainder of the packet to recover the plaintext transport-layer segment.

Transport-mode operation provides privacy for any application that uses it, thus avoiding the need to implement privacy in every individual application. This mode of operation is also reasonably efficient, adding little to the total length of the IP packet. One drawback to this mode is that it is possible to do traffic analysis on the transmitted packets. Figure 18.23a illustrates the protection provided by transport-mode operation.

### Tunnel-Mode ESP

Tunnel-mode ESP is used to encrypt an entire IP packet. For this mode, the ESP is prefixed to the packet, and then the packet plus a trailing portion of the ESP header is encrypted. This method can be used to counter traffic analysis.

Because the IP header contains the destination address and possibly source routing directives and hop-by-hop option information, it is not possible to simply transmit the encrypted IP packet prefixed by the ESP header. Intermediate routes would be unable to process such a packet. Therefore, it is necessary to encapsulate the entire block (ESP header plus encrypted IP packet) with a new IP header that will contain sufficient information for routing but not for traffic analysis.

Whereas the transport-mode is suitable for protecting connections between hosts that support the ESP feature, the tunnel-mode is useful in a configuration that

(a) Transport-level security

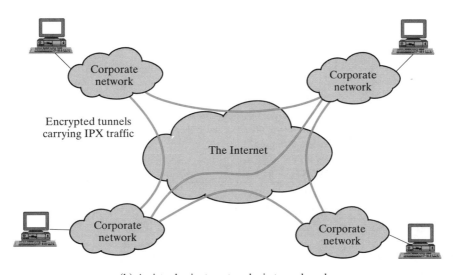

(b) A virtual private network via tunnel mode

**FIGURE 18.23**  Applications of encapsulating security payload [DOTY95].

includes a firewall or other sort of security gateway that protects a trusted network from external networks. In this latter case, encryption occurs only between an external host and the security gateway, or between two security gateways; this relieves hosts on the internal network of the processing burden of encryption and also simplifies the key distribution task by reducing the number of needed keys; further, it thwarts traffic analysis based on ultimate destination.

Consider a case in which an external host wishes to communicate with a host on an internal network protected by a firewall, and in which ESP is implemented in the external host and the firewalls. The following steps occur for transfer of a transport-layer segment from the external host to the internal host:

1.  The source prepares an inner IP packet with a destination address of the target internal host. This packet is prefixed by an ESP header; then the packet

and a portion of the ESP header are encrypted. The resulting block is encapsulated with a new IP header (base header plus optional extensions such as routing and hop-by-hop options) whose destination address is the firewall; this forms the outer IP packet (Figure 18.22b).

2. The outer packet is routed to the destination firewall. Each intermediate router needs to examine and process the outer IP header plus any outer IP extension headers, but does not need to examine the ciphertext.

3. The destination firewall examines and processes the outer IP header plus any outer IP extension headers. Then, on the basis of the SPI in the ESP header, the destination node decrypts the remainder of the packet to recover the plaintext inner IP packet. This packet is then transmitted in the internal network.

4. The inner packet is routed through zero or more routers in the internal network to the destination host.

Figure 18.23b shows how tunnel-mode operation can be used to set up a virtual private network. In this example, an organization has four private networks interconnected across the Internet. Hosts on the internal networks use the Internet for transport of data but don't interact with other Internet-based hosts. By terminating the tunnels at the security gateway to each internal network, the configuration allows the hosts to avoid implementing the security capability.

### The ESP DES-CBC Transform

All implementations that claim conformance with the ESP specification must implement the DES-CBC (Data Encryption Standard-Cipher Block Chaining) method of encryption.

Figure 18.24 shows the format of the ESP header plus payload using DES-CBC, and indicates which portions are encrypted. The fields are

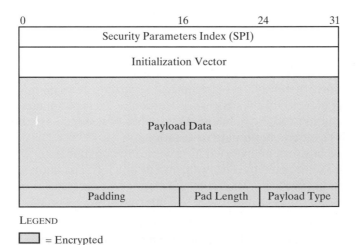

LEGEND

☐ = Encrypted

**FIGURE 18.24**  Encapsulating security payload format.

- **Security Parameters Index (32 bits).** Identifies a security association.
- **Initialization Vector (variable).** Input to the CBC algorithm, and a multiple of 32 bits.
- **Payload Data (variable).** Prior to encryption, this field contains the block of data to be encrypted, which may be a transport-layer segment (transport mode) or an IP packet (tunnel mode).
- **Padding.** Prior to encryption, filled with unspecified data to align Pad Length and Payload Type fields at a 64-bit boundary.
- **Pad Length (8 bits).** The size of the unencrypted padding field.
- **Payload Type (8 bits).** Indicates the protocol type of the Payload Data field (e.g., IP, TCP).

Note that the Initialization Vector is transmitted in plaintext. As was mentioned in our description of DES-CBC, this is not the most secure approach. However, for the purposes of this application, it should provide acceptable security.

### Authentication Plus Privacy

The two IP security mechanisms can be combined in order to transmit an IP packet that has both privacy and authentication. There are two approaches that can be used, based on the order in which the two services are applied.

**Encryption Before Authentication**

Figure 18.25a illustrates the case of encryption applied before authentication. In this case, the entire transmitted IP packet is authenticated, including both

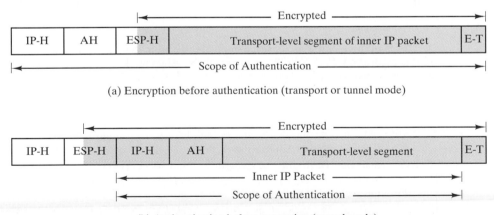

(a) Encryption before authentication (transport or tunnel mode)

(b) Authentication before encryption (tunnel mode)

LEGEND

IP-H    = IP base header plus extentions headers    E-T = Encapsulating Security Payload trailing fields
ESP-H = Encapsulating Security Payload header    AH = Authentication header

**FIGURE 18.25**   Combining privacy and authentication.

encrypted and unencrypted parts. In this approach, the user first applies ESP to the data to be protected, then prepends the authentication header and the plaintext IP header(s). There are actually two subcases:

- **Transport-Mode ESP**. Authentication applies to the entire IP packet delivered to the ultimate destination, but only the transport-layer segment is protected by the privacy mechanism (encrypted).
- **Tunnel-Mode ESP**. Authentication applies to the entire IP packet delivered to the outer IP destination address (e.g., a firewall), and authentication is performed at that destination. The entire inner IP packet is protected by the privacy mechanism, for delivery to the inner IP destination.

### Authentication Before Encryption

Figure 18.25b illustrates the case of authentication applied before encryption. This approach is only appropriate for tunnel-mode ESP. In this case, the authentication header is placed inside the inner IP packet. This inner packet is both authenticated and protected by the privacy mechanism.

As we have just seen, the functions of authentication and encryption can be applied in either order for tunnel-mode ESP. The use of authentication prior to encryption might be preferable for several reasons. First, because the AH is protected by ESP, it is impossible for anyone to intercept the message and alter the AH without detection. Secondly, it may be desirable to store the authentication information with the message at the destination for later reference. It is more convenient to perform this storage if the authentication information applies to the unencrypted message; otherwise, the message would have to be re-encrypted to verify the authentication information.

## 18.6 RECOMMENDED READING

The topics in this chapter are covered in greater detail in [STAL95]. For coverage of cryptographic algorithms, [SCHN96] is an essential reference work; it contains descriptions of virtually every cryptographic algorithm and protocol published in the last 15 years. Two very good collections of papers are [SIMM92], which provides a rigorous, mathematical treatment of cryptographic protocols and algorithms, and [ABRA95], which deals with the issues at more of a system level.

ABRA95   Abrams, M, Jajodia, S. and Podell, H. eds. *Information Security*. Los Alamitos, CA: IEEE Computer Society Press, 1995.

SCHN96   Schneier, B. *Applied Cryptography*. New York: Wiley, 1996.

SIMM92   Simmons, G., ed. *Contemporary Cryptology: The Science of Information Integrity*. Piscataway, NJ: IEEE Press, 1992.

STAL95   Stallings, W. *Network and Internetwork Security: Principles and Practice*. Upper Saddle River, NJ: Prentice-Hall, 1995.

 Recommended Web Site

- http://www.tansu.com.au/Info/security.html: Contains pointers to FAQs, documents, USENET groups, and other web sites related to security.

# 18.7  PROBLEMS

**18.1**  One of the simplest forms of encryption is a substitution cipher. A substitution cipher is an encryption technique in which the letters of plaintext are replaced by other letters or by numbers or symbols. In a famous story by Edgar Allen Poe, the following ciphertext was generated using a simple substitution algorithm:

53‡‡†305))6*;4826)4‡.)4‡);806*;48†8¶60))85;;]8*;:‡*8†83
(88)5*†;46(;88*96*?;8)*‡(;485);5*†2:*‡(;4956*2(5*—4)8¶8*
;4069285);)6†8)4‡‡;1(‡9;48081;8:8‡1;48†85;4)485†528806*81
(‡9;48;(88;4(‡?34;48)4‡;161;:188;‡?;

Decrypt this message. Hints:
a. As you know, the most frequently occurring letter in English is e. Therefore, the first or second (or perhaps third?) most common character in the message is likely to stand for e. Also, e is often seen in pairs (e.g., meet, fleet, speed, seen, been, agree, etc.). Try to find a character in the ciphertext that decodes to e.
b. The most common word in English is "the." Use this fact to guess the characters that stand for t and h.
c. Decipher the rest of the message by deducing additional words.

**Warning**: the resulting message is in English but may not make much sense on a first reading.

**18.2**  One way to solve the key distribution problem is to use a line from a book that both the sender and the receiver possess to generate the key for a substitution cipher. Typically, at least in spy novels, the first sentence of a book serves as the key. The particular scheme discussed in this problem is from one of the best suspense novels involving secret codes, *Talking to Strange Men*, by Ruth Rendell. Work this problem without consulting that book!

Consider the following message:

SIDKHKDM AF HCRKIABIE SHIMC KD LFEAILA

This ciphertext was produced using the first sentence of *The Other Side of Silence* (a book about the spy Kim Philby):

The snow lay thick on the steps and the snowflakes driven by the wind looked black in the headlights of the cars.
a. What is the encryption algorithm?
b. How secure is it?
c. To make the key distribution problem simple, both parties can agree to use the first or last sentence of a book as the key. To change the key, they simply need to agree on a new book. The use of the first sentence would be preferable to the use of the last.

Why?

**18.3**  In one of his cases, Sherlock Holmes was confronted with the following message.

534 C2 13 127 36 31 4 17 21 41
DOUGLAS 109 293 5 37 BIRLSTONE
26 BIRLSTONE 9 127 171

Although Watson was puzzled, Holmes was able to immediately deduce the type of encryption algorithm. Can you?

**18.4**  Let $\pi$ be a permutation of the integers $1, 2, \ldots 2^n - 1$, such that $\pi(m)$ gives the permuted value of $m$, $0 \leq m \leq 2^n$. Put another way, $\pi$ maps the set of $n$-bit integers into itself and no two integers map into the same integer. DES is such a permutation for 64-bit integers. We say that $\pi$ has a fixed point at $m$ if $\pi(m) = m$. That is, if $\pi$ is an encryption mapping, then a fixed point corresponds to a message that encrypts to itself. We are interested in the probability that $\pi$ has no fixed points. Show the somewhat unexpected result that over 60% of mappings will have at least one fixed point.

18.5 Consider a block encryption algorithm that encrypts blocks of length $N = 2^n$. Say we have $t$ plaintext/ciphertext pairs $P_i$, $C_i = E_K[P_i]$, where we assume that the key K selects one of the $N!$ possible mappings. Imagine that we wish to find K by exhaustive search. We could generate key K' and test whether $C_i = E_{K'}(P_i)$ for $1 \leq i \leq t$. If K' encrypts each $P_i$ to its proper $C_i$, then we have evidence that K = K'. However, it may be the case that the mappings $E_K(\cdot)$ and $E_{K'(\cdot)}$ exactly agree on the $t$ plaintext/ciphertext pairs $P_i$, $C_i$ and agree on no other pairs.
   a. What is the probability that $E_K(\cdot)$ and $E_{K'}(\cdot)$ are, in fact, distinct mappings?
   b. What is the probability that $E_K(\cdot)$ and $E_{K'}(\cdot)$ agree on another $t'$ plaintext/ciphertext pair where $0 \leq t' \leq N–k$?

18.6 Suppose that someone suggests the following way to confirm that the two of you are both in possession of the same secret key. You create a random bit string that is the length of the key, XOR it with the key, and send the result over the channel. Your partner XORs the incoming block with the key (which should be the same as your key) and sends it back. You check, and if what you receive is your original random string, you have verified that your partner has the same secret, yet neither of you has ever transmitted the key. Is there a flaw in this scheme?

18.7 Consider the following scheme:
   a. Pick an odd number, $E$.
   b. Pick two prime numbers, $P$ and $Q$, where $(P–1)(Q–1) –1$ is evenly divisible by $E$.
   c. Multiply $P$ and $Q$ to get $N$.
   d. Calculate $D = \dfrac{(P-1)(Q-1)(E-1) + 1}{E}$

   Is this scheme equivalent to RSA? Show why or why not.

18.8 Perform encryption and decryption using the RSA algorithm, as in Figure 4.8, for the following:
   a. $p = 3$; $q = 11$, $d = 7$; $M = 5$
   b. $p = 5$; $q = 11$, $e = 3$; $M = 9$
   c. $p = 7$; $q = 11$, $e = 17$; $M = 8$
   d. $p = 11$; $q = 13$, $e = 11$; $M = 7$
   e. $p = 17$; $q = 31$, $e = 7$; $M = 2$. Hint: Decryption is not as hard as you think; use some finesse.

18.9 Construct a 32-bit checksum function as the concatenation of two 16-bit functions: XOR, and RXOR, defined in Figure 18.13 as "two simple hash functions."
   a. Will this checksum detect all errors caused by an odd number of error bits? Explain.
   b. Will this checksum detect all errors caused by an even number of error bits? If not, characterize the error patterns that will cause the checksum to fail.
   c. Comment on the effectiveness of this function for use as a hash function for authentication.

18.10 Consider using an encryption algorithm to construct a one-way hash function. Consider using RSA with a known key. Then, process a message consisting of a sequence of blocks as follows: Encrypt the first block, XOR the result with the second block and encrypt again, etc. Show that this scheme is not secure by solving the following problem. Consider a two-block message B1, B2, and its hash:

$$\text{RSAH(B1, B2)} = \text{RSA (RSA(B1)} \oplus \text{B2)}$$

Given an arbitrary block C1, choose C2 so that RSAH(C1, C2) = RSAH(B1, B2).

# CHAPTER 19

# DISTRIBUTED APPLICATIONS

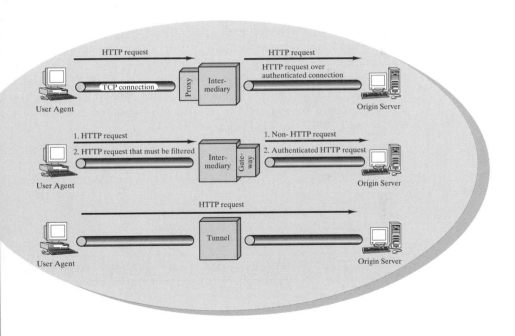

A ll of the protocols and functions described so far in Part Four are geared toward one objective: the support of distributed applications that involve the interaction of multiple independent systems. In the OSI model, such applications occupy the application layer and are directly supported by the presentation layer. In the TCP/IP protocol suite, such applications typically rely on TCP or UDP for support.

We begin this chapter with an introduction to Abstract Syntax Notation One (ASN.1), which has become an important universal language for defining representations of data structures and protocol formats, and which has gained wide use for defining application-level protocols.

Next, we examine a number of quite different applications that give the reader a feel for the range and diversity of applications supported by a communications architecture. The first, *network management*, is itself a support-type application, designed to assure the effective monitoring and control of a distributed system. The specific protocol that is examined is the Simple Network Management Protocol, version 2 (SNMPv2), which is designed to operate in both the TCP/IP and OSI environments. Next, electronic mail applications are considered, with the SMTP and MIME standards as examples; SMTP provides a basic email service, while MIME adds multimedia capability to SMTP. Finally, we look at HTTP, which is the support application on which the World Wide Web (WWW) operates; in discussing HTTP, we need to first look at the concept of Uniform Resource Locators and Universal Resource Identifiers. Figure 19.1 highlights the position of these protocols within the TCP/IP protocol suite.

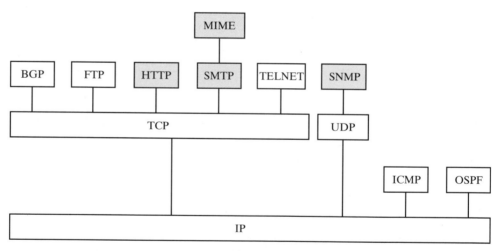

**FIGURE 19.1**   Application-level protocols discussed in this chapter.

## 19.1   ABSTRACT SYNTAX NOTATION ONE (ASN.1)

One of the most significant developments in computer communications in recent years is the development of ASN.1, which is now widely used in the development of both OSI-related standards and TCP/IP-related standards. It is used to define the format of protocol data units (PDUs), the representation of distributed information, and operations performed on transmitted data. A basic understanding of ASN.1 is essential for those who wish to study and work in this field.

Before examining the details of ASN.1, we need to introduce the concept of an abstract syntax. Then, we will look at the fundamentals of ASN.1. Next, a special and important facility, the ASN.1 macro facility, is examined.

### Abstract Syntax

Table 19.1 defines some key terms that are relevant to a discussion of ASN.1, and Figure 19.2 illustrates the underlying concepts.

For purposes of this discussion, a communications architecture in an end system can be considered to have two major components. The data transfer component is concerned with the mechanisms for the transfer of data between end systems. In the case of the TCP/IP protocol suite, this component would consist of TCP or UDP on down. In the case of the OSI architecture, this component would consist of the session layer on down. The application component is the user of the data transfer component and is concerned with the end user's application. In the case of the TCP/IP protocol suite, this component would consist of an application, such as SNMP, FTP, SMTP, or TELNET. In the case of OSI, this component actually consists of the application layer, which is composed of a number of application service elements, and the presentation layer.

As we cross the boundary from the application to the data transfer component, there is a significant change in the way that data are viewed. For the data transfer component, the data received from an application are specified as the binary value of a sequence of octets. This binary value can be directly assembled into service data units (SDUs) for passing between layers, and into protocol data units (PDUs) for passing between protocol entities within a layer. The application component, however, is concerned with a user's view of data. In general, that view is one of a structured set of information, such as text in a document, a personnel file, an integrated data base, or a visual display of image information. The user is primarily concerned with the semantics of data. The application component must provide a representation of this data that can be converted to binary values; that is, it must be concerned with the syntax of the data.

**TABLE 19.1**   Terms relevant to ASN.1.

| | |
|---|---|
| Abstract Syntax | Describes the generic structure of data independent of any encoding technique used to represent the data. The syntax allows data types to be defined and values of those types to be specified. |
| Data Type | A named set of values. A type may be simple, which is defined by specifying the set of its values, or structured, which is defined in terms of other types. |
| Encoding | The complete sequence of octets used to represent a data value. |
| Encoding Rules | A specification of the mapping from one syntax to another. Specifically, encoding rules determine algorithmically, for any set of data values defined in an abstract syntax, the representation of those values in a transfer syntax. |
| Transfer Syntax | The way in which data are actually represented in terms of bit patterns while in transit between presentation entities. |

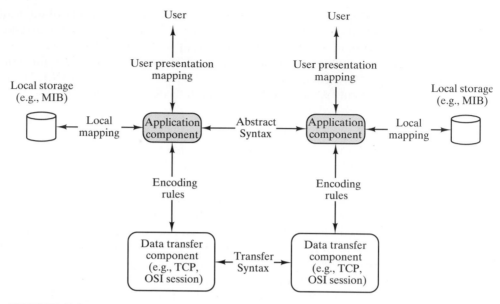

**FIGURE 19.2** The use of abstract and transfer syntaxes.

The approach illustrated in Figure 19.2 to support application data is as follows. For the application component, information is represented in an abstract syntax that deals with data types and data values. The abstract syntax formally specifies data independently from any specific representation. Thus, an abstract syntax has many similarities to the data-type definition aspects of conventional programming languages such as Pascal, C, and Ada, and to grammars such as Backus-Naur Form (BNF). Application protocols describe their PDUs in terms of an abstract syntax.

This abstract syntax is used for the exchange of information between application components in different systems. The exchange consists of application-level PDUs, which contain protocol control information and user data. Within a system, the information represented using an abstract syntax must be mapped into some form for presentation to the human user. Similarly, this abstract syntax must be mapped into some local format for storage. For example, such a mapping is used in the case of network management information. In addition, it is becoming common to use an abstract syntax to define the data elements in local storage. Thus, the abstract syntax notation is employed by a user to define network management information; the application must then convert this definition to a form suitable for local storage.

The component must also translate between the abstract syntax of the application and a transfer syntax that describes the data values in a binary form, suitable for interaction with the data transfer component. For example, an abstract syntax may include a data type of character; the transfer syntax could specify ASCII or EBCDIC encoding.

The transfer syntax thus defines the representation of the data to be exchanged between data-transfer components. The translation from abstract syntax to the transfer syntax is accomplished by means of encoding rules that specify the representation of each data value of each data type.

This approach for the exchange of application data solves the two problems that relate to data representation in a distributed, heterogeneous environment:

- There is a common representation for the exchange of data between differing systems.
- Internal to a system, an application uses some particular representation of data. The abstract/transfer syntax scheme automatically resolves differences in representation between cooperating application entities.

The fundamental requirement for selection of a transfer syntax is that it support the corresponding abstract syntax. In addition, the transfer syntax may have other attributes that are not related to the abstract syntaxes that it can support. For example, an abstract syntax could be supported by any one of four transfer syntaxes, which are the same in all respects except that one provides data compression, one provides encryption, one provides both, and one provides neither. The choice of which transfer syntax to use would depend on cost and security considerations.

## ASN.1 Concepts

The basic building block of an ASN.1 specification is the module. We begin this section by looking at the top-level structure of the module. Then, we introduce some lexical conventions used in ASN.1 definitions. Next, the data types defined in ASN.1 are described. Finally, examples of the use of ASN.1 are given.

### Module Definition

ASN.1 is a language that can be used to define data structures. A structure definition is in the form of a named module. The name of the module can then be used to reference the structure. For example, the module name can be used as an abstract syntax name; an application can pass this name to the presentation service to specify the abstract syntax of the application PDUs that the application wishes to exchange with a peer application entity.

Modules have the basic form,

```
<modulereference> DEFINITIONS ::=
    BEGIN
        EXPORTS
        IMPORTS
        AssignmentList
    End
```

The modulereference is a module name followed optionally by an object identifier to identify the module. The EXPORTS construct indicates which definitions in this module may be imported by other modules. The IMPORTS construct indicates which type and value definitions from other modules are to be imported into this module. Neither the IMPORTS or EXPORTS constructs may be included unless the object identifier for the module is included. Finally, the assignment list consists of type assignments, value assignments, and macro definitions. Macro definitions are discussed later in this section. Type and value assignments have the form,

```
<name>::=<description>
```

The easiest way to describe the syntax is by example. First, we need to specify some lexical conventions.

## Lexical Conventions

ASN.1 structures, types, and values are expressed in a notation similar to that of a programming language. The following lexical conventions are followed:

1. Layout is not significant; multiple spaces and blank lines can be considered as a single space.
2. Comments are delimited by pairs of hyphens (--) at the beginning and end of the comment, or by a pair of hyphens at the beginning of the comment and the end of the line as the end of the comment.
3. Identifiers (names of values and fields), type references (names of types), and module names consist of upper- and lowercase letters, digits, and hyphens.
4. An identifier begins with a lowercase letter.
5. A type reference or a module name begins with an uppercase letter.
6. A built-in type consists of all capital letters and is a commonly used type for which a standard notation is provided.

## Abstract Data Types

ASN.1 is a notation for abstract data types and their values. A type can be viewed as a collection of values. The number of values that a type may take on may be infinite. For example, the type INTEGER has an infinite number of values.

We can classify types into four categories:

- **Simple.** These are atomic types, with no components.
- **Structured.** A structured type has components.
- **Tagged.** These are types derived from other types.
- **Other.** This category includes the CHOICE and ANY types, defined later in this section.

Every ASN.1 data type, with the exception of CHOICE and ANY, has an associated tag. The tag consists of a class name and a nonnegative integer tag number. There are four classes of data types, or four classes of tag:

- **Universal.** Generally useful, application-independent types and construction mechanisms; these are defined in the standard and are listed in Table 19.2.
- **Application-wide.** Relevant to a particular application; these are defined in other standards.

TABLE 19.2   Universal class tag assignments.

| Tag | Type Name | Set of Values |
|---|---|---|
| | | **Basic Types** |
| UNIVERSAL 1 | BOOLEAN | TRUE or FALSE |
| UNIVERSAL 2 | INTEGER | The positive and negative whole numbers, including zero |
| UNIVERSAL 3 | BIT STRING | A sequence of zero or more bits |
| UNIVERSAL 4 | OCTET STRING | A sequence of zero or more octets |
| UNIVERSAL 9 | REAL | Real numbers |
| UNIVERSAL 10 | ENUMERATED | An explicit list of integer values that an instance of a data type may take |
| | | **Object Types** |
| UNIVERSAL 6 | OBJECT IDENTIFIER | The set of values associated with information objects |
| UNIVERSAL 7 | Object descriptor | Each value is human-readable text providing a brief description of an information object. |
| | | **Object Types** |
| UNIVERSAL 18 | NumericString | Digits 0 through 9, space |
| UNIVERSAL 19 | PrintableString | Printable characters |
| UNIVERSAL 20 | TeletexString | Character set defined by CCITT Recommendation T.61 |
| UNIVERSAL 21 | VideotexString | Set of alphabet and graphical characters defined by CCITT Recommendations T.100 and T.101. |
| UNIVERSAL 22 | IA5String | International alphabet five (equivalent to ASCII) |
| UNIVERSAL 25 | GraphicsString | Character set defined by ISO 8824 |
| UNIVERSAL 26 | VisibleString | Character set defined by ISO 646 (equivalent to ASCII) |
| UNIVERSAL 27 | GeneralString | General character string |
| | | **Miscellaneous Types** |
| UNIVERSAL 5 | NULL | The single value NULL. Commonly used where several alternatives are possible but none of them apply. |
| UNIVERSAL 8 | EXTERNAL | A type defined in some external document. It need not be one of the valid ASN.1 types. |
| UNIVERSAL 23 | UTCTime | Consists of the date, specified with a two-digit year, a two-digit month and a two-digit day, followed by the time, specified in hours, minutes, and optionally seconds, followed by an optional specification of the local time differential from universal time. |
| UNIVERSAL 24 | GeneralizedTime | Consists of the date, specified with a four-digit year, a two-digit month and a two-digit day, followed by the time, specified in hours, minutes, and optionally seconds, followed by an optional specification of the local time differential from universal time. |
| UNIVERSAL 11–15 | Reserves | Reserved for addenda to the ASN.1 standard |
| UNIVERSAL 28– | Reserved | Reserved for addenda to the ASN.1 standard |

(*Continued*)

**TABLE 19.2** (*Continued*)

| | | Structured Types |
|---|---|---|
| UNIVERSAL 16 | SEQUENCE and SEQUENCE-OF | Sequence: defined by referencing a fixed, ordered list of types; each value is an ordered list of values, one from each component type.<br>Sequence-of: defined by referencing a single existing type; each value is an ordered list of zero or more values of the existing type. |
| UNIVERSAL 17 | SET and SET-OF | Set: defined by referencing a fixed, unordered list of types, some of which may be declared optional; each value is an unordered list of values, one from each component type.<br>Set-of: defined by referencing a single existing type; each value is an unordered list of zero or more values of the existing type. |

- **Context-specific.** Also relevant to a particular application, but applicable in a limited context.
- **Private.** Types defined by users and not covered by any standard.

A data type is uniquely identified by its tag. ASN.1 types are the same if and only if their tag numbers are the same. For example, UNIVERSAL 4 refers to OctetString, which is of class UNIVERSAL and has tag number 4 within the class.

A **simple type** is one defined by directly specifying the set of its values. We may think of these as the atomic types; all other types are built up from the simple types. The simple data types in the UNIVERSAL class can be grouped into several categories, as indicated in Table 19.2; these are not "official" categories in the standard but are used here for convenience.

The first group of simple types can be referred to, for want of a better word, as basic types. The Boolean type is straightforward. The Integer type is the set of positive and negative integers and zero. In addition, individual integer values can be assigned names to indicate a specific meaning. The BitString is an ordered set of zero or more bits; individual bits can be assigned names. The actual value of a BitString can be specified as a string of either binary or hexadecimal digits. Similarly, an OctetString can be specified as a string of either binary or hexadecimal digits. The Real data type consists of numbers expressed in scientific notation (mantissa, base, exponent); that is,

$$M \times B^E$$

The mantissa ($M$) and the exponent ($E$) may take on any integer values, positive or negative; a base ($B$) of 2 or 10 may be used.

Finally, the Enumerated type consists of an explicitly enumerated list of integers, together with an associated name for each integer. The same functionality can be achieved with the Integer type by naming some of the integer values; but, because of the utility of this feature, a separate type has been defined. Note, however, that although the values of the enumerated type are integers, they do not have integer semantics. That is, arithmetic operations should not be performed on enumerated values.

Object types are used to name and describe information objects. Examples of information objects are standards documents, abstract and transfer syntaxes, data structures, and managed objects. In general, an information object is a class of information (e.g., a file format) rather than an instance of such a class (e.g., an individual file). The Object identifier is a unique identifier for a particular object. Its value consists of a sequence of integers. The set of defined objects has a tree structure, with the root of the tree being the object referring to the ASN.1 standard. Starting with the root of the object identifier tree, each object identifier component value identifies an arc in the tree. The Object descriptor is a human-readable description of an information object.

ASN.1 defines a number of character-string types. The values of each of these types consists of a sequence of zero or more characters from a standardized character set.

There are some miscellaneous types that have also been defined in the UNIVERSAL class. The Null type is used in places in a structure where a value may or may not be present. The Null type is simply the alternative of no value being present at that position in the structure. An External type is one whose values are unspecified in the ASN.1 standard; it is defined in some other document or standard and can be defined using any well-specified notation. UTCTime and Generalized-Time are two different formats for expressing time. In both cases, either a universal or local time may be specified.

**Structured types** are those consisting of components. ASN.1 provides four structured types for building complex data types from simple data types:

- SEQUENCE
- SEQUENCE-OF
- SET
- SET-OF

The Sequence and Sequence-of types are used to define an ordered list of values of one or more other data types; this is analogous to the record structure found in many programming languages, such as COBOL. A Sequence consists of an ordered list of elements, each specifying a type and, optionally, a name. The notation for defining the sequence type is as follows:

SequenceType ::= SEQUENCE {ElementTypeList} | SEQUENCE { }

ElementTypeList ::= ElementType | ElementTypeList, ElementType

ElementType ::=
      NamedType                       |
      NamedType  OPTIONAL      |
      NamedType  DEFAULT Value   |
      COMPONENTS OF Type

A NamedType is a type reference with or without a name. Each element definition may be followed by the keyword OPTIONAL or DEFAULT. The

OPTIONAL keyword indicates that the component element need not be present in a sequence value. The DEFAULT keyword indicates that, if the component element is not present, then the value specified by the DEFAULT clause will be assigned. The COMPONENTS OF clause is used to define the inclusion, at this point in the ElementTypeList, of all the ElementType sequences appearing in the referenced type.

A Sequence-of consists of an ordered, variable number of elements, all of one type. A Sequence-of definition has the following form:

SequenceOfType ::= SEQUENCE OF Type | SEQUENCE

The notation SEQUENCE is to be interpreted as SEQUENCE-OF ANY; the type ANY is explained in a later subsection.

A Set is similar to a Sequence, except that the order of the elements is not significant; the elements may be arranged in any order when they are encoded into a specific representation. A Set definition has the following form:

SetType ::= SET {ElementTypeList} | SET { }

Thus, a set may include optional, default, and component-of clauses.

A Set-of is an unordered, variable number of elements, all of one type. A Set-of definition has the following form:

SetOfType ::= SET OF Type | SET

The notation SET is to be interpreted as SET OF ANY; the type ANY is explained in a later subsection.

The term *tagged type* is somewhat of a misnomer, as all data types in ASN.1 have an associated tag. The ASN.1 standard defines a tagged type as follows:

> A type defined by referencing a single existing type and a tag; the new type is isomorphic to the existing type, but is distinct from it. In all encoding schemes, a value of the new type can be distinguished from a value of the old type.

Tagging is useful to distinguish types within an application. It may be desired to have several different type names, such as Employee_name and Customer_name, which are essentially the same type. For some structures, tagging is needed to distinguish component types within the structured type. For example, optional components of a SET or SEQUENCE type are typically given distinct context-specific tags to avoid ambiguity.

There are two categories of tagged types: implicitly tagged types and explicitly tagged types. An implicitly tagged type is derived from another type by *replacing* the tag (old class name, old tag number) of the old type with a new tag (new class name, new tag number). For purposes of encoding, only the new tag is used.

An explicitly tagged type is derived from another type by *adding* a new tag to the underlying type. In effect, an explicitly tagged type is a structured type with one component: the underlying type. For purposes of encoding, both the new and old tags must be reflected in the encoding.

An implicit tag results in shorter encodings, but an explicit tag may be necessary to avoid ambiguity if the tag of the underlying type is indeterminate (e.g., if the underlying type is CHOICE or ANY).

The **CHOICE** and **ANY** types are data types without tags; the reason for this is that when a particular value is assigned to the type, then a particular type must be assigned at the same time. Thus, the type is assigned at "run time."

The CHOICE type is a list of alternative known types. Only one of these types will actually be used to create a value. It was stated earlier that a type can be viewed as a collection of values. The CHOICE type is the union of the sets of values of all of the component types listed in the CHOICE type. This type is useful when the values to be described can be of different types depending on circumstance, and all the possible types are known in advance.

The notation for defining the CHOICE type is as follows:

ChoiceType ::= CHOICE {AlternativeTypeList}
AlternativeTypeList ::= NamedType | AlternativeTypeList, NamedType

The ANY type describes an arbitrary value of an arbitrary type. The notation is simply

AnyType ::= ANY

This type is useful when the values to be described can be of different types but the possible types are not known in advance.

## Subtypes

A subtype is derived from a parent type by restricting the set of values defined for a parent type. That is, the set of values for the subtype are a subset of the set of values for the parent type. The process of subtyping can extend to more than one level: that is, a subtype may itself be a parent of an even more restricted subtype.

Six different forms of notation for designating the values of a subtype are provided in the standard. Table 19.3 indicates which of these forms can be applied to particular parent types. The remainder of this subsection provides an overview of each form.

A *single-value subtype* is an explicit listing of all of the values that the subtype may take on. For example,

SmallPrime ::= INTEGER ( 2 | 3 | 5 | 7 | 11 | 13 | 17 | 19 | 23 | 29 )

In this case, SmallPrime is a subtype of the built-in type INTEGER. As another example,

Months ::= ENUMERATED { january (1),
                        february (2),
                        march (3),
                        april (4),
                        may (5),
                        june (6),
                        july (7),
                        august (8),
                        september (9),
                        october (10),
                        november (11),
                        december (12) }

**TABLE 19.3**  Applicability of subtype value sets.

| Type (or derived from such a type by tagging) | Single Value | Contained Subtype | Value Range | Size Constraint | Permitted Alphabet | Inner Subtyping |
|---|---|---|---|---|---|---|
| Boolean | ✔ | ✔ | | | | |
| Integer | ✔ | ✔ | ✔ | | | |
| Enumerated | ✔ | ✔ | | | | |
| Real | ✔ | ✔ | ✔ | | | |
| Object Identifier | ✔ | ✔ | | | | |
| Bit String | ✔ | ✔ | | ✔ | | |
| Octet String | ✔ | ✔ | | ✔ | | |
| Character String Types | ✔ | ✔ | | ✔ | ✔ | |
| Sequence | ✔ | ✔ | | | | ✔ |
| Sequence-of | ✔ | ✔ | | ✔ | | ✔ |
| Set | ✔ | ✔ | | | | ✔ |
| Set-of | ✔ | ✔ | | ✔ | | ✔ |
| Any | ✔ | ✔ | | | | |
| Choice | ✔ | ✔ | | | | ✔ |

> First-quarter ::= Months ( january | february | march )
> Second-quarter ::= Months ( april | may | june )

First-quarter and Second-quarter are both subtypes of the enumerated type Months.

A *contained subtype* is used to form new subtypes from existing subtypes. The contained subtype includes all of the values of the subtypes that it contains. For example,

> First-half ::= Months ( INCLUDES First-quarter | INCLUDES Second-quarter )

A contained subtype may also include listing explicit values:

> First-third ::= Months ( INCLUDES First-quarter | april )

A *value-range subtype* applies only to INTEGER and REAL types; it is specified by giving the numerical values of the endpoints of the range. The special values PLUS-INFINITY and MINUS-INFINITY may be used. Also, the special values MIN and MAX may be used to indicate the minimum and maximum allowable values in the parent. Each endpoint of the range is either closed or open. When open, the specification of the endpoint includes the less-than symbol (<). The following are equivalent definitions:

> PositiveInteger ::= INTEGER (0<..PLUS-INFINITY)
> PositiveInteger ::= INTEGER (1..PLUS-INFINITY)
> PositiveInteger ::= INTEGER (0<..MAX)
> PositiveInteger ::= INTEGER (1..MAX)

The following are equivalent:

NegativeInteger ::= INTEGER (MINUS-INFINITY..<0)
NegativeInteger ::= INTEGER (MINUS-INFINITY..–1)
NegativeInteger ::= INTEGER (MIN..<0)
NegativeInteger ::= INTEGER (MIN..–1)

The **permitted-alphabet constraint** may only be applied to character string types. A permitted-alphabet type consists of all values (strings) that can be constructed using a subalphabet of the parent type. Examples are

TouchToneButtons ::= IA5String ( FROM
  ( "0" | "1" | "2" | "3" | "5" | "6" | "7" | "8" | "9" | "*" | "#" ) )
DigitString ::= IA5String ( FROM
  ( "0" | "1" | "2" | "3" | "5" | "6" | "7" | "8" | "9" ) )

A **size constraint** limits the number of items in a type. It can only be applied to the string types (bit string, octet string, character string) and to Sequence-of and Set-of types. The item that is constrained depends on the parent type, as follows:

| Type | Unit of Measure |
| --- | --- |
| bit string | bit |
| octet string | octet |
| character string | character |
| sequence-of | component value |
| set-of | component value |

As an example of a string type, Recommendation X.121 specifies that international data numbers, which are used for addressing end systems on public data networks, including X.25 networks, should consist of at least 5 digits but not more than 14 digits; this could be specified as follows:

ItlDataNumber ::= DigitString ( SIZE ( 5..14 ) )

Now consider a parameter list for a message that may include up to 12 parameters:

ParameterList ::= SET SIZE ( 0..12 ) OF Parameter

An **inner-type constraint** can be applied to the sequence, sequence-of, set, set-of, and choice types. An inner subtype includes in its value set only those values from the parent type that satisfy one or more constraints on the presence and/or values of the components of the parent type. This is a rather complex subtype, and only a few examples are given here.

Consider a protocol data unit (PDU) that may have four different fields, in no particular order:

PDU ::= SET { alpha    [0]   INTEGER,
              beta     [1]   IA5String  OPTIONAL,
              gamma    [2]   SEQUENCE OF Parameter,
              delta    [3]   BOOLEAN }

To specify a test that requires the Boolean to be false and the integer to be negative,

TestPDU ::= PDU ( WITH COMPONENTS { ..., delta (FALSE), alpha (MIN...<0)})

To further specify that the beta parameter is to be present and either 5 or 12 characters in length,

FurtherTestPDU ::= TestPDU (WITH COMPONENTS {..., beta (SIZE (5 | 12) PRESENT})

As another example, consider the use of inner subtyping on a sequence-of construct

Text-block ::= SEQUENCE OF VisibleString

Address ::= Text-block ( SIZE (1..6) | WITH COMPONENT (SIZE (1..32)))

The above indicates that the address consists of from 1 to 6 text blocks, and that each text block is from 1 to 32 characters in length.

### PDU Example

As an example, consider the ASN.1 specification of the format of the protocol data units for the SNMPv2 protocol (described later in this chapter). The specification from the standard is reproduced in Figure 19.3.

The top-level construct uses the CHOICE type to describe a variable selected from a collection. Thus, any instance of the type PDUs will be one of eight alternative types. Note that each of the choices is labeled with a name. All of the PDUs

```
SNMPv2-PDU DEFINITIONS ::= BEGIN
PDUs ::= CHOICE {get-request              GetRequest-PDU,
                 get-next-request         GetNextRequest-PDU,
                 get-bulk-request         GetBulkRequest-PDU,
                 response                 Response-PDU,
                 set-request              SetRequest-PDU,
                 inform-request           InformRequest-PDU,
                 snmp V2-trap             SNMPv2-Trap-PDU,
                 report                   Report-PDU      }

—PDUs

GetRequest-PDU        ::=   [0] IMPLICIT PDU
GetNextRequest-PDU    ::=   [1] IMPLICIT PDU
Response-PDU          ::=   [2] IMPLICIT PDU
SetRequest-PDU        ::=   [3] IMPLICIT PDU
GetBulkRequest-PDU    ::=   [5] IMPLICIT BulkPDU
InformRequest-PDU     ::=   [6] IMPLICIT PDU
SNMPv2-Trap-PDU       ::=   [7] IMPLICIT PDU
Report-PDU            ::=   [8] IMPLICIT PDU

max-bindings  INTEGER ::= 2147483647
```

**FIGURE 19.3**   SNMPv2 PDU format definitions. (*Continued on next page*)

```
PDU ::= SEQUENCE {request-id Integer32,
                    error-status INTEGER {                              —sometimes ignored
                                    NoError (0),
                                    tooBig (1),
                                    noSuchName (2),            —for proxy compatibility
                                    badValue (3),             —for proxy compatibility
                                    readOnly (4),             —for proxy compatibility
                                    genError (5),
                                    noAccess (6),
                                    wrongType (7),
                                    wrongLength (8),
                                    wrongEncoding (9),
                                    wrongValue (10),
                                    noCreation (11),
                                    inconsistentValue (12),
                                    resourceUnavailable (13),
                                    commitFailed (14),
                                    undoFailed (15),
                                    authorizationError (16),
                                    notWritable (17),
                                    inconsistentName (18)   },
                    error-Index INTEGER (0..max-bindings),      —sometimes ignored
                    variable-binding VarBindList   }          —values are sometimes ignored
BulkPDU ::= SEQUENCE {                            —Must be identical in structure to PDU
                    request-id              Integer32,
                    non-repeaters           INTEGER (0..max-bindings),
                    max-repetitions         INTEGER (0..max-bindings),
                    variable-binding        VarBindList   }          --values are ignored

--variable binding

VarBind ::= SEQUENCE {name  ObjectName,
            CHOICE {value                       ObjectSyntax,
                    unspecified                 NULL,        --in retrieval requests
                                                --exceptions in responses:
                    noSuchObject [0]            IMPLICIT NULL,
                    noSuchInstance [1]          IMPLICIT NULL,
                    endOfMibView [2]            IMPLICIT NULL   }   }
--variable-binding list

VarBindList ::= SEQUENCE (SIZE (0..max-bindings)) OF VarBind

END
```

**FIGURE 19.3**  (*Continued*)

defined in this fashion have the same format but different labels, with the exception of GetBulkRequest-PDU. The format consists of a sequence of four elements. The second element, error-status, enumerates 18 possible integer values, each with a label. The last element, variable-binding, is defined as having syntax VarBindList, which is defined later in the same set of definitions.

The BulkPDU definition is also a sequence of four elements, but differs from the other PDUs.

VarBindList is defined as a Sequence-of construct consisting of some number of elements of syntax VarBind, with a size constraint of up to 2147483647, or $2^{31}-1$, elements. Each element, in turn, is a sequence of two values; the first is a name, and the second is a choice among five elements.

## ASN.1 Macro Definitions

Included in the ASN.1 specification is the ASN.1 macro notation. This notation allows the user to extent the syntax of ASN.1 to define new types and their values. The subject of ASN.1 macros is a complex one, and this section serves only to introduce the subject.

Let us begin with several observations:

1. There are three levels that must be carefully distinguished:
   - The macro notation, used for defining macros.
   - A macro definition, expressed in the macro notation and used to define a set of macro instances.
   - A macro instance, generated from a macro definition by substituting values for variables.
2. A macro definition functions as a Super Type, generating a class of macro instances that function exactly like a basic ASN.1 type.[1]
3. A macro definition may be viewed as a template that is used to generate a set of related types and values.
4. The macro is used to extend the ASN.1 syntax but does not extend the encoding. Any type defined by means of a macro instance is simply an ASN.1 type, and is encoded in the usual manner.
5. In addition to the convenience of defining a set of related types, the macro definition enables the user to include semantic information with the type.

### Macro Definition Format

A macro definition has the following general form:

```
<macroname> MACRO ::=
BEGIN
    TYPE NOTATION ::=  <new-type-syntax>
    VALUE NOTATION ::= <new-value-syntax>
    <supporting-productions>
END
```

The macroname is written in all uppercase letters. A new ASN.1 type is defined by writing the name of the type, which begins with a capital letter, followed by the macroname, followed by a definition of the type dictated by the form of the macro body.

The type and value notations, as well as the supporting productions, are all specified using Backus-Naur Form (BNF). The new-type-syntax describes the new type. The new-value-syntax describes the values of the new type. The supporting-

---

[1] The ASN.1 standard uses the term *basic ASN.1 type* to refer to any ASN.1 type that is not a macro instance.

productions provide any additional grammar rules for either the type or value syntax; that is, any nonterminals within the new-type-syntax and/or new-value-syntax are expanded in the supporting-productions.

When specific values are substituted for the variables or arguments of a macro definition, a macro instance is formed. This macro instance has two results. First, it generates a representation of a basic ASN.1 type, called the *returned type*. Second, it generates a representation of a generic ASN.1 value—that is, a representation of the set of values that the type may take. This generic value is called the *returned value*.

## Macros Versus Defined Types

The ASN.1 macro facility provides tools for

1. Defining new types
2. Representing those types
3. Representing values of those types
4. Encoding specific values of those types

A similar capability already exists within ASN.1, which allows for the construction of defined types, either from built-in types or, recursively, from built-in types and defined types. The macro facility differs from the ASN.1 defined type capability in the following respects:

1. The macro facility allows the definition of a family of types. Each new type generated by a macro definition (a macro instance) is closely related to other types generated from the same macro. In contrast, there is no particular relationship between one basic ASN.1 defined type and other defined types.
2. A defined type is represented in a set way from the strings symbolizing the types from which it is constructed. A macro instance is represented in whatever way the writer of the macro chooses. Thus, the syntax of a type defined via macro instance can be chosen to correspond closely to the notation used within the particular application for which the macro was written. Furthermore, the macro instance may include commentary or semantic narrative. In this way, types defined by a macro may be more readable and more writeable.
3. In basic ASN.1, the representation of a value of a type is derived from the representation of the type in a relatively straightforward manner. The two representations are isomorphic; that is, they have similar or identical structure. This isomorphism is not required with a macro definition. The returned type and the returned generic value may have quite different syntaxes. Again, this allows for more readable and writable values.

### SNMPv2 OBJECT-TYPE Macro

An example of a macro is illustrated in Figure 19.4. This macro is defined in the SNMPv2 standard, and is used to define management objects. A management object is an individual variable or item of management information stored in a man-

OBJECT-TYPE MACRO ::= BEGIN

TYPE NOTATION ::= "SYNTAX" Syntax
                    UnitsPart
                    "MAX-ACCESS" Access
                    "STATUS" Status
                    "DESCRIPTION" Text
                    ReferPart
                    IndexPart
                    DefValPart

VALUE NOTATION ::= value (VALUE ObjectName)
Syntax ::= type(ObjectSyntax) | "BITS" "{" Kibbles "}"
Kibbles ::= Kibble | Kibbles "," Kibble
Kibble ::= identifier "(" nonNegativeNumber ")"
UnitsPart ::= "UNITS" Text | empty
Access ::= "not-accessible" | "accessible-for-notify" | "read-only" | "read-write" | "read-write" | "read-create"
Status ::= "current" | "deprecated" | "obsolete"
ReferPart ::= "REFERENCE" Text | empty
IndexPart ::= "INDEX" "{" IndexTypes "}" | "AUGMENTS" "{" Entry "}" | empty
IndexTypes ::= IndexType | IndexTypes "," IndexType
IndexTypes ::= "IMPLIED" Index | Index
Index ::= value (indexobject ObjectName)      --use the SYNTAX value of the
                                              --correspondent OBJECT-TYPE invocation

Entry ::= value (entryobject ObjectName)      --use the INDEX value of the
                                              --correspondent OBJECT-TYPE invocation
DefValPart ::= "DEFVAL" "{" value (Defval ObjectSyntax) "}" | empty
—uses the NVT ASCII character set
Text ::= """"string""""

END

**FIGURE 19.4**  SNMPv2 macro for object definition.


agement information base. Thus, this is an example of the use of ASN.1 to specify
the syntax of locally maintained data that is used by a distributed application.

    The type notation portion of this macro consists of eight parts:

- The SYNTAX clause specifies the ASN.1 syntax type of this object. Object-
  Syntax defines a subset of ASN.1 types that may be used to define managed
  objects; its definition is not shown.
- The UNITS clause can be used to specify what units a numerical value has.
- The MAX-ACCESS clause is used to specify the access privileges for this
  object. Some objects are not accessible by remote users, but are used by the
  local system for data-structuring purposes. Other objects may be read-only,
  read-write, or read-create.
- The STATUS clause indicates the current status of this object with respect to
  whether it is part of the most recent standard.
- The DESCRIPTION clause is used to provide a textual description of the
  object.
- The REFERENCE clause is used to provide a cross-reference to another portion of the management information base.

- The INDEX clause is used if this object refers to a tabular structure. The clause lists the object or objects that serve as indexes into the table.
- The AUGMENTS clause is used to specify that this object refers to a tabular structure that is to be appended to another tabular structure.
- The DEFVAL clause is used to provide a default value for this object, to be supplied upon creation of the object by the local system.

The value of an object is an identifier, ObjectName, that provides a unique reference for the object.

An example of the use of this macro is the following SNMPv2 object definition:

```
ifTestResult  OBJECT-TYPE
    SYNTAX   INTEGER {
            none(1),   -- no test yet requested
            success(2),
            inProgress(3),
            notSupported(4),
            unAbleToRun(5),   -- due to state of system
            aborted(6),
            failed(7)
          }
    MAX-ACCESS  read-only
    STATUS   current
    DESCRIPTION
        "This object contains the result of the most recently
        requested test, or the value none(1) if no tests have
        been requested since the last reset. Note that this
        facility provides no provision for saving the results
        of one test when starting another, as could be
        required if used by multiple managers concurrently."
    ::= { ifTestEntry 4 }
```

## 19.2  NETWORK MANAGEMENT—SNMPv2

Networks and distributed processing systems are of critical and growing importance in business, government, and other organizations. Within a given organization, the trend is toward larger, more complex networks supporting more applications and more users. As these networks grow in scale, two facts become painfully evident:

- The network and its associated resources and distributed applications become indispensable to the organization.
- More things can go wrong, disabling the network or a portion of the network, or degrading performance to an unacceptable level.

A large network cannot be put together and managed by human effort alone. The complexity of such a system dictates the use of automated network management tools. The urgency of the need for such tools is increased, and the difficulty of supplying such tools is also increased, if the network includes equipment from multiple vendors. In response, standards that deal with network management have been developed, covering services, protocols, and management information base.

This section begins with an introduction to the overall concepts of standardized network management; the remainder is devoted to a discussion of SNMPv2, which is an extension of SNMP, the most widely used network management standard.

## Network Management Systems

A network management system is a collection of tools for network monitoring and control that is integrated in the following senses:

- A single operator interface with a powerful but user-friendly set of commands for performing most or all network management tasks.
- A minimal amount of separate equipment. That is, most of the hardware and software required for network management are incorporated into the existing user equipment.

A network management system consists of incremental hardware and software additions implemented among existing network components. The software used in accomplishing the network management tasks resides in the host computers and communications processors (e.g., front-end processors, terminal cluster controllers). A network management system is designed to view the entire network as a unified architecture, with addresses and labels assigned to each point and the specific attributes of each element and link known to the system. The active elements of the network provide regular feedback of status information to the network control center.

A network management system incorporates the following key elements:

- Management station, or manager
- Agent
- Management information base
- Network management protocol

The *management station* is typically a stand-alone device, but may be a capability implemented on a shared system. In either case, the management station serves as the interface for the human network manager into the network management system. The management station will have, at minimum,

- A set of management applications for data analysis, fault recovery, and so on.
- An interface by which the network manager may monitor and control the network.

- The capability of translating the network manager's requirements into the actual monitoring and control of remote elements in the network.
- A database of network management information extracted from the databases of all the managed entities in the network.

The other active element in the network management system is the *agent*. Key platforms, such as hosts, bridges, routers, and hubs, may be equipped with agent software so that they may be managed from a management station. The agent responds to requests for information from a management station, responds to requests for actions from the management station, and may asynchronously provide the management station with important but unsolicited information.

The means by which resources in the network may be managed entails representing these resources as objects. Each object is, essentially, a data variable that represents one aspect of the managed agent. The collection of objects is referred to as a *management information base* (MIB). The MIB functions as a collection of access points at the agent for the management station. These objects are standardized across systems of a particular class (e.g., bridges all support the same management objects). A management station performs the monitoring function by retrieving the value of MIB objects. Also, a management station can cause an action to take place at an agent, or it can change the configuration settings of an agent by modifying the value of specific variables.

The management station and agents are linked by a *network management protocol*. The protocol used for the management of TCP/IP networks is the simple network management protocol (SNMP). For OSI-based networks, the common management information protocol (CMIP) is being developed. An enhanced version of SNMP, known as SNMPv2, is intended for both TCP/IP- and OSI-based networks. Each of these protocols includes the following key capabilities:

- **Get:** Enables the management station to retrieve the value of objects at the agent.
- **Set:** Enables the management station to set the value of objects at the agent.
- **Notify:** Enables an agent to notify the management station of significant events.

In a traditional centralized network management scheme, one host in the configuration has the role of a network management station; there may be possibly one or two other management stations in a backup role. The remainder of the devices on the network contain agent software and a MIB, to allow monitoring and control from the management station. As networks grow in size and traffic load, such a centralized system is unworkable. Too much burden is placed on the management station, and there is too much traffic, with reports from every single agent having to wend their way across the entire network to headquarters. In such circumstances, a decentralized, distributed approach works best (e.g., Figure 19.5). In a decentralized network management scheme, there may be multiple top-level management stations, which might be referred to as management servers. Each such server might directly manage a portion of the total pool of agents. However, for many of the

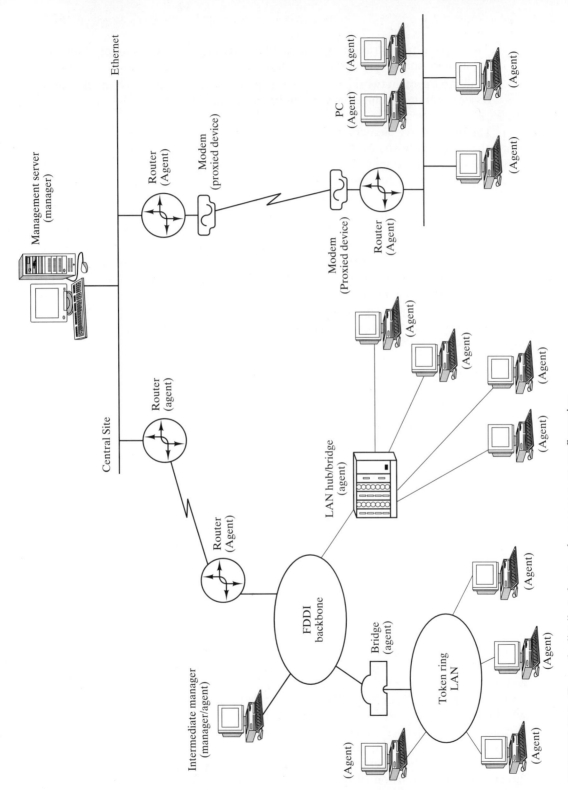

**FIGURE 19.5** Example distributed network management configuration.

agents, the management server delegates responsibility to an intermediate manager, which plays the role of manager to monitor and control the agents under its responsibility; it also plays an agent role to provide information and accept control from a higher-level management server. This type of architecture spreads the processing burden and reduces total network traffic.

## Simple Network Management Protocol Version 2 (SNMPv2)

In August of 1988, the specification for SNMP was issued and rapidly became the dominant network management standard. A number of vendors offer stand-alone network management workstations based on SNMP, and most vendors of bridges, routers, workstations, and PCs offer SNMP agent packages that allow their products to be managed by an SNMP management station.

As the name suggests, SNMP is a simple tool for network management. It defines a limited, easily implemented management information base (MIB) of scalar variables and two-dimensional tables, and it defines a streamlined protocol to enable a manager to get and set MIB variables and to enable an agent to issue unsolicited notifications, called **traps**. This simplicity is the strength of SNMP; it is easily implemented and consumes modest processor and network resources. Also, the structure of the protocol and the MIB are sufficiently straightforward that it is not difficult to achieve interoperability among management stations and agent software from a mix of vendors.

With its widespread use, the deficiencies of SNMP became increasingly apparent: functional deficiencies and lack of a security facility. As a result, an enhanced version, known as SNMPv2, was issued in 1993, with a revised version issued in 1996 (RFCs). SNMPv2 has quickly gained support, and a number of vendors announced products within months of the issuance of the standard.

### The Elements of SNMPv2

Surprisingly, SNMPv2 does not provide network management at all! SNMPv2 instead provides a framework on which network management applications can be built. Those applications, such as fault management, performance monitoring, accounting, and so on, are outside the scope of the standard.

What SNMPv2 does provide is, to use a contemporary term, the infrastructure for network management. Figure 19.6 is an example of a configuration that illustrates that infrastructure.

The essence of SNMPv2 is a protocol that is used to exchange management information. Each "player" in the network management system maintains a local database of information relevant to network management, known as the management information base. The SNMPv2 standard defines the structure of this information and the allowable data types; this definition is known as the structure of management information (SMI); we can think of this as the language for defining management information. The standard also supplies a number of MIBs that are

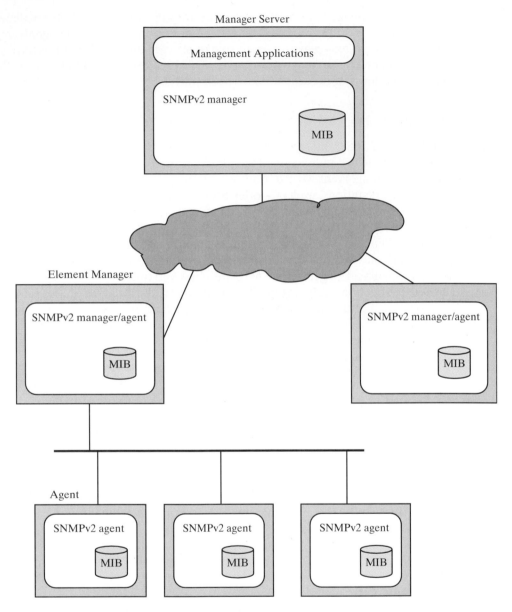

**FIGURE 19.6** SNMPv2-managed configuration.

generally useful for network management.[2] In addition, new MIBs may be defined by vendors and user groups.

---

[2]There is some ambiquity implicit in the term MIB. In its singular form, the term can be used to refer to the entire database of management information at either a manager or an agent. It can also be used in singular or plural form to refer to a specific defined collection of management information that is part of an overall MIB. Thus, the SNMPv2 standard includes the definition of several MIBs and incorporates, by reference, MIBs defined in SNMPv1.

At least one system in the configuration must be responsible for network management. It is here that any network management applications are housed. There may be more than one of these management stations, to provide redundancy or simply to split up the duties in a large network. Most other systems act in the role of agent. An agent collects information locally and stores it for later access by a manager. The information includes data about the system itself and may also include traffic information for the network or networks to which the agent attaches.

SNMPv2 will support either a highly centralized network management strategy or a distributed one. In the latter case, some systems operate both in the role of manager and of agent. In its agent role, such a system will accept commands from a superior management system. Some of those commands relate to the local MIB at the agent. Other commands require the agent to act as a proxy for remote devices. In this case, the proxy agent assumes the role of manager to access information at a remote agent, and then assumes the role of an agent to pass that information on to a superior manager.

All of these exchanges take place using the SNMPv2 protocol, which is of the simple request/response type. Typically, SNMPv2 is implemented on top of the user datagram protocol (UDP), which is part of the TCP/IP protocol suite; it can also be implemented on top of the ISO transport protocol.

### Structure of Management Information

The SMI defines the general framework within which an MIB can be defined and constructed. The SMI identifies the data types that can be used in the MIB, and how resources within the MIB are represented and named. The philosophy behind SMI is to encourage simplicity and extensibility within the MIB. Thus, the MIB can store only simple data types: scalars and two-dimensional arrays of scalars, called *tables*. The SMI does not support the creation or retrieval of complex data structures. This philosophy is in contrast to that used with OSI-systems management, which provides for complex data structures and retrieval modes to support greater functionality. SMI avoids complex data types and structures to simplify the task of implementation and to enhance interoperability. MIBs will inevitably contain vendor-created data types and, unless tight restrictions are placed on the definition of such data types, interoperability will suffer.

There are actually three key elements in the SMI specification. At the lowest level, the SMI specifies the data types that may be stored. Then, the SMI specifies a formal technique for defining objects and tables of objects. Finally, the SMI provides a scheme for associating a unique identifier with each actual object in a system, so that data at an agent can be referenced by a manager.

Table 19.4 shows the data types that are allowed by the SMI. This is a fairly restricted set of types. For example, real numbers are not supported; however, it is rich enough to support most network management requirements.

The SNMPv2 specification includes a template, known as an ASN.1 (Abstract Syntax Notation One) macro, which provides the formal model for defining objects. That template was illustrated in Figure 19.4. Figure 19.7 is an example of how this template is used to define objects and tables of objects.

**TABLE 19.4**   Allowable data types in SNMPv2.

| Data Type | Description |
|---|---|
| INTEGER | Integers in the range of $-2^{21}$ to $2^{31} - 1$. |
| UInteger32 | Integers in the range of 0 to $2^{32} - 1$. |
| Counter32 | A non-negative integer which may be incremented modulo $2^{32}$. |
| Counter64 | A non-negative integer which may be incremented modulo $2^{64}$. |
| Gauge 32 | A non-negative integer which may increase or decrease, but shall not exceed a maximum value. The maximum value can not be greater than $2^{32} - 1$. |
| TimeTicks | A non-negative integer which represents the time, modulo $2^{32}$, in hundredths of a second. |
| OCTET STRING | Octet strings for arbitrary binary or texual data; may be limited to 255 octets. |
| IpAddress | A 32-bit internet address. |
| Opaque | An arbitrary bit field. |
| BIT STRING | An enumeration of named bits. |
| OBJECT IDENTIFIER | Administratively assigned name to object or other standardized element. Value is a sequence of up to 128 non-negative integers. |

The first three productions serve to define a table, grokTable, stored at an agent. As with all SNMPv2 tables, grokTable is organized as a sequence of rows, or entries, each of which has the same sequence of objects; in this case, each row consists of four objects. The INDEX clause specifies that the object grokIndex serves as an index into the table; each row of the table will have a unique value of grokIndex.

The access type of grokIPAddress is read-create, which means that the object is read-write and that the object may be assigned a value by a manager at the time that the row containing this object is created by a manager. Each row of the table maintains a counter for the number of grok packets sent to the grokIPAddress specified for that row. The grokCount object is read-only; its value cannot be altered by a manager but is maintained by the agent within which this table resides. The grokStatus object is used in the process of row creation and deletion; for which the algorithm is rather complex. In essence, a RowStatus type of object is used to keep track of the state of a row during the process of creation and deletion.

Each object definition includes a value, which is a unique identifier for that object; for example, the value for grokEntry is {grokTable 1}, which means that the identifier for grokEntry is the concatenation of the identifier for grokTable and 1. The objects in a MIB are organized in a tree structure, and the identifier of an object is found by walking the tree from its root to the position of the object in that tree structure. For scalar objects, this scheme provides a unique identifier for any given object instance. For objects in tables, there is one instance of each object for

grokTable OBJECT-TYPE
    SYNTAX    SEQUENCE OF GrokEntry
    MAX-ACCESS    not-accessible
    STATUS    current
    DESCRIPTION
        "The (conceptual) grok table."
    ::= { adhocGroup 2 }

grokEntry OBJECT-TYPE
    SYNTAX    GrokEntry
    MAX-ACCESS    not-accessible
    STATUS    current
    DESCRIPTION
        "An entry (conceptual row) in the
        grok table."
    INDEX    { grokIndex }
    ::= { grokTable 1 }

GrokEntry ::= SEQUENCE {
        grokIndex    INTEGER,
        grokIPAddress    IpAddress,
        grokCount    Counter32,
        grokStatus    RowStatus }

grokIndex OBJECT-TYPE
    SYNTAX    INTEGER
    MAX-ACCESS    not-accessible
    STATUS    current
    DESCRIPTION
        "The auxiliary variable used for
        identify instances of the columnar
        objects in the grok table."
    ::= { grokEntry 1 }

grokIPAddress OBJECT-TYPE
    SYNTAX    IpAddress
    MAX-ACCESS    read-create
    STATUS    current
    DESCRIPTION
        "The Ip address to send grok packets
        to."
    ::= { grokEntry 2 }

grokCount OBJECT-TYPE
    SYNTAX    Counter32
    MAX-ACCESS    read-only
    STATUS    current
    DESCRIPTION
        "The total number of grok packets
        sent so far."
    DEFVAL { 0 }
    ::= { grokEntry 3 }

grokStatus OBJECT-TYPE
    SYNTAX    RowStatus
    MAX-ACCESS    read-create
    STATUS    current
    DESCRIPTION
        "The status object used for creating,
        modifying, and deleting a conceptual
        row instance in the grok table."
    DEFVAL { active }
    ::= { grokEntry 4 }

**FIGURE 19.7**    An example of an SNMPv2 table.

each row of the table, so a further qualification is needed; what is done is to concatenate the value of the INDEX object to the identifier of each object in the table.

## Protocol Operation

The heart of the SNMPv2 framework is the protocol itself. The protocol provides a straightforward, basic mechanism for the exchange of management information between manager and agent.

The basic unit of exchange is the message, which consists of an outer message wrapper and an inner protocol data unit (PDU). The outer message header deals with security and is discussed later in this section.

Eight types of PDUs may be carried in an SNMP message. The general formats for these are illustrated informally in Figure 19.8; the formal ASN.1 definition was provided in Figure 19.3. Several fields are common to a number of PDUs. The request-id field is an integer assigned such that each outstanding request can be uniquely identified. This process enables a manager to correlate incoming responses

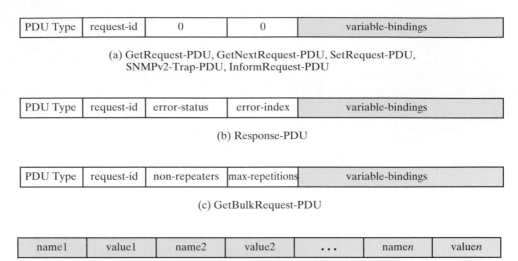

| PDU Type | request-id | 0 | 0 | variable-bindings |
|----------|-----------|---|---|-------------------|

(a) GetRequest-PDU, GetNextRequest-PDU, SetRequest-PDU,
SNMPv2-Trap-PDU, InformRequest-PDU

| PDU Type | request-id | error-status | error-index | variable-bindings |
|----------|-----------|--------------|-------------|-------------------|

(b) Response-PDU

| PDU Type | request-id | non-repeaters | max-repetitions | variable-bindings |
|----------|-----------|---------------|-----------------|-------------------|

(c) GetBulkRequest-PDU

| name1 | value1 | name2 | value2 | . . . | name$n$ | value$n$ |
|-------|--------|-------|--------|-------|---------|----------|

(d) variable-bindings

**FIGURE 19.8**   SNMPv2 PDU formats.

with outstanding requests; it also enables an agent to cope with duplicate PDUs generated by an unreliable transport service. The variable-bindings field contains a list of object identifiers; depending on the PDU, the list may also include a value for each object.

The GetRequest-PDU, issued by a manager, includes a list of one or more object names for which values are requested. If the get operation is successful, then the responding agent will send a Response-PDU. The variable-bindings list will contain the identifier and value of all retrieved objects. For any variables that are not in the relevant MIB view, its identifier and an error code are returned in the variable-bindings list. Thus, SNMPv2 permits partial responses to a GetRequest, which is a significant improvement over SNMP. In SNMP, if one or more of the variables in a GetRequest is not supported, the agent returns an error message with a status of noSuchName. In order to cope with such an error, the SNMP manager must either return no values to the requesting application, or it must include an algorithm that responds to an error by removing the missing variables, resending the request, and then sending a partial result to the application.

The GetNextRequest-PDU also is issued by a manager and includes a list of one or more objects. In this case, for each object named in the variable-bindings field, a value is to be returned for the object that is next in lexicographic order, which is equivalent to saying next in the MIB in terms of its position in the tree structure of object identifiers. As with the GetRequest-PDU, the agent will return values for as many variables as possible. One of the strengths of the GetNextRequest-PDU is that it enables a manager entity to discover the structure of an MIB view dynamically—a useful ability if the manager does not know *a priori* the set of objects that are supported by an agent or that are in a particular MIB view.

One of the major enhancements provided in SNMPv2 is the GetBulkRequest PDU. The purpose of this PDU is to minimize the number of protocol exchanges required to retrieve a large amount of management information. The GetBulkRequest PDU allows an SNMPv2 manager to request that the response be as large as possible given the constraints on message size.

The GetBulkRequest operation uses the same selection principle as the GetNextRequest operation; that is, selection is always of the next-object instance in lexicographic order. The difference is that, with GetBulkRequest, it is possible to specify that multiple lexicographic successors be selected.

In essence, the GetBulkRequest operation works in the following way. The GetBulkRequest includes a list of $(N + R)$ variable names in the variable-bindings list. For each of the first $N$ names, retrieval is done in the same fashion as for GetNextRequest. That is, for each variable in the list, the next variable in lexicographic order, plus its value, is returned; if there is no lexicographic successor, then the named variable and a value of endOfMibView are returned. For each of the last $R$ names, multiple lexicographic successors are returned.

The GetBulkRequest PDU has two fields not found in the other PDUs: non-repeaters and max-repetitions. The non-repeaters field specifies the number of variables in the variable-binding list for which a single lexicographic successor is to be returned. The max-repetitions field specifies the number of lexicographic successors to be returned for the remaining variables in the variable binding list. To explain the algorithm, let us define the following:

$L$ = number of variable names in the variable-bindings field of the GetBulkRequest PDU

$N$ = the number of variables, starting with the first variable in the variable-bindings field, for which a single lexicographic successor is requested

$R$ = the number of variables, following the first $N$ variables, for which multiple lexicographic successors are requested

$M$ = the number of lexicographic successors requested for each of the last $R$ variables

The following relationships hold:

$N = \text{MAX} [ \text{MIN} (\text{non-repeaters}, L), 0]$

$M = \text{MAX} [ \text{max-repetitions}, 0 ]$

$R = L–N$

The effect of the MAX operator is that if the value of either non-repeaters or max-repetitions is less than zero, a value of 0 is substituted.

If $N$ is greater than 0, then the first $N$ variables are processed as for GetNextRequest. If $R$ is greater than 0 and $M$ is greater than 0, then for each of the last $R$ variables in the variable bindings list, the $M$ lexicographic successors are retrieved. That is, for each variable,

• Obtain the value of the lexicographic successor of the named variable.
• Obtain the value of the lexicographic successor to the object instance retrieved in the previous step.

- Obtain the value of the lexicographic successor to the object instance retrieved in the previous step.
- And so on, until M object instances have been retrieved.

If, at any point in this process, there is no lexicographic successor, then the endOfMibView value is returned, paired with the name of the last lexicographic successor or, if there were no successors, with the name of the variable in the request.

Using these rules, the total number of variable-binding pairs that can be produced is $N + (M \times R)$. The order in which the last $(M \times R)$ of these variable-binding pairs are placed in the Response PDU can be expressed as follows:

> **for** $i := 1$ **to** $M$ **do**
> > **for** $r := 1$ **to** $R$ **do**
> > > retrieve $i$-th successor of $(N + r)$-th variable;

The effect of this definition is that the successors to the last $R$ variables are retrieved row by row, rather than retrieving all of the successors to the first variable, followed by all of the successors to the second variable, and so on; this matches with the way in which conceptual tables are lexicographically ordered, so that if the last $R$ values in the GetBulkRequest are columnar objects of the same table, then the Response will return conceptual rows of the table.

The GetBulkRequest operation removes one of the major limitations of SNMP, which is its inability to efficiently retrieve large blocks of data. Moreover, this use of this operator can actually enable reducing the size of management applications that are supported by the management protocol, realizing further efficiencies. There is no need for the management application to concern itself with some of the details of packaging requests. It need not perform a trial-and-error procedure to determine the optimal number of variable bindings to put in a request-PDU. Also, if a request is too big, even for GetBulkRequest, the agent will send back as much data as it can, rather than simply sending a tooBig error message. Thus, the manager simply has to retransmit the request for the missing data; it does not have to figure out how to repackage the original request into a series of smaller requests.

The SetRequest-PDU is issued by a manager to request that the values of one or more objects be altered. The receiving SNMPv2 entity responds with a Response-PDU containing the same request-id. The SetRequest operation is atomic: either all of the variables are updated or none are. If the responding entity is able to set values for all of the variables listed in the incoming variable-bindings list, then the Response-PDU includes the variable-binding field, with a value supplied for each variable. If at least one of the variable values cannot be supplied, then no values are returned, and no values are updated. In the latter case, the error-status code indicates the reason for the failure, and the error-index field indicates the variable in the variable-bindings list that caused the failure.

The SNMPv2-Trap-PDU is generated and transmitted by a SNMPv2 entity acting in an agent role when an unusual event occurs. It is used to provide the management station with an asynchronous notification of some significant event. The variable-bindings list is used to contain the information associated with the trap message. Unlike the GetRequest, GetNextRequest, GetBulkRequest, SetRequest, and InformRequest PDUs, the SNMPv2-Trap-PDU does not elicit a response from the receiving entity; it is an unconfirmed message.

The InformRequest-PDU is sent by an SNMPv2 entity acting in a manager role, on behalf of an application, to another SNMPv2 entity acting in a manager role, to provide management information to an application using the latter entity. As with the SNMPv2-Trap-PDU, the variable-binding field is used to convey the associated information. The manager receiving an InformRequest acknowledges receipt with a Response-PDU.

For both the SNMPv2-Trap and the InformRequest, various conditions can be defined that indicate when the notification is generated; and the information to be sent is also specified.

## 19.3   ELECTRONIC MAIL—SMTP AND MIME

The most heavily used application in virtually any distributed system is electronic mail. From the start, the Simple Mail Transfer Protocol (SMTP) has been the workhorse of the TCP/IP protocol suite. However, SMTP has traditionally been limited to the delivery of simple text messages. In recent years, there has been a demand for the delivery mail to be able to contain various types of data, including voice, images, and video clips. To satisfy this requirement, a new electronic mail standard, which builds on SMTP, has been defined: the Multi-Purpose Internet Mail Extension (MIME). In this section, we first examine SMTP, then look at MIME.

### Simple Mail Transfer Protocol (SMTP)

SMTP is the standard protocol for transferring mail between hosts in the TCP/IP protocol suite; it is defined in RFC 821.

Although messages transferred by SMTP usually follow the format defined in RFC 822, described later, SMTP is not concerned with the format or content of messages themselves, with two exceptions. This concept is often expressed by saying that SMTP uses information written on the **envelope** of the mail (message header), but does not look at the **contents** (message body) of the envelope. The two exceptions are

1. SMTP standardizes the message character set as 7-bit ASCII.
2. SMTP adds log information to the start of the delivered message that indicates the path the message took.

### Basic Electronic Mail Operation[3]

Figure 19.9 illustrates the overall flow of mail in a typical system. Although much of this activity is outside the scope of SMTP, the figure illustrates the context within which SMTP typically operates.

---

[3] The discussion in this section is based partly on a description by Paul Mockapetris, published in [STAL90].

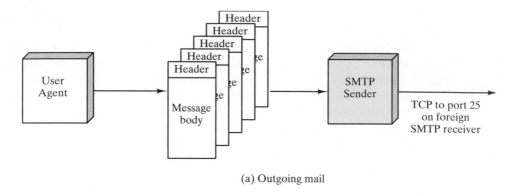

(a) Outgoing mail

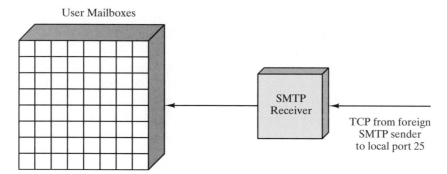

**FIGURE 19.9**   SMTP mail flow.

To begin, mail is created by a user-agent program in response to user input. Each created message consists of a header that includes the recipient's email address and other information, and a body containing the message to be sent. These messages are then queued in some fashion and provided as input to an SMTP Sender program, which is typically an always-present server program on the host.

Although the structure of the outgoing-mail queue will differ depending on the host's operating system, each queued message, conceptually, has two parts:

1. The message text, consisting of
   - The RFC 822 header: the message envelope, which includes an indication of the intended recipient or recipients.
   - The body of the message, composed by the user.
2. A list of mail destinations.

The list of mail destinations for the message is derived by the user agent from the 822 message header. In some cases, the destination, or destinations, are literally specified in the message header. In other cases, the user agent may need to expand mailing list names, remove duplicates, and replace mnemonic names with actual mailbox names. If any blind carbon copies (BCC) are indicated, the user agent needs to prepare messages that conform to this requirement. The basic idea is that the multiple formats and styles preferred by humans in the user interface are replaced by a standardized list suitable for the SMTP send program.

The **SMTP sender** takes messages from the outgoing mail queue and transmits them to the proper destination host via SMTP transactions over one or more TCP connections to port 25 on the target hosts. A host may have multiple SMTP senders active simultaneously if it has a large volume of outgoing mail, and it should also have the capability of creating SMTP receivers on demand so that mail from one host cannot delay mail from another.

Whenever the SMTP sender completes delivery of a particular message to one or more users on a specific host, it deletes the corresponding destinations from that message's destination list. When all destinations for a particular message are processed, the message is deleted from the queue. In processing a queue, the SMTP sender can perform a variety of optimization. If a particular message is sent to multiple users on a single host, the message text need be sent only once. If multiple messages are ready to send to the same host, the SMTP sender can open a TCP connection, transfer the multiple messages, and then close the connection, rather than opening and closing a connection for each message.

The SMTP sender must deal with a variety of errors. The destination host may be unreachable, out of operation, or the TCP connection may fail while mail is being transferred. The sender can requeue the mail for later delivery, but give up after some period rather then keep the message in the queue indefinitely. A common error is a faulty destination address, which can occur due to user-input error or because the intended destination user has a new address on a different host. The SMTP sender must either redirect the message, if possible, or return an error notification to the message's originator.

The **SMTP protocol** is used to transfer a message from the SMTP sender to the SMTP receiver over a TCP connection. SMTP attempts to provide reliable operation but does not guarantee to recover from lost messages. No end-to-end acknowledgment is returned to a message's originator that a message is successfully delivered to the message's recipient, and error indications are not guaranteed to be returned either. However, the SMTP-based mail system is generally considered reliable.

The **SMTP receiver** accepts each arriving message and either places it in the appropriate user mailbox or copies it to the local outgoing mail queue if forwarding is required. The SMTP receiver must be able to verify local mail destinations and deal with errors, including transmission errors and lack of disk file capacity.

The SMTP sender is responsible for a message up to the point where the SMTP receiver indicates that the transfer is complete; however, this simply means that the message has arrived at the SMTP receiver, not that the message has been delivered to and retrieved by the intended recipient. The SMTP receiver's error-handling responsibilities are generally limited to giving up on TCP connections that fail or are inactive for very long periods. Thus, the sender has most of the error-recovery responsibility. Errors during completion indication may cause duplicate, but not lost, messages.

In most cases, messages go directly from the mail originator's machine to the destination machine over a single TCP connection. However, mail will occasionally go through intermediate machines via an SMTP forwarding capability, in which case the message must traverse multiple TCP connections between source and destination; one way for this to happen is for the sender to specify a route to the destination in the form of a sequence of servers. A more common event is forwarding required because a user has moved.

It is important to note that the SMTP protocol is limited to the conversation that takes place between the SMTP sender and the SMTP receiver. SMTP's main function is the transfer of messages, although there are some ancillary functions dealing with mail destination verification and handling. The rest of the mail-handling apparatus depicted in Figure 19.9 is beyond the scope of SMTP and may differ from one system to another.

We now turn to a discussion of the main elements of SMTP.

### SMTP Overview

The operation of SMTP consists of a series of commands and responses exchanged between the SMTP sender and receiver. The initiative is with the SMTP sender, who establishes the TCP connection. Once the connection is established, the SMTP sender sends commands over the connection to the receiver. Each command generates exactly one reply from the SMTP receiver.

Table 19.5 lists the **SMTP commands**. Each command consists of a single line of text, beginning with a four-letter command code followed in some cases by an argument field. Most replies are a single line, although multiple-line replies are possible. The table indicates those commands that all receivers must be able to recognize. The other commands are optional and may be ignored by the receiver.

**TABLE 19.5**   SMTP commands

| Name | Command Form | Description |
|------|--------------|-------------|
| HELO | HELO <SP> <domain> <CRLF> | Send identification |
| MAIL | MAIL <SP> FROM:<reverse-path> <CRLF> | Identifies originator of mail |
| RCPT | RCPT <SP> TO:<forward-path> <CRLF> | Identifies recipient of mail |
| DATA | DATA <CRLF> | Transfer message text |
| RSET | RSET <CRLF> | Abort current mail transaction |
| NOOP | NOOP <CRLF> | No operation |
| QUIT | QUIT <CRLF> | Close TCP connection |
| SEND | SEND <SP> FROM:<reverse-path> <CRLF> | Send mail to terminal |
| SOML | SOML <SP> FROM:<reverse-path> <CRLF> | Send mail to terminal if possible; otherwise to mailbox |
| SAML | SAML <SP> FROM:<reverse-path> <CRLF> | Send mail to terminal and mailbox |
| VRFY | VRFY <SP> <string> <CRLF> | Confirm user name |
| EXPN | EXPN <SP> <string> <CRLF> | Return membership of mailing list |
| HELP | HELP [<SP> <string>] <CRLF> | Send system-specific documentation |
| TURN | TURN <CRLF> | Reverse role of sender and receiver |

<CRLF> = carriage return, line feed
<SP> = space
square brackets denote optional elements
shaded commands are optional in a conformant SMTP implementation

**TABLE 19.6**  SMTP replies

| Code | Description |
|------|-------------|
| | Positive Completion Reply |
| 211 | System status, or system help reply |
| 214 | Help message (Information on how to use the receiver or the meaning of a particular non-standard command; this reply is useful only to the human user) |
| 220 | <domain> Service ready |
| 221 | <domain> Service closing transmission channel |
| 250 | Requested mail action okay, completed |
| 251 | User not local; will forward to <forward-path> |
| | Positive Intermediate Reply |
| 354 | Start mail input; end with <CRLF>.<CRLF> |
| | Transient Negative Completion Reply |
| 421 | <domain> Service not available, losing transmission channel (This may be a reply to any command if the service knows it must shut down) |
| 450 | Requested mail action not taken: mailbox unavailable (e.g., mailbox busy) |
| 451 | Requested action aborted: local error in processing |
| 452 | Requested action not taken: insufficient system storage |
| | Permanent Negative Completion Reply |
| 500 | Syntax error, command unrecognized (This may include errors such as command line too long) |
| 501 | Syntax error in parameters or arguments |
| 502 | Command not implemented |
| 503 | Bad sequence of commands |
| 504 | Command parameter not implemented |
| 550 | Requested action not taken: mailbox unavailable (e.g., mailbox not found, no access) |
| 551 | User not local; please try <forward-path> |
| 552 | Requested mail action aborted: exceeded storage allocation |
| 553 | Requested action not taken: mailbox name not allowed (e.g., mailbox syntax incorrect) |
| 554 | Transaction failed |

**SMTP replies** are listed in Table 19.6. Each reply begins with a three-digit code and may be followed by additional information. The leading digit indicates the category of the reply:

- **Positive Completion reply.** The requested action has been successfully completed. A new request may be initiated.
- **Positive Intermediate reply.** The command has been accepted, but the requested action is being held in abeyance, pending receipt of further information. The sender-SMTP should send another command specifying this information. This reply is used in command sequence groups.
- **Transient Negative Completion reply.** The command was not accepted, and the requested action did not occur. However, the error condition is temporary and the action may be requested again.

- **Permanent Negative Completion reply.** The command was not accepted and the requested action did not occur.

Basic SMTP operation occurs in three phases: connection setup, exchange of one or more command-response pairs, and connection termination. We examine each phase in turn.

## Connection Setup

An SMTP sender will attempt to set up a TCP connection with a target host when it has one or more mail messages to deliver to that host. The sequence is quite simple:

1. The sender opens a TCP connection with the receiver.
2. Once the connection is established, the receiver identifies itself with "220 Service Ready".
3. The sender identifies itself with the HELO command.
4. The receiver accepts the sender's identification with "250 OK".

If the mail service on the destination is unavailable, the destination host returns a "421 Service Not Available" reply in step 2, and the process is terminated.

## Mail Transfer

Once a connection has been established, the SMTP sender may send one or more messages to the SMTP receiver. There are three logical phases to the transfer of a message:

1. A MAIL command identifies the originator of the message.
2. One or more RCPT commands identify the recipients for this message.
3. A DATA command transfers the message text.

The **MAIL command** gives the reverse-path, which can be used to report errors. If the receiver is prepared to accept messages from this originator, it returns a "250 OK" reply. Otherwise, the receiver returns a reply indicating failure to execute the command (codes 451, 452, 552), or an error in the command (codes 421, 500, 501).

The **RCPT command** identifies an individual recipient of the mail data; multiple recipients are specified by multiple use of this command. A separate reply is returned for each RCPT command, with one of the following possibilities:

1. The receiver accepts the destination with a 250 reply; this indicates that the designated mailbox is on the receiver's system.
2. The destination will require forwarding, and the receiver will forward (251).
3. The destination requires forwarding, but the receiver will not forward; the sender must resend to the forwarding address (551).
4. A mailbox does not exist for this recipient at this host (550).

5. The destination is rejected due to some other failure to execute (codes 450, 451, 452, 552, 553), or an error in the command (codes 421, 500, 501, 503).

The advantage of using a separate RCPT phase is that the sender will not send the message until it is assured that the receiver is prepared to receive the message for at least one recipient, thereby avoiding the overhead of sending an entire message only to learn that the destination is unknown. Once the SMTP receiver has agreed to receive the mail message for at least one recipient, the SMTP sender uses the **DATA command** to initiate the transfer of the message. If the SMTP receiver is still prepared to receive the message, it returns a 354 message; otherwise, the receiver returns a reply indicating failure to execute the command (codes 451, 554), or an error in the command (codes 421, 500, 501, 503). If the 354 reply is returned, the SMTP sender proceeds to send the message over the TCP connection as a sequence of ASCII lines. The end of the message is indicated by a line containing only a period. The SMTP receiver responds with a "250 OK" reply if the message is accepted, or with the appropriate error code (451, 452, 552, 554).

An example, taken from RFC 821, illustrates the process:

S: MAIL FROM:<Smith@Alpha.ARPA>
R: 250 OK

S: RCPT TO:<Jones@Beta.ARPA>
R: 250 OK

S: RCPT TO:<Green@Beta.ARPA>
R: 550 No such user here

S: RCPT TO:<Brown@Beta.ARPA>
R: 250 OK

S: DATA
R: 354 Start mail input; end with <CRLF>.<CRLF>
S: Blah blah blah...
S: ...etc. etc. etc.
S: <CRLF>.<CRLF>
R: 250 OK

The SMTP sender is transmitting mail that originates with the user Smith@Alpha.ARPA. The message is addressed to three users on machine Beta.ARPA, namely, Jones, Green, and Brown. The SMTP receiver indicates that it has mailboxes for Jones and Brown but does not have information on Green. Because at least one of the intended recipients has been verified, the sender proceeds to send the text message.

## Connection Closing

The SMTP sender closes the connection in two steps. First, the sender sends a QUIT command and waits for a reply. The second step is to initiate a TCP close operation for the TCP connection. The receiver initiates its TCP close after sending its reply to the QUIT command.

## RFC 822

RFC 822 defines a format for text messages that are sent using electronic mail. The SMTP standard adopts RFC 822 as the format for use in constructing messages for transmission via SMTP. In the RFC 822 context, messages are viewed as having an envelope and contents. The envelope contains whatever information is needed to accomplish transmission and delivery. The contents compose the object to be delivered to the recipient. The RFC 822 standard applies only to the contents. However, the content standard includes a set of header fields that may be used by the mail system to create the envelope, and the standard is intended to facilitate the acquisition of such information by programs.

An RFC 822 message consists of a sequence of lines of text, and uses a general "memo" framework. That is, a message consists of some number of header lines, which follow a rigid format, followed by a body portion consisting of arbitrary text.

A header line usually consists of a keyword, followed by a colon, followed by the keyword's arguments; the format allows a long line to be broken up into several lines. The most frequently used keywords are From, To, Subject, and Date. Here is an example message:

> Date: Tue, 16 Jan 1996 10:37:17 (EST)
> From: "William Stallings" <ws@host.com>
> Subject: The Syntax in RFC 822
> To: Smith@Other-host.com
> Cc: Jones@Yet-Another-Host.com

> Hello. This section begins the actual message body, which is
> delimited from the message heading by a blank line.

Another field that is commonly found in RFC 822 headers is Message-ID. This field contains a unique identifier associated with this message.

### Multipurpose Internet Mail Extensions (MIME)

MIME is an extension to the RFC 822 framework that is intended to address some of the problems and limitations of the use of SMTP and RFC 822 for electronic mail. [MURP95] lists the following limitations of the SMTP/822 scheme:

1. SMTP cannot transmit executable files or other binary objects. A number of schemes are in use for converting binary files into a text form that can be used by SMTP mail systems, including the popular UNIX UUencode/UUdecode scheme. However, none of these is a standard or even a de facto standard.
2. SMTP cannot transmit text data that includes national language characters, as these are represented by 8-bit codes with values of 128 decimal or higher, and SMTP is limited to 7-bit ASCII.
3. SMTP servers may reject mail message over a certain size.
4. SMTP gateways that translate between ASCII and the character code EBCDIC do not use a consistent set of mappings, resulting in translation problems.

5. SMTP gateways to X.400 electronic mail networks cannot handle non-textual data included in X.400 messages.
6. Some SMTP implementations do not adhere completely to the SMTP standards defined in RFC 821. Common problems include the following:
   - Deletion, addition, or reording of carriage return and linefeed.
   - Truncating or wrapping lines longer than 76 characters.
   - Removal of trailing white space (tab and space characters).
   - Padding of lines in a message to the same length.
   - Conversion of tab characters into multiple-space characters.

MIME is intended to resolve these problems in a manner that is compatible with existing RFC 822 implementations. The specification is provided in RFC 1521 and 1522.

## Overview

The MIME specification includes the following elements:

1. Five new message header fields are defined, which may be included in an RFC 822 header. These fields provide information about the body of the message.
2. A number of content formats are defined, thus standardizing representations that support multimedia electronic mail.
3. Transfer encodings are defined that enable the conversion of any content format into a form that is protected from alteration by the mail system.

In this subsection, we introduce the five message header fields. The next two subsections address content formats and transfer encodings.

The five header fields defined in MIME are

- **MIME-version.** Must have the parameter value 1.0. This field indicates that the message conforms to RFC 1521 and 1522.
- **Content-type.** Describes the data contained in the body with sufficient detail that the receiving user agent can pick an appropriate agent or mechanism to represent the data to the user or otherwise handle the data in an appropriate manner.
- **Content-transfer-encoding.** Indicates the type of transformation that has been used to represent the body of the message in a way that is acceptable for mail transport.
- **Content-id.** Used to uniquely identify MIME entities in multiple contexts.
- **Content-description.** A plain-text description of the object with the body; this is useful when the object is not readable (e.g., audio data).

Any or all of these fields may appear in a normal RFC 822 header. A compliant implementation must support the MIME-Version, Content-Type, and Content-Transfer-Encoding fields; the Content-ID and Content-Description fields are optional and may be ignored by the recipient implementation.

### MIME Content Types

The bulk of the MIME specification is concerned with the definition of a variety of content types; this reflects the need to provide standardized ways of dealing with a wide variety of information representations in a multimedia environment.

Table 19.7 lists the content types specified in RFC 1521. There are seven different major types of content and a total of 14 subtypes. In general, a content type declares the general type of data, and the subtype specifies a particular format for that type of data.

For the *text type* of body, no special software is required to get the full meaning of the text, aside from support of the indicated character set. RFC 1521 defines only one subtype: plain text, which is simply a string of ASCII characters or ISO 8859 characters. An earlier version of the MIME specification included a *richtext* subtype, that allows greater formatting flexibility. It is expected that this subtype will reappear in a later RFC.

The *multipart type* indicates that the body contains multiple, independent parts. The Content-Type header field includes a parameter, called a boundary, that defines the delimiter between body parts. This boundary should not appear in any parts of the message. Each boundary starts on a new line and consists of two hyphens followed by the boundary value. The final boundary, which indicates the

**TABLE 19.7** MIME content types.

| Type | Subtype | Description |
|------|---------|-------------|
| Text | Plain | Unformatted text; may be ASCII or ISO 8859. |
| Multipart | Mixed | The different parts are independent but are to be transmitted together. They should be presented to the receiver in the order that they appear in the mail message. |
| | Parallel | Differs from Mixed only in that no order is defined for delivering the parts to the receiver. |
| | Alternative | The different parts are alternative versions of the same information. They are ordered in increasing faithfulness to the original and the recipient's mail system should display the "best" version to the user. |
| | Digest | Similar to Mixed, but the default type/subtype of each part is message/rfc822 |
| Message | rfc822 | The body is itself an encapsulated message that conforms to RFC 822. |
| | Partial | Used to allow fragmentation of large mail items, in a way that is transparent to the recipient. |
| | External-body | Contains a pointer to an object that exists elsewhere. |
| Image | jpeg | The image is in JPEG format, JFIF encoding. |
| | gif | The image is in GIF format. |
| Video | mpeg | MPEG format. |
| Audio | Basic | Single-channel 8-bit ISDN mu-law encoding at a sample rate of 8 kHz. |
| Application | PostScript | Adobe Postscript |
| | octet-stream | General binary data consisting of 8-bit bytes. |

end of the last part, also has a suffix of two hyphens. Within each part, there may be an optional, ordinary MIME header.

Here is a simple example of a multipart message, containing two parts, both consisting of simple text (taken from RFC 1521):

From: Nathaniel Borenstein <nsb@bellcore.com>
To: Ned Freed <ned@innosoft.com>
Subject: Sample message
MIME-Version: 1.0
Content-type: multipart/mixed; boundary="simple boundary"

This is the preamble. It is to be ignored, though it is a handy place for mail composers to include an explanatory note to non–MIME-conformant readers.
--simple boundary

This is implicitly-typed plain ASCII text. It does NOT end with a linebreak.
--simple boundary
Content-type: text/plain; charset=us-ascii

This is explicitly-typed plain ASCII text. It DOES end with a linebreak.

--simple boundary--
This is the epilogue. It is also to be ignored.

There are four subtypes of the multipart type, all of which have the same over-all syntax. The *multipart/mixed subtype* is used when there are multiple independent body parts that need to be bundled in a particular order. For the *multipart/parallel subtype*, the order of the parts is not significant. If the recipient's system is appropriate, the multiple parts can be presented in parallel. For example, a picture or text part could be accompanied by a voice commentary that is played while the picture or text is displayed.

For the *multipart/alternative subtype*, the various parts are different representations of the same information. The following is an example:

From: Nathaniel Borenstein <nsb@bellcore.com>
To: Ned Freed <ned@innosoft.com>
Subject: Formatted text mail
MIME-Version: 1.0
Content-Type: multipart/alternative; boundary=boundary42

--boundary42

Content-Type: text/plain; charset=us-ascii

   ...plain-text version of message goes here....
--boundary42
Content-Type: text/richtext

   .... RFC 1341 richtext version of same message goes here ...
--boundary42--

In this subtype, the body parts are ordered in terms of increasing preference. For this example, if the recipient system is capable of displaying the message in the richtext format, this is done; otherwise, the plain-text format is used.

The *multipart/digest subtype* is used when each of the body parts is interpreted as an RFC 822 message with headers. This subtype enables the construction of a message whose parts are individual messages. For example, the moderator of a group might collect email messages from participants, bundle these messages, and send them out in one encapsulating MIME message.

The *message type* provides a number of important capabilities in MIME. The *message/rfc822 subtype* indicates that the body is an entire message, including header and body. Despite the name of this subtype, the encapsulated message may be not only a simple RFC 822 message, but any MIME message.

The *message/partial subtype* enables fragmentation of a large message into a number of parts, which must be reassembled at the destination. For this = subtype, three parameters are specified in the Content-Type: Message/Partial field:

- **Id.** A value that is common to each fragment of the same message, so that the fragments can be identified at the recipient for reassembly, but which is unique across different messages.
- **Number.** A sequence number that indicates the position of this fragment in the original message. The first fragment is numbered 1, the second 2, and so on.
- **Total.** The total number of parts. The last fragment is identified by having the same value for the number and total parameters.

The rules for fragmenting a message are as follows:

1. Divide the body of the original message into $N$ parts.
2. The first fragment begins with a header that has no Content-Transfer-Encoding field; the default of 7-bit ASCII is used. The header has a Content-Type of Message/Partial, with a unique id, number = 1, and total = $N$. The remaining fields of the header are copied from the original message header.
3. The body of the first fragment is an encapsulated MIME message that has the Content-Type and Content-Transfer-Encoding of the original message body. The Message-ID field of the encapsulated header must differ from that of the enclosing header.
4. The remaining fragments include header fields from the outer header of the first fragment. The Message-ID field must be unique. The Content-Type field has the same id and total values as the outer header of the first fragment, as well as the appropriate number value. There is no Content-Transfer-Encoding field.

The rules for reassembly are as follows:

1. The fields for the header of the reassembled message are taken from the outer header of the first fragment, with the following exceptions. The Content-Type,

Content-Transfer-Encoding, and Message-ID fields are taken from the inner header of the first fragment.

2. All of the header fields from the second and any subsequent fragments are ignored.

3. The body parts of the messages, not including the inner header of the first part, are reassembled in order to form the body of the reassembled message.

Figure 19.10 illustrates a message that is transferred in two fragments.

The *message/external-body subtype* indicates that the actual data to be conveyed in this message are not contained in the body. Instead, the body contains the information needed to access the data. As with the other message types, the message/external-body subtype has an outer header and an encapsulated message with its own header. The only necessary field in the outer header is the Content-Type field, which identifies this as a message/external-body subtype. The inner header is the message header for the encapsulated message.

The Content-Type field in the outer header must include an access-type parameter, which has one of the following values:

- **FTP.** The message body is accessible as a file using the file transfer protocol (FTP). For this access type, the following additional parameters are mandatory: *name*, indicating the name of the file; and *site*, indicating the domain name of the host where the file resides. Optional parameters are *directory*, the directory in which the file is located; and *mode*, which indicates how FTP

```
From: Bill@host.com
To: joe@otherhost.com
Subject: Audio mail
Message-ID: <id1@host.com>
MIME-Version: 1.0
Content-type: message/partial;
  id="ABC@host.com"; number=1; total=2
Message-ID: <anotherid@foo.com>
MIME-Version: 1.0
Content-type: audio/basic
Content-transfer-encoding: base64

... first half of encoded audio data goes here ...
```

**(a) First of Two Fragments**

```
From: Bill@host.com
To: joe@otherhost.com
Subject: Audio mail
MIME-Version: 1.0
Message-ID: <id2@host.com>
Content-type: message/partial;
  id="ABC@host.com"; number=2; total=2

... second half of encoded audio data goes here ...
```

**(b) Second of Two Fragments**

```
From: Bill@host.com
To: joe@otherhost.com
Subject: Audio mail
Message-ID: <anotherid@foo.com>
MIME-Version: 1.0
Content-type: audio/basic
Content-transfer-encoding: base64
  ... first half of encoded audio data goes here ...
  ... second half of encoded audio data goes here ...
```

**(c) Reassembled Message**

FIGURE 19.10   Message fragmentation and reassembly.

should retrieve the file (e.g., ASCII, image). Before the file transfer can take place, the user will need to provide a user id and password; these are not transmitted with the message for security reasons.

- **TFPT.** The message body is accessible as a file using the trivial file transfer protocol (TFTP). The same parameters as for FTP are used, and the user id and password must also be supplied.
- **Anon-FTP.** Identical to FTP, except that the user is not asked to supply a user id and password. The parameter name supplies the name of the file.
- **Local-File.** The message body is accessible as a file on the recipient's machine.
- **AFS**. The message body is accessible as a file via the global AFS (Andrew File System). The parameter name supplies the name of the file.
- **Mail-Server.** The message body is accessible by sending an email message to a mail server. A server parameter must be included that gives the email address of the server. The body of the original message, known as the phantom body, should contain the exact command to be sent to the mail server.

The *image type* indicates that the body contains a displayable image. The subtype, jpeg or gif, specifies the image format. In the future, more subtypes will be added to this list.

The *video type* indicates that the body contains a time-varying picture image, possibly with color and coordinated sound. The only subtype so far specified is mpeg.

The *audio type* indicates that the body contains audio data. The only subtype, basic, conforms to an ISDN service known as "64-kbps, 8-kHz Structured, Usable for Speech Information," with a digitized speech algorithm referred to as $\mu$-law PCM (pulse-code modulation). This general type is the typical way of transmitting speech signals over a digital network. The term $\mu$-law refers to the specific encoding technique; it is the standard technique used in North America and Japan. A competing system, known as A-law, is standard in Europe.

The *application type* refers to other kinds of data, typically either uninterpreted binary data or information to be processed by a mail-based application. The *application/octet-stream subtype* indicates general binary data in a sequence of octets. RFC 1521 recommends that the receiving implementation should offer to put the data in a file or use it as input to a program.

The *application/postscript subtype* indicates the use of Adobe Postscript.

### MIME Transfer Encodings

The other major component of the MIME specification, in addition to content-type specification, is a definition of transfer encodings for message bodies. The objective is to provide reliable delivery across the largest range of environments.

The MIME standard defines two methods of encoding data. The Content-Transfer-Encoding field can actually take on six values, as listed in Table 19.8. However, three of these values (7bit, 8bit, and binary) indicate that no encoding has been done, but they do provide some information about the nature of the data. For SMTP transfer, it is safe to use the 7bit form. The 8bit and binary forms may be

**TABLE 19.8**   MIME transfer encodings.

| | |
|---|---|
| 7bit | The data are all represented by short lines of ASCII characters. |
| 8bit | The lines are short, but there may be non-ASCII characters (octets with the high-order bit set). |
| binary | Not only may non-ASCII characters be present but the lines are not necessarily short enough for SMTP transport. |
| quoted-printable | Encodes the data in such a way that if the data being encoded are mostly ASCII text, the encoded form of the data remains largely recognizable by humans. |
| base64 | Encodes data by mapping 6-bit blocks of input to 8-bit blocks of output, all of which are printable ASCII characters. |
| x-token | A named non-standard encoding. |

usable in other mail-transport contexts. Another Content-Transfer-Encoding value is *x*-token, which indicates that some other encoding scheme is used, for which a name is to be supplied; this could be a vendor-specific or application-specific scheme. The two actual encoding schemes defined are quoted-printable and base64. Two schemes are defined to provide a choice between a transfer technique that is essentially human-readable and one that is safe for all types of data in a way that is reasonably compact.

The *quoted-printable* transfer encoding is useful when the data consist largely of octets that correspond to printable ASCII characters (see Table 2.1). In essence, it represents non-safe characters by the hexadecimal representation of their code and introduces reversible (soft) line breaks to limit message lines to 76 characters. The encoding rules are as follows:

1. General 8-bit representation: This rule is to be used when none of the other rules apply. Any character is represented by an equal sign, followed by a two-digit hexadecimal representation of the octet's value. For example, the ASCII form-feed, which has an 8-bit value of decimal 12, is represented by "=0C".

2. Literal representation: Any character in the range decimal 33 ("!") through decimal 126 ("~"), except decimal 61, ("=") is represented as that ASCII character.

3. White space: Octets with the values 9 and 32 may be represented as ASCII tab and space characters, respectively, except at the end of a line. Any white space (tab or blank) at the end of a line must be represented by rule 1. On decoding, any trailing white space on a line is deleted; this eliminates any white space added by intermediate transport agents.

4. Line breaks: Any line break, regardless of its initial representation, is represented by the RFC 822 line break, which is a carriage-return/line-feed combination.

5. Soft line breaks: If an encoded line would be longer than 76 characters (excluding <CRLF>), a soft line break must be inserted at or before character position 75. A soft line break consists of the hexadecimal sequence 3D0D0A, which is the ASCII code for an equal sign followed by carriage return line feed.

The *base64 transfer encoding*, also known as radix-64 encoding, is a common one for encoding arbitrary binary data in such a way as to be invulnerable to the processing by mail-transport programs. For example, both PGP (Pretty Good Privacy) and PEM (Privacy Enhanced Mail) secure electronic-mail schemes make use of base64; this technique maps arbitrary binary input into printable character output. The form of encoding has the following relevant characteristics:

1. The range of the function is a character set that is universally representable at all sites, not a specific binary encoding of that character set. Thus, the characters themselves can be encoded into whatever form is needed by a specific system. For example, the character "E" is represented in an ASCII-based system as hexadecimal 45 and in an EBCDIC-based system as hexadecimal C5.

2. The character set consists of 65 printable characters, one of which is used for padding. With $2^6 = 64$ available characters, each character can be used to represent 6 bits of input.

3. No control characters are included in the set. Thus, a message encoded in radix 64 can traverse mail-handling systems that scan the data stream for control characters.

4. The hyphen character ("-") is not used. This character has significance in the RFC 822 format and should therefore be avoided.

Table 19.9 shows the mapping of 6-bit input values to characters. The character set consists of the alphanumeric characters plus "+" and "/". The "=" character is used as the padding character.

Figure 19.11 illustrates the simple mapping scheme. Binary input is processed in blocks of 3 octets, or 24 bits. Each set of 6 bits in the 24-bit block is mapped into

TABLE 19.9   Radix-64 encoding.

| 6-bit value | character encoding | 6-bit value | character encoding | 6-bit value | character encoding | 6-bit value | character encoding |
|---|---|---|---|---|---|---|---|
| 0 | A | 16 | Q | 32 | g | 48 | w |
| 1 | B | 17 | R | 33 | h | 49 | x |
| 2 | C | 18 | S | 34 | i | 50 | y |
| 3 | D | 19 | T | 35 | j | 51 | z |
| 4 | E | 20 | U | 36 | k | 52 | 0 |
| 5 | F | 21 | V | 37 | l | 53 | 1 |
| 6 | G | 22 | W | 38 | m | 54 | 2 |
| 7 | H | 23 | X | 39 | n | 55 | 3 |
| 8 | I | 24 | Y | 40 | o | 56 | 4 |
| 9 | J | 25 | Z | 41 | p | 57 | 5 |
| 1 | K | 26 | a | 42 | q | 58 | 6 |
| 11 | L | 27 | b | 42 | r | 59 | 7 |
| 12 | M | 28 | c | 44 | d | 60 | 8 |
| 13 | N | 29 | d | 45 | t | 61 | 9 |
| 14 | O | 30 | e | 46 | u | 62 | + |
| 15 | P | 31 | f | 47 | v | 63 | / |
| | | | | | | (pad) | = |

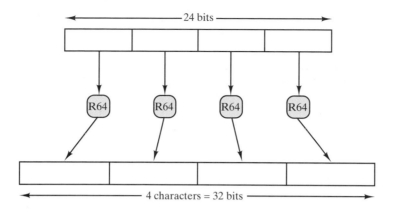

**FIGURE 19.11**  Printable encoding of binary data into radix-64 format.

a character. In the figure, the characters are shown encoded as 8-bit quantities. In this typical case, each 24-bit input is expanded to 32 bits of output.

One important feature of this mapping is that the least significant 6 bits of the representation of these 65 characters is the same in all commonly used character sets. For example, as was mentioned, "E" in 7-bit ASCII is 0100 0101 and in 8-bit EBCDIC is 1100 0101. The rightmost 6 bits are the same in both cases. Thus, the reverse mapping from radix 64 to binary is simply a matter of extracting the least significant 6 bits of each character.

For example, the sequence "H52Q" in ASCII is

$$1001000\ 0110101\ 0110010\ 1010001$$

The extracted 6-bit values are 8, 53, 50, 17:

$$001000\ 110101\ 110010\ 010001$$

The resulting 24-bit value can be expressed in hexadecimal as 235C91.

**A Multipart Example**

Figure 19.12, taken from RFC 1521, is the outline of a complex multipart message. The message has five parts to be displayed serially: two introductory plain text parts, an embedded multipart message, a richtext part, and a closing encapsulated text message in a non-ASCII character set. The embedded multipart message has two parts to be displayed in parallel: a picture and an audio fragment.

## 19.4  UNIFORM RESOURCE LOCATORS (URL) AND UNIVERSAL RESOURCE IDENTIFIERS (URI)

Before turning to a description of the Hypertext Transfer Protocol (HTTP), we need to examine two important concepts: the Uniform Resource Locator (URL) and the Universal Resource Identifier (URI).

MIME-Version: 1.0
From: Nathaniel Borenstein <nsb@bellcore.com>
To: Ned Freed <ned@innosoft.com>
Subject: A multipart example
Content-Type: multipart/mixed;
  boundary=unique-boundary-1

This is the preamble area of a multipart message. Mail readers that understand multipart format should ignore this preamble. If you are reading this text, you might want to consider changing to a mail reader that understands how to properly display multipart messages. --unique-boundary-1

   ... Some text appears here ...
[Note that the preceding blank line means no header fields were given and this is text, with charset US ASCII. It could have been done with explicit typing as in the next part.]

--unique-boundary-1
Content-type: text/plain; charset=US-ASCII

This could have been part of the previous part, but illustrates explicit versus implicit typing of body parts.

--unique-boundary-1
Content-Type: multipart/parallel;
  boundary=unique-boundary-2

--unique-boundary-2
Content-Type: audio/basic
Content-Transfer-Encoding: base64

   ... base64-encoded 8000 Hz single-channel
      mu-law-format audio data goes here ...

--unique-boundary-2
Content-Type: image/gif
Content-Transfer-Encoding: base64

   ... base64-encoded image data goes here ...

--unique-boundary-2—

--unique-boundary-1
Content-type: text/richtext

This is <>bold><italic>richtext<>/italic></bold><smaller>as defined in RFC
1341</smaller><nl><snl>Isn't it <bigger><bigger>cool?</bigger></bigger>

--unique-boundary-1
Content-Type: message/rfc822

From: (mailbox in US-ASCII)
To: (address in US-ASCII)
Subject: (subject in US-ASCII)
Content-Type: Text/plain; charset=ISO-8859-1
Content-Transfer-Encoding: Quoted-printable

   ... Additional text in ISO-8859-1 goes here ...

--unique-boundary-1--

**FIGURE 19.12**   Example MIME message structure.

## Uniform Resource Locator

A key concept in the operation of the World-Wide Web (WWW) is that of Uniform Resource Locator (URL). In the defining documents (RFC 1738, 1808), the URL is characterized as follows:

> A Uniform Resource Locator (URL) is a compact representation of the location and access method for a resource available via the Internet. URLs are used to locate resources by providing an abstract identification of the resource location. Having located a resource, a system may perform a variety of operations on the resource, as might be characterized by such words as access, update, replace, and find attributes. In general, only the access method needs to be specified for any URL scheme.

A *resource* is any object that can be accessed by the Internet, and includes file directories, files, documents, images, audio or video clips, and any other data that may be stored on an Internet-connected computer. The term *resource* in this context also includes electronic mail addresses, the results of a finger or archie command, USENET newsgroups, and individual messages in a USENET newsgroup.

With the exception of certain dynamic URLs, such as the email address, we can think of a URL as a networked extension of a filename. The URL provides a pointer to any object that is accessible on any machine connected to the Internet. Furthermore, because different objects are accessible in different ways (e.g., via Web, FTP, Gopher, etc., the URL also indicates the access method that must be used to retrieve the object.

The general form of a URL is as follows:

<scheme>:<scheme-specific-part>

The URL consists of the name of the access scheme being used, followed by a colon, and then by an identifier of a resource whose format is specific to the scheme being used.

Although the scheme-specific formats differ, they have a number of points in common, as we will see. In particular, many of the access schemes support the use of hierarchical structures, similar to the hierarchical directory and file structures common to file systems such as UNIX. For the URL, the components of the hierarchy are separated by a "/", similar to the UNIX approach.

RFC 1738 defines URL formats for the following access schemes:

| | |
|---|---|
| ftp | File Transfer Protocol |
| http | Hypertext Transfer Protocol |
| gopher | The Gopher Protocol |
| mailto | Electronic mail address |
| news | USENET news |
| nntp | USENET news using NNTP access |
| telnet | Reference to interactive sessions |
| wais | Wide-Area Information Servers |
| file | Host-specific file names |
| prospero | Prospero Directory Service |

Table 19.10 shows the general format of each of these schemes.

**TABLE 19.10** Uniform resource locator (URL) schemes.

| Scheme | Default Port | Syntax |
|---|---|---|
| ftp | 21 | ftp://<user>:<password>@<host>:<port>/<cwd1>/<cwd2>/.../<cwdN>/<name>; type=<typecode> |
| http | 80 | http://<host>:<port>/<path>?<searchpart> |
| gopher | 70 | gopher://<host>:<port>/<selector> or |
| | | gopher://<host>:<port>/<selector>%09<search> or |
| | | gopher://<host>:<port>/<selector>%09<search>%09<gopher+_string> or |
| mailto | — | mailto:<rfc822-addr-spec> |
| news | — | news:<newsgroup-name> or |
| | | news:<message-id> |
| nntp | 119 | nntp://<host>:<port>/<newsgroup-name>/<article-number> |
| telnet | 23 | telnet://<user>:<password>@<host>:<port> |
| wais | 210 | wais://<host>:<port>/<database> or |
| | | wais://<host>:<port>/<database>?<search> or |
| | | wais://<host>:<port>/<database>/<wtype>/<wpath> or |
| file | — | file://<host>/<path> |
| prospero | 1525 | prospero://<host>:<port>/<hsoname>;<field>=<value> |

### File Transfer Protocol (FTP)

The FTP URL scheme designates files and directories accessible using the FTP protocol. In its simplest form, an FTP URL has the following format:

> ftp://<host>/<directoryname>/<filename>

where <host> is the name on an Internet host or a dotted decimal IP address of the host (e.g., acm.org).

As an example, consider the document named Index.README on the anonymous FTP server rtfm.mit.edu in directory pub. The URL for this file is

> ftp://rtfm.mit.edu/pub/Index.README

The URL for the directory is

> ftp://rtfm.mit.edu/pub/

And the URL for the ftp site itself is simply

> ftp://rtfm.mit.edu

The most general form of the ftp URL is

> ftp://<user>:<password>@<host>:<port>/<cwd1>/<cwd2>/.../<cwdN>/
> <name>;type=<typecode>

Some FTP sites require that the user provide a user id and a password; these are provided in the form <user>:<password> and the @ symbol, preceding the <host> value. The next new item in the format is <port>. Most access schemes, including ftp, designate protocols that have a default port number; for ftp, it is 21. Another port number may be optionally used and, if so, is supplied by a colon and the port number following the <host> value.

After the specification of the host, with an optional user-ID and password, and a port number, a slash indicates the beginning of the file designation. Each of the <cwd> elements is a directory name, or, more precisely, an argument to a CWD (change working directory) command, such as is used in UNIX. The <name> value, if present, is the name of a file. Finally, the <typecode> value can be used to designate a particular type of file; otherwise, the type defaults in an implementation-dependent way.

## Hypertext Transfer Protocol (HTTP)

The HTTP URL scheme designates accessible Internet resources, using the HTTP protocol, and, in particular, designates web sites. In its simplest form, an HTTP URL has the following format:

> http://<host>:<port>/<path>

The default port number for HTTP is 80. If the <path> portion is omitted, then the URL points to the top level resource, such as a home page. For example,

> http://www.shore.net

points to the home page of the Internet site "www.shore.net." A more complex path points to hierarchically subordinate pages. For example,

> http://www.shore.net/~ws

points to the author's home page on the shore.net computer. An HTTP URL can also point to a document available via the web, such as

> http://www.w3.org/pub/WWW/Addressing/rfc1738.txt

This is the URL for RFC 1738, available through the web site of the WWW consortium.

The ?<searchpart> portion of an HTTP URL is optional. When present, it designates a query that will be invoked when the resource is accessed.

## The Gopher Protocol

The FTP URL scheme designates files and directories accessible using the FTP protocol. A Gopher URL takes the form:

> gopher://<host>:<port>/<gopher-path>

where <gopher-path> is one of the following:

> <gophertype><selector>
> <gophertype><selector>%09<search>
> <gophertype><selector>%09<search>%09<gopher+_string>

The default port is 70. The first form selects a Gopher site, or a directory or file at the Gopher site. For example,

> gopher://mitdir.mit.edu:105/2

Selects the Gopher-accessible telephone directory at M.I.T. This directory is searchable by keyword. A user who accesses this directory can then interactively enter a key word to initiate a search. Alternatively, this can be part of the URL; for example

> gopher://mitdir.mit.edu:105/2?chomsky

will access the directory and search it for the word "chomsky."

A URL can also be used to access a more-general Gopher search engine and initiate a search by supplying the string %09<search>, where %09 refers to the tab. URLs for Gopher+ have a second tab and a Gopher+ string. Gopher+ is a set of extensions to the original Gopher protocol.

### Electronic Mail Address

The mailto URL scheme designates the Internet mailing address of an individual or service. When invoked by a web client, it triggers the creation of an email message to be sent by Internet electronic mail. For example,

> mailto:webmaster@w3.org

designates the email address of the webmaster for the WWW consortium web site.

### USENET News

The news URL scheme designates either a news group or the individual articles of USENET news. For example,

> news:comp.dcom.cell-relay

designates the ATM newsgroup, and

> news:4bs62n$10le@usenetw1.news.prodigy.com

refers to a message in that newsgroup

### USENET News Using NNTP Access

The NNTP URL scheme is an alternative way of designating news articles, useful for specifying articles from NNTP servers. The general form is

> nntp://<host>:<port>/<newsgroup-name>/<article-number>

This technique designates a particular location for the news server, whereas the news:// scheme does not. Because most NNTP servers are configured to allow access only from local clients, the news form of the URL is preferred.

### Reference to Interactive Sessions (TELNET)

The TELNET URL scheme designates interactive services accessible by the TELNET protocol. Thus, this URL does not designate a data object but a service.

### Wide Area Information Servers (WAIS)

The WAIS URL scheme designates WAIS databases, searches, or individual documents available from a WAIS database. A WAIS takes one of the following forms:

wais://<host>:<port>/<database>
wais://<host>:<port>/<database>?<search>
wais://<host>:<port>/<database>/<wtype>/<wpath>

The first form designates a WAIS database. The second form designates a search submitted to a database. The third form designates a particular document within a database, where <wtype> is the WAIS designation of the document type.

### Host-Specific File Names

The file URL scheme differs from other URL schemes in that it does not designate an Internet-accessible object or service. It provides a way of uniquely identifying a directory or file on an Internet-addressable host, but does not designate an access protocol. Thus, it has limited utility in a network context.

### Prospero Directory Service

The Prospero URL scheme designates resources that are accessed via the Prospero Directory Service. A prospero URL takes the form

prospero://<host>:<port>/<hsoname>;<field>=<value>

where <hsoname> is the host-specific object name in the Prospero protocol. The optional clause <field>=<value> serves to identify a particular target entry.

## Universal Resource Identifier

Universal Resource Identifier (URI) is a term for a generic WWW identifier. The URI specification (RFC 1630) defines a syntax for encoding arbitrary naming or addressing schemes, and provides a list of such schemes. The concept of a URI, and in particular its details, are still evolving. The URL is a type of URI, in which an access protocol is designated and a specific Internet address is provided.

The potential advantage of the URI is that it decouples the name of a resource from its location and even from its access method. With the URL, a specific instance of a resource at a specific location is designated. If there are multiple instances, and that specific instance is unavailable at the time of a request, then a requester must determine an alternative URL and try that. In principle, with a URI, this process could be automated. In practice, documents such as the HTTP specification refer to the use of URIs, but are currently implemented using only URLs.

## 19.5  HYPERTEXT TRANSFER PROTOCOL (HTTP)

The Hypertext Transfer Protocol (HTTP) is the foundation protocol of the world-wide web (WWW) and can be used in any client-server application involving hypertext. The name is somewhat misleading in that HTTP is not a protocol for transferring hypertext; rather, it is a protocol for transmitting information with the efficiency necessary for making hypertext jumps. The data transferred by the protocol can be plain text, hypertext, audio, images, or any Internet-accessible information.

We begin with an overview of HTTP concepts and operation and then look at some of the details.[4] A number of important terms defined in the HTTP specification are summarized in Table 19.11; these will be introduced as the discussion proceeds.

## HTTP Overview

HTTP is a transaction-oriented client/server protocol. The most typical use of HTTP is between a web browser and a web server. To provide reliability, HTTP

**TABLE 19.11**   Key terms related to HTTP.

Cache
    A program's local store of response messages and the subsystem that controls its message storage, retrieval, and deletion. A cache stores cacheable responses in order to reduce the response time and network bandwidth consumption on future, equivalent requests. Any client or server may include a cache, though a cache cannot be used by a server while it is acting as a tunnel.

Client
    An application program that establishes connections for the purpose of sending requests.

Connection
    A transport layer virtual circuit established between two application programs for the purposes of communication.

Entity
    A particular representation or rendition of a data resource, or reply from a service resource, that may be enclosed within a request or response message. An entity consists of entity headers and an entity body.

Gateway
    A server that acts as an intermediary for some other server. Unlike a proxy, a gateway receives requests as if it were the original server for the requested resource; the requesting client may not be aware that it is communicating with a gateway. Gateways are often used as server-side portals through network firewalls and as protocol translators for access to resources stored on non-HTTP systems.

Message
    The basic unit of HTTP communication, consisting of a structured sequence of octets transmitted via the connection.

Origin Server
    The server on which a given resource resides or is to be created.

Proxy
    An intermediary program that acts as both a server and a client for the purpose of making requests on behalf of other clients. Requests are serviced internally or by passing them, with possible translation, on to other servers. A proxy must interpret and, if necessary, rewrite a request message before forwarding it. Proxies are often used as client-side portals through network firewalls and as helper applications for handling requests via protocols not implemented by the user agent.

Resource
    A network data object or service that can be identified by a URI.

Server
    An application program that accepts connections in order to service requests by sending back responses.

Tunnel
    A tunnel is an intermediary program that is acting as a blind relay between two connections. Once active, a tunnel is not considered a party to the HTTP communication, though the tunnel may have been initiated by an HTTP request. A tunnel ceases to exist when both ends of the relayed connections are closed. Tunnels are used when a portal is necessary and the intermediary cannot, or should not, interpret the relayed communication.

User Agent
    The client that initiates a request. These are often browsers, editors, spiders, or other end-user tools.

---

[4] This section is based on the most recent (at the time of this writing) specification, HTTP 1.1, which is the first version to be put on the IETF standards track.

makes use of TCP. Nevertheless, HTTP is a "stateless" protocol: Each transaction is treated independently. Accordingly, a typical implementation will create a new TCP connection between client and server for each transaction and then terminate the connection as soon as the transaction completes, although the specification does not dictate this one-to-one relationship between transaction and connection lifetimes.

The stateless nature of HTTP is well-suited to its typical application. A normal session of a user with a web browser involves retrieving a sequence of web pages and documents. The sequence is, ideally, performed rapidly, and the locations of the various pages and documents may be a number of widely distributed servers.

Another important feature of HTTP is that it is flexible in the formats that it can handle. When a client issues a request to a server, it may include a prioritized list of formats that it can handle, and the server replies with the appropriate format. For example, a Lynx browser cannot handle images, so a web server need not transmit any images on web pages. This arrangement prevents the transmission of unnecessary information and provides the basis for extending the set of formats with new standardized and proprietary specifications.

Figure 19.13 illustrates three examples of HTTP operation. The simplest case is one in which a *user agent* establishes a direct connection with an *origin server*. The *user agent* is the client that initiates the request, such as a web browser being run on behalf of an end user. The *origin server* is the server on which a resource of interest resides; an example is a web server at which a desired web home page resides. For this case, the client opens a TCP connection that is end-to-end between the client and the server. The client then issues an HTTP request. The request consists of a specific command, referred to as a method, a URL, and a MIME-like message containing request parameters, information about the client, and perhaps some additional content information.

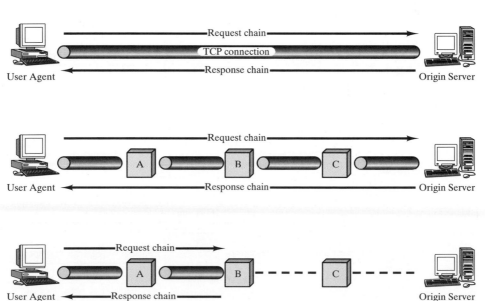

**FIGURE 19.13**  Examples of HTTP operation.

When the server receives the request, it attempts to perform the requested action and then returns an HTTP response. The response includes status information, a success/error code, and a MIME-like message containing information about the server, information about the response itself, and possible body content. The TCP connection is then closed.

The middle part of Figure 19.13 shows a case in which there is not an end-to-end TCP connection between the user agent and the origin server. Instead, there are one or more intermediate systems with TCP connections between logically adjacent systems. Each intermediate system acts as a relay, so that a request initiated by the client is relayed through the intermediate systems to the server, and the response from the server is relayed back to the client.

Three forms of intermediate systems are defined in the HTTP specification: *proxy*, *gateway*, and *tunnel*, all of which are illustrated in Figure 19.14.

## Proxy

A proxy acts on behalf of other clients and presents requests from other clients to a server. The proxy acts as a server in interacting with a client, and as a client in interacting with a server. There are several scenarios that call for the use of a proxy:

1. **Security intermediary.** The client and server may be separated by a security intermediary such as a firewall, with the proxy on the client side of the firewall. Typically, the client is part of a network secured by a firewall, and the server is external to the secured network. In this case, the server must authenticate itself to the firewall to set up a connection with the proxy. The proxy accepts responses after they have passed through the firewall.

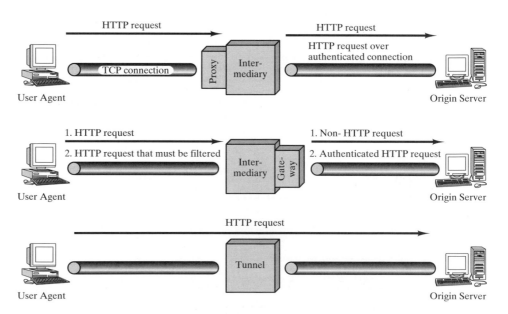

**FIGURE 19.14** Intermediate HTTP systems.

   2. **Different versions of HTTP.** If the client and server are running different versions of HTTP, then the proxy can implement both versions and perform the required mapping.

   In summary, a proxy is a forwarding agent, receiving a request for a URL object, modifying the request, and forwarding that request toward the server identified in the URL.

### Gateway

A gateway is a server that appears to the client as if it were an origin server. It acts on behalf of other servers that may not be able to communicate directly with a client. There are several scenarios in which servers can be used:

   1. **Security intermediary.** The client and server may be separated by a security intermediary such as a firewall, with the gateway on the server side of the firewall. Typically, the server is connected to a network protected by a firewall, with the client external to the network. In this case, the client must authenticate itself to the proxy, which can then pass the request on to the server.
   2. **Non-HTTP server.** Web browsers have built into them the capability to contact servers for protocols other than HTTP, such as FTP and Gopher servers. This capability can also be provided by a gateway. The client makes an HTTP request to a gateway server. The gateway server then contacts the relevant FTP or Gopher server to obtain the desired result. This result is then converted into a form suitable for HTTP and transmitted back to the client.

### Tunnel

Unlike the proxy and the gateway, the tunnel performs no operations on HTTP requests and responses. Instead, a tunnel is simply a relay point between two TCP connections, and the HTTP messages are passed unchanged as if there were a single HTTP connection between user agent and origin server. Tunnels are used when there must be an intermediary system between client and server, but it is not necessary for that system to understand the contents of messages. An example is a firewall in which a client or server external to a protected network can establish an authenticated connection, and which can then maintain that connection for purposes of HTTP transactions.

### Cache

Returning to Figure 19.13, the lowest portion of the figure shows an example of a cache. A cache is a facility that may store previous requests and responses for handling new requests. If a new request arrives that is the same as a stored request, then the cache can supply the stored response rather than accessing the resource indicated in the URL. The cache can operate on a client or server, or on an intermediate system other than a tunnel. In the figure, intermediary B has cached a request/response transaction, so that a corresponding new request from the client need not travel the entire chain to the origin server, but is handled by B.

Not all transactions can be cached, and a client or server can dictate that a certain transaction may be cached only for a given time limit.

## Messages

The best way to describe the functionality of HTTP is to describe the individual elements of the HTTP message. HTTP consists of two types of messages: requests from clients to servers, and responses from servers to clients. The general structure of such messages is shown in Figure 19.15. More formally, using enhanced BNF (Backus-Naur Form) notation (Table 19.12), we have

HTTP-Message = Simple-Request | Simple-Response | Full-Request | Full-
               Response
Full-Request = Request-Line
               *( General-Header | Request-Header | Entity-Header )
               CRLF
               [ Entity-Body ]
Full-Response = Status-Line
               *( General-Header | Response-Header | Entity-Header )
               CRLF
               [ Entity-Body ]
Simple-Request = "GET" SP Request-URI CRLF
Simple-Response = [ Entity-Body ]

The Simple-Request and Simple-Response messages were defined in HTTP/0.9. The request is a simple GET command with the requested URI; the response is simply a block containing the information identified in the URI. In

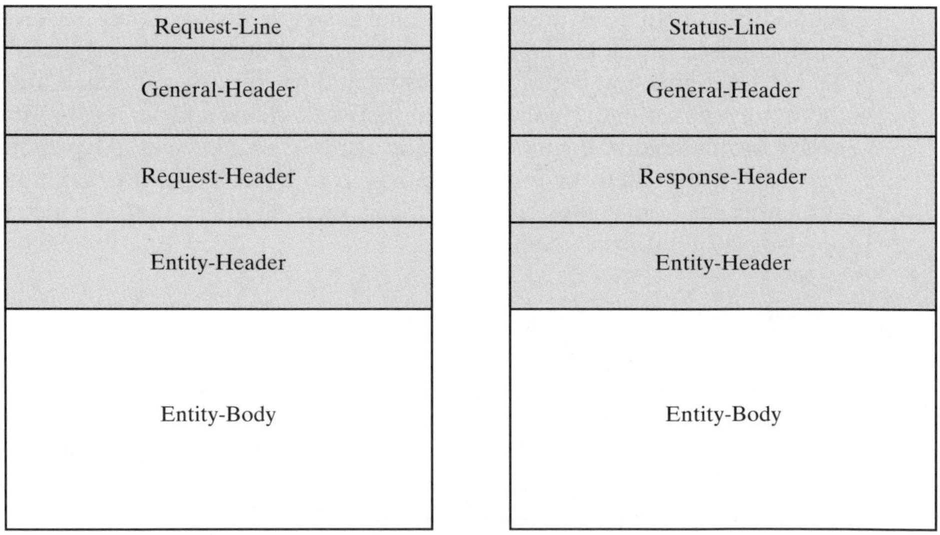

| Request-Line | Status-Line |
|:---:|:---:|
| General-Header | General-Header |
| Request-Header | Response-Header |
| Entity-Header | Entity-Header |
| Entity-Body | Entity-Body |

**FIGURE 19.15**   General structure of HTTP messages.

**TABLE 19.12** Augmented BNF notation used in URL and HTTP specifications.

- Words in lower case represent variables or names of rules.
- A rule has the form

  name = definition

- DIGIT is any decimal digit; CRLF is carriage return, line feed; SP is one or more spaces.
- Quotation marks enclose literal text.
- Angle brackets, "<" ">", may be used within a definition to enclose a rule name when their presence will facilitate clarity.
- Elements separated by bar ("|") are alternatives.
- Ordinary parentheses are used simply for grouping.
- The character "*" preceding an element indicates repetition. The full form is

  <I>*<J>element

indicating at least I and at most J occurrences of the element. *element allows any number, including 0; 1*element requires at least one element; and 1*2element allows 1 or 2 elements; <N>element means exactly *N* elements.
- Square brackets, "[ "]", enclose optional elements.
- The construct "#" is used to define, with the following form,

  <I>#<J>element

indicating at least *I* and at most *J* elements, each separated by a comma and optional linear white space.
- A semicolon at the right of a rule starts a comment that continues to the end of the line.

HTTP/1.1, the use of these simple forms is discouraged because it prevents the client from using content negotiation and the server from identifying the media type of the returned entity.

With full requests and responses, the following fields are used:

- **Request-line.** Identifies the message type and the requested resource.
- **Response-line.** Provides status information about this response.
- **General-header.** Contains fields that are applicable to both request and response messages, but which do not apply to the entity being transferred.
- **Request-header.** Contains information about the request and the client.
- **Response-header.** Contains information about the response.
- **Entity-header.** Contains information about the resource identified by the request and information about the entity body.
- **Entity-body.** The body of the message.

All of the HTTP headers consist of a sequence of fields, following the same generic format as RFC 822 (described in Section 19.3). Each field begins on a new line and consists of the field name followed by a colon and the field value.

Although the basic transaction mechanism is simple, there are a large number of fields and parameters defined in HTTP; these are listed in Table 19.13. In the remainder of this section, we look at the general header fields. Succeeding sections describe request headers, response headers, and entities.

**TABLE 19.13** HTTP elements.

| ALL MESSAGES | | | |
|---|---|---|---|
| **GENERAL HEADER FIELDS** | | **ENTITY HEADER FIELDS** | |
| Cache-Control | Keep-Alive | Allow | Derived-From |
| Connection | MIME-Version | Content-Encoding | Expires |
| Data | Pragma | Content-Language | Last-Modified |
| Forwarded | Upgrade | Content-Length | Link |
| | | Content-MD5 | Title |
| | | Content-Range | Transfer-Encoding |
| | | Content-Type | URI-Header |
| | | Content-Version | extension-header |

| REQUEST MESSAGES | | | |
|---|---|---|---|
| **REQUEST METHODS** | | **REQUEST HEADER FIELDS** | |
| OPTIONS | MOVE | Accept | If-Modified-Since |
| GET | DELETE | Accept-Charset | Proxy-Authorization |
| HEAD | LINK | Accept-Encoding | Range |
| POST | UNLINK | Accept-Language | Referer |
| PUT | TRACE | Authorization | Unless |
| PATCH | WRAPPED | From | User-Agent |
| COPY | extension-method | Host | |

| RESPONSE MESSAGES | | | |
|---|---|---|---|
| **RESPONSE STATUS CODES** | | | **RESPONSE HEADER FIELDS** |
| Continue | Moved Temporarily | Request Timeout | Location |
| Switching Protocols | See Other | Conflict | Proxy-Authenticate |
| OK | Not Modified | Gone | Public |
| Created | Use Proxy | Length Required | Retry-After |
| Accepted | Bad Request | Unless True | Server |
| Non-Authoritative Information | Unauthorized | Internal Server Error | WWW-Authenticate |
| No Content | Payment Required | Not Implemented | |
| Reset Content | Forbidden | Bad Gateway | |
| Partial Content | Not Found | Service Unavailable | |
| Multiple Choices | Method Not Allowed | Gateway Timeout | |
| Moved Permanently | None Acceptable | extension code | |
| | Proxy Authentication Required | | |

## General Header Fields

General header fields can be used in both request and response messages. These fields are applicable in both types of messages and contain information that does not directly apply to the entity being transferred. The fields are the following:

- **Cache-Control.** Specifies directives that must be obeyed by any caching mechanisms along the request/response chain; the purpose is to prevent a cache from adversely interfering with this particular request or response.

- **Connection.** Contains a list of keywords and header-field names that only apply to this TCP connection between the sender and the nearest non-tunnel recipient.
- **Data.** Data and time at which the message originated.
- **Forwarded.** Used by gateways and proxies to indicate intermediate steps along a request or response chain. Each gateway or proxy that handles a message may attach a Forwarded field that gives its URI.
- **Keep-Alive.** May be present if the Keep-Alive keyword is present in an incoming Connection field, to provide information to the requester of the persistent connection. This field may indicate a maximum time that the sender will keep the connection open while waiting for the next request or the maximum number of additional requests that will be allowed on the current persistent connection.
- **MIME-Version.** Indicates that the message complies with the indicated version of MIME.
- **Pragma.** Contains implementation-specific directives that may apply to any recipient along the request/response chain.
- **Upgrade.** Used in a request to specify what additional protocols the client supports and would like to use; used in a response to indicate which protocol will be used.

Two of these fields warrant further elaboration: Cache-Control and Connection.

## Cache-Control

A Cache-Control field can be attached to either a request or a response. Any caching mechanisms that receive a message with this header must follow the directives in the header, which may mean deviating from the default caching action. This field has the following format:

```
Cache-Control    = "Cache-Control" ":" 1#cache-directive
cache-directive  = "cachable"
                   | "max-age" "=" delta-seconds
                   | "private" [ "=" <"> 1#field-name <"> ]
                   | "no-cache" [ "=" <"> 1#field-name <"> ]
```

That is, this field consists of the phrase "Cache-Control:" followed by one or more directives.

A *cachable* directive is included in a response to indicate that the server generating the response declares it to be cachable. Any caching mechanism that forwards this response may cache it for future use.

A *max-age* directive is used in a request to inform any caching mechanism en route that it may use a cached response to this message only if it has a cached response that is no older than the age specified. A server may include this directive in a response to inform any caching mechanism en route that it may cache this response for future requests up to the max-age time limit.

A *private* directive in a response indicates that parts of the response message are intended for a single user and must not be cached except within a non-shared cache controlled by the user agent. If no field names are listed, the entire message is private.

A *no-cache* directive in a request forces that request to be forwarded to the origin server and not answered by an intermediate cache. This directive allows a client to request an authoritative response or to refresh a suspect cache. The list of field names is not used in a request message. In a response, the no-cache directive indicates that part or all of the message must not be cached for future use.

### Connection

A Connection field can be attached to either a request or a response. It is used to communicate from one end point of a TCP connection to the other end point. Thus, this field is not end-to-end at the HTTP level. When an intermediary system receives and forwards a message containing this field, that system must remove the field prior to forwarding.

The body of this field may include one or more field names for fields included in this message. These fields are to be processed by the recipient and not forwarded with the rest of the message. Alternatively, the body may consist of one or more keywords. At present, only the Keep-Alive keyword is defined in version 1.1 of HTTP; this indicates that the sender would like a persistent TCP connection (one that remains open beyond the current transaction).

## Request Messages

A full-request message consists of a status line followed by one or more general, request, and entity headers, followed by an optional entity body.

### Request Methods

A full request message always begins with a Request-Line, which has the following format:

Request-Line = Method SP Request-URI SP HTTP-Version CRLF

The Method parameter indicates the actual request command, called a *method* in HTTP. Request-URI is the URI of the requested resource, and HTTP-Version is the version number of HTTP used by the sender.

The following request methods are defined in HTTP/1.1:

- **OPTIONS.** A request for information about the options available for the request/response chain identified by this URI.
- **GET.** A request to retrieve the information identified in the URI and return it in an entity body. A GET is conditional if the If-Modified-Since header field is included, and is partial if a Range header field is included.
- **HEAD.** This request is identical to a GET, except that the server's response must not include an entity body; all of the header fields in the response are the same as if the entity body were present; this enables a client to get information about a resource without transferring the entity body.

- **POST.** A request to accept the attached entity as a new subordinate to the identified URI. The posted entity is subordinate to that URI in the same way that a file is subordinate to a directory containing it, a news article is subordinate to a newsgroup to which it is posted, or a record is subordinate to a database.
- **PUT.** A request to accept the attached entity and store it under the supplied URI. This may be a new resource with a new URI, or a replacement of the contents of an existing resource with an existing URI.
- **PATCH.** Similar to a PUT, except that the entity contains a list of differences from the content of the original resource identified in the URI.
- **COPY.** Requests that a copy of the resource identified by the URI in the Request-Line be copied to the location(s) given in the URI-Header field in the Entity-Header of this message.
- **MOVE.** Requests that the resource identified by the URI in the Request-Line be moved to the location(s) given in the URI-Header field in the Entity-Header of this message; equivalent to a COPY followed by a DELETE.
- **DELETE.** Requests that the origin server delete the resource identified by the URI in the Request-Line.
- **LINK.** Establishes one or more link relationships from the resource identified in the Request-Line. The links are defined in the Link field in the Entity-Header.
- **UNLINK.** Removes one or more link relationships from the resource identified in the Request-Line. The links are defined in the Link field in the Entity-Header.
- **TRACE.** Requests that the server return whatever is received as the entity body of the response; this can be used for testing and diagnostic purposes.
- **WRAPPED.** Allows a client to send one or more encapsulated requests. The requests may be encrypted or otherwise processed. The server must unwrap the requests and process accordingly.
- **Extension-method.** Allows additional methods to be defined without changing the protocol, but these methods cannot be assumed to be recognizable by the recipient.

## Request Header Fields

Request header fields function as request modifiers, providing additional information and parameters related to the request. The following fields are defined in HTTP/1.1:

- **Accept.** A list of media types and ranges that are acceptable as a response to this request.
- **Accept-charset.** A list of character sets acceptable for the response.
- **Accept-encoding.** List of acceptable content encodings for the entity body. Content encodings are primarily used to allow a document to be compressed or encrypted. Typically, the resource is stored in this encoding and only decoded before actual use.

- **Accept-language.** Restricts the set of natural languages that are preferred for the response.
- **Authorization.** Contains a field value, referred to as *credentials*, used by the client to authenticate itself to the server.
- **From.** The Internet e-mail address for the human user who controls the requesting user agent.
- **Host.** Specifies the Internet host of the resource being requested.
- **If-modified-since.** Used with the GET method. This header includes a date/time parameter; the resource is to be transferred only if it has been modified since the date/time specified. This feature allows for efficient cache update. A caching mechanism can periodically issue GET messages to an origin server, and will receive only a small response message unless an update is needed.
- **Proxy-authorization.** Allows the client to identify itself to a proxy that requires authentication.
- **Range.** For future study. The intent is that, in a GET message, a client can request only a portion of the identified resource.
- **Referer.** The URI of the resource from which the Request-URI was obtained. This enables a server to generate lists of back-links.
- **Unless.** Similar in function to the If-Modified-Since field, with two differences: (1) It is not restricted to the GET method, and (2) comparison is based on any Entity-Header field value rather than a date/time value.
- **User-agent.** Contains information about the user agent originating this request. This is used for statistical purposes, the tracing of protocol violations, and automated recognition of user agents for the sake of tailoring responses to avoid particular user agent limitations.

## Response Messages

A full-response message consists of a status line followed by one or more general, response, and entity headers, followed by an optional entity body.

### Status Codes

A full-response message always begins with a Status-Line, which has the following format:

Status-Line = HTTP-Version SP Status-Code SP Reason-Phrase CRLF

The HTTP-Version value is the version number of HTTP used by the sender. The Status-Code is a 3-digit integer that indicates the response to a received request, and the Reason-Phrase provides a short textual explanation of the status code.

There are a rather large number of status codes defined in HTTP/1.1; these are listed in Table 19.14, together with a brief definition. The codes are organized into the following categories:

**TABLE 19.14**  HTTP status codes.

| | Informational |
|---|---|
| Continue | Initial part of request received; client may continue with request. |
| Switching Protocols | Server will switch to requested new application protocol. |

| | Successful |
|---|---|
| OK | Request has succeeded and the appropriate response information is included. |
| Created | Request fulfilled and a new resource has been created; the URI(s) are included. |
| Accepted | Request accepted but processing not completed. The request may or may not eventually be acted upon. |
| Non-Authoritative Information | Returned contents of entity header is not the definitive set available from origin server, but is gathered from a local or third-party copy. |
| No Content | Server has fulfilled request but there is no information to send back. |
| Reset Content | Request has succeeded and the user agent should reset the document view that caused the request to be generated. |
| Partial Content | Server has fulfilled the partial GET request and the corresponding information is included. |

| | Redirection |
|---|---|
| Multiple Choices | Requested resource is available at multiple locations and a preferred location could not be determined. |
| Moved Permanently | Requested resource has been assigned a new permanent URI; future reference should use this URI |
| Moved Temporarily | Requested resource resides temporarily under a different URI. |
| See Other | Response to the request can be found under a different URI and should be retrieved using a GET on that resource. |
| Not Modified | The client has performed a conditional GET, access is allowed, and the document has not been modified since the date/time specified in the request. |
| Use Proxy | Requested resource must be accessed through the proxy indicated in the Location field. |

| | Client Error |
|---|---|
| Bad Request | Malformed syntax in request. |
| Unauthorized | Request requires user authentication. |
| Payment Required | Reserved for future use. |
| Forbidden | Server refuses to fulfill request; used when server does not wish to reveal why the request was refused. |
| Not Found | Requested URI not found. |
| Method Not Allowed | Method (command) not allowed for the requested resource. |
| None Acceptable | Resource found that matches requested URI, but does not satisfy conditions specified in the request. |
| Proxy Authentication Required | Client must first authenticate itself with the proxy. |
| Request Timeout | Client did not produce a request within the time that the server was prepared to wait. |
| Conflict | Request could not be completed due to a conflict with the current state of the resource. |
| Gone | Requested resource no longer available at the server and no forwarding address is known. |
| Length Required | Server refuses to accept request without a defined content length. |
| Unless True | Condition given in the Unless field was true when tested on server. |

*(Continued)*

**TABLE 19.14**    (*Continued*)

| Server Error | |
|---|---|
| Internal Server Error | Server encountered an unexpected condition that prevented it from fulfilling the request. |
| Not Implemented | Server does not support the functionality required to fulfill the request. |
| Bad Gateway | Server, while acting as a gateway or proxy, received an invalid response from the upstream server it accessed to fulfill the request. |
| Service Unavailable | Server unable to handle request due to temporary overloading or maintenance of the server. |
| Gateway Timeout | Server, while acting as a gateway or proxy, did not receive a timely response from the upstream server it accessed to fulfill the request. |

- **Informational.** The request has been received and processing continues. No entity body accompanies this response.
- **Successful.** The request was successfully received, understood, and accepted. The information returned in the response message depends on the request method, as follows:

  —GET: The contents of the entity-body corresponds to the requested resource.

  —HEAD: No entity body is returned.

  —POST: The entity describes or contains the result of the action.

  —TRACE: The entity contains the request message.

  —Other methods: The entity describes the result of the action.

- **Redirection.** Further action is required to complete the request.
- **Client error.** The request contains a syntax error or the request cannot be fulfilled.
- **Server error.** The server failed to fulfill an apparently valid request.

### Response Header Fields

Response header fields providing additional information related to the response that cannot be placed in the Status-Line. The following fields are defined in HTTP/1.1:

- **Location.** Defines the exact location of the resource identified by the Request-URI.
- **Proxy-authenticate.** Included with a response that has a status code of Proxy Authentication Required. This field contains a "challenge" that indicates the authentication scheme and parameters required.
- **Public.** Lists the non-standard methods supported by this server.
- **Retry-after.** Included with a response that has a status code of Service Unavailable, and indicates how long the service is expected to be unavailable.
- **Server.** Identifies the software product used by the origin server to handle the request.

- **WWW-authenticate.** Included with a response that has a status code of Unauthorized. This field contains a challenge that indicates the authentication scheme and parameters required.

## Entities

An entity consists of an entity header and an entity body in a request or response message. An entity may represent a data resource, or it may constitute other information supplied with a request or response.

### Entity Header Fields

Entity header fields provide optional information about the entity body or, if no body is present, about the resource identified by the request. The following fields are defined in HTTP/1.1:

- **Allow.** Lists methods supported by the resource identified in the Request-URI. This field must be included with a response that has a status code of Method Not Allowed and may be included in other responses.
- **Content-encoding.** Indicates what content encodings have been applied to the resource. The only encoding currently defined is zip compression.
- **Content-language.** Identifies the natural language(s) of the intended audience of the enclosed entity.
- **Content-length.** The size of the entity body in octets.
- **Content-MD5.** For future study. MD5 refers to the MD5 hash code function, described in Chapter 18.
- **Content-range.** For future study. The intent is that this designation will indicate a portion of the identified resource that is included in this response.
- **Content-type.** Indicates the media type of the entity body.
- **Content-version.** A version tag associated with an evolving entity.
- **Derived-from.** Indicates the version tag of the resource from which this entity was derived before modifications were made by the sender. This field and the Content-Version field can be used to manage multiple updates by a group of users.
- **Expires.** Date/time after which the entity should be considered stale.
- **Last-modified.** Date/time that the sender believes the resource was last modified.
- **Link.** Defines links to other resources.
- **Title.** A textual title for the entity.
- **Transfer-encoding.** Indicates what type of transformation has been applied to the message body to safely transfer it between the sender and the recipient. The only encoding defined in the standard is *chunked*. The chunked option defines a procedure for breaking an entity body into labeled chunks that are transmitted separately.
- **URI-header.** Informs the recipient of other URIs by which the resource can be identified.

- **Extension-header.** Allows additional fields to be defined without changing the protocol, but these fields cannot be assumed to be recognizable by the recipient.

### Entity Body

An entity body consists of an arbitrary sequence of octets. HTTP is designed to be able to transfer any type of content, including text, binary data, audio, images, and video. When an entity body is present in a message, the interpretation of the octets in the body is determined by the entity header fields Content-Encoding, Content-Type, and Transfer-Encoding. These define a three-layer, ordered encoding model:

$$\text{entity-body} := \text{Transfer-Encoding( Content-Encoding( Content-Type ( data ) ) )}$$

The data are the contents of a resource identified by a URI. The Content-Type field determines the way in which the data are interpreted. A Content-Encoding may be applied to the data and stored at the URI instead of the data. Finally, on transfer, a Transfer-Encoding may be applied to form the entity body of the message.

### Access Authentication

HTTP/1.1 defines a simple challenge-response technique for authentication. This definition does not restrict HTTP clients and servers from using other forms of authentication, but the current standard only covers this simple form.

Two authentication exchanges are defined: one between a client and a server, and one between a client and a proxy. Both types of exchange use a challenge-response mechanism. The challenge, issued by a server or proxy, is of the form

```
challenge = auth-scheme 1*SP realm *( "," auth-param )
auth-scheme = token
auth-param = token "=" quoted-string
realm = "realm" "=" realm-value
realm-value = quoted-string
```

Auth-scheme is the name of a particular authentication scheme. The realm defines a particular *protection space*, which is simply a conceptual partition of the resource, with its own authentication scheme and authorization database. For example, a resource may define several realms, one for end users and one for network managers. The latter realm may have more privileges and requires a more powerful authentication scheme.

In response to an authentication challenge, a client must provide credentials. These are of the form

```
credentials = basic-credentials | auth-scheme *("," auth-param )
```

Basic credentials are covered below. In the general case, the user would return the name of the authentication scheme and a set of parameters required to authenticate itself.

### Client-Server Authentication

A user agent that wishes to authenticate itself with a server may do so by including an Authorization field in the request header; an agent may do this when initially sending the request. An alternative, which may be more common, is that a client sends a Request message without an Authorization field and is then required to return an authorization by the server. Figure 19.16 illustrates this scenario, which involves three steps:

1. The client sends a request, such as a GET request to the server, with no Authorization field in the request header.
2. The server returns a response with a status code in the Status line of Unauthorized and a WWW-Authenticate field in the response header. The WWW-Authenticate field consists of a challenge that indicates the type of authentication required and may include other parameters. No entity body is returned.
3. The client repeats the request but includes an Authorization field that contains the authorization data needed by the server.

If authentication succeeds, the server returns a response with some other status code and without a WWW-Authenticate field. If authentication fails, the server can initiate a new authentication sequence by returning a response with a status of Unauthorized and a WWW-Authenticate field containing the (possibly new) challenge. The entity body should explain the reason for the refusal.

In client-server authentication, any proxy or gateway must be transparent, as far as authentication is concerned. That is, the WWW-Authenticate and Authorization fields must be forwarded unmodified, and the response to a request containing an Authorization field must not be cached. This latter requirement dictates that the authentication always takes place between client and server and does not simply replay the server's prior acceptance of authentication.

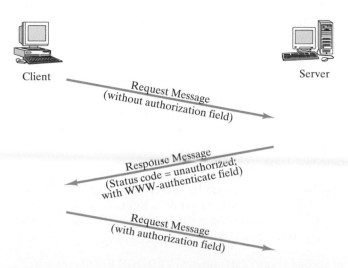

**FIGURE 19.16**   HTTP access-authentication scenario.

## Proxy Authentication

A proxy may be configured so that a client must first authenticate itself to the proxy before being granted access to an origin server. The sequence is similar to that described for client-server authentication. In this case, the authentication information is carried in the Proxy-Authorization field in the request header. A client may authenticate itself when first issuing a Request message. Alternatively, a scenario similar to Figure 19.16 occurs:

1. The client sends a request, such as a GET request to the server, with no Proxy-Authorization field in the request header.
2. The proxy does not forward the request, but returns a response with a status code in the Status line of Proxy-Authentication Required and a Proxy-Authenticate field in the response header.
3. The client repeats the request but includes a Proxy-Authorization field that contains the authorization data needed by the proxy.

If the request is authenticated, then the proxy may forward the request to a server, but will omit the Proxy-Authorization field. The proxy could also return a cached response.

## Basic Authentication Scheme

For the basic authentication scheme, a user agent authenticates itself within a particular realm by supplying a user ID and a password. This is the simplest form of authentication, comparable to logging on to a system. Within HTTP, there is no provision for protecting the user ID or password with encryption, so this method provides minimal security. The form of the credentials for basic authentication are

```
basic-credentials  = " Basic" SP basic-cookie
basic-cookie = <base64 [7] encoding of userid-password, except not limited to
                    76 char/line>
userid-password    = [ token ] ":" *TEXT
```

The combination of user ID and password is an arbitrary string of textual characters, transmitted in base-64 encoding. For example, consider a server that has an end-user realm and that receives a Request message without an Authorization field. The server sends a Response message with a status code of Unauthorized and this WWW-Authenticate field:

WWW-Authenticate: Basic-realm="UserSpace"

where "UserSpace" is the string assigned by the server to identify the protection space of the Request-URI. The client then sends a Request message that includes an Authorization field that base-64 encodes the user ID of "Aladdin" and the password "open sesame." The field looks like this:

Authorization: Basic QWxhZGRpbjpvcGVuIHNlc2FtZQ==

## 19.6 RECOMMENDED READING

A thorough presentation of ASN.1 is to be found in [STEE90]. Two quite useful documents are [KALI91] and [GAUD89]. [STAL96] provides a comprehensive and detailed examination of SNMP and SNMPv2; the book also provides an overview of network-management technology. One of the few textbooks on the subject of network management is [TERP92]. [ROSE93] provides a book-length treatment of electronic mail, including some coverage of SMTP and MIME.

GAUD89  Gaudette, P. *A Tutorial on ASN.1*. Technical Report NCSL/SNA-89/12. Gaithersburg, MD: National Institute of Standards and Technology, 1989.

KALI91  Kaliski, B. *A Layman's Guide to a Subset of ASN.1, BER, and DER. Report SEC-SIG-91-17*. Redwood City, CA: RSA Data Security Inc. 1991.

ROSE93  Rose, M. *The Internet Message: Closing the Book with Electronic Mail*. Englewood Cliffs, NJ: Prentice Hall, 1993.

STAL96  Stallings, W. *SNMP, SNMPv2, and RMON: Practical Network Management,* Reading, MA: Addison-Wesley, 1996.

STEE90  Steedman, D. *ASN.1: The Tutorial and Reference*. London: Technology Appraisals, 1990.

TERP92  Terplan, K. *Communication Networks Management*. Englewood Cliffs, NJ: Prentice Hall, 1992.

### Recommended Web Sites

- http://snmp.cs.utwente.nl: Exhaustive source of information on SNMP.
- http://www.w3.org/pub/WWW: Web site of the World Wide Web Consortium, containing up-to-date information on HTTP.
- http://www.inria.fr/rodeo/personnel/hoschka/asn1.html: ASN.1 web site, contains tutorial information, links to software tools, ASN.1-based applications and products, and standards information.

## 19.7 PROBLEMS

19.1  a.  Consider the following definitions:
```
      ExpeditedDataAcknowledgement ::= SET {
      destRef                        [0]        Reference,
      yr-tu-nr                       [1]        TPDUnumber,
      checkSum                       [2]        CheckSum OPTIONAL }
      NormalEA ::= ExpeditedDataAcknowledgement
      ( WITH COMPONENTS {
                        destRef,
                        yr-tu-nr (0..127) }
```
Find an equivalent expression for defining NormalEA.

b.  Consider the following definition
```
      ExtendedEA ::= ExpeditedDataAcknowledgement
      ( WITH COMPONENTS {..., checkSum PRESENT } )
```
Find an equivalent expression for defining ExtendedEA.

c.  Define a new type, EA, based on ExpeditedDataAcknowledgement, with the restriction that either the checksum is absent, in which case yr-tu-nr must be in the range of 0 to 127, or the checksum is present, in which case there is no additional constraint on yr-tu-nr.

19.2    Given the following definition,
        TypH ::= SEQUENCE {
        r                               INTEGER,
        s                               BOOLEAN,
        t                               INTEGER OPTIONAL }

        Which of the following values are valid?
        valH1 TypH ::= { r –5, s TRUE, t 0}
        valH2 TypH ::= {10, FALSE}
        valH3 TypH ::= { t 1, r 2, s TRUE}

19.3    Given the following definitions,
        T1 ::= SEQUENCE { X1,
                             b BOOLEAN }
        X1 ::= CHOICE {y INTEGER, z REAL }

        Would the identifiers for T1 be: y, z, b?

19.4    Define an IA5String-based type that contains only either "A" or "B" characters and is restricted to a maximum length of 10 chars.

19.5    The original (version 1) specification of SNMP has the following definition of a new type:
        Gauge ::= [APPLICATION 2] IMPLICIT INTEGER (0..4294967295)

        The standard includes the following explanation of the semantics of this type:

        This application-wide type represents a non-negative integer, which may increase or decrease, but which latches at a maximum value. This standard specifies a maximum value of $2^{32}-1$ (4294967295 decimal) for Gauges.

        Unfortunately, the word latch is not defined, and has resulted in two different interpretations. The SNMPv2 standard cleared up the ambiguity with the following definition:

        The value of a Gauge has its maximum value whenever the information being modeled is greater than or equal to that maximum value; if the information being modeled subsequently decreases below the maximum value, the Gauge also decreases.

        a. What is the alternative interpretation?
        b. Discuss the pros and cons of the two interpretations.

19.6    Electronic mail systems differ in the manner in which multiple recipients are handled. In some systems, the originating user agent or mail sender makes all the necessary copies, and these are sent out independently. An alternative approach is to determine the route for each destination first. Then a single message is sent out on a common portion of the route, and copies are only made when the routes diverge; this process is referred to as mail-bagging. Discuss the relative advantages and disadvantages of the two methods.

# APPENDIX A

# ISDN AND BROADBAND ISDN

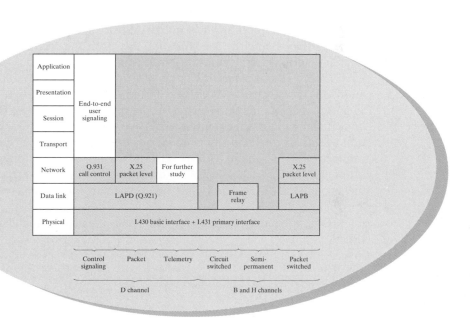

Rapid advances in computer and communication technologies have resulted in the increasing merging of these two fields. The lines have blurred among computing, switching, and digital transmission equipment, and the same digital techniques are being used for data, voice, and image transmission. Merging and evolving technologies, coupled with increasing demands for efficient and timely collection, processing, and dissemination of information, are leading to the development of integrated systems that transmit and process all types of data. The ultimate goal of this evolution is the integrated services digital network (ISDN).

The ISDN is intended to be a worldwide public telecommunications network to replace existing public telecommunications networks and deliver a wide variety of services. The ISDN is defined by the standardization of user interfaces and is implemented as a set of digital switches and paths supporting a broad range of traffic types and providing value-added processing services. In practice, there are multiple networks, implemented within national boundaries, but from the user's point of view, there will be a single, uniformly accessible, worldwide network.

The impact of ISDN on both users and vendors will be profound. To control ISDN evolution and impact, a massive effort at standardization is underway. Although ISDN standards are still evolving, both the technology and the emerging implementation strategy are well understood.

Despite the fact that ISDN has yet to achieve the hoped for universal deployment, it is already in its second generation. The first generation, sometimes referred to as *narrowband ISDN*, is based on the use of a 64-kbps channel as the basic unit of switching and has a circuit-switching orientation. The major technical contribution of the narrowband ISDN effort has been frame relay. The second generation, referred to as *broadband ISDN* (B-ISDN), supports very high data rates (100s of Mbps) and has a packet-switching orientation. The major technical contribution of the broadband ISDN effort has been asynchronous transfer mode (ATM), also known as cell relay.

This appendix provides an overview of narrowband ISDN and broadband ISDN.

## A.1 OVERVIEW OF ISDN

### ISDN Concept

The concept of ISDN is best introduced by considering it from several different viewpoints:

- Principles of ISDN
- The user interface
- Objectives
- Services

#### Principles of ISDN

Standards for ISDN have been defined by ITU-T (formerly CCITT), a topic that we explore later in this section. Table A.1, which is the complete text of one of the

TABLE A.1 Recommendation I.120 (1988).

1 Principles of ISDN

1.1 The main feature of the ISDN concept is the support of a wide range of voice and nonvoice applications in the same network. A key element of service integration for an ISDN is the provision of a range of services (see Part II of the I-Series in this Fascicle) using a limited set of connection types and multipurpose user-network interface arrangements (see Parts III and IV of the I-Series in Fascicle III.8).

1.2 ISDNs support a variety of applications including both switched and non-switched connections. Switched connections in an ISDN include both circuit-switched and packet-switched connections and their concatenations.

1.3 As far as practicable, new services introduced into an ISDN should be arranged to be compatible with 64 kbit/s switched digital connections.

1.4 An ISDN will contain intelligence for the purpose of providing service features, maintenance and network management functions. This intelligence may not be sufficient for some new services and may have to be supplemented by either additional intelligence within the network, or possibly compatible intelligence in the user terminals.

1.5 A layered protocol structure should be used for the specification of the access to an ISDN. Access from a user to ISDN resources may vary depending upon the service required and upon the status of implementation of national ISDNs.

1.6 It is recognized that ISDNs may be implemented in a variety of configurations according to specific national situations.

2 Evolution of ISDNs

2.1 ISDNs will be based on the concepts for telephone IDNs and may evolve by progressively incorporating additional functions and network features including those of any other dedicated networks such as circuit-switching and packet-switching for data so as to provide for existing and new services.

2.2 The transition from an existing network to a comprehensive ISDN may require a period of time extending over one or more decades. During this period arrangements must be developed for the networking of services on ISDNs and services on other networks (see Part V).

2.3 In the evolution towards an ISDN, digital end-to-end connectivity will be obtained via plant and equipment used in existing networks, such as digital transmission, time-division multiplex switching and/or space-division multiplex switching. Existing relevant recommendations for these constituent elements of an ISDN are contained in the appropriate series of recommendations of CCITT and of CCIR.

2.4 In the early stages of the evolution of ISDNs, some interim user-network arrangements may need to be adopted in certain countries to facilitate early penetration of digital service capabilities. Arrangements corresponding to national variants may comply partly or wholly with I-Series Recommendations. However, the intention is that they not be specifically included in the I-Series.

2.5 An evolving ISDN may also include at later stages switched connections at bit rates higher and lower than 64 kbit/s.

ISDN-related standards, states the principles of ISDN from the point of view of CCITT. Let us look at each of these points in turn:

1. *Support of voice and nonvoice applications using a limited set of standardized facilities.* This principle defines both the purpose of ISDN and the means of achieving it. The ISDN supports a variety of services related to voice communications (telephone calls) and nonvoice communications (digital data exchange). These services are to be provided in conformance with standards

(ITU-T recommendations) that specify a small number of interfaces and data transmission facilities.

2. *Support for switched and nonswitched applications.* ISDN supports both circuit switching and packet switching. In addition, ISDN supports nonswitched services in the form of dedicated lines.

3. *Reliance on 64-kbps connections.* ISDN provides circuit-switched and packet-switched connections at 64 kbps; this is the fundamental building block of ISDN. This rate was chosen because, at the time, it was the standard rate for digitized voice, and, hence, was being introduced into the evolving integrated digital networks (IDNs). Although this data rate is useful, it is unfortunately restrictive to rely solely on it. Future developments in ISDN will permit greater flexibility.

4. *Intelligence in the network.* An ISDN is expected to be able to provide sophisticated services beyond the simple setup of a circuit-switched call.

5. *Layered protocol architecture.* The protocols for user access to ISDN exhibit a layered architecture and can be mapped into the OSI model. This procedure has a number of advantages:

    • Standards already developed for OSI-related applications may be used on ISDN. An example is X.25 level 3 for access to packet-switching services in ISDN.

    • New ISDN-related standards can be based on existing standards, reducing the cost of new implementations. An example is LAPD, which is based on LAPB.

    • Standards can be developed and implemented independently for various layers and functions within a layer; this allows for the gradual implementation of ISDN services at a pace appropriate for a given provider or a given customer base.

6. *Variety of configurations.* More than one physical configuration is possible for implementing ISDN; this allows for differences in national policy (single-source versus competition), in the states of technology, and in the needs and existing equipment of the customer base.

## The User Interface

Figure A.1 is a conceptual view of the ISDN from a user, or customer, point of view. The user has access to the ISDN by means of a local interface to a "digital pipe" of a certain bit rate. Pipes of various sizes are available to satisfy differing needs. For example, a residential customer may require only sufficient capacity to handle a telephone and a videotex terminal. An office will undoubtedly wish to connect to the ISDN via an on-premise digital PBX, and will require a much higher capacity pipe.

At any given point in time, the pipe to the user's premises has a fixed capacity, but the traffic on the pipe may be a variable mix up to the capacity limit. Thus, a user may access circuit-switched and packet-switched services, as well as other services, in a dynamic mix of signal types and bit rates. To provide these services, the ISDN requires rather complex control signals to instruct it how to sort out the time-

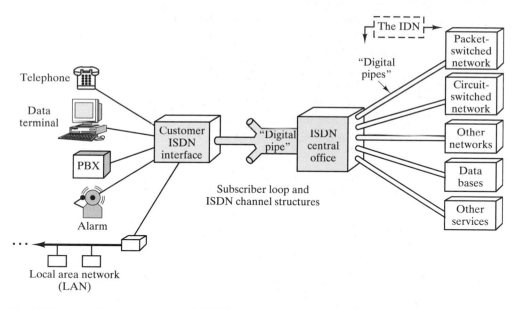

**FIGURE A.1**   Conceptual view of ISDN connection features.

multiplexed data and provide the required services. These control signals are also multiplexed onto the same digital pipe.

An important aspect of the interface is that the user may, at any time, employ less than the maximum capacity of the pipe, and will be charged according to the capacity used rather than "connect time." This characteristic significantly diminishes the value of current user design efforts that are geared to optimize circuit utilization by use of concentrators, multiplexers, packet switches, and other line-sharing arrangements.

## Objectives

Activities currently under way are leading to the development of a worldwide ISDN. This effort involves national governments, data processing and communications companies, standards organizations, and other agencies. Certain common objectives are, by and large, shared by this disparate group. We list here the key objectives:

- **Standardization.** It is essential that a single set of ISDN standards be provided to permit universal access and to permit the development of cost-effective equipment.
- **Transparency.** The most important service to be provided is a transparent transmission service, thereby permitting users to develop applications and protocols with the confidence that they will not be affected by the underlying ISDN.
- **Separation of competitive functions.** It must be possible to separate out functions that could be provided competitively as opposed to those that are fun-

damentally part of the ISDN. In many countries, a single, government-owned entity provides all services. Some countries desire (in the case of the United States, require) that certain enhanced services be offered competitively (e.g., videotex, electronic mail).

- **Leased and switched services.** The ISDN should provide dedicated point-to-point services as well as switched services, thereby allowing the user to optimize implementation of switching and routing techniques.
- **Cost-related tariffs.** The price for ISDN service should be related to cost, and should be independent of the type of data being carried. One type of service should not be in the position of subsidizing others.
- **Smooth migration.** The conversion to ISDN will be gradual, and the evolving network must coexist with existing equipment and services. Thus, ISDN interfaces should evolve from current interfaces, and provide a migration path for users.
- **Multiplexed support.** In addition to providing low-capacity support to individual users, multiplexed support must be provided to accommodate user-owned PBX and local network equipment.

There are, of course, other objectives that could be named. Those listed above are certainly among the most important and widely accepted, and each helps to define the character of the ISDN.

### Architecture

Figure A.2 is a block diagram of ISDN. ISDN supports a new physical connecter for users, a digital subscriber loop (link from end user to central or end office), and modifications to all central office equipment.

The area to which most attention has been paid by standards organizations is that of user access. A common physical interface has been defined to provide, in essence, a DTE-DCE connection. The same interface should be usable for telephone, computer terminal, and videotex terminal. Protocols are needed for the exchange of control information between user device and the network. Provision must be made for high-speed interfaces to, for example, a digital PBX or a LAN.

The subscriber loop portion of today's telephone network consists of twisted pair links between the subscriber and the central office, carrying 4-kHz analog signals. Under the ISDN, one or two twisted pairs are used to provide a basic full-duplex digital communications link.

The digital central office connects the numerous ISDN subscriber loop signals to the IDN. In addition to providing access to the circuit-switched network, the central office provides subscriber access to dedicated lines, packet-switched networks, and time-shared, transaction-oriented computer services. Multiplexed access via digital PBX and LAN must also be accommodated.

### Standards

The development of ISDN is governed by a set of recommendations issued by ISDN, called the I-series Recommendations. These Recommendations, or stan-

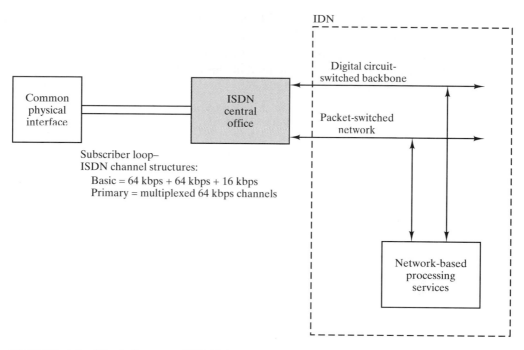

**FIGURE A.2**  Block diagram of ISDN functions.

dards, were first issued in 1984. A more complete set was issued in 1988. Most of the Recommendations have been updated, at irregular intervals, since that time. The bulk of the description of ISDN is contained in the I-series Recommendations, with some related topics covered in other Recommendations. The characterization of ISDN contained in these Recommendations is centered on three main areas:

1. The standardization of services offered to users, so as to enable services to be internationally compatible.
2. The standardization of user-network interfaces, so as to enable terminal equipment to be portable, and to assist in (1).
3. The standardization of ISDN capabilities to the degree necessary to allow user-network and network-network interworking, and thus achieve (1) and (2).

The I-series Recommendations are broken up into six main groupings, labeled I.100 through I.600.

### I.100 Series—General Concepts

The I.100 series serves as a general introduction to ISDN. The general structure of the ISDN recommendations is presented as well as a glossary of terms. I.120 provides an overall description of ISDN and the expected evolution of ISDNs. I.130 introduces terminology and concepts that are used in the I.200 series to specify services.

### I.200 Series—Service Capabilities

The I.200 series is in a sense the most important part of the ITU-T ISDN recommendations. Here, the services to be provided to users are specified. We may look on this as a set of requirements that the ISDN must satisfy. In the ISDN glossary (I.112), the term *service* is defined as

> That which is offered by an Administration or recognized private operating agency (RPOA) to its customers in order to satisfy a specific telecommunication requirement.

Although this is a very general definition, the term "service" has come to have a very specific meaning in ITU-T, a meaning that is somewhat different from the use of that term in an OSI context. For ITU-T, a standardized service is characterized by

- Complete, guaranteed end-to-end compatibility
- ITU-T–standardized terminals, including procedures
- Listing of the service subscribers in an international directory
- ITU-T–standardized testing and maintenance procedures
- Charging and accounting rules

There are three fully standardized ITU-T services: telegraphy, telephony, and data. There are four additional *telematic* services in the process of being standardized: teletex, facsimile, videotex, and message handling. The goal with all of these services is to ensure high-quality international telecommunications for the end user, regardless of the make of the terminal equipment and the type of network used nationally to support the service.

### I.300 Series—Network Aspects

Whereas the I.200 series focuses on the user, in terms of the services provided, the I.300 series focuses on the network, in terms of how the network goes about providing those services. A protocol reference model is presented that, while based on the 7-layer OSI model, attempts to account for the complexity of a connection that may involve two or more users (e.g., a conference call) plus a related common-channel signaling dialogue. Issues such as numbering and addressing are covered. There is also a discussion of ISDN connection types.

### I.400 Series—User-Network Interfaces

The I.400 series deals with the interface between the user and the network. Three major topics are addressed:

- **Physical configurations.** The issue of how ISDN functions are configured into equipment. The standards specify functional groupings and define reference points between those groupings.
- **Transmission rates.** The data rates and combinations of data rates to be offered to the user.
- **Protocol specifications.** The protocols at OSI layers 1 through 3 that specify the user-network interaction.

### I.500 Series—Internetwork Interfaces

ISDN supports services that are also provided on older circuit-switched and packet-switched networks. Thus, it is necessary to provide interworking between an ISDN and other types of networks to allow communications between terminals belonging to equivalent services offered through different networks. The I.500 series deals with the various network issues that arise in attempting to define interfaces between ISDN and other types of networks.

### I.600 Series—Maintenance Principles

This series provides guidance for maintenance of the ISDN subscriber installation, the network portion of the ISDN basic access, primary access, and higher data-rate services. Maintenance principles and functions are related to the reference configuration and general architecture of ISDN. A key function that is identified in the series is loopback. In general, loopback testing is used for failure localization and verification.

## A.2  ISDN CHANNELS

The digital pipe between the central office and the ISDN user is used to carry a number of communication channels. The capacity of the pipe, and therefore the number of channels carried, may vary from user to user. The transmission structure of any access link is constructed from the following types of channels:

- B channel: 64 kbps
- D channel: 16 or 64 kbps
- H channel: 384(H0), 1536(H11), and 1920 (H12) kbps

The *B channel* is the basic user channel. It can be used to carry digital data, PCM-encoded digital voice, or a mixture of lower-rate traffic, including digital data and digitized voice encoded at a fraction of 64 kbps. In the case of mixed traffic, all traffic must be destined for the same endpoint. Four kinds of connections can be set up over a B channel:

- **Circuit-switched.** This is equivalent to switched digital service available today. The user places a call, and a circuit-switched connection is established with another network user. An interesting feature is that call-establishment dialogue does not take place over the B channel, but is done over the D, as explained below.
- **Packet-switched.** The user is connected to a packet-switching node, and data are exchanged with other users via X.25.
- **Frame mode.** The user is connected to a frame relay node, and data are exchanged with other users via LAPF.

- **Semipermanent.** This is a connection to another user set up by prior arrangement, and not requiring a call-establishment protocol; this is equivalent to a leased line.

The designation of 64 kbps as the standard user channel rate highlights the fundamental contradiction in standards activities. This rate was chosen as the most effective for digitized voice, yet the technology has progressed to the point at which 32 kbps, or even less, produces equally satisfactory voice reproduction. To be effective, a standard must freeze the technology at some defined point. Yet by the time the standard is approved, it may already be obsolete.

The *D channel* serves two purposes. First, it carries signaling information to control circuit-switched calls on associated B channels at the user interface. In addition, the D channel may be used for packet-switching or low-speed (e.g., 100 bps) telemetry at times when no signaling information is waiting. Table A.2 summarizes the types of data traffic to be supported on B and D channels.

*H channels* are provided for user information at higher bit rates. The user may employ such a channel as a high-speed trunk, or the channel may be subdivided according to the user's own TDM scheme. Examples of applications include fast facsimile, video, high-speed data, high-quality audio, and multiple information streams at lower data rates.

These channel types are grouped into transmission structures that are offered as a package to the user. The best-defined structures at this time are the basic channel structure (basic access) and the primary channel structure (primary access), which are depicted in Figure A.3.

*Basic access* consists of two full-duplex 64-kbps B channels and a full-duplex 16-kbps D channel. The total bit rate, by simple arithmetic, is 144 kbps. However, framing, synchronization, and other overhead bits bring the total bit rate on a basic access link to 192 kbps. The frame structure for basic access was shown in Figure 7.10. Each frame of 48 bits includes 16 bits from each of the B channels and 4 bits from the D channel.

The basic service is intended to meet the needs of most individual users, including residential and very small offices. It allows the simultaneous use of voice and several data applications, such as packet-switched access, a link to a central

TABLE A.2  ISDN Channel functions.

| B Channel (64 kbps) | D Channel (16 kbps) |
| --- | --- |
| Digital voice | Signaling |
|   64 kbps PCM |   Basic |
|   Low bit rate (32 kbps) |   Enhanced |
| High-speed data | Low-speed data |
|   Circuit-switched |   Videotex |
|   Packet-switched |   Teletex |
| Other |   Terminal |
|   Facsimile | Telemetry |
|   Slow-scan video |   Emergency services |
| |     Energy management |

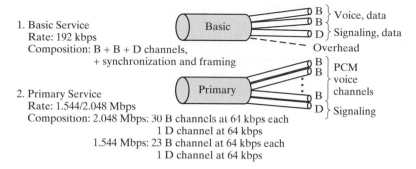

1. Basic Service
   Rate: 192 kbps
   Composition: B + B + D channels,
                + synchronization and framing

2. Primary Service
   Rate: 1.544/2.048 Mbps
   Composition: 2.048 Mbps: 30 B channels at 64 kbps each
                           1 D channel at 64 kbps
                1.544 Mbps: 23 B channel at 64 kbps each
                           1 D channel at 64 kbps

**FIGURE A.3**    ISDN channel structures.

alarm service, facsimile, videotex, and so on. These services could be accessed through a single multifunction terminal or several separate terminals. In either case, a single physical interface is provided. Most existing two-wire local loops can support this interface.

In some cases, one or both of the B channels remain unused; this results in a B+D or D interface, rather than the 2B+D interface. However, to simplify the network implementation, the data rate at the interface remains at 192 kbps. Nevertheless, for those subscribers with more modest transmission requirements, there may be a cost savings in using a reduced basic interface.

*Primary access* is intended for users with greater capacity requirements, such as offices with a digital PBX or a local network. Because of differences in the digital transmission hierarchies used in different countries, it was not possible to get agreement on a single data rate. The United States, Canada, and Japan make use of a transmission structure based on 1.544 Mbps; this corresponds to the T1 transmission facility using the DS-1 transmission format. In Europe, 2.048 Mbps is the standard rate. Both of these data rates are provided as a primary interface service. Typically, the channel structure for the 1.544-Mbps rate is 23 B channels plus one 64-kbps D channel and, for the 2.048-Mbps rate, 30 B channels plus one 64-kbps D channel. Again, it is possible for a customer with lower requirements to employ fewer B channels, in which case the channel structure is $n$B+D, where $n$ ranges from 1 to 23, or 1 to 30 for the two primary services. Also, a customer with high data-rate demands may be provided with more than one primary physical interface. In this case, a single D channel on one of the interfaces may suffice for all signaling needs, and the other interfaces may consist solely of B channels (24B or 31B). The frame structure for primary access was shown in Figure 7.11.

The primary interface may also be used to support H channels. Some of these structures include a 64-kbps D channel for control signaling. When no D channel is present, it is assumed that a D channel on another primary interface at the same subscriber location will provide any required signaling. The following structures are recognized:

- **Primary rate interface H0 channel structures.** This interface supports multiple 384-kbps H0 channels. The structures are 3H0 + D and 4H0 for the 1.544-Mbps interface, and 5H0 + D for the 2.048-Mbps interface.

- **Primary rate interface H1 channel structures.** The H11 channel structure consists of one 1536-kbps H11 channel. The H12 channel structure consists of one 1920-kbps H12 channel and one D channel.
- **Primary rate interface structures for mixtures of B and H0 channels.** This interface consists of 0 or 1 D channels plus any possible combination of B and H0 channels, up to the capacity of the physical interface (e.g., 3H0 + 5B + D and 3H0 + 6B).

## A.3  USER ACCESS

To define the requirements for ISDN user access, an understanding of the anticipated configuration of user premises equipment and of the necessary standard interfaces is critical. The first step is to group functions that may exist on the user's premises. Figure A.4 shows the CCITT approach to this task, using

- **Functional groupings.** Certain finite arrangements of physical equipment or combinations of equipment.
- **Reference points.** Conceptual points used to separate groups of functions.

The architecture on the subscriber's premises is broken up functionally into groupings separated by reference points. This separation permits interface standards to be developed at each reference point; this effectively organizes the standards work and provides guidance to the equipment providers. Once stable interface standards exist, technical improvements on either side of an interface can be

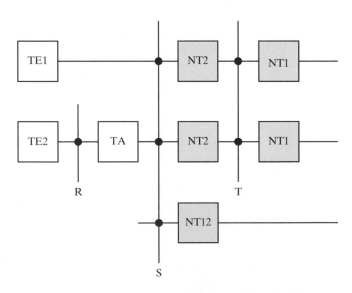

**FIGURE A.4**  ISDN reference points and functional groupings.

made without impacting adjacent functional groupings. Finally, with stable interfaces, the subscriber is free to procure equipment from different suppliers for the various functional groupings, so long as the equipment conforms to the relevant interface standards.

*Network termination 1* (NT1) includes functions associated with the physical and electrical termination of the ISDN on the user's premises; these correspond to OSI layer 1. The NT1 may be controlled by the ISDN provider and forms a boundary to the network. This boundary isolates the user from the transmission technology of the subscriber loop and presents a physical connector interface for user device attachment. In addition, the NT1 performs line maintenance functions such as loopback testing and performance monitoring. The NT1 supports multiple channels (e.g., 2B + D); at the physical level, the bit streams of these channels are multiplexed together, using synchronous time-division multiplexing. Finally, the NT1 interface might support multiple devices in a multidrop arrangement. For example, a residential interface might include a telephone, personal computer, and alarm system, all attached to a single NT1 interface via a multidrop line.

*Network termination 2* (NT2) is an intelligent device that can perform switching and concentration functions; it may include functionality up through layer 3 of the OSI model. Examples of NT2 are a digital PBX, a terminal controller, and a LAN. An example of a switching function is the construction of a private network using semipermanent circuits among a number of sites, each of which could include a PBX that acts as a circuit switch, or a host computer that acts as a packet switch. The concentration function simply means that multiple devices, attached to a digital PBX, LAN, or terminal controller, may transmit data across an ISDN.

*Network termination 1, 2* (NT12) is a single piece of equipment that contains the combined functions of NT1 and NT2; this points out one of the regulatory issues associated with ISDN interface development. In many countries, the ISDN provider will own the NT12 and provide full service to the user. In the United States, there is a need for a network termination with a limited number of functions to permit competitive provision of user premises equipment. Hence, the user premises network functions are split into NT1 and NT2.

Terminal equipment refers to subscriber equipment that makes use of ISDN; two types are defined. *Terminal equipment type 1* (TE1) refers to devices that support the standard ISDN interface. Examples are digital telephones, integrated voice/data terminals, and digital facsimile equipment. Terminal equipment type 2 (TE2) encompasses existing non-ISDN equipment. Examples are terminals with a physical interface, such as EIA-232-E, and host computers with an X.25 interface. Such equipment requires a terminal adapter (TA) to plug into an ISDN interface.

The definitions of the functional groupings also define, by implication, the reference points. *Reference point T* (terminal) corresponds to a minimal ISDN network termination at the customer's premises; it separates the network provider's equipment from the user's equipment. *Reference point S* (system) corresponds to the interface of individual ISDN terminals and separates user terminal equipment from network-related communications functions. *Reference point R* (rate) provides a non-ISDN interface between user equipment that is not ISDN-compatible and adapter equipment. Typically, this interface will comply with an older interface standard, such as EIA-232-E.

## A.4 ISDN PROTOCOLS

### ISDN Protocol Architecture

Figure A.5 illustrates, in the context of the OSI model, the protocols defined or referenced in the ISDN documents. As a network, ISDN is essentially unconcerned with user layers 4–7. These are end-to-end layers employed by the user for the exchange of information. Network access is concerned only with layers 1–3. Layer 1, defined in I.430 and I.431, specifies the physical interface for both basic and primary access. Because B and D channels are multiplexed over the same physical interface, these standards apply to both types of channels. Above this layer, the protocol structure differs for the two channels.

For the D channel, a new data link layer standard, LAPD (Link Access Protocol, D channel) has been defined. This standard is based on HDLC, modified to meet ISDN requirements. All transmission on the D channel is in the form of LAPD frames that are exchanged between the subscriber equipment and an ISDN switching element. Three applications are supported: control signaling, packet-switching, and telemetry. For **control signaling**, a call control protocol has been

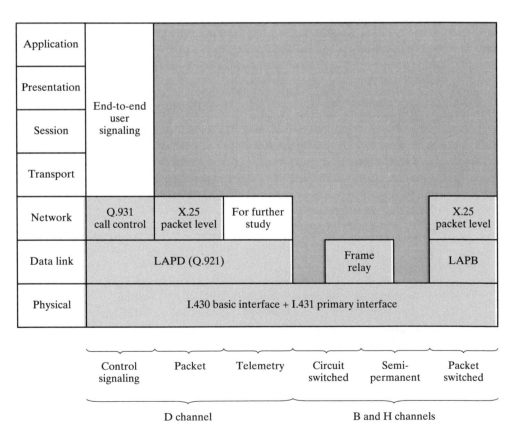

**FIGURE A.5** ISDN protocols at the user-network interface.

defined (I.451/Q.931). This protocol is used to establish, maintain, and terminate connections on B channels; thus, it is a protocol between the user and the network. Above layer 3, there is the possibility for higher-layer functions associated with user-to-user control signaling. These functions are a subject for further study. The D channel can also be used to provide *packet-switching* services to the subscriber. In this case, the X.25 level-3 protocol is used, and X.25 packets are transmitted in LAPD frames. The X.25 level-3 protocol is used to establish virtual circuits on the D channel to other users and to exchange packetized data. The final application area, *telemetry*, is a subject for further study.

The B channel can be used for circuit switching, semipermanent circuits, and packet-switching. For *circuit switching*, a circuit is set up on a B channel, on demand. The D-channel call control protocol is used for this purpose. Once the circuit is set up, it may be used for data transfer between the users. A *semipermanent circuit* is a B-channel circuit that is set up by prior agreement between the connected users and the network. As with a circuit-switched connection, it provides a transparent data path between end systems.

With either a circuit-switched connection or a semipermanent circuit, it appears to the connected stations that they have a direct, full-duplex link with each other. They are free to use their own formats, protocols, and frame synchronization. Hence, from the point of view of ISDN, layers 2 through 7 are not visible or specified.

In the case of *packet-switching*, a circuit-switched connection is set up on a B channel between the user and a packet-switched node using the D-channel control protocol. Once the circuit is set up on the B channel, the user may employ X.25 layers 2 and 3 to establish a virtual circuit to another user over that channel and to exchange packetized data. As an alternative, the frame relay service may be used. Frame relay can also be used over H channels and over the D channel.

Some of the protocols shown in Figure A.5 are summarized in the remainder of this section. First, we look at the way in which packet-switched and circuit-switched connections are set up. Next, we examine the control-signaling protocol and then LAPD. Finally, the physical-layer specifications are reviewed.

## ISDN Connections

ISDN provides four types of service for end-to-end communication:

- Circuit-switched calls over a B channel.
- Semipermanent connections over a B channel.
- Packet-switched calls over a B channel.
- Packet-switched calls over the D channel.

### Circuit-Switched Calls

The network configuration and protocols for circuit switching involve both the B and D channels. The B channel is used for the transparent exchange of user data. The communicating users may employ any protocols they wish for end-to-end communication. The D channel is used to exchange control information between the user and the network for call establishment and termination, as well as to gain access to network facilities.

The B channel is serviced by an NT1 or NT2 using only layer-1 functions. On the D channel, a three-layer network access protocol is used and is explained below. Finally, the process of establishing a circuit through ISDN involves the cooperation of switches internal to ISDN to set up the connection. These switches interact by using an internal protocol: Signaling-System Number 7.

## Semipermanent Connections

A semipermanent connection between agreed points may be provided for an indefinite period of time after subscription, for a fixed period, or for agreed-upon periods during a day, a week, or some other interval. As with circuit-switched connections, only Layer-1 functionality is provided by the network interface. The call-control protocol is not needed because the connection already exists.

## Packet-Switched Calls over a B Channel

The ISDN must also permit user access to packet-switched services for data traffic (e.g., interactive) that is best serviced by packet switching. There are two possibilities for implementing this service: Either the packet-switching capability is furnished by a separate network, referred to as a packet-switched public data network (PSPDN), or the packet-switching capability is integrated into ISDN. In the former case, the service is provided over a B channel. In the latter case, the service may be provided over a B or D channel. We first examine the use of a B channel for packet-switching.

When the packet-switching service is provided by a separate PSPDN, the access to that service is via a B channel. Both the user and the PSPDN must therefore be connected as subscribers to the ISDN. In the case of the PSPDN, one or more of the packet-switching network nodes, referred to as packet handlers, are connected to ISDN. We can think of each such node as a traditional X.25 DCE supplemented by the logic needed to access ISDN. That is, the ISDN subscriber assumes the role of an X.25 DTE, the node in the PSPDN to which it is connected functions as an X.25 DCE, and the ISDN simply provides the connection from DTE to DCE. Any ISDN subscriber can then communicate, via X.25, with any user connected to the PSPDN, including

- Users with a direct, permanent connection to the PSPDN.
- Users of the ISDN that currently enjoy a connection, through the ISDN, to the PSPDN.

The connection between the user (via a B channel) and the packet handler with which it communicates may be either semipermanent or circuit-switched. In the former case, the connection is always there and the user may freely invoke X.25 to set up a virtual circuit to another user. In the latter case, the D channel is involved, and the following sequence of steps occurs (Figure A.6):

1. The user requests, via the D-channel call-control protocol (I.451/Q.931), a circuit-switched connection on a B channel to a packet handler.
2. The connection is set up by ISDN, and the user is notified via the D channel call-control protocol.

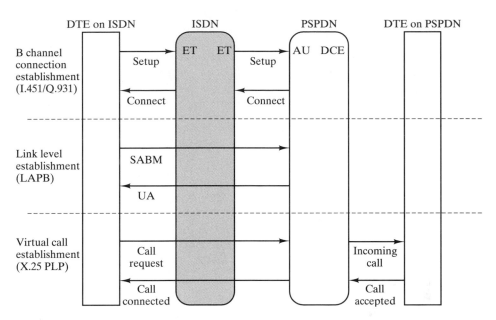

**FIGURE A.6** Virtual call setup.

3. The user sets up a virtual circuit to another user via the X.25 call establishment procedure on the B channel (described in Section 3.2). This step requires first that a data link connection, using LAPB, must be set up between the user and the packet handler.

4. The user terminates the virtual circuit, using X.25 on the B channel.

5. After one or more virtual calls on the B channel, the user is done and signals via the D channel to terminate the circuit-switched connection to the packet-switching node.

6. The connection is terminated by ISDN.

Figure A.7 shows the configuration involved in providing this service. In the figure, the user is shown to employ a DTE device that expects an interface to an X.25 DCE. Hence, a terminal adapter is required. Alternatively, the X.25 capability can be an integrated function of an ISDN TE1 device, dispensing with the need for a separate TA.

When the packet-switching service is provided by ISDN, the packet-handling function is provided within the ISDN, either by separate equipment or as part of the exchange equipment. The user may connect to a packet handler either by a B channel or the D channel. On a B channel, the connection to the packet handler may be either switched or semipermanent, and the same procedures described above apply for switched connections. In this case, rather than establish a B-channel connection to another ISDN subscriber that is a PSPDN packet handler, the connection is to an internal element of ISDN that is a packet handler.

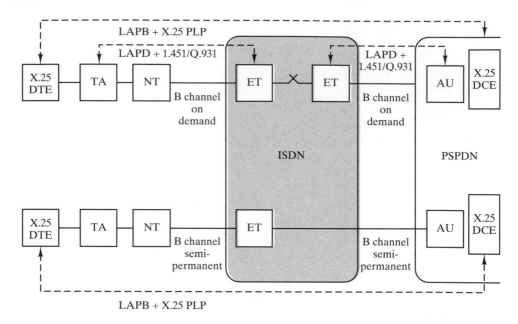

LEGEND

AU = ISDN access unit            ET      = Exchange termination
TA = Terminal adapter               PLP     = Packet-level procedure
NT = Network termination 2 and/or 1     PSPDN = Packet-switched public data network

**FIGURE A.7**  Access to PSPDN for packet-mode service.

## Packet-Switched Calls over a D Channel

When the packet-switching service is provided internal to the ISDN, it can also be accessed on the D channel. For this access, ISDN provides a semipermanent connection to a packet-switching node within the ISDN. The user employs the X.25 level-3 protocol, as is done in the case of a B-channel virtual call. Here, the level-3 protocol is carried by LAPD frames. Because the D channel is also used for control signaling, some means is needed to distinguish between X.25 packet traffic and ISDN control traffic; this is accomplished by means of the link-layer addressing scheme, as explained below.

Figure A.8 shows the configuration for providing packet-switching within ISDN. The packet-switching service provided internal to the ISDN over the B and D channels is logically provided by a single packet-switching network. Thus, virtual calls can be set up between two D-channel users, two B-channel users, and between a B and D channel user. In addition, it will be typical to also provide access to X.25 users on other ISDNs and PSPDNs by appropriate interworking procedures.

### Common Channel Signaling at the ISDN User-Network Interface

ITU-T has developed a standard, I.451, for common channel signaling. The primary application of this standard is for the Integrated Services Digital Network. In OSI terms, I.451 is a layer-3, or network-layer, protocol. As Figure A.9 indicates, I.451

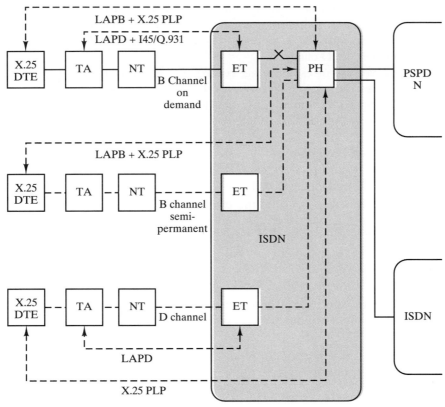

LEGEND

TA = Terminal adapter
NT = Network termination 2 and/or 1
ET = Exchange termination

PLP   = Packet-level procedure
PSPDN = Packet-switched public data network
PH    = Packet handling function

**FIGURE A.8**  Access to ISDN for packet-mode service.

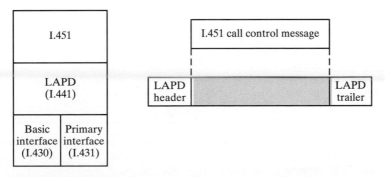

**FIGURE A.9**  Call control communications architecture.

relies on a link layer protocol to transmit messages over the D channel. I.451 specifies procedures for establishing connections on the B channels that share the same physical interface to ISDN as the D channel. It also provides user-to-user control signaling over the D channel.

The process of establishing, controlling, and terminating a call occurs as a result of control-signaling messages exchanged between the user and the network over a D channel. A common format is used for all messages defined in I.451, illustrated in Figure A.10a. Three fields are common to all messages:

- **Protocol discriminator.** Used to distinguish messages for user-network call control from other message types. Other sorts of protocols may share the common signaling channel.
- **Call reference.** Identifies the user-channel call to which this message refers. As with X.25 virtual circuit numbers, it has only local significance. The call reference field comprises three subfields. The length subfield specifies the length of the remainder of the field in octets. This length is one octet for a basic-rate interface, and two octets for a primary-rate interface. The flag indicates which end of the LAPD logical connection initiated the call.
- **Message type.** Identifies which I.451 message is being sent. The contents of the remainder of the message depend on the message type.

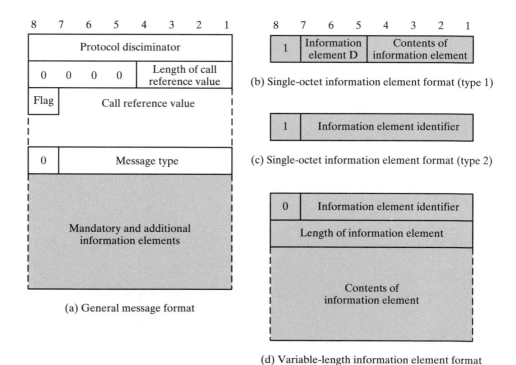

(a) General message format

(b) Single-octet information element format (type 1)

(c) Single-octet information element format (type 2)

(d) Variable-length information element format

**FIGURE A.10**   I.451 formats.

Following these three common fields, the remainder of the message consists of a sequence of zero or more information elements, or parameters. These contain additional information to be conveyed with the message. Thus, the message type specifies a command or response, and the details are provided by the information elements. Some information elements must always be included with a given message (mandatory), and others are optional (additional). Three formats for information elements are used, as indicated in Figure A.10b through d.

Table A.3 lists the I.451 messages. The messages can be grouped along two dimensions. Messages apply to one of four applications: circuit-mode control, packet-mode access connection control, user-to-user signaling not associated with circuit-switched calls, and messages used with the global call reference. In addition, messages perform functions in one of four categories: call establishment, call information, call clearing, and miscellaneous.

*Circuit-mode control* refers to the functions needed to set up, maintain, and clear a circuit-switched connection on a user channel. This function corresponds to call control in existing circuit-switching telecommunications networks. *Packet-mode access connection control* refers to the functions needed to set up a circuit-switched connection (called an access connection in this context) to an ISDN packet-switching node; this connects the user to the packet-switching network provided by the ISDN provider. *User-to-user signaling messages* allow two users to communicate without setting up a circuit-switched connection. A temporary signaling connection is established and cleared in a manner similar to the control of a circuit-switched connection. Signaling takes place over the signaling channel and thus does not consume user-channel resources. Finally, global call reference refers to the functions that enable either user or network to return one or more channels to an idle condition.

*Call establishment messages* are used to initially set up a call. This group includes messages between the calling terminal and the network, and between the network and the called terminal. These messages support the following services:

- Set up a user-channel call in response to user request.
- Provide particular network facilities for this call.
- Inform calling user of the progress of the call establishment process.

Once a call has been set up, but prior to the disestablishment (termination) phase, *call-information* phase messages are sent between user and network. One of the messages in this group allows the network to relay, without modification, information between the two users of the call. The nature of this information is beyond the scope of the standard, but it is assumed that it is control signaling information that can't or should not be sent directly over the user-channel circuit. The remainder of the messages allow users to request both the suspension and later resumption of a call. When a call is suspended, the network remembers the identity of the called parties and the network facilities supporting the call, but it deactivates the call so that no additional charges are incurred and so that the corresponding user channel is freed up. Presumably, the resumption of a call is quicker and cheaper than the origination of a new call.

**TABLE A.3** I.451/Q.931 messages for circuit-mode connection control.

| Message | Significance | Direction | Function |
|---|---|---|---|
| Call establishment messages | | | |
| ALERTING | global | both | Indicates that user alerting has begun |
| CALL PROCEEDING | local | both | Indicates that call establishment has been initiated |
| CONNECT | global | both | Indicates call acceptance by called TE |
| CONNECT ACKNOWLEDGE | local | both | Indicates that user has been awarded the call |
| PROGRESS | global | both | Reports progress of a call |
| SETUP | global | both | Initiates call establishment |
| SETUP ACKNOWLEDGE | local | both | Indicates that call establishment has been initiated but requests more information |
| Call information phase messages | | | |
| RESUME | local | u → n | Requests resumption of previously suspended call |
| RESUME ACKNOWLEDGE | local | n → u | Indicates requested call has been reestablished |
| RESUME REJECT | local | n → u | Indicates failure to resume suspended call |
| SUSPEND | local | u → n | Requests suspension of a call |
| SUSPEND ACKNOWLEDGE | local | n → u | Call has been suspended |
| SUSPEND REJECT | local | n → u | Indicates failure of requested call suspension |
| USER INFORMATION | access | both | Transfers information from one user to another |
| Call clearing messages | | | |
| DISCONNECT | global | both | Sent by user to request connection clearing; sent by network to indicate connection clearing |
| RELEASE | local | both | Indicates intent to release channel and call reference. |
| RELEASE COMPLETE | local | both | Indicates release of channel and call reference |
| Miscellaneous messages | | | |
| CONGESTION CONTROL | local | both | Sets or releases flow control on USER INFORMATION messages |
| FACILITY | local | both | Requests or acknowledges a supplementary service |
| INFORMATION | local | both | Provides additional information |
| NOTIFY | access | both | Indicates information pertaining to a call |
| STATUS | local | both | Sent in response to a STATUS ENQUIRY or at any time to report an error |
| STATUS ENQUIRY | local | both | Solicits STATUS message |

*Call-clearing messages* are sent between user and network in order to terminate a call. Finally, there are some *miscellaneous messages* that may be sent between user and network at various stages of the call. Some may be sent during call setup; others may be sent even though no calls exist. The primary function of these messages is to negotiate network features (supplementary services).

## LAPD

All traffic over the D channel employs a link-layer protocol known as LAPD (Link Access Protocol-D Channel).

### LAPD Services

The LAPD standard provides two forms of service to LAPD users: the unacknowledged information-transfer service and the acknowledged information-transfer service. The *unacknowledged information-transfer service* simply provides for the transfer of frames containing user data with no acknowledgment. The service does not guarantee that data presented by one user will be delivered to another user, nor does it inform the sender if the delivery attempt fails. The service does not provide any flow control or error-control mechanism. This service supports both point-to-point (deliver to one user) or broadcast (deliver to a number of users); it allows for fast data transfer and is useful for management procedures such as alarm messages and messages that need to be broadcast to multiple users.

The *acknowledged information-transfer* is the more common service, and is similar to that offered by LAP-B and HDLC. With this service, a logical connection is established between two LAPD users prior to the exchange of data.

### LAPD Protocol

The LAPD protocol is based on HDLC. Both user information and protocol-control information and parameters are transmitted in frames. Corresponding to the two types of service offered by LAPD, there are two types of operation:

- **Unacknowledged operation.** Layer-3 information is transferred in unnumbered frames. Error detection is used to discard damaged frames, but there is no error control or flow control.
- **Acknowledged operation.** Layer-3 information is transferred in frames that include acknowledged sequence numbers. Error control and flow control procedures are included in the protocol. This type is also referred to in the standard as multiple-frame operation.

These two types of operation may coexist on a single D channel, and both make use of the frame format illustrated in Figure A.11. This format is identical to that of HDLC (Figure 6.10), with the exception of the address field.

To explain the address field, we need to consider that LAPD has to deal with two levels of multiplexing. First, at the subscriber site, there may be multiple user devices sharing the same physical interface. Second, within each user device, there may be multiple types of traffic: specifically, packet-switched data and control signaling. To accommodate these levels of multiplexing, LAPD employs a two-part

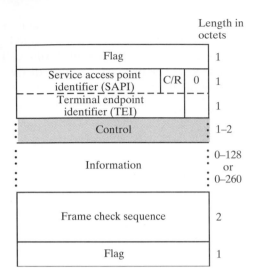

**FIGURE A.11** LAP-D format.

address, consisting of a terminal endpoint identifier (TEI) and a service access point identifier (SAPI).

Typically, each user device is given a unique *terminal endpoint identifier* (TEI). It is also possible for a single device to be assigned more than one TEI; this might be the case for a terminal concentrator. TEI assignment occurs either automatically when the equipment first connects to the interface, or manually by the user. In the latter case, care must be taken that multiple equipment attached to the same interface do not have the same TEI. The advantage of the automatic procedure is that it allows the user to change, add, or delete equipment at will without prior notification to the network administration. Without this feature, the network would be obliged to manage a data base for each subscriber that would need to be updated manually. Table A.4a shows the assignment of TEI numbers.

The *service access point identifier* (SAPI) identifies a layer-3 user of LAPD, and thus corresponds to a layer-3 protocol entity within a user device. Four specific values have been assigned, as shown in Table A.4b. A SAPI of 0 is used for call-control procedures for managing B-channel circuits; the value 16 is reserved for packet-mode communication on the D channel using X.25 level 3; and a value of 63 is used for the exchange of layer-2 management information. Finally, values in the range 32 to 62 are reserved to support frame-relay connections.

For acknowledged operation, LAPD follows essentially the same procedures described for HDLC in Chapter 6. For unacknowledged operation, the user information (UI) frame is used to transmit user data. When a LAPD user wishes to send data, it passes the data to its LAPD entity, which passes the data in the information field of a UI frame. When this frame is received, the information field is passed up to the destination user. There is no acknowledgment returned to the other side. However, error detection is performed, and frames in error are discarded.

**TABLE A.4**   SAPI and TEI assignments.

(a) TEI Assignments

| TE1 value | User type |
|-----------|-----------|
| 0–63<br>64–126<br>127 | Nonautomatic TEI assignment user equipment<br>Automatic TEI assignment user equipment<br>Used during automatic TEI assignment |

(b) SAPI Assignments

| SAPI value | Related protocol or management entity |
|------------|---------------------------------------|
| 0<br>16<br>32–61<br>63<br>All others | Call control procedures<br>Packet communication conforming to X.25 level 3<br>Frame relay communication<br>Layer 2 management procedures<br>Reserved for future standardization |

## Physical Layer

The ISDN physical layer is presented to the user at either reference point S or T (Figure A.4). The mechanical interface was described in Chapter 5.

The electrical specification depends on the specific interface. For the basic-access interface, pseudoternary coding is used (Figure 4.2). Recall that with pseudoternary, the line signal may take one of three levels; this is not as efficient as a two-level code, but it is reasonably simple and inexpensive. At the relatively modest data rate of the basic-access interface, this is a suitable code.

For the higher-speed, primary-access interface, a more efficient coding scheme is needed. For the 1.544-Mbps data rate, the B8ZS code is used, while for the 2.048-Mbps data rate, the HDB3 code is used (Figure 4.6). There is no particular advantage of one over the other; the specification reflects historical usage.

The functional specification for the physical layer includes the following functions:

- Full-duplex transmission of B-channel data
- Full-duplex transmission of D-channel data
- Full-duplex transmission of timing signals
- Activation and deactivation of physical circuit
- Power feeding from the network termination to the terminal
- Terminal identification
- Faulty-terminal isolation
- D-channel–contention access

The final function is required when multiple TE1 terminals share a single physical interface (i.e., a multipoint line). In that case, no additional functionality is needed to control access in the B channels, as each channel is dedicated to a particular circuit at any given time. However, the D channel is available for use by all the devices for both control signaling and for packet transmission. For incoming data, the LAPD addressing scheme is sufficient to sort out the proper destination for each data unit. For outgoing data, some sort of contention resolution protocol is needed to assure that only one device at a time attempts to transmit. The D-channel, contention-resolution algorithm was described in Chapter 7.

## A.5  BROADBAND ISDN

In 1988, as part of its I-series of recommendations on ISDN, CCITT issued the first two recommendations relating to broadband (B-ISDN): I.113, Vocabulary of Terms for Broadband Aspects of ISDN; and I.121, Broadband Aspects of ISDN. These documents provided a preliminary description and a basis for future standardization and development work, and from those documents a rich set of recommendations has been developed. Some of the important notions developed in these documents are presented in Table A.5.

**TABLE A.5**   Noteworthy statements in I.113 and I.121.

Broadband: A service or a system requiring transmission channels capable of supporting rates greater than the primary rate.

The term B-ISDN is used for convenience in order to refer to and emphasize the broadband aspects of ISDN. The intent, however, is that there be one comprehensive notion of an ISDN which provides broadband and other ISDN services.

Asynchronous transfer mode (ATM) is the transfer mode for implementing B-ISDN and is independent of the means of transport at the Physical Layer.

B-ISDN will be based on the concepts developed for ISDN and may evolve by progressively incorporating directly into the network additional B-ISDN functions enabling new and advanced services.

Since the B-ISDN is based on overall ISDN concepts, the ISDN access reference configuration is also the basis for the B-ISDN reference configuration.

CCITT modestly defines B-ISDN as "a service requiring transmission channels capable of supporting rates greater than the primary rate." Behind this innocuous statement lie plans for a network and a set of services that will have far more impact on business and residential customers than ISDN. With B-ISDN, services, especially video services, requiring data rates in excess of those that can be delivered by ISDN will become available. To contrast this new network and these new services to the original concept of ISDN, that original concept is now being referred to as narrowband ISDN.

### Broadband ISDN Architecture

B-ISDN differs from a narrowband ISDN in a number of ways. To meet the requirement for high-resolution video, an upper channel rate of approximately

150 Mbps is needed. To simultaneously support one or more interactive and distributive services, a total subscriber line rate of about 600 Mbps is needed. In terms of today's installed telephone plant, this is a stupendous data rate to sustain. The only appropriate technology for widespread support of such data rates is optical fiber. Hence, the introduction of B-ISDN depends on the pace of introduction of fiber subscriber loops.

Internal to the network, there is the issue of the switching technique to be used. The switching facility has to be capable of handling a wide range of different bit rates and traffic parameters (e.g., burstiness). Despite the increasing power of digital circuit-switching hardware and the increasing use of optical fiber trunking, it is difficult to handle the large and diverse requirements of B-ISDN with circuit-switching technology. For this reason, there is increasing interest in some type of fast packet-switching as the basic switching technique for B-ISDN. This form of switching readily supports ATM at the user-network interface.

## Functional Architecture

Figure A.12 depicts the functional architecture of B-ISDN. As with narrowband ISDN, control of B-ISDN is based on common-channel signaling. Within the network, an SS7, enhanced to support the expanded capabilities of a higher-speed network, is used. Similarly, the user-network control-signaling protocol is an enhanced version of I.451/Q.931.

B-ISDN must, of course, support all of the 64-kbps transmission services, both circuit-switching and packet-switching, that are supported by narrowband ISDN;

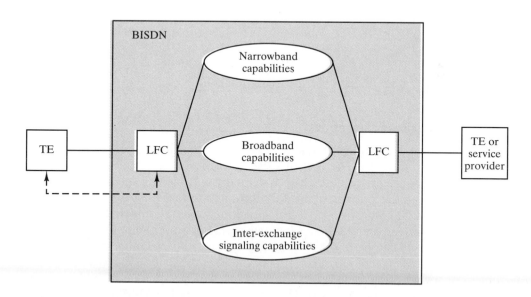

LEGEND

LFC  =  local function capabilities        TE = terminal equipment

**FIGURE A.12**    BISDN architecture.

this protects the user's investment and facilitates migration from narrowband to broadband ISDN. In addition, broadband capabilities are provided for higher data-rate transmission services. At the user-network interface, these capabilities will be provided with the connection-oriented asynchronous transfer mode (ATM) facility.

### User-Network Interface

The reference configuration defined for narrowband ISDN is considered general enough to be used for B-ISDN. Figure A.13, which is almost identical to Figure A.4, shows the reference configuration for B-ISDN. In order to clearly illustrate the broadband aspects, the notations for reference points and functional groupings are appended with the letter B (e.g., B-NT1, TB). The broadband functional groups are equivalent to the functional groups defined for narrowband ISDN, and are discussed below. Interfaces at the R reference point may or may not have broadband capabilities.

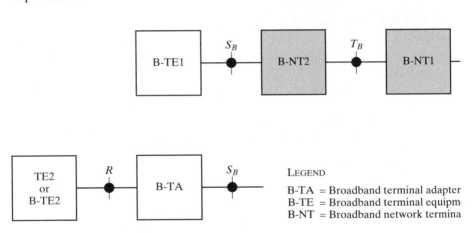

**FIGURE A.13** B ISDN reference configurations.

### Transmission Structure

In terms of data rates available to B-ISDN subscribers, three new transmission services are defined. The first of these consists of a full-duplex 155.52-Mbps service. The second service defined is asymmetrical, providing transmission from the subscriber to the network at 155.52 Mbps, and in the other direction at 622.08 Mbps; and the highest-capacity service yet defined is a full-duplex, 622.08-Mbps service.

A data rate of 155.52 Mbps can certainly support all of the narrowband ISDN services. That is, such a rate readily supports one or more basic- or primary-rate interfaces; in addition, it can support most of the B-ISDN services. At that rate, one or several video channels can be supported, depending on the video resolution and the coding technique used. Thus, the full-duplex 155.52-Mbps service will probably be the most common B-ISDN service.

The higher data rate of 622.08 Mbps is needed to handle multiple video distribution, such as might be required when a business conducts multiple simultaneous videoconferences. This data rate makes sense in the network-to-subscriber direction. The typical subscriber will not initiate distribution services and thus would still be able to use the lower, 155.52-Mbps service. The full-duplex, 622.08-Mbps service would be appropriate for a video-distribution provider.

## Broadband ISDN Protocols

The protocol architecture for B-ISDN introduces some new elements not found in the ISDN architecture, as depicted in Figure A.14. For B-ISDN, it is assumed that the transfer of information across the user-network interface will use ATM.

The decision to use ATM for B-ISDN is a remarkable one; it implies that B-ISDN will be a packet-based network, certainly at the interface, and almost certainly in terms of its internal switching. Although the recommendation also states that B-ISDN will support circuit-mode applications, this will be done over a packet-based transport mechanism. Thus, ISDN, which began as an evolution from the circuit-switching telephone network, will transform itself into a packet-switching network as it takes on broadband services.

The protocol reference model makes reference to three separate planes:

- **User Plane.** Provides for user-information transfer, along with associated controls (e.g., flow control, error control).
- **Control Plane.** Performs call-control and connection-control functions.
- **Management Plane.** Includes plane management, which performs management functions related to a system as a whole and provides coordination between all the planes, and layer management, which performs management functions relating to resources and parameters residing in its protocol entities.

Table A.6 highlights the functions to be performed at each sublayer.

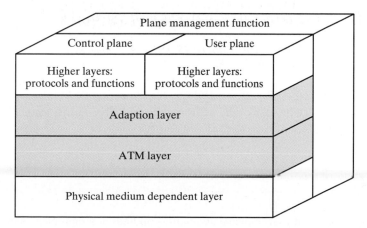

**FIGURE A.14**    B-ISDN protocol model for ATM.

TABLE A.6   Functions of the B-ISDN layers.

| | Higher-layer functions | Higher layers | |
|---|---|---|---|
| | Convergence | CS | |
| | Segmentation and reassembly | SAR | AAL |
| Layer Management | Generic flow control<br>Cell header generation/extraction<br>Cell VPI/VCI translation<br>Cell multiplex and demultiplex | ATM | |
| | Cell rate decoupling<br>HEC header sequence generation/verification<br>Cell delineation<br>Transmission frame adaptation<br>Transmission frame generation/recovery | TC | Physical layer |
| | Bit timing<br>Physical medium | PM | |

CS = Covergence sublayer
SAR = Segmentation and reassembly sublayer
AAL = ATM adaptation layer
ATM = Asynchronous transfer mode
TC = Transmission control sublayer
PM = Physical medium sublayer

## A.6   RECOMMENDED READING

A detailed technical treatment of ISDN and broadband ISDN can be found in [STAL95a]. Other book-length treatments include [KESS93] and [HELG91].

HELG91   Helgert, H. *Integrated Services Digital Networks: Architectures, Protocols, and Standards*. Reading, MA: Addison-Wesley, 1991.

KESS93   Kessler, G. *ISDN: Concepts, Facilities, and Services*. New York: McGraw-Hill, 1993.

STAL95a   Stallings, W. *ISDN and Broadband ISDN, with Frame Relay and ATM*. Upper Saddle River, NJ: Prentice Hall, 1995.

**Recommended Web Site**

* http:/alumni.caltech.edu/~dank/isdn: Information on ISDN tariffs, standards status, and links to vendors.

## A.7   PROBLEMS

A.1   It was mentioned that user-implemented multidrop lines and multiplexers may disappear. Explain why.

A.2   An ISDN customer has offices at a number of sites. A typical office is served by two 1.544-Mbps digital pipes. One provides circuit-switched access to the ISDN; the other is a leased line connecting to another user site. The on-premises equipment consists of a PBX aligned with packet-switching node logic. The user has three requirements:

- Telephone service
- A private packet-switched network for data
- Video teleconferencing at 1.544 Mbps

How might the user allocate capacity optimally to meet these requirements?

A.3   An ISDN basic access frame has 32 B bits and 4 D bits. Suppose that more bits were used—say 160 B bits and 20 D bits per frame. Would this reduce the percentage overhead and therefore the basic-access bit rate? If so, discuss any potential disadvantages.

A.4   Under what circumstances would user layer 3 on the B channel not be null?

A.5   Compare the addressing schemes in HDLC, LLC, and LAPD:
    a. Are the SAPI of LAP-D and the SAP of LLC the same thing?
    b. Are the TEI of LAP-D and the MAC-level address of IEEE 802 the same thing?
    c. Why are two levels of addressing needed for LAP-D and LLC, but only one level for HDLC?
    d. Why does LLC need a source address, but LAP-D and HDLC do not?

A.6   What is the percentage overhead on the basic channel structure?

A.7   From Figure A.5, it would appear that layers 4–7 of the OSI model are little affected by ISDN. Would you expect this? Why or why not?

A.8   X.25 and most other layer-3 protocols provide techniques for flow control and error control. Why are such features not provided in I.451?

# Appendix B

# RFCs Cited
# in This Book

| RFC Number | Title | Date |
|---|---|---|
| 768 | User Datagram Protocol (UDP) | August 1980 |
| 791 | Internet Protocol (IP) | September 1981 |
| 792 | Internet Control Message Protocol (ICMP) | September 1981 |
| 793 | Transmission Control Protocol (TCP) | September 1981 |
| 821 | Simple Mail-Transfer Protocol (SMTP) | August 1982 |
| 822 | Standard for the Format of ARPA Internet Text Messages | August 1982 |
| 1321 | The MD5 Message-Digest Algorithm | April 1992 |
| 1521 | MIME (Multipurpose Internet Mail Extensions) Part One: Mechanisms for Specifying and Describing the Format of Internet Message Bodies | September 1993 |
| 1522 | MIME (Multipurpose Internet Mail Extensions) Part Two: Message Header Extensions for Non-ASCII Text | September 1993 |
| 1583 | OSPF Version 2 | March 1994 |
| 1630 | Universal Resource Identifiers in WWW | June 1994 |
| 1738 | Uniform Resource Locators (URL) | December 1994 |
| 1752 | The Recommendation for the IP Next-Generation Protocol | January 1995 |
| 1771 | A Border Gateway Protocol 4 (BGP-4) | March 1995 |
| 1808 | Relative Uniform Resource Locators | June 1995 |
| 1809 | Using the Flow Label in IPv6 | June 1995 |
| 1825 | Security Architecture for the Internet Protocol | August 1995 |
| 1826 | IP Authentication Header | August 1995 |
| 1827 | IP Encapsulating Security Payload (ESP) | August 1995 |
| 1828 | IP Authentication Using Keyed MD5 | August 1995 |
| 1829 | The ESP DES-CBC Transform | August 1995 |
| 1883 | Internet Protocol, Version 6 Specification | December 1995 |
| 1884 | IP Version-6 Addressing Architecture | December 1995 |
| 1885 | Internet Control Message Protocol (ICMPv6) for the Internet Protocol Version-6 (IPv6) Specification | December 1995 |
| 1886 | DNS Extensions to Support IP Version 6 | December 1995 |
| 1887 | An Architecture for IPv6 Unicast Address Allocation | December 1995 |
| 1901 | Introduction to Community-Based SNMPv2 | January 1996 |
| 1902 | Structure of Management Information for SNMPv2 | January 1996 |
| 1903 | Textual Conventions for SNMPv2 | January 1996 |
| 1904 | Conformance Statements for SNMPv2 | January 1996 |
| 1905 | Protocol Operations for SNMPv2 | January 1996 |
| 1906 | Transport Mappings for SNMPv2 | January 1996 |
| 1907 | Management Information Base for SNMPv2 | January 1996 |
| 1908 | Coexistence Between Version 1 and Version 2 of the Internet-Standard Network Management Framework | January 1996 |

# GLOSSARY

Some of the definitions in this glossary are from the *American National Standard Dictionary of Information Technology*, ANSI Standard X3.172, 1995; these are marked with an asterisk.

**Abstract Syntax Notation One (ASN.1)**  A formal language used to define syntax. In the case of SNMP, ASN.1 notation is used to define the format of SNMP protocol data units and of objects.

**Aloha**  A medium access control technique for multiple-access transmission media. A station transmits whenever it has data to send. Unacknowledged transmissions are repeated.

**Amplitude**  The size or magnitude of a voltage or current waveform.

**Amplitude modulation***  A form of modulation in which the amplitude of a carrier wave is varied in accordance with some characteristic of the modulating signal.

**Amplitude-shift keying**  Modulation in which the two binary values are represented by two different amplitudes of the carrier frequency.

**Analog data***  Data represented by a physical quantity that is considered to be continuously variable and whose magnitude is made directly proportional to the data or to a suitable function of the data.

**Analog signal**  A continuously varying electromagnetic wave that may be propagated over a variety of media.

**Analog transmission**  The transmission of analog signals without regard to content. The signal may be amplified, but there is no intermediate attempt to recover the data from the signal.

**Angle modulation***  Modulation in which the angle of a sine wave carrier is varied. Phase and frequency modulation are particular forms of angle modulation.

**Application layer**  Layer 7 of the OSI model. This layer determines the interface of the system with the user.

**Asymmetric encryption**  A form of cryptosystem in which encryption and decryption are performed using two different keys, one of which is referred to as the public key and one of which is referred to as the private key. Also known as public-key encryption.

**Asynchronous transfer mode (ATM)**   A form of packet transmission using fixed-size packets, called cells. ATM is the data transfer interface for B-ISDN. Unlike X.25, ATM does not provide error control and flow control mechanisms.

**Asynchronous transmission**   Transmission in which each information character is individually synchronized (usually by the use of start elements and stop elements).

**Attenuation**   A decrease in magnitude of current, voltage, or power of a signal in transmission between points.

**ATM adaptation layer (AAL)**   The layer that maps information transfer protocols onto ATM.

**Authentication***   A process used to verify the integrity of transmitted data, especially a message.

**Automatic repeat request**   A feature that automatically initiates a request for retransmission when an error in transmission is detected.

**Balanced transmission**   A transmission mode in which signals are transmitted as a current that travels down one conductor and returns on the other. For digital signals, this technique is known as differential signaling, with the binary value depending on the voltage difference.

**Bandlimited signal**   A signal, all of whose energy is contained within a finite frequency range.

**Bandwidth***   The difference between the limiting frequencies of a continuous frequency spectrum.

**Baseband**   Transmission of signals without modulation. In a baseband local network, digital signals (1s and 0s) are inserted directly onto the cable as voltage pulses. The entire spectrum of the cable is consumed by the signal. This scheme does not allow frequency-division multiplexing.

**Bit stuffing**   The insertion of extra bits into a data stream to avoid the appearance of unintended control sequences.

**Bridge***   A functional unit that interconnects two local area networks (LANs) that use the same logical link control protocol but may use different medium access control protocols.

**Broadband**   The use of coaxial cable for providing data transfer by means of analog (radio-frequency) signals. Digital signals are passed through a modem and transmitted over one of the frequency bands of the cable.

**Broadcast**   The simultaneous transmission of data to a number of stations.

**Broadcast address**   An address that designates all entities within a domain (e.g., network, internet).

**Broadcast communication network**   A communication network in which a transmission from one station is broadcast to and received by all other stations.

**Bus\*** One or more conductors that serve as a common connection for a related group of devices.

**Carrier** A continuous frequency capable of being modulated or impressed with a second (information carrying) signal.

**CATV** Community Antenna Television. CATV cable is used for broadband local networks, and broadcast TV distribution.

**Cell relay** The packet-switching mechanism used for the fixed-size packets called cells. ATM is based on cell relay technology.

**Checksum** An error-detecting code based on a summation operation performed on the bits to be checked.

**Ciphertext** The output of an encryption algorithm; the encrypted form of a message or data.

**Circuit switching** A method of communicating in which a dedicated communications path is established between two devices through one or more intermediate switching nodes. Unlike packet switching, digital data are sent as a continuous stream of bits. Bandwidth is guaranteed, and delay is essentially limited to propagation time. The telephone system uses circuit switching.

**Coaxial cable** A cable consisting of one conductor, usually a small copper tube or wire, within and insulated from another conductor of larger diameter, usually copper tubing or copper braid.

**Codec (Coder-decoder)** Transforms analog data into a digital bit stream (coder), and digital signals into analog data (decoder).

**Collision** A condition in which two packets are being transmitted over a medium at the same time. Their interference makes both unintelligible.

**Common carrier** In the United States, companies that furnish communication services to the public. The usual connotation is for long-distance telecommunications services. Common carriers are subject to regulation by federal and state regulatory commissions.

**Common channel signaling** Technique in which network control signals (e.g., call request) are separated from the associated voice or data path by placing the signaling from a group of voice or data paths on a separate channel dedicated to signaling only.

**Communications architecture** The hardware and software structure that implements the communications function.

**Communication network** A collection of interconnected functional units that provides a data communications service among stations attached to the network.

**Connectionless data transfer** A protocol for exchanging data in an unplanned fashion and without prior coordination (e.g., datagram).

**Connection-oriented data transfer** A protocol for exchanging data in which a logical connection is established between the endpoints (e.g., virtual circuit).

**Contention** The condition when two or more stations attempt to use the same channel at the same time.

**Conventional encryption** Symmetric encryption.

**Crosstalk\*** The phenomenon in which a signal transmitted on one circuit or channel of a transmission system creates an undesired effect in another circuit or channel.

**CSMA (Carrier Sense Multiple Access)** A medium access control technique for multiple-access transmission media. A station wishing to transmit first senses the medium and transmits only if the medium is idle.

**CSMA/CD (Carrier Sense Multiple Access with collision detection)** A refinement of CSMA in which a station ceases transmission if it detects a collision.

**Current-mode transmission** A transmission mode in which the transmitter alternately applies current to each of two conductors in a twisted pair to represent logic 1 or 0. The total current is constant and always in the same direction.

**Cyclic redundancy check** An error detecting code in which the code is the remainder resulting from dividing the bits to be checked by a predetermined binary number.

**Data circuit-terminating equipment (DCE)** In a data station, the equipment that provides the signal conversion and coding between the data terminal equipment (DTE) and the line. The DCE may be separate equipment, or an integral part of the DTE, or of intermediate equipment. The DCE may perform other functions that are normally performed at the network end of the line.

**Datagram\*** In packet switching, a packet, independent of other packets, that carries information sufficient for routing from the originating data terminal equipment (DTE) to the destination DTE without the necessity of establishing a connection between the DTEs and the network.

**Data link layer\*** In OSI, the layer that provides service to transfer data between network layer entities, usually in adjacent nodes. The data link layer detects and possibly corrects errors that may occur in the physical layer.

**Data terminal equipment (DTE)\*** Equipment consisting of digital end instruments that convert the user information into data signals for transmission, or reconvert the received data signals into user information.

**Decibel** A measure of the relative strength of two signals. The number of decibels is 10 times the log of the ratio of the power of two signals, or 20 times the log of the ratio of the voltage of two signals.

**Decryption** The translation of encrypted text or data (called ciphertext) into original text or data (called plaintext). Also called deciphering.

**Delay distortion** Distortion of a signal occurring when the propagation delay for the transmission medium is not constant over the frequency range of the signal.

**Demand-assignment multiple access**   A technique for allocating satellite capacity, based on either FDM or TDM, in which capacity is granted on demand.

**Differential encoding**   A means of encoding digital data on a digital signal such that the binary value is determined by a signal change rather than a signal level.

**Digital data**   Data consisting of a sequence of discrete elements.

**Digital signal**   A discrete or discontinuous signal, such as voltage pulses.

**Digital signature**   An authentication mechanism that enables the creator of a message to attach a code that acts as a signature. The signature guarantees the source and integrity of the message.

**Digital switch**   A star-topology local network. Usually refers to a system that handles only data, but not voice.

**Digital transmission**   The transmission of digital data, using either an analog or digital signal, in which the digital data are recovered and repeated at intermediate points to reduce the effects of noise.

**Digitize***   To convert an analog signal to a digital signal.

**Encapsulation**   The addition of control information by a protocol entity to data obtained from a protocol user.

**Encrypt***   To convert plain text or data into unintelligible form by the use of a code in such a manner that reconversion to the original form is possible.

**Error detecting code***   A code in which each expression conforms to specific rules of construction, so that if certain errors occur in an expression, the resulting expression will not conform to the rules of construction, and thus the presence of the errors is detected.

**Error rate***   The ratio of the number of data units in error to the total number of data units.

**Flow control**   The function performed by a receiving entity to limit the amount or rate of data that is sent by a transmitting entity.

**Frame**   A group of bits that includes data plus one or more addresses, and other protocol control information. Generally refers to a link layer (OSI layer 2) protocol data unit.

**Frame check sequence**   An error-detecting code inserted as a field in a block of data to be transmitted. The code serves to check for errors upon reception of the data.

**Frame relay**   A form of packet switching based on the use of variable-length, link-layer frames. There is no network layer, and many of the basic functions have been streamlined or eliminated to provide for greater throughput.

**Frequency**   Rate of signal oscillation in hertz.

**Frequency-division multiplexing**   The division of a transmission facility into two or more channels by splitting the frequency band transmitted by the facility into narrower bands, each of which is used to constitute a distinct channel.

**Frequency modulation**   Modulation in which the frequency of an alternating current is the characteristic varied.

**Frequency-shift keying**   Modulation in which the two binary values are represented by two different frequencies near the carrier frequency.

**Full-duplex transmission**   Data transmission in both directions at the same time.

**Half-duplex transmission**   Data transmission in either direction, one direction at a time.

**Hash function**   A function that maps a variable-length data block or message into a fixed-length value called a hash code. The function is designed in such a way that, when protected, it provides an authenticator to the data or message. Also referred to as a message digest.

**HDLC (high-level data link control)**   A very common, bit-oriented data link protocol (OSI layer 2) issued by ISO. Similar protocols are LAPB, LAPD, and LLC.

**Header**   System-defined control information that precedes user data.

**Impulse noise**   A high-amplitude, short-duration noise pulse.

**Integrated services digital network**   A planned worldwide telecommunication service that will use digital transmission and switching technology to support voice and digital data communication.

**Intermediate system (IS)**   A device attached to two or more subnetworks in an internet and that performs routing and relaying of data between end systems. Examples of intermediate systems are bridges and routers.

**Intermodulation noise**   Noise due to the nonlinear combination of signals of different frequencies.

**Internetwork**   A collection of packet-switching and broadcast networks that are connected together via routers.

**Internet protocol**   An internetworking protocol that provides connectionless service across multiple packet-switching networks.

**Internetworking**   Communication among devices across multiple networks.

**Layer***   A group of services, functions, and protocols that is complete from a conceptual point of view, that is one out of a set of hierarchically arranged groups, and that extends across all systems that conform to the network architecture.

**Local area network**   A communication network that provides interconnection of a variety of data communicating devices within a small area.

**Local loop**   Transmission path, generally twisted pair, between the individual subscriber and the nearest switching center of the public telecommunications network.

**Longitudinal redundancy check**   The use of a set of parity bits for a block of characters, such that there is a parity bit for each bit position in the characters.

**Manchester encoding**   A digital signaling technique in which there is a transition in the middle of each bit time. A 1 is encoded with a high level during the first half of the bit time; a 0 is encoded with a low level during the first half of the bit time.

**Medium access control (MAC)**   For broadcast networks, the method of determining which device has access to the transmission medium at any time. CSMA/CD and token are common access methods.

**Microwave**   Electromagnetic waves in the frequency range of about 2 to 40 GHz.

**Modem (Modulator/Demodulator)**   Transforms a digital bit stream into an analog signal (modulator), and vice versa (demodulator).

**Modulation***   The process, or result of the process, of varying certain characteristics of a signal, called a carrier, in accordance with a message signal.

**Multicast address**   An address that designates a group of entities within a domain (e.g., network, internet).

**Multiplexing**   In data transmission, a function that permits two or more data sources to share a common transmission medium such that each data source has its own channel.

**Multipoint**   A configuration in which more than two stations share a transmission path.

**Network layer**   Layer 3 of the OSI model. Responsible for routing data through a communication network.

**Network terminating equipment**   Grouping of ISDN functions at the boundary between the ISDN and the subscriber.

**Noise**   Unwanted signals that combine with and, hence, distort the signal intended for transmission and reception.

**Nonreturn to zero**   A digital signaling technique in which the signal is at a constant level for the duration of a bit time.

**Octet**   A group of eight bits, usually operated upon as an entity.

**Open systems interconnection (OSI) reference model**   A model of communications between cooperating devices. It defines a seven-layer architecture of communication functions.

**Optical fiber**   A thin filament of glass or other transparent material, through which a signal-encoded light beam may be transmitted by means of total internal reflection.

**Packet**   A group of bits that include data plus control information. Generally refers to a network layer (OSI layer 3) protocol data unit.

**Packet switching**   A method of transmitting messages through a communication network, in which long messages are subdivided into short packets. The packets are then transmitted as in message switching.

**Parity bit***   A check bit appended to an array of binary digits to make the sum of all the binary digits, including the check bit, always odd or always even.

**PBX**   Private branch exchange. A telephone exchange on the user's premises. Provides a switching facility for telephones on extension lines within the building as well as access to the public telephone network.

**Phase**   The relative position in time within a single period of a signal.

**Phase modulation**   Modulation in which the phase angle of a carrier is the characteristic varied.

**Phase-shift keying**   Modulation in which the phase of the  carrier signal is shifted to represent digital data.

**Physical layer**   Layer 1 of the OSI model. Concerned with the electrical, mechanical, and timing aspects of signal transmission over a medium.

**Piggybacking**   The inclusion of an acknowledgment to a previously received packet in an outgoing data packet.

**Plaintext**   The input to an encryption function or the output of a decryption function.

**Point-to-point**   A configuration in which two stations share a transmission path.

**Poll and select**   The process by which a primary station invites  secondary stations, one at a time, to transmit (poll), and by which a primary station requests that a secondary receive data (select).

**Presentation layer***   Layer 6 of the OSI model. Provides for the selection of a common syntax for representing data and for transformation of application data into and from the common syntax.

**Private key**   One of the two keys used in an asymmetric encryption system. For secure communication, the private key should only be known to its creator.

**Propagation delay**   The delay between the time a signal enters a channel and the time it is received.

**Protocol**   A set of rules that govern the operation of functional units to achieve communication.

**Protocol control information***   Information exchanged between entities of a given layer, via the service provided by the next lower layer, to coordinate their joint operation.

**Protocol data unit (PDU)***   A set of data specified in a protocol of a given layer and consisting of protocol control information of that layer, and possibly user data of that layer.

**Public data network** A government-controlled or national-monopoly packet-switched network. This service is publicly available to data processing users.

**Public key** One of the two keys used in an asymmetric encryption system. The public key is made public, to be used in conjunction with a corresponding private key.

**Public-key encryption** Asymmetric encryption.

**Pulse code modulation** A process in which a signal is sampled, and the magnitude of each sample with respect to a fixed reference is quantized and converted by coding to a digital signal.

**Residual error rate** The error rate remaining after attempts at correction are made.

**Ring** A local-network topology in which stations are attached to repeaters connected in a closed loop. Data are transmitted in one direction around the ring, and can be read by all attached stations.

**Router** An internetworking device that connects two computer networks. It makes use of an internet protocol and assumes that all of the attached devices on the networks use the same communications architecture and protocols. A router operates at OSI layer 3.

**Routing** The determination of a path that a data unit (frame, packet, message) will traverse from source to destination.

**Service access point** A means of identifying a user of the services of a protocol entity. A protocol entity provides one or more SAPs for use by higher-level entities.

**Session layer** Layer 5 of the OSI model. Manages a logical connection (session) between two communicating processes or applications.

**Simplex transmission** Data transmission in one preassigned direction only.

**Sliding-window technique** A method of flow control in which a transmitting station may send numbered packets within a window of numbers. The window changes dynamically to allow additional packets to be sent.

**Space-division switching** A circuit-switching technique in which each connection through the switch takes a physically separate and dedicated path.

**Spectrum** Refers to an absolute range of frequencies. For example, the spectrum of CATV cable is now about 5 to 400 MHz.

**Star** A topology in which all stations are connected to a central switch. Two stations communicate via circuit switching.

**Statistical time-division multiplexing** A method of TDM in which time slots on a shared transmission line are allocated to I/O channels on demand.

**Stop-and-wait** A flow control protocol in which the sender transmits a block of data and then awaits an acknowledgment before transmitting the next block.

**Subnetwork** Refers to a constituent network of an internet; this avoids ambiguity because the entire internet, from a user's point of view, is a single network.

**Switched communication network** A communication network consisting of a network of nodes connected by point-to-point links. Data are transmitted from source to destination through intermediate nodes.

**Symmetric encryption** A form of cryptosystem in which encryption and decryption are performed using the same key. Also known as conventional encryption.

**Synchronous time-division multiplexing** A method of TDM in which time slots on a shared transmission line are assigned to I/O channels on a fixed, predetermined basis.

**Synchronous transmission** Data transmission in which the time of occurrence of each signal representing a bit is related to a fixed time frame.

**Telematics** User-oriented information transmission services. Includes Teletex, Videotex, and facsimile.

**Thermal noise** Statistically uniform noise due to the temperature of the transmission medium.

**Time-division multiplexing** The division of a transmission facility into two or more channels by allotting the facility to several different information channels, one at a time.

**Time-division switching** A circuit-switching technique in which time slots in a time-multiplexed stream of data are manipulated to pass data from an input to an output.

**Token bus** A medium access control technique for bus/tree. Stations form a logical ring, around which a token is passed. A station receiving the token may transmit data and then must pass the token on to the next station in the ring.

**Token ring** A medium access control technique for rings. A token circulates around the ring. A station may transmit by seizing the token, inserting a packet onto the ring, and then retransmitting the token.

**Topology** The structure, consisting of paths and switches, that provides the communications interconnection among nodes of a network.

**Transmission medium** The physical path between transmitters and receivers in a communications system.

**Transport layer** Layer 4 of the OSI model. Provides reliable, transparent transfer of data between endpoints.

**Tree** A local network topology in which stations are attached to a shared transmission medium. The transmission medium is a branching cable emanating from a headend, with no closed circuits. Transmissions propagate throughout all branches of the tree, and are received by all stations.

**Twisted pair**    A transmission medium consisting of two insulated wires arranged in a regular spiral pattern.

**Unbalanced transmission**    A transmission mode in which signals are transmitted on a single conductor. Transmitter and receiver share a common ground.

**Value-added network**    A privately-owned, packet-switching network whose services are sold to the public.

**Virtual circuit**    A packet-switching service in which a connection (virtual circuit) is established between two stations at the start of transmission. All packets follow the same route; they need not carry a complete address, and they arrive in sequence.

# REFERENCES

ABRA95    Abrams, M., Jajodia, S., and Podell, H., eds. *Information Security*. Los Alamitos, CA: IEEE Computer Society Press, 1995.

ABSX92    Apple Computer, Bellcore, Sun Microsystems, and Xerox. *Network Compatible ATM for Local Network Applications, Version 1.01*. October 19, 1992 (available at parcftp.xerox.com/pub/latm).

ANSI85    American National Standards Institute. *Financial Institution Key Management (Wholesale)*. ANS X9.17, 1985.

ARMI93    Armitage, G. and Adams, K. "Packet Reassembly During Cell Loss." *IEEE Network*, September 1993.

ASH90    Ash, G. "Design and Control of Networks with Dynamic Nonhierarchical Routing." *IEEE Communications Magazine*, October 1990.

ATM95    ATM Forum. *LAN Emulation over ATM Specification—Version 1.0*. 1995.

BANT94    Bantz, D. and Bauchot, F. "Wireless LAN Design Alternatives." *IEEE Network*, March/April, 1994.

BELL90    Bellcore (Bell Communications Research). *Telecommunications Transmission Engineering*. Three volumes. 1990.

BELL91    Bellamy, J. *Digital Telephony*. New York: Wiley, 1991.

BENE87    Benedetto, S., Biglieri, E., and Castellani, V. *Digital Transmission Theory*. Englewood Cliffs, NJ: Prentice Hall, 1987.

BERG91    Bergman, W. "Narrowband Frame Relay Congestion Control." *Proceedings of the Tenth Annual Phoenix Conference of Computers and Communications*, March 1991.

BERT92    Bertsekas, D. and Gallager, R. *Data Networks*. Englewood Cliffs, NJ: Prentice Hall, 1992.

BIRD94    Bird, D. *Token Ring Network Design*. Reading, MA: Addison-Wesley, 1994.

BLAC93    Black, U. *Data Link Protocols*. Englewood Cliffs, NJ: Prentice Hall, 1993.

BLAC94    Black, U. *Frame Relay Networks: Specifications and Implementations*. New York: McGraw-Hill, 1994.

BLAC95a    Black, U. *Physical Level Interfaces and Protocols*. Los Alamitos, CA: IEEE Computer Society Press, 1995.

BLAC95b    Black, U. *The V Series Recommendations: Standards for Data Communications Over the Telephone Network*. New York: McGraw-Hill, 1995.

BOUD92    Boudec, J. "The Asynchronous Transfer Mode: A Tutorial." *Computer Networks and ISDN Systems*, May 1992.

BRAD96    Bradner, S. and Mankin, A. *IPng: Internet Protocol Next Generation*. Reading, MA: Addison-Wesley, 1996.

BURG91    Burg, J. and Dorman, D. "Broadband ISDN Resource Management: The Role of Virtual Paths." *IEEE Communications Magazine*, September 1991.

CHEN89    Chen, K., Ho, K., and Saksena, V. "Analysis and Design of a Highly Reliable Transport Architecture for ISDN Frame-Relay Networks." *IEEE Journal on Selected Areas in Communications*, October 1989.

COME94a    Comer, D. and Stevens, D. *Internetworking with TCP/IP, Volume II: Design Implementation, and Internals*. Englewood Cliffs, NJ: Prentice Hall, 1994.

COME94b    Comer, D. and Stevens, D. *Internetworking with TCP/IP, Volume III: Client-Server Programming and Applications*. Englewood Cliffs, NJ: Prentice Hall, 1994.

COME95    Comer, D. *Internetworking with TCP/IP, Volume I: Principles, Protocols, and Architecture*. Englewood Cliffs, NJ: Prentice Hall, 1995.

COUC95    Couch, L. *Modern Communication Systems: Principles and Applications*. Englewood Cliffs, NJ: Prentice Hall, 1995.

DAVI89    Davies, D. and Price, W. *Security for Computer Networks*. New York: Wiley, 1989.

DAVI95    Davis, P. and McGuffin, C. *Wireless Local Area Networks*. New York: McGraw-Hill, 1995.

DIFF76    Diffie, W. and Hellman, M. "New Directions in Cryptography." *IEEE Transactions on Information Theory*, November 1976.

DIJK59    Dijkstra, E. "A Note on Two Problems in Connection with Graphs." *Numerical Mathematics*, October 1959.

DIXO94    Dixon, R. *Spread Spectrum Systems with Commercial Applications*. New York: Wiley, 1994.

DOSH88    Doshi, B. and Nguyen, H. "Congestion Control in ISDN Frame-Relay Networks." *AT&T Technical Journal*, November/December 1988.

DOTY95    Doty, T. "Towards Real Internet Security." *Connexions*, December 1995.

FCA94    Fibre Channel Association. *Fibre Channel: Connection to the Future*. Austin, TX: Fibre Channel Association, 1994.

FORD62    Ford, L. and Fulkerson, D. *Flows in Networks*. Princeton, NJ: Princeton University Press, 1962.

FREE91    Freeman, R. *Telecommunication Transmission Handbook*. New York: Wiley, 1991.

FREE94    Freeman, R. *Reference Manual for Telecommunications Engineering*. New York: Wiley, 1994.

FREE96    Freeman, R. *Telecommunication System Engineering*. New York: Wiley, 1996.

GAUD89    Gaudette, P. *A Tutorial on ASN.1*. Technical Report NCSL/SNA-89/12. Gaithersburg, MD: National Institute of Standards and Technology, 1989.

GERS91    Gersht, A. and Lee, K. "A Congestion Control Framework for ATM Networks." IEEE Journal on Selected Areas in Communications, September 1991.

GILL95    Gilligan, R. and Callon, R. "IPv6 Transition Mechanisms Overview." *Connexions*, October 1995.

GIRA90    Girard, A. *Routing and Dimensioning in Circuit-Switched Networks*. Reading, MA: Addison-Wesley, 1990.

GORA95    Goralski, W. Introduction to ATM Networking. New York: McGraw-Hill, 1995.

GREE93    Green, P. *Fiber Optic Networks*. Englewood Cliffs, NJ: Prentice Hall, 1993.

HAMM86    Hammond, J. and O'Reilly, P. *Performance Analysis of Local Computer Networks*. Reading, MA: Addison-Wesley, 1986.

HAND94    Handel, R., Huber, N., and Schroder, S. *ATM Networks: Concepts, Protocols, Applications*. Reading, MA: Addison-Wesley, 1994.

HALS96   Halsall, F. *Data Communications, Computer Networks, and Open Systems*. Reading, MA: Addison-Wesley, 1996.

HARB92   Harbison, R. "Frame Relay: Technology for Our Time." *LAN Technology*, December 1992.

HAYK94   Haykin, S. *Communication Systems*. New York: Wiley, 1994.

HEGE93   Hegering, H. and Lapple, A. *Ethernet: Building a Communications Infrastructure*. Reading, MA: Addison-Wesley, 1993.

HELG91   Helgert, H. *Integrated Services Digital Networks: Architectures, Protocols, and Standards*. Reading, MA: Addison-Wesley, 1991.

HIND83   Hinden, R., Haverty, J., and Sheltzer, A. "The DARPA Internet: Interconnecting Heterogeneous Computer Networks with Gateways." *Computer*, September 1983.

HIND95   Hinden, R. "IP Next Generation Overview." *Connexions*, March 1995.

HUIT95   Huitema, C. *Routing in the Internet*. Englewood Cliffs, NJ: Prentice Hall, 1995.

JAIN93   Jain, B. and Agrawala, A. *Open Systems Interconnection*. New York: McGraw-Hill, 1993.

JEFF94   Jeffries, R. "ATM LAN Emulation: The Inside Story." *Data Communications*, September 21, 1994.

KALI91   Kaliski, B. *A Layman's Guide to a Subset of ASN.1, BER, and DER*. Report SEC-SIG-91-17, Redwood City, CA: RSA Data Security Inc., 1991.

KAVA95   Kavak, N. "Data Communication in ATM Networks." *IEEE Network*, May/June 1995.

KESS92   Kessler, G. and Train, D. *Metropolitan Area Networks: Concepts, Standards, and Services*. New York: McGraw-Hill, 1992.

KESS93   Kessler, G. *ISDN: Concepts, Facilities, and Services*. New York: McGraw-Hill, 1993.

KHAN89   Khanna, A. and Zinky, J. "The Revised ARPANET Routing Metric." *Proceedings, SIGCOMM '89 Sypmosium*, 1989.

KLEI76   Kleinrock, L. *Queueing Systems, Volume II: Computer Applications*. New York: Wiley, 1976.

LANG95   Lang, L. "Using Multilayer Switches to Connect Legacy LANs and the ATM Backbone." *Telecommunications*, March 1995.

LEUT94   Leutwyler, K. "Superhack." *Scientific American*, July 1994.

MADR94   Madron, T. *Local Area Networks: New Technologies, Emerging Standards*. New York: Wiley, 1994.

MART90   Martin, J. *Telecommunications and the Computer*. Englewood Cliffs, NJ: Prentice Hall, 1990.

MART94   Martin, J., Chapman, K., and Leben, J. *Local Area Networks: Architectures and Implementations*. Englewood Cliffs, NJ: Prentice Hall, 1994.

MCDY95   McDysan, D. and Spohn, D. *ATM: Theory and Application*. New York: McGraw-Hill, 1995.

MCQU80   McQuillan, J., Richer, I., and Rosen, E. "The New Routing Algorithm for the ARPANET." *IEEE Transactions on Communications*, May 1980.

MEEK90   Meeks, F. "The Sound of Lamarr." *Forbes*, May 1990.

MILL95   Mills, A. *Understanding FDDI*. Englewood Cliffs, NJ: Prentice Hall, 1995.

MURP95   Murphy, E., Hayes, S., and Enders, M. *TCP/IP: Tutorial and Technical Overview*. Englewood Cliffs, NJ: Prentice Hall, 1995.

NECH92   Nechvatal, J. "Public Key Cryptography." [SIMM92].

NIST94   National Institute of Standards and Technology. *Data Encryption Standard*. FIPS-PUB 46-2, June 1994.

NEWM94   Newman, P. "ATM Local Area Networks." *IEEE Communications Magazine*, March 1994.

ONVU94   Onvural, R. *Asynchronous Transfer Mode Networks: Performance Issues*. Boston: Artech House, 1994.

PAHL95a   Pahlavan, K., Probert, T., and Chase, M. "Trends in Local Wireless Networks." *IEEE Communications Magazine*, March 1995.

PAHL95b   Pahlavan, K. and Levesque, A. *Wireless Information Networks*. New York: Wiley, 1995.

PARK92   Park, Y. et al. "2.488 Gb/s-318 km Repeaterless Transmission Using Erbium-Doped Fiber Amplifiers in a Direct-Detection System." *IEEE Photonics Technology Letters*, February 1992.

PART88   Partridge, C. *Innovations in Internetworking*. Norwood, MA: Artech House, 1988.

PEAR92   Pearson, J. *Basic Communication Theory*. Englewood Cliffs, NJ: Prentice Hall, 1992.

PEEB87   Peebles, P. *Digital Communication Systems*. Englewood Cliffs, NJ: Prentice Hall, 1987.

PERL92   Perlman, R. *Interconnections: Bridges and Routers*. Reading, MA: Addison-Wesley, 1992.

PETE61   Peterson, W. and Brown, D. "Cyclic Codes for Error Detection." *Proceedings of the IRE*, January 1961.

PETE95   Peterson, R., Ziemer, R., and Borth, D. *Introduction to Spread Spectrum Communications*. Englewood Cliffs, NJ: Prentice Hall, 1995.

POWE90   Powers, J. and Stair, H. *Megabit Data Communications*. Englewood Cliffs, NJ: Prentice Hall, 1990.

PROA94   Proakis, J. and Salehi, M. *Communication Systems Engineering*. Englewood Cliffs, NJ: Prentice Hall, 1994.

PRYC93   Prycker, M. *Asynchronous Transfer Mode: Solutions for Broadband ISDN*. New York: Ellis Horwood, 1993.

REEV95   Reeve, W. *Subscriber Loop Signaling and Transmission Handbook*. Piscataway, NJ: IEEE Press, 1995.

REGN90   Regnier, J. and Cameron, W. "State-Dependent Dynamic Traffic Management for Telepone Networks." *IEEE Communications Magazine*, October 1990.

RIVE78   Rivest, R., Shamir, A., and Adleman, L. "A Method for Obtaining Digital Signatures and Public Key Cryptosystems." *Communications of the ACM*, February 1978.

ROSE93   Rose, M. *The Internet Message: Closing the Book with Electronic Mail*. Englewood Cliffs, NJ: Prentice Hall, 1993.

SADI95   Sadiku, M. *Metropolitan Area Networks*. Boca Raton, FL: CRC Press, 1995.

SANT94   Santamaria, A. and Lopez-Hernandez, F., eds. *Wireless LAN Systems*. Boston MA: Artech House, 1994.

SATO90   Sato, K., Ohta, S., and Tokizawa, I. "Broad-band ATM Network Architecture Based on Virtual Paths." *IEEE Transactions on Communications*, August 1990.

SATO91   Sato, K., Ueda, H., and Yoshikai, M. "The Role of Virtual Path Crossconnection." *IEEE LTS*, August 1991.

SCHN91   Schneier, B. "One-Way Hash Functions." *Dr. Dobb's Journal*, September 1991.

SCHN96   Schneier, B. *Applied Cryptography*. New York: Wiley, 1996.

SCHW77   Schwartz, M. *Computer-Communication Network Design and Analysis*. Englewood Cliffs, NJ: Prentice Hall, 1977.

SHAH94   Shah, A. and Ramakrishnan, G. *FDDI: A High-Speed Network*. Englewood Cliffs, NJ: Prentice Hall, 1994.

SEYE91   Seyer, M. *RS-232 Made Easy: Connecting Computers, Printers, Terminals, and Modems*. Englewood Cliffs, NJ: Prentice Hall, 1991.

SIMM92   Simmons, G., ed. *Contemporary Cryptology: The Science of Information Integrity*. Piscataway, NJ: IEEE Press, 1992.

SKLA88   Sklar, B. *Digital Communications: Fundamentals and Applications*. Englewood Cliffs, NJ: Prentice Hall, 1988.

SMIT93   Smith, P. *Frame Relay: Principles and Applications*. Reading, MA: Addison-Wesley, 1993.

SPOH93   Spohn, D. *Data Network Design*. New York: McGraw-Hill, 1994.

SPRA91   Spragins, J., Hammond, J., and Pawlikowski, K. *Telecommunications Protocols and Design*. Reading, MA: Addison-Wesley, 1991.

SPUR95   Spurgeon, C. *Quick Reference Guide to Ethernet*. Austin, TX: Harris Park Press, 1995.

STAL90   Stallings, W. *Handbook of Computer Communications Standards, Volume 3: The TCP/IP Protocol Suite, Second Edition*. Englewood Cliffs, NJ: Prentice Hall, 1990.

STAL95a   Stallings, W. *ISDN and Broadband ISDN, with Frame Relay and ATM, Third Edition*. Englewood Cliffs, NJ: Prentice Hall, 1995.

STAL95b   Stallings, W. *Network and Internetwork Security: Principles and Practice*. Englewood Cliffs, NJ: Prentice Hall, 1995.

STAL96   Stallings, W. *Computer Organization and Architecture, Fourth Edition*. Upper Saddle River, NJ: PrenticeHall, 1996.

STAL97   Stallings, W. *Local and Metropolitan Area Networks, Fifth Edition*. Upper Saddle River, NJ: Prentice Hall, 1997.

STEE90   Steedman, D. *ASN.1: The Tutorial and Reference*. London: Technology Appraisals, 1990.

STEE95   Steenstrup, M. *Routing in Communications Networks*. Englewood Cliffs, NJ: Prentice-Hall, 1995.

STEV94   Stevens, W. *TCP/IP Illustrated, Volume 1: The Protocols*. Reading, MA: Addison-Wesley, 1994.

STEV96   Stevens, W. *TCP/IP Illustrated, Volume 3: TCP for Transactions, HTTP, NNTP, and the UNIX(R) Domain Protocol*. Reading, MA: Addison-Wesley, 1996.

STER93   Sterling, D. *Technician's Guide to Fiber Optics*. Albany, NY: Delmar Publications, 1993.

STUC85   Stuck, B. and Arthurs, E. *A Computer Communications Network Performance Analysis Primer*. Englewood Cliffs, NJ: Prentice Hall, 1985.

SUZU94   Suzuki, T. "ATM Adaptation Layer Protocol." *IEEE Communications Magazine*, April 1994.

TANE88   Tanenbaum, A. *Computer Networks*. Englewood Cliffs, NJ: Prentice Hall, 1988.

TERP92   Terplan, K. *Communication Networks Management*. Englewood Cliffs, NJ: Prentice Hall, 1992.

TRUO95   Truong, H. et al. "LAN Emulation on an ATM Network." *IEEE Communications Magazine*, May 1995.

TSUD92   Tsudik, G. "Message Authentication with One-Way Hash Functions." *Computer Communications Review*, October, 1992

TUCH79   Tuchman, W. *Hellman Presents No-Shortcut Solutions to DES. IEEE Spectrum*, July 1979.

VALK93   Valkenburg, M. ed. *Reference Data for Engineers: Radio, Electronics, Computer, and Communications*. Carmel, IN: Prentice Hall/SAMS, 1993.

VALE92   Valenzano, A., DeMartini, C., and Ciminiera, L. *MAP and TOP Communications: Standards and Applications*. Reading, MA: Addison-Wesley, 1992.

WIDM83   Widmer, A. and Franaszek, P. "A DC-Balanced, Partitioned, 8B/10B Transmission Code." *IBM Journal of Research and Development*, September 1983.

WIEN93   Wiener, M. *Efficient DES Key Search. Proceedings, Crypto '93*. Springer-Verlag, 1993.

WRIG95   Wright, G. and Stevens, W. *TCP/IP Illustrated, Volume 2: The Implementation*. Reading, MA: Addison-Wesley, 1995.

YEN83   Yen, C. and Crawford, R. "Distribution and Equalization of Signal on Coaxial Cables Used in 10-Mbits Baseband Local Area Networks." *IEEE Transactions on Communications*, October 1983.

# INDEX

# ACRONYMS

| | |
|---|---|
| AAL | ATM Adaptation Layer |
| AM | Amplitude Modulation |
| AMI | Alternate Mark Inversion |
| ANS | American National Standard |
| ANSI | American National Standard Institute |
| ARQ | Automatic Repeat Request |
| ASCII | American Standard Code for Information Interchange |
| ASK | Amplitude-Shift Keying |
| ATM | Asynchronous Transfer Mode |
| B-ISDN | Broadband ISDN |
| BOC | Bell Operating Company |
| CBR | Constant Bit Rate |
| CCITT | International Consultative Committee on Telegraphy and Telephony |
| CIR | Committed Information Rate |
| CRC | Cyclic Redundancy Check |
| CSMA/CD | Carrier Sense Multiple Access with Collision Detection |
| DCE | Data Circuit-Terminating Equipment |
| DES | Data Encryption Standard |
| DTE | Data Terminal Equipment |
| FCC | Federal Communications Commission |
| FCS | Frame Check Sequence |
| FDDI | Fiber Distributed Data Interface |
| FDM | Frequency-Division Multiplexing |
| FSK | Frequency-Shift Keying |
| FTP | File Transfer Protocol |
| FM | Frequency Modulation |
| HDLC | High-Level Data Link Control |
| HTTP | Hypertext Transfer Protocol |
| ICMP | Internet Control Message Protocol |
| IDN | Integrated Digital Network |
| IEEE | Institute of Electrical and Electronics Engineers |
| IETF | Internet Engineering Task Force |
| IP | Internet Protocol |
| IPng | Internet Protocol - Next Generation |
| ISDN | Integrated Services Digital Network |
| ISO | International Organization for Standardization |
| ITU | International Telecommunication Union |
| ITU-T | ITU Telecommunication Standardization Sector |

| | |
|---|---|
| LAN | Local Area Network |
| LAPB | Link Access Procedure–Balanced |
| LAPD | Link Access Procedure on the D Channel |
| LAPF | Link Access Procedure for Frame Mode Bearer Services |
| LLC | Logical Link Control |
| MAC | Medium Access Control |
| MAN | Metropolitan Area Network |
| MIME | Multi-Purpose Internet Mail Extension |
| NRZI | Nonreturn to Zero, Inverted |
| NRZL | Nonreturn to Zero, Level |
| NT | Network Termination |
| OSI | Open Systems Interconnection |
| PBX | Private Branch Exchange |
| PCM | Pulse-Code Modulation |
| PDU | Protocol Data Unit |
| PSK | Phase-Shift Keying |
| PTT | Postal, Telegraph, and Telephone |
| PM | Phase Modulation |
| QOS | Quality of Service |
| QPSK | Quadrature Phase Shift Keying |
| RBOC | Regional Bell Operating Company |
| RF | Radio Frequency |
| RSA | Rivest, Shamir, Adleman Algorithm |
| SAP | Service Access Point |
| SDH | Synchronous Digital Hierarchy |
| SDU | Service Data Unit |
| SMTP | Simple Mail Transfer Protocol |
| SONET | Synchronous Optical Network |
| TCP | Transmission Control Protocol |
| TDM | Time-Division Multiplexing |
| TE | Terminal Equipment |
| UNI | User-Network Interface |
| URI | Universal Resource Identifier |
| URL | Uniform Resource Locator |
| VAN | Value-Added Network |
| VBR | Variable Bit Rate |
| VCC | Virtual Channel Connection |
| VPC | Virtual Path Connection |
| WWW | World Wide Web |